Lecture Notes in Business Information Processing 571

LNBIP reports state-of-the-art results in areas related to business information systems and industrial application software development – timely, at a high level, and in both printed and electronic form.

The type of material published includes

- Proceedings (published in time for the respective event)
- Postproceedings (consisting of thoroughly revised and/or extended final papers)
- Other edited monographs (such as, for example, project reports or invited volumes)
- Tutorials (coherently integrated collections of lectures given at advanced courses, seminars, schools, etc.)
- Award-winning or exceptional theses

LNBIP is abstracted/indexed in DBLP, EI and Scopus. LNBIP volumes are also submitted for the inclusion in ISI Proceedings.

José Barateiro · Andrey Rivkin ·
Jelena Zdravkovic · José Borbinha ·
Miguel Mira da Silva
Editors

Enterprise Design, Operations, and Computing

EDOC 2025 Workshops

Forum, Doctoral Consortium, EA4AI, iRESEARCH, SoEA4EE
Tool Presentations, Lisbon, Portugal, September 9–12, 2025
Revised Selected Papers

Springer

Editors
José Barateiro
Nova LINCS and University of Algarve
Lisbon, Portugal

Andrey Rivkin
Technical University of Denmark
Kongens Lyngby, Denmark

Jelena Zdravkovic
Stockholm University
Stockholm, Sweden

José Borbinha
Universidade de Lisboa
Lisbon, Portugal

Miguel Mira da Silva
Universidade de Lisboa
Lisbon, Portugal

ISSN 1865-1348 ISSN 1865-1356 (electronic)
Lecture Notes in Business Information Processing
ISBN 978-3-032-16233-5 ISBN 978-3-032-16234-2 (eBook)
https://doi.org/10.1007/978-3-032-16234-2

This Springer imprint is published by the registered company Springer Nature Switzerland AG
The registered company address is: Gewerbestrasse 11, 6330 Cham, Switzerland

Preface

CBI-EDOC 2025 represented the second edition of a joint initiative that brings together two long-established conferences: the IEEE Conference on Business Informatics (CBI) and the IEEE Conference on Enterprise Design, Operations, and Computing (EDOC). Building on the success of their first combine devent in Vienna in 2024, this year's conference continued the collaboration under a single, integrated program, hosted in Lisbon, Portugal, from 9 to 12 September 2025.

CBI-EDOC 2025 offered a rich and varied program that reflected the breadth and maturity of two communities united by a shared commitment to advancing research and practice in enterprise and information systems. Alongside the main research program, the conference featured a Forum, a Doctoral Consortium (DC), a Tools and Demonstrations track, and three specialized workshops, each providing unique opportunities for presentation, discussion, and collaboration across academia and industry. Together, these venues created a dynamic environment where established scholars, early-stage researchers, and practitioners could exchange ideas, explore emerging topics, and strengthen the foundations for future innovation.

The Forum sessions brought together applied research, industrial case studies, and project reports, offering a bridge between conceptual advances and realworld implementation. The Tools and Demonstrations track showcased innovative software solutions and prototypes that illustrate how theoretical principles can be operationalized to support enterprise and information systems design.

The three workshops, each with its own thematic community, broadened the reach of the joint program and encouraged in-depth discussion on specialized and emerging topics across enterprise computing and business informatics. The Doctoral Consortium maintained its essential role in supporting the next generation of researchers, offering mentoring, constructive feedback, and networking opportunities for PhD students exploring diverse aspects of business informatics and enterprise systems.

Altogether, CBI-EDOC 2025 reaffirmed the strength and relevance of this joint platform for advancing theory and practice across the intersecting domains of modeling, architecture, operations, data, and digital transformation. The conference program was further enriched by keynote lectures, joint panels, and social events that stimulated dialogue beyond disciplinary boundaries and fostered a shared vision for the future of enterprise information systems.

These proceedings collect the contributions presented in the Forum, the Tools and Demonstrations track, the three Workshops, and the Doctoral Consortium. They comprise 33 papers, selected from a total of 67 contributions (45 submitted directly to the respective tracks, and 22 initially submitted to EDOC 2025 or CBI 2025, not accepted there but recommended for additional review in this volume, of which 6 were accepted). This collection represents the collaborative effort of authors, reviewers, and organizers who ensured the scientific quality, diversity, and coherence of the conference content. In addition, this volume includes one extended abstract from the Tools and Demonstrations session and three adapted abstracts from the Journal-First session. The latter complemented the main program by featuring presentations of recently published, high-impact papers from leading journals, whose adapted abstracts are reproduced here.

We extend our heartfelt thanks to all members of the organizing and program committees, to the workshop chairs and doctoral consortium mentors for their dedication to fostering community engagement, and to the local organizing team at INESC-ID and Instituto Superior Técnico, whose professionalism and hospitality ensured a smooth and welcoming experience for all participants.

Finally, we express our sincere appreciation to all authors, reviewers, and attendees for their contributions and active participation. Their collective effort made CBI-EDOC 2025 a vibrant and memorable event that continued to strengthen the collaboration between the business informatics and enterprise computing communities.

As this joint initiative evolves, we hope that the work presented in these proceedings, together with the ideas exchanged during the conference, will inspire further research, foster new collaborations, and shape the development of future enterprise and information systems.

November 2025

José Barateiro
Andrey Rivkin
Jelena Zdravkovic
José Borbinha
Miguel Mira da Silva

Organization

General Chairs

José Borbinha	INESC-ID, IST, Universidade de Lisboa, Portugal
Miguel Mira da Silva	INOV, IST, Universidade de Lisboa, Portugal

Program Committee Chairs

Alessandro Gianola	INESC-ID, IST, Universidade de Lisboa, Portugal
Renata Guizzardi	University of Twente, Netherlands

Forum Chairs

Andrey Rivkin	Technical University of Denmark, Denmark
Jelena Zdravkovic	Stockholm University, Sweden

Workshop Chairs

Cláudia Antunes	IST, Universidade de Lisboa, Portugal
Andrea Marrella	Sapienza University of Rome, Italy

Doctoral Consortium Chairs

Selmin Nurcan	Université Paris 1 Panthéon–Sorbonne, France
Raimundas Matulevicius	University of Tartu, Estonia

Industry and Case Reports Chairs

Zoran Milosevic	Deontik, Australia
Rui Dinis Sousa	University of Minho, Portugal

Tools and Demos Chairs

Luis Sousa	INESC-ID, IST, Universidade de Lisboa, Portugal
Simone Agostinelli	Sapienza – Università di Roma, Italy

Journal-First Chairs

Faiza Bukhsh	University of Twente, Netherlands
Marco Montali	Free University of Bozen-Bolzano, Italy

Proceedings Chair

José Barateiro	NOVA-LINCS, Universidade do Algarve, Portugal

Publicity Chairs

Rob Bemthuis	University of Twente, Netherlands
André Vasconcelos	INESC-ID, IST, Universidade de Lisboa, Portugal

Steering Committee

Alan Wee-Chung Liew	Griffith University, Australia
Colin Atkinson	University of Mannheim, Germany
Dimka Karastoyanova	University of Groningen, The Netherlands
Georg Grossmann	University of South Australia, Australia
Giancarlo Guizzardi	University of Twente, The Netherlands
Henderik A. Proper	TUWien, Austria
João Paulo A. Almeida	Federal University of Espírito Santo, Brazil
Manfred Reichert	University of Ulm, Germany
Marten van Sinderen	University of Twente, The Netherlands
Remco Dijkman	Eindhoven University of Technology, The Netherlands
Selmin Nurcan (Chair)	Paris 1 Panthéon-Sorbonne University, France
Sylvain Hallé	Université du Québec ‘a Chicoutimi, Canada
Zoran Milosevic	Deontik, Australia

Report from the Doctoral Consortium Chairs

Selmin Nurcan[1] and Raimundas Matulevičius[2]

[1] Université Paris 1 Panthéon – Sorbonne, Paris, France
nurcan@univ-paris1.fr
[2] University of Tartu, Tartu, Estonia

The EDOC Doctoral Consortium has been initiated during the 2019 edition of the International EDOC conference series. Since 2024, it has been organised as a joint EDOC + CBI Doctoral Consortium.

The joint EDOC + CBI 2025 Doctoral Consortium aims to offer a supportive learning opportunity for doctoral students in the early stage of their research project, i.e., typically in their first or second year, to discuss their work in progress and to receive feedback and guidance from senior researchers and the audience. A panel of senior researchers serve as mentors during the Doctoral Consortium sessions. The Doctoral Consortium also offers opportunities to establish a social network with peers in CBI and EDOC conferences and to engage with some industry participants.

This year, the Doctoral Consortium received nine submissions. They have all been reviewed by three members of the Doctoral Consortium Program Committee. Six papers were selected for presentation at the conference and inclusion in the LNBIP proceedings.

The accepted papers cover several topics within the scope of the conference and were structured in two sessions, having three papers each. Over the course of two sessions, the "IT-based Enterprise Reengineering" session, with Benjamin Nast, Han Bingbing, and Vânia Sousa and the "Knowledge Management and Reference Model" session with Edwin de Haan, Anca Moldovan, and Marcel Pertenbreiter, the PhD candidates presented and discussed their research with the mentors. The presenters received the feedback, advice, and recommendations to further improve their PhD research plans.

We want to thank all participating PhD candidates for their presentations, as well as all Doctoral Consortium Program Committee members who were involved in the reviewing process and the mentors who served as discussants during the on-site presentations. Also, we thank the CBI-EDOC 2025 general chairs, Professor José Borbinha and Professor Miguel Mira da Silva, for supporting the organisation of the Doctoral Consortium.

Doctoral Consortium Program Chairs

- Raimundas Matulevičius, University of Tartu, Estonia
- Selmin Nurcan, Université Paris 1 Panthéon-Sorbonne, France

Doctoral Consortium Program Committee

- Saïd Assar, Institut Mines-Telecom Business School, France
- Colin Atkinson, University of Mannheim, Germany
- Rob Bemthuis, University of Twente, Netherlands
- Georg Grossmann, University of South Australia, Australia
- Giancarlo Guizzardi, University of Twente, Netherlands
- Sylvain Hallé, Université du Québec à Chicoutimi, Canada
- Dimka Karastoyanova, University of Groningen, Netherlands
- Andreas Opdahl, University of Bergen, Norway
- Oscar Pastor, Universidad Politécnica de Valencia, Spain
- Jean Paul Sebastian Piest, University of Twente, Netherlands
- Jolita Ralyté, University of Geneva, Switzerland
- Marcela Ruiz, Zurich Universities of Applied Sciences and Arts, Switzerland

Doctoral Consortium Mentors

- João Paulo Almeida, Federal University of Espírito Santo, Brazil
- Ilja Bider, Stockholm University, Sweden
- José Borbinha, Universidade de Lisboa, Portugal
- Raimundas Matulevičius, University of Tartu, Estonia
- Selmin Nurcan, Université Paris 1 Panthéon-Sorbonne, France
- Henderik Proper, TU Wien, Austria

Report from the EA4AI Workshop Chair

Asif Qumer Gill[1], Anastasija Nikiforova[2], and Madhushi Bandara[1]

[1] University of Technology Sydney, Sydney, Australia
asif.gill@uts.edu.au
[2] University of Tartu, Tartu, Estonia

Artificial intelligence systems are perceived to replicate or automate human intelligence or capabilities. Augmented intelligence (AI) goes beyond human capability replication or automation and focuses on enhancing or augmenting human capabilities [1]. However, the challenge is that Isolated or individual AI applications, models, proof-of-concepts (PoCs) and protype developments often fail to integrate with or scale at the enterprise level as production ready enterprise systems [2]. For instance, how will applications and models share data with each other? How to ensure that models have controlled access to the right data based on their permission or need to know basis? How to avoid vendor lock-in where enterprise depend on different agents developed or provided by different service providers across the heterogeneous multi-cloud and on premises computing environment? How to ensure communication and coordination across such heterogeneous multi-agent AI systems? How to orchestrate, operate and manage such multi-agent environment at the enterprise and federated ecosystem levels.

There is a lot of focus on AI Engineering or AI Development, however, there is a significant gap around the topic of AI Architecture, which is critical for scaling AI at enterprise level [3]. Therefore, International Workshop on Enterprise Architecture for Augmented Intelligence (EAA4I) focuses on this challenge of "Scalable Enterprise AI Systems". This workshop was organised as a part of the CBI-EDOC 2025 conference and accepted three papers after the peer review process.

AI, in the modern context, can use large language models (LLMs) for generating artifacts such as business capability models and process models. One of the accepted papers "LLM4BPMN: A Prompting Approach with LLMs for BPMN Model Generation" presented a prompting approach coupled with LLMs for automatically generating the Business Process Model and Notation (BPMN) models. This research provided architecture and tool as solutions, which seems to augment the human capability for modelling complex processes. A model is an abstraction or representation of reality and could be considered as the digital twin of a physical world such as the intelligent digital twin of an organisation (DTO) in the context of modern enterprise architecture [4].

The second contribution "Designing a Predictive Digital Twin Architecture for Smart Bridge Maintenance" provided a structured approach and its application using the ArchiMate modelling language for architecting the intelligent and predictive digital twins for the smart civil infrastructure such as the bridge maintenance.

AI Architecture can be implemented by using the low-code platform for AI Engineering.

Low-code platforms enable rapid application development; however, they also face several challenges such as poor software traceability and knowledge due to no or limited documentation [5]. Third and final paper addressed this challenge and presented "CLAIR: Generating On-Demand Low-Code Application Documentation through Knowledge Graph and LLM-based Multi-Agent System Integration". This AI/LLM driven documentation augments the low-code application development capability and provided a solid foundation to support the reusable and maintainable AI systems and solutions.

In summary, this workshop provided opportunities to researchers, enterprise architects, business and IT thought leaders to share, network and learn from each other through the presentation of applied research and innovation.

References

1. Tarafdar, M., Beath, C.M., Ross, J.W.: Using AI to enhance business operations. MIT Sloan Manag. Rev. **60**(4) (2019)
2. Haefner, N., Parida, V., Gassmann, O., Wincent, J.: Implementing and scaling artificial intelligence: a review, framework, and research agenda. Technol. Forecast. Soc. Change, 122878 (2023)
3. Rittelmeyer, J.D., Sandkuhl, K.: Effects of artificial intelligence on enterprise architectures - a structured literature review. In: 2021 IEEE 25th International Enterprise Distributed Object Computing Workshop (EDOCW), pp. 130–137. IEEE (2021)
4. Riss, U.V., Maus, H., Javaid, S., Jilek, C.: Digital twins of an organization for enterprise modeling. In: IFIP Working Conference on the Practice of Enterprise Modeling, pp. 25–40. Springer, Cham (2020)
5. Luo, Y., Liang, P., Wang, C., Shahin, M., Zhan, J.: Characteristics and challenges of low-code development: the practitioners' perspective. In: Proceedings of the 15th ACM/IEEE International Symposium on Empirical Software Engineering and Measurement (ESEM), pp. 1–11. ACM (2021). https://doi.org/10.1145/3475716.3475782

Report from the iRESEARCH 2025 Workshop Chairs

Rob Bemthuis, Faiza Bukhsh, and Maya Daneva

University of Twente, Enschede, The Netherlands
f.a.bukhsh@utwente.nl

Empirical inquiry sits at the heart of how our community learns what truly works in Enterprise Architecture (EA) and Service-Oriented Computing (SOC). Building on the spirit of earlier editions, this year's iRESEARCH workshop continues to foreground industry-relevant studies, rigorous methods, and reflective practice. The workshop's mission is twofold: (1) to keep open an interdisciplinary debate on the fast-moving frontiers of empirical methodologies that support EA and SOC research projects; and (2) to expand the network of scholars who design and conduct such studies, so that cross-fertilization between EA/SOC and empirical research methods happens by design, not by accident.

Concretely, iRESEARCH seeks outcomes along four lines: (i) clear ways to evaluate and compare methods, processes, and tools "in context"; (ii) the surfacing of emerging and hybrid research methods; (iii) new collaboration patterns with industry partners that make empirical work more feasible and impactful; and (iv) sharper criteria for when and how empirical results transfer to practice. These outcomes echo the workshop's established focus on evidence-building, from design science and case studies to interview- and survey-based work, and its commitment to problems that matter to organizations operating amid AI-enabled enterprise computing, IoT, digital ecosystems, digital twins, and cloud/green computing.

This year, iRESEARCH received 9 submissions; 4 papers were accepted for presentation (44% acceptance rate). All accepted contributions underwent peer review and were selected for novelty, methodological soundness, and practical relevance, continuing the workshop's emphasis on empirical quality and industry connectedness.

The workshop sessions were chaired by F.A. Bukhsh and R.H. Bemthuis. The discussions surfaced shared challenges and highlighted promising directions for joint empirical studies and benchmark datasets.

Acknowledgments. We warmly thank all authors for their submissions, the reviewers for their timely and constructive evaluations, and our colleagues across the CBI–EDOC organization for their support. The community's engagement keeps iRESEARCH a focused, hands-on forum for advancing empirical EA/SOC scholarship and practice.

Workshop Chairs

- Rob Bemthuis, University of Twente, the Netherlands
- Faiza Bukhsh, University of Twente, the Netherlands

- Maya Daneva, University of Twente, the Netherlands

Programme Committee

- Jelena Zdravkovic, Stockholm University, Sweden
- Saïd Assar, IMT Business School, France
- Pnina Soffer, University of Haifa, Israel
- Hajo Reijers, Utrecht University, The Netherlands
- Jeewanie Jayasinghe Arachchige, University of Amsterdam, The Netherlands
- Oscar Pastor, Universidad Politécnica de Valencia, Spain
- Hans Weigand, Tilburg University, The Netherlands
- Selmin Nurcan, Université de Paris 1 Panthéon-Sorbonne, France
- Dimka Karastoyanova, University of Groningen, The Netherlands
- Claudia Negri Ribalta, University of Luxembourg, Luxembourg
- Sybren de Kinderen, Eindhoven University of Technology, The Netherlands
- Marite Kirikova, Riga Technical University, Latvia
- Yves Wautelet, Katholieke Universiteit Leuven, Belgium
- Patrizio De Alencar Silva, Universidade Federal de Pernambuco, Brazil
- Tharaka Ilayperuma, Staffordshire University, United Kingdom
- Nacir Bouali, University of Twente, The Netherlands
- Iqbal Yulizar Mukti, Telkom University, Indonesia

Report from the SoEA4EE'2025 Workshop Chairs

Selmin Nurcan[1] and Rainer Schmidt[2]

[1] Université Paris 1 Panthéon Sorbonne, Paris, France
nurcan@univ-paris1.fr
[2] Munich University of Applied Sciences, Munich, Germany

The SoEA4EE workshop focuses on encapsulating digital resources and capacities as services for enterprise architecture. The workshop aims to develop concepts and methods to assist the engineering and management of service-oriented enterprise architectures (SoEA) and the software systems supporting them in the Computing Continuum.

Since its foundation in 2009 [1], the SoEA4EE workshop has complemented well-established topics of the EDOC conferences, such as service-oriented architectures and enterprise service architectures, by addressing the coupling of business processes and services and the alignment of business and IT. The SoEA4EE workshop also includes topics such as Business Process Management, Enterprise Service Architectures, Analytics, Big Data, Networked Enterprise Solutions, and their connections.

According to [2], smart companies define how they (will) do business (using an operating model) and design processes and infrastructure critical to their current and future operations using enterprise architecture (EA). Enterprise Engineering (EE) is the application of engineering principles to the design of enterprise architectures. This enables the derivation of the EA from the enterprise goals and strategy and aligns it with the enterprise resources. EA [2] maps enterprise goals and strategies to the enterprise's resources (actors, assets, IT supports) and supports the evolution of this mapping.

Different paradigms exist for creating enterprise architectures. In the SoEA4EE series, the one that is considered as the most promising is to encapsulate the functionalities of IT resources as services. This makes it possible to clearly describe the contributions of IT in terms of functionality and quality and to define a service-oriented enterprise architecture (SoEA).

Two special journal issues [3, 4] have been published in the International Journal of Information Systems in the Service Sector (IJISSS), the first with invited papers from SoEA4EE 2010, 2011, and 2012, and the second with invited papers from SoEA4EE 2013, 2014, and 2015. The extended papers underwent a systematic review process again, and the accepted papers were included in those special issues.

Five research themes have been pursued in this edition:

1. Digital enterprises, Industry 4.0, and Platforms in the Computing Continuum
2. SoEA and influence of Artificial Intelligence, social information systems, and big data in Enterprise Engineering
3. Alignment of the enterprise goals and strategy with the SoEA
4. Design of SoEA
5. Governance of SoEA

Organization

The 16th Service-oriented Enterprise Architecture for Enterprise Engineering (SoEA4EE'2025) workshop was organized in conjunction with EDOC'2025 and CBI'2025. We received eight submissions from authors in seven countries (Austria, Canada, Colombia, Germany, Netherlands, Portugal, and Sweden). All submissions were peer-reviewed by at least three members of the International Program Committee. Four papers were selected for presentation at the conference and inclusion in the LNBIP proceedings.

We wish to thank all authors for sharing their work with us, the members of the SoEA4EE'2025 Program Committee for their efforts in reviewing submissions, and the organizers of EDOC + CBI 2025 for their help with the organization of the workshop.

Workshop Chairs

Selmin Nurcan – University Paris 1 Panthéon Sorbonne, France.
Rainer Schmidt – Munich University of Applied Sciences, Germany.

Progamme Committee

Khalid Benali - LORIA, Nancy, France
Kahina Bessai – Telecom Paris, France
Mohamad Gharib - University of Tartu, Estonia
Jānis Grabis, Riga Technical University, Latvia
Sung-Kook Han - Won Kwang University, South Korea
Zoran Milosevic - Deontik, Australia
Michael Möhring – Reutlingen University, Germany
Jean Paul Sebastian Piest - University of Twente, The Netherlands
Flavia Santoro, Universidade do Estado do Rio de Janeiro, Brazil
Ulrike Steffens - Hamburg University of Applied Sciences, Germany

References

1. Nurcan, S., Schmidt, R.: Service-Oriented Enterprise-Architecture for enterprise engineering introduction. In: 2009 13th Enterprise Distributed Object Computing Conference Workshops, pp. 247–253 (2009)
2. Ross, J.W., Weill, P., Robertson, D.: Enterprise Architecture as Strategy: Creating a Foundation for Business Execution. Harvard Business School Press (2006)
3. Nurcan, S., Schmidt, R.: Special Issue Selected Papers from the SoEA4EE 2010, 2011, and 2012 on "Service-oriented Enterprise Architecture on Enterprise Engineering. Int. J. Inf. Syst. Serv. Sector (IJISSS) **7**(1) (2015)
4. Nurcan, S.: Special Issue Selected Papers from the SoEA4EE Workshops 2013, 2014, and 2015 on "Service-oriented Enterprise Architecture on Enterprise Engineering. Int. J. Inf. Syst. Serv. Sector (IJISSS) **10**(3) (2018)

Report from the Tools and Demos Chairs

José Borbinha[1], Luís Moreira de Sousa[1], and Simone Agostinelli[2]

[1] INESC-ID, IST, Universidade de Lisboa, Lisbon, Portugal
{jlb,luis.moreira.de.sousa}@tecnico.ulisboa.pt
[2] Sapienza – Università di Roma, Rome, Italy

The session on Tools and Demos featured four presentations, three of which are published here as regular papers. The fourth, describing an established commercial tool, is included as an extended abstract.

The demo "FEM Viewer Version 2: How Much Functionality Should Be Given to the Experts?" presents the new version of the "FEM Viewer", a web-based tool supporting the Fractal Enterprise Model (FEM). The tool now allows business experts, not only modeling specialists, to annotate and modify models using color codes representing agreed meanings (e.g., performance or ease of replacement). This controlled editing capability enables domain experts to participate directly in enterprise analysis without technical modeling skills, extending the practical usability of the tool.

The "DISME (Dynamic Information System Modeller and Executor)" is a "low-code/no-code" platform that operationalises enterprise models based on the Design and Engineering Methodology for Organisations (DEMO). It allows domain experts to model, configure, and execute organisational processes in real time, unifying modelling and implementation. DISME combines a visual modeller with a live execution engine, supports REST API integration, real-time dashboards, and has shown through case studies significant gains in development efficiency and usability.

The demo "KPI-driven Visualizations for Root Cause Analysis in Manufacturing Processes" introduces an interactive dashboard supporting process-mining-based anomaly detection. It visualises production data using scatter plots and process graphs to reveal deviations in key indicators such as lead time, malfunction duration, rejections, and OEE. Built with PM4Py, Graphviz and the Mercury Framework, the dashboard enables manufacturing professionals to detect inefficiencies and understand causes without data science expertise. Expert evaluations confirmed its clarity, usefulness, and potential applicability to other domains.

Finally, "Atlas: The Enterprise Cartography Tool" is a commercial tool by Link Consulting for maintaining live, descriptive enterprise representations. Focusing on the "as-is" and "emerging as-is" views, Atlas integrates data from transformation project pipelines to automatically compute evolving architectural states over time. It supports temporal navigation, semantic model import (BPMN, ArchiMate), and LLM-based automation of BPMN workflows. Atlas reduces manual modeling effort, ensuring continuously updated, actionable enterprise models.

Contents

Forum

Tool Presentations

Journal-first Papers

Forum

Designing an Observable Human-Centric Agentic AI System Architecture for Decision-Making

Asif Qumer Gill(✉) and Yanjun Zhang

Faculty of Engineering and IT, School of Computer Science, University of Technology Sydney, Sydney, NSW 2007, Australia
asif.gill@uts.edu.au

Abstract. Human decision-making is an arduous activity requiring the complex processing of data, information, knowledge and rules for given context and constraints when choosing between two or more options. AI systems claim to provide capabilities for automating and improving human decision-making. However, AI systems and decision-automation often suffered from explainability and trust issues requiring resilience and observability by design. The challenge is: how to do so? This paper proposes the observable human-centric Agentic Neuro-symbolic (ANS) AI system architecture pattern to address this challenge. ANS AI pattern is organized into five layers: human, ANS AI system, environment, resilience and observability. Human layer interacts with the ANS AI system layer for AI powered decision-making. Based on trimodal thinking, ANS AI system contains integrated three types of AI components: intuitive, rational, and control components. ANS AI system influences or is influenced by the environment layer. Finally, resilience and observability layers are integrated into the architecture pattern for enhancing the explainability and trustworthiness of AI powered decision-making. It is anticipated that the proposed ANS AI system architecture pattern and underpinning modelling elements seem useful to support explainable and trustworthy AI powered decision-making.

Keywords: AI system architecture · Agentic AI · Neuro-symbolic AI · Decision-making · Observability · Resilience

1 Introduction

Humans exhibit several types of behaviors such as conducting business, processing information, making decisions, and engaging in different personal social and professional activities [7]. Software systems have been developed and evolved over time to support human needs. Most recently, there is a significant interest in using AI systems for augmenting human needs [22, 23]. Human decision-making is one of the needs or behaviors that can be automated and augmented by AI systems. Human decision-making can be described as a complex cognitive process that deals with uncertain circumstances when selecting a particular option from two or more options or alternatives [12]. This

J. Barateiro et al. (Eds.): EDOC 2025 Workshops, LNBIP 571, pp. 3–17, 2026.
https://doi.org/10.1007/978-3-032-16234-2_1

decision could be a high-level strategic, mid-level tactical or a low-level operational decision [8]. For instance, (1) strategic decisions could be around setting up a new insurance business or investing in a certain business area or technology, (2) tactical decisions could be around the on-going management of a certain business area, projects or team, and (3) operational decisions could be around on-going execution of business operations or processes such as on-boarding insurance customers, processing and paying their claims. Thus, humans, whether as individuals or as a part of an organization or group, need to make decisions [18]. While decision-making is a permanent and on-going feature of our life and work. However, making quality decisions is not an easy task. It requires complex processing of data, information, knowledge and rules for given context and constraints [17]. Further, human decision-making may experience the challenges of judgements, biases, errors and noise that can compromise the quality of decisions and resultant outcomes [10, 19].

There are a range of decision support systems (DSS) that have been used to support human decision-making needs such as business intelligence and reporting systems, enterprise information systems, expert systems and knowledge-based systems. Most recently, there is a significant interest in the AI-based DSS to meet contemporary human decision-making needs for complex scenarios [20]. AI system is "a machine-based system that, for explicit or implicit objectives, infers, from the input it receives, how to generate outputs such as predictions, content, recommendations, or decisions that can influence physical or virtual environments. Different AI systems vary in their levels of autonomy and adaptiveness after deployment" [9]. As per definition, AI systems claim to provide capabilities for automating and improving human decision-making. While AI systems seem useful, however, they also suffer from explainability and trust issues [29]. Lack of trust or over trust may harm the believability of decisions made or assisted by AI systems. AI systems are complex in nature thus it is not easy to explain their design and inner working or logic used for decision-making. Lack of explainability leads to trust issues. This draws our attention to the following overarching challenge:

Research Question. How can we design an observable human-centric AI system architecture to support explainable and trustworthy AI powered decision-making?

Theoretical Foundation and Key Contribution. To address the above-mentioned research question, based on trimodal thinking for architecting human-centric AI systems (intuitive, rational, and control components) [30], this paper proposes the integrated Agentic Neuro-symbolic (ANS) AI system architecture pattern with embedded resilience and observability for enhancing explainability and trustworthiness. Most recently, there is a significant interest in (1) Agentic AI [15], (2) Neural AI and its integration with (3) Symbolic AI (Neuro-symbolic AI) [4] for architecting and engineering the AI systems. For instance, Agentic AI refers to the use of intelligent or AI agents for decision automation. AI agents can plan and orchestrate other agents (control), can invoke different AI models for supporting decision-making needs such as Neural AI (intuitive) and Symbolic AI (rational) models. The complex inner working of the Neural AI models (e.g. deep learning, Generative AI) can be interpreted, analyzed and explained by using the human readable Symbolic AI models (e.g. knowledge representation, reasoning, rules). While the ANS approach provides the internal configuration of the AI systems. However, the central subject of interest is the "human" and "decision-making". Based on the adaptive

EA [7, 8], the proposed ANS AI system architecture pattern included the human layer with a view to understanding and explaining humans and their interactions with the AI system layer (e.g. Human-AI partnership). Furthermore, it also includes the environment layer. AI agents interact with each other and their dynamic operating environment. This environment provides the context and data for decision-making. ANS AI system inner working and decision-making needs to demonstrate trustworthiness (e.g. accountability, fairness, transparency, ethics, privacy, security, proof). Further, ANS AI system needs to be resilient in response to attacks by adversaries (e.g. data poisoning, model poisoning, model stealing etc.). Hence, resilience and observability need to be designed in the ANS AI system architecture for enhancing trustworthiness. Thus, resilience and observability layers have been added to the ANS AI system architecture pattern to support the overall explainable and trustworthy AI powered decision-making. Given this paper focuses on "observability" modelling in human-centric ANS AI system, thus, it also proposes the E2C4 model. The E2C4 model extends the well-known C4 model [31] to provide the modeling of observability elements (events, logs, metrics, profiles, spans and traces). Modelling notation is beyond the scope of this paper. However, it is worth mentioning here that the agile system development lifecycle (SDLC) can be used for developing and deploying the ANS AI system architecture pattern for decision automation including post-deployment AI system adaptation as noted in [8].

This paper is organized as follows. Firstly, it discusses the research problem and scope. Secondly, it discusses the ANS AI system architecture pattern. Thirdly, it discusses the observability and example scenario to demonstrate the application of the proposed pattern. Finally, it concludes with key insights and future research directions.

2 Research Problem and Scope

Beyond traditional DSS or rule-based expert systems [17], machine learning techniques enabled data-driven decision-making. Most recently, AI and large language models (LLMs), such as OpenAI's GPT series and Google's Gemini, which utilize vast amounts of textual data and sophisticated architectures to perform complex cognitive tasks. LLMs excel in natural language understanding and generation, making them suitable for a wide range of decision-making applications, from customer service chatbots to strategic business analysis across a variety of areas such as healthcare, finance, legal and business operations [22]. The increasing reliance on LLMs for automating or augmenting decision-making has led to significant advancements in capability but also introduced substantial concerns regarding observability and trustworthiness. These concerns arise from intrinsic limitations in the decision-making behavior of AI/LLM, which often operate as "black boxes" whose internal logic is not often transparent to developers, users, or auditors [9, 29]. Observability is critical to establish trustworthiness via understanding and validating the internal state of an AI system for decision-making. Three primary challenges undermine the ability to observe and explain AI-driven decision-making processes (Table 1):

- **Non-determinism in AI decision-making.** LLMs generate outputs using stochastic sampling methods, leading to non-deterministic behavior. Identical inputs may yield different results at different times, making it difficult to reproduce, trace, or justify decisions in critical domains. This inherent variability complicates validation, reducing stakeholders' confidence in AI-assisted decisions [5].

- **Context sensitivity of system behavior**. The behavior of LLMs is highly context-sensitive, shaped not only by the immediate prompt but also by preceding interactions and embedded conversational history. Minor variations in phrasing or timing can significantly influence decision outcomes. This creates challenges for observability because the underlying context that drives decision changes is often implicit and hard to reconstruct post hoc [14, 28].
- **Dynamic evolution of models**. Modern LLM models are not static. They evolve dynamically based on runtime evaluations, human feedback, and continuous learning loops. While this adaptability enhances personalization and task efficiency, it introduces concept drift and makes long-term system behavior less predictable. The absence of mechanisms to trace these adaptations raises concerns about safety, accountability, and quality assurance over the AI lifecycle [6].

Architectural Response: The ANS AI System. To address the above challenges, this paper proposes the ANS AI System Architecture modelling pattern, which integrates Agentic AI (e.g. controlling and orchestrating purposeful, perceptive, and adaptive agents) with Neuro-symbolic AI (for combining statistical learning with symbolic reasoning). Further, to support trustworthiness into the fabric of AI-powered decision-making systems, the ANS architecture introduces dedicated resilience and observability layers that capture and structures system telemetry (e.g., events, logs, metrics, profiles, traces and spans) in a manner that supports real-time diagnostics, post-decision auditing, and lifecycle oversight. Symbolic reasoning elements enhance explainability by translating neural inferences into interpretable decision rules or knowledge graphs, while agents provide control, modularity and traceability across tasks. In this way, the ANS AI system responds holistically to the demands of transparent, accountable, and adaptable decision automation.

3 Agentic Neuro-Symbolic AI System: Architecture Pattern

ANS AI system architecture pattern is organized into five layers. The top layer highlights humans and their interactions with the ANS AI system. The core middle layer highlights the integrated ANS AI system components or elements. Bottom three layers highlight the ANS AI system environment, resilience and observability elements. Overall, the integrated ANS AI system architecture pattern has the necessary modelling components to support the explainable and trustworthy AI powered decision-making.

Human. Human users can interact with the ANS AI system via the typical user request and system response model. They can use ANS AI system prompts or client software for sending their decision queries or questions to ANS AI system agent(s). For instance, prompt frameworks such as Chain of Thoughts, Chain of Density, ReACT, RISEN, RODES or Tree-of-Thoughts [13, 28] can be tailored, implemented and used by humans for interacting with the ANS AI system agents. Human-AI interactions could be semi-automatic, automatic or autonomous in nature.

Table 1. Summary of challenges in AI-driven decision-making and architectural response.

Challenge	Description	Proposed Architectural Solution
Non-determinism in AI decision-making	LLMs use stochastic sampling, leading to non-deterministic, irreproducible outputs that reduce confidence in AI decisions	Integration of symbolic reasoning with neural networks to provide interpretable outputs and improved reproducibility
Context sensitivity of system behavior	Behavior of LLMs is heavily influenced by prior interactions and slight prompt variations, making decision outcomes unpredictable	Capture and structure system telemetry to trace decision-making context and history, enhancing transparency
Dynamic evolution of models	Models evolve at runtime with feedback and continuous learning, introducing concept drift and making long-term behavior less predictable	Introduce observability layer for real-time diagnostics and post-decision audits to track dynamic model changes

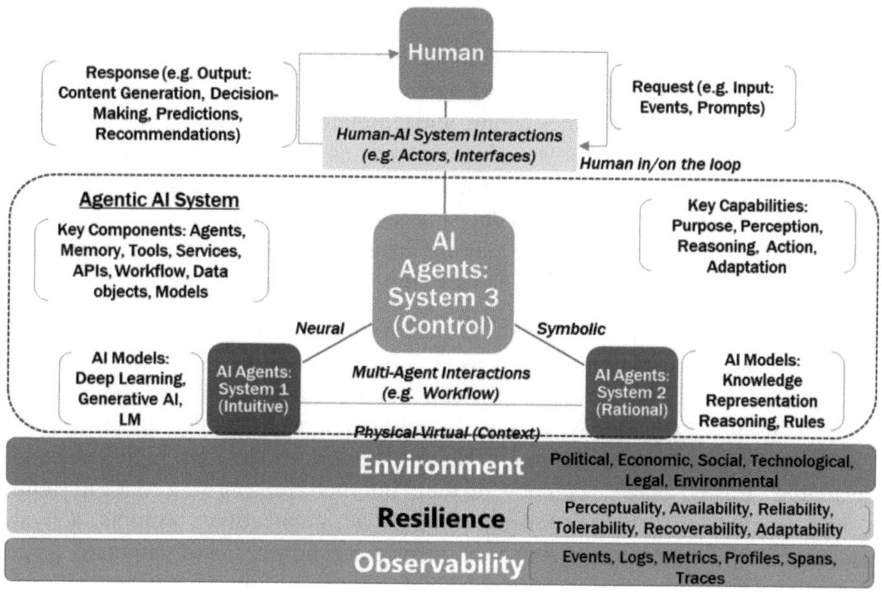

Fig. 1. Agentic Neuro-symbolic AI System Architecture Pattern.

Agentic AI System. Agentic AI is a multiagent AI system, where an AI agent has Purpose, Perception, Reasoning, Action and Adaptation capabilities [11, 15]. Contrary to traditional non-AI agents, AI powered, or intelligent agents have (1) purpose such as goals, the ability to function or act independently such as (2) perception, (3) reasoning, (4) action, and the pervasive property of (5) adaptation to achieve their purpose without intensive or constant human intervention. Hayes-Roth [11] defines the three key integrated capabilities of an intelligent or AI agent: "**Perception** of dynamic conditions in the environment; **actions** to affect conditions in the environment; and **reasoning** to interpret perceptions, solve problems, draw inferences, and determine actions".

Perception is about scanning and sensing data from the environment (input), which is pre-processed (e.g. filtering, sorting) before it is sent to the reasoning function for further analysis and interpretation (e.g. AI models). Based on the reasoning function results, actions (e.g. decision actions, control actions) are planned and executed for achieving the desired purpose and adaptations [7]. AI agent capabilities, including adaptations, can be implemented for a specific purpose by using different types of components. There are also many ways to configure and orchestrate those components for responding to human decision-making requests or queries. For instance, they can use RAG (Retrieval Augmented Generation) with LLM (Large Language Model) for planning, executing and generating intelligent responses, and Memory (e.g. short term and long term) for keeping the record of interactions and related patterns [14]. For example, based on the decision-making request query, they can use RAG to retrieve relevant information and documents from relevant repositories (e.g. knowledge base), embed the retrieved information in the user request query, and then forward it to LLM for generating responses.

AI agents can use additional components for further processing and refining the generated response as per decision requirements [8]. For instance, they can use other Agents, APIs, Services, Templates and Tools to process human requests and generate intelligent responses (e.g. decisions). AI agents can use other agents, their APIs and services for pre-processing and messaging, and templates for prompting and formulating responses. They can also use tools such as extensions for accessing the external APIs (e.g. server-side executable payment history APIs), functions (e.g. self-contained client-side modules for batch processing and decision review tasks), data stores (e.g. additional related data, files and documents for making decisions) [28]. Agentic AI can also use Neural-symbolic AI models via APIs for specific decision-making needs.

Neuro-symbolic AI. Neuro-symbolic AI possess the power of Neutral AI plus Symbolic AI for integrated Data Driven Deep Learning, Statistics, Symbolic Knowledge Representation, Reasoning and Rules for explainable and trustworthy decision-making [3–5]. For instance, Agentic AI can use specific Neural AI models to process large datasets via deep learning + statistics. Neural network models are highly dependent on available "trusted data", accuracy of their internal working (e.g. data normalization, nodes, input layer, hidden layers, output layer, connections, weights, activation functions, feed forward, backpropagation, error, learning rate), and outputs (e.g. decision, predictions). Thus, their complexity and outputs are not easy to understand by humans. Such limitations can be mitigated by integrating Neural AI with Symbolic AI models (e.g. Neural-symbolic AI). For instance, Symbolic AI models can represent neural network and domain knowledge in a human understandable symbol (e.g. semantic enterprise knowledge graphs). Knowledge can be processed via probabilistic reasoning models (e.g. Bayesian networks) and rules (e.g. Rule-based classifiers) for supporting explainable and trustworthy decision-making.

Environment. AI system is attached to the context via their environment. As noted earlier, AI agents' perception capability can scan and sense data from their environment, which is then further processed by the reasoning capability and results are forwarded to the action capability. Based on the results, action capability can make decisions, which may change the environment. Environment is characterized by Political, Economic, Social, Technological, Legal and Environment elements or factors that can influence the overall decision-making and related data and AI models.

Resilience and Observability. AI system may face several challenges such as bias, misconfiguration, data portioning, model inversion, model stealing and outages; and may also malfunction or initiate attacks such as deepfake identities, password staling, and ransomware distribution [1, 25–27]. AI system needs to be resilient by design beyond typical reactive system security, safety and privacy. It should implement proactive Perceptuality (e.g. anticipate, predict, and plan for disruptions), Availability (e.g. uptime and downtime metrics), Reliability (e.g. performance as intended), Tolerability (e.g. protection and resistance to attacks), Recoverability (e.g. response and recovery from distributions), Adaptability (e.g. corrective actions and learnings) [2, 6]. Resilience depends on the availability of the AI system data, which can be enabled by AI system observability. The focus of the paper is on the "observability" of the ANS AI system architecture pattern, which will be discussed in detail in the following section.

4 Observable ANS AI System Architecture Design

The ANS AI system should be observable and provide data and analysis to the resilience layer. ANS AI systems can use Open Telemetry [24] for capturing Events, Logs, Metrics, Profiles, Spans and Traces (Fig. 1) for explainable and trustworthy AI powered decision-making (main research question).

- **Events**: Human-AI interactions, requests and responses, changes and updates.
- **Logs**: Records of events e.g. human-AI interactions and decisions logs (ADL).
- **Metrics**: Numerical representation of logs and events for detecting different performance metrics such as decision quality, AI model and system performance.
- **Profiles**: Resource profile for supporting detailed understanding, explainability and diagnostic such as agent profiling, data proofing and model profiling.
- **Traces**: Complete trace of human-AI interaction such as request/response decision journeys across different agents, data flows and AI models.
- **Spans**: Specific operation or module execution within each trace such as stepwise operations within decision workflows.

This paper extends the C4 Model [31] based approach, adds additional two levels of E1:Ecosystem and E2: Enterprise, to decompose the "observability" details of the proposed ANS AI system architecture stack at 6 levels (E2C4) - from high to low detailed levels: (E1) Ecosystem, (E2) Enterprise, (C1) AI System, (C2) Container, (C3) Component and (C4) Code. Table 2 provides a mapping of the observable ANS AI system architecture using E2C4 Model and six observability modelling elements. Each E2C4 layer is elaborated with its observability element, telemetry types, and potential example tools, which are subject to further evaluation and research.

- **E1: Ecosystem**. Observability at the ecosystem level involves monitoring interactions between the human and AI systems operating across different enterprises and decision networks, including cross organisation agents, data inflows/outflows, decision-making, regulatory compliance checks, external APIs, and external environmental factors. Capturing events and logs across the ecosystem is critical to observing federated ecosystem agents, data sources and decisions.
- **E2: Enterprise**. Observability at the enterprise level focuses on how different AI systems are integrated within the enterprise systems, processes, decision workflows, and governance structures. It includes audit logs of data, decision-making workflows, performance metrics (e.g., SLAs), usage telemetry, and user access audits for accountability and traceability across business units within an enterprise.
- **C1: AI Software System (Context)**. Observability at the individual AI software system entails collecting structured telemetry about events, logs, performance metrics (response times, error rates), data and decision-making traces at the integrated AI software system level.
- **C2: Container**. Observability at the individual container level involves collecting and analyzing data about applications, data and model server of an AI systems—e.g., multiagent application container, database container such as the vector database and graph database, and AI model container.
- **C3: Component**. Observability at the individual component level involves collecting and analyzing data about individual agents, memory, tools, services, APIs, workflows, data objects, AI models (e.g., LLM, Knowledge Graph reasoners). For instance, Neuro-symbolic model artifacts like LLM and decision tree inputs and outputs are observed and logged at this level.
- **C4: Code**. Observability at the code-level captures function-level traces, debug logs, execution spans, and performance profiles. Code coverage reports, unit/integration test logs, and continuous integration telemetry are also captured. Ensures traceability and quick diagnosis of failures down to the source code and library.

Table 2. E2C4 model and observability elements.

E2C4	Observability	Telemetry Types for Observability	Example Tools
Ecosystem	Events	Federated ecosystem data and decision flows, third-party API and tools interactions, model interactions, federated user consents and query submissions	OpenTelemetry, EventBridge
	Logs	Federated ecosystem user, agent application, data, model and decision logs e.g. access attempts from external systems, federated decision logs, explainability provenance logs, robustness evaluation logs, consent and privacy logs	ELK Stack, Loki

(*continued*)

Table 2. (*continued*)

E2C4	Observability	Telemetry Types for Observability	Example Tools
	Metrics	Federated ecosystem performance metrics such as latency, response time, and availability of external services	Prometheus, Grafana
	Profiles	Federated ecosystem resource profiling such as multi-agency agents, data sources and models for detailed analysis	Py-spy, pprof
	Traces	Federated ecosystem end-to-end tracing of user input, internal and external decision chains including underpinning agents, data sources and models for explainability and evidence	Jaeger, Zipkin
	Spans	Federated ecosystem request and response spans at sub-task level across different enterprises	OpenTelemetry SDKs, Jaeger
Enterprise	Events	Internal enterprise interactions, data and decision flows including decision approval events and their annotations and robustness validation	Camunda, Zeebe
	Logs	User access logs, decision workflow execution logs, explainability audit logs, fairness and bias logs, privacy impact logs	Splunk, ELK Stack
	Metrics	Enterprise level SLA adherence, decision fairness, explainability coverage metrics, decision robustness metrics under varying operational conditions, data minimization metrics	Prometheus, Grafana
	Profiles	Enterprise resource profiling such as enterprise AI systems	Py-spy, Dynatrace
	Traces	Enterprise level tracing of decision, agents, data sources, models explainability and evidence collection	Jaeger, Zeebe
	Spans	Internal enterprise level sub-tasks within the trace across different units	OpenTelemetry, Jaeger
AI software system	Events	AI system level interactions, agent orchestration, data flows, models and decisions	Model management logs, XAI logs
	Logs	AI system events and decision logs	Structured logging pipelines

(*continued*)

Table 2. (*continued*)

E2C4	Observability	Telemetry Types for Observability	Example Tools
	Metrics	AI system performance metrics (response times, error rates), model metrics (accuracy, precision, recall, F1-score, robust accuracy), explainability fidelity scores, privacy leakage risk metrics, robustness metrics	Model performance and trustworthiness monitoring
	Profiles	AI system resource profiling and configuration across integrated applications, data and models	AI model profilers, XAI profilers
	Traces	AI system level request and response tracing such as agentic orchestration and communication	Model and orchestration trace instrumentation
	Spans	AI system and sub-system level tasks such as reasoning steps, agentic orchestration decision points	OpenTelemetry spans with XAI/Robustness
Container	Events	Containers such as individual agentic application and data lifecycle events, model serving instances with explainability components	Kubernetes, FluentBit
	Logs	Individual application, data and model logs, XAI components	Fluentd, Loki
	Metrics	Container level performance metrics for serving explainability and robustness modules	Prometheus, Grafana
	Profiles	Container resource profiling including explainability generation loads, robustness test resource consumption	cAdvisor, Py-spy
	Traces	Application, data and model communication traces including	Istio, Jaeger, Linkerd
	Spans	Inter-service spans for inference, explanation, and robustness services	OpenTelemetry SDKs
Component	Events	API calls, model inference triggers (LLM, Knowledge Graph), explanation generation triggers, robustness validation triggers, prompt tracking events, vector database interactions	Kong, MLflow

(*continued*)

Table 2. (*continued*)

E2C4	Observability	Telemetry Types for Observability	Example Tools
	Logs	Inference logs, explanation generation logs, robustness evaluation outputs, prompt tracking logs, neuro-symbolic artifact logs (Knowledge Graphs, decision trees), feature drift detection logs	Kong, ELK Stack
	Metrics	API response times, model inference throughput, explanation generation latency, robustness success rate, feature drift detection statistics	Prometheus, Grafana
	Profiles	Profiling model inference, explanation generation times, robustness evaluation profiling, feature drift monitoring overhead	Py-spy, pprof
	Traces	Input-output-explanation-robustness flows, tracing across agentic workflows including model contributions (LLM, Knowledge Graph)	Jaeger, Zipkin
	Spans	Specific application or data operations or model execution within each trace within decision workflows	OpenTelemetry SDKs
Code	Events	Code execution events, explanation function calls, robustness checks	Jaeger, Zipkin, Sentry
	Logs	Code debug logs, error records, explainability and robustness function logs	Log4j, Winston, ELK Stack
	Metrics	Code execution time, function call frequency for explanation and robustness methods	Prometheus, OpenTelemetry
	Profiles	CPU/memory profiling of algorithmic decision code explanation	Py-spy, cProfile, Perf
	Traces	Full call stack tracing including explanation and robustness logic	Jaeger, Zipkin
	Spans	Function spans for decision, explanation, and robustness evaluation	OpenTelemetry SDKs, Jaeger

5 Application

To demonstrate the practical application of the proposed observable ANS AI System Architecture, we consider a scenario in the domain of **autonomous insurance claim approval**—a decision-making process requiring explainability, robustness, and privacy assurances. In this scenario, customers submit their car damage insurance claims through an online portal. The ANS AI system autonomously processes the claims, determines the validity, and makes payout decisions with minimal human intervention. Given the high stakes involved, the system must ensure decisions are explainable, robust against adversarial manipulation (e.g., fraudulent claims), resistance to backdoor attacks, and compliant with privacy standards. A basic claim processing workflow is as follows:

1. **Request**: A customer (*human*) submits a claim through a web portal. The ANS AI system (*control agent*) captures the request and initiates the decision-making.
2. **Data retrieval and preprocessing**: The ANS AI system (*control agent*) retrieves and preprocesses customer profile, claim history, and policy data.
3. **Model invocation**: The ANS AI system selects an appropriate agent with deep neural network model (*neurol intelligence or intuitive agent)* for validating damaged car image. Based on the successful damage validation, the ANS AI system (*control agent*) invokes an appropriate agent with policy rules model (*symbolic intelligence or rational agent*) for determining the payout. The rule-based model evaluates the claim data and produces a classification (e.g., approve/reject) along with the payout amount, if applicable.
4. **Response:** The ANS AI system (*control agent*) sends the response back to the customer (*human*).

OpenTelemetry can be used to observe the events and log the events (e.g. user request, model invocation, decisions, response). Further, each claim request can be traced from request to response where intermediate operations and decisions can be captured as spans. OpenTelemetry data can be used to measure the decision quality and system performance. Customer profile, agents' profile, insurance data profile and models' profile can be captured for understating the configuration of these resources. In addition to OpenTelemetry tool, explainability tools such as Grad-CAM, SHAP, and LIME can be applied to generate interpretable explanations. Symbolic reasoning can be used to augment explanations, for instance by mapping model outputs to knowledge graph nodes representing policy rules. The system can evaluate the robustness of the decision by checking for adversarial manipulations. Robust accuracy is computed to assess whether small perturbations in input would alter the model's decision. The system can monitor activations and detect potential backdoor attacks that might misclassify maliciously crafted claims. Membership likelihood ratio can be calculated to assess whether the model is leaking sensitive training data, ensuring privacy protection. The ANS AI system can consolidate the result, explainability artifacts, robustness and privacy assessments into structured logs. The decision and an accompanying explanation can be presented to the customer via the web user interface. In case of appeal, human auditors can review the decision logs and explanations for transparency.

6 Discussion and Future Research

This paper proposed an approach to designing the observable ANS AI system architecture to support explainable and trustworthy AI powered decision-making. The application of the proposed approach is demonstrated with the help of a simple insurance claim processing example. It is anticipated that observability can be systematically embedded in the design of the ANS AI systems architecture using the E2C4 Model layers and observability elements before, during development and post deployment phases of the AI systems. Before development it can be planned and emebded in the design requirements. During development including the training and testing, it can be implemented using the proposed tools such as OpenTelemetry etc.

It is important to note there that observability can be specified at the broader ecosystem level to ensure that federated decisions and data sourced from external providers—such as third-party claim validation services—is accurately recorded and verifiable. Logs confirm data provenance and external API interactions, metrics track data ingestion volumes and service reliability, while traces and spans map the flow of data from external sources into the model pipeline. At the enterprise level, observability ensures alignment and integration with internal requirements and systems. Within the AI software system, observability captures integrated system telemetry. The AI system is made of containers and underpinning components. This can include agent or model performance metrics such as model accuracy, precision, recall, and F1 scores, along with robustness evaluations (e.g., adversarial accuracy) and privacy leakage indicators (e.g., membership inference scores). Finally, code-level observability monitors function execution paths during development, training and testing.

In summary, this paper presented the combination of the E2C4 model and observability elements to address the main research question: how to design an observable human-centric AI system architecture to support explainable and trustworthy AI powered decision-making? While this paper lays a good foundation, however, much more work is required to further understand the observability elements for different types of AI systems and underpinning models. Further research may focus on developing specific metrics for specific types of models and decision-making with desired quality outcomes. Research in modelling may introduce specific notation whether visual or mathematical to represent the observability of an ANS AI systems. Finally, research could be conducted in evaluating the observability tools outlined in this research.

7 Conclusion

This paper presented an integrated conceptual or meta observable ANS AI system architecture pattern. This conceptual pattern can be tailored, configured and detailed (logical pattern) for a specific business context and decision-making needs. For instance, it can be used for a range of decision-making cases with little to no human intervention such as autonomous customer order placement, problem resolution, notification, delivery, automatic credit approval, insurance claim approval and payout decisions etc. The proposed ANS AI system architecture pattern can be implemented by using a range of technologies. For instance, LangChain, Vector DB, LLM, Microsoft's AuthoGen and Semantic

Kernel, Salesforce Agentforce, Python, Java and OpenTelemetry can be used for implementing the various components of the proposed ANS AI system architecture pattern along observability. It is important to note here that there are several ways to slice and dice the AI system architecture. The future work will report on the implementations of the proposed pattern for different decision-making applications.

Disclosure of Interests. The authors have no competing interests to declare that are relevant to the content of this article.

References

1. Baxter, C.: Resilient architecture. ISACA J. (2024)
2. Blair, R., Wilson, B., Bangera, M.: IT Resilience — 7 tips for improving reliability, tolerability and disaster recovery. Gartner (2024)
3. Colelough, B.C., Regli, W.: Neuro-Symbolic AI in 2024: A Systematic Review (2025). arXiv: 2501.05435v1 [cs.AI]
4. Dingli, A., Farrugia, D.: Neuro-Symbolic AI: Design transparent and trustworthy systems that understand the world as you do. Packt Publishing (2023)
5. Garcez, A.D., Lamb, L.C.: Neurosymbolic AI: the 3rd wave. Artif. Intell. Rev. **56**, 12387–12406 (2023)
6. Gill, A.Q., Chew, E.: Configuration information system architecture: Insights from applied action design research. Inf. Manage. **56**(4) (2019)
7. Gill, A.Q.: Adaptive enterprise architecture as information: Architecting intelligent enterprises. World Scientific Publishing, Singapore (2022)
8. Gill, A.Q.: Agile System Development Lifecycle for AI Systems: Decision Architecture. arXiv e-prints, pp.arXiv-2501 (2025)
9. Grobelnik, M., Perset, K., Russell, S.: What is AI? Can you make a clear distinction between AI and non-AI systems? OECD (2024)
10. Hastie, R., Dawes, R.M.: Rational Choice in an Uncertain World: the Psychology of Judgment and Decision Making. Sage Publications, California (2001)
11. Hayes-Roth, B.: An architecture for adaptive intelligent systems. AI, **72**, 329–365 (1995)
12. Howard, R.A., Abbas A.E.: Foundations of Decision Analysis. Pearson (2016)
13. Kremb, M.: 5 prompt frameworks to level up your prompts: RTF, RISEN, RODES, Chain of thought and Chain of density (2023). https://www.thepromptwarrior.com/p/5-prompt-frameworks-level-prompts
14. Mittal, A.: Building LLM Agents for RAG from Scratch and Beyond: A Comprehensive Guide (2024). https://www.unite.ai/building-llm-agents-for-rag-from-scratch-and-beyond-a-comprehensive-guide/
15. Purdy, M.: What Is Agentic AI, and How Will It Change Work? HBR (2024)
16. Sarker, I.H., Janicke, H., Mohsin, A., Gill, A., Maglaras, L.: Explainable AI for cybersecurity automation, intelligence and trustworthiness in digital twin: methods, taxonomy, challenges and prospects. ICT Express (2024)
17. Schoemaker, P., Russo, J.E.: A pyramid of decision approaches. Calif. Manage. Rev. **36**, 9–31 (1993)
18. Simon, H.A.: Administrative Behavior: A Study of Decision-Making Processes in Administrative Organization, The Oxford Handbook of Classics in Public Policy and Administration, second edition, New York, 1957 (1957)
19. Soll, J.B., Milkman, K.L., Payne, J.W.: A user's guide to debiasing. In: The Wiley Blackwell Handbook of Judgment and Decision Making, vol. II. Oxford: Blackwell Publishing (2015)

20. Soori, M., Jough, F.K.G., Dastres, R., Arezoo, B.: AI-Based decision support systems in industry 4.0, a review. J. Econ. Technol. (2024)
21. Sospeter, O., Finke, M., Belke, J., Dyck, F., Kürpick, C.: Use Case Catalog and Assessment for AI Applications in Intralogistics of Manufacturing Companies. Procedia CIRP, vol. 118, pp. 74–79 (2023)
22. Tarafdar, M., Beath, C.M., Ross, J.W.: Using AI to enhance business operations. MIT Sloan Manage. Rev. **60**(4) (2019)
23. Tekic, Z., Füller, J.: Managing innovation in the era of AI. Technol. Soc. **73** (2023). https://doi.org/10.1016/j.techsoc.2023.102254
24. Open Telemetry. High-quality, ubiquitous, and portable telemetry to enable effective observability (2024). https://opentelemetry.io/
25. Uptime report. 2024. Annual Outage Analysis (2024). https://uptimeinstitute.com/resources/research-and-reports/annual-outage-analysis-2024
26. Verma, S.: Securing the future: mitigating data security concerns in AI models. ISACA J. (2024)
27. White, K.: Real-Life Examples of How AI Was Used to Breach Businesses. Business Productivity, Security (2024). https://oxen.tech/blog/real-life-examples-of-how-ai-was-used-to-breach-businesses-omaha-ne/
28. Wiesinger, J., Marlow, P., Vuskovic, V.: Agents. Google (2024). https://medium.com/@penkow/summary-of-googles-ai-white-paper-agents-d5670ae495c9
29. Zerilli, J., Knott, A., Maclaurin, J., Gavaghan, C.: Transparency in algorithmic and human decision-making: is there a double standard? Philos. Technol. **32**, 661–683 (2019)
30. Gill, A.Q.: Trimodal thinking for architecting human-centric ai systems: fast, slow, and control. IEEE Trans. Technol. Soc. (2025)
31. C4 Model. The C4 model for visualising software architecture. https://c4model.com/

Enhancing Business Dashboards with Explanatory Analytics

Emiel Caron(✉) and Thi Hoang Anh Tran

Tilburg University, 5037 AB Tilburg, The Netherlands
{e.a.m.caron,t.h.a.tran}@tilburguniversity.edu

Abstract. Business dashboards are a popular tool for descriptive analytics, significantly aiding the decision-making process in business and management. This study examines the possibility of enhancing data analytics in business dashboards with AI integration. With the growth in data volume and complexity, explanatory models for automatic diagnostic analytics have been developed. We extend the explanation formalism by Daniels and Feelders (2001) by employing Generative AI to transform the explanatory analytics process from manual data aggregation to conversation analysis. The prototype, Explanatory Text Generator, handles both descriptive and diagnostic questions from users and provides human-digestible answers. It is evaluated using a cognitive walkthrough of a case study related to business accounting, demonstrating its capability to transform data figures into a comprehensible text format. This study contributes to the fields of information management and business intelligence by presenting a human-centric design combining existing explanatory models with AI. This approach bridges the gap between data analysis and decision-making, providing comprehensible explanations of data trends and anomalies.

Keywords: Business Intelligence · Generative AI · Business dashboards · Explanatory analytics · Descriptive analytics

1 Introduction

1.1 Problem Context

The growing sophistication of big data technologies, coupled with advances in machine learning, has led to increased interest in business intelligence (BI) from both industry practitioners and academic researchers [4]. Recent developments in BI and analytics are particularly notable, with a growing number of organizations incorporating features such as explanatory analytics to support and improve decision-making processes. As a result, business dashboards have gained prominence as essential tools for visually presenting key performance indicators (KPIs) and assisting managerial decision-making [15]. Explanatory analytics further support managers by automatically identifying and presenting the underlying causes of trends and anomalies. Despite their widespread use, dashboards

J. Barateiro et al. (Eds.): EDOC 2025 Workshops, LNBIP 571, pp. 18–34, 2026.
https://doi.org/10.1007/978-3-032-16234-2_2

often fall short in one critical area: the automated generation of explanations for observed data patterns [12]. This study addresses this limitation by proposing an AI-integrated approach to explanatory analytics. The goal is to simplify the communication of insights for end users and enhance the overall quality of data-driven decision-making.

1.2 Contribution

The incorporation of Artificial Intelligence (AI) into the existing explanatory analytics framework within business dashboards introduces business implications. This integration provides users with nuanced insights and contextualised explanations, enhancing intepretability of analytics results. Decision-makers can make informed choices based on a thorough understanding of the underlying data, contributing to contextually aware decision support. Furthermore, the integration of AI enhances communication by generating human-readable explanations. This improvement in communication makes it easier for stakeholders to comprehend and act upon the insights presented in business dashboards, fostering a more collaborative and informed decision-making environment.

The scientific relevance of this study lies in contributing to existing research on explanatory analytics and, more broadly, to the field of BI. While the development of data analysis systems has become increasingly transparent, these systems often remain too complex for lay users to effectively interpret and utilize [11]. This research aims to enhance explanatory analytics through the integration of AI, with the goal of achieving a more granular understanding of observed phenomena. Such increased granularity supports the interpretability of analytical outcomes and helps reveal underlying factors behind trends and results. By comparing traditional explanatory analytics with AI-enhanced approaches, this study identifies both the limitations and advantages introduced by AI integration. The central research question guiding this study is:
"How can the integration of AI techniques enhance the explanatory analytics capabilities of business dashboards to improve business decision-making?"

This paper is structured as follows: Sect. 2 provides an overview of existing studies on explanation models and technologies in explanatory analytics. Based on this, we discuss the methodology and the design Explanation Text Generator in Sect. 3. The tool is evaluated by a case study in Sect. 4, in which we compare the manual explanation with the AI-generated explanation. Section 5 provides conclusions of the study and recommendations for future research.

2 Related Work

Explanatory analytics, also referred to as explanation generation, aims to uncover the underlying causes of observed events, positioning it as a subset of diagnostic analytics. Causal explanations are particularly valuable, as they reveal the factors driving specific outcomes, thereby enhancing the relevance and interpretability of the findings [7]. *Diagnostic analytics* is a data analysis methodology focused on identifying causal relationships within datasets. By employing techniques from statistics, econometrics, and machine learning, it provides a structured framework for establishing causation—an essential component for making reliable decisions and designing effective interventions. This approach moves beyond surface-level correlations to address the deeper question of why particular patterns or outcomes occur. In a business context, diagnostic analytics plays a critical role in explaining performance outcomes and operational phenomena. It enables organizations to understand the root causes behind key metrics, thereby reducing the risk of decisions based on misleading or oversimplified interpretations of the data.

This section explores the models and technologies employed in explanatory analytics within the context of business dashboards: Explanation formalism (see Sect. 2.1) and Generative AI - GPT-4 (see Sect. 2.2).

2.1 Explanation Formalism

Explanation generation [3,6] is a structured approach to provide causal explanations for observed events in multidimensional databases. This method is particularly useful in OLAP (Online Analytical Processing) systems and business dashboards, where the goal is to diagnose and explain deviations from expected values. Typical comparisons include those with historical data and industry benchmarks. These reference values are derived through various normative models [3]. Explanations are defined as:

$$\langle a, F, r \rangle \text{ because } C^{+}, \text{ despite } C^{-}. \tag{1}$$

Here, $\langle a, F, r \rangle$ represents the event to be explained, where a is the actual value, F is the property showing deviation from the reference object r. C^{+} is the collection of contributing causes, and C^{-} is the collection of counteracting causes. In diagnostic contexts, the explanation is simplified to:

$$\delta y = q \text{ occured because } C^{+}, \text{ despite } C^{-}. \tag{2}$$

Contributing causes (C^{+}) are those driving the deviation of y, and counteracting causes (C^{-}) are those mitigating the deviation. Feelders and Daniels (2001) assert that an explanation relies upon fundamental principles that describe relationships such as causality or interdependencies among variables. These relationships can be depicted through a business model M. It represents relevant financial and operating variables. Using equations such as $y = f(\mathbf{x})$, where $\mathbf{x} = \{x_1, x_2, ..., x_n\}$. A business model M can be visualised as an explanatory graph, showing dependencies between causes. Quantitative explanations use these equations to measure the impact of one variable on another, aiding in decision-making by computing outcomes of changes in key variables. In 2, the qualitative difference between the actual value y^a and reference value y^r, has values like $q = \{low, normal, high\}$, e.g. if $y^a > y^r$ then $\delta y = \{high\}$.

A measure of influence is defined to assess the impact of the contributing as well as the counteracting causes. The *influence measure* for an individual variable is:

$$\inf(x_i, y) = f(\mathbf{x}^r_{-i}, x^a_i) - y^r. \quad (3)$$

It signifies the difference between the actual value and the normal value of y if only x_i differs from the norm, thereby adhering to the *ceteris paribus* principle. This implies that the analysis assumes that all other variables remain unchanged while x_i varies. The x_i's are regarded as the causes of y. This metric enables the operationalisation of the concepts of contributing and counteracting causes.

The *parsimonious set of causes* (C_p) includes only the most significant causes that explain an event, those exceeding a certain threshold of influence T^+. Contributing parsimonious (C_p^+) and counteracting parsimonious (C_p^-) causes require a certain influence on y to exceed a fraction T. In this fraction, T has values between 0 and 1, which are set by the analyst typically close to 1. Parsimonious causes are computed as:

$$\frac{\inf(C_p^+, y)}{\inf(C^+, y)} >= T^+. \quad (4)$$

Maximal explanation: A one-level explanation identifies the most basic causes of $\delta y = q$. Finding a comprehensive explanation that thoroughly accounts for δy involves repeatedly identifying the set of *contributing parsimonious causes (C_p^+)*. This process starts by pinpointing the contributing and counteracting causes, then selecting the simplest set among them. If a variable acts as a counteracting cause, it moves in the opposite direction of δy. Since the objective is to explain δy, counteracting causes are not investigated further. The procedure continues to elucidate all contributing parsimonious variables until no additional contributing parsimonious causes remain. In other words, only the significant causes are incorporated into the tree to ensure the explanation remains clear and robust.

2.2 Generative AI as Explanatory Model

Generative AI refers to a subset of AI that focuses on creating new data instances from existing ones. Unlike traditional AI models that are designed for specific tasks, generative AI models operate in an unsupervised or semi-supervised manner, enabling them to generate content autonomously [1]. Natural Language Processing (NLP), a subfield of AI, has witnessed significant progress with the advent of models like OpenAI's GPT (Generative Pre-trained Transformer) or Google's Gemini [9]. These models leverage large-scale pre-training on vast text corpora to generate coherent and contextually relevant text across a wide range of tasks, including language translation, summarising, and dialogue generation [2]. Generative AI can be used as an explanatory model due to its ability to analyse large volumes of tables and texts to uncover hidden patterns that might not be immediately apparent through traditional analytical methods. By leveraging techniques such as neural networks, these models can process and learn from vast datasets, identifying intricate relationships and correlations [16].

In [13], the ability of ChatGPT to generate and assess hypotheses—a process known as explanatory inference—is examined. The study introduces benchmarks to evaluate ChatGPT's performance, showing that it is proficient across domains such as science, medicine, law, and technology. ChatGPT exhibits creativity by proposing novel hypotheses and analogies, and it evaluates them effectively using criteria such as explanatory breadth, simplicity, and predictive power. Moreover, [13] discusses conceptual issues surrounding explanation, understanding, causality, meaning, and creativity, arguing that ChatGPT's emergent abilities, developed through extensive training, enable it to perform sophisticated explanatory inferences and thus extend the scope of intelligent reasoning to AI systems.

There is a concern regarding the phenomenon of "hallucination", wherein models produce content that diverges from the data distribution and creates instances that do not accurately represent reality [10]. Hallucination can occur due to various factors, including inherent biases in the training data, limitations in the model architecture, or insufficient diversity in the training samples [19].

Prompt engineering is a way to deal with hallucinations [14]. In the context of ChatGPT, a prompt is an input text that a user provides to initiate a response or reaction from the model [5]. The prompt sets the stage for the interaction, guiding the AI on what to focus on and how to respond based on the language and context it is given. The prompt signals what the user is looking for, whether it's an answer, a continuation of a text, a specific action, or a creative piece. Since the output heavily relies on the input of a prompt, it is crucial to understand the correct characteristics to achieve the desired outcome. Research by [17,18,20] point out characteristics of a good prompt, namely: clarity and specificity, length and detail, directness, bias and framing, intent, and adaptability.

AI is used in commercial solutions for querying data or diagnostic analytics. For example, in Power BI, the "Natural language Q&A"[1] feature allows users to query the data with natural language. This feature can supports wide range of questions, including: asking natural questions e.g. "Which sales has the highest revenue?", using complex aggregations e.g. "Show me median sales by product", comparing data e.g. "Show me date by total sales vs total cost", sorting results e.g. "Show me top 10 countries/regions by sales ordered by country/region code", etc. In addition, the "Decomposition Tree"[2] provides visual answers for ad-hoc diagnostic questions by users. The tree has an "AI Split" function suggesting users with the next dimension to drill down for root cause analysis.

3 Design: Explanatory Text Generator

3.1 Design Requirements

We propose an artefact, the *Explanatory Text Generator* (ETG), designed to provide textual responses to analytical questions within a dashboard environment. ETG is intended to address two primary types of questions: *descriptive*

[1] https://learn.microsoft.com/en-us/power-bi/natural-language/q-and-a-intro.

[2] https://learn.microsoft.com/en-us/power-bi/visuals/power-bi-visualization-decomposition-tree.

questions (e.g., "What happened?") and *explanatory questions* (e.g., "What factors contributed to this event?"). In this context, the terms *questions* and *queries* are used interchangeably.

To support this functionality, we define the following requirements and use cases for the artefact:

- A text input box that allows users to submit their queries.
- A classifier to distinguish between descriptive and explanatory queries.
- For *descriptive queries*, the system requires: (1) Access to the relevant database (e.g., Excel file); (2) Access to the underlying business model; (3) Integration with the OpenAI API to analyze and generate text-based answers.
- For *explanatory queries*, the system requires: (1) A mechanism to generate explanatory data; (2) A pipeline to convert the explanatory data into text using GPT-4; (3) Support for user-defined parameters when using explanation formalism (see Sect. 2.1); (4) The ability to identify parsimonious sets of contributing factors, resulting in a *maximal explanation* by excluding counteracting causes; (5) Generation of an explanation report based on the derived maximal explanation; and (6) A display component to present the generated textual output for both query types.

The artefact is implemented in Python and leverages both the explanation formalism outlined in Sect. 2.1 and the GPT-4 model to fulfill its objectives. A detailed explanation of the implementation follows in the next section.

3.2 Explanatory Text Generator Design

This section focuses on the design of the artefact. Figures 1 and 2 illustrate the artefact workflow. It starts with the Business Analyst asking a question (query) via the GUI. The question is classified by 'QueryClassifier' (descriptive or explanatory query), followed by additional data fetching and processing depending on the type of query. The final output is delivered in textual form, incorporating relevant data and explanations if needed.

ETG Workflow for a Descriptive Query: If the query qualifies as a 'Descriptive Query', it sends the query to the 'OpenAI API' to fetch an answer. Upon receiving this request, the 'OpenAI API' retrieves and analyses the necessary data from the 'Dashboard Database', generates a textual answer and returns it to the 'GUI'. The 'GUI' delivers the answer to the Business Analyst.
ETG Workflow for Explanatory Query: If the question is classified as an Explanatory Query, additional parameters are needed; the 'GUI' requests these parameters from the Business Analyst. The Business Analyst sets the parameters, and the 'GUI' sends them to the 'Explanation Formalism Algorithm'. Further explanation data is processed to compute influences and causes, generating explanatory tables which are put into text by the OpenAI API. These detailed explanations are then returned to the Business Analyst through the GUI.
ETG GUI: Each query type is supported by two dedicated modules—one handling the graphical user interface, and the other focusing on the back-end logic

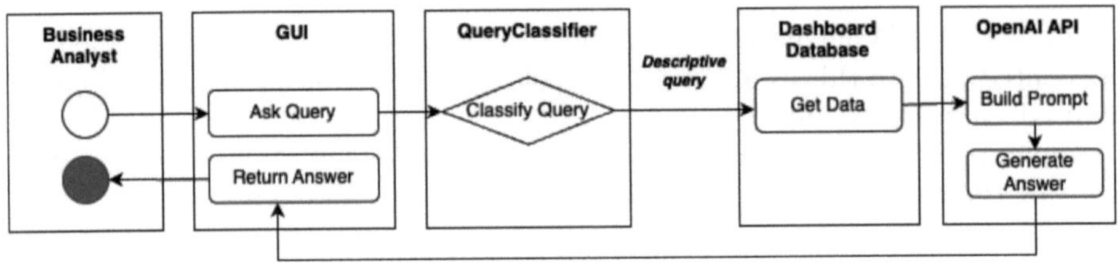

Fig. 1. UML Activity diagram for a descriptive query.

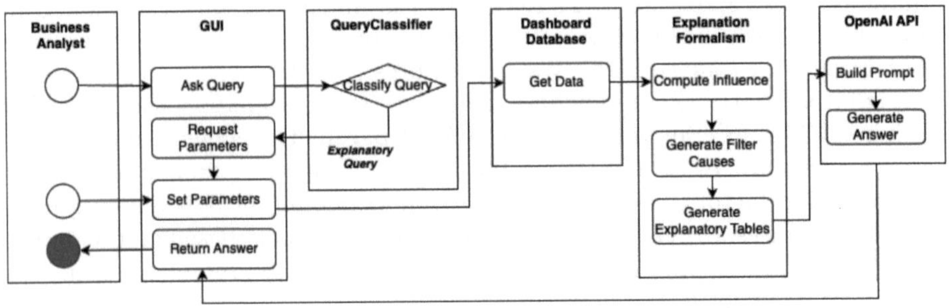

Fig. 2. UML Activity diagram for an explanatory query.

for generating responses. These modules ensure a seamless interaction between users and the system, facilitating accurate and user-friendly query responses. The Descriptive Query GUI is built using the Python package Tinker[3]. The Descriptive Query GUI is interpreted as a chatbot, where users can input descriptive queries, and the interface subsequently displays the corresponding textual answers. There is no visual GUI for the Explanatory Query. Instead, it consists of a list of selectable variables.

Prompt builder: Final explanations are generated using the black-box OpenAI API, which requires constructed prompts to ensure accurate and contextually appropriate responses. Each prompt consists of the following components:

1. *Constraints:* A fixed portion of the prompt designed to ensure consistency in generated responses and to mitigate the risk of hallucinations, as discussed in Sect. 2. For descriptive queries, the constraint focuses on scope: the model is restricted to the provided dataset and formulas, preventing data drift (see Listing 1.1). For explanatory queries, the constraint structures the output according to the explanatory table variables, i.e., translating the table into textual explanations, thereby reducing hallucinations caused by narrative drift. This approach is reflected in the prompt template shown in Listing 1.2.
2. *Query:* The question posed by the user (e.g., a business analyst), which drives the interaction with the system. This can take the form of either a descriptive or explanatory query, depending on the user's objectives.

[3] https://docs.python.org/3/library/tkinter.html.

3. *Dashboard data:* The relevant information displayed on the dashboard that serves as the basis for the user's inquiry.
4. *Business model equations:* The formal equations underpinning the business logic. These are essential for contextualizing dashboard data and supporting accurate interpretation. Examples of such equations are presented in Sect. 4.
5. *Explanatory tables:* These tables include computed influence values and parsimonious sets for each business variable (see Table 2). They are essential for generating responses to explanatory queries. The explanatory tables are produced using the explanation formalism algorithm illustrated in Fig. 2. This algorithm enables users to define parameters such as dimensionality, filtering thresholds, and the direction of change, allowing for customized output tailored to specific scenarios. Such flexibility helps users explore alternative explanations and gain deeper insights.

Listing 1.1. Extracted source code of promt for descriptive queries

```
analysis_prompt = f"You are given the following data. Use only the provided data and the
    formulas, it is important to give only the information that is asked to keep the answer
     as short as possible, e.g. when the factors for ROA are asked only return PM and TA
    and not anything more!!. :\n{data_prompt}\n\n{self.formulas}"
```

Listing 1.2. Extracted source code of promt for explanatory queries

```
"content": f"""Explain, without mentioning the table or measure of influence, why the
    variable is high or low by indicating the contributing and counteracting factors from
    the table. Note that the first variable is the selected variable and that all other
    tables when referring to contributing or counteracting refer to the influence on the
    selected variable. When generating the explanation please use one! paragraph per
    explained variable and put that as a header in bold above it. Everytime you mention
    another variable in the text you make them italic. This is all the information that is
    required. This is the table:\n\n{report}\n\nExplanation:"""}
```

The sequence in which the prompt is constructed is critical. Providing context—through constraints, the query, dashboard data, and business model equations—prior to presenting explanatory tables ensures that the model processes the task instructions before analyzing detailed data. This ordering enhances the coherence and relevance of the responses.

4 Evaluation

4.1 Case Study: Business Accounting

A case study related to business accounting is used to evaluate the ETG design. This case study originates from the book "Interfirm Comparison" [8], involving a comparison of nine firms in the mechanical engineering industry. The case study shows how management can use interfirm comparison in a business dashboard to diagnose the strengths and weaknesses of its business. The dataset in Table 5 and business equations from 5 - 16 were reused in the study [6] to illustrate the explanation formalism method. These equations describe both quantitative and qualitative relationships between variables in the dataset, describing the business model M (see Sect. 2.1).

$$\text{ROA} = \text{PM} \times \text{TA} \tag{5}$$
$$\text{PM} = 1 - (\text{AC} + \text{PC} + \text{RDC} + \text{DMC}) \tag{6}$$
$$\text{TA} = \frac{1}{\text{OA}} \tag{7}$$
$$\text{OA} = \text{CA} + \text{FA} \tag{8}$$
$$\text{PC} = \text{MC} + \text{WLC} + \text{WS} + \text{OPC} \tag{9}$$
$$\text{CA} = \text{FGS} + \text{DEB} + \text{MS} + \text{WIP} \tag{10}$$
$$\text{FA} = \text{LB} + \text{PAM} + \text{OFA} \tag{11}$$
$$\text{WIP} \leftarrow \{\text{SPP} : \text{neg}\} \tag{12}$$
$$\text{MC} \leftarrow \{(\text{MU} : \text{pos}), (\text{BC} : \text{pos})\} \tag{13}$$
$$\text{DMC} \leftarrow \{(\text{SPP} : \text{pos}), (\text{EX} : \text{pos})\} \tag{14}$$
$$\text{FGS} \leftarrow \{(\text{SPP} : \text{pos})\} \tag{15}$$
$$\text{DEB} \leftarrow \{(\text{EX} : \text{pos})\} \tag{16}$$

The explanation formalism is used in the ETG workflow (see Fig. 2) to generate the explanatory tables. Here, maximal explanation (see 2.1) starts by computing the influence of variables on the top variable Return on Assets (ROA) variable in M for a firm, considering δROA is relatively "high" or "low" compared to the industry average. The ETG prototype is evaluated based on two types of queries: descriptive query and explanatory query.

4.2 Descriptive Query Evaluation

For the descriptive query, three type of questions are used: involving value query (Q1), comparison query (Q2), and computation query (Q3), as shown Table 1 (Column 1). These questions aim to provide factual information about a specific subject or dataset related to the business model. It typically involves summarising or describing variable characteristics, such as averages or distributions, without delving into deeper reasons or causes behind the data. The questions were entered into the chatbot (Descriptive Query GUI module). Subsequently, the chatbot provided answers, as shown in Fig. 3a. ETG provides the same answers as the expectation (Column 3) and additional context by explicitly stating that the value represents the industry average ROA (Q3).

Table 1 shows the comparison between Descriptive Query ETG answers and pre-defined answers for the test queries. Descriptive Query ETG effectively answers descriptive queries and provides additional context. As demonstrated in Fig. 3a, it can also address more complex, i.e. explanatory, queries such as identifying the factors that contribute to the ROA.

4.3 Explanatory Query Evaluation

We evaluate the Explanation Query by comparing the text answer generated by ETG using OpenAI API, as in Fig. 2 and the visualisation explanation, i.e.

Table 1. Evaluation ETG – Descriptive Query

Question	Pre-defined answer	ETG answer
Q1: *What is the ROA of firm 1?*	0.251	ROA of firm 1 is 0.251.
Q2: *Which firm has the highest ROA?*	Firm 1 (ROA = 0.251)	Firm 1 has the highest ROA (0.251).
Q3: *What is the average ROA in the data set?*	0.137	The average industry ROA is 0.137.

Explanatory Tree as in [6]. Both ETG and Explanatory Tree require similar inputs for generating the final explanations, including parsimonious sets of variables, and the type of causes. Thus, the evaluation process is divided into two sub-processes: the validation of the inputs of the explanation generator and the validation of the final output. Input validation is required to ensure that ETG's explanation algorithm generates the same results as the manual calculation [6]. These inputs are checked through (one-level) analysis on various variables and a multi-level analysis on variable ROA. Next, the explanation report generated by ETG is compared to the explanatory tree to see if it contains the correct information. The remaining section presents detailed evaluation results.

Multi-level (max) analysis: Here we provide an answer to the explanatory business question: "*Why is firm 2's return on operating assets (ROA) relatively high, compared to the industry average?*" by means of maximal (multi-level) explanation. The event to be explained is $\langle$firm 2, δROA = 'high', industry average$\rangle$ (see Eq. 1) with threshold $T^+ = T^- = 0.85$ (see Eq. 4). The example below is a walk-through of the calculation. We compare the result with the explanation formalism and the explanatory tables for ETG. Computation starts with Table 2, and contributing parsimonious variables are further investigated in Table 3, Table 4, and related equations in M. The final conclusion was the same as the explanatory table generated by the module, as shown in Fig. 3b.

Table 2. Data for explanation of δROA = $\{high\}$, $T^+ = T^- = 0.85$ (1/3)

Firm 2	Ind. avg	Actual	Inf	**Causes**
ROA	0.137	0.239		
PM	0.12	0.199	$0.199 \times 1.14 - 0.137 = 0.089$	C_p^+
TA	1.14	1.2	$0.12 \times 1.2 - 0.137 = 0.007$	C^+

In Table 2 comparison is made between the ROA of firm 2 and the norm value (industry average). From the data it follows that C^+ = {PM,TA}, and C_p^+ ={PM}, since only PM is needed to explain the desired fraction of inf(C^+, ROA). Evidently, $C_p^- = \emptyset$, so only PM, the contributing parsimonious cause, is investigated further. The model does not mention that the Turnover of Assets (TA) is below average. The reason is that its contribution to the overall contributing influence (inf(C^+,ROA) = 0.007) on ROA is negligible.

Table 3. Data for explanation of δPM = $\{high\}$, $T^+ = T^- = 0.85$ (2/3)

Firm 2	Ind. avg	Actual	Inf	Causes
PM	0.12	0.199		
AC	0.079	0.04	$1-(0.04+0.722+0.007+0.072)-0.12=0.039$	C_p^+
PC	0.722	0.635	$1-(0.079+0.635+0.007+0.072)-0.12=0.087$	C_p^+
RDC	0.007	0.01	$1-(0.079+0.722+0.01+0.072)-0.12=-0.003$	C^-
DMC	0.072	0.116	$1-(0.079+0.722+0.007+0.116)-0.12=-0.044$	C_p^-

Analogous to the previous example, the event to be explained is given by $\langle$firm 2, δPM = 'high', industry average$\rangle$. PM is computed by Eq. 6 and the explanation computation is shown in Table 3. The table provides the model results for the explanation of firm 2's relatively high profit margin. From the data in the table it follows that C_p^+ ={AC, PC} since both AC and PC contributed to the difference between norm and actual value, and both are needed to explain the desired fraction of inf(C^+, PM). The explanatory model also mentions counteracting influences, by indicating distribution and marketing costs are relatively high by C_p^- ={DMC}. Research and development costs are filtered out because its contribution to the overall counteracting influence is insignificant. Among the parsimonious causes, only PC is further investigated as it is supported by eq. 9. DMC is a counteracting cause and, therefore, is not investigated further.

Table 4. Data for explanation of δPC = $\{low\}$, $T^+ = T^- = 0.85$ (3/3)

Firm 2	Ind. avg	Actual	Inf	Causes
PC	0.722	0.635		
MC	0.333	0.287	$(0.287+0.234+0.027+0.127)-0.722=0.047$	C_p^+
WLC	0.234	0.221	$(0.333+0.221+0.027+0.127)-0.722=0.014$	C_p^+
WS	0.027	0	$(0.333+0.234+0+0.127)-0.722=0.028$	C_p^+
OPC	0.127	0.127	$(0.333+0.234+0.027+0.127)-0.722=0.001$	C^+

The explanation computation for $\langle$firm 2, δPC = 'low', industry average$\rangle$ is depicted in Table 4. From the data in the table it follows that C_p^+ ={MC, WLC,

WS}, since this combination of variables is necessary to explain the selected fraction T^+. OPC is filtered out of the explanation as its influence is marginal. So, the lower costs on average for production costs are explained by lower costs on average for materials, works labour, and work sub-contracted.

The material costs (MC) are further investigated with event ⟨firm 2, δMC = 'low', industry average⟩, since it is the only contributing parsimonious cause that has an equation (see Eq. 13). The qualitative equation says that a firm whose costs of bought-out components is high in relation to its total material cost, will have a high MC ratio, and that this ratio is also affected by the costs of the metals used.

- For MU, the firm's actual value is lower than the industry average (1 vs. 1.44), thus, it is a contributing variable for a low MC, i.e. C_p^+ ={MU}.
- For BC, the firm's actual value is (slightly) higher than the industry average (0.39 vs. 0.38), thus, BC is a counteracting variable, i.e. C_p^- ={BC}.

The previous examples of one-level explanations in Firm 2 are now joined together to form a full explanation in Fig. 4a, where dashed lines indicate counteracting causes. This figure shows the maximal explanation for δROA = $\{high\}$. The explanation tree is an answer to the business question in the dashboard.

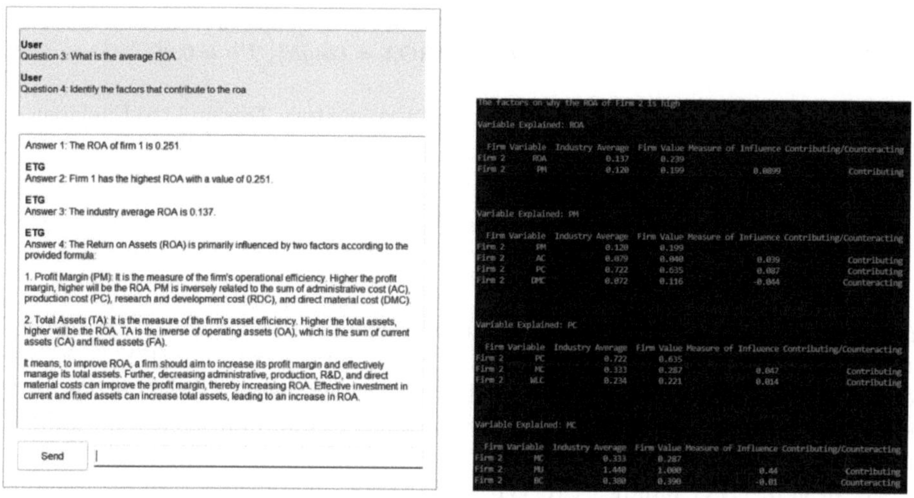

(a) Interface Descriptive Query

(b) Explanatory table for firm 2, δROA = $\{high\}$, $T^+ = 0.85$ generated by ETG

Fig. 3. Output of ETG: (a) GUI Descriptive Query and (b) Explanatory table.

Evaluating explanatory outputs:

ETG's final output is a textual explanation, i.e. an explanation report, where the explanation tree is converted by a prompt to a full-text representation. Again we generate outputs for the event ⟨firm 2, δROA = 'high', industry average⟩. The explanatory text depicted in Fig. 4b shows the explanation generated by the ETG, based on (part of) the input data for explanation as shown in Fig 3b.

The outputs were assessed by simply verifying if the variables identified in the tree were also present in the text and whether the same contributing and counteracting variables were recognised. As can be seen from the two figures, the textual explanation consistently identifies the same variables, including significant contributing and counteracting factors.

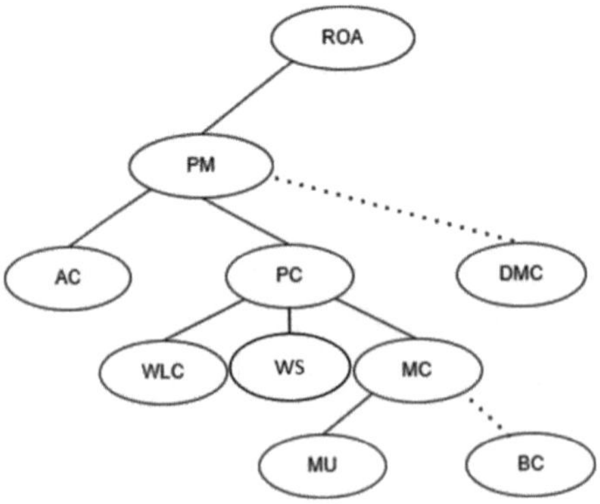

(a) Explanatory Tree: Firm 2, δROA = $\{high\}$, $T^{+} = 0.85$, using method by [6]

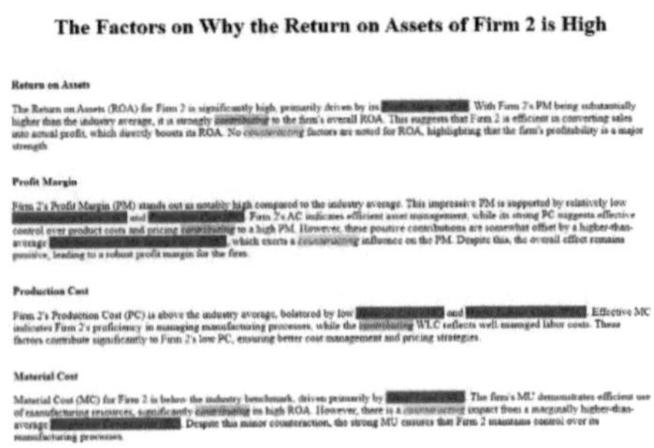

The Factors on Why the Return on Assets of Firm 2 is High

Return on Assets

The Return on Assets (ROA) for Firm 2 is significantly high, primarily driven by its [redacted]. With Firm 2's PM being substantially higher than the industry average, it is strongly contributing to the firm's overall ROA. This suggests that Firm 2 is efficient in converting sales into actual profit, which directly boosts its ROA. No counteracting factors are noted for ROA, highlighting that the firm's profitability is a major strength.

Profit Margin

Firm 2's Profit Margin (PM) stands out as notably high compared to the industry average. This impressive PM is supported by relatively low [redacted] and [redacted]. Firm 2's AC indicates efficient asset management, while its strong PC suggests effective control over product costs and pricing contributing to a high PM. However, these positive contributions are somewhat offset by a higher-than-average [redacted], which exerts a counteracting influence on the PM. Despite this, the overall effect remains positive, leading to a robust profit margin for the firm.

Production Cost

Firm 2's Production Cost (PC) is above the industry average, bolstered by low [redacted] and [redacted]. Effective MC indicates Firm 2's proficiency in managing manufacturing processes, while the contributing WLC reflects well managed labor costs. These factors contribute significantly to Firm 2's low PC, ensuring better cost management and pricing strategies.

Material Cost

Material Cost (MC) for Firm 2 is below the industry benchmark, driven primarily by [redacted]. The firm's MU demonstrates efficient use of manufacturing resources, significantly contributing to high ROA. However, there is a counteracting impact from a marginally higher-than-average [redacted]. Despite this minor counteraction, the strong MU ensures that Firm 2 maintains control over its manufacturing processes.

(b) ETG Explanatory Report: Firm 2, δROA = $\{high\}$, $T^{+} = 0.85$

Fig. 4. Comparison of explanatory outputs: (a) Explanatory Tree and (b) Explanatory Report (ETG).

4.4 Discussion of Findings

In this study, we combined the explanation formalism (see Sect. 2.1) with Generative AI (GPT-4) to build an explanatory analytic prototype (ETG). In this prototype, the explanation model was chosen because the input and output could be closely monitored, and GPT-4 plays the role of communicating the explanation to final users.

By design, ETG handles two types of queries, descriptive and explanatory queries. The nature of ETG is a prompt builder, thus, prompt quality determines the quality of the answer. Key components of the prompt include the context of the query, the specific details required, and the intended use of the information. The prototype shows constraints in prompt template to reduce hallucination.

ETG's Descriptive Query GUI is useful for business users (i.e. who are familiar with the business model) to quickly get the statistics of the interested KPI without manually calculating or querying the dashboard. Thanks to the business models in the prompt context, the API can handle simple diagnosis questions by reasoning based on the business model. Diagnosis analytics at a deeper level leverages ETG's Explanatory Query pipeline. We built the prototype separately from the descriptive GUI above. The walk-through case study in Sect. 4.3 confirms the consistency between model-generated results and manual calculation. Again, the consistency in the results is attributed to prompt construction with valid explanatory tables, context data and constraints in the right sequence.

The ETG's textual explanatory output offers comprehensive, clear, and nuanced information with detailed context for each factor. However, this text-heavy format can be time-consuming to read and potentially overwhelming for dashboard users seeking quick insights.

Explanatory trees offer advantages as visual explanations in dashboards: they clearly show relationships between factors, provide quick insights into contributing and counteracting elements, and can be made interactive. However, they also have limitations: they may lack depth, require familiarity with the format and business context to interpret correctly, and can present counterintuitive interactions between factors.

Thus, the choice between an explanation tree and explanatory text depends on the specific needs and preferences of the users. An explanation tree is ideal for quick insights and visual learners, while explanatory text is more suitable for those who require detailed, contextual information. Combining both can offer a balanced approach, particularly when the text is optional, to ensure quick insights and provide comprehensive information when needed. However, this approach requires careful design to maintain usability and coherence.

5 Conclusion

5.1 Limitation of the Study

The study has some limitations. The prototype does not include a classifier to determine whether a query is descriptive or explanatory. As a result, the artefact was not an integrated solution but rather comprised two separate modules. Additionally, the artefact is a prototype and has not been tested extensively in real-world business environments, limiting its applicability and scalability. The evaluations were conducted in controlled settings, which do not fully represent real-world complexities and variabilities, thus affecting the generalisability of the findings. Finally, GPT-4 was the only AI model used in this study, and no other AI models were tested, which may limit the understanding of how different models could perform under similar conditions.

5.2 Future Research

Future research should focus on several areas to enhance the current artefact. Developing a classifier to better manage the queries would improve the system's effectiveness in creating an integrated system. Expanding the system to handle qualitative relations more effectively would provide a more comprehensive analysis of business scenarios, capturing the full context and underlying causes. Conducting real-world testing is essential to validate the artefact's performance and adaptability in diverse business environments, ensuring its robustness and scalability. Additionally, the necessity of integrating textual explanations should be tested by users. It might turn out that users prefer visual explanations.

Moreover, as AI continues to evolve, and GPT shows potential in handling specific areas of expertise such as business intelligence, data analysis, or economics, it would be interesting to explore building AI models with domain-specific explanations. Such advancements could enhance the precision and relevance of AI-generated insights. This approach could lead to more effective integration of AI in the explanatory analytics domain.

In conclusion, while the current artefact shows promising results in enhancing explanatory analytics with AI, further research and development are needed to fully realise its potential in real-world applications.

5.3 Conclusion

This study examines the possibility of enhancing explanatory analytics in business dashboards with AI integration. We developed a prototype, Explanation Text Generator, using an explanation formalism in combination with Generative AI to transform the explanatory analytics process from manual data aggregation to conversations. In this design, AI can handle descriptive queries on its own, making it a versatile tool for straightforward information needs. Richer explanations require input from the explanation formalism. By integrating existing explanatory models with GPT-4, AI can generate coherent and contextually relevant textual explanations alongside visualizations. This feature is particularly beneficial for dashboard users who may lack data analysis expertise or domain-specific knowledge. It enhances the interpretability of complex data patterns, supports more informed decision-making, and helps bridge the gap between data presentation and actionable insights. The developed artefact demonstrates the potential of AI to support business decision-makers by delivering intuitive, accessible explanations in response to questions that arise during dashboard use.

Acknowledgments. The authors thank Aaro Askala and Jeroen Valkenburgh for their contributions to this work.

Disclosure of Interests. The authors have no competing interests to declare that are relevant to the content of this article.

A Appendix

Table 5. Data used for the ETG prototype, derived from [6]. The dataset includes financial variables for nine firms.

Variables	Definition	Firm 1	Firm 2	Firm 3	Firm 4	Firm 5	Firm 6	Firm 7	Firm 8	Firm 9	Avg.
ROA	Return On Assets	0.251	0.239	0.189	0.161	0.133	0.132	0.088	0.079	0.041	0.137
PM	Profit Margin	0.19	0.199	0.151	0.099	0.103	0.115	0.087	0.089	0.047	0.12
TA	Turnover of Assets	1.32	1.2	1.25	1.63	1.29	1.15	1.01	0.9	0.87	1.14
OA	Operating Assets	0.758	0.833	0.8	0.77	0.869	0.809	0.754	0.774	1.149	0.877
PC	Production Cost	0.628	0.635	0.711	0.747	0.725	0.719	0.754	0.774	0.802	0.722
RDC	Research and Development Costs	0.005	0.01	0.009	0.007	0.007	0.011	0.014	0	0.002	0.007
DMC	Distribution and Marketing Cost	0.109	0.116	0.047	0.072	0.062	0.058	0.073	0.046	0.064	0.072
AC	Administrative Costs	0.068	0.04	0.082	0.075	0.103	0.097	0.072	0.091	0.085	0.079
MC	Material Cost	0.32	0.287	0.339	0.301	0.397	0.316	0.336	0.347	0.358	0.333
WLC	Works Labour Costs	0.165	0.221	0.232	0.283	0.157	0.241	0.248	0.274	0.289	0.234
OPC	Other Production Costs	0.143	0.127	0.14	0.092	0.104	0.113	0.114	0.153	0.155	0.127
WS	Work Sub-contracted	0	0	0	0.071	0.067	0.049	0.056	0	0	0.027
CA	Utilization rate of Current assets	0.465	0.481	0.412	0.35	0.369	0.449	0.549	0.582	0.608	0.474
FA	Utilization rate of Fixed assets	0.293	0.352	0.388	0.263	0.406	0.42	0.441	0.529	0.541	0.404
MS	Materials Stock	0.08	0.11	0.081	0.079	0.068	0.092	0.1	0.101	0.082	0.088
WIP	Work In Progress	0.043	0.04	0.063	0.062	0.083	0.106	0.188	0.225	0.245	0.117
FGS	Finished Goods Stock	0.132	0.102	0.047	0.037	0.039	0.045	0.044	0.053	0.057	0.062
DEB	Debtors	0.21	0.229	0.221	0.172	0.179	0.206	0.217	0.203	0.224	0.207
LB	Land and Buildings	0.13	0.158	0.194	0.169	0.208	0.214	0.311	0.277	0.268	0.214
PAM	Plant and Machinery	0.16	0.189	0.19	0.089	0.194	0.203	0.123	0.246	0.264	0.184
OFA	Other Fixed Assets	0.003	0.005	0.004	0.005	0.004	0.003	0.007	0.006	0.009	0.005
EX	Export Sales	0.16	0.4	0.15	0	0.25	0.23	0.1	0.12	0.3	0.19
SPP	Sales/Production Policy	2	2	1	1	1	1	1	1	1	1.22
BC	Bought-out Components	0.32	0.39	0.29	0.33	0.56	0.35	0.4	0.37	0.43	0.38
MU	Metal Used	2	1	2	1	2	1	1	2	1	1.44

References

1. Brynjolfsson, E., Li, D., Raymond, L.R.: Generative ai at work. Tech. Rep. 31161, National Bureau of Economic Research (2023). https://doi.org/10.3386/w31161, https://www.nber.org/papers/w31161. Accessed 01 Apr 2025
2. Cambria, E., White, B.: Jumping NLP curves: a review of natural language processing research [review article]. IEEE Comput. Intell. Mag. **9**(2), 48–57 (2014). https://doi.org/10.1109/MCI.2014.2307227
3. Caron, E.: Explanation of Exceptional Values in Multi-dimensional Business Databases. Ph.D. thesis, Erasmus University Rotterdam (2013). http://hdl.handle.net/1765/50005. Accessed 01 Apr 2025
4. Chen, H., Chiang, R.H.L., Storey, V.C.: Business intelligence and analytics: from big data to big impact. MIS Quart. **36**(4), 1165–1188 (2012). http://www.jstor.org/stable/41703503

5. Dong, X., et al.: C3: Zero-shot text-to-sql with chatgpt (2023). https://arxiv.org/abs/2307.07306
6. Feelders, A.J., Daniels, H.A.M.: A general model for automated business diagnosis. Europ. J. Oper. Res. **130**(3), 623–637 (May 2001). https://ideas.repec.org/a/eee/ejores/v130y2001i3p623-637.html
7. Friedman, M.: Explanation and scientific understanding. J. Philos. **71**(1), 5–19 (1974). https://doi.org/10.2307/2024924
8. Ingham, H., Harrington, L.T., for Interfirm Comparison, C.: Interfirm comparison. The Heinemann accountancy and administration series, Heinemann, London (1980)
9. Kang, Y., Cai, Z., Tan, C.W., Huang, Q., H.L.: Natural language processing (nlp) in management research: a literature review. J. Manage. Anal. **7**(2), 139–172 (2020). https://doi.org/10.1080/23270012.2020.1756939
10. McIntosh, T.R., Liu, T., Susnjak, T., Watters, P., Ng, A., Halgamuge, M.N.: A culturally sensitive test to evaluate nuanced GPT hallucination. IEEE Trans. Artif. Intell. **5**(6), 2739–2751 (2024). https://doi.org/10.1109/TAI.2023.3332837
11. Montavon, G., Samek, W., Müller, K.R.: Methods for interpreting and understanding deep neural networks. Digital Signal Process. **73**, 1–15 (2018). https://doi.org/10.1016/j.dsp.2017.10.011, https://www.sciencedirect.com/science/article/pii/S1051200417302385
12. Pauliuk, S.: Critical appraisal of the circular economy standard bs 8001:2017 and a dashboard of quantitative system indicators for its implementation in organizations. Resources, Conserv. Recycl. **129**, 81–92 (2018). https://doi.org/10.1016/j.resconrec.2017.10.019, https://www.sciencedirect.com/science/article/pii/S0921344917303531
13. Thagard, P.: Can chatgpt make explanatory inferences? benchmarks for abductive reasoning. ArXiv **abs/2404.18982** (2024). https://api.semanticscholar.org/CorpusID:269457635
14. Tonmoy, S., et al.: A comprehensive survey of hallucination mitigation techniques in large language models **6**, arXiv:2401.01313 (2024)
15. Walchshofer, C., Dhanoa, V., Streit, M., Meyer, M.: Transitioning to a commercial dashboarding system: Socio-technical observations and opportunities. IEEE Trans. Visual. Comput. Graph. **30**(1), 381–391 (Jan 2024). https://doi.org/10.1109/TVCG.2023.3326525, https://doi.org/10.1109/TVCG.2023.3326525, epub 2023 Dec 25. Accessed 01 Apr 2025
16. Wang, Z., Wang, J., Wang, Y.: An intelligent diagnosis scheme based on generative adversarial learning deep neural networks and its application to planetary gearbox fault pattern recognition. Neurocomputing **310**, 213–222 (2018). https://doi.org/10.1016/j.neucom.2018.05.024, https://www.sciencedirect.com/science/article/pii/S0925231218305617
17. Wei, J., et al.: Chain-of-thought prompting elicits reasoning in large language models. In: Proceedings of the 36th International Conference on Neural Information Processing Systems. NIPS '22, Curran Associates Inc., Red Hook, NY, USA (2022)
18. White, J., et al.: A prompt pattern catalog to enhance prompt engineering with chatgpt (2023). https://arxiv.org/abs/2302.11382
19. Zhang, Y., et al.: Siren's song in the ai ocean: a survey on hallucination in large language models (2023). https://arxiv.org/abs/2309.01219
20. Zhou, D., et al.: Least-to-most prompting enables complex reasoning in large language models (2023). https://arxiv.org/abs/2205.10625

ProA: A Bottom-Up Process Architecture Approach for Automated Generation of Process Maps Based on BPMN Process Models

Philipp Hehnle[1,2(✉)], Katharina Paulick[1], and Manfred Reichert[2]

[1] envite consulting GmbH, Stuttgart, Germany
{philipp.hehnle,katharina.paulick}@envite.de
[2] Institute of Databases and Information Systems, Ulm University, Ulm, Germany
{philipp.hehnle,manfred.reichert}@uni-ulm.de

Abstract. Improving business processes separately may entail limited success with respect to the overall performance of an organisation. Interfaces (i.e. dependencies) among business processes must be investigated and improved as well. Process maps are diagrams that can be used to illustrate business processes and their dependencies. Literature recommends a top-down process architecture approach, which implies first investigating interfaces and creating process maps before modelling business processes. In practice, organisations often first model business processes and then inspect their dependencies. Consequently, in this paper, a bottom-up approach is presented, which allows automatically generating process maps by importing process models expressed in terms of the Business Process Model and Notation 2.0. A proof-of-concept tool illustrates the approach. Two case studies and expert interviews attest our approach usefulness and ease of use.

Keywords: Business Process Management · Process Map · Process Landscape · Process Overview · Process Architecture · Process Dependencies

1 Introduction

Common activities of Business Process Management (BPM), which are widely considered the BPM lifecycle, include designing process models, implementing and executing/enacting them (e.g. by policies or using a workflow management system), and analysing them in order to improve the business process during its (re-) design in another iteration [29,31]. Business processes are traditionally improved with respect to *time*, *cost*, and *quality* [26], and sometimes *ecology* [13].

Due to dependencies (e.g. required inputs form other business processes), business processes cannot always be improved individually, e.g. improving the interfaces among business processes may reduce inefficiencies and thereby reduce

J. Barateiro et al. (Eds.): EDOC 2025 Workshops, LNBIP 571, pp. 35–52, 2026.
https://doi.org/10.1007/978-3-032-16234-2_3

time, which results in an improved overall performance of an organisation [31]. Predicting the effects of a change in one business process on others is another challenge with respect to business process dependencies [30].

To organise business processes modelled on different levels of abstraction, frequently, a hierarchical structure with layers is used, with the upper layers comprising more abstract representations. This structure is referred to as *process architecture* with varying number of layers depending on the approach [11,30].

Dependencies and relations among business processes can be visualised in a diagram, which is called *process map* [15,30] or *process landscape* [23,31] and is commonly considered the most abstract representation of business processes and hence corresponds to the top layer of a process architecture. In this paper, the term *process map*[1] is used to refer to a diagram visualising business processes and their dependencies and relations.

1.1 Problem Statement

Frequently, literature advises to first investigate process dependencies and specify inputs/outputs of processes (i.e. create a process map), and then create the process models [11,31]. In practice, many times, we observed companies modelling business processes first and then trying to identify the dependencies among them, which is cumbersome and error-prone when dealing with lots of process models. When trying to get a holistic view about the business processes, the creation of a process map based on the process models is necessary. According to a literature review about process maps [12], current research lacks a systematic approach for the identification of business process relations and tool support.

1.2 Contribution

This work addresses the aforementioned challenges of systematically identifying dependencies among process models as well as tool-supported and automated creation of process maps. In line with other researchers [6,10,14], we consider BPMN 2.0 [21] being the de-facto standard for process modelling in industry. Therefore, our approach presumes the use of BPMN 2.0 process models. Our contribution is mainly twofold with a third intermediate result:

1. Pairs of elements of BPMN 2.0 process models are identified that may represent an interaction between two business processes and consequently correspond to a relation or dependency among those business processes.
2. A bottom-up approach is defined to analyse the dependencies of process models of a lower level of a process architecture and derive a process map based on the identified pairs of elements. A proof-of-concept tool for automatically generating process maps illustrates the approach.

[1] Note that the terms *process map*, *process landscape*, and *process architecture* are not used uniformly and consistently in the literature, the terms are sometimes used as synonyms, or the definitions differ. See [22] for a detailed comparison.

(3) A first draft of a new modelling notation is presented to depict the process map, as existing notations did not meet our requirements. This modelling notation can be considered an intermediate result. While the evaluation provided good results, an exhaustive study on the intuitiveness (i.e. semantic transparency, e.g. [24]) and cognitive effectiveness (e.g. [18,25]) is pending.

1.3 Outline

In Sect. 2, related work with respect to process architectures and maps is presented. The bottom-up approach for automatically generating process maps is introduced and discussed in Sect. 3. The approach is evaluated in case studies and expert interviews in Sect. 4. Section 5 concludes the paper and provides and outlook on open challenges and further research topics.

2 Related Work

This section presents related work regarding process architectures and maps.

2.1 Process Architecture

A *process architecture* is commonly understood as an approach to organise business processes on different layers (i.e. different levels of abstraction/details), whereby the top level comprises a process map illustrating an overview of the business processes with their relations and dependencies [11,30]. An example of a process architecture is presented in Fig. 1.

The process architecture in [11] consists of three layers. The top layer corresponds to the process map, which is decomposed to abstract process models in the second layer. Layer three contains detailed process models.

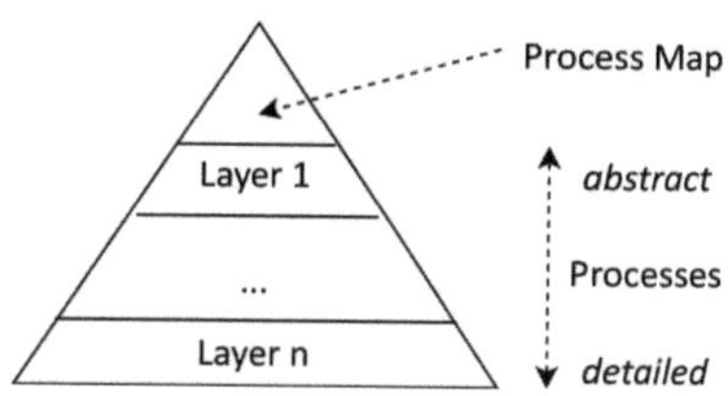

Fig. 1. Process Architecture

In contrast, the approach presented in [30] does not only decompose the process map into process models but also decomposes the process models into activities and tasks in lower layers. Furthermore, the approach proposes views that allow showing, for instance, the corresponding responsibilities or domains. The authors propose a round-tripping approach (i.e. both top-down and bottom-up), i.e. if a dependency is introduced at a lower level it needs to be propagated upwards and vice versa. However, the approach lacks systematics and tool support for automated dependency propagation among the levels.

The framework introduced in [8] proposes a process architecture including structuring principles. First, business functions (i.e. the capabilities of an organisation) are decomposed in a hierarchy. Then, business processes are structured in a matrix with respect to their business functions and objects. Although the authors do not denote the top level of the process architecture as such, it shows the characteristics of a process map (e.g. sequence relations among processes).

2.2 Process Maps

Process maps have been subject to research with respect to meta-models, languages, and quality characteristics. Figure 2 depicts an example of a process map illustrating `Support`, `Core`, and `Management` processes (i.e. categories of processes), which have sequence ordering (e.g. `Sales` process after `Development` process) and are decomposed into subprocesses (e.g. `Innovate` is a subprocess of `Development`).

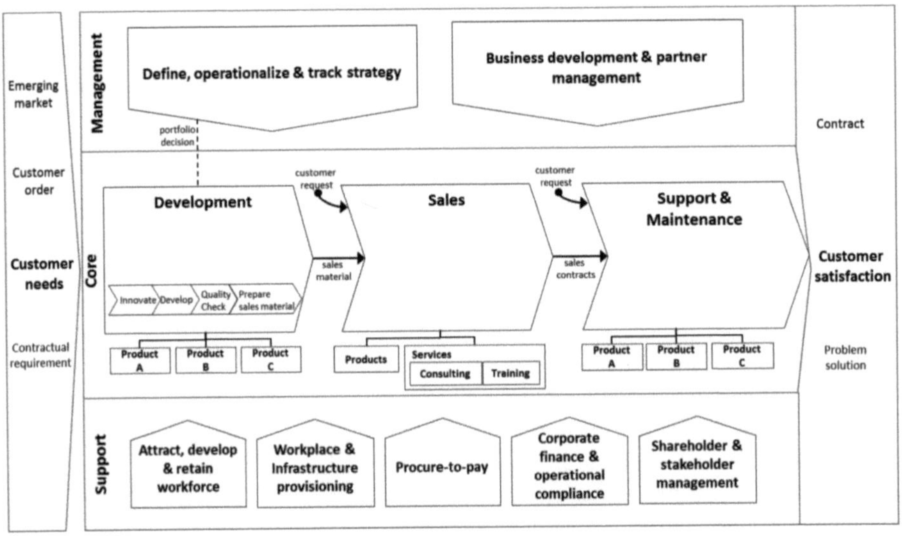

Fig. 2. Example Process Map [15].

In [16,17], a meta-model for process maps is presented, i.e. a model comprising all components that can or need to be present in a process map. These components include business processes, their relations, actors, resources, and categories (i.e. core processes creating value for the customer, support processes supporting the core processes, and management processes aligning the core processes with the company's strategy). The authors studied process maps from literature, case studies, and industry and found that these maps are modelled with varying degree of detail.

In [22], a meta-model for process maps within a process architecture is proposed, i.e. business processes are depicted as black boxes in a process map with their relations (i.e. sequence, grouping) including relations spanning several layers of abstractions (i.e. decomposition, specialisation).

The work presented in [19] uses the meta-model introduced in [16,17] for a semantic mapping and argues that for certain process map concepts there is no equivalent concept in BPMN. Therefore, [15] introduced a proprietary notation (cf. Fig. 2). In contrast, BPMN-L [23] is an extension of BPMN, which allows modelling process maps addressing the deficiencies discovered in [19].

During case studies in the public sector, crucial characteristics for a process map modelling method could be identified like a simple representation, comparable, analysable, and maintainable models [3].

Furthermore, process map languages have been evaluated with respect to their cognitive effectiveness (i.e. how fast, easy, and accurately is the notation understood). Most process maps in industry do not comply with the nine principles of cognitively effective visual notations (cf. [20]), which may result in ambiguity [18]. The results of an empirical survey indicate that a lack of semiotic clarity (i.e. similar/same visualisations represent different concepts) may impact how accurately a process map is understood [25].

Another study on the intuitiveness (i.e. semantic transparency) comparing various process map languages revealed that chevrons (i.e. arrow-shaped rectangles) are better recognised as processes in a process map than other symbols and that BPMN experts understand process maps containing elements transferred from BPMN (e.g. sequence flow and message flow) better than participants without respective experience [24].

Process Mining [27] is a method to analyse and improve processes harnessing event logs and includes bottom-up process discovery [28] as a data-driven alternative to traditional process modelling by identifying local patterns in activities. Process Mining also includes performance analysis and the identification of deviations between modelled and observed behaviour (i.e. conformance checking)[27,28]. In case studies, the interpretation of process mining results could be improved by integrating contextual factors (e.g. region of executed process) and real-time event data, and thereby business value could be created [1].

Although process mining is a bottom-up approach, it rather focuses on individual business processes. In [2], process mining is leveraged to automatically discover relations (i.e. trigger and information flow) among business processes. However, the authors acknowledge that a process mining expert might be necessary. Besides, a recent study revealed that the most cited challenges in process mining are related to event logs (i.e. quality, size, and complexity) [9].

3 Automated Generation of a Process Map

In this section, we present an approach and a proof-of-concept for automatically generating process maps. First, the requirements are elicited. Then, the approach is described satisfying the requirements. Subsequently, our proof-of-concept is introduced implementing the approach. Finally, the approach and proof-of-concept are discussed, and limitations are presented.

3.1 Requirements

During multiple projects, in which we digitalised business processes for different customers from industry and large organisations, we faced the recurring challenge of keeping track of the dependencies among the business processes. In contrast to best practices, organisations frequently start modelling and digitalising business processes independently without taking into account the dependencies. To get a better understanding of the challenge, we conducted unstructured interviews with various customers including a pharmaceutical company (>100,000 employees), two insurance companies (~5,000 employees and ~700 employees), and a software vendor for trade, customs management, and logistics (>650 employees).

In the following, we outline the starting base in the projects of our customers we encountered and their objectives.

Starting Base: The surveyed customers uniformly have a repository full of process models of which some are digitalised. To manage the dependencies, they manually create process maps often relying on Microsoft PowerPoint or Value Chains. While some of the modelling tools are able to show dependencies when the elements are manually linked, this requires substantial discipline during modelling and also knowledge about the dependencies in advance. Due to poor data quality or missing data, process mining cannot be applied.

Objectives: The customers surveyed mainly have two objectives when creating a process map. 1) They need an up-to-date process map to document the dependencies in order to predict the effects of changes to one business process on other business processes and to be able to holistically improve the overall performance of the organisation by improving process chains. As the process models evolve, the process map needs to be updated automatically. 2) The process map is supposed to reveal quality flaws in the process models, e.g. if a dependency is missing in the process map, it is likely that the corresponding process models are not modelled adequately.

Based on our observations and the unstructured interviews we conducted, the following requirements for our approach could be deduced:

- *R1:* The BPMN elements need to be identified that may constitute an interface to another business process and thereby introduce a dependency.
- *R2:* The approach needs to allow detecting dependencies among business processes based on the identified BPMN elements constituting interfaces among business processes (cf. Requirement *R1*).
- *R3:* The dependencies among the business processes need to be visualised. The types of dependencies need to be distinguished.

3.2 Approach

Relations among business processes have been investigated in literature to some extent. For instance, in [22], *sequence*, *decomposition*, *grouping*, and *specialisation* are identified as relations. Furthermore, *data flow*, *support*, and *manage* constitute relations [16,17]. However, these abstract relations have not yet been systematically and explicitly mapped to elements of BPMN.

To tackle this challenge systematically, we analysed the BPMN 2.0 notation and identified element pairs that pose an interaction and thereby create a dependency among business processes. Subsequently, we compared our findings with business processes from our customers and confirmed our conclusions.

In the following, the types of dependencies we have identified are listed :

- *D1:* Business processes may be connected via end/start event, i.e. the end (event) may be the start (event) of another business process.
- *D2:* Business processes may call other business processes (i.e. via a call activity), so that the called business process can be reused by multiple business processes.
- *D3:* Business processes may be connected via intermediate events (e.g. message/signal, throw/catch events).
- *D4:* Business processes may interact by accessing the same data (store).
- *D5:* There can be dependencies between business processes indicated by message flows between pools of which one might even be collapsed within the same BPMN file.

Examples 1, 2, 3 and 4 describe in a simplified way processes of one of our customers, which will then be used to demonstrate the approach.

Example 1. Figure 3 depicts an order process. An incoming order initiates the process, followed by activities to handle the order including a subprocess `Product Availability Check` and a message throw event `Payment necessary`.

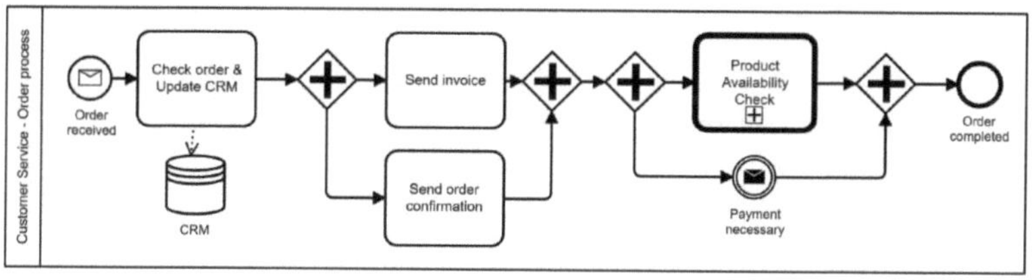

Fig. 3. order-process.bpmn

Example 2. The collaboration between the `Warehouse` and the `Supplier` is illustrated in the business process `Product Availability Check` in Fig. 4, which is either called by the parent process or instantiated on its own. If the product is not available, it is reordered from the supplier. Thus, communication with the supplier is shown, who is represented as a collapsed pool.

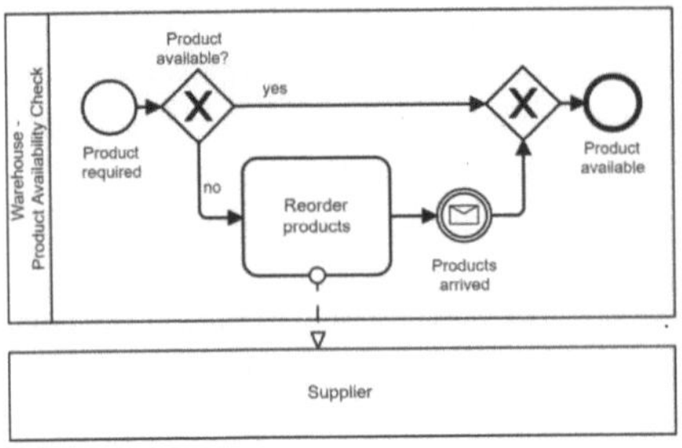

Fig. 4. availability-check-process.bpmn.

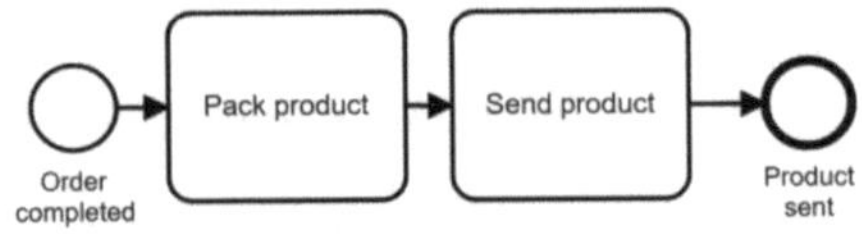

Fig. 5. shipment-process.bpmn.

Example 3. Figure 5 sketches the shipment process, which starts after the order is completed and includes the activities of packing and sending the product.

Example 4. Figure 6 imposes the invoice process carried out by the finance department. If the due date is exceeded before the payment is received, the customer gets reminded and the `Dunning Process` is started.

We deliberately embed some of the processes in pools whereas others are not contained in pools as this mix can be found in practice.

Listing 1.1. Pseudo Code for the Approach of Identifying Process Dependencies

```
var newElements = Extract elements D1–D5 from BPMN model
for(var newElement : newElements){
  if(exists(newElement.name) &&
     matchesTypeWithExistingElement(newElement) {
    create dependency
  }
}
Persist process model
Persist dependencies
```

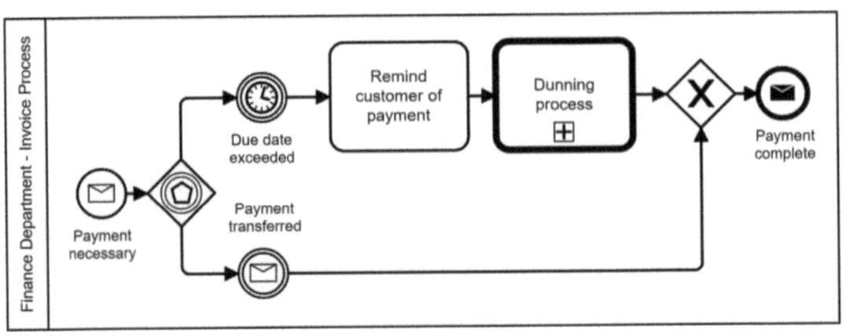

Fig. 6. invoice-process.bpmn.

Listing 1.1 illustrates the approach of identifying dependencies among business processes as pseudo code. First, all BPMN elements identified in *D1-D5* are extracted from a given BPMN process model. Subsequently, it is checked whether the labels of the elements are already known from previously analysed process models and whether the types match, i.e. whether the types of the two elements correspond to one of the identified element pairs *D1-D5*.

When applying the presented approach to the business processes described in Figs. 3, 4, 5 and 6, the following dependencies can be identified: When the `Order process` completes, the `Shipment process` starts (i.e. end/start dependency, cf. *D1*). Furthermore, during the execution of the `Order process`, the `Product Availability Check` is called as a subprocess (cf. *D2*). Besides, when reaching the event `Payment necessary`, the `Invoice process` is started (i.e. intermediate event dependency, cf. *D3*). The `Order process` accesses the CRM data store. Although not included in the examples due to limited space, another business process sending newsletters might also access the CRM data. When analysing the newsletter process it might become relevant to know where the data is captured, which can be analysed using our approach (cf. *D4*). Finally, there is a dependency within the process model `availability-check-process.bpmn`, namely the message flow between the `Warehouse` and the `Supplier` (cf. *D5*).

3.3 ProA: Proof-of-Concept

We implemented the presented approach (cf. Listing 1.1) in a proof-of-concept tool to which we refer as *ProA*[2] (short for Process Analysis). While the meta-models and notations for process maps found in literature include concepts like process categories, actors, and relations spanning multiple layers of abstraction of a process architecture (e.g. specialisation), they do not encompass all relations we identified. The abstract process relations sequence and decomposition can be mapped to end/start relation (cf. *D1*) and call/subprocess relation (cf. *D2*). However, the remaining relations we identified in BPMN cannot be mapped to concepts found in literature. Consequently, we cannot adopt a process map language from literature. Note that during the interviews with customers we found that other concepts from literature including process category and actors are not relevant in that layer of abstraction. Consequently, we omit them in our process map. Based on these observations, we created a first draft of a process map language (cf. the legend in Fig. 7 for an overview of the symbols of the language). The black-box processes are represented by chevrons, which are also used by Value Chains, BPMN-L [23], and the language introduced in [23] (cf. [25] for a comparison). The BPMN elements identified in *D1-D5* are attached to the black-box processes to act as a trigger or receiver of a dependency. Each type of element is only attached once representing all elements of that type in one business process to reduce complexity. The elements are linked by sequence flows and message flows also known from BPMN and partially adopted by the aforementioned process map languages. Consequently, widely known elements of BPMN/process maps are combined. According to [24], this will increase the likelihood that our notation will be comprehensible to experts already familiar with

[2] https://github.com/envite-consulting/ProA.

BPMN or process maps. In line with the results in [25], semiotic clarity is ensured (i.e. one symbol represents one concept) to improve cognitive effectiveness.

When importing BPMN process models to ProA, their XML content is analysed and all elements with their `name` attribute are identified and stored in a database. For entire processes contained in a pool, first the corresponding process name is checked and stored in the database. If the process name is empty, first, the participant name is checked and finally the participant ID used as name to identify a process. For each identified BPMN element, the corresponding element with the same name is searched in the database, e.g. an end event of an imported process model triggers a search for a start event with the same name in the database. If a corresponding element in another BPMN process model is found, a new dependency is stored in a separate table referencing the two process models including the two elements that constitute the dependency.

Figure 7 shows the process map generated by ProA when importing the example processes (i.e. Figs. 3, 4 and 5) reflecting the dependencies sketched at the end of Sect. 3.2.

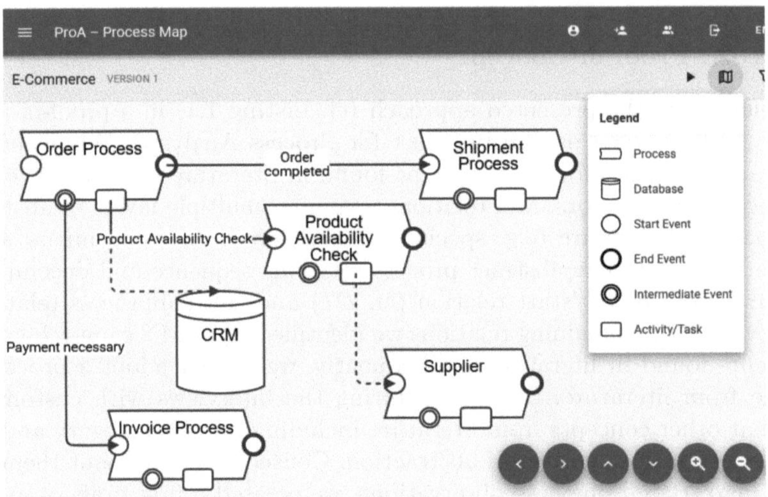

Fig. 7. Full Process Map in ProA.

In line with the approach presented in [30], ProA allows creating different views. Figure 8 shows the process map after filtering, i.e. hiding all non-essential connections apart from end/start event connections allowing for end-to-end process visibility on a high level for executives. Note that ProA has a technical interface to a commercial workflow management system, which allows importing process models directly from its cloud modelling tool and fetch runtime data, i.e. the number of running instances per process is shown in blue circles (cf. Fig. 8). Consequently, simple forecasts become possible, e.g. if currently three orders are processed, in the near future, these three orders need to be shipped. Obviously, in more complex scenarios in which not every instance of a business process will trigger the same subsequent process, forecasts are not equally simple. Therefore, in future, we want to leverage the capabilities of Predictive Process Monitoring (PPM) [7], which corresponds to a machine learning model that is trained with process history data to predict aspects of running process instances (e.g. next activity or remaining time of the process instance). While PPM currently focuses on single processes, it might be extended and applied to the process map in ProA to predict the next process or the remaining time of a whole process chain (i.e. processes that have dependencies).

3.4 Discussion

We identified BPMN element pairs that constitute a cross-process interaction and listed them as Dependencies *D1-D5*, which satisfies Requirement *R1*. ProA is able to identify corresponding elements in two process models and visualises the dependencies in a process map, which meets Requirements *R2*. The BPMN elements that may be the trigger/receiver of a relation are attached to the black-box processes. Therefore, it becomes possible to distinguish the types of relations (cf. *R3*).

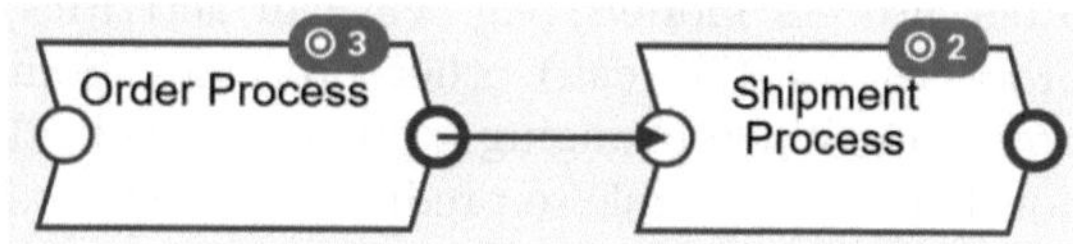

Fig. 8. Filtered Process Map in ProA with Runtime Data

3.5 Limitations

While ProA currently encompassed two layers, i.e. the first layer corresponds to the process map and the second layer corresponds to the imported process models, in future, ProA will be able to manage more layers with different levels of abstraction to correspond to a more complete version of a process architecture. Furthermore, in addition to the number of running process instances, more runtime data will be imported, to fully support the BPM lifecycle phase *evaluation*.

Currently detecting dependencies solely relies on the names of the BPMN elements, whereas in future, technical links created by the most commonly used modelling tools will be considered. Besides, ProA will be more tolerant by ignoring spelling mistakes (e.g. using Levenshtein distance) or word orders, e.g. events labelled with `order completed` / `completed order` will be treated equally.

4 Evaluation

We evaluated our approach and the proof-of-concept tool *ProA* by conducting two case studies with organisations from the public and private sector. Furthermore, we conducted expert interviews. Finally, we discuss threats to validity.

4.1 Case Studies

As part of the case studies, 24 process models of a pharmaceutical company and 11 process models of a German federal agency have been imported into ProA to depict the dependencies among the process model visualised as a process map. While the models of the pharmaceutical company only document the business processes, the process models of the German federal agency are executed on a process engine.

Results. After having imported the process models, the employees of the German federal agency were quite satisfied with the process map affirming having gained the ability to keep track of the dependencies, which allows predicting how a change to one process model may affect other process models. This is vital, especially when the process models are executed by a process engine (like in the case of this federal agency) and various process models are reused by multiple other process models (e.g. via call activities). The process map shows which processes use (i.e. call) other processes. Some processes are used by multiple processes. When changing a process model called by multiple other processes, it now becomes possible to predict the effects as it is now apparent which processes are affected. ProA also allows the agency to evolve the process models and keep track of different versions that might be in use (e.g. development server, test server). The agency is currently considering the permanent usage of ProA.

As anticipated, the employees of the pharmaceutical company noticed missing dependencies among business processes after importing the corresponding models into ProA. Due to careless modelling resulting in poor and non-compliant naming of process elements, ProA could not detect all dependencies. Furthermore, the employees found dependencies in the generated process map they were unaware of, some of which are wrong or duplicates. These findings are now the basis to improve the quality of the process models and a permanent use of ProA is under consideration.

In our case study, we could confirm that all connection types (i.e. end/start event, intermediate events, call activities, data store, message flows) are used in practice.

Lessons Learnt. During the development of ProA, we closely collaborated with and used process models of the pharmaceutical company as examples to test our tool. Using these example process models, some challenges could be unveiled and eventually solved.

The first problem we encountered when importing the example processes were the different namespace prefixes in the XML of the BPMN files depending on the modelling tool used to create the process models, which we fixed eventually by ignoring the prefix. Then, different graph layouting algorithms were evaluated to best depict the process map with minimal overlap of visualised dependencies. Furthermore, it became necessary to allow users to rearrange elements of the process map (e.g. processes, data stores) to better meet the aesthetic perception of the users. The rearranged process map is saved. Besides, clarity suffered when importing lots of processes (>15). To mitigate this challenge, filter options were introduced (e.g. hide data stores, dependency labels, message flows). Finally, we could resolve performance issues when importing lots of process models (>20) with multiple pools and numerous elements (>60) by replacing the Java library that was responsible for analysing the process models by solely relying on plain Java (i.e. `javax.xml.parsers.DocumentBuilderFactory`).

4.2 Expert Interviews

In this section, we evaluate our approach with respect to 1) whether the challenge we identified is widespread and 2) our approach mitigates this challenge. We conducted expert interviews with 11 BPM practitioners from industry to access hands-on experience. Table 1 shows an anonymised overview of the experts. All the experts have multiple years of professional experience with BPM some of which bringing up to several decades of total professional experience which makes us confident to get profound feedback. None of the experts is employed by the affiliation of the authors ensuring independent and neutral feedback.

With each expert, we conducted an online meeting. After an introduction, we presented ProA. Then, we started a discussion based on a predefined interview guideline consisting of open questions and statements for which the experts could express their disagreement or agreement on a 5-point Likert scale ("strongly disagree" to "strongly agree"). Each question and statement could be discussed and clarified to prevent misunderstandings. The experts were allowed to skip a question or statement if they did not feel fit to answer. The extent to which the experts agree to the presented statements is visualised in Table 2 as a bar diagram. On the right-hand side of the bar, the number of experts is shown who either agree or strongly agree. On the left hand side of the bar, the number of experts is shown who either disagree or strongly disagree. The number of experts who gave feedback is shown in parentheses next to respective statement.

Table 1. Expert panel overview

ID	Job Title	YoE[1]	Country
A	Business Analyst	8 (8)	Canada
B	Senior Business Process Architect	15 (25)	Australia
C	Head of Process Excellence Team	18 (18)	USA
D	Author/Podcast Producer (BPM)	28 (39)	USA
E	Business Analyst/Team Lead	10 (16)	Saudi Arabia
F	Principal Business Architect	15 (18)	Brazil
G	Process Manager	10 (10)	Germany
H	BPM Consultant/Aris Architect	10 (25)	Belgium
I	CEO	15 (17)	Germany
J	Process Manager	7 (11)	Germany
K	Consultant	11 (13)	Germany

[1] Years of professional experience with BPM (total)

In the following, the results of the interviews are evaluated. As can be seen in Table 2, the experts uniformly strongly agree that keeping track of dependencies among business processes is important. Furthermore, a majority agrees or strongly agrees that it is also challenging to keep track of these dependencies. The neutral stance of Experts B and D reflects the conflict between theory and practice as Expert D acknowledges that, in contrast to literature, the challenge can be found in companies in practice, which may benefit from our approach. According to Expert B, organisations should agree on hand-offs between business processes and ensure rare changes.

In line with the Technology Acceptance Model [4,5], we gathered information with respect to the Perceived Usefulness (PU) and Perceived Ease-Of-Use (PEOU) of ProA (cf. Table 2). The experts uniformly agreed or strongly agreed that ProA seems useful to detect, visualise, and keep track of dependencies among business processes. Furthermore, a majority agrees or strongly agrees that ProA seems easy to use. Expert E is neutral towards the Perceived Ease-Of-Use as ProA is still in early stages and does not provide many features. Furthermore, he argues that it is necessary to be able to edit the process models within ProA. Even though Expert J strongly agrees that ProA is useful, she indicates that the elements of their process model are linked by a technical identifier (ID) instead of labels, which ProA needs to be able to handle during import in the future.

Table 2. Results of the Conducted Expert Interviews

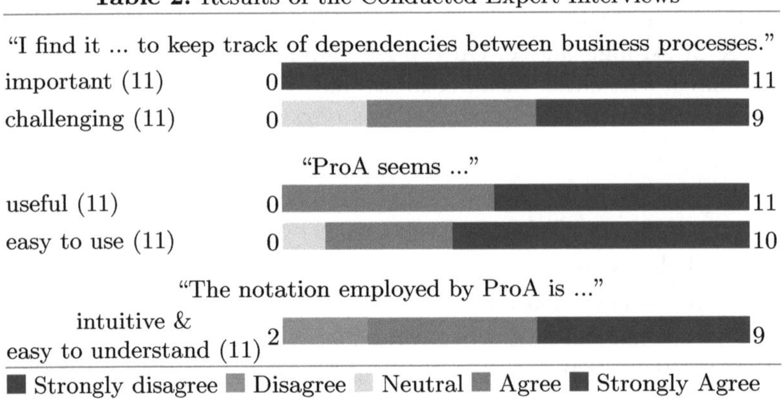

Table 2 shows that a majority of the experts agrees or strongly agrees that the notation employed by ProA is intuitive and easy to understand. Expert F highlights that the filter option of ProA allows showing and hiding certain elements of the process map, which makes it suitable for different target groups (e.g. domain experts, management) with different needs for abstraction. Only Experts E and H disagree. While Expert E argues that a widely known standard notation (e.g. BPMN) should be adopted, Expert H suggests improving the notation, e.g. by using colours to distinguish the connections. In contrast, Expert I explicitly highlights that BPMN is not suitable for displaying process maps.

Experts D and H both emphasize that business process modelling and management tools exist to create a process map, e.g. both experts explain that the tool Aris allows reusing elements in different business processes, which links them and allows generating a process map. Furthermore, Expert H has integrated a custom script in Aris to generate process maps based on the labels of the elements, i.e. similar to our approach. This shows that we identified a challenge that concerns process experts and for which there is no systematic approach yet as Aris requires the user to manually link the elements or write a custom script.

Expert E and G independently propose for future work a form/table with basic information (e.g. start/end event) which can be filled for processes for which there is no model yet. Then, these information can be used to generate the process map even though some business processes have not yet been modelled. For future work, Expert I suggests also providing other presentations like process dependency matrices and a digitalisation maturity level (based on service/manual tasks) and also allow creating process capability maps.

In summary, the data gathered during the interviews suggest that 1) the challenge we identified in this paper is widespread and 2) our approach is able to mitigate it. Furthermore, ProA is perceived to be useful and easy to use.

4.3 Threats to Validity

In line with [32], common threats to validity are discussed:

To mitigate *threats to internal validity* (i.e. false conclusions about causality), we encouraged the experts to share their thoughts. For instance, some experts were not agreeing that keeping track of process dependencies is challenging. We could clarify that they acknowledge that the challenge does exist in practice but believe it should not exist due to best practices.

An *external threat to validity* is the lack of generalisability. While we cannot generalise the approach to all process initiatives, we are confident that lots of organisations can benefit from our approach as this was confirmed by two case studies and a variety of experts coming from all around the world. However, when looking for experts, we explicitly mentioned the topic. Consequently, only experts participated in the interview who are interested in the topic or have already encountered the challenge, which might impact generalisability.

Threats to construct validity refer to the design of study or social threats. To mitigate the risk of ambiguity, we discussed and test-run the questions and statements of the interview with colleagues. Furthermore, we deliberately conducted face-to-face interviews to ensure that the experts understand the approach and can give valid feedback. We have assured the experts anonymity to alleviate perceived pressure to answer the questions according to what they believed was expected, which is a social threat. When experts reveal their identity, it becomes possible to make sure the answers are based on professional experience, which outweighs the social threat. Finally, with respect to the intuitiveness of the notation employed by ProA the experts reported their impression, which is subjective. In future, a more objective measurement will become necessary.

5 Conclusion and Outlook

In ideal BPM initiatives, a top-down approach is adopted, in which a process map comprising all processes including their dependencies is created before modelling the processes in detail. In practice, organisations often start modelling and digitalising individual processes separately. When the BPM initiative is growing, dependencies among the business processes need to be tediously identified.

Therefore, in this work, we present a bottom-up process architecture approach for generating process maps based on identified pairs of BPMN elements that may correspond to an interaction among process models. The proof-of-concept tool, ProA, implements the approach by visualising the dependencies among business processes by using a newly introduced notation. The approach is evaluated in two case studies with organisations, which are currently considering using ProA permanently. Furthermore, results of experts interviews suggest that our approach is useful and easy-to-use.

While a majority of the experts attests to the intuitiveness of our notation, an exhaustive study is necessary to investigate the cognitive effectiveness of the notation, in future work. Finally, we are working on supporting a full process architecture including multiple layers and the BPM lifecycle phase *evaluation* by integrating more runtime data (e.g. from process engines, process mining, provided by users) to create cross-process forecasts and simulations. Despite open issues, based on the insights gathered during the case studies and expert interviews, we are confident that lots of organisations can benefit from our approach.

Acknowledgments. This research is a joint effort of envite consulting GmbH and MINAUTICS GmbH. The authors explicitly thank Björn Richerzhagen, who was one of the initiators of the research contributing ideas, concepts, and the vision.

Disclosure of Interests. The authors have no competing interests to declare that are relevant to the content of this article.

References

1. Badakhshan, P., Wurm, B., Grisold, T., Geyer-Klingeberg, J., Mendling, J., vom Brocke, J.: Creating business value with process mining. J. Strateg. Inf. Syst. **31**(4), 101745 (2022)
2. Bano, D., Nikaj, A., Weske, M.: Discovering business process architectures from event logs. In: Polyvyanyy, A., Wynn, M.T., Van Looy, A., Reichert, M. (eds.) BPM 2021. LNBIP, vol. 427, pp. 162–177. Springer, Cham (2021). https://doi.org/10.1007/978-3-030-85440-9_10
3. Becker, J., Pfeiffer, D., Räckers, M., Fuchs, P.: Business process management in public administrations - the PICTURE approach. In: 11th Pacific-Asia Conference on Information Systems (PACIS) (2007)

4. Davis, F.D.: A technology acceptance model for empirically testing new end-user information systems : theory and results. doctoral dissertation, Massachusetts Institute of Technology, Sloan School of Management, Cambridge (1986)
5. Davis, F.D.: Perceived usefulness, perceived ease of use, and user acceptance of information technology. MIS Q. **13**(3), 319 (1989)
6. Delgado, A., Calegari, D., García, F., Weber, B.: Model-driven management of BPMN-based business process families. Softw. Syst. Model. **21**(6), 2517–2553 (2022)
7. Di Francescomarino, C., Ghidini, C.: Predictive process monitoring. In: Process Mining Handbook, LNBIP, vol. 448, pp. 320–346. Springer International Publishing (2022)
8. Dijkman, R., Vanderfeesten, I., Reijers, H.A.: Business process architectures: overview, comparison and framework. Enterprise Inform. Syst. **10**(2), 129–158 (2014)
9. Dinkowski, T.G., Avila, D.T., Thom, L.H.: Fifteen years of process mining in Brazil: Current contributions, most used techniques, and challenges. In: Anais do XXI Simpósio Brasileiro de Sistemas de Informação (SBSI 2025), pp. 409–418. Sociedade Brasileira de Computação (2025)
10. Döhring, M., Zimmermann, B.: vBPMN: event-aware workflow variants by weaving bpmn2 and business rules. In: Enterprise, Business-Process and Information Systems Modeling, Lecture Notes in Business Information Processing, vol. 81, pp. 332–341. Springer (2011)
11. Dumas, M., La Rosa, M., Mendling, J., Reijers, H.A.: Fundamentals of Business Process Management. Springer (2013)
12. Gonzalez-Lopez, F., Bustos, G.: Business process architecture design methodologies - a literature review. Bus. Process. Manag. J. **25**(6), 1317–1334 (2019)
13. Hehnle, P., Behrendt, M., Weinbrecht, L., Corea, C.: Carbon-aware process execution for green business process management. In: Proceedings of the 26th International Conference on Enterprise Information Systems, pp. 659–666. SCITEPRESS - Science and Technology Publications (2024)
14. Zhang, H., Han, W., Ouyang, C.: Extending BPMN for configurable process modeling. In: Proceedings of the 21st ISPE Inc. International Conference on Concurrent Engineering, pp. 317–330. IOS Press (2014)
15. Malinova, M.: A Language for Designing Process Maps. Ph.D. thesis, Vienna University of Economics and Business (2016)
16. Malinova, M., Leopold, H., Mendling, J.: A meta-model for process map design. In: CEUR (ed.) International Conference on Advanced Information Systems Engineering - CAiSE Forum, pp. 25–32. CEUR Workshop Proceedings (2014)
17. Malinova, M., Leopold, H., Mendling, J.: An explorative study for process map design. In: Nurcan, S., Pimenidis, E. (eds.) CAiSE Forum 2014. LNBIP, vol. 204, pp. 36–51. Springer, Cham (2015). https://doi.org/10.1007/978-3-319-19270-3_3
18. Malinova, M., Mendling, J.: The effect of process map design quality on process management success. In: ECIS 2013 - Proceedings of the 21st European Conference on Information Systems (2013)
19. Malinova, M., Mendling, J.: Why is BPMN not appropriate for process maps? In: International Conference on Interaction Sciences (2015)
20. Moody, D.: The "Physics" of Notations: Toward a scientific basis for constructing visual notations in software engineering. IEEE Trans. Softw. Eng. **35**(6), 756–779 (2009)
21. Object Management Group: Business Process Model and Notation (BPMN): Version 2.0.2 (2013). https://www.omg.org/spec/BPMN/2.0.2/PDF

22. Poels, G., García, F., Ruiz, F., Piattini, M.G.: Architecting business process maps. Comput. Sci. Inf. Syst. **17**, 117–139 (2020)
23. Polančič, G.: BPMN-L: A BPMN extension for modeling of process landscapes. Comput. Ind. **121**, 103276 (2020)
24. Polančič, G., Brin, P., Heloisa Thom, L., Sosa, E., Kocbek Bule, M.: An empirical investigation of the intuitiveness of process landscape designs. In: Enterprise, Business-Process and Information Systems Modeling, Lecture Notes in Business Information Processing, vol. 387, pp. 209–223. Springer International Publishing (2020)
25. Polančič, G., Kous, K.: High-level process modeling–an experimental investigation of the cognitive effectiveness of process landscape diagrams. Mathematics **12**(9), 1376 (2024)
26. van der Aalst, W.M.P.: Business process management: a comprehensive survey. ISRN Softw. Eng. **2013**, 1–37 (2013)
27. van der Aalst, W.M.P.: Foundations of process discovery. In: Process Mining Handbook, LNBIP, vol. 448, pp. 37–75. Springer International Publishing (2022)
28. van der Aalst, W.M.P.: Process mining: a 360 degree overview. In: Process Mining Handbook, LNBIP, vol. 448, pp. 3–34. Springer International Publishing (2022)
29. van der Aalst, W.: Business process management: a personal view. Business Process Manage. J. **10**(2) (2004)
30. van Nuffel, D., de Backer, M.: Multi-abstraction layered business process modeling. Comput. Ind. **63**(2), 131–147 (2012)
31. Weske, M.: Business Process Manage. Springer, Berlin, Heidelberg (2024)
32. Wohlin, C., Runeson, P., Höst, M., Ohlsson, M.C., Regnell, B., Wesslén, A.: Experimentation in Software Engineering. Springer, Berlin, Heidelberg (2024)

Impact and Implications of Generative AI for Enterprise Architects in Agile Environments: A Systematic Literature Review

Stefan Julian Kooy(✉), Jean Paul Sebastian Piest, and Rob Henk Bemthuis

University of Twente, Drienerlolaan 5, 7522 NB, The Netherlands
s.j.kooy@student.utwente.nl, {j.p.s.piest,r.h.bemthuis}@utwente.nl

Abstract. Generative AI (GenAI) is reshaping enterprise architecture work in agile software organizations, yet evidence on its effects remains scattered. We report a systematic literature review (SLR), following established SLR protocols of Kitchenham and PRISMA, of 1,697 records, yielding 33 studies across enterprise, solution, domain, business, and IT architect roles. GenAI most consistently supports (i) design ideation and trade-off exploration; (ii) rapid creation and refinement of artifacts (e.g., code, models, documentation); and (iii) architectural decision support and knowledge retrieval. Reported risks include opacity and bias, contextually incorrect outputs leading to rework, privacy and compliance concerns, and social loafing. We also identify emerging skills and competencies, including prompt engineering, model evaluation, and professional oversight, and organizational enablers around readiness and adaptive governance. The review contributes with (1) a mapping of GenAI use cases and risks in agile architecting, (2) implications for capability building and governance, and (3) an initial research agenda on humanâĂŞAI collaboration in architecture. Overall, the findings inform responsible adoption of GenAI that accelerates digital transformation while safeguarding architectural integrity

Keywords: Generative AI · Enterprise Architect · Agile · Scrum · Systematic Literature Review

1 Introduction

Organizations face persistent challenges in developing and delivering digital products and services. Agile methods such as Scrum and frameworks like the Scaled Agile Framework (SAFe) have reshaped how teams conceive, build, and deploy solutions, emphasizing flexibility and rapid feedback to meet changing market needs [30]. In parallel, the adoption of generative artificial intelligence (GenAI) is accelerating across manufacturing, healthcare, finance, telecommunications, and the public sector [13,17,39,47]. GenAI refers to the class of Artificial

J. Barateiro et al. (Eds.): EDOC 2025 Workshops, LNBIP 571, pp. 53–69, 2026.
https://doi.org/10.1007/978-3-032-16234-2_4

Intelligence (AI) models that emulate the structure and characteristics of input data to generate synthetic content, such as text, images, audio, or video, rather than merely classifying or predicting existing data [11]. GenAI is increasingly used to streamline operations, support customer interaction, and enable new forms of innovation, making it a practical enabler for modernizing industrial practice.

Enterprise Architecture (EA) offers guidance for aligning digital solutions, from cloud-native platforms to data, Internet of Things (IoT), and Artificial Intelligence (AI), with strategic objectives. In this paper, "architects" includes enterprise, solution, domain, business, and IT architects. Practitioners frequently rely on frameworks such as TOGAF or Zachman to support businessâĂŞIT alignment and strategic decision making. However, traditional approaches can fall short in agile settings due to "big design upfront" practices and slower feedback cycles [61]. Prior work indicates that AI can improve decision making within established architecture frameworks, a foundation for organizational agility [38], yet integrating AI into these frameworks remains challenging [6].

This paper examines how GenAI affects the role, skills, and responsibilities of architects in large-scale agile software development. We conduct a systematic literature review (SLR) to assess how GenAI may address current challenges and to identify the capabilities relevant to architecture work (e.g., generating design alternatives, accelerating documentation, supporting architectural decisions). We also consider potential risks and trade-offs. Our goal is to clarify whether GenAI can contribute to architectural agility and operational efficiency, and under what conditions.

The remainder of the paper is organized as follows. Section 2 outlines the background on EA, agile methodologies, and GenAI. Section 3 introduces the methodology. Section 4 presents the key results and findings of the SLR. Section 5 discusses the implications of the results and findings, and Sect. 6 concludes with a summary, limitations, and directions for future research.

2 Background

This section defines key concepts: EA as the structure for aligning business and technology, common EA frameworks, agile methods for software delivery, and GenAI.

2.1 Enterprise Architecture

EA provides a structured approach to designing and governing systems, technologies, and processes so they align with business objectives and operate effectively in dynamic environments [35,54]. EA spans multiple architectural viewpoints (enterprise, business, IT, domain, solution) that share key responsibilities: stakeholder communication, strategic alignment, risk management, and governance [20]. As an organizational blueprint, EA helps ensure that technology investments support business goals, improve agility, and address regulatory and cybersecurity concerns while reducing complexity [20,37,54]. Standardized processes and consistent documentation also support digital transformation, including the adoption of AI-enabled capabilities [14,22].

2.2 Architecture Frameworks

The Zachman Framework [63,64] and The Open Group Architecture Framework (TOGAF) [24] offer widely used approaches for implementing EA. Zachman organizes architectural artifacts across the "What, How, Where, Who, When, Why" perspectives and role-based rows to support comprehensive documentation and cross-functional collaboration. TOGAF's Architecture Development Method (ADM) defines iterative phases for aligning business and IT, managing change, and governing execution. While effective for long-term planning, these phase-driven approaches can conflict with the fast feedback cycles and flexibility emphasized by agile methods [49].

2.3 Agile Methodologies

Agile methodologies, such as Scrum, and frameworks, such as SAFe, promote iterative development, short feedback loops, and cross-functional collaboration [4,8,50]. Scrum is common in small teams that work in short sprints with frequent stakeholder input and incremental releases. SAFe scales agile practices across the enterprise via "Agile Release Trains" and formal architecture roles (enterprise, solution, and system) that help maintain strategic alignment and architectural integrity [46,51–53]. Despite these benefits, agile practices can strain traditional EA processes that rely on upfront design and rigid governance [49].

2.4 Generative AI

AI aims to build systems that perform tasks requiring human-level capabilities such as pattern recognition, language understanding, and decision making [62]. Machine learning and deep learning learn from data rather than explicit rules. GenAI focuses on producing new content. Using models such as GANs, VAEs, Transformers, and latent diffusion models, GenAI can generate text, code, and images from learned distributions [7,16].

GenAI may help bridge the structure of EA with the iterative nature of agile work. It can automate routine documentation and augment design ideation, potentially easing common bottlenecks. This review therefore studies GenAI's impact on architectural roles and responsibilities in agile environments, with attention to implications for practice, decision making, and governance.

3 Methodology

We followed Kitchenham's guidelines [32] and PRISMA [43] to plan, conduct, and report this SLR. The sections below describe how we defined the research questions (RQs), designed the search strategy, applied inclusion and exclusion criteria, extracted and synthesized data, and assured quality. The full protocol is available at [45].

3.1 Research Questions

The study examines the impact of GenAI on EA in agile development contexts. Our main research question is: *How does GenAI influence the evolving role, skills, and responsibilities of architects in large-scale agile software development environments?*

To operationalize the main RQ, we formulated five sub-questions:

1. Which technical characteristics of GenAI create opportunities and challenges for architects in agile environments?
2. Which current GenAI use cases influence architectural practices and decision making in agile organizations?
3. How does GenAI affect traditional roles, tasks, and required skills of architects in agile digital transformations?
4. What organizational and technological factors influence the adoption trajectory of GenAI in architecture practices?
5. What governance and capability adaptations are needed to integrate GenAI into architecture practices?

3.2 Search Strategy

The search was performed on 17th of February, 2025, in two electronic databases, IEEE Xplore and Scopus. These databases provide complementary coverage of computing research and practitioner-oriented literature. Guided by the RQs, we designed English-language queries addressing (1) GenAI characteristics, (2) architectural roles and skills, (3) agile architecture, and (4) AI governance and adoption.

Four query sets (Table 1) returned 1,697 records. Title screening excluded 1,529 irrelevant items. Abstract screening removed a further 96 records (including 16 duplicates). We assessed 72 full texts and selected 33 papers for data extraction (Fig. 1).

The mapping between RQs and query sets is many-to-many. Each query captures a facet of the topic, with intentional overlap (Table 3). For example, Q1 targets GenAI characteristics (supporting RQ1); Q2–Q3 emphasize architectural roles, skills, and agile contexts (informing RQ2–RQ3); Q4 focuses on governance and maturity (supporting RQ4–RQ5). We synthesize insights across all queries to answer the five RQs.

3.3 Inclusion and Exclusion Criteria

We defined criteria based on topical relevance, publication type, year, and language (Table 2). To reflect the recent emergence of GenAI, we applied a stricter recency threshold to GenAI-specific work.

Table 1. Overview of search queries and results.

Query	Generic Search String, Specifics In [45]	Total Found	Selected
Q1	`"Generative AI" AND agile AND (characteristics OR capabilities OR features OR opportunities OR challenges)`	369	11
Q2	`("enterprise architect" OR "domain architect" OR "solution architect" OR "business architect" OR "IT architect") AND (role OR task OR skill)`	871	15
Q3	`("enterprise architect" OR "domain architect" OR "solution architect" OR "business architect" OR "IT architect") AND (agile OR Scrum OR SAFe OR DevOps)`	390	3
Q4	`(("Generative AI" OR "generative artificial intelligence") AND governance) OR ("AI" AND "maturity model")`	67	4

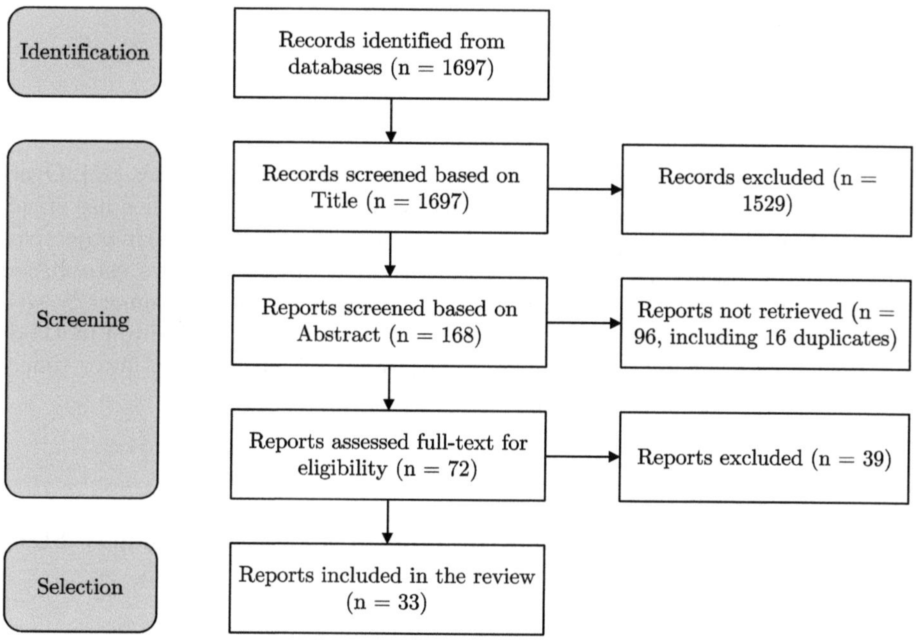

Fig. 1. Screening and selection process, as adopted by [32,43].

3.4 Data Extraction and Synthesis

We extracted data against the RQs (Table 3). We then performed mapping and thematic analysis to identify cross-study patterns and synthesize findings.

Table 2. Inclusion and exclusion criteria.

Inclusion Criteria	Exclusion Criteria
Studies addressing at least one of the RQs	Studies focusing on non-GenAI (e.g., rule-based systems, traditional ML, robotics)
Subject areas: computer science, social sciences, engineering, decision science	Studies from domains (e.g., medicine, agriculture) lacking relevant GenAI use cases for EA
Publication types: journal articles, SLRs, meta-analyses, conference papers or books	Articles published in languages other than English
Published prior to 2015 only if foundational for EA or agile contexts	—
Published in 2015 or later (for studies related to EA, agile methods, or architect roles)	—
Published in 2022 or later (for studies related to GenAI)	—

3.5 Quality Assurance

We assessed methodological rigor, transparency, and potential biases [45]. Overall, the included literature provides a basis for analysis. Many studies use structured methods (e.g., SLRs, case studies, empirical designs) with clear objectives and analytical frameworks. Rigor is strongest in work that follows established guidance (e.g., PRISMA), and data collection and analysis are generally well documented. Some papers exhibit partial outcome reporting or limited methodological detail (e.g., [3,25,27]). Several conceptual papers provide fewer reflections on assumptions and limitations (e.g., [20,26]).

4 Results

We report findings by the five RQs. In total, 33 studies were included. Study methods are summarized in Table 4.

4.1 Opportunities and Challenges of GenAI for Architects

This subsection addresses RQ1 by identifying the technical characteristics of GenAI that present opportunities and challenges for architects operating in agile software development environments. Table 5 summarizes the main opportunities and challenges.

GenAI introduces capabilities that can reshape architecture work in agile settings. Key opportunities include content generation, design ideation, rapid prototyping, and targeted knowledge retrieval. These align with agile practices such as

Table 3. Relevance of studies to research questions.

ID	RQ1	RQ2	RQ3	RQ4	RQ5	Ref.
1	x				x	[60]
2	x	x				[44]
3	x	x		x		[27]
4	x					[26]
5	x				x	[23]
6	x	x		x	x	[2]
7	x			x		[18]
8	x	x				[42]
9					x	[36]
10	x	x				[28]
11	x	x				[5]
12		x	x			[55]
13			x			[31]
14			x			[10]
15			x			[59]
16		x	x			[9]
17	x		x			[33]
18			x			[15]
19			x			[48]
20				x		[29]
21			x			[34]
22			x			[19]
23			x			[56]
24			x			[12]
25			x			[20]
26			x			[21]
27			x			[58]
28			x			[57]
29			x			[25]
30	x			x	x	[1]
31	x				x	[3]
32				x	x	[40]
33	x					[41]

iterative delivery and frequent feedback. LLMs (e.g., ChatGPT) can accelerate the creation of architectural artifacts (documentation, diagrams, and code) and

Table 4. Study methods of included articles.

Method	Count (n)	References
Survey	3	[23,29,60]
Literature review	5	[2,19,26,41,42]
Systematic literature / mapping study	2	[1,25]
Case study (single, multiple, or mixed-methods)	8	[9,10,12,15,56–59]
Conceptual / Theoretical / Descriptive analysis	6	[21,28,31,44,48,55]
Exploratory / Qualitative / Reflective study	6	[5,18,27,33,34,40]
Quantitative (e.g., PLS-SEM)	1	[3]
Data / Content analysis	2	[20,36]

Table 5. Opportunities and challenges of GenAI for architects.

Opportunities	Challenges
Automated generation of code, models, and documentation accelerates delivery [27,44]	GenAI systems often function as "black boxes", limiting transparency and traceability [2,26]
Supports fast design ideation and exploration of alternative solutions [44]	Risk of generating biased, inappropriate, or low-quality outputs [23,42]
Enhances collaboration (e.g. during agile sprints) [27]	Over-reliance on AI may impact architects' analytical judgment and design skills [33]
Improves requirements analysis and specification via NLP capabilities [42]	Limited context windows reduce effectiveness in large-scale enterprise modeling [26]
Enables architectural decision support through scenario simulation [5,28]	Raises concerns about security, privacy, and regulatory compliance [23]
Assists in retrieving and organizing architectural and technical knowledge [18,26]	Lack of standardization in GenAI outputs complicates reuse and interoperability [18]

improve cross-role communication [1,18,27,44]. This, in turn, allows enterprise and solution architects to complete tasks more quickly and align IT capabilities with evolving business strategies, while remaining responsive to stakeholder needs [3,33]. GenAI also supports architectural decision making by suggesting alternative solutions and enabling comparative evaluations [28,44].

These gains come with risks. A prominent technical challenge is the opacity of GenAI systems; many function as "black boxes" whose internal reasoning processes are inaccessible [60]. This can undermine the transparency, interpretability, and traceability required for sound architectural governance [2,26]. Additionally, concerns exist around biased or low-quality outputs, data privacy risks when using sensitive inputs, and a low output reliability, often stemming from hallucinations, where the model generates plausible yet factually incorrect responses. These challenges raise substantial implications for regulatory compliance and architectural integrity [18,23,41,42].

Excessive dependence on GenAI can also erode critical thinking skills among architects, weakening their ability to recognize systemic trade-offs or perform nuanced risk assessments. Furthermore, many LLMs often exhibit limited effectiveness in large-scale enterprise contexts on input length and lack of embedded domain knowledge [5,41]. This limitation reduces their utility in end-to-end architectural reasoning [26,59,60].

4.2 GenAI Use Cases for Architectural Decision Making

This section is related to RQ2 and discusses GenAI use cases for decision making.

Our findings suggest that GenAI proves particularly impactful during the early phases of agile development, including ideation, trade-off analysis, and requirements engineering. In these stages, GenAI can facilitate the exploration of alternative design paths, enabling architects to balance competing quality attributes, such as scalability, performance, and maintainability [44]. This can be valuable in volatile and complex enterprise environments, where decision latency should be minimized [55].

GenAI also improves team collaboration by simplifying complex technical concepts in accessible terms. By bridging gaps between diverse stakeholders, such as developers, product owners, and business analysts, it strengthens the architect's integrative and coordination roles [9,27].

Additional use cases involve classifying, prioritizing, and clustering stakeholder requirements, generating architectural diagrams (e.g., UML), and visualizing dependencies early in the design process [2,42]. These functionalities contribute to faster and more informed architectural decision making.

Nonetheless, human oversight remains key. Given the probabilistic nature of LLMs, their outputs are neither guaranteed to be optimal nor contextually precise, and studies highlight the importance of validating GenAI-derived suggestions before implementation [5,27,28].

4.3 Evolving Role, Tasks, and Required Skills of the Architect

Addressing RQ3, this subsection examines how GenAI can alter the roles, tasks, and competencies of enterprise architects in agile environments.

The capabilities of GenAI influence the professional identity and skill composition of architects in agile enterprises. As discussed in previous sections, GenAI can enable tasks such as natural language-based code generation, real-time feedback, and architectural synthesis. These functionalities alleviate (parts of) the cognitive workload traditionally carried out by architects during design decision making, affecting the architect's role [9]. Recent research on on-demand architectural knowledge systems supports this view, showing how GenAI can deliver generated suggestions, structured knowledge, and reflective prompts to assist in complex architectural evaluations [48]. Consequently, architects increasingly operate as curators and validators of GenAI outputs, rather than primary creators of design artifacts. This shift requires a reconfiguration of core architectural competencies.

There are many different types of architects. While each type has its own responsibilities, they share overlap in tasks and required competencies [20]. In addition to foundational skills of architects such as technical expertise, stakeholder communication, strategic thinking, and governance oversight [21,34,55,59], architects increasingly require proficiency in prompt engineering, model governance, professional judgement, and human oversight of AI-generated content. These emerging competencies are aligned with the need for fast validation, continuous iteration, and collaborative judgment in dynamic software environments [25,31,57].

In large-scale agile programs, architects are expected to engage more closely with development teams and operational workflows [19]. Prior research shows that architectural practices are increasingly defined by facilitation, negotiation, and design adjudication across multiple agile teams [56,58]. As GenAI capabilities integrate into these workflows, architects assume multi-faceted roles. Depending on the context, they may act as strategic advisors, technical coaches, reviewers, or even crisis managers [10,12,57]. This development expands the architectural role from one of high-level oversight to active participation in lower-level software delivery, which could address persistent communication gaps experienced between higher and lower levels [15].

While traditionally these roles required extensive experience in abstract modeling, stakeholder communication, and standardization across domains [33], these competencies are now augmented, rather than replaced, by AI-driven assistance. Rather than reducing the architect's contribution, GenAI supports their role in contextualizing AI outputs, aligning them with enterprise objectives, and supporting collaborative decision making in agile environments.

4.4 Factors Influencing GenAI Adoption Trajectory

In response to RQ4, this subsection identifies the organizational and technological factors that affect GenAI adoption in architectural practices.

Key enablers include targeted education programs, GenAI literacy, and organizational culture. Absent sufficient investments in upskilling (particularly in areas such as prompt engineering, GenAI evaluation, and responsible AI use), organizations may struggle to realize the promised productivity gains [2,18]. These training efforts are especially important in agile contexts, where architects must adapt to fast feedback loops and evolving stakeholder needs. Additionally, two behavioral challenges are identified during human-AI collaboration: a steep learning curve for mastering GenAI tools, and social loafing, where individuals may rely too much on AI and reduce their own effort [27]. These findings reinforce the importance of comprehensive education and awareness programs.

Governance maturity also plays a key role. Organizations with formalized AI policies, ethical oversight, and traceability mechanisms are more likely to integrate GenAI into architecture workflows effectively [40]. A maturity model could range from "Initial" to "Optimizing", where higher levels are characterized by continuous monitoring, defined responsibilities, and established safeguards [40]. In contrast, underdeveloped governance frameworks lead to accountability gaps and undermine trust in AI-generated outputs, particularly in high-stakes architectural decision making.

Finally, organizational readiness is key. This encompasses resource availability, technology proficiency, regulatory compatibility (e.g., GDPR compliance), strategic-operational alignment, and the overall coherence between strategic goals and GenAI deployment plans [1,29]. Readiness can be categorized into four domains: infrastructure and skilled personnel, data governance maturity, legal and system compatibility, and strategic alignment [1]. These collectively contribute to whether GenAI can effectively be integrated into architecture work. In relation to this, research suggests that organizations with greater awareness of agile principles tend to support more adaptive architecture practices, thereby creating more favorable conditions for GenAI integration [29].

4.5 Adaptations Required for GenAI Integration

In response to RQ5, this subsection identifies governance and capability adaptations required to support responsible and effective integration of GenAI in architectural work.

To support GenAI's potential while mitigating associated risks, organizations should adopt dynamic governance frameworks that evolve with model performance and regulatory change [60]. Nakayama et al.'s governance lifecycle proposes an iterative approach that embeds principles such as fairness, transparency, and accountability into GenAI management practices [40]. Architects require well-defined policies for handling sensitive data, interpret model outputs, and apply GenAI tools responsibly. Organizations should also revise data-handling protocols to comply with emerging AI standards and introduce privacy-preserving measures and audit trails to support legal compliance and system transparency [1,2,23].

Building organizational capabilities remains a priority. Training programs on GenAI risks and best practices can reduce the likelihood of misuse and support cultural acceptance. Employees with strong data-governance awareness are more likely to use GenAI tools in an ethically responsible manner [3].

Lastly, trust-building measures, such as open communication and responsible usage guidelines, are key to reducing public skepticism and supporting responsible GenAI adoption within architectural communities [36].

5 Discussion

This review indicates that GenAI is reshaping roles, workflows, and governance expectations for enterprise architects in agile settings. On the opportunity side, GenAI can support the generation, analysis, and communication of complex information, strengthening the architect's integrative and decision-making functions within cross-functional teams. On the risk side, limited explainability, contextual misalignment, reliability issues (e.g., hallucinations), and overreliance on automation raise concerns for governance and professional judgement.

These dynamics suggest a shift from an "architect-as-creator" model toward an "architect-as-curator" role. New competencies, including prompt design, model oversight, and ethical judgement, complement, rather than replace, existing skills. Adoption is not purely technical. Organizations need capability-building, structured evaluation, and support mechanisms, together with governance maturity, ethical frameworks, and cross-team learning.

A practical implication is tighter integration of GenAI into enterprise architecture platforms to streamline modeling and artifact generation. Theoretically, the findings point to co-adaptive humanâĂŞAI collaboration. Practically, they emphasize disciplined experimentation, clear data-governance practices, and explicit humanâĂŞAI task allocation.

The review remains exploratory. Rapid developments in GenAI limit generalizability. Nonetheless, the review offers guidance for enterprise architects to understand and navigate the implications of GenAI for their evolving roles and practices.

6 Conclusion

Based on a structured synthesis of 33 peer-reviewed articles, this SLR concludes that GenAI is influencing the roles, skills, and work practices of architects in agile software development. It augments productivity in ideation, artifact generation (code, diagrams, documentation), and architectural decision support, while introducing risks related to explainability, privacy, and potential erosion of professional judgement through overreliance. Addressing these issues requires targeted education, training, and robust governance.

The contribution of this review is twofold: it organizes emerging evidence on how architectural roles are evolving with GenAI, and it outlines practical considerations for responsible, context-aware adoption. It also identifies organizational enablers and barriers that inform governance design and strategy for bringing GenAI into agile environments.

Several limitations apply. Restricting searches to two databases may reduce coverage, although recurring themes across diverse sources suggest stability of the main insights. With many studies being conceptual or exploratory, the review structures early discussions rather than offering definitive causal claims. The term "architects" was used broadly (enterprise, domain, solution, business, IT), which may blur role-specific nuances. Transferability is uncertain and likely depends on enterprise size, maturity, and sector. Finally, the field of research is nascent and evolving, which constrains the strength of conclusions.

Future work should pursue empirical studies on the longitudinal effects of GenAI on architectural roles, inter-team collaboration, and enterprise agility. Promising methods include multi-site case studies, ethnographic fieldwork, and controlled experiments. A concrete agenda is to develop principles and patterns that guide architects' effective and responsible use of GenAI.

Acknowledgments. The authors thank Martin van Capelleveen for the constructive discussions.

Disclosure of Interests. The authors have no competing interests to declare that are relevant to the content of this article.

References

1. Al-Kfairy, M.: Strategic integration of generative ai in organizational settings: applications, challenges and adoption requirements. IEEE Eng. Manage. Rev. (2025). https://doi.org/10.1109/EMR.2025.3534034
2. Alenezi, M., Akour, M.: Ai-driven innovations in software engineering: a review of current practices and future directions. Appl. Sci. **15**(3) (2025). https://doi.org/10.3390/app15031344
3. Amendi, R., Halim, E., Hartono, H.: Exploring ethical implications: unraveling factors influencing data governance awareness behavior in generative AI chatbot. In: 2024 2nd International Conference on Technology Innovation and Its Applications (ICTIIA). IEEE, Jakarta, Indonesia (2024). https://doi.org/10.1109/ICTIIA61827.2024.10761290
4. Andrei, B.A., Casu-Pop, A.C., Gheorghe, S.C., Boiangiu, C.A.: A study on using waterfall and agile methods in software project management. J. Inform. Syst. Oper. Manage. 125–135 (2019)
5. Bahi, A., Gharib, J., Youssef, G., Belkadi, L.: Integrating generative AI for advancing Agile software development and mitigating project management challenges. Int. J. Adv. Comput. Sci. Appl. **15**(3) (2024). https://doi.org/10.14569/IJACSA.2024.0150306
6. Bakar, N.A.A., Suib, A.H., Othman, A., Amdan, A.A., Hassan, M.A.A., Hussein, S.S.: Artificial intelligence in enterprise architecture: Innovations, integration challenges, and ethics. In: Proceedings of the International Conference on Innovation & Entrepreneurship in Computing, Engineering & Science Education (InvENT 2024), pp. 578–588 (2024). https://doi.org/10.2991/978-94-6463-589-8_54
7. Banh, L., Strobel, G.: Generative artificial intelligence. Electron. Mark. **33**(1), 63 (2023). https://doi.org/10.1007/s12525-023-00680-1
8. Beck, K., et al.: Manifesto for Agile software development (2001). https://agilemanifesto.org/. Accessed 24 Mar 2025
9. van den Berg, M., van Vliet, H.: The decision-making context influences the role of the enterprise architect. In: Proceedings of the IEEE 20th International Enterprise Distributed Object Computing Workshop (EDOCW), pp. 1–7 (2016). https://doi.org/10.1109/EDOCW.2016.7584389
10. van den Berg, M., van Vliet, H.: Enterprise architects should play different roles. In: Proceedings of the IEEE International Conference on Enterprise Distributed Object Computing Workshop (EDOCW), pp. 1–7. IEEE (2016). https://doi.org/10.1109/CBI.2016.56

11. Booth, H., Souppaya, M., Vassilev, A., Ogata, M., Stanley, M., Scarfone, K.: Secure software development practices for generative AI and dual-use foundation models: An SSDF community profile. Tech. Rep. NIST Special Publication (SP) 800-218A, National Institute of Standards and Technology (2024). https://doi.org/10.6028/NIST.SP.800-218A
12. Breithaupt, C., Vieracker, J., Chircu, A., Cox, S., Sultanow, E.: The enterprise architect as a crisis manager: Insights from Lufthansa. In: INFORMATIK 2020. Lecture Notes in Informatics (LNI), Gesellschaft für Informatik (2021). https://doi.org/10.18420/inf2020_14
13. Bright, J., Enock, F., Esnaashari, S., Francis, J., Hashem, Y., Morgan, D.: Generative AI is already widespread in the public sector: Evidence from a survey of UK public sector professionals. Digital Government: Research and Practice **6**(1) (2025). https://doi.org/10.1145/3700140
14. Bughin, J.: What drives the corporate payoffs of using generative artificial intelligence? Struct. Chang. Econ. Dyn. **71**, 658–668 (2024). https://doi.org/10.1016/j.strueco.2024.09.011
15. Canat, M., Català, N.P., Jourkovski, A., Petrov, S., Wellme, M., Lagerström, R.: Enterprise architecture and agile development: Friends or foes? In: 2018 IEEE 22nd International Enterprise Distributed Object Computing Workshop (EDOCW), pp. 176–182. IEEE (2018). https://doi.org/10.1109/EDOCW.2018.00033
16. Chahal, A., Gulia, P.: Machine learning and deep learning. Int. J. Innov. Technol. Explor. Eng. (IJITEE) **8**(12), 4910–4914 (2019). https://doi.org/10.35940/ijitee.L3550.1081219
17. Chui, M., Yee, L., Hall, B., Singla, A., Sukharevsky, A.: The state of AI in 2023: Generative AI's breakout year (2023). https://www.mckinsey.com/capabilities/quantumblack/our-insights/the-state-of-ai-in-2023-generative-ais-breakout-year. Accessed 24 Mar 2025
18. Di Rocco, J., Di Ruscio, D., Di Sipio, C., Nguyen, P.T., Rubei, R.: On the use of large language models in model-driven engineering. Softw. Syst. Model. (2025). https://doi.org/10.1007/s10270-025-01263-8
19. Gellweiler, C.: Collaboration of solution architects and project managers. Int. J. Human Capital Inform. Technol. Profess. **10**(4), 1–15 (2019). https://doi.org/10.4018/IJHCITP.2019100101
20. Gellweiler, C.: Types of IT architects: a content analysis on tasks and skills. J. Theor. Appl. Electron. Commer. Res. **15**, 15–37 (2020). https://doi.org/10.4067/S0718-18762020000200103
21. Gellweiler, C.: IT architects and IT-business alignment: a theoretical review. Proc. Comput. Sci. **196**, 13–20 (2022). https://doi.org/10.1016/j.procs.2021.11.067
22. Georgiev, D., Antonova, A.: Enhancing knowledge sharing processes via automated software documentation management systems using Gen AI software tools. In: Proceedings of the IEEE Conference. IEEE (2024). https://doi.org/10.1109/MMA62616.2024.10817681
23. Golda, A., et al.: Privacy and security concerns in generative ai: a comprehensive survey. IEEE Access **12**, 48126–48149 (2024). https://doi.org/10.1109/ACCESS.2024.3381611
24. Group, T.O.: Togaf 9.2 documentation (2025). https://pubs.opengroup.org/architecture/togaf9-doc/arch/index.html
25. Guo, H., Smite, D., Li, J., Gao, S.: Enterprise architecture and agility: a systematic mapping study. In: Business Modeling and Software Design (BMSD 2021), Lecture Notes in Business Information Processing. vol. 422, pp. 296–305. Springer (2021). https://doi.org/10.1007/978-3-030-79976-2_18

26. Hagos, D.H., Battle, R., Rawat, D.B.: Recent advances in generative ai and large language models: current status, challenges, and perspectives. IEEE Trans. Artif. Intell. **5**(1) (2024). https://doi.org/10.1109/TAI.2024.3444742
27. Hamza, M., Siemon, D., Akbar, M.A., Rahman, T.: Human-ai collaboration in software engineering: lessons learned from a hands-on workshop. In: ACM/IEEE International Workshop on Software-intensive Business (2024). https://doi.org/10.1145/3643690.3648236
28. Handler, A., Larsen, K.R., Hackathorn, R.: Large language models present new questions for decision support. Int. J. Inform. Manage. **79** (2024). https://doi.org/10.1016/j.ijinfomgt.2024.102811
29. Kaddoumi, T., Watfa, M.: A foundational framework for agile enterprise architecture. Int. J. Lean Six Sigma **13**(1), 136–155 (2022). https://doi.org/10.1108/IJLSS-03-2021-0057
30. Kalenda, M., Hyna, P., Rossi, B.: Scaling agile in large organizations: practices, challenges, and success factors. J. Softw.: Evol. Process **30**(10), e1954 (2018). https://doi.org/10.1002/smr.1954
31. Kempegowda, S.M., Chaczko, Z.: Essential skill of enterprise architect practitioners for digital era. In: Proceedings of the International Conference on Electrical and Data Engineering. IEEE (2020). https://doi.org/10.1109/ICSENG.2018.8638210
32. Kitchenham, B., Charters, S.: Guidelines for performing systematic literature reviews in software engineering (2007)
33. Krishnamurthy, R.: Breezing my way as a solution architect: a retrospective on skill development and use. IEEE Softw. **34**(3), 9–13 (2017). https://doi.org/10.1109/MS.2017.83
34. Kurnia, S., Kotusev, S., Shanks, G., Dilnutt, R., Taylor, P., Milton, S.K.: Enterprise architecture practice under a magnifying glass: Linking artifacts, activities, benefits, and blockers. Commun. Assoc. Inform. Syst. **49**, 668–698 (2021). https://doi.org/10.17705/1CAIS.04936
35. Lankhorst, M.: Enterprise architecture at work: Modelling, communication and analysis. The Enterprise Engineering Series, Springer (2017). https://doi.org/10.1007/978-3-662-53933-0
36. Mahmoud, A.B., Kumar, V., Spyropoulou, S.: Identifying the public's beliefs about generative artificial intelligence: a big data approach. IEEE Trans. Eng. Manage. (2025). https://doi.org/10.1109/TEM.2025.3534088
37. Mulder, J.: Modern enterprise architecture: Using DevSecOps and cloud-native in large enterprises. Apress (2023). https://doi.org/10.1007/978-1-4842-9066-8
38. Nafei, W.: Organizational agility: the key to improve organizational performance. Int. Bus. Res. **9**(3), 97–104 (2016). https://doi.org/10.5539/ibr.v9n3p97
39. Nah, F.F.H., Zheng, R., Cai, J., Siau, K., Chen, L.: Generative AI and ChatGPT: applications, challenges, and AI-human collaboration. J. Inform. Technol. Case Appl. Res. **25**(3), 277–304 (2023). https://doi.org/10.1080/15228053.2023.2233814
40. Nakayama, M., Wan, Y., Alvino, F.: Balancing potential and prudence: An ongoing study on organizational policymaking for generative AI adoption. In: Proceedings of the 2024 Artificial Intelligence for Business (AIxB). IEEE (2024). https://doi.org/10.1109/AIxB62249.2024.00014
41. Nidhisree, C., Paul, A., Venunadh, A., Bhowmick, R.S.: Generative AI under scrutiny: assessing the risks and challenges in diverse domains. In: 2024 IEEE 6th International Conference on Cybernetics, Cognition and Machine Learning Applications (ICCCMLA), pp. 243–246. IEEE (2024). https://doi.org/10.1109/ICCCMLA63077.2024.10871350

42. Norheim, J.J., Rebentisch, E., Xiao, D., Draeger, L., Kerbrat, A., de Weck, O.L.: Challenges in applying large language models to requirements engineering tasks. Design Sci. J. **10** (2024). https://doi.org/10.1017/dsj.2024.8
43. Page, M., et al.: The PRISMA 2020 statement: an updated guideline for reporting systematic reviews. BMJ **372**, n71 (2021). https://doi.org/10.1136/bmj.n71
44. Paliwal, G., Donvir, A., Gujar, P., Panyam, S.: Accelerating time-to-market: The role of generative AI in product development (2024). https://doi.org/10.1109/COLCOM62950.2024.10720255, white paper or preprint
45. Piest, J.P.S., Kooy, S.J., Bemthuis, R.: Impact and implications of GenAI on enterprise architects (2025). https://doi.org/10.17605/OSF.IO/DH2AS
46. Putta, A., Paasivaara, M., Lassenius, C.: Adopting Scaled Agile Framework (SAFe): a multivocal literature review. In: XP '18 Companion. ACM (2018). https://doi.org/10.1145/3234152.3234164
47. Rashid, A.B., Kausik, A.K.: AI revolutionizing industries worldwide: a comprehensive overview of its diverse applications. Hybrid Adv. **7**(100277), 100277–100277 (2024). https://doi.org/10.1016/j.hybadv.2024.100277
48. Razavian, M., Paech, B., Tang, A.: The vision of on-demand architectural knowledge systems as a decision-making companion. J. Syst. Softw. **198** (2023). https://doi.org/10.1016/j.jss.2022.111560
49. Rouhani, B.D., Mahrin, M.N.M., Nikpay, F., Ahmad, R., Nikfard, P.: A systematic literature review on enterprise architecture implementation methodologies. Inf. Softw. Technol. **62**, 1–20 (2015). https://doi.org/10.1016/j.infsof.2015.01.012
50. Sassa, A.C., de Almeida, I.A., Fernandes Pereira, T.N., de Oliveira, M.S.: Scrum: a systematic literature review. Int. J. Adv. Comput. Sci. Appl. **14**(4), 173–184 (2023). https://doi.org/10.14569/IJACSA.2023.0140420
51. Scaled Agile, Inc.: Enterprise architect (2023). https://scaledagileframework.com/enterprise-architect/. Accessed 24 Mar 2025
52. Scaled Agile, Inc.: Solution architect (2023). https://scaledagileframework.com/solution-architect/. Accessed 24 Mar 2025
53. Scaled Agile, Inc.: System architect/engineer (2023). https://scaledagileframework.com/system-architect-engineer/. Accessed 24 Mar 2025
54. Strano, C., Rehmani, Q.: The role of the enterprise architect. IseB **5**(4), 379–396 (2007). https://doi.org/10.1007/s10257-007-0053-1
55. Ullrich, A., Bertheau, C., Wiedmann, M., Sultanow, E., Körppen, T., Bente, S.: Roles, tasks and skills of the enterprise architect in the vuca world. In: 2021 IEEE 25th International Enterprise Distributed Object Computing Workshop (EDOCW), pp. 261–270 (2021). https://doi.org/10.1109/EDOCW52865.2021.00057
56. Ömer Uludağ, Kleehaus, M., Matthes, F., Schneider, J.: What to expect from enterprise architects in large-scale Agile development: a multiple-case study. In: Proceedings of the Americas Conference on Information Systems (AMCIS) (2019)
57. Ömer Uludağ, Matthes, F.: Investigating the role of enterprise architects in supporting large-scale agile transformations: A multiple-case study. In: Proceedings of the Americas Conference on Information Systems (AMCIS). Salt Lake City, USA (2020). https://aisel.aisnet.org/amcis2020/digital_agility/digital_agility/2/
58. Ömer Uludağ, Matthes, F.: Large-scale agile development patterns for enterprise and solution architects. In: Proceedings of the European Conference on Pattern Languages of Programs (EuroPLoP). ACM (2020). https://doi.org/10.1145/3424771.3424895

59. Wagner, H.T., Moshtaf, J.: Individual it roles in business–it alignment and it governance. In: Proceedings of the 2016 European Conference on Information Systems (ECIS) (2016). https://doi.org/10.1109/HICSS.2016.610
60. Wang, Y., Pan, Y., Yan, M., Su, Z., Luan, T.H.: A survey on ChatGPT: AI–generated contents, challenges, and solutions. IEEE Open J. Comput. Society (2023). https://doi.org/10.1109/OJCS.2023.3300321
61. Waterman, M., Noble, J., Allan, G.: How much up-front? A grounded theory of Agile architecture. In: IEEE Xplore (2015). https://doi.org/10.1109/ICSE.2015.54
62. Williams, C.: A brief introduction to artificial intelligence. In: Proceedings OCEANS '83, pp. 94–99 (1983). https://doi.org/10.1109/OCEANS.1983.1152096
63. Zachman, J.A.: A framework for information systems architecture. IBM Syst. J. **26**(3), 276–292 (1987). https://doi.org/10.1147/sj.263.0276
64. Zachman, J.A.: The framework for enterprise architecture: Background, description and utility (2000). https://zachman-feac.com/the-framework-for-enterprise-architecture-background-description-and-utility

Reuse and Guidance for Generative AI Solution Development and Implementation: Knowledge Management Perspective

Dmitry Kudryavtsev(✉), Umair Ali Khan, Jukka Remes, and Janne Kauttonen

Haaga-Helia University of Applied Sciences, Ratapihantie 13, 00520 Helsinki, Finland
{dmitry.kudryavtsev,umairali.khan,jukka.remes, janne.kauttonen}@haaga-helia.fi

Abstract. Despite the high potential of Generative AI (GenAI) for increasing the productivity of knowledge work, the business value derived from GenAI remains limited. Reusable building blocks and guidelines for GenAI solution development and implementation may help companies. Various artefacts provide such reuse and guidance, including GenAI playbooks and guides, frameworks and platforms with reusable building blocks for GenAI systems, reference architectures and design patterns for GenAI solutions, and GenAI adoption frameworks. Existing reuse and guidance frameworks and tools for GenAI development and implementation have certain limitations. We suggest a knowledge management (KM) perspective for scoping and structuring GenAI development and implementation activities. This perspective applies knowledge processes such as knowledge capture, synthesis, access for organizing GenAI solution building blocks, fostering reuse and guiding development and implementation. The paper suggests a preliminary vision of the toolkit, which combines reusable and guiding artefacts to develop and implement GenAI solutions for leveraging organizational knowledge assets and processes.

Keywords: generative AI · knowledge management · software reuse · knowledge reuse · AI adoption

1 Introduction

Generative AI has significant potential to increase the productivity of knowledge work. This claim is supported by experiments in controlled settings (Dell'Acqua, 2023) and cases from business practice, such as customer-support agents at a large firm selling business-process software, who demonstrated a 15% productivity increase when assisted by generative AI (Brynjolfsson, 2025). At the same time, tangible business value from Generative AI implementation projects is still limited. BCG's report states that "only 26% of companies have advanced beyond the proof-of-concept stage to generate value" (de Bellefonds et al., 2024). While the recent MIT study makes an even more impressive claim that "Despite $30–40 billion in enterprise investment into GenAI, this report uncovers a surprising result in that 95% of organizations are getting zero return." (Challapally et al., 2025).

J. Barateiro et al. (Eds.): EDOC 2025 Workshops, LNBIP 571, pp. 70–83, 2026.
https://doi.org/10.1007/978-3-032-16234-2_5

Adopting Generative AI and creating value from it is especially challenging for small and medium-sized enterprises (SMEs), which lack the technical expertise and capabilities to implement GenAI solutions effectively. The literature review of Oldemeyer et al. (2024) identified the following three most frequent challenges for SMEs in the AI implementation in the industrial sector: knowledge, costs, and the low maturity level in digitalization.

We assume that knowledge and software reuse, accompanied by the corresponding guidance, can enhance GenAI adoption in business, especially by SMEs. The existing resources—such as GenAI playbooks, adoption frameworks, reference architectures, and modular development platforms—offer partial support by enabling reuse in both business and technical contexts. However, these resources often exhibit limitations: some are overly generic, others are narrowly focused on specific applications (e.g., chatbots), and many are vendor-specific (e.g., Microsoft Copilot). Furthermore, most existing solutions address either the business or technical dimension in isolation, whereas successful GenAI implementation requires integrated efforts across both domains.

This paper proposes a knowledge management (KM) perspective to structure and guide GenAI development and implementation. By organizing reusable solution elements around key knowledge processes (e.g., knowledge capture, synthesis, and access), this approach fosters reuse and provides a coherent, holistic framework for implementation. KM perspective emphasizes the role of the company's own knowledge assets and GenAI ability to leverage them. Additionally, KM enablers define crucial dimensions for planning GenAI initiatives.

The paper introduces a preliminary vision for a toolkit designed to support the development and deployment of GenAI solutions that enhance organizational knowledge processes and leverage the company's information resources.

2 Existing Reuse Support and Guidance for GenAI Solution Development and Implementation

2.1 General Overview of Knowledge and Software Reuse

The reuse of existing knowledge by individuals and organizations plays a critical role in addressing novel tasks and challenges. As outlined by Markus (2001), knowledge reuse occurs in various contexts, including reuse by original knowledge creators, practitioners engaged in similar work, novices seeking expertise, and secondary users extracting knowledge for new applications. To facilitate such reuse, diverse strategies and methodologies have been developed for structuring and presenting documented knowledge. These include ontologies, reusable tasks, problem-solving methods, various types of patterns (e.g. task, design, ontology, and workflow patterns), rules, decision models (e.g., trees), reference models, best practice cases, and documented lessons learned (Musen, 1992; Sandkuhl, 2014). In some domains, particularly enterprise architecture management, this reusable knowledge is conceptualized as "building blocks," exemplified by architecture and solution building blocks (The Open Group, 2022).

2.2 General Overview of Software Reuse Methods

Software development rarely involves building systems from scratch entirely. In practice, a substantial portion of software artefacts—such as source code and design documentation—are often replicated and modified to accommodate new requirements. Software reuse refers to the systematic process of developing software systems by leveraging existing software components, rather than initiating development from scratch.

Sommerville identified and described various software reuse approaches (Sommerville, 2010): design patterns, architectural patterns, software product lines, component-based software engineering, service-oriented systems, application frameworks, application system integrations, ERP systems, systems of systems, configurable application systems, legacy system wrapping, model-driven engineering, aspect-oriented software engineering, program generators, and program libraries.

2.3 Overview of the Existing Reuse Support and Guidance for GenAI Solution Development and Implementation

Guidance and reuse opportunities at both business and technical levels increasingly support the development and deployment of GenAI solutions (Fig. 1). At the business level, GenAI adoption & implementation are in focus. GenAI playbooks and guides, GenAI product development life-cycle, organizational AI implementation capability models exist at this level. At the technical level, modular development software frameworks (e.g., LangChain, Llamalndex), No-code platforms (e.g., Flowise, LangFlow), reference architectures, patterns, and principles for GenAI system engineering can be found.

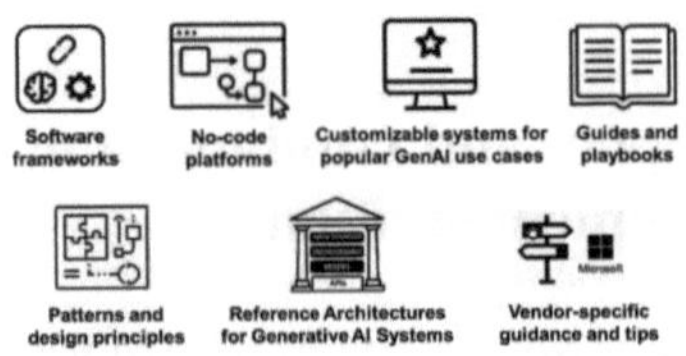

Fig. 1. Overview of the existing reuse support and guidance for GenAI solution development and implementation

2.4 Existing Reuse Support for GenAI Solution Development and Implementation

Software Frameworks. Several software frameworks and platforms enable developers to orchestrate and manage components of large language model (LLM)-based applications (Khan et al., 2025, b).

LangChain[1] is an open-source software framework designed to make it easier to build applications powered by large language models (LLMs). LangChain is built around reusable software components, enabling developers to assemble complex language-model-powered applications using pre-defined, interchangeable building

[1] https://www.langchain.com/

blocks. LangChain introduces modular components that can be reused across different applications and chains, providing customizable, use-case-specific pipelines (Topsakal, Akinci, 2023).

LlamaIndex[2] is a simple, flexible framework for building knowledge assistants using LLMs connected to enterprise data. From a software reuse perspective, LlamaIndex exemplifies modular, reusable software design by enabling the ingestion, indexing, and querying of diverse data types in a manner that supports composability, encapsulation, and interoperability. LlamaIndex is structured around discrete, interoperable modules—each responsible for a specific function in the data-to-LLM pipeline.

No-Code Generative AI Platforms and Software Reuse. The emergence of no-code platforms such as Flowise[3] and LangFlow[4] has significantly lowered the technical barriers associated with developing Generative AI (GenAI) applications. These platforms, built on top of frameworks like LangChain, provide visual, modular environments that enable the construction of AI workflows through drag-and-drop interfaces. GenAI extensions are growing in established no-code platforms, such as n8n. From a software engineering perspective, particularly in the context of software reuse, these platforms embody core principles of modularity, abstraction, and configurability.

Customizable Systems for Popular Business Use Cases. MaxKB[5] (Max Knowledge Brain) positions itself as an easy-to-use AI assistant that integrates Retrieval-Augmented Generation (RAG) pipelines, supports robust workflows, and provides advanced MCP tool-use capabilities. MaxKB can be applied in scenarios such as intelligent customer service, corporate internal knowledge bases, etc.

2.5 Existing Guidance for GenAI Solution Development and Implementation

Guides. Nika M. (2025) suggested the AI Product Development Lifecycle and associated guidelines. This life cycle involves transitioning from a business problem to an AI solution that addresses that problem. It consists of five stages: ideation, opportunity, developing a concept/prototype, testing and analysis, and rollout. This process primarily addresses the business side of GenAI solution development and is complemented by the more technical AI system lifecycle. Consulting companies actively suggest their guides or playbooks. A couple of examples below: Futurice developed the GenAI Playbook to help companies transform their business with AI (Futurice, 2024); KPMG provided a guide for identifying GenAI use cases along various business functions (marketing, sales, procurement etc.) and aligning GenAI with the transformation of these functions.

Reference Architectures for Generative AI Systems. Grau et al. (2025) provided a Reference Architecture for Generative AI Systems with corresponding design requirements for such systems. (Bucaioni et al., 2025) suggest a Functional Software Reference Architecture for LLM-Integrated Systems starting from architectural concerns (similar

[2] https://www.llamaindex.ai/
[3] https://flowiseai.com/
[4] https://www.langflow.org/
[5] https://github.com/1Panel-dev/MaxKB.

to the requirements in the previous paper). The authors also map three open-source LLM-integrated systems (including MaxKB, see above) to the proposed preliminary functional software reference architecture. A Reference Architecture for Designing Foundation Model-Based Systems is suggested in (Lu et al., 2023).

Patterns, Design Principles etc. A collection of architectural patterns for foundation model-based agents is suggested in (Liu et al., 2025). This catalogue links agent components with the relevant design patterns. (Zhou et al., 2024) suggested a decision-making model of architectural decisions for creating foundation model-based agents and analyzing trade-offs between various options for each type of architectural element. (Zhang et al., 2024) introduces a layered architecture that organizes LLM software system development into distinct layers, each characterized by specific attributes. By aligning capabilities with these layers, the framework encourages the systematic implementation of capabilities in effective and efficient ways that ultimately support desired functionalities and qualities. Design principles for generative AI applications are suggested in (Weisz et al., 2024).

Vendor-Specific Guidance and Reuse Support. Big players develop elaborate guidelines and recommendations for their own software products. For example, Microsoft developed Microsoft Scenario Library[6], which helps companies to define and implement Microsoft Copilot and other supporting products. Guidelines are structured by function and industry. For each function and industry, a scenario kit is provided. Such scenario kits describe possible GenAI use cases, including corresponding KPIs, benefits, workflows supported by Microsoft products, prompts for each step etc.

2.6 Limitations of Existing Frameworks, Methods and Tools

Existing reuse and guidance frameworks and tools for GenAI development and implementation have certain limitations:

- Some of them are too general, while others support only fragmented solution types (e.g. customer support chatbots).
- Some of them are vendor-specific – e.g. for Microsoft Copilot and Azure.
- They address only one of the business or technical levels, while successful AI implementation requires efforts at both levels.
- Proprietary solutions from consulting companies.

3 Knowledge Management Perspective for GenAI Solution Development and Implementation

The KM perspective can be used for scoping and structuring GenAI development and implementation activities. This perspective applies knowledge processes for organizing GenAI solution building blocks, fostering reuse and guiding development and implementation. Other KM insights can be applied for organizing and planning Gen AI implementation: knowledge services can be used for identifying building blocks, organizational knowledge assets should be considered as a key strategic resource of the company, and well-known KM enablers can define planning dimensions.

[6] https://adoption.microsoft.com/en-us/scenario-library.

3.1 GenAI as a Lever for Knowledge Processes

Recent publications highlight the role of Generative AI in knowledge processes (Alavi et al., 2024; Benbya et al., 2024; Murphy, 2023). Example roles of GenAI for knowledge processes are presented below. Extraction of needed information from business materials (including texts, videos, voice recordings) and guided knowledge elicitation from experts provide new opportunities for capturing knowledge. Intelligent search, chatbots and recommendation mechanisms for accessing organizational knowledge, including document repositories, databases, wikis, and CRMs. Automatic generation of business reports, sales proposals, and marketing materials as an example of synthesizing new organizational knowledge.

It is important to frame these roles within a paradigm of human-AI collaboration where humans contribute oversight, creativity, and strategic judgment while AI provides computational power, automation, and analytical insights (Frenette, 2024). For instance, in Knowledge Creation, a GenAI system might generate a draft report from multiple data sources, but the human expert provides critical judgment, contextual nuance, and final validation. This perspective positions GenAI not as a replacement for the knowledge worker but as an augmentation tool that handles cognitive heavy lifting, allowing humans to focus on higher-order tasks.

Knowledge processes provide an additional viewpoint on knowledge-intensive business processes. For example, sales business processes can be viewed as knowledge capture about customers and their needs, knowledge access to existing customer proposals and product descriptions, knowledge creation within customer proposal development, etc. The links between knowledge processes and business processes are established in the works (Heisig, 2006; Strohmaier, Tochtermann, 2005).

3.2 Knowledge Services for Specifying GenAI Solution Building Blocks

To specify the GenAI support for knowledge processes in a way that would help to design and develop GenAI-based solutions, the role of GenAI can be represented as knowledge services (Maier et al., 2009). Such a service-based approach helps business users easily understand the functionality of KM solutions and gives IT specialists an understanding of what information systems should do. Such generic services allow to see similarities across application domains and create reusable solutions that can be used in various application areas. These knowledge services correspond to activities, behaviors, or means supporting knowledge conveyance and transformation processes in ISO 30401:2018 (ISO, 2018; Carlucci et al., 2022).

The examples of GenAI-based knowledge services for the main knowledge processes:

1. Knowledge Creation: document/report synthesis service; idea generation service.
2. Knowledge Capture: capturing knowledge through voice service; information extraction service; automated categorization and tagging service.
3. Knowledge Access: conversational interface (chatbot) service; advanced/enhanced search service; personalized recommendations service.

This list of knowledge processes and services can be extended, e.g. by adding knowledge curation services for maintaining organizational knowledge base.

3.3 Leveraging Organizational Knowledge via Generative AI

KM perspective also emphasizes the role of company's own knowledge assets and GenAI's ability to leverage them. "Most users realize that GenAI systems are primarily trained on internet-based information and can't respond to prompts or questions regarding proprietary content or knowledge." So GenAI should be connected to the company's own information (Davenport, Alavi, 2023). Some companies have already implemented AI to leverage their knowledge assets. McKinsey recently introduced Lilli, their new generative AI tool: "Lilli aggregates our knowledge and capabilities in one place for the first time and will allow us to spend more time with clients activating those insights and recommendations and maximizing the value we can create," says Erik Roth, a senior partner with McKinsey who leads the firm's development of Lilli and integrating generative AI technologies into the company's work (McKinsey 2023).

3.4 KM Enablers as a Checklist for Planning GenAI Implementation

By adopting the KM perspective, GenAI implementation initiatives can also utilize ISO-compliant requirements for establishing, implementing and maintaining knowledge management systems (KMS) (ISO, 2018; Kudryavtsev, Sadykova, 2019; Carlucci et al., 2022). According to the ISO 30401:2018, the organizational KMS shall include and integrate elements of all the following enablers: human capital, processes, technology and infrastructure, governance and culture.

4 The Knowledge-Focused GenAI Development and Implementation Toolkit for SMEs

To enable reuse and guide the development and implementation of GenAI, we are creating a knowledge-focused toolkit for SMEs within the GAIK project (Kudryavtsev et al., 2025). This toolkit applies a KM perspective for GenAI solution development and implementation by helping to leverage the company's own knowledge assets and improve knowledge processes (capture, synthesis, and access). The toolkit will include software components (modules and code libraries), guidelines, process models, templates, and reusable knowledge models, enabling companies and technology providers to develop easy-to-deploy knowledge management solutions using business data.

4.1 Methodology for the GenAI Toolkit Development

The project[7] employs the action design research methodology (Sein et al., 2011) to develop and evaluate the GenAI toolkit (the instance of IT-based artefact). The GenAI toolkit development is a cooperation between industry and academia – the consortium includes three academic partners and five companies. The companies provide the use cases and testbeds for the R&D activities (Kudryavtsev et al., 2025). Within the project, we combine toolkit development with solution development for specific companies.

[7] GAIK (Generative AI-enhanced Knowledge Management in Business) project, https://gaik.ai/.

The company-specific solutions help to validate requirements, provide sample data, and enable testing and validation.

The toolkit development goes from two intertwined directions. The review of existing literature and technologies, as well as the top-down design of the toolkit vision, represent one direction. Identification of commonalities and reusable building blocks within the development of company-specific solutions represents another bottom-up direction.

4.2 Requirements for a GenAI Toolkit (Based on GAIK and FAIR Projects)

We defined the preliminary requirements based on the previous research (Kudryavtsev et al., 2024) and insights from the advisory experience within the Finnish AI Region (FAIR) European Digital Innovation Hub (EDIHs)[8] (Khan et al., 2025, a). The previous research included interviews and co-creation workshops with over 20 companies. FAIR EDIH experience includes approximately 50 + consultancy cases related to GenAI (by Aug 2025). The preliminary requirements include:

A. Business-level support: GenAI solution should generate value for the company and provide a reasonable return-on-investment, so business-level guidelines and building blocks are needed.
B. Technical guidance and reuse are needed to answer these questions: how to develop GenAI-based software system? What components can be reused?
C. Support for the whole life-cycle: requirements analysis, development, implementation & operation.
D. Suitability for SMEs with low AI maturity and limited tech expertise.

4.3 Preliminary Scope of the GenAI Toolkit

The scope of the toolkit extends the requirements. The generic and company-specific use cases define the scope of the toolkit, and identification of these use cases is described in more detail in (Kudryavtsev et al., 2024). For knowledge capture, the generic use case is speech-to-structured document conversion. For knowledge access, companies need GenAI assistants to support the employees' interaction with the company's knowledge and systems. For knowledge synthesis, GenAI assistants are required to produce documents or reports from various data sources. We also defined company-specific use cases for each generic one based on the needs of partner companies (Table 1).

Although Table 1 associates each company-specific case with a single generic use case and knowledge process, it often happens that a company-specific case requires multiple knowledge processes and corresponding knowledge services. For example, incident reporting requires not only knowledge synthesis but also the capture of knowledge from various sources and formats. It is shown in Table 2, which also demonstrates two similar company-specific cases and their abstraction into a generic use case "Structured report generation from speech, images and text". The solution for such a generic use case can be considered as a software product line (see Sect. 2).

[8] https://www.fairedih.fi/en/

Table 1. Generic and company-specific use cases.

Generic use cases	Company-specific use cases
1. From speech, images and texts to structured documents. **K-Capture**	a. Creation of closed captions and spoken translations in the Nordic and English languages for educational videos and podcasts in Finnish b. Creating construction site diaries from speech, images and text c. Building inspections report creation assistant
2. Report and document creation assistant **K-Synthesis**	a. Purchase order processing assistant (converts customer purchase orders into structured data for the ERP system) b. Incident reporting assistant c. Customer experience reporting
3. AI assistant to talk to your company data and systems. **K-Access**	a. Customer support assistant, Q&A based on the ticket history b. Sales and customer onboarding assistant for a complex, customizable software product c. Search and recommendation mechanisms for the library of educational videos and podcasts

Table 2. Generalization over the set of similar company-specific cases

Use cases	Knowledge capture	Knowledge synthesis
Company-specific use cases		
Incident reporting assistant (Company A)	Captures voice-recorded observations and site photos from employees, then transcribes and processes them to extract information	Assembling a structured incident report
Creating construction site diaries (Company B)	Captures project manager's voice-recorded site observations, voice calls and photos	Assembling structured construction site diaries
Generalized use-cases		
Structured report generation from speech, images and text	Capturing needed information from speech, text, and photos	Assembling information from various sources into a report with the needed structure

4.4 Preliminary GenAI Toolkit Development Design Principles

To satisfy the defined requirements (see Sect. 4.2) and the needed scope (see Sect. 4.3), we suggested a preliminary set of design principles for the GenAI toolkit:

1. Knowledge processes and services are used for scoping and organizing building blocks for GenAI solution development and implementation.
2. Knowledge of the company, its customers and partners should be leveraged by GenAI solutions (utilization of LLMs' general knowledge is insufficient).
3. Combination of no-code building blocks with code-based components.
4. Architecture as the backbone for a GenAI toolkit development and utilization. Generic implementation-independent architecture/blueprints specification with links to implementation-specific components.
5. Value-based approach for WHY-aspect analysis of GenAI solutions.
6. Core assets of a GenAI toolkit should address the complete solution development life-cycle and include requirements, architecture, components, testing and evaluation tools.
7. Combination of component-based software development (Lau, Cola, 2018) with software product lines (Northrop et al., 2012), which implies that components are not only grouped by knowledge process but also assembled into typical solutions for generic business needs.
8. Inclusion of process and decision models to guide reuse-based GenAI solution development and implementation.
9. Guidance and reuse address various GenAI solution enablers: human capital, processes, technology and infrastructure, governance and culture.
10. Unified language for specifying both business- and technical-level building blocks (workflows, software components), human- and machine-readable, "design-as-code".
11. Separate processes for component-based software development for reuse (1) and with reuse (2).
12. Human-in-the-Loop workflows: The toolkit's components should be designed to facilitate human oversight, review, and refinement of AI-generated outputs. This principle treats GenAI as a collaborative partner rather than a fully autonomous agent, ensuring accuracy, contextual relevance, and user trust in the knowledge processes it supports.

4.5 GenAI Toolkit Architecture Vision

The toolkit is structured across three levels (Fig. 2). At the business layer, the focus is on identifying business value and use cases, as well as defining the solution's business logic. The technical layer provides reusable software components to support system development, guides the system development lifecycle, and includes the selection and evaluation of large language models. Finally, the GenAI implementation layer outlines the process for developing and deploying solutions, while also addressing AI readiness assessment and preparation.

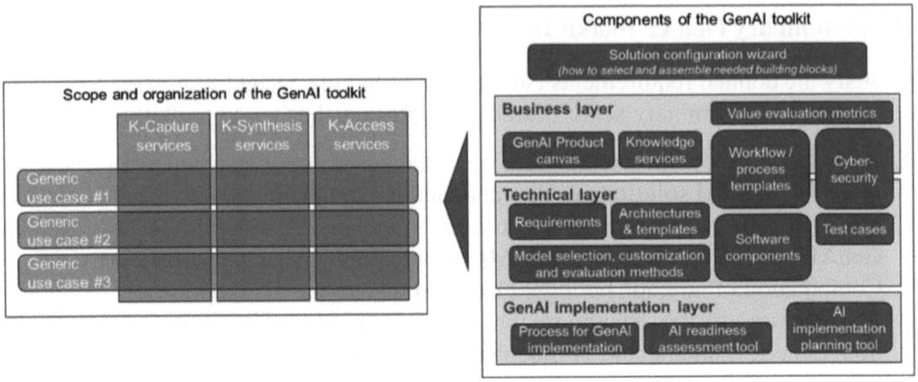

Fig. 2. High-level architecture of the GenAI toolkit for SMEs

5 Conclusions

This study explored the potential of a KM perspective to enhance reuse and guidance in GenAI solution development and implementation, particularly for SMEs. By analyzing existing frameworks and tools, the paper identified key limitations in current approaches and argued for the integration of the KM perspective into GenAI solution development and implementation. To enable reuse and guide the development and implementation of GenAI, the paper suggests a knowledge-focused toolkit for SMEs. Future work will focus on elaborating the requirements, vision, and architecture of the GenAI toolkit; defining a comprehensive list of generic knowledge services to be supported; and identifying key reusable assets for the toolkit. These steps aim to operationalize the KM perspective and facilitate practical, scalable GenAI adoption for SMEs.

Acknowledgments. The present work is part of the Generative AI-Enhanced Knowledge Management in Business (GAIK) project, which is co-funded by the European Union (European Regional Development Fund).

Disclosure of Interests. The authors have no competing interests to declare that are relevant to the content of this article.

References

Alavi, M., Leidner, D.E., Mousavi, R.A.: Knowledge management perspective of generative artificial intelligence. J. Assoc. Inf. Syst. **25**(1), 1–12 (2024). https://doi.org/10.17705/1jais.00859

Benbya, H., Strich, F., Tamm, T.: Navigating generative artificial intelligence promises and perils for knowledge and creative work. J. Assoc. Inf. Syst. **25**(1), 23–36 (2024). https://doi.org/10.17705/1jais.00861

Brynjolfsson, E., Li, D., Raymond, L.: Generative AI at work. Q. J. Econ. **140**(2), 889–942 (2025). https://doi.org/10.1093/qje/qjae044

Bucaioni, A., Weyssow, M., He, J., Lyu, Y., Lo, D.: A functional software reference architecture for LLM-integrated systems. In: 2025 IEEE 22nd International Conference on Software Architecture Companion (ICSA-C), pp. 1–5. IEEE (2025). https://doi.org/10.1109/ICSA-C65153.2025.00006

Carlucci, D., Kudryavtsev, D., Santarsiero, F., Lagrutta, R., Garavelli, A.C.: The ISO 30401 knowledge management systems: a new frame for managing knowledge. Conceptualisation and practice. Knowl. Manag. Res. Pract. **20**(6), 975–986 (2022). https://doi.org/10.1080/14778238.2022.2118637

Challapally, A., Pease, C., Raskar, R., Chari, P.: The GenAI Divide - State of AI in Business 2025. MIT Nanda (2025)

Davenport, T., Alavi, M.: How to Train Generative AI Using Your Company's Data (2023). https://hbr.org/2023/07/how-to-train-generative-ai-using-your-companys-data

Dell'Acqua, F., et al.: Navigating the jagged technological frontier: field experimental evidence of the effects of AI on knowledge worker productivity and quality. Harvard Business School Technology & Operations Mgt. Unit Working Paper No. 24–013 (2023). https://doi.org/10.2139/ssrn.4573321

de Bellefonds, et al.: Where's the Value in AI? BCG report (2024). https://www.bcg.com/publications/2024/wheres-value-in-ai

Frenette, J.: Human-AI collaboration models: frameworks for effective integration of human oversight and AI insights in business processes. Int. J. Res. Appl. Sci. Eng. Technol. **12**(12), 1475–1487 (2024). https://doi.org/10.22214/ijraset.2024.66051

Futurice. Generative AI Playbook: Transform your business with AI (2024). https://www.futurice.com/downloads/en-generative-ai-business-playbook

Heisig, P.: The GPO-WM® method for the integration of knowledge management into business processes. In: International Conference on Knowledge Management, Graz, Austria, pp. 331–337 (2006)

International Organization for Standardization (ISO): ISO 30401:2018 Knowledge management systems – Requirements. International Organization for Standardization – ISO (2018)

Grau, M.C., Reinhard, P., Bauer-Hänsel, I., Blohm, I.: Rethinking AI Design Practices: A Reference Architecture for Generative AI Systems. ECIS 2025 (2025). https://aisel.aisnet.org/ecis2025/des_research/des_research/6

Khan, U.A., Kauttonen, J., Kudryavtsev, D.: AI adoption in finnish SMEs: key findings from AI consultancy at a european digital innovation hub. In: 2025 IEEE 23rd World Symposium on Applied Machine Intelligence and Informatics (SAMI), pp. 000465–000470. IEEE (2025a). https://doi.org/10.1109/SAMI63904.2025.10883271

Khan, U.A., et al.: Evaluating generative AI technology choices and software frameworks for developing AI solutions in business. In: 26th European Conference on Knowledge Management (ECKM 2025), Lahti, Finland, pp. 1289–1294 (2025b). https://doi.org/10.34190/eckm.26.2.3809

KPMG: AI & generative AI in functional transformation: A practical guide to the opportunity for AI across the front, middle and back office (2024). https://assets.kpmg.com/content/dam/kpmgsites/uk/pdf/2024/06/ai-and-generative-ai-in-functional-transformation.pdf

Kudryavtsev, D., Sadykova, D.: Towards architecting a knowledge management system: requirements for an ISO compliant framework. In: The Practice of Enterprise Modeling: 12th IFIP Working Conference, PoEM 2019, Luxembourg, Luxembourg, 27–29 November 2019, Proceedings 12, pp. 36–50. Springer (2019). https://doi.org/10.1007/978-3-030-35151-9_3

Kudryavtsev, D., Khan, U., Kauttonen, J.: Transforming knowledge management using generative AI: from theory to practice. In: Proceedings of the 16th International Joint Conference on Knowledge Discovery, Knowledge Engineering and Knowledge Management - Volume 3: KMIS; ISBN 978-989-758-716-0, SciTePress, pp. 362–370 (2024). https://doi.org/10.5220/0013071400003838

Kudryavtsev, D., et al.: Building a generative AI toolkit for leveraging knowledge processes: the GAIK project report. In: 26th European Conference on Knowledge Management (ECKM 2025), Lahti, Finland, pp. 1317–1321 (2025). https://doi.org/10.34190/eckm.26.2.3701

Lau, K.K., Cola, S.D.: An introduction to component-based software development. World Scientific (2018). https://doi.org/10.1142/10486

Liu, Y., et al.: Agent design pattern catalogue: a collection of architectural patterns for foundation model-based agents. J. Syst. Softw. **220**, 112278 (2025). https://doi.org/10.1016/j.jss.2024.112278

Lu, Q., Zhu, L., Xu, X., Xing, Z., Whittle, J.: Towards responsible AI in the era of generative AI: a reference architecture for designing foundation model-based systems. IEEE Softw. (2024). https://doi.org/10.1109/MS.2024.3406333

Maier, R., Hädrich, T., Peinl, R.: Enterprise Knowledge Infrastructures. Springer (2009)

Markus, L.M.: Toward a theory of knowledge reuse: types of knowledge reuse situations and factors in reuse success. J. Manag. Inf. Syst. **18**(1), 57–93 (2001)

McKinsey & Company: Meet Lilli, our generative AI tool that's a researcher, a time saver, and an inspiration (2023). https://www.mckinsey.com/about-us/new-at-mckinsey-blog/meet-lilli-our-generative-ai-tool

Murphy, T.: How generative AI can improve knowledge management. TechTarget (2023). https://www.techtarget.com/searchcontentmanagement/feature/How-generative-AI-can-improve-knowledge-management

Musen, M.: Dimensions of knowledge sharing and reuse. Comput. Biomed. Res. **25**(5), 435–467 (1992)

Nika, M.: Building AI-Powered Products: The Essential Guide to AI and GenAI Product Management. O'Reilly Media (2025)

Northrop, L.M., Clements, P.C., Krut, R., Little, R., McGregor, J., O'Brien, L.: A framework for software product line practice, version 5.0 (2012)

Oldemeyer, L., Jede, A., Teuteberg, F.: Investigation of artificial intelligence in SMEs: a systematic review of the state of the art and the main implementation challenges. Manag. Rev. Q. **75**(2), 1185–1227 (2024). https://doi.org/10.1007/s11301-024-00405-4

Sandkuhl, K.: Knowledge reuse: survey of existing techniques and classification approach. In: Business Intelligence, vol. 205, pp. 126–148. Springer, Berlin (2014). https://doi.org/10.1007/978-3-319-17551-5_5

Sein, M.K., Henfridsson, O., Purao, S., Rossi, M., Lindgren, R.: Action design research. MIS Q. 37–56 (2011). https://aisel.aisnet.org/misq/vol35/iss1/5/

Sommerville, I.: Software Engineering, 10th edn. Pearson Education Limited (2010)

Strohmaier, M., Tochtermann, K.: B-KIDE: a framework and a tool for business process-oriented knowledge infrastructure development. Knowl. Process. Manag. **12**(3), 171–189 (2005)

The Open Group: Section 5. Building Blocks in Architecture Content, The TOGAF Standard (2022). https://goodelearning.com/togaf-framework-what-is-a-building-block-in-togaf/

Topsakal, O., Akinci, T.C.: Creating large language model applications utilizing langchain: a primer on developing LLM apps fast. In: International Conference on Applied Engineering and Natural Sciences, vol. 1, no. 1, pp. 1050–1056 (2023). https://doi.org/10.59287/icaens.1127

Weisz, J.D., He, J., Muller, M., Hoefer, G., Miles, R., Geyer, W.: Design principles for generative AI applications. In: Proceedings of the 2024 CHI Conference on Human Factors in Computing Systems, pp. 1–22 (2024). https://doi.org/10.1145/3613904.3642466

Zhang, D., Xu, X., Wang, C., Xing, Z., Mao, R.: A Layered Architecture for Developing and Enhancing Capabilities in Large Language Model-based Software Systems. arXiv preprint arXiv:2411.12357 (2024). https://doi.org/10.48550/arXiv.2411.12357

Zhou, J., et al.: A taxonomy of architecture options for foundation model-based agents: Analysis and decision model. arXiv preprint arXiv:2408.02920 (2024). https://doi.org/10.48550/arXiv.2408.02920

Enhancing Process Model Comprehension Through Animations: A Comparative Study of Tokens vs. Highlighting

Ilia Maslov[1(✉)], Stephan Poelmans[1], and Banu Aysolmaz[2]

[1] KU Leuven, Warmoesberg 26, 1000 Brussels, Belgium
ilia.maslov@kuleuven.be
[2] Eindhoven University of Technology, 5612 AZ Eindhoven, Netherlands

Abstract. Process modeling involves creating diagrammatic representations of business processes, commonly employed for collaborative efforts, information exchange, and documentation. Considerable challenges hinder the training and learning of process modeling in comprehending process models, primarily due to the absence of systematic teaching approaches. Although various visualization and animation techniques, such as tokens and highlighting, exhibit significant potential in enhancing the guidance of modelers, this area remains underexplored. This research delves into an in-depth exploration of animated process model comprehension by novice modelers with a focus on comparing the two animation features. The study compares the effects of tokens and highlighting in process models on their comprehension by novice modelers, measuring their objective comprehension (correct answers, time to completion), subjective comprehension (subjective cognitive load and technology acceptance) and interactions (NASA-TLX survey and semi-structured feedback on survey questions). The paper confirms similarity in using both types of animation to improve the comprehension of novice modelers and suggests pedagogical implications for using animations to improve novice modelers' comprehension and learning outcomes.

Keywords: Process modelling · Token-animated process models · Highlighting in process models · Process model comprehension · Process modeling education · Survey-based experimentation

1 Introduction

Process Modeling (PM) typically entails converting textual specifications into graphical representations, with the goal of enhancing dialogue between business and IT, clarifying employee responsibilities, optimizing or redesigning workflows, or facilitating automation via enterprise software solutions. Business Process Model and Notation (BPMN) has emerged as the industry standard, necessitating proficient PM practitioners [1, 2].

The clarity and comprehensibility of process models are among their most critical attributes [3], significantly influencing how individuals interpret and navigate models [4]. For beginners, understanding process models accurately is challenging due to possible

J. Barateiro et al. (Eds.): EDOC 2025 Workshops, LNBIP 571, pp. 84–98, 2026.
https://doi.org/10.1007/978-3-032-16234-2_6

complex behaviors a process model can represent through elements such as gateways, which may not be explicit to the student through a static model [4, 5]. Educators face difficulties in effectively teaching process modelling concepts, as they lack the tools to depict process model behavior that improve reading behaviors and comprehension strategies of students [2]. Beginners often navigate process paths in a linear manner, display more frequent fixations, and require additional time to interpret information, suggesting a higher cognitive load [4]. Reading intensity correlates with lower knowledge, implying increased re-reads and cognitive load. Experienced users concentrate on critical decision nodes and optimize their reading strategies [6].

One approach to improving process model comprehension is through dynamic visualization techniques implementing ***token-based*** or ***highlighting*** animations [5, 7, 8]. Highlighting animation colors (highlights) the process activities and gateways leaves a trace of the followed process flow by immediately coloring the activated paths and it can effectively communicate the sequence of PM activities and clarify the interactions and behaviors of various model elements [5]. Tokens progress through the workflow, moving from one activity to the next as colored dots, taking time to go through the sequence flows and can also explain the interactions and behaviors of various model elements, but do not leave an explicit trace [8]. While both aim to aid understanding, they may differ in how they guide perception due to different visualization methods. Tokens show the current state of the process instance and are suggested to better indicate the frequency of certain task activations, whereas highlighting may indicate better the process instance execution path.

To the best of the authors' knowledge, no research has been conducted comparing directly in an empirical setting the effectiveness of highlighting and token animations in improving process model comprehension. Although both techniques arguably have different impacts on how process instance behavior is visualized, their comparative effects remain unexplored. By comparing the two techniques, one could potentially identify their better fit to improve comprehension or learning of certain topics, such as specific patterns, such as teaching specific patterns via a specific technique [9]. This necessitates the following research question (RQ):

RQ1: *How do the effect of token-based and highlighting animations compare in improving PM comprehension?*

Furthermore, despite the promise of animations to enhance comprehension and learning, systematic research on human-model interactions with animations remains limited, especially in the educational context [5, 8, 10–12]. These interactions depend on both the modeler's process modeling skills and the animation features used, which may need to be adapted to the learner's level [5]. Learners might even choose to ignore animations if the task feels too simple [8, 10, 13]. Still, animations can enrich learning contexts—such as flipped classrooms—by supporting instructors and enabling more engaging, interactive model exploration [8, 10, 11, 13]. The lack of empirical comparison between animation types prevents further understanding into how to best employ animations to improve comprehension and learning outcomes of novice modelers, a recent initiative [5, 8, 13]. Different animation techniques may promote the different use and acceptance of the animation techniques [14]. This underscores the need for understanding human-model interactions with animated process models, differentiated based on the animation technique. To this end, we propose the following RQ:

RQ2: *How do human-model interactions differ between token-based and highlighting animated process models?*

To answer the RQs, the paper implements survey-based experimentation methodology using previously validated BPMN process models for comparing the effect of two types of animations on PM comprehension [5, 8] via (semi-)controlled surveying of novice modelers in a higher education context. By controlling for other comprehension factors—such as modeler expertise, layout, and task type—we isolate the animation type to examine its impact on human-model interaction and resulting comprehension.

The paper is structured as follows: Sect. 2 provides a literature review of existing research. Section 3 outlines the applied experimentation methodology. Section 4 presents findings from the objective and perceived comprehension results of the experiment, and Sect. 5 discusses the results, limitations, threats to validity, and future research directions.

2 Background and Related Work

Process Modeling (PM) involves externalizing mental representations into graphical models to facilitate shared understanding [15, 16]. Despite this, interpretation discrepancies persist, underscoring the importance of comprehension [1]. PM is composed of reading and designing models, where clarity and interpretability take precedence over mere syntactic or semantic accuracy [3].

In the learning context, PM engages various cognitive processes, including abstracting, conceptualizing, associating, contextualizing, visualizing, interpreting, sense-making, judging, evaluating, and, in group settings, communicating, discussing, and reaching agreements [12, 17]. Recent studies on PM education emphasize flipped and project-based learning approaches, highlighting their benefits in enhancing student engagement, comprehension, and practical PM skills, while also identifying challenges such as the need for direct instructor support and structured guidance to balance autonomy and learning outcomes [12, 18].

This study focuses on reading and understanding process models, as a pre-requisite for further learning [18]. Comprehension can be measured objectively by the number of correct answers and time taken to answer, and subjectively by perceived difficulty [4]. Factors affecting PM comprehension include (1) individual (modeler) factors, (2) model characteristics, and (3) human-model interactions, such as model reading behaviors [4, 8, 19].

Individual factors typically include internal cognitive aspects crucial to comprehension, such as cognitive load capacity, which is influenced by an individual's working memory [4]. Higher education levels improve comprehension scores [11], familiarity with a domain reduces cognitive load [4], and age affects fixation count [2, 13].

Model factors also impact comprehension. These factors include the modeling language [4], model size [5], and semantic richness provided by features like task descriptions [4]. Complex logic, defined by numerous uncommon elements causing deviations from standard flow, can obstruct understanding [5]. Still, the explicit articulation of business rules within models boosts precision and diminishes cognitive load [20]. The arrangement of process tasks, including bending and modularization, is critical in their legibility and ease of interpretation [21].

Furthermore, visual cues, including task coloring, lower cognitive demands and support the assimilation of information [6]. Such cues are related to animations that can improve comprehension [5], which is the focus of this research. Animated process models offer substantial cognitive benefits, as dynamic visual representations are easier to process than purely static notation [5, 7]. Animations clarify model elements, making them more intuitive, while also providing real-time feedback on model correctness [4, 5, 7].

By directing attention to pertinent model elements and the way they are connected, animations can assist in reducing cognitive load and expanding working memory capacity [4, 5]. There are two most promising animation techniques: token-based and highlighting. Token-based animation is where colored indicators (tokens) dynamically traverse a process model, mirroring its execution logic [8]. Highlighting of a process path animation technique is signifying the behavior of an underlying process instance by coloring activated process paths [5]. Other animation features exist, such as 3D, VR-based visualizations [22], though they often are only developed and used by a select research group largely for research purposes, and unlike tokens, lack widespread adoption in the industry.

The integration of **Visualization, Animation, and Simulation (VAS)** features in PM enhances both process model comprehension and PM learning [4, 5, 8, 13]. Though often inseparable and interrelated, it is good to make attempt at separating the meaning of Visualization, Animation, and Simulation (VAS) features contained in process models. *Visualization* is understood as making process information more accessible by presenting it in a graphical format. *Animation* introduces motion, aiding in understanding the flow of process elements. *Simulation* generates hypothetical or real-world process instances using the underlying process model semantics, allowing for "what-if" scenario analysis, though within animation context, typically at the individual process instance level [8, 10]. This understanding of Simulation in process model can differ from BPM community, where it is understood as large-scale simulations over many instances [1], though we argue, the two definitions could aim at the same underlying phenomena but studied at individual ("qualitative") or large-scale ("quantitative") degree. Distinguishing can be relevant for instance in this case: Highlighting animation and Token animation both provide dynamic element but both animation techniques are visualized using different approaches (highlight coloring of BPMN elements or colored token). The study uses Visualization, Animation and Simulation interchangeably to refer to VAS features of token-based or highlighting animation.

Finally, **human-model interactions** factor is understood as *"the way the reader interacts with the model."* According to the distributed cognition theory, the intrinsic (individual's factors) and extrinsic (model's factors) must be aligned to result in an effectively arranged interaction: it is critical to improve the efficiency of interaction to improve comprehension and learning outcomes in PM [4, 8, 19]. Different model reading strategies can influence comprehension, which is determined by the modeler's experience and the model's layout [21]. Eye-tracking studies showed, for instance, that novice process modelers may need more support, especially in learning contexts [2]. Animations support dynamic interaction with process models, enhancing comprehension and knowledge acquisition through interactive learning experiences [10, 11]. Studying human-model interactions with animations is essential for tailoring animation use to learners' modeling skills and optimizing learning outcomes across educational contexts, such as flipped classrooms [5, 8, 10].

3 Methodology

To answer the RQs and explore the differences in the effects of token-based and highlighting animation types on BPMN process model comprehension and to study the differences in human-model interactions between the two animation types, we conducted a between-subjects experiment with random assignment to the condition. Survey-based experiment on process model comprehension is one of the empirical methods, and among the most effective at validating hypotheses [2, 5, 8]. Building upon the work of [8] and [5], we adopt their experimentation design and material to answer the RQs, which are available in the appendix[1]. The following section describes experimental design, participants, and materials.

All student participants were explicitly informed that their survey, interaction, and performance data would be used for research purposes, and written informed consent was obtained prior to any data collection; participation was voluntary, withdrawal was possible at any time without consequence, and all data were anonymized/pseudonymized in line with GDPR.

The online experiment was held at one of the sessions of the course on business process management in an engineering master's program at a Dutch university. Participants were offered individualized feedback on their performance in a survey in preparation for their summative evaluations at the end of the semester. 38 students participated, 11 females and 27 males. Some students were given an option to answer the survey at home given their promise of not using any other material when answering the survey. We distributed the invitations to token and highlighting surveys by random condition assignment, resulting in 19 participants in the token condition, and 19 in the highlighting condition.

Participants first filled in the pre-survey containing demographic and knowledge questions. Then the participants were given 6 process models in separate pages together with 4 multiple choice questions per process model. The correct score to multiple choice questions and time to answer are one of the most used measures in measuring process model objective comprehension [4, 5]. The students were asked to give feedback about the animations in a semi-structured approach.

The average age was 23 (*SD* = *1.34*). All participants were taught BPMN, and a small proportion knew other process modelling languages: PetriNets (31%) and Activity Diagrams (13%). The business profile of the novice modeler participants matches the profile of the industry professionals in the future [9].

[1] For videos with animations, questionnaire items and anonymized dataset, please consult openly accessible Appendix via https://zenodo.org/records/17167264.

Based on a combined measure of the number of models read, created and the time since process modelling was learned [5], participants can be considered as relatively experienced process modelers undergoing advanced training at the university (M = 8.97 out of 15; SD = 1.73). Participants were somewhat knowledgeable of the idea of tokens (an animation feature). In a pre-test to measure BPMN knowledge, participants (experiment procedure described below) gave on average 80% correct score on the basic semantics and syntax questions, and down to 20% on the more complex topics. We thus rate the participant sample as rather homogeneous in terms of its educational background and process modelling expertise, who are somewhat proficient in process modelling and are currently undergoing further training (Fig. 1).

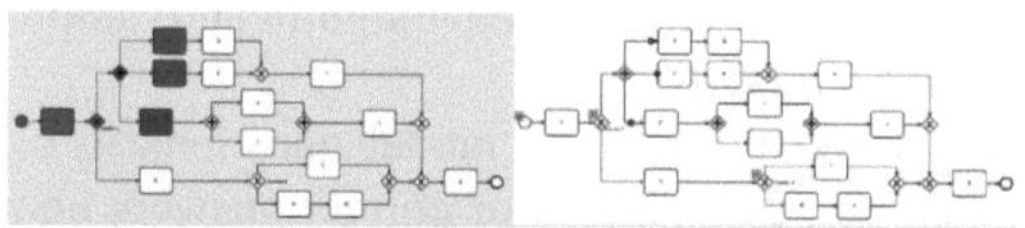

Fig. 1. Screenshots of the same model animated with highlighting (left) and token-based animation (right).

Using the BPMN 2.0 standard in Camunda Modeler, we generated 6 abstract models that had 20 to 30 nodes, with 4 multiple-choice questions per model, adapted from [5]. "Abstract model" means that task activities and conditions don't represent semantic meaning, by using abstract labels such as task "A" or "Condition A". This minimizes the effect of domain and English knowledge on process model comprehension [5].

The models were then animated using openly available PM animator tools Camunda Simulator (for token version) and PRIME animator (for highlighting, developed in [5]). Tokens appear at the start events and disappear at the end event in the process model. Meanwhile, tokens progress through the workflow, moving from one activity to the next. However, BPMN does not account for the actual time a token takes to travel along the sequence flow between 2 consecutive activities or events. In a bigger model, it could take a token up to a few seconds to traverse the sequence flow. According to the BPMN standard, however, an activity should start immediately once the previous step is completed, meaning that a token leaving a task should instantly appear in the next activity without delay. In other words, the time it takes for tokens to move along the sequence flows is not in line with BPMN that assumes no duration of the sequence flows.

Highlighting the process activities and gateways leaves a trace of the followed process flow by immediately coloring the activated paths in green aligning better with the semantics of the BPMN standard). Highlighting also shows the paths that can be activated by coloring in grey. When re-activating, highlighting re-colors the BPMN element in green. Unlike tokens, highlighting is more faithful to the BPMN, suggesting immediate activation of process tasks and gateways and assuming no duration of the sequence flows.

Process scenarios were adapted to fit the question (i.e., an animation depicted the more relevant flow of the process instance to help answer the questions, which relied on the correct semantic understanding of these relevant parts of the model). Four models had a single animation video to help answer all four questions. Two models had three and four videos, specific to the questions. The only difference was the method of animation, while the animated process instance and the underlying BPMN model remained the same.

These animated models were recorded via screen-capture software, resulting in videos that showed the same process scenario via tokens and highlighting animation features. These videos hence represent low-interaction animation, as defined by [5], since a modeler could not select his/her own scenarios. In the survey, animations were automatically started and looped through as a participant went through the question models.

We decided not to have a control condition with a static process model, as past research indicated that both animation types have significantly improved comprehension with respect to static process models [5, 8].

Participants first answered the process model questions to measure participants' *objective comprehension*, i.e., the number of correct answers about the models (also called effectiveness of comprehension), the time it took for them to answer (efficiency of comprehension) [4] to compare between the two animation types. Then, participants answered questions measuring subjective comprehension.

Subjective comprehension is a subjective difficulty (for instance, experienced as "cognitive effort" or challenge expensed to read a model) of performing process modelling tasks [4]. Subjective comprehension is typically measured by the cognitive load scale [4] and Technology Acceptance Model (TAM) constructs, which, according to [23], can measure not only intention to adopt Information Systems, but also the *subjective comprehension* of process models.

Hence, to measure subjective comprehension, we first used the cognitive load scale survey measuring modelers' intrinsic, extraneous and germane loads, adapted from [24, 25]. Then, we further used the Technology Acceptance Model (TAM) adapted to PM context using the study of [8] to gauge modelers' perceptions on the utility of animations in improving understandability and ease of understanding the process models, along with their preference to use animated models in the future.

To measure the *efficiency of human-model interactions*, a critical component especially in the context of determining the success of animations on process model comprehension and learning [5, 8, 10, 13], we employed NASA Task Load Index (NASA-TLX). NASA-TLX is a widely used, subjective, multidimensional assessment tool that rates perceived workload to assess a task, system, or team's effectiveness or other aspects of performance, used in the study of human factors and it is used to study experiences and interactions in human-model interactions in process modelling context [26]. We used NASA-TLX adapted from [26].

To further study human-model interactions, the survey concluded with questions pertaining to the modelers' feedback on how they used the animations and their general qualitative feedback on the animations for improving comprehension and PM learning [8]. Specifically, we asked participants to mention advantages, disadvantages, and their recommendations for improving PM learning via animations. Answers were recorded, transcribed, and analyzed inductively to generate thematic codes using a qualitative analysis assistance software [27].

In the following section, we present the general descriptives of the data and the quantitative and qualitative analysis of the *objective comprehension* (analysing correct answers and time to answer), *subjective comprehension* (analysing cognitive load and TAM constructs) and human-*model interactions* (analysing NASA-TLX constructs and semi-structured feedback).

4 Data Analysis Results

4.1 Objective Comprehension: Number of Correct Answers and Time to Answer

We first analyse objective comprehension scores. Using an independent t-test (with a 5% significance level), we did not find any significant differences between the two animation types in either the individual model scores or the total score. Table 1 shows the descriptive statistics.

Table 1. Descriptive statistics comparing objective comprehension between techniques.

Model	Tokens (n = 19)				Highlighting (n = 19)			
	Correct answers		Time to completion (sec)		Correct answers		Time to completion (sec)	
	Mean	SD	Mean	SD	Mean	SD	Mean	SD
1	0,84	0,15	150,72	62,26	0,78	0,18	150,43	57,53
2	0,91	0,17	174,51	100,06	0,89	0,19	167,25	45,61
3	0,79	0,28	148,02	62,76	0,88	0,19	147,53	51,22
4	0,64	0,17	112,53	50,87	0,70	0,18	121,01	33,25
5	0,66	0,29	185,90	289,09	0,80	0,16	124,85	24,90
6	0,95	0,10	92,21	25,01	0,87	0,21	108,61	36,72
Total	0,80	0,10	863,90	426,24	0,82	0,10	819,68	169,11

4.2 Subjective Comprehension: TAM and Cognitive Load

Table 2 below presents the combined descriptive statistics of both measurements, as they are means across all individual participants' responses. There were no statistically significant differences in the 8 factors of the two surveys: both animation types had a comparable effect on subjective comprehension.

Table 2. Descriptive statistics comparing subjective comprehension between techniques.

Survey	Survey Factor	Tokens (n = 19)		Highlighting (n = 19)		Total (n = 38)	
		Mean	SD	Mean	SD	Mean	SD
Cognitive Load Scale (CLS)	Intrinsic Cognitive Load (ICL)	3,0	1,0	3,1	1,0	3,0	1,0
	Extraneous Cognitive Load (ECL)	2,2	0,7	2,6	0,8	2,4	0,7
	Germane Cognitive Load (GCL)	4,0	0,8	4,0	0,8	4,0	0,8
Technology Acceptance Model (TAM)	Perceived Ease of Use (PEOU)	4,8	1,0	4,9	0,6	4,8	0,8
	Perceived Usefulness (PU)	4,8	0,9	4,6	0,8	4,7	0,9
	Perceived Enjoyment (PENJ)	4,5	1,3	4,3	0,8	4,4	1,0
	Learning Opportunities (LO)	4,6	1,0	4,5	0,9	4,6	0,9
	Preference (PREF)	4,9	0,8	4,7	0,8	4,8	0,8

4.3 Human-Modeler Interactions: NASA-TLX and Semi-Structured Feedback

The descriptive statistics of NASA-TLX are in Table 3. We do not find any differences in how the participants evaluate their interaction behaviors using a NASA-TLX survey, besides that highlighting had a lower degree of insecurity, discouragement, irritation ($p = 0.01$).

Table 3. Descriptive statistics comparing NASA-TLX responses between techniques.

Survey Factor	Tokens (n = 19)		Highlighting (n = 19)		Total (n = 38)	
	Mean	SD	Mean	SD	Mean	SD
Use frequency of animations	3,3	0,9	3,5	1,0	3,4	1,0
How mentally demanding	2,2	1,0	2,5	1,3	2,3	1,2

(continued)

Table 3. (*continued*)

Survey Factor	Tokens (n = 19)		Highlighting (n = 19)		Total (n = 38)	
	Mean	SD	Mean	SD	Mean	SD
How physically demanding	2,9	1,1	3,1	1,4	3,0	1,3
How hurried or rushed	4,3	0,7	4,2	0,8	4,2	0,8
How successful in accomplishing	3,4	0,9	3,2	1,1	3,3	1,0
How hard had to work	2,7	0,9	2,6	1,5	2,7	1,3
How insecure, discouraged, irritated, stressed, and annoyed	4,4	1,1	3,2	1,6	3,8	1,5

Otherwise, we find that participants used animations somewhat often, and that the tokens were somewhat more physically demanding than mentally demanding ($p < 0.01$), which may necessitate further investigation into the body-mind research in the human-model interactions as the novice modelers interact with the process models. Participants found that they were somewhat hurried or rushed (which may come because of attending the experimentation in the class setting). They were somewhat modest about self-evaluating the successes of their responses and found that it was not particularly hard to work with reading the models.

In semi-structured questions, we first asked participants to select in multiple choice options reasons for using animation. We adapted a list of reasons from our previous work on a qualitative analysis of novice modelers' feedback about their interactions with the token-animated process models [11, 14]. The most common motivations across both techniques were "confirm my answers" (68% overall; 74% tokens vs. 63% highlighting), "find the exact answer" (58% overall; 74% vs. 42%), and "get a global overview of the model" (47% for both); only the "find the exact answer" difference reached statistical significance ($p = .05$). More targeted uses clustered around one third to two fifths of respondents: understanding iterations (39% overall; 53% tokens vs. 26% highlighting), the behavior of XOR gateways (39% overall; 42% vs. 37%) and AND gateways (29% overall; 32% vs. 26%), comprehending how several elements work together (37% overall; 47% vs. 26%), improving concentration (37% overall; 42% vs. 32%), comparing process scenarios (37% overall; 42% vs. 32%), and reducing perceived complexity (32% for both). Overall, tokens tended to be chosen more often than highlighting for pinpointing answers and reasoning about iterations or multi-element interactions, while both techniques were used equally for gaining a global overview and reducing complexity.

We also asked participants to give their feedback about the fact that the animations automatically started (i.e., when opening a survey webpage with the model animation and the question), animation being looped (i.e. showing the animation repeatedly) and whether they preferred one scenario per question, or one scenario for all questions. We found that participants on average preferred slightly more when it's one animated video per one question rather than a single video for all questions (total $M = 2.3$, $SD = 1.35$).

This can suggest that participants would expect an adapted animation specific to their question or modelling task.

14 respondents found the **auto-start feature** beneficial, stating that it helped them engage with the content immediately. 4 respondents indicated that the automatic start was distracting or overwhelming. 18 participants expressed a desire for more control over when animations start, suggesting options to pause, rewind, or manually begin the animations. Additionally, 2 responses reflected a neutral stance, with participants either noticing the feature or finding it insignificant.

29 participants found the **looping feature** beneficial, stating that it allowed them to review the animations without manually restarting them. No responses explicitly mentioned the looping as distracting or unnecessary. 7 participants expressed a desire for more control over looping, such as the ability to pause or manually restart the animations. Interestingly, no participants provided a neutral stance, indicating that most had a clear preference regarding the feature.

Finally, we also asked qualitative questions at the end of the survey about their perceptions of advantages, disadvantages and the recommendations for using animations in PM education.

The **advantages** of animations in understanding BPMN models were mentioned in several key themes. 13 participants emphasized that animations provide a clearer representation of process flows, making it easier to see how different elements interact. Also, 12 responses highlighted that animations enhance comprehension by dynamically illustrating process behaviors. 4 participants found that animations help in following the sequence of tasks and navigating through complex processes. 4 participants indicated that animations help in visualizing how gateways function, aiding in decision-making processes. 2 participants specifically mentioned that animations help in tracking the movement of tokens, improving the understanding of execution flow. Token animations were more frequently cited as aiding in tracing specific execution sequences, while highlighting animations were described as more intuitive for understanding overall process behavior.

The following **disadvantages** of using animations were identified. 7 participants stated that they did not perceive any disadvantages, indicating that they found animations useful or neutral in their learning experience. 2 participants mentioned that animations could lead to cognitive overload, making it difficult to process information effectively. Similarly, 2 respondents highlighted that animations can be distracting, drawing attention away from essential process elements. 2 participants pointed out that animations hinder retention, making it harder to recall process details. Additionally, one response indicated concerns about the speed of animations, stating that they may be too fast or too slow, affecting comprehension.

The **improvement suggestions** in BPMN teaching using animations revealed that 2 participants emphasized the need for better explanations, suggesting that teachers should clarify animation details to improve comprehension. 1 response indicated that incorporating more hands-on exercises or interactive practice would enhance learning. Additionally, 3 participants did not suggest any improvements, indicating satisfaction with the current approach.

5 Discussion: Results, Limitations, and Future Work

This research presents the results of an experiment to compare the effect of two process model animation types. Our study confirmed the positive effects of both animation types, which have been shown in previous studies, and largely found that there are no significant differences.

The results reinforce that animations in general serve as effective scaffolding tools, helping to externalize complex BPMN logic in a way that is more accessible to novice modelers. We thus find that token and highlighting animations can provide semantical information that is similarly better than the one provided by a static process model. We conclude and suggest that animations, as a method of visualization, are a suitable external cognition resource, as indicated by the distributed cognition theory [10, 19], reinforcing existing internal mental models of the given processes [15, 16].

The study contributes towards exploring objective and subjective comprehension and human-model interactions, including uses of animations, with the aim to contribute towards understanding of the use and perceptions of both types of animations by novice modelers in comprehension and PM learning. Overall, the findings suggest that animations significantly contribute to BPMN model comprehension by improving clarity, aiding navigation, and facilitating decision-making processes. The most frequently mentioned benefits revolve around making the processes more visual and easier to follow. Most frequent uses of animation follow the four proposed by [13]: (1) tracing the animation (e.g., to understand a certain element), (2) answering questions (e.g., by verifying one's own understanding), (3) comprehending the models (getting a global understanding of a model), and (4) imagining new scenarios by relying on existing animations (e.g., by comparing possible or pre-existing answers with the model).

A particularly noteworthy finding is that participants exhibited a strong preference for having individualized control over animations, including the ability to pause, rewind, and replay animations at their own pace. This supports the argument that passive viewing of animations may be less effective than interactive engagement, especially when modelers are more experienced. The qualitative evaluation results from this study confirm with the experimental results of the need for high interactivity in certain situations [5]. However, low-interactive pre-recorded videos can be used in other situations, e.g., to introduce the concepts initially or to balance the degree of external cognitive aid offered to the modelers [5].

Participants use animations to make BPMN rules and behavior of collaborating elements (patterns) explicit, thus improving the initial identification and comprehension of the BPMN elements and patterns. This can be employed in course materials to ease the understanding of novice modelers. Animations can be used in e-learning to support independent learning by exploiting the simulation feature of the scenarios, allowing them to find and verify novice modelers' answers about a model [28]. It is critical that the satisfaction of novice modelers as learners be maintained [29] and the animations may improve learners' enjoyment and engagement. Furthermore, it is critical that novice modelers accept and adopt the use of animations to realize their comprehension and learning outcomes [14]. Different animation types may be suited to different pedagogical goals, tokens potentially being more beneficial for understanding execution paths and instance-based behaviors, while highlighting may be better suited for high-level pattern recognition and process navigation. For instance, different process patterns that are better suited to be explained via specific techniques [9]. Future research should explore whether combining both techniques could yield synergistic effects in PM learning. Furthermore, the positive effects of animations on comprehension and learning may be facilitated with the use of generative AI, such as by providing the targeted recommendations by the AI on how to better visualize and hence validate the model by the novice modelers [30].

Despite our efforts to keep the study valid and reliable, some limitations and threats to validity may still exist [27]. The limited sample size (N = 38) may have impacted statistical significance results. Also, the way the animations were designed may influence comprehension. While highlighting instantly marks an activity as active when the preceding activity (or event) is executed, tokens take some time to travel through the sequence flow before reaching the next task. Therefore, the highlighting technique aligns more closely with the BPMN standard. The time required for a token to move forward can be an issue for instance, especially when depicting parallel tasks that should start simultaneously but may instead begin sequentially with tokens due to variations in the length of their incoming sequence flows. Feedback on experiences using software in process modelling context can be misleading [31].

We make available data along with experiment data to address typical threats to the validity of qualitative research and for improving research transparency and replicability [27]. The study relied on low-interactivity pre-recorded animations, which, while effective, do not fully replicate the dynamic interaction possibilities available in BPMN simulation tools used in practice (such as Camunda Simulator). We attempted to use mixed methods to avoid participants' biases at response [27, 31].

The study's between-subjects design limits inference: a counterbalanced within-subjects experiment (e.g., randomizing model order, using mirrored variants/technique manipulations) would likely have provided greater power than the present largely descriptive analyses, which therefore yield only tentative insights. Moreover, animation effects should be judged against an explicit "no-animation" baseline and, ideally, a fourth condition combining token replay with highlighting.

Our findings may inform future design and instructional approaches for BPMN modeling tools and education, emphasizing the importance of interactive animations that scaffold the viewer's cognitive processes. In future research, the human-model interaction strategies can be further developed and decomposed, and techniques such as eye-tracking comparative analysis could be employed to study the human-model interactions [2]. High-interactive animation tools should be considered instead of the present low-interactivity pre-recorded tools [5] and can be used in experiments.

Disclosure of Interests. The authors have no competing interests to declare that are relevant to the content of this article.

References

1. Dumas, M., La Rosa, M., Mendling, J., Reijers, H.A.: Fundamentals of business process management (2018)

2. Winter, M., Neumann, H., Pryss, R., Probst, T., Reichert, M.: Defining gaze patterns for process model literacy–exploring visual routines in process models with diverse mappings. Expert Syst. Appl. **213**, 119217 (2023)
3. Moody, D.L., Shanks, G.G.: Improving the quality of data models: empirical validation of a quality management framework. Inf. Syst. **28**, 619–650 (2003)
4. Figl, K.: Comprehension of procedural visual business process models: a literature review. Bus. Inf. Syst. Eng. **59**, 41–67 (2017)
5. Aysolmaz, B., Reijers, H.A.: Animation as a dynamic visualization technique for improving process model comprehension. Inf. Manag. **58** (2021)
6. Petrusel, R., Mendling, J., Reijers, H.A.: How visual cognition influences process model comprehension. Decis. Support. Syst. **96**, 1–16 (2017)
7. Emens, R., Vanderfeesten, I., Reijers, H.A.: The dynamic visualization of business process models: a prototype and evaluation. In: BPM 2016 Conference, pp. 559–570. Springer (2016)
8. Maslov, I., Poelmans, S.: Facilitating the comprehension of business process models for unexperienced modelers using token-based animations. Inf. Mngmt. **61**, 103967 (2024)
9. Maslov, I., Poelmans, S., Mandeelburger, M.M., Proper, H.: Teaching Process Patterns in BPMN to Novice Modelers via Token Animations (2025)
10. Maslov, I., Poelmans, S.: Advancing the BPMN 2.0 Standard with an Extended Animated Notation: A Research Program for Token-Based Process Modeling Education. BIR (2023)
11. Maslov, I.: Towards empirically validated process modelling education using a BPMN formalism. In: International Conference on Research Challenges in Information Science, pp. 803–810. Springer (2022)
12. Maslov, I., Poelmans, S., Rosenthal, K.: Conceptual modeling education: a bibliometric literature review and avenues for future research. BISE 1–33 (2025)
13. Maslov, I., Poelmans, S.: Comprehension of (business) process models via tokens: an eye-tracking approach. In: BPM 2024 Conference, pp. 375–385. Springer (2024)
14. Maslov, I., Poelmans, S., Wautelet, Y., Gailly, F.: Novice modelers' subjective comprehension and interaction with token-animated process Models. J. Com. Lang. 101350 (2025)
15. Aysolmaz, B., Reijers, H.A.: Towards an integrated framework for invigorating process models: a research agenda. In: BPM 2016 Conference, pp. 552–558. Springer (2016)
16. Moody, D.: The physics of notations: toward a scientific basis for constructing visual notations in software engineering. IEEE Trans. Softw. Eng. **35**, 756–779 (2009)
17. Ternes, B., Rosenthal, K., Strecker, S.: User interface design research for modeling tools: a literature study. EMISAJ **16**, 1–4 (2021)
18. Rosenthal, K., Ternes, B., Strecker, S.: Learning conceptual modeling: structuring overview, research themes and paths for future research. In: 27th European Conference on Information Systems - Information Systems for a Sharing Society, ECIS 2019 (2020)
19. Bardone, E., Secchi, D.: Distributed cognition: a research agenda for management. Curr. Top. Manag. 183–208 (2018)
20. Wang, W., Chen, T., Indulska, M., Sadiq, S., Weber, B.: Business process and rule integration approaches—an empirical analysis of model understanding. Inf. Syst. (2022)
21. Lübke, D., Ahrens, M., Schneider, K.: Influence of diagram layout and scrolling on understandability of BPMN processes: an eye tracking experiment with BPMN diagrams. Inf. Technol. Manage. **22**, 99–131 (2021)
22. Stein Dani, V., Dal Sasso Freitas, C.M., Thom, L.H.: Ten years of visualization of business process models: a systematic literature review. Comput. Stand. Interfaces **66** (2019)
23. Dikici, A., Turetken, O., Demirors, O.: Factors influencing the understandability of process models: a systematic literature review. Inf. Softw. Technol. **93**, 112–129 (2018)
24. Leppink, J., Paas, F., Van der Vleuten, C.P.M., Van Gog, T., Van Merriënboer, J.J.G.: Development of an instrument for measuring different types of cognitive load. Behav. Res. Methods **45**, 1058–1072 (2013)

25. Klepsch, M., Schmitz, F., Seufert, T.: Development and validation of two instruments measuring intrinsic, extraneous, and germane cognitive load. Front. Psychol. **8**, 1997 (2017)
26. Henriques, H., Lourenço, H., Amaral, V., Goulão, M.: Improving the developer experience with a low-code process modelling language. In: Proceedings of the 21th ACM/IEEE International Conference on Model Driven Engineering Languages and Systems, pp. 200–210 (2018)
27. Saunders, M., Lewis, P., Thornhill, A.: Research methods for business students. Pearson Education (2009)
28. Maslov, I., Nikou, S., Hansen, P.: Exploring user experience of learning management system. Int. J. Inf. Learn. Technol. **38**, 344–363 (2021)
29. Nikou, S., Kim, S., Lim, C., Maslov, I.: Satisfaction with e-Learning Systems during the COVID-19 Pandemic–A Comparative Study. ITS (2021)
30. Maslov, I., Poelmans, S., Wautelet, Y., Rosenthal, K.: Generative AI's aid in business process modeling instructional design: a case study. In: BPM 2025, pp. 343–357. Springer (2025)
31. Maslov, I., Poelmans, S., Wautelet, Y.: Measuring Internal Validity in Mixed Methods User Feedback Survey by Finding Inconsistencies with sentimentR and ChatGPT-4 (2024)

Process Visualizations for Object-Centric Process Mining: An Evaluation Taxonomy

Florian Eckhard(✉), Holger Wittges, and Stefanie Rinderle-Ma

Technical University of Munich, School of Computation, Information and Technology, Boltzmannstr. 3, 85748 Garching, Germany
{florian.eckhard,holger.wittges,stefanie.rinderle-ma}@tum.de

Abstract. Object-centric Process Mining (OCPM) is a new approach integrating objects into the process mining model. This offers a more realistic view of real word processes. Since OCPM is an upcoming topic in research and industry, we expect an increasing number of visualizations in the coming years. To evaluate the usability of these approaches for different process mining use cases, it is essential to have a taxonomy offering a structure about relevant visualization aspects. This paper presents a first proposal of such a taxonomy based on the what-why-how visualization framework. First, we developed the taxonomy based on visualization and interaction theory as well as existing OCPM tools. As the second step, we applied the taxonomy to two existing OCPM tools. The evaluation results show the usefulness of our taxonomy, covering relevant capabilities in existing tools and offering directions for future research. The existing tools offer valuable initial approaches to process discovery visualization, but several research directions remain open. For future work, we propose multiple directions on how to extend OCPM visualizations based on this taxonomy. This includes new visualization approaches, adding new process mining attributes, and improving the exploration capabilities of OCPM tools.

Keywords: Visualization · Object-centric Process Mining · Evaluation Taxonomy

1 Introduction

Object-centric Process Mining (OCPM) is a new approach in the area of process mining with a combined view of objects and activities. Because most processes include more than one object, this enables analyses that are closer to reality [3]. While case-centric process mining is a widely used approach in research and industry, OCPM is still in its infancy. By incorporating objects into the process model and thus also the visualization, the views become more complex, and new opportunities and challenges arise. While multiple visualizations have already been developed for case-centric process mining, OCPM visualizations raise new research questions [12]. To develop and compare visualizations, it is helpful to

J. Barateiro et al. (Eds.): EDOC 2025 Workshops, LNBIP 571, pp. 99–116, 2026.
https://doi.org/10.1007/978-3-032-16234-2_7

have a taxonomy giving an overview of relevant visualization dimensions and characteristics. To design an evaluation taxonomy and check its usefulness for current OCPM tools, this work answers the following two research questions:

1. What should a taxonomy constitute to support analyzing and classifying OCPM process visualizations?
2. Which dimensions and characteristics from the taxonomy should be focused for the further development of OCPM process visualizations?

To answer the first research question, we develop a taxonomy based on visualization and interaction theory as well as existing OCPM visualizations. The taxonomy is evaluated and refined in an iterative process. The second research question focuses on identifying areas for future research. During the evaluation of the taxonomy we apply it to two OCPM visualizations to check its usefulness for analyzing and classifying OCPM tools. Based on these results we identify areas that are currently under-researched and need more consideration from the authors point of view. To the best of our knowledge, such a taxonomy for OCPM visualizations currently does not exist. Previous works from Rehse et al. [24] and Häge and Rehse [15] focused on conformance checking for case-centric process mining. In Rehse et al., a systematic study analyzing process mining tools regarding their conformance checking functionalities is presented. The paper from Häge and Rehse presents a taxonomy for the characteristics of conformance checking visualizations. In contrast to these two publications, this work focuses not exclusively on conformance checking but on OCPM process visualizations. Besides conformance checking, some other papers give a comprehensive overview of the current state of event sequence data visualization [13,31]. However, they do not provide details on how visualization elements are used. Additionally, they focus more on event sequence data in general and not on (object-centric) process mining.

This paper is separated into six sections. After the introduction, we define relevant process mining terms and concepts, followed by an overview of selected tools offering OCPM visualization. The taxonomy design process is described in the third section. Based on this process, the developed evaluation taxonomy is presented in Sect. 4. In the fifth section, we present our results from applying our taxonomy at the example of two OCPM tools. Our conclusion and discussion will be presented in Sect. 6.

2 Object-Centric Process Mining and Visualization

Process mining is a discipline at the intersection of machine learning/data mining and process modeling/process analysis [1]. As input process mining requires an event log. An event log lists activities recorded in a system during their execution. Each element in the event log is usually assigned to a case and includes the activity name, a timestamp, and optional additional properties [1,2]. The three primary process mining types are process discovery, conformance checking and process enhancement [1,2]. Van der Aalst [4] further extended this list by introducing a fourth type, operational support. In the context of this work, we define operational support as equivalent to process monitoring and will hereafter use only the term process monitoring [10]. Besides process mining types, there is a further classification by process mining perspective. A perspective describes additional attributes that could be used for analysis. The perspectives defined in the process mining manifesto [2] are control flow, time, case, and organizational perspective. The control flow, for example, describes the ordering of the activities, while the time perspective covers the timing and frequency of events [1,2,4].

Case-centric process mining focuses on a single object. An object for an hiring process could be for example an application or vacancy. Limitations of case-centric process mining are convergence and divergence problems. To explain these we will consider an hiring process with five activities: apply (100), interview (10), open a vacancy (5), hire (4), close a vacancy (5) and two object types: application (100) and vacancy (5). The number behind the elements indicating the frequencies of activities and object types. If we examine the process from the perspective of the *application* and incorporate the *open/close* events into the process model, these events will be shown 100 times for each *application* instead of 5. This is because a *vacancy* can pertain to multiple *applications*. This scenario illustrates the convergence problem. When look at the process from the perspective of the *vacancy* and including the *apply* and *interview* events, an issue with the activity sequence arises. Since there is no distinction between the different *applications*, it may happen that an *apply* event follows an *interview* event, or loops may occur that do not exist in the real process. This is referred to as the divergence problem. To overcome these issues OCPM was proposed. The event log is extended by object attributes, and all objects in a process are connected to their corresponding activities. This creates a unified data model and enables new analysis capabilities [3].

Independently of the type of process mining, visualization is an essential aspect. Current process mining visualization research is focused on case-centric process mining. As modeling notation, most approaches use the Directly-Follows Graph (DFG) or present new visualization approaches. Regarding process mining types, there is a focus on process discovery and process monitoring. Considering process mining perspectives, the focus lies on control flow and time perspective. While new visualization approaches have been presented in the last years, these do not take sufficient account of OCPM requirements [12].

OCPM Visualization Tools: The leading event log standard for OCPM is Object-centric Event Log (OCEL) [16]. The OCEL standard defines relevant elements in an OCPM event log and the relations between them. Therefore, we focus our evaluation on tools supporting the OCEL standard or explicitly listed on the OCEL website. We have also included the tools Mehrwerk mpmx[1] and Noreja[2], which also implement OCPM concepts, even if they are not listed on the OCEL website, to give a broader overview of available OCPM tools.

[1] https://mpmx.com.

[2] https://noreja.com.

Table 1. OCPM Modeling Tool Support (✓ = supported; - = not supported)

Software - Event Log based	OC-DFG	OC-Petri Net	OC-BPMN	Chevron Diagram	Causal Event Graph
OCPM (JS)	✓	✓	✓	-	-
OCPM (ProM)	✓	✓	-	-	-
Celonis	✓	-	-	-	-
Mehrwerk mpmx	✓	-	-	-	-
Library - Event Log based	**OC-DFG**	**OC-Petri Net**	**OC-BPMN**	**Chevron Diagram**	**Causal Event Graph**
ocpa (incl. ocpi)	-	✓	-	✓	-
pm4js	-	-	-	-	-
pm4py	✓	✓	-	-	-
Rust4PM	-	-	-	-	-
Software - Causal Process Mining	**OC-DFG**	**OC-Petri Net**	**OC-BPMN**	**Chevron Diagram**	**Causal Event Graph**
Noreja	-	-	-	-	✓

In Table 1, an overview of the tools and the supported modeling types is given. The available tools are separated between software solutions/libraries and if they support classic event logs or are based on causal process mining. The software solutions include a user interface that can also be used by end users to analyze processes. In contrast, the library tools only offer an API. Causal process mining renounces the use of traditional event logs, using direct access to the data storage and building an event graph as event log replacement [30]. Regarding Celonis[3], two remarks are important. (1) Although Celonis is listed on the OCEL website, it does not currently support the standard. However, it has been included due to Celonis' extensive support of OCPM. (2) The visualization used by Celonis is a custom approach that is partly inspired by DFG. For the scope of this research, we will consider it as a DFG visualization and make no further distinction. Additionally, we excluded the tools Oracle EBS, Ocelot.pm and OCPQ from the analysis. These tools do not offer a process visualization, but can be used for data extraction respectively as a data viewer and are therefore not in the scope of this paper. As we can see in Table 1, OC-DFG and OC-Petri Nets are the most supported visualizations with 5 and 4 tools, respectively. For causal process mining we only identified Noreja as an available tool. In contrast to other tools identified, Noreja visualizes the cardinalities in a process flow, instead of integration multiple objects in the visualization [23].

3 Taxonomy Design Methodology

This section describes the research methodology used to develop the taxonomy and gives an overview of the literature grounding. The research process, shown in Fig. 1, is based on the taxonomy development method from Nickerson et al. [21] and Kundisch et al. [18]. In contrast to the taxonomy definition of Nickerson et al., we define it as possible that an object has more than one characteristic per dimension. We make this modification because multiple characteristics can

[3] https://www.celonis.com.

be used for the visualization of a dimension. The process is separated into five phases. (1) We start with the *Identify problem and motivate* phase to define the context for our taxonomy. Our taxonomy supports process mining researchers and practitioners by analyzing and classifying existing OCPM visualizations as well as giving remarks what needs to be considered if developing a new visualization. (2) To define the objectives of the taxonomy we ground it in scientific literature. Additionally we define the following meta-characteristic: *Identify visualization-related elements and use cases for OCPM processes.* As a second step the ending conditions and evaluation goals are defined. For the ending conditions, we adopt the criteria from Nickerson et al. As evaluation goals our taxonomy should support users in analyzing and classifying OCPM visualizations [18]. (3) For taxonomy building we use conceptual-to-empirical and empirical-to-conceptual approaches as proposed by Kundisch et al. After designing new taxonomy elements we create/revise the taxonomy accordingly. If the ending conditions are fulfilled we continue with the next phase, otherwise the next iterations starts. (4) After defining the first taxonomy draft, we apply it to two existing OCPM tools to verify its usefulness. This is also an iterative process to improve the taxonomy characteristics based on the evaluation results. (5) The process is complete after successful evaluation, ending with the taxonomy reporting.

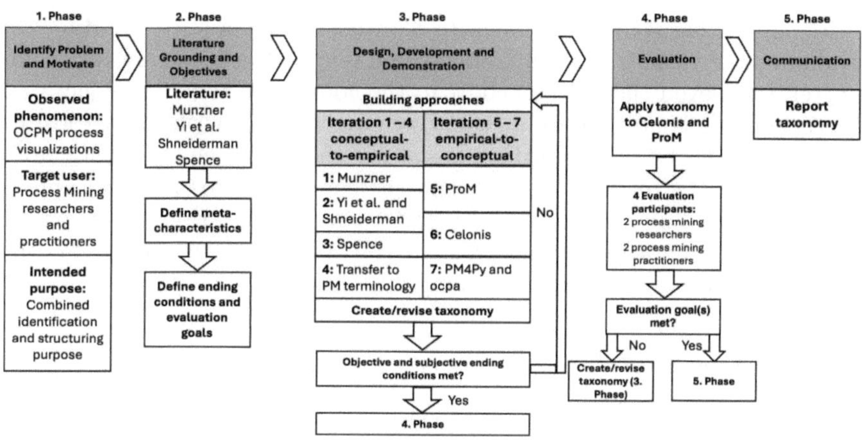

Fig. 1. Research process

4 Evaluation Taxonomy

This section presents the *design and development* results (phase 3), as shown in Fig. 1. The output of this stage is an evaluation taxonomy draft, which has passed the ex ante evaluation [18]. The taxonomy *design and development* phase consists of seven iterations. In the first three cycles we follows an conceptual-to-empirical approach based on the literature grounding. In the first round we identified relevant characteristics and dimensions from Munzner [20]. In Munzner, three questions relevant to visualizations are defined. The first question, *what* considers which data is displayed to the user. This is followed by *why* focusing on the user's intention in using the visualization. Finally, *how* defines the visual encoding and interaction idioms that are defined to visualize the data. We assign all dimensions to one of these questions. In the second iteration we include the visualization contributions from Yi et al. [32] and Shneiderman [26], because of their high citation count, indicating their impact and recognition within the visualization community. Since interaction is also an essential part of process mining visualizations, in the third iteration we include Spence [27], which has a broader focus on interaction in visualizations. As the previous two works we chose Spence because of their high citation count. For usage in the context of process mining the existing characteristics and dimensions are transferred to process mining terminology, in iteration four. The main objective of this iteration is checking if a characteristics or dimensions is relevant for process mining and what is the corresponding terminology.

Starting iteration five we switched to an empirical-to-conceptual approach. Four different OCPM tools were considered for this purpose. We used (1) ProM[4], as a widely used open source software, (2) Celonis as a leading commercial offering in the area of OCPM, (3) PM4Py[5] and ocpa[6] are open source software libraries supporting OCPM. To identify relevant characteristics and dimensions we evaluated the visualization capabilities and revised the taxonomy accordingly. After iteration seven the authors come to the conclusion that the objective and subjective ending condition are met and we can continue with the ex post evaluation [18] (see Sect. 5). The authors are aware that "null" characteristic are not recommended in taxonomies [21]. Due to the conceptual-to-empirical approach in taxonomy building and the novelty of OCPM visualization, we recommend these characteristic for future development [18]. We therefore remove this objective ending condition from our taxonomy evaluation.

4.1 What-Question

The result for the *what-question* is shown in Fig. 2. For clarity, we provide an example in Fig. 3 that illustrates a simplified procure-to-payment process [22] from the perspective of the *what-question.* We will reuse this process throughout all three questions. We group the elements into four dimensions. For *process/data modeling*, we mainly use the types that are currently supported by OCPM tools. Furthermore, we consider displaying *single models* and *model comparisons.* Additionally, we add modeling notations for univariate and multi-dimensional data as well as new visualizations. Univariate data includes all kinds of numbers,

[4] https://promtools.org.
[5] https://github.com/process-intelligence-solutions/pm4py.
[6] https://github.com/ocpm/ocpa/tree/ocel2.

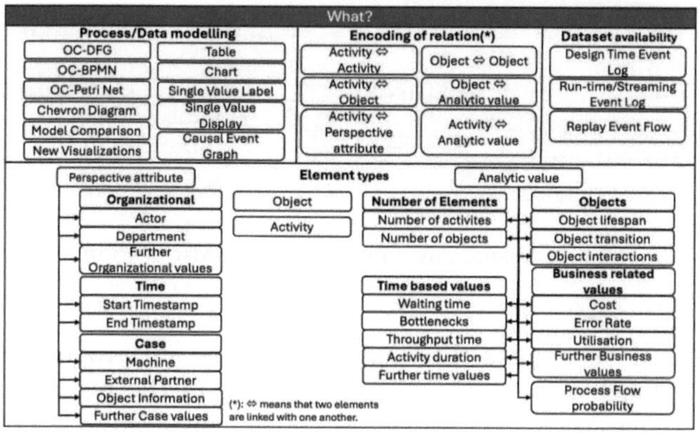

Fig. 2. Visualization taxonomy: What-question

like process performance indicators or values added to a label in a diagram. Multi-dimensional data covers all data that goes beyond a pure number (one dimension), for example tables representing two dimensions. We added *tables* and *charts* as visualization options. Since we expect further visualizations for OCPM, as can be observed in case-centric process mining and process visualization in general [12,28,31], *new visualizations* was included as a placeholder characteristic. This should be used as a substitute until new approaches are available. In Fig. 3 we used an *OC-DFG* to visualize the process flow and a *single value label* to present the *throughput time.*

The second dimension focuses on the encoding of relations. As OCPM additionally contains objects, it is important to consider how all shown elements are connected. This includes intra-element connections (e.g., activity to activity) and inter-element connections (e.g., object to activity).

Visualizations often show the current state of the available data, which is called *design time* visualization. However, new technologies allow the continuous generation and processing of data. Therefore, it is relevant to determine whether a visualization can process a *design time* or *streaming event log* [20,25]. A special case is a visualization of event flows (*Replay Event Flow* in Fig. 2), which shows the historical sequence of process cases in the visualization without accessing live data (e.g., ProM Inductive Miner [19]).

The last dimension contains the element types. We focus on elements that are part of the OCEL specification [6]. The two main characteristic are *objects* and *activities* (see Fig. 3). We also add *perspective attributes* that can extend them. As an example we added *payment provider* as external partner (case perspective) in Fig. 3. The last characteristic is *analytic value*, which includes information that can be calculated based on other attributes. For example, the *throughput time*, as shown in Fig. 3, can be determined using timestamp information. For better differentiation, the *perspective attributes* and *analytical values* are categorized according to their respective process mining perspectives in Fig. 2. To cover new

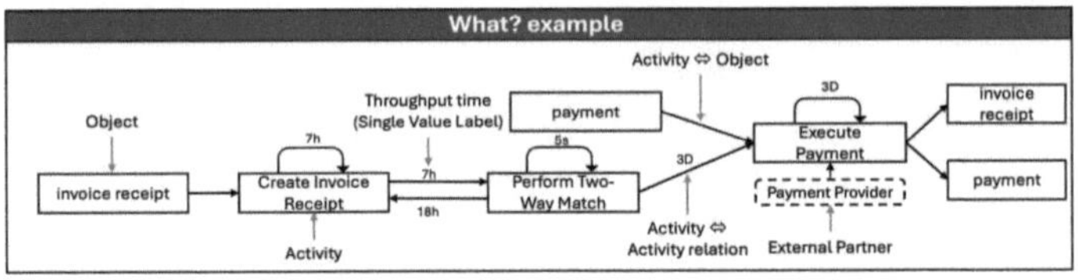

Fig. 3. Visualization example: What-question

possibilities based on objects three *analytic values* are proposed: (1) **Object lifespan**: How much time is the object involved in the process? (2) **Object transition**: In how many activities is the object involved? (3) **Object interactions**: With how many other objects is the object in contact with? Object specific *analytic values* are an open research question and there is no proposal for such values. For the three proposed *analytic values*, we examine which information is relevant for activities in case-centric process mining and how this can be transferred to objects. For the *object lifespan*, we consider the runtime of activities. By examining the lifespan of an object within a process, we can assess the relevance of an object in relation to the overall duration of the entire process. For *object transition*, we use bottleneck analysis and utilization as references. The aim is to illustrate how central an object is to a process, based on the number of activities it is involved in and what impact a problem with this object could have. For the final attribute, *object interaction*, we derive it from the process flow representation, which illustrates the connections between activities. We consider this relevant to assess how many dependencies an object has with other objects and how potential process improvements can be derived from this. In processes with many object dependencies, it could be examined in which process phases these dependencies exist and whether an adjustment to the process flow could improve, e.g., waiting times.

4.2 Why-Question

To identify relevant process mining use cases for visualization, we use the work from Ailenei et al. [5] as a starting point. To get a broader overview of different intents, we additionally add literature from the Business Process Management Cases book series, publications describing process mining use cases, and process reengineering research [7,8,17,25,29]. The Business Process Management Cases book series gives a good overview about applying process mining in different domains and use cases. The result is shown in Fig. 4.

The process mining use cases are categorized based on their process mining types. A further annotation is added based on the use case intents. In this context, intent is defined as the goal the user wants to achieve with its visualization usage. While the terms *consume* and *produce* are being used in the visualization literature, we decided to change *consume* to *discover* and *produce* to *analyze* [20]. Instead of *consume*, *discover* is a more common term in the context of

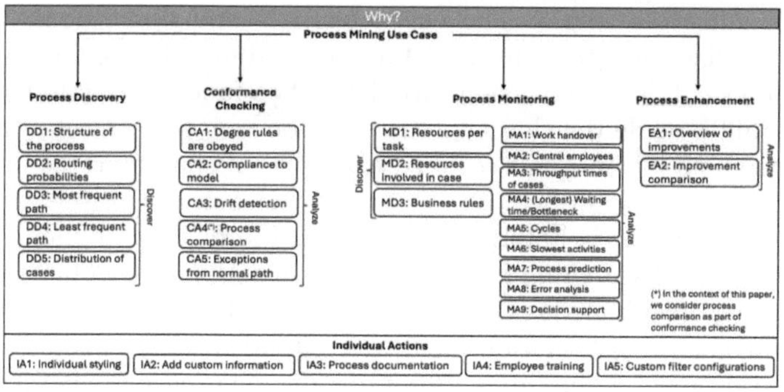

Fig. 4. Visualization taxonomy: Why-question

process mining (e.g. process discovery). We additionally assume that most use cases are more about producing results based on existing data (*analyze*) instead of producing completely new data [11]. Besides use cases assigned to a process mining type, we also define individual actions that are relevant for process mining visualizations. This includes adding *individual styling* options, *adding custom information* to extend existing visualizations or creating *process documentation* based on process mining results.

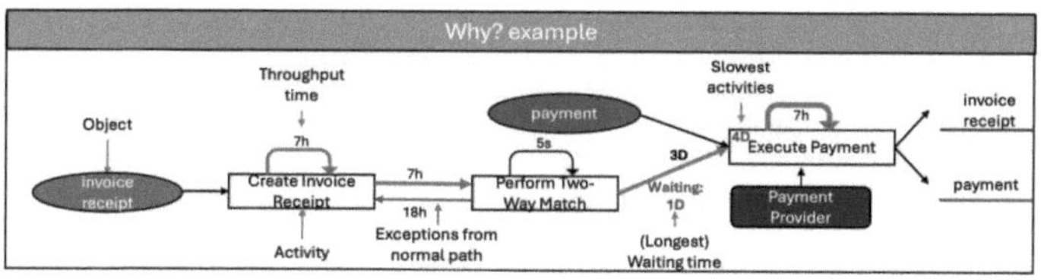

Fig. 5. Visualization example: Why-question.

An example of an visualization that can be used for different use cases, is shown in Fig. 5. From *process discovery* the use cases *DD1* and *DD3* are presented. *DD1* is represented by the overview about process objects, activities and their connections. For *DD3* the most frequent path is visualized by bold connection lines. For *conformance checking* the use case *CA5* is shown by a red line indicating an exception from normal path. The use cases *MA3, MA4* and *MA6* are covered for the *process monitoring* type. All three use cases are related to the time perspective and visualized by single values added to the relations or activities.

4.3 How-Question

The last category is the *how-question*, which is shown in Fig. 6. The category comprises eight dimensions; seven include visualization aspects, and one is about handling visualization issues. The characteristics and dimensions are defined based on visualization literature and functions from existing OCPM tools, as described in Sect. 4. The dimensions are defined as function requirements that a tool should fulfill, while the characteristics can be seen as features implementing these requirements [9]. In Fig. 7 selected examples of characteristic implementations are shown.

The first dimension is about *selection* and *interaction*. It includes aspects about *modifying* and *searching* for elements or *changing labels*. This is not limited to elements, but also includes the lines connecting them. For example in Fig. 7 the *create invoice receipt* relation label was extended with custom information. A more general aspect is the *interaction type*. The difference is whether the result of an interaction is displayed continuously or only after, for example, an apply button has been clicked.

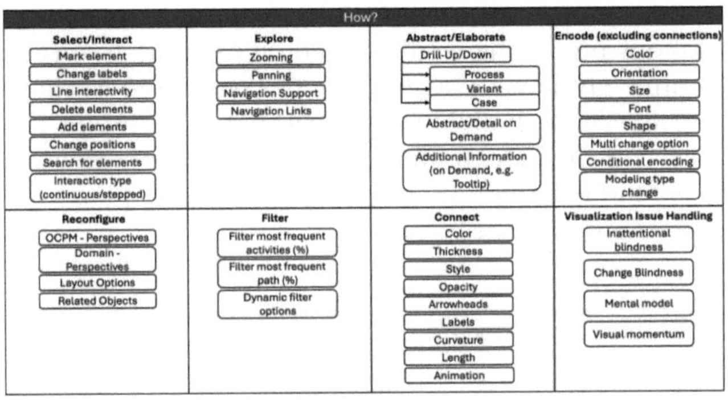

Fig. 6. Visualization taxonomy: How-question

Another central aspect of process mining visualizations is the *explore* dimension. Since complex process models often do not fit in one screen, *explore* functions are a central feature. Besides widely used functions like *zooming* (see Fig. 7 +/- options in the left down corner) and *panning*, further approaches from the visualization literature were adopted. This includes functions to *support navigation* and *navigation links*. *Navigation support* includes all functions that make it easier to navigate through the visualization, for example, the option to jump to relevant points (e.g., process start or points of interest). *Navigation links* mean, for example, the possibility to jump back to the previous presentation or view when an adjustment has been made.

Process mining can be viewed from different levels (process, variant, case) and with different details, the ability to *abstract/elaborate* is relevant. The dimension contains three relevant functions. First, a *drill-up/down* characteristic. This characteristic is inspired by OLAP operations from the data mining domain [14]. This enables users to start with an overview of the whole process and seamlessly drill-down to a variant and a single case. The second characteristic is *abstract/detail*

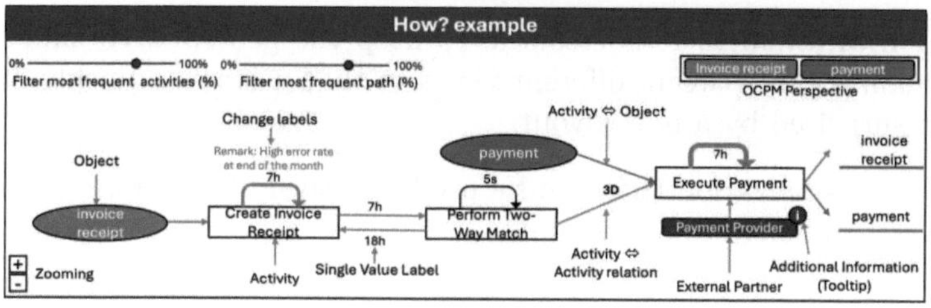

Fig. 7. Visualization example: How-question

on demand. Although this characteristic is similar to *drill-up/down*, drill-down focuses on changing the process mining level, while *abstract/detail on demand* combines or separates activities and objects to provide an overview or detailed view, maintaining the current level. *Additional information* extends the visualization by more details, for example, time perspective information. In Fig. 7 an example regarding the *payment provider* indicated by an information icon is shown.

Two dimensions that are similar but have different focuses are *connect* and *encode.* While *connect* only focuses on the lines between elements, *encode* considers the visualization of all elements shown in the visualization. Basic *color*, *size*, or *style* modifications are relevant for both dimensions. For *encode*, we add additional modification options. This includes *multi change* for changing several elements simultaneously, *conditional encoding* to control encoding based on rules, and the option to *change the modeling type.* In Fig. 7 we mainly used *color* and *shape* features to differentiate activities and objects.

The last two visualization dimensions are *reconfigure* and *filter.* While both are partially linked, they have a different focus regarding updating the visualization. The *filter* dimension can be used to *filter activities* and *paths* in the current view (see Fig. 7 sliders on the top left). The difference is that all filter operations are related to the current view. In contrast, the *reconfigure* operation transfers or replaces the current view with an updated version. This includes showing different *OCPM perspectives* (see Fig. 7 object selection on the top right), changing the *visualization layout*, or focusing only on *related objects* based on a selected activity. We also add the handling of visualization issues to the *how-question.* These issues include [27]:

- **Inattentional blindness**: Users overlook parts of the visualization because they focus on other parts.
- **Change blindness**: Users have problems recognizing changes in a visualization if these are not highlighted.
- **Mental model**: When switching from an old view to a new view, the user may lose their reference to the visualization if, for example, there is no animation to facilitate the transition. This can happen because users form a mental model of visualization, which can be disturbed by a change.

- **Visual momentum**: It is essential to keep the general style and layout of the visualization between different views so that users can quickly orient and are not surprised by a new layout.

To develop a visualization that can be used effectively by users, it is important to take these challenges into account.

5 Results

Based on the results presented in Sect. 4, we apply our taxonomy to two OCPM tools. This section represents phase 4 of our development methodology.

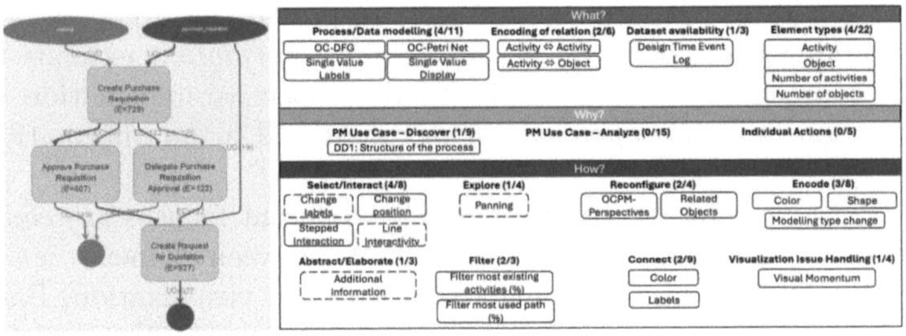

(a) ProM OC-DFG (b) ProM taxonomy results

Fig. 8. ProM evaluation

As output, the analysis generates an overview of how the included visualizations were evaluated using the taxonomy. The objective is to decide if the taxonomy generates a meaningful assessment of the tool's visualization capabilities. For evaluation, we use the criteria proposed by Kundisch et al. [18]: completeness, simplicity, understandability and robustness. If the evaluation goal is met, the taxonomy is assessed as final, and the process ends with phase 5. If dimensions are discovered that are currently not sufficiently considered or other taxonomy issues are identified, we go back to phase 3 to refine the taxonomy. The evaluation is conducted by two process mining researchers and two process mining practitioners. One of the process mining researchers is part of the authors, while the remaining three participants are independent from the taxonomy creation.

Our evaluation focuses on the OCEL Standard Plugin for ProM[7] and the Celonis Studio View[8]. ProM was selected because it is a widely used open-source tool, while Celonis is a established commercial product in the area of OCPM. The result of the evaluation from ProM is shown in Fig. 8b. The figure is separated according to the three main questions. Under each question, the dimensions are shown with the available characteristics, respectively, for which

[7] Version: ProM 6.14 (https://promtools.org/).

[8] Celonis Academic Edition available as of April 2025.

intents the visualization can be used. Characteristics with a dashed frame indicate that the property is present but with limitations. An excerpt from the evaluated visualization is shown in Fig. 8a. ProM offers two options for presenting the process model: *OC-DFG* and *OC-Petri Net.* In addition, univariate data are shown as *single value displays* or *labels. Activities, objects*, and *analytic values* are visualized in both modeling notations, including the connections between *activities* and *objects. Analytical values* have limited support, only showing the number of *activities/objects.* ProM expects a static event log as input. Based on the defined intents, only *DD1: Structure of the process* is supported. The *how-question* also shows that only a few features have been implemented. Considering object *encoding* and *connect*, only 3/8 and 2/9 characteristics are used, respectively. For *encoding* features like *color*, there is the problem that they cannot be configured, and some very bright colors are not easily recognizable. Also, the *interaction* and *exploration* options are limited, with only *panning* available. *Select and interact* have 50% supported activities, but two have limited support. For example, it is possible to change a label, but the change is lost as soon as another operation (e.g., filtering) is performed. Two well-supported categories are *reconfigure* and *filter*. However, functions for *layout modification* and *domain perspectives* are not available. The last two categories, *abstract/elaborate* and *visualization issue handling*, are only partially covered. Especially the visualization issues, e.g., *change blindness*, are not considered, resulting in a higher cognitive effort while working with the visualization.

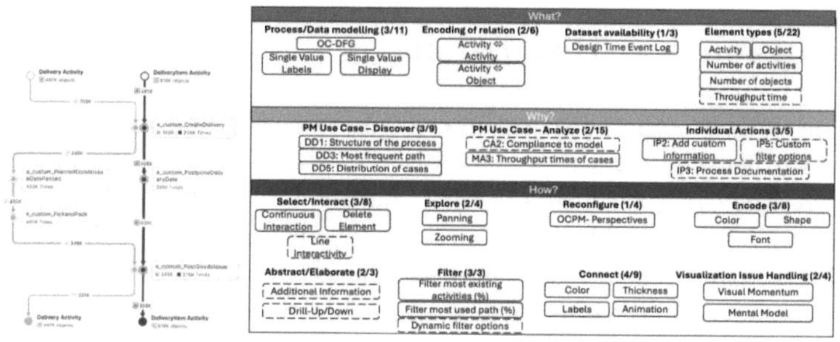

(a) Celonis OCPM (b) Celonis taxonomy results

Fig. 9. Celonis evaluation

Besides ProM we also applied our taxonomy to Celonis. The result is shown in Fig. 9b and an example in Fig. 9a. Looking at the *what-question*, Celonis is only offering *OC-DFG.* We observe similar results for all other dimensions except for the *element types* where Celonis offers *throughput time* as additional time-related information. A more extensive difference is recognizable for the *why-question.* While ProM supports one process mining use case, we identified seven supported use cases for Celonis. This includes three use cases from *process discovery*, two *analyze* annotated (one *conformance checking* and one *process monitoring*), and two *individual actions*. The use cases *CA2*, *IP3* and *IP5* are considered as only partially fulfilled. For *CA2*, the decision was made because only the deviation is visualized in the DFG, and the two processes cannot be compared directly. Additionally, this function is only available in the Process Adherence Manager and not directly in the Celonis Studio View[9]. *IP5* was considered partially because some custom filter options are available but need to be added manually and are not offered as the Studio default view. For the *how-question* we see broader coverage of visualization elements. Celonis feels more fluent through *continuous interaction* while offering *zooming* and *panning* options for exploration. However, the visualization offers few options for individual intervention, such as *adjusting labels* or *arranging elements*. Another significant difference is in the *connect* category. By including *animation* and *thickness*, the pre- and post-follower activities are more clearly highlighted, and the metrics shown in the labels are clarified.

In summary, ProM offers more freedom in changing the visualizations but is currently more limited regarding visualization elements. Celonis supports more process mining use cases and uses more visualization elements. Nevertheless, Celonis currently only offers one modeling type, and fewer elements are covered in the *select/interact* and *reconfigure* categories compared to ProM. With respect to our taxonomy, it can be shown that it provides a good starting point for evaluating OCPM visualizations. Analysts can adopt the systematic approach by breaking the analysis down into three key questions and their corresponding dimensions. This structured approach provides valuable insights into the potential for further visualization development.

6 Conclusion and Discussion

This section presents the main results of our research and explores their implications for future studies.

Evaluation Taxonomy: Our research mainly focuses on proposing an evaluation taxonomy for OCPM process visualization. In the first taxonomy building iterations, generic dimensions and visualization characteristics were defined, based on a conceptual-to-empirical approach. In the following iterations, the results were transferred into the process mining terminology and expanded through an empirical-to-conceptual approach based on existing OCPM tools.

Regarding the *what-question*, only limited visualization approaches are currently available for OCPM. We expect this number will increase in the future, as seen for case-centric process mining [12]. Another under-researched area is the *perspective attributes*. Although analyzing *case* and *organizational* information is essential to process mining, it is currently not supported in the OCPM visualizations. The same is also recognizable for *analytical values*. While most *analytical values*, like *waiting time*, *bottlenecks*, or *cost*, are well known, we do not see support in the tools we used for the taxonomy evaluation. To exploit the

[9] OCPM Process Adherence Manager is not part of the Celonis Academic Edition. We, therefore, had to refer to documentation and other external sources for the analysis.

analytical potential of object information, this work proposes three object-based analytical values as a starting point.

For the *why-question*, we identified process mining use cases and intents that could be covered by visualizations, but only limited support exists, especially for *analyze* annotated use cases. This is comprehensible because *process discovery/discover* annotated use cases are sometimes a prerequisite for *analyze* use cases. However, we see greater value for the *analyze* use cases in the future. As these use cases often require data from other process mining perspectives, implementation is not always possible, as research in the area of data modeling is still ongoing, for example with causal process mining [30]. However, it is helpful to start research on how to visualize these use cases so that they can be implemented as soon as the data provisioning is sufficient.

For the *how-question*, we have adopted elements from visualization literature into process mining terminology. Considering current tool support, we identified a focus on presenting OCPM process flows. While Celonis offers a good design for process flows, areas like *exploring*, *interacting*, and *reconfiguring* have improvement potential. It is also essential to focus on new opportunities and challenges regarding the integration of objects in the process model. One example is the increasing model complexity, which requires *exploration* or *abstraction* strategies to guide users in working with the visualization.

In summary, we consider OCPM visualizations in their infancy. Although there are first process visualizations, they only support a limited number of process mining use cases. With respect to our taxonomy, we see a good coverage of existing and potential future visualizations. This could help process mining developers have a starting point for what are relevant aspects for OCPM visualizations.

Limitations: One limitation of our study concerns the evaluations based on our taxonomy. Currently, the taxonomy offers a general evaluation scope and a set of relevant properties for OCPM visualization. Still, it does not yet give a mapping of which visualization elements are essential for which *what-* and *why-question* categories. Analyzing the significance of visualization features for these questions and their categories is a relevant field for future research. A second limitation arises from the limited availability of OCPM visualization tools. If new visualizations are developed, new visualization elements and currently not considered requirements could arise. However, we assume that the taxonomy can be extended with ease.

Future Research: We propose future research areas for OCPM visualization based on the gaps identified using our taxonomy and the authors assumption that a category is mandatory to enable further OCPM use case. For the *what-question*, the focus should be on developing *new visualizations*, *model comparison*, *perspective attributes*, and *analytical values. Model comparison* is important to compare processes based on different criteria and can also be reused in conformance checking. To enable more process mining use cases, the integration of more element types is also essential. The limited support for the case and organizational perspective is not limited to OCPM but is also recognizable in case-centric process mining [12]. We especially emphasize the integration of object-related metrics and information to increase the value of the object-centric data model. Regarding the *why-question*, we recommend starting with *process discovery* use cases. This process mining type was selected because a good process model visualization is the basis for further use cases like process monitoring. Due to the increasing complexity in OCPM process models, we propose the areas *explore*, *abstract/elaborate* and *reconfigure* as the next research fields in the *how-question*. These were selected to give users the opportunity to get an overview of the processes and to offer a suitable level of visualization depending on the target group. For *reconfigure*, we propose especially considering *domain perspectives*, like customer, organization, and production [25] and how these perspectives influence visualization development. Our next step is to investigate ways to improve the *abstract* and *reconfigure* categories in the *how-question*.

Disclosure of Interests. The authors have no competing interests to declare that are relevant to the content of this article.

References

1. van der Aalst, W.: Process Mining. Springer Berlin Heidelberg (2016). https://doi.org/10.1007/978-3-662-49851-4
2. van der Aalst, W., et al.: Process mining manifesto (2021). https://www.tf-pm.org/resources/manifesto. Accessed 25 Oct 2024
3. van der Aalst, W.M.P.: Object-Centric Process Mining: Dealing with Divergence and Convergence in Event Data, pp. 3–25. Springer International Publishing (2019). https://doi.org/10.1007/978-3-030-30446-1_1
4. van der Aalst, W.M.: Process discovery from event data: Relating models and logs through abstractions. WIREs Data Mining Knowl. Discov. **8**(3) (Feb 2018). https://doi.org/10.1002/widm.1244
5. Ailenei, I., Rozinat, A., Eckert, A., van der Aalst, W.M.: Definition and validation of process mining use cases. In: Business Process Management Workshops: BPM 2011 International Workshops, Clermont-Ferrand, France, August 29, 2011, Revised Selected Papers, Part I 9, pp. 75–86. Springer (2012). https://doi.org/10.1007/978-3-642-28108-2_7
6. Berti, A., et al.: Ocel (object-centric event log) 2.0 specification (Mar 2024). https://doi.org/10.48550/ARXIV.2403.01975
7. vom Brocke, J., Mendling, J. (eds.): Business Process Management Cases. Springer International Publishing (2018). https://doi.org/10.1007/978-3-319-58307-5
8. vom Brocke, J., Mendling, J., Rosemann, M. (eds.): Business Process Management Cases Vol. 3: Implementation in Practice. Springer Nature Switzerland (2025). https://doi.org/10.1007/978-3-031-80793-0
9. Du, F., Shneiderman, B., Plaisant, C., Malik, S., Perer, A.: Coping with volume and variety in temporal event sequences: strategies for sharpening analytic focus. IEEE Trans. Visual Comput. Graph. **23**(6), 1636–1649 (2017). https://doi.org/10.1109/tvcg.2016.2539960
10. Dumas, M.: Fundamentals of Business Process Management. Springer, Berlin, second edition edn (2018)

11. van Eck, M.L., Lu, X., Leemans, S.J.J., van der Aalst, W.M.P.: PM2: A Process Mining Project Methodology, pp. 297–313. Springer International Publishing (2015). https://doi.org/10.1007/978-3-319-19069-3_19
12. Eckhard, F., Wittges, H., Rinderle-Ma, S.: Exploring the role of visualization in process mining: a systematic literature review. In: Węcel, K. (ed.) Business Information Systems, pp. 165–178. Springer Nature Switzerland, Cham (2025)
13. Guo, Y., Guo, S., Jin, Z., Kaul, S., Gotz, D., Cao, N.: Survey on visual analysis of event sequence data. IEEE Trans. Visual Comput. Graphics **28**(12), 5091–5112 (2022). https://doi.org/10.1109/tvcg.2021.3100413
14. Han, J.: Data mining. Morgan Kaufmann series in data management systems, Morgan Kaufmann/Elsevier, Waltham, MA, 3rd ed. edn. (2012)
15. Häge, M.C., Rehse, J.R.: A taxonomy for conformance checking visualizations, pp. 507–519. Springer Nature Switzerland (2025). https://doi.org/10.1007/978-3-031-82225-4_37
16. Koren, I., Adams, J.N., Berti, A., van der Aalst, W. (eds.): OCEL 2.0 Resources – www.ocel-standard.org, vol. 3648 (2023)
17. Kubrak, K., Milani, F., Nolte, A.: A visual approach to support process analysts in working with process improvement opportunities. Bus. Process. Manag. J. **29**(8), 101–132 (2023). https://doi.org/10.1108/bpmj-10-2021-0631
18. Kundisch, D., et al.: An update for taxonomy designers: methodological guidance from information systems research. Business Inform. Syst. Eng. **64**(4), 421–439 (Oct 2021). https://doi.org/10.1007/s12599-021-00723-x
19. Leemans, S.J., Fahland, D., Van Der Aalst, W.M.: Process and deviation exploration with inductive visual miner. CEUR Workshop Proceedings, vol. 1295, p. 46 – 50 (2014)
20. Munzner, T.: Visualization Analysis and Design. A K Peters/CRC Press (Dec 2014)
21. Nickerson, R.C., Varshney, U., Muntermann, J.: A method for taxonomy development and its application in information systems. Eur. J. Inf. Syst. **22**(3), 336–359 (2013). https://doi.org/10.1057/ejis.2012.26
22. Park, G., Leah Tacke, g.U.: Procure-to-payment (p2p) object-centric event log in ocel 2.0 standard (2023). https://doi.org/10.5281/ZENODO.8412919
23. Pfahlsberger, L.: Cardinalities: How your business processes split and combine. Online (Jan 2024). https://noreja.com/en/cardinalities/. Accessed June 05 2025
24. Rehse, J.R., Pufahl, L., Grohs, M., Klein, L.M.: Process mining meets visual analytics: the case of conformance checking. In: Proceedings of the Annual Hawaii International Conference on System Sciences, vol. 2023-January, pp. 5452 – 5461 (2023)
25. Rinderle-Ma, S., Stertz, F., Mangler, J., Pauker, F.: Process Mining—Discovery, Conformance, and Enhancement of Manufacturing Processes, pp. 363–383. Springer Berlin Heidelberg (2023). https://doi.org/10.1007/978-3-662-65004-2_15
26. Shneiderman, B.: The eyes have it: A task by data type taxonomy for information visualizations. In: The craft of information visualization, pp. 364–371. Elsevier (2003)
27. Spence, R.: Information visualization. Pearson/Prentice Hall, Harlow, 2. ed. edn. (2007), includes bibliographical references and index. - Previous ed.: 2001
28. Stein Dani, V., Dal Sasso Freitas, C.M., Thom, L.H.: Ten years of visualization of business process models: a systematic literature review. Comput. Stand. Interfaces **66**, 103347 (2019). https://doi.org/10.1016/j.csi.2019.04.006

29. Stertz, F., Mangler, J., Scheibel, B., Rinderle-Ma, S.: Expectations vs. Experiences – Process Mining in Small and Medium Sized Manufacturing Companies, pp. 195–211. Springer International Publishing (2021). https://doi.org/10.1007/978-3-030-85440-9_12
30. Waibel, P., Pfahlsberger, L., Revoredo, K., Mendling, J.: Causal process mining from relational databases with domain knowledge (Feb 2022). https://doi.org/10.48550/ARXIV.2202.08314
31. Yeshchenko, A., Mendling, J.: A survey of approaches for event sequence analysis and visualization. Inf. Syst. **120**, 102283 (2024). https://doi.org/10.1016/j.is.2023.102283
32. Yi, J.S., Kang, Y.A., Stasko, J.T., Jacko, J.A.: Toward a deeper understanding of the role of interaction in information visualization. IEEE Trans. Visual Comput. Graph. **13**(6), 1224–1231 (2007). https://doi.org/10.1109/TVCG.2007.70515

Visualising and Monitoring Object-Centric Processes with Complex Object Interdependencies

Lisa Arnold(✉), Maurice Cordts, and Manfred Reichert

Institute of Databases and Information Systems, Ulm University, Ulm, Germany
{lisa.arnold,maurice.cordts,manfred.reichert}@uni-ulm.de

Abstract. Sunburst charts are an appropriate method for visualising a hierarchically structured process. In particular, they seem to be well-suited for visualising and monitoring object-centric processes, which consist of multiple interacting object lifecycles. In our previous work, we identified two challenges when mapping object-centric processes to sunburst charts: (1) the representation of object dependencies beyond one-to-many and (2) the handling of objects that are assigned to multiple hierarchy levels within the overall process structure. This paper presents advanced variants of sunburst charts designed to address these challenges. An empirical study was conducted with 154 participants to evaluate the understandability, readability and suitability of the designed sunburst chart variants for object-centric processes. A key observation of the study is a clear preference among participants for the aggregation of multiple objects in one entity, a strategy that significantly enhances readability.

Keywords: Process monitoring · Process visualisation · Dashboard · Object-centric processes · Sunburst chart · Empirical study

1 Introduction

In today's dynamic business world, object-centric processes have emerged as a pivotal aspect of managing the intricacies and adaptability inherent in contemporary organisations. Each object represents a specific entity or resource within the process and can generate any number of instances at runtime based on its cardinalities. Object-centric processes, therefore, consist of a large number of loosely coupled, interacting object instances. These can act independently of each other while still interacting in a common context. This enables a high degree of modularity and adaptability, which are essential for responding to shifting market conditions. The high level of flexibility inherent in large, complex object-centric processes [1] constitutes a significant challenge when designing a monitoring dashboard and selecting suitable diagrams. These diagrams are required to present a broad spectrum of information in a lucid, systematic and succinct

J. Barateiro et al. (Eds.): EDOC 2025 Workshops, LNBIP 571, pp. 117–133, 2026.
https://doi.org/10.1007/978-3-032-16234-2_8

manner [4]. From the end user's perspective, the diagrams must be readable and comprehensible. The value offered to the end user by the dashboard [12] and its diagrams is critical to their usefulness. It is vital to maintain smooth operations, minimise risks, comply with regulations and achieve long-term success by monitoring highly complex object-centric processes.

The utilisation of sunburst charts [10, 14] appears to be an efficacious methodology to surmount these hurdles. In this context, sunburst charts [9, 18] are employed to visualise hierarchically structured data present in object-centric processes [8]. In particular, sunburst diagrams appear to be a valuable way of visualising the current status and progress of multiple interacting business objects and their instances at runtime. In preliminary work [2], we attempted to generate sunburst charts for object-centric processes. However, this approach exposed two challenges that were identified during the generation of 150 automatically generated object-centric processes and their integration into our monitoring framework. First, it was not possible to present object dependencies beyond one-to-many. Second, business objects that are assigned to multiple hierarchy levels of a process structure cannot be mapped. To exemplify, consider the following example: if B is the parent object of D and E, and D is the parent object of E, E may be associated with multiple hierarchy levels (cf. Figure 2b level 3 and 4). Consequently, the use of advanced charts is essential. This paper proposes sophisticated sunburst charts that successfully overcome the identified challenges. Furthermore, an empirical study is conducted. The primary objective of this study is to analyse and evaluate the understandability, readability and suitability of the designed sunburst chart variants for object-centric processes.

The structure of the remainder of this paper is as follows: Related work is discussed in Sect. 2. Section 3 provides a summary of the characteristics of object-centric processes as well as the procedure [2] for generating sunburst charts for object-centric processes. Moreover, the challenges of mapping object-centric processes to sunburst charts are discussed in Sect. 4. Afterwards, Sect. 5 presents advanced sunburst charts that address the challenges above. In Sect. 6, the research design of the empirical study investigating the sunburst charts is explained. Section 7 analyses, evaluates and discusses the empirical research with its 154 participants. Section 8 concludes the paper.

2 Related Work

In [6, 14], an overview of data visualisation methods, including the sunburst chart, is provided. This emphasises the suitability of sunburst charts for visualising hierarchical data, as demonstrated in this work. In [10], a comparison of visualisation methods for large and small hierarchies is presented. Sunburst charts were found to be particularly well-suited to the visualisation of large hierarchical structures. This insight suggests that our work is also applicable to large and complex processes, despite our study focusing on relatively minor scenarios. Research has also been conducted in the field of object-centric process monitoring. In [11], an object-centric approach for operational process monitoring

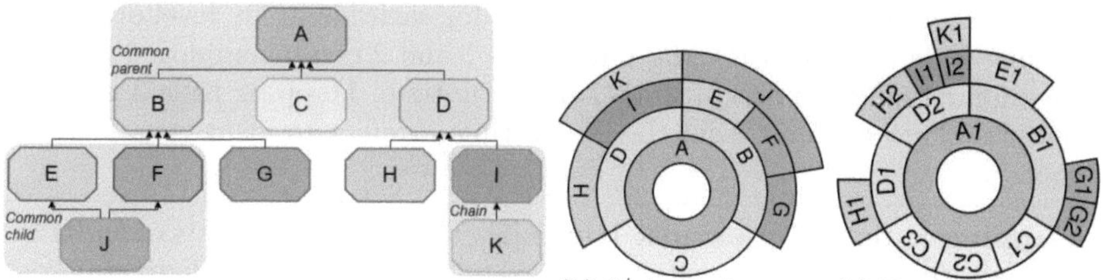

(a) A RPS with three patterns. **(b)** Sunburst chart at design time. **(c)** Example of a sunburst chart instance at runtime.

Fig. 1. Sunburst Charts derived from an RPS.

using Object-Centric Event Logs (OCELs) is presented that handles the issues caused by the presence of single-case notions in event logs. Moreover, object-centric predictive process monitoring seeks to ascertain the ongoing behaviour of running object instances. Consequently, OCELs have been shown to enhance prediction accuracy in various contexts [5]. In conclusion, to the best of our knowledge, there are no existing works that deal with visualising object-centric process monitoring.

3 Background

This section introduces fundamental concepts of object-centric processes and sunburst charts to ensure this work is comprehensible.

Object-centric Process. An object-centric process consists of interacting business objects These interactions can be organised in a *Relational Process Structure* (RPS), which represents both the object relations and the object hierarchy [16]. Consider Fig. 1a: A is the top-level object and B to K are lower-level objects. The RPS also includes the cardinalities between objects. At runtime, object instances (*instances* for short) are created from the objects established in the RPS. The runtime behaviour of each object is defined by its lifecycle process, which may comprise several states. In turn, each state is refined by several steps, with each step corresponding to an update of an object attribute [15]. Finally, the interaction between multiple lifecycle processes is defined in a coordination process [17].

Sunburst Charts Mapping Rules. Sunburst charts are a promising candidate for monitoring the execution of object-centric processes (cf. Fig. 1). They are particularly well-suited for representing hierarchically structured data, with the rings of the chart arranged according to a defined hierarchy. Concerning the RPS of an object-centric process, the top-level object(s) can be mapped to the innermost ring of the sunburst chart. In previous work [2], we presented three mapping rules to derive a sunburst chart from an RPS automatically. This derivation begins with the innermost ring, which is created from the top-level objects of the RPS (Mapping Rule 1). The subsequent creation of the additional rings of the sunburst chart occurs iteratively for each hierarchy level of the RPS (Mapping Rule 2). Note that Mapping Rules 1 and 2 can be employed to generate a sunburst chart at design time. During runtime, Mapping Rule 3 generates a sunburst chart instance from the design time artefact to visualise all running instances.

Mapping Rule 1 (Innermost Ring) [2]. The top-level objects of an RPS are mapped to the innermost ring of the sunburst chart. Two distinct cases need to be distinguished:

RPS with one top-level object. The top-level object represents the innermost ring of the sunburst chart.

RPS with more than one top-level object. The innermost ring comprises all top-level objects in equal parts.

An example of an RPS is shown in Fig. 1a. The sunburst charts derived from this RPS are displayed in Fig. 1b (at design time) and 1c (at runtime). The given RPS (cf. Fig. 1a) comprises a single top-level object (i.e. *Object A*), which represents the innermost ring of the depicted chart (cf. Fig. 1b). Subsequently, in accordance with the hierarchical order, the remaining objects are then mapped to additional rings through the application of Mapping Rule 2, starting from the second-level objects.

Mapping Rule 2 (Additional Rings) [2]. For each hierarchy level of the RPS, from the highest to the lowest, an additional outer ring is added to the corresponding sunburst chart. For this purpose, the following three patterns can be applied:

Pattern 1 (Chain). A child object is added on the top of the parent object, forming the next ring.

Pattern 2 (Common parent). Child objects are added on top of their common parent object as the next outer ring, sharing the parent object's fraction ring equally.

Pattern 3 (Common child). The child object is added on top of all its parent objects as the next outer ring.

No child: If there is no child object, no additional ring will be added.

Multiple instances of each object may be generated at runtime. Mapping Rule 3 can be employed to generate a sunburst chart instance (cf. Fig. 1c) that encompasses all instances of a running object-centric process based on the sunburst chart created at design time.

Mapping Rule 3 (Runtime) [2]. The design time sunburst chart can be employed to generate a sunburst chart representing the instances of the process at runtime. The design time chart is transformed into a runtime artefact, beginning with the innermost ring. Each (fraction of a) ring is then divided into parts that are equal in number to the instances of the object. If no instances of an object exist, the (fraction of a) ring is deemed to be empty.

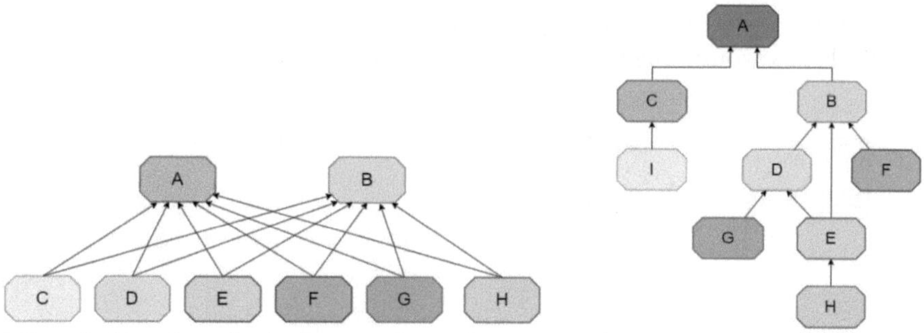

(a) Several object dependencies between the top-level objects A to B and their child objects C to H.

(b) Object E is associated with multiple hierarchy levels.

Fig. 2. Two RPS to demonstrate the challenges.

4 Problem Statement

Monitoring object-centric processes during runtime is challenging due to the unknown number of object instances and their dynamic changes. As supported by PHILharmonicFlows [1], for example, their behaviour may vary significantly. The challenge pertains to facilitating the monitoring of process structures that are characterised by dynamic evolution and variability. These structures may encompass hundreds or thousands of interacting object lifecycle processes. It is essential to note that this is not a straightforward task, as an ambiguous or unreadable visualisation will not be accepted by end-users. To incorporate sunburst charts into a monitoring framework, the following two challenges must be addressed first.

Challenge 1 (Object Dependencies Beyond One-to-Many). Both at design and at runtime, complex and multiple object dependencies that exceed a one-to-many relation are possible. These cannot be visualised with the described approach and mapping rules. At design time, it is feasible for a minimum of two objects to be associated with more than two other objects. As illustrated in Fig. 2a, an RPS with two parent objects A and B is demonstrated, each of which exhibits a relationship with the child objects C to H. Furthermore, a many-to-many relation between two objects (for example, Object X and Y) can be defined. During runtime, this may result in the creation of multiple instances of Object X, with each instance being dependent on all instances of Object Y. To overcome this challenge, it is necessary to design advanced sunburst charts, as standard versions are unable to display these complex dependencies.

Challenge 2 (Multiple Hierarchy Levels). An object may be assigned to multiple hierarchical levels. For example, consider the RPS shown in Fig. 2b with B being the parent of D and E, and D being the parent of E. In this case, E may be associated with hierarchy levels 3 and 4. Note that this scenario is not covered by the described mapping rules, as an object that is assigned to multiple hierarchy levels would need to be placed in multiple rings.

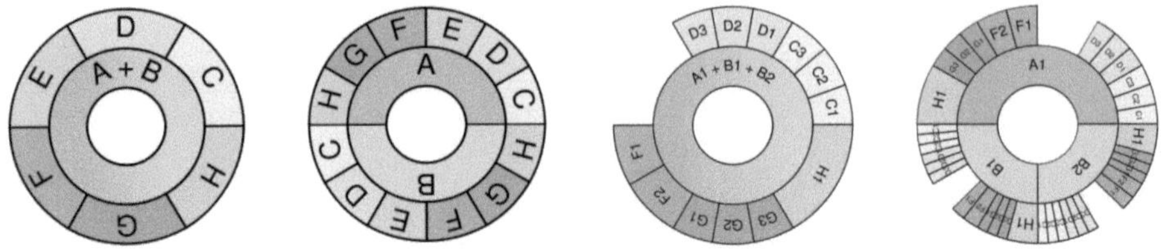

(a) VAR 1.1.1. **(b)** VAR 1.1.2. **(c)** VAR 1.2.1. **(d)** VAR 1.2.2.

Fig. 3. Variations of sunburst charts at design and runtime for Challenge 1.

5 Designing Advanced Sunburst Charts

Advanced sunburst charts must be designed to overcome the existing complex object dependencies that extend beyond one-to-many object relations or cardinalities (Challenge 1) and objects that are assigned to one hierarchy level only (Challenge 2). This section addresses the two challenges described above and presents several design choices to overcome them. Concerning the nomenclature of the variants, the following conventions have been established: The first digit indicates the number of the challenge, the second digit shows whether the sunburst chart is at design time (i.e., Number 1) or at runtime (i.e., Number 2), and the last digit distinguishes the different conditions.

Coping with Object Dependencies Beyond One-to-Many (Challenge 1). The visualisation of object dependencies beyond one-to-many object relations or cardinalities (i.e., many-to-many) is not possible when using two-dimensional sunburst charts with the defined mapping rules.

There are two variants (VAR for short) to deal with object dependencies beyond one-to-many object relations at design time:

VAR 1.1.1: The parent objects are merged into one entity, concatenating their labels with the symbol '+'.

VAR 1.1.2: Each parent object is displayed separately. The common child objects are displayed multiple times, once for each of their parent object.

The sunburst charts depicted in Figs. 3a and 3b are generated from the RPS[1] depicted in Fig. 2a with A and B being the parent objects and C to H being

[1] The RPS and sunburst charts are available on Researchgate: https://www.researchgate.net/publication/377727125_Visualising_and_Monitoring_Object-centric_Processes_with_Complex_Object_Interdependencies.

the corresponding common child objects. Each child object is related to both parent objects, forming an object dependency beyond one-to-many object relations. VAR 1.1.1 combines the common parent objects (e.g., A and B in Fig. 3a) by linking the object labels with '+'. Consequently, each of the common child objects is displayed exactly once. For VAR 1.1.2, the common child objects of A and B would be displayed multiple times (cf. Fig. 3b), with one occurrence per parent object. Consequently, the greater the number of parent objects is, the more frequently a child object will appear.

There are two variants to deal with object dependencies beyond one-to-many cardinalities at runtime:

VAR 1.2.1: The instances of the parent objects are merged into one entity, concatenating their labels with the symbol '+'.
VAR 1.2.2: Each parent object instance is displayed separately. The common child object instances are displayed multiple times, once for each parent instance.

The sunburst charts depicted in Figs. 3c and 3d were generated from the same RPS(see footnote 1) (cf. Fig. 2a) with A1, B1, and B2 being the parent object instances and C1 to C3, D1 to D3, F1 to F2, G1 to G3, and H1 being their common child object instances. Each child object instance has a relation to every parent object instance. VAR 1.2.1 concatenates all instances of common parent objects using the symbol '+' to link instance labels (cf. Fig. 3c). Furthermore, each of the common child instances is displayed once. In contrast, VAR 1.2.2 displays all parent object instances separately and the instances of the common child objects multiple times (cf. Fig. 3d).

Coping with Multiple Hierarchy Levels (Challenge 2). The described mapping rules preclude the use of sunburst charts when assigning objects to multiple hierarchy levels of the RPS.

There are two variants to deal with objects that are assigned to multiple hierarchy levels at design time:

VAR 2.1.1: Objects that are assigned to multiple hierarchy levels are displayed spanning all associated levels of the sunburst chart.
VAR 2.1.2: Objects that are assigned to multiple hierarchy levels and their child objects are displayed in each associated level of the sunburst chart (i.e. several times) separately.

The sunburst charts shown in Fig. 4 were generated from an RPS(see footnote 1) depicted in Fig. 2b with E being the child object of both B (Level 2) and D (Level 3). Consequently, E can be assigned to hierarchy levels 3 and 4. VAR 2.1.1 merges the objects into one object spanning over multiple hierarchy levels (cf. Fig. 4a). In contrast, VAR 2.1.2 shows the object and its child objects separately in each hierarchy level (cf. Fig. 4b). There are three variants to deal with objects that are assigned to multiple hierarchy levels at runtime:

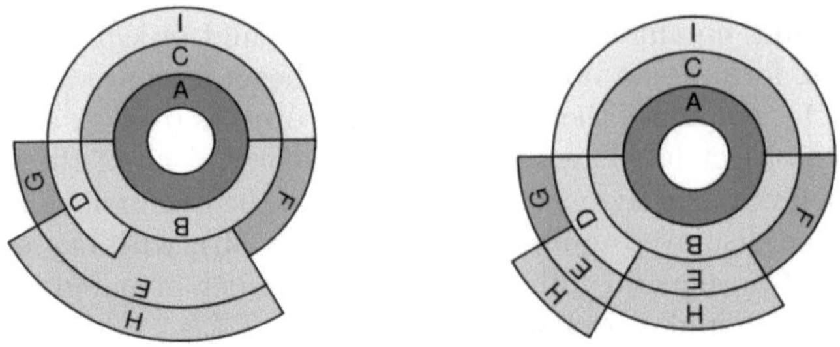

a VAR 2.1.1. **b** VAR 2.1.2.

Fig. 4. Variations of sunburst charts at design time for Challenges 2.

VAR 2.2.1: Object instances that are assigned to multiple hierarchy levels are merged into one entity spanning all associated levels of the sunburst chart. In its outermost level, the labels of the instances are separated by lines.

VAR 2.2.2: Object instances that are assigned to multiple hierarchy levels are merged into one entity spanning all associated levels of the sunburst chart. In its outermost level, the labels of the instances are concatenated with the symbol '+'.

VAR 2.2.3: Object instances that are assigned to multiple hierarchy levels, as well as their child object instances, are displayed at each associated level of the sunburst chart (i.e. several times) separately.

The sunburst charts depicted in Fig. 5 were generated from an RPS(see footnote 1) (cf. Fig. 2b) with E1 and E2 being the child object instances of B1 (Level 2) and D1 (Level 3). Consequently, object instances E1 and E2 can be assigned to levels 3 and 4. Moreover, object instances H1 to H3 are child object instances of the object instances E1 and E2, which are assigned to multiple hierarchy levels. VAR 2.2.1 (cf. Fig. 5a) and VAR 2.2.2 (cf. Fig. 5b) merge the object instances E1 and E2 into one entity spanning multiple hierarchy levels, with different labelling. In contrast, VAR 2.2.3 displays the instances and their child instances in each hierarchy level separately (cf. Fig. 5c).

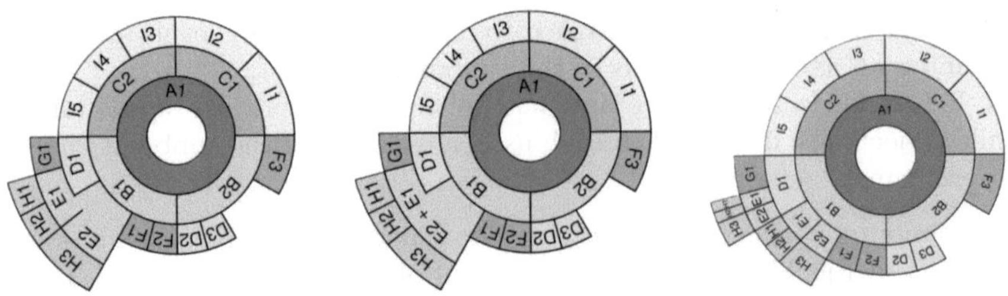

(a) VAR 2.2.1. **(b)** VAR 2.2.2. **(c)** VAR 2.2.3.

Fig. 5. Variations of sunburst charts at runtime for Challenges 2.

6 Study Design

To assess the different sunburst chart variants for visualising and monitoring object-centric processes, an empirical study was conducted. Given that these charts serve as an interface for engaging process stakeholders, the study focused on the understandability, readability, and suitability of these advanced sunburst charts.

6.1 Data Collection Method

The study is based on an online questionnaire[2] completed anonymously. The data were collected using the web-based tool `Unipark`. The study was available in both English (in the original version) and German (in a translated version, presented in grey and brackets). The structure, layout and content of the questionnaire were found to be consistent across both language options. The questionnaire was available for one month.

6.2 Questionnaire Structure

The questionnaire is divided into three parts. The first one focuses on collecting demographic data and assessing the level of experience in process models and monitoring. In the second part, sunburst charts are introduced using three alternative documents with varying levels of detail, specifically pertaining to the training phase. The third part of the questionnaire addresses the understandability, readability, and suitability of the advanced sunburst charts. The questionnaire comprises a total of 62 questions, of which 18 are displayed depending on the answers given to the preceding questions.

Demographics and Experience. The first questionnaire part comprises eight questions. The four demographic questions collect information about the participant's gender, age, current professional status and area of expertise. Furthermore, four dichotomous questions address the participants' experience levels concerning tools for process modelling, data modelling, and (business process) monitoring tools.

Training Phase. The second part of the questionnaire introduces participants to the creation of sunburst charts from object-centric processes. To investigate the appropriate level of knowledge required for these introductions(see footnote 2), we have established three different extensive introductions, which are then randomly assigned to each participant. The first one (*Intro 1* for short) offers a concise synopsis of sunburst charts, accompanied by a fundamental exposition of the mapping of objects to the components of sunburst charts. The second one (*Intro 2* for short) builds upon the first one and incorporates an exposition of the three mapping rules. The third one (*Intro 3* for short) builds upon the

[2] The questionnaire and responses are also available on Researchgate.

second one, but additionally includes the example of the RPS from Fig. 1a and its corresponding sunburst chart from Fig. 1b.

Sunburst Chart Variants. The main part of the study investigates the advanced sunburst chart variants. The structure of the questionnaire is as follows: First, the designed sunburst charts are investigated to overcome object dependencies that extend beyond one-to-many object relations (at design time), and second, the sunburst charts are examined to overcome many-to-many cardinalities (at runtime). Third, the designed sunburst charts are investigated for overcoming objects (at design time) and fourth, instances (at runtime) that are assigned to multiple hierarchy levels. These four main pages are structured identically and include the following five sections.

1. A description of the investigated challenge.
2. The RPS serves as the origin of the sunburst charts.
3. The designed sunburst charts are displayed to assess their understandability and readability (i.e., Statement 1; $S_{U/R}$ for short) and suitability (i.e., Statement 2; S_{Suit} for short). A five-point Likert scale was employed for the survey, with responses ranging from 1 (completely false) to 3 (neutral) to 5 (completely true).

$S_{U/R}$: The illustrated sunburst chart is intuitively understandable and readable.
S_{Suit}: The illustrated sunburst chart is suitable.

4. An optional question that asks for additional variants that overcome the respective challenge.
5. A question to establish a ranking of the variants according to their suitability.
6. A context- and scenario-independent question to investigate the variants in the case of large sunburst charts.

6.3 Data Analysis Method

To analyse and evaluate the collected data, we adopted methodologies presented in [3,20]. Study participants were recruited at Ulm University. Additionally, the study was published on social media to find young participants with a wide range of backgrounds. The creation of participant groups enabled the comparison of the results. A range of statistical analyses was conducted to assess the usability, readability, and suitability of the individual variants in relation to the demographics and experience of the participants. These analyses included both descriptive statistics and inferential statistics. The identification of the most appropriate statistical test for the data set under investigation was achieved by the *Which Stats Test*, developed by *Sage Research Methods*[3]. The *Shapiro-Wilk test* was employed to evaluate the normality of the data. The findings of the study indicated that the data for most items did not adhere to a normal distribution ($p < .0001$). However, it is important to note that non-normality is a prevalent phenomenon in Likert-type data, as responses are ordinally scaled and thus may exhibit skewness towards one extreme of the scale. In case of

[3] https://methods.sagepub.com/which-stats-test.

non-normality and more than two groups (i.e., comparison between variants), a *Kruskal-Wallis test* (KW) was conducted. The validity of this test extends to non-normality distributed and non-parametric between-subjects data. In light of the non-normality of the data and the non-paired nature of the variables, *Dunn's test* was identified as the optimal approach for the analysis of the differences between the variants. The effect sizes for *Dunn's test* were calculated using the *rank biserial correlation*. The *rank biserial correlation* is a measure of the effect size for non-parametric tests [7]. The following interpretation of the values is proposed: The value 0.2 is indicative of a small effect, 0.5 of a medium effect, and 0.8 of a large effect [19]. When comparing only two groups (i.e., experts vs. non-experts), the subsequent test after the *Shapiro-Wilk test* was a *Mann-Whitney U test* (MWU), since the data did not meet the criteria for normality in any case. In addition, an exploratory analysis utilising *cross tabulations* is employed to facilitate the comparison of the quantitative results obtained for each participant group. The results have been coloured to ease readability. For this, values less than 3.0 were assigned a red colour, those between 3.0 and 3.5 were assigned yellow, and those greater than 3.5 were assigned green.

7 Study Results

Demographics and Experience: A total of 154 participants completed the questionnaire: 96 male participants (62.3%), 56 female participants (36.4%), and two diverse participants (1.3%). The mean age of the participants was 23.8 years, with the majority (137 | 89.0%) falling within the 18-28 age bracket. The age of one participant has been excluded from the mean age calculation due to an erroneous entry. The majority of participants (125 | 81.2%) are students. The remainder are academics (21 | 13.6%) and other categories (8 | 5.2%). Most of the participants (89 | 57.8%) are studying economics, while 48 (31.2%) are studying STEM (science, technology, engineering, and mathematics). The majority of participants (91 | 59.1%) have prior experience in the creation of process models, 82 participants (53.2%) have experience in data modelling. In contrast, only a minority of the participants (38 | 24,7%) have experience in monitoring, and even fewer (24 | 15.6%) have experience in business process monitoring. To analyse the influence of experience, a group (25 | 16.2%) of experts (*E* for short) with familiarity in process models, data modelling, and monitoring is defined. The non-experts (*NE* for short) lack all the requisite experience (43 | 27.9%). In addition, this evaluation compares the two professional field groups, Economics and STEM, as well as the three groups with different introductions.

Object Dependencies Beyond One-to-Many (Challenge 1). To overcome the challenge posed by complex object dependencies, the design of two variants of sunburst charts (VAR 1.1.1 and 1.1.2) at design time has enabled the handling of objects. Furthermore, two further variants (VAR 1.2.1 and 1.2.2) have been designed at runtime to facilitate the visualisation of object instances. Table 1 presents the mean score on a five-point Likert scale for each participant group with respect to the understandability and readability (cf. $S_{U/R}$) and suitability (cf. S_{Suit}) of VAR 1.1.1 to VAR 1.2.2.

Table 1. Mean of five-point Likert scale regarding Challenge 1. Any significant disparities between two groups for a particular variant are highlighted in grey.

	VAR 1.1.1		VAR 1.1.2		VAR 1.2.1		VAR 1.2.2	
	$S_{U/R}$	S_{Suit}	$S_{U/R}$	S_{Suit}	$S_{U/R}$	S_{Suit}	$S_{U/R}$	S_{Suit}
Total (154)	4.1	3.7	3.9	3.6	3.6	3.5	3.0	3.1
E (25)	3.8	3.2	4.0	3.9	3.7	3.4	3.1	3.5
NE (43)	4.3	4.0	3.9	3.7	3.6	3.3	2.8	2.9
Economics (89)	4.2	3.8	3.8	3.7	3.5	3.6	2.9	3.1
STEM (48)	4.0	3.5	3.8	3.6	3.7	3.3	3.2	3.2
Intro 1 (45)	4.2	3.8	3.6	3.5	3.6	3.3	2.9	3.1
Intro 2 (56)	4.0	3.6	3.9	3.6	3.6	3.5	3.1	3.3
Intro 3 (53)	4.3	3.9	4.0	3.7	3.6	3.5	3.0	3.1

`Ranking`: The results indicate that VAR 1.1.1 (i.e., merging the labels) is the preferred variant for the majority of the participants (60.4%), across all groups (54.2% to 68.9%) at design time. This is supported by the results (cf. Table 2) of a *Kruskal-Wallis test* (KW: $S_{U/R}$: H = 6.31; p = 0.012; RBC = 0.156). However, except for the experts, who demonstrated a clear preference for VAR 1.1.2 (i.e., separating the labels) (68.8%). At runtime, a greater proportion of participants (63.0%) indicated a preference for VAR 1.2.1 (i.e., merging the labels), which merges the common parents into one, in comparison to VAR 1.2.2 (i.e., separating the labels).

Table 2. Statistical results between variants over all participants.

	S_{Suit}				$S_{U/R}$					
Variant	1.2.1	1.2.2	2.1.1	2.1.2	1.1.1	1.1.2	1.2.1	1.2.2	2.1.1	2.1.2
Mean	3.45	3.15	3.84	3.49	4.14	3.86	3.62	2.99	3.86	3.50
SD	1.10	1.22	1.12	1.17	0.99	1.06	1.11	1.21	1.09	1.17
Kruskal-Wallis	H=4.83, p=0.028		H=7.54, p=0.006		H=6.31, p=0.012		H=21.26, p<0.0001		H=8.11, p=0.004	
Effect size (RBC)	0.140		0.175		0.156		0.294		0.180	

`Likert-Scale`: The participants of each group (except the expert group) evaluated $S_{U/R}$ and S_{Suit}, which concatenate the labels of the parent objects (i.e.,

VAR 1.1.1) or instances (i.e., VAR 1.2.1), higher than the other variant. For VAR 1.1.1, a *Mann-Whitney U test* revealed that experts assigned a significantly lower rating to the understandability, readability, and suitability than non-experts (MWU: $S_{U/R}$: U = 382.0; p = 0.034; RBC = -0.29 | MWU: S_{Suit}: U = 342.0; p = 0.010; RBC = -0.36), both reflecting a small effect size. At design time, experts evaluated VAR 1.1.2 as more understandable and suitable. However, at runtime, they exhibited a distinct preference for the merging of common parent object instances into a single entity (i.e., VAR 1.2.1). This finding suggests that objects that have been consolidated into a single entity are perceived as unfamiliar by experts and, as a result, are less favoured. At runtime in VAR 1.2.2, S_{Suit} is rated significantly higher by experts than by non-experts (U = 708.5; p = 0.024; RBC = 0.318). Both $S_{U/R}$ and S_{Suit} are rated significantly higher during design time compared to at runtime across all participants ($S_{U/R}$: H = 21.26; p < 0.0001; RBC = 0.294 | S_{Suit}: H = 4.83; p = 0.028; RBC = 0.140) as shown in Table 2. This phenomenon can be attributed to the increased complexity present during runtime, where an object is instantiated on multiple occasions. This observation is also corroborated by both rankings.

`Satisfaction Score and Frequency Analysis:` In the case of the sunburst charts at design time, the satisfaction score for $S_{U/R}$ is consistently high across all groups, with an average of 4.0±0.1. The mean score for S_{Suit} is 3.7±0.1. The mean satisfaction score for both $S_{U/R}$ and S_{Suit} is 3.3±0.1 for the sunburst charts at runtime across all groups. Regarding the frequency analysis, non-experts have been observed to rate design time variants with a score of 4 or 5. In contrast, runtime variants are predominantly rated with a score of 2 due to their higher complexity. Both at design and runtime, experts frequently assign a rating of 4 or 5 on a five-point Likert scale for all sunburst chart variants.

`Complex Scenario:` Furthermore, a mere 7.8% of respondents indicated that they would have altered their decision if the complex relation had been extended over a small fraction of a ring rather than the entire ring. This finding suggests that the preferred variant of the majority does not depend on the complexity of the scenario.

`Discussion:` The findings indicate that non-experts possess the capacity to comprehend and evaluate concise, intelligible examples during design time. However, at runtime, an example comprising only 39 instances (cf. Fig. 3d) is perceived as challenging to interpret and comprehend. In the context of an exhaustive process comprising hundreds or thousands of instances, the merging of parent instances into one entity is paramount to the generation of a comprehensible sunburst chart, thus ensuring the prevention of superfluous instance duplication.

Multiple Hierarchy Levels (Challenge 2). To overcome the challenge posed by multiple hierarchy levels, the design of two variants of sunburst charts (VAR 2.1.1 and 2.1.2) at design time has enabled the handling of multiple hierarchy objects. Furthermore, three further variants (VAR 2.2.1 and 2.2.3) have been designed at runtime to facilitate the visualisation of multiple hierarchy object instances. Table 3 presents the mean score on a five-point Likert scale for each participant group with respect to the understandability and readability (cf. $S_{U/R}$) and suitability (cf. S_{Suit}) of VAR 2.1.1 to VAR 2.2.3.

Table 3. Mean of five-point Likert scale regarding Challenge 2. Any significant disparities between two groups for a particular variant are highlighted in grey.

	VAR 2.1.1		VAR 2.1.2		VAR 2.2.1		VAR 2.2.2		VAR 2.2.3	
	$S_{U/R}$	S_{Suit}	$S_{U/R}$	S_{Suit}	$S_{U/R}$	S_{Suit}	$S_{U/R}$	S_{Suit}	$S_{U/R}$	S_{Suit}
Total (154)	3.9	3.8	3.5	3.5	3.3	3.3	3.5	3.4	3.3	3.4
E (25)	4.1	4.0	3.8	3.9	3.6	3.7	3.3	3.1	3.5	3.8
NE (43)	3.7	3.7	3.2	[illegible]	[illegible]	[illegible]	3.5	3.3	3.1	3.3
Economics (89)	3.7	3.7	[illegible]	3.4	3.1	3.2	3.4	3.3	3.2	3.3
STEM (48)	4.0	3.9	3.8	3.7	3.4	3.5	3.3	3.4	3.5	3.6
Intro 1 (45)	3.7	3.7	[illegible]	[illegible]	3.3	3.3	[illegible]	3.1	3.1	3.3
Intro 2 (56)	3.9	3.9	3.4	3.4	3.1	3.3	3.6	3.5	3.2	3.5
Intro 3 (53)	4.0	3.8	3.8	3.7	3.4	3.3	3.6	3.4	3.5	3.5

`Ranking:` The majority of the participant groups (except for the participant group with Intro 1) demonstrate a preference for VAR 2.1.1 (i.e., displaying multiple times) (ranging from 56.0% to 67.4%) in comparison to VAR 2.1.2 (i.e., spanning over multiple hierarchy levels) during the design time. At runtime, only experts and participants with Intro 2 expressed a preference for VAR 2.2.1 (i.e., merging the labels with '|'). Moreover, the STEM group indicated that they considered VAR 2.2.2 (i.e., merging the labels with '+') to be the most suitable variant, with a percentage of 47.9%. In contrast, only 18.8% of respondents indicated a preference for VAR 2.2.1, and 33.3% expressed a preference for VAR 2.2.3 (i.e., displaying multiple times). When comparing both $S_{U/R}$ and S_{Suit}, the STEM group indicates that VAR 2.2.3 is marginally more favourable than VAR 2.2.2 (cf. Table 3). This phenomenon may be attributable to the fact that the STEM group has greater familiarity with this type of visualisation, due to their experience with other types of variants that also use this type [13]. However, 42.2% of all participants indicated that VAR 2.2.3 is the least suitable variant. Due to the uneven group sizes, the results could be skewed towards non-experts.
`Likert-Scale:` At design time, both $S_{U/R}$ and S_{Suit} elicit a significantly more favourable response across all participants for VAR 2.1.1 in comparison to VAR 2.1.2 (KW: $S_{U/R}$: H = 8.11; p = 0.004; RBC = 0.180 | KW: S_{Suit}: H = 7.54; p = 0.006; RBC = 0.175 cf. Table 2), which supports the assumption of the ranking results, that 60.4% of participants have a marked preference for VAR 2.1.1. Moreover, among those who had completed Intro 3 compared to Intro 1, VAR 2.1.2 was regarded as significantly more understandable, readable, and suitable (MWU: $S_{U/R}$: U = 1467.5; p = 0.042; RBC = 0.231 | MWU: S_{Suit}: U = 1501.0; p = 0.024; RBC = 0.259). In addition, the experts also rated the suitability of VAR 2.1.2 as significantly higher than that given by non-experts (MWU:

S_{Suit}: U = 342.5; p = 0.027; RBC = 0.32). Similarly, STEM participants rated the understandability and readability of VAR 2.1.2 as significantly higher than those given by economics (MWU: $S_{U/R}$: U = 2581.0; p = 0.037; RBC = 0.21). At runtime, experts rated both $S_{U/R}$ and S_{Suit} of VAR 2.2.1 significantly higher than non-experts (MWU: $S_{U/R}$: U = 667.0; p = 0.022; RBC = 0.323 | MWU: S_{Suit}: U = 680.0; p = 0.015; RBC = 0.35). Similar to the observation at design time, Intro 2 has a significantly higher rating than Intro 1 at runtime (MWU: $S_{U/R}$: U = 964.0; p = 0.036; RBC = 0.235), and Intro 3 has also a significantly higher rating than Intro 1 (MWU: $S_{U/R}$: U = 885.0; p = 0.024; RBC = 0.258). The present results from both design time and runtime suggest that participants with greater experience, who have undergone more extensive training or possess a higher level of process modelling competence, tend to rate the criteria of suitability, understandability, and readability higher than inexperienced participants.

`Satisfaction Score and Frequency Analysis:` In the case of the sunburst charts at design time, the satisfaction score of each participant group for $S_{U/R}$ and S_{Suit} is 3.7±0.2. In the case of the sunburst charts at runtime, the satisfaction score for $S_{U/R}$ remains at 3.3 compared to Challenge 1, with a slightly higher standard deviation of 0.2 for all participant groups. Conversely, the satisfaction score for S_{Suit} exhibited an increase to 3.4±0.2. A frequency analysis of the data reveals that participants assess sunburst charts with a mean rating of 4, except VAR 2.1.2, which obtained a mean rating of 5.

`Complex Scenario:` Furthermore, in cases where an object (or instance) spans more than two hierarchical levels, only 8.4% of participants change their preference to one of the other variants. This suggests that for the majority of participants, the preferred variant is not contingent on the number of levels over which a multi-hierarchical object (or instances) spans.

`Discussion:` In order to reduce the complexity of large object-centric processes, most participants expressed a preference for merging various instances of a multiple hierarchical object into a single entity at the sunburst chart, in preference to displaying the instances on multiple occasions. However, the findings of the study do not provide any significant indication of which labelling type (i.e. '+' or '|') is preferred for the entities displayed on the charts.

Limitation of the Study. The objective of this empirical study was to gain initial insights into the understandability and suitability of the developed variants. However, this work is subject to certain limitations. Of particular significance is the preponderance of student subjects within the sample population. The absence of individuals with extensive professional experience has the potential to compromise the validity of the study, potentially leading to the oversight of significant design considerations, challenges and potential discrepancies between the variants. Moreover, a technical implementation, such as a prototype, with which participants can interact, is not provided. Furthermore, the employment of sunburst charts is contingent upon data that is not aligned with actual business data. This is due to the fact that, to prioritise the presentation variety over the inherent business data itself, users of the runtime engine and the integrated monitoring component generally lack such knowledge as well. This generalisation poses a threat to validity and should be investigated in more detail in future research.

8 Summary and Outlook

This paper addresses two challenges inherent to the automatic derivation of sunburst charts from object-centric processes. To address these challenges, a series of sunburst chart variants has been developed and subjected to empirical evaluation involving 154 participants. With regard to Challenge 1, two distinct variants were identified that appear to address complex and multiple object dependencies that exceed a one-to-many relation. At design time, experts prefer the display of each parent object separately and the common child objects multiple times. However, at runtime, participants with experience tend to favour the variant that merges the parent object instances to reduce complexity. To address Challenge 2, two design time variants and three runtime variants have been designed to represent objects (or instances) that are assigned to multiple hierarchy levels. The majority of participants preferred representing such objects (or instances) that spanned across multiple levels, as opposed to displaying the objects (or instances) multiple times. Nevertheless, there is only a discrepancy in the preferred labelling of the merged objects (or instances) between the individual participant groups. In future work, the implementation of the sunburst charts will be incorporated in the PHILharmonicFlows monitoring tool. Furthermore, an empirical eye-tracking study will be conducted to examine the sunburst charts in the context of large business processes and potential interactions, to enhance readability. Finally, the sunburst diagram will be adapted for runtime components (e.g., progress, risk management or current status) to fulfil specific tasks and examine their suitability directly in a monitoring dashboard.

Acknowledgements. This work is part of the ProcMape project, funded by the KMU Innovativ Program of the Federal Ministry of Education and Research, Germany (F. No. 01IS23045B).

Disclosure of Interests. The authors have no competing interests to declare that are relevant to the content of this article.

References

1. Andrews, K., Steinau, S., Reichert, M.: Enabling runtime flexibility in data-centric and data-driven process execution engines. Inf. Syst. **101**, 101447 (2021)
2. Arnold, L., Breitmayer, M., Reichert, M.: Monitoring object-centric business processes: an empirical study. International Conference on Research Challenges in Information Science, pp. 327–342 (2023)
3. Brace, I.: Questionnaire design: How to plan, structure and write survey material for effective market research. Kogan Page Publishers (2018)

4. Claes, J., Vanderfeesten, I., Pinggera, J., Reijers, H.A., Weber, B., Poels, G.: A visual analysis of the process of process modeling. IseB **13**, 147–190 (2015)
5. Gherissi, W., El Haddad, J., Grigori, D.: Object-centric predictive process monitoring. In: International Conference on Service-Oriented Computing, pp. 27–39. Springer (2022)
6. Hofer, P., Perkhofer, L., Mayr, A.: Interactive big data visualizations: potential for management reporting: A summary of empirical studies on the selection, use, and design of novel visualization types. The Digitalization of Management Accounting: Use Cases from Theory and Practice, pp. 143–169 (2023)
7. Kerby, D.S.: The simple difference formula: an approach to teaching nonparametric correlation. Comprehen. Psychol. **3**, 11–IT (2014)
8. Künzle, V.: Object-aware process management. Ulm University (2013)
9. Leite, J., Mantovani, J., Kezunovic, M.: Use of distribution network topological fractality and sunburst charts in the online risk assessment. ISGT - LA pp. 1–6 (2019)
10. Macquisten, A., Smith, A.M., Fernstad, S.J.: Hierarchical visualization for exploration of large and small hierarchies. In: Integrating Artificial Intelligence and Visualization for Visual Knowledge Discovery, pp. 587–612 (2022)
11. Park, G., van der Aalst, W.M.: Operational process monitoring: an object-centric approach. Comput. Ind. **164**, 104170 (2025)
12. Sarikaya, A., Correll, M., Bartram, L., Tory, M., Fisher, D.: What do we talk about when we talk about dashboards? IEEE Trans. Visual Comput. Graphics **25**(1), 682–692 (2018)
13. Sathiyanarayanan, M., Mulling, T.: Wellformedness properties in Euler diagrams: an eye tracking study for visualisation evaluation. arXiv preprint arXiv:1611.06587 (2016)
14. Srinivas, T.A.S., Sravanthi, Y., Kumar, Y.K., Srihith, I.D.: From charts to dashboards: an overview of data visualization methods. Adv. Comput. Technol. Appl. **7**(1), 1–14 (2023)
15. Steinau, S., Andrews, K., Reichert, M.: Executing lifecycle processes in object-aware process management. In: SIMPDA, pp. 25–44 (2017)
16. Steinau, S., Andrews, K., Reichert, M.: The relational process structure. In: International Conference on Advanced Information Systems Engineering (CAiSE), pp. 53–67 (2018)
17. Steinau, S., Andrews, K., Reichert, M.: Coordinating large distributed relational process structures. Softw. Syst. Model. **20**(5), 1403–1435 (2021). https://doi.org/10.1007/s10270-020-00835-0
18. Sun, G., Li, F., Jiang, W.: Brief talk about big data graph analysis and visualization. J. Big Data **1**(1), 25 (2019)
19. Tomczak, M., Tomczak, E.: The need to report effect size estimates revisited. An overview of some recommended measures of effect size (2014)
20. Wieringa, R.: Design Science Methodology for Information Systems and Software Engineering. Springer-Verlag, Berlin Heidelberg (2014)

DMN-Guided Prompting: A Framework for Controlling LLM Behavior

Shaghayegh Abedi[1] and Amin Jalali[2(✉)]

[1] Politecnico di Torino, Turin, Italy
s309894@studenti.polito.it
[2] Stockholm University, Stockholm, Sweden
aj@dsv.su.se

Abstract. Large Language Models (LLMs) have shown considerable potential in automating decision logic within knowledge-intensive processes. However, their effectiveness largely depends on the strategy and quality of prompting. Since decision logic is typically embedded in prompts, it becomes challenging for end users to modify or refine it. Decision Model and Notation (DMN) offers a standardized graphical approach for defining decision logic in a structured, user-friendly manner. This paper introduces a DMN-guided prompting framework that breaks down complex decision logic into smaller, manageable components, guiding LLMs through structured decision pathways. We implemented the framework in a graduate-level course where students submitted assignments. The assignments and DMN models representing feedback instructions served as inputs to our framework. The instructor evaluated the generated feedback and labeled it for performance assessment. Our approach demonstrated promising results, outperforming chain-of-thought (CoT) prompting in our case study. Students also responded positively to the generated feedback, reporting high levels of perceived usefulness in a survey based on the Technology Acceptance Model.

Keywords: Large Language Models · Decision Model and Notation · Automated Feedback · Prompt Engineering

1 Introduction

Large Language Models (LLMs) have shown considerable potential in automating decision logic within knowledge-intensive processes [13]. Their capabilities are increasingly leveraged across multiple domains where complex decisions must be made. However, the effectiveness of LLMs critically depends on the quality of their instructions, also known as prompts. Developing such prompts (commonly known as prompt engineering) is often a trial-and-error process, requiring technical expertise and posing challenges related to transparency, reusability, and maintenance [16,20]. As decision logics evolve, their instructional prompts must also be adapted - a task often non-trivial for business users lacking technical proficiency in developing or adjusting prompts.

To address these challenges, we propose a novel framework that integrates Decision Model and Notation (DMN) into prompt template definitions. DMN is a standardized

J. Barateiro et al. (Eds.): EDOC 2025 Workshops, LNBIP 571, pp. 134–148, 2026.
https://doi.org/10.1007/978-3-032-16234-2_9

graphical notation for modeling decision logic [1,6]. By leveraging DMN to modularize and guide prompt structures, our strategy enables LLMs to follow structured decision pathways, breaking down complex logic into interpretable and manageable components. This approach reduces the dependency on ad hoc changes of prompts, making it easier to understand, modify, and maintain - particularly in settings where clarity, consistency, and collaboration are essential.

We implemented our proposed framework as a DMN-guided prompting framework configured in a graduate-level course to automatically support generating feedback for students' assignments while having the instructor in the loop. Students submitted graphical models representing domain-specific decisions. These models were transformed into natural texts, which are given to our framework in addition to instructional DMN rules defined by the course instructor. The framework generated feedback, which was given to students after the instructor labeled them, so students could distinguish between correct and incorrect feedback. These labeled data were used to evaluate the approach, and the results show that DMN-guided prompting outperformed equivalent prompts defined purely using chain-of-thought prompting [21]. In addition, students reported high levels of perceived usefulness, as measured through a survey designed based on the Technology Acceptance Model (TAM) [5].

The remainder of the paper is organized as follows. Section 2 provides a brief background on Decision Model and Notation (DMN) and prompt engineering, outlining their relevance for guiding the behavior of Large Language Models. Section 3 introduces the proposed DMN-guided prompting framework. Section 4 presents the case study conducted in a graduate-level course, explaining the implementation process, reporting evaluation results, and discussing the strengths and limitations observed in the study. Finally, Sect. 5 concludes the paper and introduces future directions.

2 Background

2.1 Decision Model and Notation

Decision Model and Notation (DMN) is a standard developed by the Object Management Group (OMG) to represent decision logic in a clear, structured, and interpretable format [1]. It is widely used in business process management to separate decision logic from process flows [3], enabling organizations to formalize and automate operational decisions transparently. A key advantage of DMN is its accessibility to both business professionals and technical users. It offers graphical and tabular notations that help bridge the gap between informal business rules and executable logic [2,15]. DMN supports decision modeling using the Decision Requirements Diagram (DRD) [1].

Figure 1 presents a sample DRD that will serve as a running example throughout this paper to illustrate our approach (for the complete DMN specification, refer to [1]). This diagram specifies the rules for a fictitious loan eligibility process, where the decision is based on the applicant's *Salary* and *Credit Score*, modeled as *input data* elements. A *decision table* element, named *Loan Approval Rule*, encodes the decision logic. The decision output is then passed to a *literal expression* element, called *Loan Approval Result*. Literal expressions represent decision logic using textual statements - in this case, defining the message to be displayed to the user based on the decision outcome.

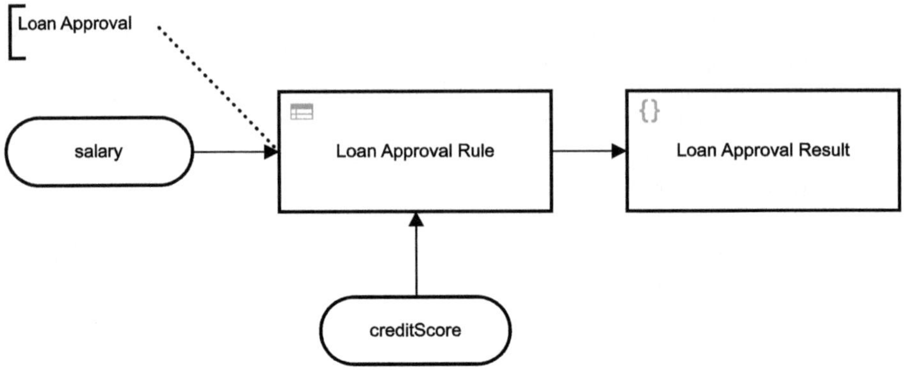

Fig. 1. A decision requirements diagram example.

Loan Approval is an annotation that does not have any semantics yet enables providing more information about elements in the DMN model.

Loan Approval Rule | **Hit policy:** Unique

	When salary (string)	And creditScore (string)	Then Is Eligible for Loan? (string)
1	> 50000	>= 700	approve
2	> 50000	[650..700[	manual_review
3	-	-	decline

Fig. 2. A decision table example.

Figure 2 illustrates how the *Loan Approval Rule* decision table specifies the decision logic. In DMN, a decision table can be used to document the rules governing a decision. Each row in this table represents an individual rule, while columns define the conditions (inputs) and their corresponding outcomes (outputs). This tabular structure is intuitive for many users, resembling familiar tools such as spreadsheets. In our example, the loan will be approved if the applicant's salary exceeds 50,000 and their credit score is greater than or equal to 700. The rules in this example are evaluated top-down, and the dash symbols in the final row represent a wildcard ("any input value"), which applies when none of the above rules evaluate to true.

Figure 3 shows how the *literal expression* is defined using the Friendly Enough Expression Language (FEEL). Based on the decision outcome, this expression determines the message to be shown to the user.

Loan Approval Result

```
approave_message = "We're pleased to inform you that your loan application has been
approved. Congratulations!".
manual_review_message = "We'd like to inform you that your application has been
processed and requires a manual review. We will update you as soon as the review is
complete.".
decline_message = "We regret to inform you that your loan application has not been
approved due to either insufficient income or credit score. If you have any questions
or would like further clarification, please feel free to contact us."
```

Fig. 3. A literal expression example.

It is important to note that we only present a simplified DMN example here to introduce the essential concepts relevant to this paper. DMN supports a variety of modeling styles, with detailed specifications provided in [1]. Overall, DMN offers a modular and interpretable framework for defining decision logic. While it has traditionally been applied in operational and compliance domains, its potential for structuring interactions between domain experts and AI-based systems such as Large Language Models (LLMs) remains largely unexplored. This study investigates how DMN can guide LLMs in generating consistent and correct feedback.

2.2 Prompt Engineering

Prompt engineering refers to designing input instructions that effectively guide the behavior of Large Language Models. Because LLMs generate output based on probabilistic patterns learned from large datasets, their responses are susceptible to the wording, structure, and context provided in the prompt. As a result, prompt engineering is critical in ensuring the relevance, accuracy, and clarity of the model's output [14,18].

A variety of prompting strategies have emerged in recent research. These include zero-shot prompting, where the model is asked to perform a task without examples; few-shot prompting, which provides the model with a few example cases; and Chain-of-Thought (CoT) prompting [21], which encourages the model to generate intermediate reasoning steps before answering. Other techniques, such as retrieval-augmented and role-based prompting, aim to inject external knowledge or frame the model's behavior through personas or task-specific instructions [7,17].

Among these strategies, Chain-of-thought prompting is reported to be effective for complex tasks as it follows the divide-and-conquer approach, decomposing a task into smaller sub-tasks and helping LLMs to follow a step-by-step approach to solve a problem. For example, instead of prompting the LLM to evaluate an assignment holistically, the task can be divided into sub-prompts that independently assess correctness, clarity, and completeness. These individual judgments are combined to form the final feedback [4]. Dividing prompts into individual parts is effective, yet some parts, like business logics, change more frequently than others, requiring the prompt engineer to refine the prompts. A framework enabling the separation of such business rules using DMN can help business people to apply the changes directly, requiring less intervention from a prompt engineer, and enabling organizations to apply changes more easily and quickly.

3 DMN-Guided Prompting

We propose a structured prompting framework in which the behavior of Large Language Models (LLMs) is guided by a formal specification based on the Decision Model and Notation (DMN) standard.

Although DMN supports multiple representations of decision logic, our approach adopts a divide-and-conquer strategy (including chain-of-thought prompting [21]) by organizing logic into modular units we refer to as triples. Each triple comprises (1) a set of input data elements, (2) a decision table, and (3) a corresponding literal expression (as illustrated early in the paper in Fig. 1, including one sample triple). These triples encapsulate logically self-contained decision-making units, each functioning as an independent sub-prompt. This modular structure enables LLMs to process each unit sequentially and coherently.

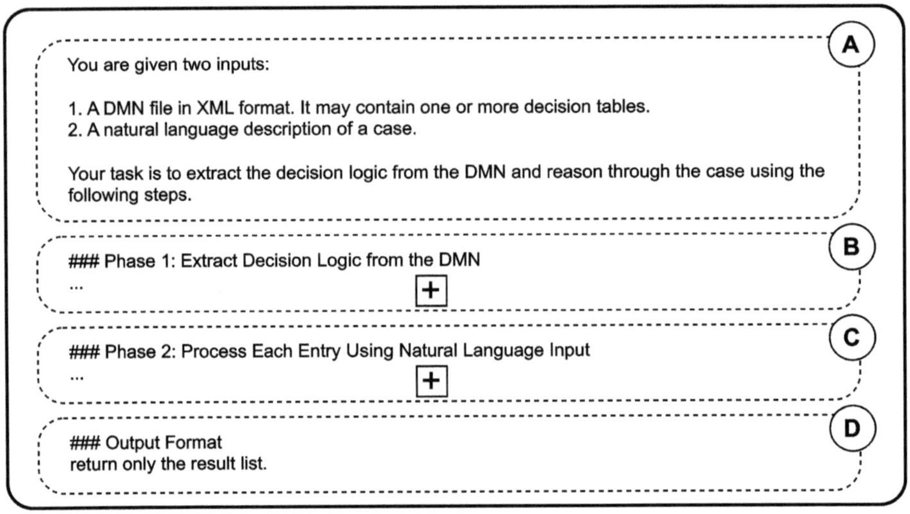

Fig. 4. The overall prompt structure used for DMN-guided evaluation.

Figure 4 outlines the full prompt template used to parse and evaluate the running example DMN file, which can be adopted for different use cases differently. Prompt templates refinement is important as it gives organizations freedom in how to design DMN models based on their needs. The process is divided into four sequential parts. While the complete contents of Part B and Part C are not shown in the figure, the roles of each part are as follows:

– *Part A:* Provides instructional and contextual data, including the DMN file and the input text to be evaluated.

- *Part B:* Instructs the LLM to parse the DMN model.
- *Part C:* Guides the LLM in evaluating the input text based on the parsed DMN logic.
- *Part D:* Directs the LLM to return only the final decision output.

In the following sections, we elaborate on *Part B* and *Part C*.

B

```
### Phase 1: Extract Decision Logic from the DMN

From the DMN file:
- Identify each decision rule (preferably using annotations as rule names).
- For each rule, extract a structured dictionary entry as follows:

```json
{
 "rule Name": {
  "input": [list of required input field names],
  "decision table": {
   "name": "<decision table name>",
   "content": "<decision table XML snippet>"
  },
  "literal expression": {
   "name": "<output name>",
   "content": "<list of outcomes and corresponding messages>"
  }
 }
}
```

Fig. 5. Instructions in Part B: parsing DMN into structured triples.

3.1 Part B: Parsing the DMN Model

Part B instructs the LLM to parse the provided DMN content, as shown in Fig. 5. The LLM is guided to extract each decision rule using explicit annotations. This approach allows our framework to support multiple decision rules within a single DMN file. For each rule, the LLM constructs a dictionary containing the following components: rule name, list of input elements, decision table (name and contents), and literal expression (name and contents). This dictionary forms the knowledge base of triples used to guide subsequent evaluations. Each triple corresponds to a logically encapsulated unit, enabling the LLM to focus on discrete decision points within a larger decision model.

3.2 Part C: Evaluating the Input Text

Figure 6 illustrates the instructions given in *Part C*, which guide the LLM in evaluating the natural language input using the previously parsed decision logic. This phase comprises four key steps applied to each entry in the extracted dictionary:

- (*C1*) *Extract Input Values:* This step instructs the LLM to extract input values from the extracted input list in the extracted dictionary. These input elements guide LLM in extracting their value from the given text (see second instruction line in C1).
```

```
C
### Phase 2: Process Each Entry Using Natural Language Input

For each extracted entry:

C1
**Step 1: Extract Input Values**
- Identify the required input fields from the input list.
- From the natural language text, extract the values for those fields (even if not in key-value format).

C2
**Step 2: Evaluate the Decision Table**
- Evaluate input values strictly according to the decision table logic, any value shall be treated accordingly (numbers below are examples):
   - [40..50] means inclusive of 40 and 50.
   - (40..50) means exclusive of both 40 and 50.
   - ]40..50[ means exclusive of both 40 and 50.
   - [40..50) means inclusive of 40, exclusive of 50 (and so on).
   - [40..50[ means inclusive of 40, exclusive of 50 (and so on).
   - Do not round or approximate values. For instance, 39 must not match [40..50].
- Identify the name of the outcome for the matching rule.

C3
**Step 3: Retrieve the Corresponding Literal Expression**
- Use the outcome name and look at the message instruction written in the `"literal expression"` entry.

C4
**Step 4: Generate the Replies**
- return the message exactly as written, without any change.
- generate a list named **result** include all generated messages, i.e., "result": [
```

Fig. 6. Instructions in Part C: evaluating input text using parsed DMN.

– (C2) *Evaluate Decision Table:* Based on the extracted input values, the LLM evaluates the decision rule using the decision table. Examples are provided to illustrate how to evaluate numeric intervals and enforce exact matching (following a few-shot prompting strategy). These examples were found to be crucial in avoiding hallucinations, particularly in boundary conditions.
– (C3) *Retrieve Literal Expression:* Once a matching decision rule is identified, the LLM retrieves the corresponding literal expression associated with the outcome.
– (C4) *Return Final Message:* The final step ensures that only the decision message (from the literal expression) is returned. The prompt instructs the LLM to avoid including intermediate data structures such as the extracted dictionary. Without this constraint, the LLM often included unnecessary reasoning traces, leading to downstream usage confusion.

3.3 Result Compilation and Final Output

After completing all sub-tasks, the LLM assembles the outputs into a single response as described in *Part D*. Each triple is evaluated independently, and the results are synthesized into a coherent final output. The full implementation, including the Python source code, the running example DMN file, and example input texts, is available on our GitHub repository[1]. It is important to emphasize that there is no need to modify the prompt if decision rules are changed. Instead, users modify the DMN model, which the LLM interprets to evaluate the logic and generate the results.

Furthermore, if customized message generation is desired, the LLM can post-process the output messages using a secondary prompt. Otherwise, the framework returns only the predefined messages specified in the DMN logic.

This framework offers several key benefits: *Modularity:* Components can be independently created, reused, or updated, supporting maintainable and scalable prompt design. *Interpretability:* Each decision rule and its corresponding output are explicit and traceable, enhancing transparency. *Collaborative design:* Domain experts can contribute directly to changing decision logic and improving quality. *Transparency:* Most significantly, it enables moving away from ad hoc prompt crafting toward systematic and auditable LLM design for complex, rule-based tasks.

4 Case Study

This case study investigates the feasibility and effectiveness of the proposed DMN-guided prompting framework for automated feedback generation in an academic context. Specifically, it examines how decision models can structure the behavior of large language models (LLMs) to evaluate student-created process models and return predefined feedback addressing common known problems in the models. We begin by describing the educational setting, followed by the implementation and evaluation methodology, and conclude with findings concerning system performance and student perceptions. Due to privacy concerns, the student submissions and responses could not be published. However, the framework and example materials are provided in our GitHub repository to help readers apply the framework to their own use cases.

4.1 Educational Setting and Study Context

The study was conducted in a graduate-level course titled Business Process Design and Intelligence at the Department of Computer and Systems Sciences (DSV), Stockholm University. A total of 24 student groups participated, each comprising approximately six members. As part of their coursework, students were tasked with designing business process models using Petri nets, implemented via the WoPeD tool [8] in an agile way [9]. The models were expected to reflect best practices in Business Process Redesign (BPR) [19], such as triage, parallelism, task elimination, automation, and resequencing. Participation in the study was voluntary, and students provided informed consent for using their anonymized submissions in this research.

4.2 Framework Deployment in the Case Study

Figure 7 depicts deploying the DMN-guided prompting framework within the course. The setup comprises four primary actors: (i) the prompt engineer defining the prompt

[1] https://github.com/Shaghayegh-Abedi/DMN-prompting-project.

template, (ii) the instructor, who encodes feedback logic using DMN triples; (iii) the student, who submits process models for evaluation; and (iv) the DMN-guided prompting system, which generates feedback based on the encoded logic for each submission.

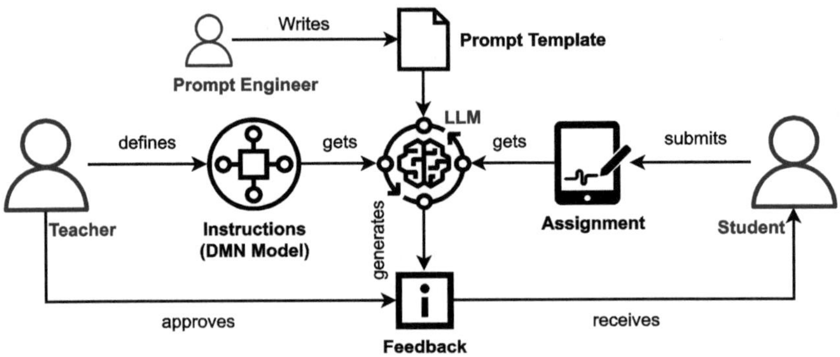

Fig. 7. Application of the DMN-Guided Prompting Framework in our case study.

To ensure reliability, the generated feedback was not directly shared with students. Instead, a human-in-the-loop mechanism was implemented: instructors manually reviewed each comment and classified it as correct or incorrect. The labeled feedback was subsequently communicated to students, reducing the risk of misleading them into assuming that the received feedback was always correct. This approach safeguarded the instructional quality and enabled an empirical evaluation of the system's predictive accuracy. The framework was executed for robustness using two LLMs - GPT-4o (via the OpenAI API) and Gemini 1.5 Pro (via Google's Gemini API). Additionally, we implemented a Chain-of-Thought (CoT) [21] prompting set up as a performance baseline, allowing us to isolate the impact of the DMN structure from general prompt engineering strategies.

4.3 Technical Implementation

We developed a software component to operationalize the framework that translates Petri net models into structured natural language descriptions. These descriptions retain critical control flow and resource semantics, enabling LLMs to interpret process models as standardized textual artifacts. The implementation is publicly available on GitHub for reuse in similar applications. The core feedback mechanism comprises nine decision rules, each encoded as a table in the Decision Model and Notation (DMN). These rules align with specific BPR principles and provide pedagogically meaningful evaluation criteria for student submissions.

4.4 Evaluation Results

Figure 8 presents an overview of instructor-labeled feedback (for GPT-4o experiment) across student groups and nine BPR rules. Each rule is assessed along two dimensions:

Group ID	Rule1	Feedback1	Rule2	Feedback2	Rule3	Feedback3	Rule4	Feedback4	Rule5	Feedback5	Rule6	Feedback6	Rule7	Feedback7	Rule8	Feedback8	Rule9	Feedback9
1	TRUE	TRUE	TRUE	TRUE	TRUE	TRUE	TRUE	TRUE	FALSE	FALSE	TRUE	TRUE	TRUE	TRUE	TRUE	TRUE	TRUE	TRUE
2	TRUE	TRUE	TRUE	FALSE	TRUE	TRUE	TRUE	TRUE	FALSE	FALSE	FALSE	FALSE	TRUE	TRUE	TRUE	TRUE	TRUE	TRUE
3	TRUE	TRUE	TRUE	TRUE	TRUE	TRUE	TRUE	TRUE	FALSE	FALSE	TRUE	FALSE	TRUE	TRUE	TRUE	TRUE	TRUE	TRUE
4	TRUE	TRUE	TRUE	FALSE	TRUE	TRUE	TRUE	TRUE	FALSE	FALSE	FALSE	FALSE	TRUE	TRUE	TRUE	TRUE	TRUE	TRUE
5	TRUE	TRUE	FALSE	FALSE	FALSE	FALSE	TRUE	TRUE	FALSE	FALSE	TRUE	FALSE	TRUE	TRUE	TRUE	TRUE	TRUE	TRUE
6	TRUE	TRUE	FALSE	FALSE	TRUE	TRUE	TRUE	TRUE	FALSE	FALSE	TRUE	TRUE	TRUE	TRUE	TRUE	TRUE	TRUE	TRUE
7	TRUE	TRUE	TRUE	TRUE	TRUE	TRUE	FALSE	TRUE	TRUE	TRUE	TRUE	TRUE	TRUE	TRUE	TRUE	TRUE	TRUE	TRUE
8	TRUE	TRUE	TRUE	TRUE	TRUE	TRUE	FALSE	FALSE	FALSE	FALSE	TRUE	TRUE	FALSE	TRUE	TRUE	TRUE	FALSE	TRUE
9	TRUE	TRUE	TRUE	TRUE	TRUE	TRUE	TRUE	FALSE	FALSE	FALSE	TRUE	TRUE	TRUE	TRUE	TRUE	TRUE	TRUE	TRUE
10	TRUE	TRUE	TRUE	TRUE	TRUE	TRUE	TRUE	TRUE	FALSE	FALSE	TRUE	FALSE	TRUE	TRUE	TRUE	TRUE	TRUE	TRUE
11	TRUE	TRUE	TRUE	TRUE	TRUE	TRUE	TRUE	TRUE	FALSE	FALSE	FALSE	FALSE	TRUE	TRUE	TRUE	TRUE	TRUE	TRUE
12	TRUE	TRUE	FALSE	FALSE	TRUE	FALSE	FALSE	FALSE	FALSE	FALSE	FALSE	FALSE	FALSE	FALSE	TRUE	FALSE	TRUE	FALSE
13	TRUE	TRUE	TRUE	TRUE	TRUE	TRUE	FALSE	FALSE	FALSE	FALSE	FALSE	FALSE	FALSE	TRUE	FALSE	FALSE	FALSE	FALSE
14	TRUE	TRUE	TRUE	TRUE	TRUE	TRUE	FALSE	TRUE	FALSE	TRUE	TRUE	TRUE	FALSE	TRUE	FALSE	TRUE	TRUE	TRUE

Fig. 8. Overview of instructor-labeled evaluations of GPT-4ogenerated feedback, presented across student groups and nine BPR rules. Each rule is assessed along two dimensions: whether the student correctly applied the principle (Rule column) and the GPT-4o feedback (Feedback column).

the student correctly applied the principle (Rule column), and the LLM-generated feedback (Feedback column). Table 1 provides a comparative analysis of four configurations: DMN-guided and CoT prompting strategies, each paired with GPT-4o and Gemini 1.5 Pro. Standard classification metrics - Precision, Recall, F1-score, and Accuracy - were computed by comparing system outputs with instructor labels.

The specified results in Table 1 show that the DMN-guided prompting generally outperforms the CoT baseline across most metrics and models. The GPT-4o + DMN configuration yielded the highest performance: 0.91 precision, 0.90 recall, 0.91 F1-score, and 0.87 accuracy. In contrast, GPT-4o + CoT achieved perfect recall (1.00) but suffered a severe drop in precision (0.36), resulting in a markedly lower F1-score of 0.53 - suggesting a high rate of false positives.

Gemini 1.5 Pro exhibited similar trends. The DMN-guided setup achieved an F1-score of 0.71, outperforming the CoT variant (F1-score: 0.62). These results confirm the value of integrating decision logic into prompt design for enhancing precision, consistency, and pedagogical alignment in automated feedback systems.

Table 1. Performance comparison of different prompting approaches.

Approach	Model	Precision	Recall	F1-score	Accuracy
DMN-guided	GPT-4o	0.91	0.90	0.91	0.87
Chain-of-Thought	GPT-4o	0.36	1.00	0.53	0.54
DMN-guided	Gemini 1.5 Pro	0.60	0.87	0.71	0.65
Chain-of-Thought	Gemini 1.5 Pro	0.55	0.71	0.62	0.52

4.5 Feedback Analysis and Rule-Specific Insights

To complement the quantitative findings, we conducted a detailed qualitative analysis to assess the system's capability to detect individual BPR principles and reveal underlying student comprehension patterns. All 14 groups correctly applied Rule 1 (triage), and the DMN-guided framework using GPT-4o flawlessly recognized these instances.

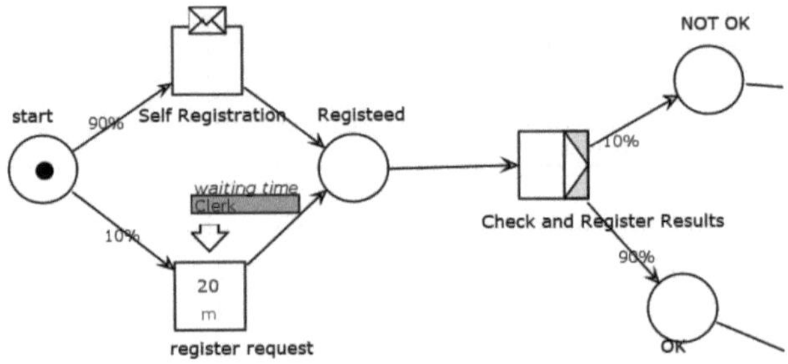

Fig. 9. Example of a merged task with ambiguous labeling, leading to DMN-Guided framework using GPT-4o feedback misclassification for Rule 2 (task composition).

Rule 2 (task composition) was correctly implemented by the majority (79%) of the groups, and the framework achieved 86% accuracy in identifying them - closely aligned with the overall accuracy. Notably, in the two misclassified cases, students labeled the merged task using unexpected phrasing (e.g., "check and register result" instead of the expected formulation indicating the task is related to *credit* check), leading to reduced model confidence in mapping the task semantics, as illustrated in Fig. 9.

For Rule 3 (knock-out), 93% of the groups modeled the principle correctly, and the framework matched this performance with a 93% accuracy rate - exceeding its overall average. This rule entails rejecting cases early based on credit score assessments (see the XOR-split after "Check and Register Result" in Fig. 9).

In contrast, Rule 5 (task resequencing) was the most challenging for students, with only one group (7%) correctly reordering tasks. Despite this, the framework successfully identified the intended logic in 93% of the cases. This rule involved moving fraud detection earlier in the process and replacing manual evaluation with a machine learning-based approach. The low implementation rate suggests students struggled with abstract dependency reasoning, signaling a need for more advanced instructional scaffolding.

Rule 6 (deferred choice and contact reduction) was correctly applied by 64% of the groups, with the framework achieving 79% accuracy. Some groups misused XOR-splits to represent deferred choices. Some groups incorrectly modeled the deferred choice pattern using an XOR-split, which is inappropriate in this context. The task required groups to redesign the process to avoid repeatedly checking the status of an external fraud detection request. According to the business-to-business agreement, the result would be received automatically within two days; otherwise, a reminder should be sent.

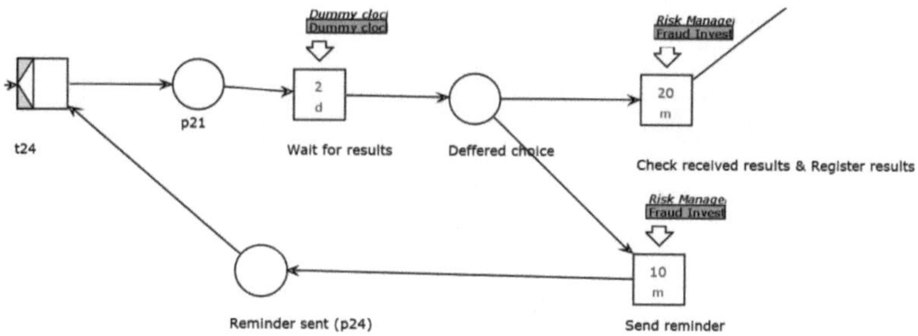

Fig. 10. Example of an incorrectly modeled deferred choice, where an unnecessary 'Wait for Result' task was added despite the presence of an automated reminder mechanism.

Figure 10 illustrates an example of a model that does not fully comply with the intended design. The group correctly identified and modeled the deferred choice between sending a reminder and receiving the result (though the automation aspect was not explicitly captured). However, they also added a separate "Wait for Result" task, introducing an unnecessary delay in the process. The DMN-guided framework using GPT-4o successfully identified this issue, even though the merged task ("Receive Result") was not clearly labeled. This may be due to defining the task to be performed manually by assigning it to the "Fraud Investigator," which likely helped the LLM interpret the intent from the surrounding context.

Regarding Rule 7 (parallelism between two automated tasks), 71% of the groups applied it correctly, and the framework reached 79% accuracy. Some confusion arose when students incorrectly applied task composition - merging two external web services into a single task- violating design control assumptions, as the process designer cannot merge such services.

Finally, for Rules 8 (parallelism of an automated and a manual task) and 9 (sequence within parallelized tasks), 86% of the groups applied them correctly, and the framework achieved an identical 86% accuracy - matching its overall performance.

4.6 Perceived Usefulness

To assess the proposed system's perceived usefulness (PU), we asked students to fill out a survey designed based on the Technology Acceptance Model (TAM) [5], a common approach to measure perceived usefulness and ease of use of information systems artifacts [10–12]. Figure 11 shows the result in aggregated and detailed levels.

At the aggregated level, the overall PU construct, calculated as the average of the six PU items, shows a high central tendency. The median value is above 5.5 on a 7-point Likert scale, indicating strong agreement among participants regarding the system's usefulness. The narrow interquartile range suggests that most responses are concentrated around the upper scale values. While a few outliers exist (e.g., ratings around 3), they do not significantly impact the overall distribution. This confirms that participants, on average, perceived the system to be highly useful.

The detailed boxplots present the distribution of responses for each PU item (PU1 to PU6). All six items reflect consistently high medians, typically at or above 5.5, reinforc-

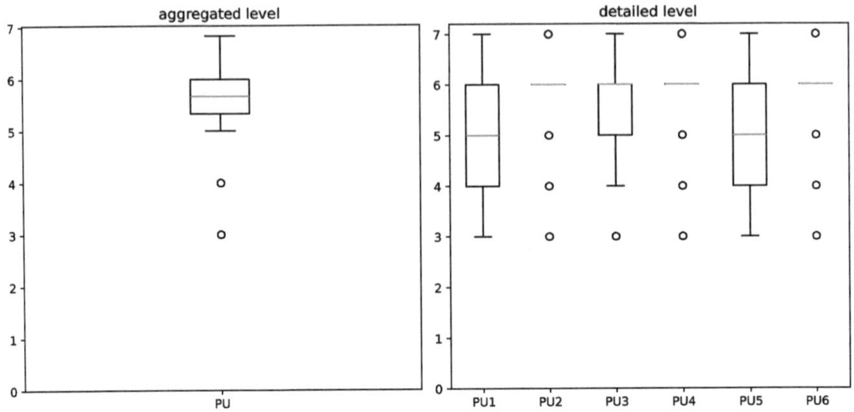

Fig. 11. Boxplots showing the distribution of Perceived Usefulness (PU) in aggregated and detailed level.

ing the aggregated findings. Some variation in spread exists across items, particularly for PU5, where responses show a slightly broader distribution. Nonetheless, even in the presence of outliers, the central tendency for all items remains strong, indicating a reliable pattern of positive user perception.

The consistency across items and low variability further support the internal reliability of the PU construct and suggest that the users evaluated the system as useful across different functional dimensions captured by the individual items.

Note on Perceived Ease of Use: Perceived Ease of Use (PEU) was not assessed, since students interacted with the system only through the university's Learning Management System (LMS). In this context, PEU would reflect the usability of the LMS rather than our system, making it irrelevant. In contrast, Perceived Usefulness (PU) was evaluated, as students could reflect on the usefulness of the feedback received.

Threats to Validity: Our study has several limitations. *Internal validity* may be affected by the manual labeling of feedback, which introduces subjectivity despite the human-in-the-loop review. *Construct validity* is constrained by the chosen metrics (precision, recall, F1, accuracy) and the survey-based perceived usefulness, which may not fully capture long-term learning outcomes. *External validity* is limited since the case study was conducted in a single graduate-level course with 24 groups and nine decision rules, reducing generalizability to other domains and contexts. Finally, *conclusion validity* may be influenced by the relatively small dataset and ceiling effects for some rules. Further studies in diverse educational and professional settings are needed to strengthen the generalizability of our findings.

5 Conclusion

This paper presented a novel prompting framework that integrates Decision Model and Notation (DMN) with Large Language Models (LLMs) to guide decision logic in a modular, interpretable, and user-friendly manner. By structuring prompts as DMN triples (each consisting of input data, decision tables, and literal expressions), our approach operationalizes a divide-and-conquer strategy for LLM behavior control. The case study conducted in a graduate-level course demonstrated that DMN-guided prompting generally outperformed chain-of-thought (CoT) methods in predictive accuracy. Regarding user-perceived usefulness, students reported high perceived value from the feedback generated by our DMN-based approach.

The results confirm the viability of DMN for LLM control in educational settings, particularly for structured feedback generation. More broadly, this work illustrates the untapped potential of DMN to encode domain-specific reasoning in a format that LLMs can interpret and execute reliably, offering a promising direction for rule-based, transparent AI systems.

Future research can expand in several directions. First, exploring how DMN-guided prompting can be adapted for other application domains, such as healthcare or compliance auditing, will help assess its generalizability. Second, combining DMN with retrieval-augmented generation (RAG) may further enhance reasoning grounded in external knowledge. Third, if customized message generation is desired, the LLM can post-process the output messages using a secondary prompt; otherwise, the framework returns only the predefined messages specified in the DMN logic. Fourth, this approach can be complemented by incorporating few-shot learning, where example inputs are used to improve LLM accuracy when interpreting or applying DMN rules. Fifth, other ways of defining DMN rules and alternative strategies for prompt construction can be explored to increase flexibility and expressiveness. Finally, investigating multi-turn interactions and conversational agents powered by DMN-guided LLMs could open new opportunities for explainable and controllable AI interfaces in decision support systems.

Acknowledgment. The computations for testing and developing our approach were enabled by resources provided by the National Academic Infrastructure for Supercomputing in Sweden (NAISS), partially funded by the Swedish Research Council through grant agreement no. 2022-06725.

Disclosure of Interests. The authors have no competing interests.

References

1. Decision Model and Notation Specification. Technical report 1.6, Object Management Group - Standards Development Organization (2024)
2. Bazhenova, E., Zerbato, F., Oliboni, B., Weske, M.: From BPMN process models to DMN decision models. Inf. Syst. **83**, 69–88 (2019)

3. Biard, T., Le Mauff, A., Bigand, M., Bourey, J.-P.: Separation of Decision Modeling from Business Process Modeling Using New Decision Model and Notation" (DMN) for Automating Operational Decision-Making. In: Camarinha-Matos, L.M., Bénaben, F., Picard, W. (eds.) PRO-VE 2015. IAICT, vol. 463, pp. 489–496. Springer, Cham (2015). https://doi.org/10.1007/978-3-319-24141-8_45
4. Cui, W., et al.: Divide-conquer-reasoning for consistency evaluation and automatic improvement of large language models. In: Empirical Methods in Natural Language Processing, pp. 334–361 (2024)
5. Davis, F.D.: Perceived usefulness, perceived ease of use, and user acceptance of information technology. MIS Q. **13**(3), 319–340 (1989)
6. De Leoni, M., Felli, P., Montali, M.: Integrating BPMN and DMN: modeling and analysis. J. Data Semant. **10**(1), 165–188 (2021)
7. Feng, G., Zhang, B., Gu, Y., Ye, H., He, D., Wang, L.: Towards revealing the mystery behind chain of thought: a theoretical perspective. NeurIPS **36**, 70757–70798 (2023)
8. Freytag, T.: Woped–workflow petri net designer. University of Cooperative Education (2005)
9. Jalali, A.: Teaching Business Process Development Through Experience-Based Learning and Agile Principle. In: Zdravkovic, J., Grabis, J., Nurcan, S., Stirna, J. (eds.) BIR 2018. LNBIP, vol. 330, pp. 250–265. Springer, Cham (2018). https://doi.org/10.1007/978-3-319-99951-7_17
10. Jalali, A.: Evaluating Perceived Usefulness and Ease of Use of CMMN and DCR. In: Augusto, A., Gill, A., Nurcan, S., Reinhartz-Berger, I., Schmidt, R., Zdravkovic, J. (eds.) BPMDS/EMMSAD -2021. LNBIP, vol. 421, pp. 147–162. Springer, Cham (2021). https://doi.org/10.1007/978-3-030-79186-5_10
11. Jalali, A.: Evaluating user acceptance of knowledge-intensive business process modeling languages. Softw. Syst. Model. **22**(6), 1803–1826 (2023)
12. Jalali, A., Maggi, F.M., Reijers, H.A.: A hybrid approach for aspect-oriented business process modeling. J. Softw. Evol. Process **30**(8), e1931 (2018)
13. Khayatbashi, S., Sjölind, V., Granåker, A., Jalali, A.: AI-enhanced business process automation: a case study in the insurance domain using object-centric process mining (2025)
14. Marvin, G., Hellen, N., Jjingo, D., Nakatumba-Nabende, J.: Prompt Engineering in Large Language Models. In: Jacob, I.J., Piramuthu, S., Falkowski-Gilski, P. (eds.) Data Intelligence and Cognitive Informatics, pp. 387–402. Springer, Singapore (2024)
15. Mertens, S., Gailly, F., Poels, G.: Enhancing Declarative Process Models with DMN Decision Logic. In: Gaaloul, K., Schmidt, R., Nurcan, S., Guerreiro, S., Ma, Q. (eds.) CAISE 2015. LNBIP, vol. 214, pp. 151–165. Springer, Cham (2015). https://doi.org/10.1007/978-3-319-19237-6_10
16. Parker, M., Anderson, C., Stone, C., Oh, Y.: A large language model approach to educational survey feedback analysis. Int. J. Artif. Intell. Edu. (2024)
17. Rama Padmaja, C.V., Lakshminarayana, S.: Enhancing language models through prompt engineering - a survey. In: 2024 IEEE International Conference on Intelligent Systems, Smart and Green Technologies (ICISSGT), pp. 117–121 (2024)
18. Ramanathan, S., Lim, L.-A., Mottaghi, N.R., Buckingham Shum, S.: When the prompt becomes the codebook: grounded prompt engineering (groproe) and its application to belonging analytics. In: LAK '25, pp. 713–725, ACM, New York, NY, USA (2025)
19. Reijers, H.A., Mansar, S.L.: Best practices in business process redesign: an overview and qualitative evaluation of successful redesign heuristics. Omega **33**(4), 283–306 (2005)
20. Sandkuhl, K.: LLM-assistance for quality control of LLM output. In: Řepa, V., Matulevičius, R., Laurenzi, E., (eds.) Business Informatics Research, vol. 529. Springer, Cham (2024). https://doi.org/10.1007/978-3-031-71333-0_3
21. Wei, J., et al.: Chain-of-thought prompting elicits reasoning in large language models. In: Neural Information Processing Systems, Curran Associates Inc, Red Hook, NY, USA (2022)

Evaluating LLM-Based Process Explanations Under Progressive Behavioral-Input Reduction

P. van Oerle, R.H. Bemthuis(✉), and F.A. Bukhsh

University of Twente, Enschede, The Netherlands
p.vanoerle@student.utwente.nl, {r.h.bemthuis,f.a.bukhsh}@utwente.nl

Abstract. Large language models (LLMs) are increasingly used to generate textual explanations of process models discovered from event logs. Producing explanations from large behavioral abstractions (e.g., directly-follows graphs or Petri nets) can be computationally expensive. This paper reports an exploratory evaluation of explanation quality under progressive behavioral-input reduction, where models are discovered from progressively smaller prefixes of a fixed log. Our pipeline (i) discovers models at multiple input sizes, (ii) prompts an LLM to generate explanations, and (iii) uses a second LLM to assess completeness, bottleneck identification, and suggested improvements. On synthetic logs, explanation quality is largely preserved under moderate reduction, indicating a practical cost-quality trade-off. The study is exploratory, as the scores are LLM-based (i.e., comparative signals rather than ground truth) and the data are synthetic. The results suggest a path toward more computationally efficient, LLM-assisted process analysis in resource-constrained settings.

Keywords: Process Mining · Large Language Models · Behavioral Abstractions · Data Efficiency

1 Introduction

Process mining extracts actionable insights from event logs by discovering process models [1,9]. Over the last two decades, tools for discovery and conformance checking have matured substantially [18,20], with applications in logistics, healthcare, and finance [21]. Recent advances in large language models (LLMs) enable automatic generation of such explanations [8,19]. However, producing explanations from behavioral abstractions derived from large logs, such as directly-follows graphs (DFGs) or Petri nets, can be computationally intensive partly due to the size and structural complexity of the input given to the model. While each event may contribute unique behavior that is, in principle, worth capturing, it remains an open question how much input is required to obtain high-quality explanations. Here, we use behavioral abstraction to denote formal

J. Barateiro et al. (Eds.): EDOC 2025 Workshops, LNBIP 571, pp. 149–160, 2026.
https://doi.org/10.1007/978-3-032-16234-2_10

structures (e.g., control-flow graphs) derived from event logs and supplied to an LLM as the basis for textual descriptions.

Despite promising results with models such as GPT-4 and Llama for insights and next-step prediction [5,12], leveraging LLMs for explanations remains challenging in data-intensive settings. Large logs require substantial computation [20], motivating behaviorally efficient approaches that reduce the size of the abstraction while retaining explanation fidelity. Prior work examines LLM capabilities in process mining but rarely studies the effect of reducing behavioral information [2]. Recent works highlight both promise and limitations across semantic awareness [17], anomaly detection, and prediction [6,11], yet to our knowledge do not quantify the trade-off between input complexity and explanation quality.

This paper reports an exploratory evaluation of explanation quality under progressive behavioral-input reduction, where process abstractions are constructed from progressively fewer events. Studying reduction is relevant for: (i) data efficiency (e.g., acceptable explanations may be achievable from smaller abstractions); (ii) non-linear payoff (e.g., quality gains may plateau beyond mid-range input sizes); (iii) robustness (e.g., omitting rare variants or later events probes resilience under constraints); and (iv) practical thresholds (e.g., organizations need guidance on input sizes that balance quality with usability).

We fix the log and vary the fraction of events used to construct the model, thereby potentially lowering the complexity of the structures provided to the LLM. Concretely, we propose a pipeline that (i) discovers process models from progressively smaller subsets of synthetic logs, (ii) prompts an LLM to produce textual explanations, and (iii) uses a second LLM to evaluate those explanations along three dimensions: completeness, bottleneck identification, and suggested improvements.

Our contributions are: (1) a pipeline for evaluating the effect of behavioral-input reduction on LLM-based process explanations; (2) an exploratory quantification of explanation quality along three dimensions (completeness, bottlenecks, improvements) under progressive behavioral reduction; and (3) empirical evidence on synthetic logs that identifies a region of favorable cost–quality trade-offs, informing resource-constrained and real-time process intelligence systems.

The remainder of this paper is structured as follows. Section 2 reviews related work. Section 3 presents our research pipeline for data reduction. Section 4 details the experimental setup. Section 5 reports and briefly discusses the results. Lastly, Sect. 6 discusses threats to validity, and Sect. 7 concludes.

2 Related Work

Recent work at the intersection of LLMs and process mining explores tasks such as semantically aware process discovery [17] and next-step prediction [5,12]. LLM-based methods can exploit contextual language cues that reveal subtle operational details. However, existing works [4,6] largely emphasize accuracy or descriptive clarity and do not explicitly study data efficiency or the robustness of explanations.

Beyond algorithmic enhancements, event log pre-processing, covering tasks such as filtering, noise removal and sampling, has long been pivotal for scalable analysis [16]. Yet little work combines such preprocessing with LLM-driven interpretation, despite growing volumes of heterogeneous logs where computation can be a bottleneck. We take a step in this direction by asking whether high quality explanations can be obtained from reduced behavioral abstractions. Online/streaming process mining addresses ingest-time scalability (e.g., single-pass or windowed processing) [20], while our focus is on how much behavioral abstraction is sufficient for high quality LLM explanations once a log (or its prefix) is available.

In parallel, LLMs have been applied to process improvement. Lashkevich et al. [14] propose a prompting method in which an LLM analyzes waiting time causes and recommends redesign options. In a user study, an enhanced prompt with a structured catalog of redesign patterns yields more relevant and actionable suggestions than a zero-shot baseline while maintaining diversity and novelty. Kubrak et al. [13] study LLM-generated explanations for process monitoring. Using a design science approach and an explainability question bank, they find dialogue-style explanations aid understanding but often fail to address the "why" and to support trust calibration. These studies indicate value for improvement and explainability, but assume full access to behavioral information and do not examine reduced abstractions.

In contrast, we study the data efficiency of LLM-generated explanations. By systematically reducing the fraction of events used to build the behavioral model and quantifying the effect on explanation quality, we extend LLM-assisted process mining to reduction regimes and surface trade-offs between model complexity and explanation quality, which may be particularly relevant for large-scale or resource-constrained process intelligence.

3 Research Pipeline

This section presents a four-stage pipeline to test whether LLMs can be applied more data-efficiently in process mining. Figure 1 summarizes the flow. We vary the behavioral input used for model discovery and measure the impact on explanation quality.

Our goal is not to reduce the number of logs, but to progressively reduce the behavioral footprint derived from a given log by selecting only a fraction of its events prior to discovery.

3.1 Event Logs and Sub-log Generation

Let L denote the full event log, represented as a time-ordered sequence of events $L = \langle e_1, e_2, \ldots, e_n \rangle$ with $|L| = n$. For $k \in \{1, \ldots, n\}$, a sub-log S_k is the prefix containing the first k events:

$$S_k = \langle e_1, e_2, \ldots, e_k \rangle, \quad k \in \{1, \ldots, n\}. \tag{1}$$

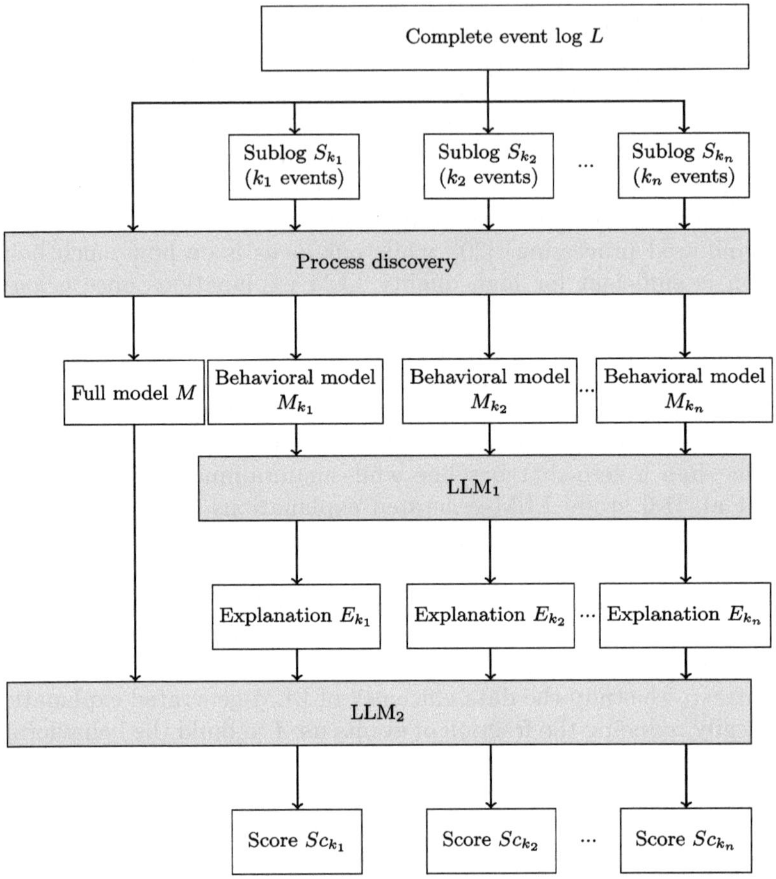

Fig. 1. Research pipeline illustrating how process models (behavioral abstractions) are derived from sublogs containing only k events. These models are explained by LLM_1 and scored by LLM_2 with the full model M as a reference.

This prefix sampling is simple and reproducible, but it may exclude infrequent variants or late-appearing behavior; we discuss implications and alternatives in Sect. 6. Other strategies (e.g., trace-based subsampling, variant-aware or stratified selection) are compatible with the pipeline and are left for future work.

3.2 Process Discovery

Process discovery maps an event log to a process model. Applying a discovery algorithm to S_k yields:

$$M_k = \text{Discover}(S_k), \tag{2}$$

and $M = \text{Discover}(L)$ for the full log. The pipeline is agnostic to the specific discovery method.

3.3 LLM_1: Explanation Generation

For each discovered model M_k, the first LLM (LLM_1) generates a textual explanation:

$$E_k = \mathrm{LLM}_1(M_k). \tag{3}$$

Each E_k is prompted to (i) describe the process, (ii) identify bottlenecks, and (iii) suggest improvements.

3.4 LLM_2: Scoring Against the Full Model

A second LLM (LLM_2) evaluates E_k with the full model M as reference:

$$\mathrm{Sc}_k = \mathrm{LLM}_2(E_k, M). \tag{4}$$

Concretely, LLM_2 assigns three scores in $[1, 10]$ (related to completeness, bottleneck identification, and improvement suggestions), then returns their average as the overall score. This setup indicates how well E_k captures salient behavior relative to M.

This pipeline enables a controlled study of how decreasing behavioral input (in M_k) affects the quality of generated explanations. While LLM-as-judge raises concerns about determinism and validity, it is practical for multi-faceted, semantically rich criteria that can be challenging to formalize.

4 Experimental Configuration

This section details the experimental setup: the case study, data preprocessing, and LLM configuration.

4.1 Case Study Introduction

We use the synthetic dataset from [3], which contains event logs generated via discrete event simulation of a job-shop scheduling problem. Each experiment provides raw results and a corresponding `.xes` log with roughly 1,000–1,500 traces (about 250,000–350,000 events). We convert logs to process models using standard tools; in our experiments we employ the Inductive Miner [15] as implemented in PM4Py [7], due to its robustness on noisy, large-scale logs.

4.2 Data Preprocessing

All `.xes` logs are processed with PM4Py [7]. From each log, we derive partial models M_k for

$$k \in \{10, 20, 50, 100, 1000, 10000, 100000\},$$

as well as the full model M. These k values span a wide range of behavioral inputs. Note that k counts events used for discovery, not traces or logs. Table 1 summarizes the datasets.

Table 1. Number of traces and events per experiment.

Experiment	Number of traces	Number of events
411	1,296	314,160
412	1,013	244,384
413	1,308	317,072
421	1,422	345,520
422	1,223	296,184

4.3 LLM Configuration

All experiments were conducted in Python. We accessed Meta's Llama 3.3-70B [10] via standard APIs. Llama was chosen for its balance of quality and cost.

For each experiment in Table 1 and for each M_k, we generate five explanations with independent runs, then score each explanation using a separate LLM instance on a 1–10 scale; we report the average per k. The generation prompt asks for: (i) a concise process description, (ii) bottleneck identification, and (iii) actionable improvement suggestions. An explanation is satisfactory if it covers the end-to-end flow, highlights inefficiencies, and proposes concrete actions.

Table 2 lists the scoring rubric. The evaluation prompt assigns three scores (completeness, bottlenecks, improvements) and returns their mean as the overall score. Code and results are publicly available[1]. Notice that the rubric serves as guidance for the evaluator LLM; we analyze scores comparatively across k rather than as absolute ground truth.

Table 2. Scoring criteria for each metric.

Score	Criteria
1-3	Major elements are not mentioned or incorrect information is given.
4-6	All main elements are mentioned, but lack detail or are incomplete.
7-9	All important elements are mentioned with minor omissions.
10	All aspects are accurately described without omissions.

5 Experimental Results

This section reports the key findings. We first describe the explanations of the LLM's responses, then examine how explanation quality varies with the size of the input data.

[1] https://github.com/oerlep/data-reduction-llm-in-pm/.

5.1 Explanations of Discovered Models

Generated explanations include: (i) a concise process overview (start/end points and major activities); (ii) control-flow structures (sequences, parallelism, loops); (iii) structural bottleneck candidates (e.g., self-loops, high-wait transitions); and (iv) actionable improvement suggestions.

High-scoring outputs reference all major activities and propose concrete improvement strategies. Low-scoring outputs typically omit key steps or provide vague recommendations (e.g., "investigating causes") without specific actions or data references.

5.2 LLM-Based Judgments

The evaluator LLM assigns three scores (1–10) per explanation: completeness, bottleneck identification, and improvement suggestions. Explanations should cover main activities, transitions, and loops; identify salient performance issues; and propose data-informed changes. Missing or unclear elements reduce the score.

LLM-based scoring is efficient but introduces variability and subjectivity. To mitigate this, we generate five explanations per k and report the average. Section 6 discusses complementary evaluation strategies.

5.3 Effect of Behavioral Input Size on Quality

Figure 2 shows the average score as a function of k. Table 3 provides per-experiment details. Here, k is the number of events used to discover the behavioral model, not the number of traces or logs. We observe:

- **Small k (10–20):** low average scores (<5.0), reflecting incomplete or imprecise explanations.
- **Mid-range k (100–1,000):** substantial quality gains, with typical averages around 6.5–7.0.
- **Large k (10,000–100,000):** further improvements and higher consistency, stabilizing near ≈ 8.0.

Across experiments, the curve shows a practical knee between k=100 and k=1,000: average scores rise from ≈ 6.5 to ≈ 6.9. From 1,000 to 10,000, gains are modest (to ≈ 7.0), suggesting diminishing returns in that range under our setup. By contrast, moving to k=100,000 yields a clearer uplift (to ≈ 7.92) and visibly narrower error bars, indicating higher consistency. The full logs provide only a marginal additional increase (≈ 7.95 on average), likely within the variability observed. Thus, $k \approx 1{,}000$ offers a stable mid-range when latency or budget constraints apply, while $k \approx 100{,}000$ can be justified in higher-stakes settings that benefit from the extra point of quality. Per-experiment trends are monotonic on average, though individual logs show slight non-monotonicity around k=10,000, illustrating the value of reporting variability. These findings remain contingent on synthetic job-shop data and may vary with real-world noise and variant structure.

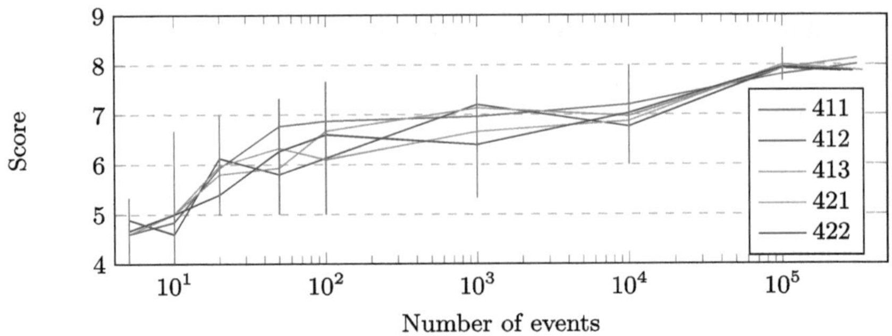

Fig. 2. Average LLM-assigned explanation scores per number of input events (k). Each line corresponds to one experiment from Table 1. Error bars represent score variability across five explanation evaluations per k.

5.4 Discussion

The results suggest that meaningful explanations can be derived from significantly reduced behavioral input, paving the way for more scalable and resource-efficient LLM-assisted process intelligence. Explanation quality improves non-linearly with input size: from very small sub-logs to mid-range values of k, we observe clear gains; between $k = 1{,}000$ and $k = 10{,}000$, improvements are modest under our setup; at $k = 100{,}000$, we see a further uplift along with reduced variance, while full logs yield only marginal additional improvement. A plausible explanation can be coverage: very small sub-logs under-sample rare variants and loop structures, resulting in under-specified models. Larger values of k capture more control-flow detail, enabling richer explanations. The precise "sweet spot" may depend on the task and domain; for example, sensitivity to rare events or tolerance for cost and latency.

We used Inductive Miner with default settings and serialized the discovered Petri nets for LLM input. Inductive Miner's block-structured nets are sound and may over-approximate behavior, which can improve readability but alter the abstraction exposed to the LLM. We expect notation and algorithm choices (e.g., DFGs or BPMN; Heuristics/Alpha Miner; intentionally unsound nets) to affect explanation quality by changing label granularity and control-flow clarity. A systematic analysis over discovery methods and model forms is an important next step.

6 Threats to Validity

This study has several limitations that may affect the generalizability, reproducibility, and interpretability of the results.

Using an LLM to grade another LLM introduces subjectivity, prompt sensitivity, and potential bias propagation. We averaged five generations per k, yet residual variability remains, and evaluator preferences (e.g., phrasing/style) may

Table 3. Per-experiment explanation scores by input event count (k). Each row reports the five scores from LLM_2 for different values of k (5 to full log), across five experiments (411–422). Each column group corresponds to a different event count; the final column in each group shows the average across the five runs.

Experiment	5 logs						10 logs						20 logs					
						Avg						*Avg*						*Avg*
411	5.0	4.3	4.3	5.0	4.3	4.6	5.2	4.3	4.3	5.7	4.7	4.8	6.3	6.0	5.3	5.7	6.3	5.9
412	5.3	5.2	4.7	4.7	4.7	4.9	4.3	5.0	4.3	4.3	5.0	4.6	6.0	7.0	6.0	6.0	5.7	6.1
413	5.0	4.3	4.3	4.7	4.7	4.6	5.7	4.3	4.3	4.7	6.0	5.0	5.3	6.3	5.7	5.3	6.3	5.8
421	5.0	4.7	4.7	5.0	4.7	4.8	5.7	4.7	4.7	5.0	4.7	5.0	6.0	6.3	6.3	6.3	5.7	6.1
422	5.0	4.7	4.7	5.3	3.7	4.7	5.7	5.7	5.0	4.7	4.0	5.0	5.3	5.3	5.0	5.3	6.0	5.4
Experiment	50 logs						100 logs						1,000 logs					
						Avg						*Avg*						*Avg*
411	7.3	7.3	5.3	7.2	6.7	6.8	7.7	7.0	7.7	6.7	5.3	6.9	5.3	7.0	7.7	7.8	7.0	7.0
412	6.7	5.3	6.0	5.0	6.0	5.8	5.0	7.0	5.3	6.7	6.7	6.1	7.3	7.5	7.7	7.5	6.0	7.2
413	6.0	6.0	6.3	6.0	5.3	5.9	7.7	7.3	6.0	7.0	5.3	6.7	6.7	7.0	7.0	7.3	7.7	7.1
421	4.0	4.7	4.3	5.3	4.7	4.6	5.3	5.3	5.7	4.3	4.3	5.0	7.3	5.7	6.7	7.0	6.7	6.7
422	6.7	5.3	6.7	7.3	5.3	6.3	6.7	7.3	6.0	4.7	7.3	6.6	6.0	6.7	6.0	7.3	6.0	6.4
Experiment	10,000 logs						100,000 logs						Full log					
						Avg						*Avg*						*Avg*
411	7.3	6.3	7.3	7.7	7.3	7.2	8.0	7.7	8.0	7.7	7.7	7.8	7.7	8.0	8.7	8.0	7.7	8.0
412	7.7	6.0	6.3	7.8	6.0	6.8	8.0	8.0	7.7	8.0	7.7	7.9	7.7	8.3	7.7	8.0	7.7	7.9
413	7.3	7.2	7.0	7.3	6.0	7.1	7.7	8.0	8.0	8.0	8.0	7.9	8.0	8.3	8.3	8.0	8.0	8.1
421	7.3	6.7	6.7	6.0	7.7	6.9	8.0	8.0	8.0	8.0	8.0	8.0	7.7	8.0	7.7	8.0	8.0	7.9
422	6.0	7.3	8.0	6.0	7.8	7.0	7.7	7.7	8.3	7.7	8.3	8.0	7.7	7.7	8.0	8.0	8.0	7.9

correlate with the generator's output. Even for full logs, no perfect (10) scores were produced, suggesting missing context or model limitations. We therefore treat scores as comparative signals, not ground truth. Future work should triangulate with (i) human ratings by process analysts, (ii) cross-model judging (e.g., different evaluator LLMs), and (iii) task-specific objective proxies (e.g., activity/edge coverage against M_k, penalties for hallucinated activities, alignment-based fitness of described paths). We plan a small expert study (think-aloud and rubric) to calibrate LLM scores and assess inter-rater agreement.

Prefix sampling (first k events) simplifies incremental comparisons but may under-sample late or rare variants, potentially inflating apparent gains at larger k. Alternative strategies (e.g., variant-aware, stratified, or trace-level sampling) could alter the curve. Prompt wording, decoding parameters, and seed control affect both generations and judgments. We report averages but acknowledge sensitivity to these settings. Results may also depend on discovery and notation choices.

With five generations per point, uncertainty persists. We did not report significance tests or confidence intervals. Replications could include dispersion (e.g., bootstrap CIs), effect sizes, and corrections for multiple comparisons across k and datasets.

Findings are based on synthetic job-shop logs, aiding control and reproducibility but not fully reflecting real-world noise, heterogeneity, or semantic ambiguity. Validation on organizational logs across domains is needed to assess robustness and to recalibrate the cost–quality frontier under realistic conditions.

Evolving LLMs (with e.g., model updates, API changes) can affect replication. We release code, prompts, and outputs, but exact reproduction may vary with model versions. Recording model identifiers, decoding parameters, and system prompts, and including stable open-weight baselines alongside proprietary models, would further improve reproducibility.

7 Conclusion

We examined whether useful LLM-based process explanations can be generated from reduced behavioral input. Using synthetic event logs, we discovered models from progressively smaller prefixes and evaluated the resulting explanations with a second LLM. Our results indicate that explanation quality improves with larger inputs but does not scale linearly, with diminishing returns once a sufficient behavioral footprint is captured. This suggests the existence of practical cost–quality trade-offs: smaller inputs may already yield adequate explanations for many scenarios, while larger inputs can provide additional consistency in settings where this is critical.

While our pipeline offers a preliminary artifact for data-efficient LLM applications in process mining, several caveats remain. This study is exploratory. Scores are produced by an LLM acting as judge and should be interpreted as comparative signals rather than ground truth. Furthermore, results are based on synthetic job-shop data and may not generalize to noisier, heterogeneous logs. The full model is used here only as an evaluation reference, not as a deployment requirement.

Future work includes validation on real-world logs; analyzing over discovery algorithms and model notations; representative sampling (e.g., variant-aware or stratified) to preserve coverage at smaller k; and human and cross-LLM evaluations alongside objective proxies (e.g., activity/edge coverage, hallucination penalties), with uncertainty reporting and runtime/cost profiles. The reduction-first pipeline can also be applied to related tasks (e.g., improvement recommendation, prescriptive monitoring explanations) to study data efficiency more broadly.

Disclosure of Interests. The authors have no competing interests to declare that are relevant to the content of this article.

References

1. van Aalst, W.M.P., et al.: Business process mining: an industrial application. Inf. Syst. **32**, 713–732 (2007)
2. Bauer, M., Senderovich, A., Gal, A., Grunske, L., Weidlich, M.: How much event data is enough? A statistical framework for process discovery. In: Advanced Information Systems Engineering, pp. 239–256 (2018)

3. Bemthuis, R., Koot, M., Mes, M.R.K., Bukhsh, F.A., Iacob, M.E., Meratnia, N.: Data underlying the paper: an agent-based process mining architecture for emergent behavior analysis. 4TU.Centre for Research Data (2021). https://doi.org/10.4121/12708839.V2
4. Berti, A., Kourani, H., van der Aalst, W.M.P.: PM-LLM-benchmark: Evaluating large language models on process mining tasks. In: International Conference on Process Mining, pp. 610–623. Springer (2024)
5. Berti, A., Kourani, H., Häfke, H., Li, C.Y., Schuster, D.: Evaluating large language models in process mining: Capabilities, benchmarks, and evaluation strategies, pp. 13–21. Springer Nature Switzerland (2024). https://doi.org/10.1007/978-3-031-61007-3_2
6. Berti, A., Qafari, M.S.: Leveraging Large Language Models (LLMs) for process mining (Technical Report) (2023). https://arxiv.org/abs/2307.12701
7. Berti, A., van Zelst, S.J., W.M.P. van der Aalst: Process Mining for Python (PM4Py): Bridging the Gap Between Process- and Data Science (2019). https://arxiv.org/abs/1905.06169
8. Chang, Y., et al.: A survey on evaluation of large language models. ACM Trans. Intell. Syst. Technol. **15**(3) (2024). https://doi.org/10.1145/3641289
9. Emamjome, F., Andrews, R., ter Hofstede, A.H.M.: A case study lens on process mining in practice. In: On the Move to Meaningful Internet Systems: OTM 2019 Conferences, pp. 127–145. Cham (2019)
10. Grattafiori, A., Dubey, A., Jauhri, A., et al.: The Llama 3 herd of models (2024). https://arxiv.org/abs/2407.21783
11. Grohs, M., Abb, L., Elsayed, N., Rehse, J.R.: Large language models can accomplish business process management tasks. In: International conference on business process management, pp. 453–465. Springer (2023)
12. Jessen, U., Sroka, M., Fahland, D.: Chit-Chat or Deep Talk: Prompt Engineering for Process Mining (2023). https://arxiv.org/abs/2307.09909
13. Kubrak, K., Botchorishvili, L., Milani, F., Nolte, A., Dumas, M.: Explanatory capabilities of large language models in prescriptive process monitoring. In: International Conference on Business Process Management, pp. 403–420. Springer (2024)
14. Lashkevich, K., Milani, F., Avramenko, M., Dumas, M.: LLM-assisted optimization of waiting time in business processes: A prompting method. In: International Conference on Business Process Management, pp. 474–492. Springer (2024)
15. Leemans, S.J.J., Fahland, D., van der Aalst, W.M.P.: Process and deviation exploration with inductive visual miner. In: 12th International Conference on Business Process Management, BPM 2014, pp. 46–50. CEUR-WS. org (2014)
16. Marin-Castro, H.M., Tello-Leal, E.: Event log preprocessing for process mining: a review. Applied Sciences 11(22) (2021). https://doi.org/10.3390/app112210556
17. Rebmann, A., Schmidt, F.D., Glavaš, G., van Der Aa, H.: Evaluating the ability of LLMs to solve semantics-aware process mining tasks. In: 2024 6th International Conference on Process Mining (ICPM), pp. 9–16. IEEE (2024)
18. Viner, D., Stierle, M., Matzner, M.: A process mining software comparison (2021). https://arxiv.org/abs/2007.14038
19. Wang, Z., Chu, Z., Doan, T.V., Ni, S., Yang, M., Zhang, W.: History, development, and principles of Large Language Models: an introductory survey. AI Ethics 1–17 (2024)

20. W.M.P. van der Aalst: Process mining in the large, pp. 353–385. Springer, Berlin Heidelberg, Berlin, Heidelberg (2016). https://doi.org/10.1007/978-3-662-49851-4_12
21. W.M.P. van der Aalst, et al.: Business process mining: an industrial application. Inform. Syst. **32**(5), 713–732 (2007). https://doi.org/10.1016/j.is.2006.05.003

Design Principles for Data Trustee Governance: Application and Validation in a Geospatial Data Space

Marius Hupperz(✉)

Fraunhofer ISST, Dortmund, Germany
marius.hupperz@isst.fraunhofer.de

Abstract. This article explores data governance design principles for data trustees within data space environments. Data spaces are emerging as novel infrastructures that enable organizations to share data while maintaining data ownership. Accessing data spaces requires significant organizational and technical effort. In our research project, focusing on a geospatial data space, the data trustee plays a central role in enabling access. While this approach appears pragmatic, no comprehensive data governance model for data trustees in data space environments has been developed to date. Building on this need, this article introduces a framework grounded in five core principles: trust, independence, compliance, value-adding services, and stewardship. These principles were derived from a systematic literature review, validated through an expert workshop, and will be applied to a real-world data trustee in a geospatial data space. As the EU continues to promote the development of domain-specific data spaces, this article offers a foundational framework for integrating data trustees into these infrastructures, ultimately enhancing the usability and inclusivity of data sharing ecosystems.

Keywords: Data trustees · data spaces · design principles · data governance

1 Introduction

In today's business world, organizations are connected through data ecosystems to share data [35]. As data sharing becomes a key driver of innovation and value creation, it enables the generation of new data insights across domains [25]. However, alongside these opportunities, there is a pressing need to establish clear rules and frameworks for governing shared data. While data governance has historically concentrated on managing data within individual organizations, current developments shift attention towards governance at the ecosystem level, where multiple stakeholders must coordinate data access, usage, and responsibilities [29]. As a driver of innovation, data sharing has brought data spaces to the forefront of the European data economy. Data spaces represent a federated infrastructure that facilitates sovereign data exchange while ensuring that data owners retain control over their data [39]. In practice, this infrastructure is used in domain-specific data space. In order to share data, as the providing or using part, data space

J. Barateiro et al. (Eds.): EDOC 2025 Workshops, LNBIP 571, pp. 161–174, 2026.
https://doi.org/10.1007/978-3-032-16234-2_11

connectors form the gateway into data spaces [19]. Data space connectors enable data sharing while allowing usage policies to be enforced, ensuring that data is always used according to the data owner's intentions [37]. As it can be a burden for organizations to build and maintain a connector [19], data trustees can support this. Data trustees are a subgroup of data intermediaries and can act as facilitators for data sharing in the European data economy [14, 48]. The motivation for this study stems from the insight that linking data across organizations can unlock new knowledge and business opportunities [20]. Therefore, an organization willing to gain new business insights, data sharing and linking data from different sources cannot be neglected [24]. When data from multiple entities, such as public authorities, private companies, and sector specialists is combined, new business cases and value chains can emerge [12]. However, sourcing such data into a data space remains complex due to heterogeneity in technical capabilities and organizational readiness [16]. In these cases, data trustees can play a pivotal role in aggregating, processing, and sharing data on behalf of the data owners [9].

This article explores the specific case of a geospatial data trustee that facilitates data sharing in a geospatial data space. A typical example involves the development of wind farms, where multiple stakeholders, including cadastral agencies, municipalities, land registries, developers, and wind energy experts, must contribute data. Not all stakeholders, however, have the capacity to provide data directly due to organizational or technological constraints [16]. To enable new data-driven business models, a data trustee can securely provision this data into the data space, under the condition that usage policies are enforced through connectors operated by the data-consuming organizations [19]. A significant initiative in this context is our project on a geospatial data space, which aims to integrate diverse geospatial datasets to enable novel applications. When organizations are unable to share their data directly, the trustee assumes responsibility for data provisioning. This requires the development of a comprehensive data governance model tailored to the trustee's role. While the concept of data intermediaries is gaining momentum, data governance frameworks for data trustees remain underdeveloped despite their anticipated importance for the European data infrastructure [14]. Accordingly, this article seeks to answer the following research question: What principles can be applied in the development of a data governance model for a data trustee in a geospatial data space?

2 Theoretical Background

2.1 Data Spaces

The European Union is heavily investing in data spaces. Data spaces represent a federated alternative to hyperscalers (large-scale data centers) from the United States and China, promoting data storage and sharing in a sovereign manner [15]. In this context, data sovereignty means that data can be shared, while the data owner maintains control over their data [4]. Data spaces enable data sovereignty with usage control, which includes both traditional access control and data sovereignty, terms of use for future data usage [8, 17]. The basic concept of data spaces is providing an infrastructure for data sharing, where no central keystone is needed, but the actual data sharing occurs directly between organizations (peer-to-peer) [17, 19, 23]. Data providers and data users are connected through both operating a data space connector, which is the gateway into a data space [39]. The data space provides essential services, such as a catalog, to search metadata and find data for the respective use [23, 39]. Building on the concept of data ecosystems and their potential to unlock value through data sharing [35], data spaces offer the necessary infrastructure to enable such exchange [39]. In this context, data intermediaries can play a key role by facilitating data sharing through the provisioning of data or value-added tools and services [15, 44].

2.2 Data Trustees

Data trustees belong to the group of data intermediaries, which connect data providers and data consumers [48]. Data trustees can be individuals or organizations, who manage access or hold data from data providers according to contracts or laws, and provide it for others [9]. The main objective of data trustees is to ensure trust in the data sharing process [27]. Therefore, they need to be independent third party [13]. Thus, the main tasks are data storage, granting access, and distributing data [18, 27, 31]. Not all of these must be accomplished, but at least one, to allow data consumers the usage of others' data. An additional form can be a data platform, where data can be obtained [47]. Besides the provisioning of data, data trustees can offer value-adding services, such as data services, financial services, or consultancy [10, 13, 31]. A data trustee's ultimate responsibility is to enable reliable data sharing while maintaining a fiduciary duty, but does not exclude the possibility for the data trustee to follow its own interests [44].

2.3 Data Governance

The term data governance is subject to various definitions and interpretations. Some define it as the assignment of decision rights and accountability for data assets within an organization [26], while others describe it as a comprehensive framework encompassing decision rights and accountabilities [51]. [38] defines it as companywide framework for assigning decision related rights and duties to be able to adequately handle data as a company asset. This article defines data governance as a framework that provides rules for how data is collected, stored, processed, and disposed of. The article distinguishes between intra-organizational and inter-organizational data governance [2]. Inter-organizational data governance exceeds organizational boundaries since it involves data sharing between organizations [42]. The overall purpose of inter-organizational data governance is to foster collaboration among multiple entities, facilitate data sharing, and prevent the formation of monopolies [29, 42]. A data trustee, obligated to provide data on behalf of data owners, must address both inter-organizational and intra-organizational dimensions within the governance model. To fulfill this role, the data trustee must ensure secure and legally compliant data sharing, along with access management, data storage, encryption, and data transmission [5]. Consequently, the data governance framework must not only define how data is collected, stored, processed, and disposed of, but also how it is shared, to maintain stakeholder trust.

2.4 Design Principles

Design principles in information systems research provide structured guidelines for the development of new instances of artifacts within the same class [49]. Therefore, knowledge from specific use cases can be used to derive design principles for practitioners to develop new solutions [6, 32]. An important distinction in the literature is that the supplier perspective may plan to supply design principles for reusability, while the actual usage is decided by the customer perspective [52]. Design principles operate at a meta-level, guiding the design process without dictating specific solutions [33]. Design principles belong to the design science research (DSR) approach. DSR is a well-established approach in IS research, ideally suited for the development and evaluation of artifacts such as models, methods, or principles [11].

3 Research Design

3.1 Structured Literature Review

Following [50], a structured literature review (SLR) was conducted to identify and synthesize research on data trustees and data governance. The SLR included 17 peer-reviewed publications retrieved from major academic databases (ACM Digital Library, AIS eLibrary, IEEE Xplore, and Scopus). Searches were run in February 2025, and the included papers were analyzed using a concept matrix.

Given the wide range of concepts and lack of consensus around the term "data trustee", the search strategy included a range of related keywords to ensure comprehensive coverage. These included: data trustee, data trust, data intermediary, and data fiduciary, with and without the prefix "data". The term "data trustee" is used variably across contexts and disciplines, which was reflected in the variety of literature identified. This structured approach ensured a transparent, replicable, and conceptually inclusive review process, forming the foundation for the development of design principles in this study.

3.2 Design Principles Generation

The artifact developed in this article consists of design principles, intended to guide practitioners in the development of data governance models for data trustees across various domains. This approach builds upon prior research in the field [6, 21, 32]. Additionally, a concrete data governance model for the geospatial data trustee project will be published separately. The research process follows the generic DSR framework outlined in [40], which synthesizes several established approaches.

Problem identification & motivation:

The initial motivation for this study arose from the research project focused on developing a data governance model for a geospatial data trustee within a data space environment. A key challenge identified in the literature is the absence of established guidelines for such governance models, highlighting a critical gap in both theory and practice.

Objectives and artifact design: The objective was to apply the DSR methodology to construct design principles as the central artifact. These principles aim to guide future implementations of data trustees in the context of data spaces. To achieve this task, two methods were used: A literature review provided theoretical grounding and insights from related research; And a collaboratively developed working document, co-developed with the project team, captured practical requirements for the governance model of the geospatial data trustee. Both streams contributed to the development of the design principles, integrating knowledge from both theory and practice.

Demonstration and evaluation: The design principles were applied in the development of the actual data governance model for the geospatial data trustee. This served as a proof of concept, demonstrating that the principles were actionable and relevant in a real-world setting. To evaluate the design principles, a workshop with domain experts was conducted. The evaluation was based on the ontological expressiveness framework [43], which assesses principles along four dimensions: Deficit, excess, redundancy, and overload. This structured approach ensured that the resulting design knowledge was robust, relevant, and practically applicable.

Communication: The results of the research are documented in this article. In addition, the data governance model developed for the geospatial data trustee will be shared as an open resource for future projects in the data space domain. The geospatial data trustee governance model will act as an instantiation of the design principles. Therefore, the collaborative developed document mentioned before will be published as a separate document.

4 Geospatial Data Space

This article was grounded in a project about a geospatial data space. Modern geodata originate from a diverse array of digital sources and serve as a critical foundation across numerous domains. Conventional geospatial base data are increasingly supplemented by georeferenced data from extensive IoT sensor networks, smartphones, vehicles, energy systems, and more. High-resolution, up-to-date geospatial and Earth observation data are essential for autonomous vehicles, efficient planning of renewable energy infrastructure, and strategies for urban heat mitigation and mobility planning.

Given the broad range of applications for geospatial data, there is a growing need for the availability of high-quality datasets. Therefore, one of the project's objectives is the development of a data trustee designed to address and overcome the organizational, technical, and legal challenges that data providers face when integrating into a data space. Along with the growing interest in data spaces and appliances for other domains, the data trustee needs to be designed largely compliant with the standards of the federated European Gaia-X[1] data sharing initiative and the International Data Spaces Association (IDSA[2]) standards (Fig. 1).

However, certain data owners may face technical or organizational barriers that prevent them from directly engaging in data space activities. In such cases, a data trustee

[1] https://gaia-x.eu/

[2] https://internationaldataspaces.org/

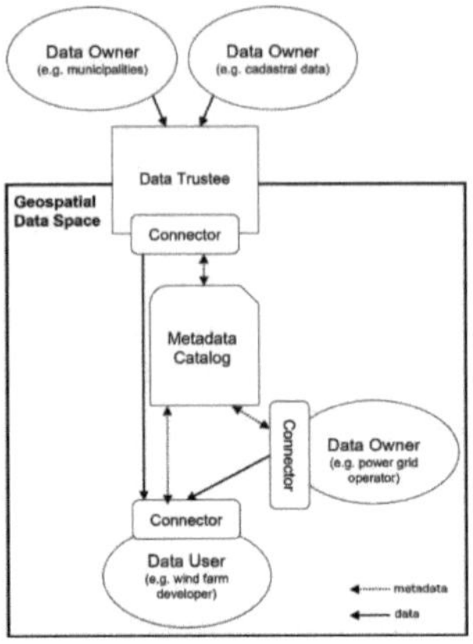

Fig. 1. Geospatial data space (own illustration).

can act on their behalf to initiate and manage the data sharing process. As illustrated, the geospatial data space provides metadata cataloging services, allowing data users to discover available datasets through metadata crawling. To enable this functionality, metadata must either be supplied directly by the data owners or provided via the services of a data trustee. Once relevant data is identified through the catalog, users can request access and receive the data directly from the data owners. When the data is provided via the data trustee, the provisioning of usage policies needs to be rooted in the data governance of the data trustee.

5 Proposed Design Principles

Despite the growing interest in data trustees the knowledge about design, especially the data governance model, for data trustees is still in its infancy. The proposed design principles introduce a novel approach to building data trustees and their data governance models.

DP 1: Trust. *To ensure users feel confident in sharing their data through the trustee.*

Trust in the context of data trustees refers to their function of ensuring and signaling reliable, accountable data handling by implementing trust-enabling mechanisms (e.g. certification) that guarantees data is handled and shared in accordance with the data owners predefined conditions [50]. They must also ensure security and confidentiality of data [30], to prevent misuse and data theft. In a data ecosystem multiple data trustees may coexist and data owners can opt-in for the trustee best fitting their preferences [51]. Thus, it enables data providers the freedom of choice for their desired data trustee and intended (service-) use (see also DP 4).

DP 2: Independence. *To foster a fair, competitive, and innovation-driven data ecosystem.*

The Data Governance Act speaks of neutrality of data intermediaries with regard to the shared data between data owner and data user [14]. Therefore, a data trustee must be an independent party between data providers and data users [13]. Data trustees are institutions tasked with the independent "trusteeship" to manage resources to enable data-driven innovation, for re-balancing power asymmetries, or to manage data use [1]. They are especially important in the European market, as they enable the free flow of high-quality data [13]. With data trustees in a data ecosystem the rise of monolith, meaning the pooling of data at large tech companies, can be prevented and thus open up the market for minor organizations [22, 39].

DP 3: Compliance. *To protect data owner interests and ensure alignment with regulatory frameworks.*

A data trustee has a fiduciary duty to prioritize the interests of data owners when making decisions about data processing and ensuring privacy [27]. This fiduciary responsibility requires trustees to act strictly in accordance with the data owner's predefined conditions, when sharing data [34]. Data sharing enhances data accessibility by breaking down data silos [28]. Data trustees play a crucial role in addressing tensions arising from imbalances in data sharing relationships, for example, by safeguarding personal data rights in line with regulatory frameworks, such as the General Data Protection Regulation (GDPR) [7, 14]. In this context, data trustees have already demonstrated their relevance and effectiveness in managing personal data rights, particularly within the healthcare sector [27, 46].

DP 4: Value-adding Services. *To offer data sharing services and remain effective and competitive.*

Their main purpose is the facilitation of mediating data sharing between data owners and their data, and data users [7]. The mediation includes the management of access to data provided in accordance with agreed usage policies and the ability to enforce these with usage control [27]. This means that the data trustee enforces usage policies when sharing data [41]. To remain effective and competitive, they can adopt strategies for data handling that go beyond the core function of enabling data sharing, by providing value-added services [50]. Examples of value-added services include data encryption and anonymization, which help protect data owners from risks associated with the misuse of personal data, such as in marketing or health-related contexts [3, 34, 52]. More general services may involve data cataloging and search, storage, pooling and aggregation, processing, or custody functions [27, 30]. Additionally, data trustees can enhance transparency, clarity, and usability by centralizing and standardizing processes, thereby enabling data owners to better manage and control data sharing [7].

DP 5: Data Stewardship. *To translate data governance principles into concrete practices.*

While data governance establishes the overarching principles, policies, and responsibilities for data access, management, and use, data stewardship translates these directives into concrete practices [45]. Data trustees, acting as stewards, manage data on behalf of data owners in accordance with stewardship principles and enforceable obligations to ensure responsible and privacy-conscious use [41]. Their responsibilities include maintaining data accuracy, ensuring security, and enforcing appropriate usage, thereby safeguarding data integrity and enabling responsible access in line with established conditions [45]. By overseeing data pooling and external sharing, data trustees ensure these practices benefit specific communities or organizations instead of concentrating control among dominant market players [13, 36]. As stewards, they are responsible for maintaining data quality, integrity, security, usage rights, and access management [52].

6 Evaluation

To evaluate the proposed design principles, five experts, whose roles and fields of expertise are outlined in Table 1, participated in a 60 min workshop and were identified through the joint research project explained in Section 4. The workshop promoted a focused and in-depth analysis of the DPs in question. Their feedback was collected and synthesized through a consensus-based approach, whereby points of agreement and divergence were identified and used to refine the design principles accordingly. Prior to the online workshop, participants received the design principles along with the ontological expressiveness assessment of [43].

Table 1. Overview of experts in the workshop.

#	Institution	Role	Focus
1	Research organization (geoinformation)	Head of department	Geoinformation management
2	Research organization (geoinformation)	Scientific employee	Tech transfer
3	Start-up (geospatial data)	Founder	Geospatial infrastructure
4	Research organization (data spaces)	Scientific employee	Data trustees
5	Research organization (AI)	Data engineer	Data spaces

DP 1 Trust: Trust is a foundational principle for data trustees in a data ecosystem. However, expert feedback emphasized that trust is not a standalone feature but touches all design principles. It intersects strongly with DP 2 and DP 3. The current definition of DP 1 focuses mostly on the technical part of trust, like trust mechanisms. Trust should be refined and add the social dimension to it, which includes aspects like communication, user experience, and network effects. Trust should not be seen as a static requirement, but as a relational process that enables data owners to confidently share their data.

DP 2 Independence: The experts unanimously agreed that independence is important for the design of a data trustee. It is a key enabler for fairness, openness, and innovation in a data ecosystem. Despite the experts' approval of DP 2, some refinements can be made. While structural and functional independence is essential, the neutral representation of data owners' interests must be assured, as well as non-discrimination. Governance mechanisms must ensure independence in practice, such as firewalls, public oversight, and transparency audits. The institutional form can demonstrate independence, such as non-profits, cooperatives, or public institutions.

DP 3 Compliance: Compliance should not be reduced to a passive legal obligation, but rather to a proactive stance. Meaning, anticipating potential regulatory shifts, implementing ethical review processes, and embedding legal expertise within their governance structure (e.g. through cooperation with legal advisor or law firms). The discussion highlighted that compliance mechanisms play a key role in building and maintaining trust (DP1), while institutional independence strengthens the credibility of compliance actions (DP2). Moreover, participants welcomed the clear distinction between legal and contractual compliance but added the need for ethical compliance.

DP 4 Value-adding Services: Value-adding services are recognized as critical for ensuring the effectiveness, usability, and competitiveness of data trustees in real-world ecosystems. The expert workshop affirmed this interpretation and stressed that data sharing alone is insufficient to establish a viable business model and attract data owners and users. Participants emphasized that value-adding services can include a broad array of functionalities, such as temporary storage, curation, anonymization, or pseudonymization. These services can enhance transparency and reduce regulatory burdens for data owners and users.

DP 5 Data Stewardship: The discussion clarified that data stewardship is closely linked to compliance. Experts emphasized that many of the practical duties associated with stewardship are directly connected to ensuring regulatory and contractual compliance (e.g. enforcing usage policies, maintaining data quality, and protecting personal data). It ensures that governance principles are effectively implemented through robust, trustworthy operational practices. By doing so, data stewardship supports compliance, protects user interests, and reinforces the legitimacy and reliability of data trustees in data ecosystems.

7 Application

The data trustee must provide streamlined, standardized processes for secure data sharing, ensuring that data owners can share their data within the data space while retaining control through their predefined usage policies. Importantly, the technical, organizational, and financial effort required for data owners to participate through the trustee should be significantly lower than that of directly joining the data space.

DP 1 Trust: Trust is foundational in enabling sovereign data sharing, especially in a data space where sensitive, high-value datasets are exchanged across organizational and sectoral boundaries. Trust must be established through a combination of technical, organizational, and social safeguards. The geospatial data space also incorporates attribute-based trust mechanisms, in which trustworthiness is derived from verifiable credentials. By combining transparency and oversight, the geospatial data trustee enables a trustworthy environment for data sharing. This empowers data owners to retain control over their data while unlocking its value across diverse use cases.

DP 2 Independence: To maintain its independence over time, the trustee's financial and operational model must be designed for long-term sustainability without reliance on any dominant market actor. Funding mechanisms may include membership fees, tiered service charges, public support, or consulting income. The trustee should also offer modular services such as secure geospatial data hosting, connector management, and interoperability support. Operationally, this involves using scalable cloud infrastructure and offering diverse computing environments for the processing and transformation of geospatial datasets.

DP 3 Compliance: The data trustee must ensure the highest standards of data protection, legal compliance, and regulatory alignment, thereby fulfilling its fiduciary duty to data owners. This includes prioritizing the data owner's conditions for data use, ensuring that all data processing activities reflect both their intentions and applicable legal obligations. Where appropriate, the trustee may facilitate transparent disclosures to data users while maintaining full compliance with data protection regulations. Additionally, the trustee bears responsibility for monitoring legal developments, updating compliance protocols, and ensuring that all data-sharing activities remain aligned with current regulatory requirements. By embracing this fiduciary and regulatory role, the geospatial data trustee not only mitigates risk but also reinforces trust among data owners and users across the data space.

DP 4 Value-adding Services: The central service of the data trustee is to facilitate secure and efficient data sharing within the data space for data owners. By providing the necessary infrastructure, tools, and compliance measures, the trustee ensures that data owners can share their geospatial data while retaining control and adhering to usage policies. The trustee needs to assure, that data is shared in the correct data standard and with the right metadata. As the data space evolves, users will indicate their preferred formats, naming conventions, data models, and projections to facilitate smooth data exchange. Standardized data formats and structures ensure that geospatial information can be efficiently stored, shared, and processed, enhancing the overall functionality of the data space.

DP 5 Data Stewardship: The role of a geospatial data trustee as a data steward is central to ensuring data sovereignty and enabling responsible data sharing within a geospatial data space. Given the sensitive and high-value nature of geospatial data, the trustee's responsibilities extend across the full data lifecycle, encompassing the creation, storage, use, modification, archiving, and deletion of geospatial datasets. As steward, the geospatial data trustee manages access to datasets under its custody. This involves defining and enforcing clear usage policies that regulate how participants within the data space can interact with specific geospatial data assets. The trustee shares responsibility with data owners for maintaining data quality. This entails regular data validation, timely updates, and the meticulous documentation of any changes.

8 Results

The article contributes a set of design principles for the development of data governance models for data trustees, grounded in insights from a newly established data space initiative. It addresses the research question: *What principles can be applied in the development of a data governance model for a data trustee in a geospatial data space?*

The expert workshop confirmed the practical relevance of the five design principles for data trustees while highlighting overlaps, tensions, and areas for refinement.

DP 1 trust should be reframed from a standalone principle into an overarching meta-principle with technical, organizational, and social dimensions. **DP 2 independence** is a foundational requirement aligned with DGA neutrality, demonstrated not just through institutional form (e.g. nonprofit, cooperative) but also via governance practices such as transparency audits, public oversight, and firewalls against conflict of interest. **DP 3 compliance** is a cornerstone, tightly interlinked with trust and independence, and should include a proactive compliance advisory function. **DP 4 value-adding services** should underpin all trustee activities, with data sharing as the core function and additional services needed to deliver clear benefits for data providers. **DP 5 data stewardship** is widely supported as a mechanism to enforce governance, closely tied to compliance; a renaming to "trusteeship" was proposed but not agreed.

Limitations include the small sample (N = 5), limited stakeholder diversity, and an emphasis on application and synthesis rather than theoretical novelty. Overall, the framework is a practical starting point that warrants broader validation and conceptual refinement in future work. The results offer a foundational basis for developing data governance models specifically tailored to data trustees. Each of the proposed design principles represents a promising starting point for future in-depth research, including empirical validation, contextual adaptation, and theoretical refinement. The structured articulation of these principles contributes to the broader academic discourse on sovereign data sharing and the role of data trustees.

Acknowledgments. This work was supported by the German Federal Ministry of Research, Technology and Space (BMFTR) and is part of the research project "InGeoDTM – Data trustee for horizontal geospatial data spaces" (16DTM310A).

Disclosure of Interests.. The author has no competing interests to declare that are relevant to the content of this article.

References

1. Aapti Institute, Open Data Institute. Enabling Data Sharing for Social Benefit Through Data Trusts. Technical Report (2021). https://gpai.ai/projects/data-governance/data-trusts/enabling-data-sharing-for-social-benefit-data-trusts-interim-report.pdf
2. Abraham, R., Schneider, J., vom Brocke, J.: Data governance. A conceptual framework, structured review, and research agenda. Int. J. Inf. Manage. **49**, 424–438 (2019). https://doi.org/10.1016/j.ijinfomgt.2019.07.008
3. Aydin, A., Bensghir, T.K.: Digital data sovereignty. Towards a conceptual framework. In: 2019 1st International Informatics and Software Engineering Conference, pp. 1–6. IEEE (2019)
4. Azkan, C., Möller, F., Ebel, M., et al.: Hunting the treasure. Modeling data ecosystem value co-creation. In: ICIS 2022 Proceedings (2022)
5. Azkan, C., Möller, F., Iggena, L., et al.: Design principles for industrial data-driven services. IEEE Trans. Eng. Manage. **71**, 2379–2402 (2024). https://doi.org/10.1109/TEM.2022.3167737
6. Barnett, S., Brand, N., Odom, W., et al.: Exploring data intermediaries as infrastructure for a human-centric data economy. In: NordiCHI 2022. The Association for Computing Machinery, New York, New York, pp. 1–20 (2022)

7. Beverungen, D., Hess, T., Köster, A., et al.: From private digital platforms to public data spaces: implications for the digital transformation. Electron Markets **32**, 493–501 (2022). https://doi.org/10.1007/s12525-022-00553-z
8. Blankertz, A., Specht-Riemenschneider, L.: Neue Modelle ermöglichen. Regulierung für Datentreuhänder, Berlin (2021)
9. Brown, C., Regan, Á., van der Burg, S.: Farming futures: perspectives of Irish agricultural stakeholders on data sharing and data governance. Agric. Hum. Values **40**, 565–580 (2023). https://doi.org/10.1007/s10460-022-10357-8
10. Chandra Kruse, L., Seidel, S., Purao, S.: Making use of design principles. In: Parsons, J., Tuunanen, T., Venable, J., et al. (eds.) Tackling Society's Grand Challenges with Design Science, vol. 9661, pp. 37–51. Springer International Publishing, Cham (2016)
11. Curry, E.: Future Research Directions for Dataspaces, Data Ecosystems, and Intelligent Systems, pp. 297–304 (2020). https://doi.org/10.1007/978-3-030-29665-0_18.pdf
12. Doan, X., Selzer, A., Rossi, A., et al.: Context, prioritization, and unexpectedness. factors influencing user attitudes about infographic and comic consent. In: Herman, I., Médini, L., Laforest, F., et al. (eds.) WWW 2022 Companion, pp. 534–545. Association for Computing Machinery, New York, NY (2022)
13. European Union. Data Governance Act. Regulation 2022/868:1–44 (2022)
14. European Commission. A European Strategy for Data, Brussels (2020)
15. Fassnacht, M.K., Benz, C., Heinz, D., et al.: Barriers to data sharing among private sector organizations. In: Proceedings of the Hawaii International Conference on Systems Sciences (HICSS-56) (2023)
16. Gelhaar, J., Groß, T., Otto, B.: A taxonomy for data ecosystems. In: Bui, T. (ed.) Proceedings of the 54th Hawaii International Conference on System Sciences. Hawaii International Conference on System Sciences (2021)
17. Ghayyur, S., Pappachan, P., Wang, G., et al.: Designing privacy preserving data sharing middleware for internet of things. In: Proceedings of the Third Workshop on Data: Acquisition to Analysis, pp. 1–6. Association for Computing Machinery, New York, NY, United States (2020)
18. Gieß, A., Hupperz, M., Schoormann, T., et al.: What does it take to connect? Unveiling characteristics of data space connectors. In: Proceedings of the 57th Hawaii International Conference on System Sciences (HICSS) (2024)
19. Guggenberger, T.M., Boualouch, K., Otto, B., et al.: Towards a unifying understanding of digital business models. In: PACIS 2020 Proceedings (2020)
20. Guggenberger, T.M., Altendeitering, M., Schlueter Langdon, C.: Design principles for quality scoring – coping with information asymmetry of data products. In: Bui, T. (ed.) Proceedings of the 57th Hawaii International Conference on System Sciences. Hawaii International Conference on System Sciences (2024)
21. Guggenberger, T.M., Schlueter Langdon, C., Otto, B.: Data spaces as meta-organisations. Eur. J. Inf. Syst. 1–21 (2025). https://doi.org/10.1080/0960085X.2025.2451250
22. Hupperz, M., Gieß, A.: The interplay of data-driven organizations and data spaces. Unlocking capabilities for transforming organizations in the era of data spaces. In: Proceedings of the 57th Hawaii International Conference on System Sciences (HICSS) (2024)
23. Hupperz, M., Gür, I., Möller, F., et al.: What is a data-driven organization? In: AMCIS 2021 Proceedings (2021)
24. Jussen, I., Schweihoff, J., Dahms, V., et al.: Data sharing fundamentals. Characteristics and definition. In: Proceedings of the Hawaii International Conference on Systems Sciences (HICSS-56) (2023)
25. Khatri, V., Brown, C.V.: Designing data governance. Commun. ACM **53**, 148–152 (2010). https://doi.org/10.1145/1629175.1629210

26. Lauf, F., Scheider, S., Friese, J., et al.: Exploring Design Characteristics of Data Trustees in Healthcare. Taxonomy and Archetypes. ECIS 2023 Research Papers (2023)
27. Lian, J., Chen, J.: Research and practice of data governance in universities based on data middleware. In: 2024 International Conference on Cloud Computing and Big Data, pp. 238–242. ACM, New York, NY, USA (2024)
28. Lis, D., Otto, B.: Data governance in data ecosystems. Insights from organizations. In: AMCIS 2020 Proceedings (2020)
29. Londońo Peláez, J.M., Echavarria Arcila, M.A., Betancur Agudelo, L., et al.: Shared-data governance frameworks. In: Callaos, N., Callaos, N., Horne, J., et al. (eds.) Proceedings ICSIT 2024. International Institute of Informatics and Cybernetics, pp. 65–70 Winter Garden, Florida, United States (2024)
30. Maaß, W.: Contract-based data-sharing for AI-based decision making on the web. In: 55th Hawaii International Conference on System (2022)
31. Möller, F., Guggenberger, T.M., Otto, B.: Towards a method for design principle development in information systems. In: Hofmann, S., Müller, O., Rossi, M. (eds.) Designing for Digital Transformation, vol. 12388, pp. 208–220. Springer International Publishing, Cham (2020)
32. Mukhametov, D.R.: Collective data governance for development of digital government. In: 2021 International Conference on Engineering Management of Communication and Technology (EMCTECH), pp. 1–5. IEEE (2021)
33. Oliveira, M.I.S., Lóscio, B.F.: What is a data ecosystem? In: Janssen, M. (ed.) Proceedings of the 19th Annual International Conference on Digital Government Research Governance in the Data Age, pp. 1–9. ACM (2018)
34. Open Data Institute. Data Trusts. Lessons From Three Pilots (2019). https://docs.google.com/document/d/118RqyUAWP3WIyyCO4iLUT3oOobnYJGibEhspr2v87jg/edit?tab=t.0#heading=h.3fngvdcfo2cs
35. Opriel, S., Möller, F., Burkhardt, U., et al.: Requirements for usage control based exchange of sensitive data in automotive supply chains. In: Bui, T. (ed.) Proceedings of the 54th Hawaii International Conference on System Sciences. Hawaii International Conference on System Sciences (2021)
36. Otto, B.: Organizing Data Governance: Findings from the Telecommunications Industry and Consequences for Large Service Providers. CAIS 29(2011). https://doi.org/10.17705/1CAIS.02903
37. Otto, B.: A federated infrastructure for European data spaces. Commun. ACM **65**, 44–45 (2022). https://doi.org/10.1145/3512341
38. Peffers, K., Tuunanen, T., Rothenberger, M.A., et al.: A design science research methodology for information systems research. J. Manag. Inf. Syst. **24**, 45–77 (2007). https://doi.org/10.2753/MIS0742-1222240302
39. Potoczny-Jones, I., Kenneally, E., Ruffing, J.: Encrypted dataset collaboration. In: Proceedings of the 2nd ACM/EIGSCC Symposium on Smart Cities and Communities, pp. 1–8. Association for Computing Machinery, New York, NY, United States (2019)
40. de Prieelle, F., de Reuver, M., Rezaei, J.: The role of ecosystem data governance in adoption of data platforms by internet-of-things data providers: case of Dutch horticulture industry. IEEE Trans. Eng. Manage. **69**, 940–950 (2022). https://doi.org/10.1109/TEM.2020.2966024
41. Recker, Rosemann, Green, et al.: Do ontological deficiencies in modeling grammars matter? MIS Q. **35**, 57 (2011). https://doi.org/10.2307/23043489
42. Richter, H.: Looking at the data governance act and beyond: how to better integrate data intermediaries in the market order for data sharing. GRUR Int. **72**, 458–470 (2023). https://doi.org/10.1093/grurint/ikad014
43. Rosenbaum, S.: Data governance and stewardship: designing data stewardship entities and advancing data access. Health Serv. Res. **45**, 1442–1455 (2010). https://doi.org/10.1111/j.1475-6773.2010.01140.x

44. Scheider, S., Lauf, F., Möller, F., et al.: A reference system architecture with data sovereignty for human-centric data ecosystems. Bus. Inf. Syst. Eng. **65**, 577–595 (2023). https://doi.org/10.1007/s12599-023-00816-9
45. Schweihoff, J., Lipovetskaja, A., Jussen-Lengersdorf, I., et al.: Stuck in the middle with you. Electron Markets **34**, 48 (2024). https://doi.org/10.1007/s12525-024-00729-9
46. Sein, M.K., Henfridsson, O., Purao, S., et al.: Action design research. MIS Q. **35**, 37 (2011). https://doi.org/10.2307/23043488
47. Stachon, M., Möller, F., Guggenberger, T.M., et al.: Understanding Data Trusts. ECIS 2023 Research-in-Progress Papers (2023)
48. van der Sloot, B., Keymolen, E.: Can we trust trust-based data governance models? Data Policy **4**, 36 (2022). https://doi.org/10.1017/dap.2022.36
49. vom Brocke, J.: Design principles for reference modeling. In: Fettke, P., Loos, P. (eds.) Reference Modeling for Business Systems Analysis, pp. 47–76. IGI Global (2007)
50. vom Brocke, J., Simons, A., Niehaves, B., et al.: Reconstructing the giant. On the importance of rigour in documenting the literature search process. In: ECIS 2009 Proceedings (2009)
51. Weber, K., Otto, B., Österle, H.: One size does not fit all – a contingency approach to data governance. J. Data Inf. Qual. **1**, 1–27 (2009). https://doi.org/10.1145/1515693.1515696
52. Winter, J.S., Davidson, E.: Investigating values in personal health data governance models. In: AMCIS 2017 Proceedings, p. 15 (2017)

FreeCAT—Towards a Framework for Resilience and Evolution by Code Analysis Tools

Simon Hacks[1(✉)], Cyrille Artho[2], Roberto Guanciale[2], Robert Künnemann[3], Diana Malakhova[1], and Emre Süren[2,4]

[1] Stockholm University, Stockholm, Sweden
{simon.hacks,diana.malakhova}@dsv.su.se
[2] KTH Royal Institute of Technology, Stockholm, Sweden
{artho,robertog,emsuren}@kth.se
[3] CISPA Helmholtz Center for Information Security, Saarbrücken, Germany
robert.kuennemann@cispa.de
[4] Cybercampus Sweden, Stockholm, Sweden
emre@cybercampus.se

Abstract. Cyber attacks are getting smarter every year, yet most security checks still happen late in the project, when fixes are hardest and costliest. To change that, we propose FreeCAT, a step-by-step "security copilot" that works from the first design sketch all the way to day-to-day operation. FreeCAT automatically turns models, documentation, and log files into easy-to-read threat maps that show which parts of a system hackers would target first. It then runs simulations to test different defenses, points human testers to the riskiest spots, and feeds every new finding back into the map so the picture stays up to date. An AI component speeds up chores such as writing audit reports or checking compliance rules. Because these activities repeat in short loops throughout development and after launch, organizations can spot weak points early, use security budgets where they matter most, and keep pace with new attack tactics without hiring an army of specialists. The current paper outlines the concept and planned building blocks; the full platform will be assembled and validated in future work.

Keywords: Cybersecurity Automation · Threat Modeling · Attack Simulations · Vulnerability Assessment

1 Introduction

In the modern digital landscape, cyber threats are evolving at an unprecedented rate, posing significant challenges to organizations, industries, and governments worldwide [4]. As cyber-attacks become more sophisticated, they exploit vulnerabilities across interconnected systems, supply chains, and the rapidly expanding Internet of Things (IoT) ecosystem [17]. The rise of supply chain attacks,

J. Barateiro et al. (Eds.): EDOC 2025 Workshops, LNBIP 571, pp. 175–188, 2026.
https://doi.org/10.1007/978-3-032-16234-2_12

where adversaries infiltrate trusted software or hardware providers to compromise entire networks, highlights the growing complexity of cybersecurity risks [2]. At the same time, the increasing integration of IoT in critical infrastructure, such as healthcare, transportation, and industrial automation, introduces new attack vectors that traditional security mechanisms struggle to address [3].

Despite advancements in cybersecurity technologies, several critical challenges remain. First, security is often addressed too late in the software and hardware development lifecycle, leading to costly, reactive measures [13]. Second, traditional security assessment methods are limited in scope, focusing on isolated aspects such as code analysis or system design without a holistic perspective. Third, the cybersecurity industry faces a shortage of skilled professionals, making it difficult for organizations to manage the growing volume of security threats [8]. These factors underscore the urgent need for a comprehensive and integrated approach to cybersecurity that proactively addresses threats throughout the development and operational stages.

To address these challenges, we suggest the cybersecurity framework for resilience and evolution by code analysis tools (FreeCAT), which integrates threat modeling, automated vulnerability assessment, and security simulation. The main objective is to integrate tools that enhance proactive cybersecurity strategies. Specifically, the framework aims to: (1) Provide a domain-specific threat modeling language; (2) Establish a state-of-the-art hacking lab to conduct controlled security testing of hardware and software components; (3) Implement simulation tools to assess and refine cybersecurity defenses; (4) Enhance code analysis to identify vulnerabilities early in development.

Several building blocks of FreeCAT are already available: the Meta Attack Language (MAL) [21] core and several domain-specific MAL dialects [10] are mature and in use for OT and IT infrastructure assessments; a research-grade Stackelberg planner [19] and the open-source symbolic-execution engine KLEE [7] likewise exist and have been validated independently; and a collection of commodity penetration-testing tools is readily deployable. FreeCAT capitalises on these assets but moves well beyond them: we will (i) craft a new MAL dialect for software architectures, (ii) hard-wire MAL semantics into the Stackelberg planner to yield full attack-defence simulations, (iii) extend KLEE so it interprets those same semantics during code execution, (iv) build an AI-assisted pipeline that converts partner documentation into executable MAL models, (v) establish an instrumented hacking lab that runs model-driven penetration campaigns, and (vi) integrate all components—together with a dashboard, cost-benefit analytics, and compliance reporting—into a cohesive cybersecurity platform.

The rest of this work is structured as follows: Sect. 2 provides an overview of the background and related work. Section 3 presents the research objectives, outlining the key security challenges addressed by the framework. Section 4 describes the research methodology. Section 5 introduces the platform approach and the structured process workflow. Section 6 concludes the paper.

2 Background

The increasing complexity of software architectures has led to developing threat modeling techniques that integrate deep learning, model-driven engineering (MDE), and comprehensive security frameworks [18]. Research in Model-Driven Security (MDS) has shown that structured, model-based approaches unify software design and security, enabling security measures to evolve alongside architectural adaptations [14]. In particular, security frameworks such as Attack Defence Trees (ADTrees) [18] have been proposed as practical tools for integrating security from the early design stages. These advancements are especially critical for safety-critical domains where integrating security with hazard analysis is essential for system reliability [12].

Alongside these modeling techniques, attack simulations have emerged to evaluate system defenses in a controlled environment. Attack simulations like those based on Evolving Behavior Trees (EBTs) [15] allow cybersecurity researchers to assess dynamic attacker-defender interactions. These simulations enable organizations to test their security postures against adversaries that modify their attack tactics mid-operation. Integrating attack simulations with data flow-based threat modeling has improved vulnerability detection by tracing potential attack paths [1]. This approach effectively identifies security gaps before real-world attacks, helping organizations implement defense strategies.

Code analysis techniques are essential to identifying vulnerabilities within software. Static analysis tools such as DrChecker, Securify, FIRMSCOPE, and Pysa have been developed to detect, e.g., memory leaks, buffer overflows, privilege escalation, and injection attacks. These tools utilize techniques like bounded path-sensitive analysis, control flow analysis, and taint tracking to identify security flaws at the code level. Integrating symbolic execution engines, such as KLEE, further enhances security assessments by verifying that all possible execution paths within the software comply with security policies.

Penetration testing is an effective method for evaluating an organization's cybersecurity posture. This process typically involves multiple phases [9], including reconnaissance, vulnerability scanning, exploitation, post-exploitation, and reporting. IoT vulnerability research methodologies [20] take a comprehensive approach, focusing on attack surface decomposition to analyze products in depth. This involves identifying relationships between vulnerabilities, leveraging findings across different attack surfaces, discovering ways to chain vulnerabilities, and systematically developing attack paths. Advancement testing methodologies [11] have emphasized automation and integration with other cybersecurity tools, such as threat modeling and attack simulations. By leveraging automated scanning tools and AI-driven vulnerability assessments, penetration testers can identify weaknesses more efficiently and provide actionable insights to improve system defenses.

Cybersecurity self-assessment tools help organizations to strengthen their security cultures and enhance regulatory compliance. Studies [6] have explored the development of interactive security assessment frameworks that allow organizations to evaluate their risk exposure systematically. These frameworks

Table 1. Research Objectives

ID	Objective	Description
O1	Automation of Security Assessments and Compliance Reporting	Streamline security documentation and reporting through automation, reducing complexity in compliance efforts.
O2	Integration of Security into Agile Software Development	Embed real-time security assessments in agile workflows, enabling continuous vulnerability detection and mitigation.
O3	Automated Threat Model Generation	Generate threat models based on existing documentation to improve security insights in development.
O4	Comprehensive Cybersecurity Framework	Integrate threat modeling, attack simulations, and security assessment tools into a unified system.
O5	Reduction of Cybersecurity Costs through Early Security Integration	Embed security in IT and software engineering processes to prevent costly late-stage fixes.
O6	Seamless Interoperability of Security Tools	Ensure automated data flow and feedback loops between security components for improved resilience.

typically incorporate AI-driven recommendations tailored to an organization's security needs. Research [5] has demonstrated that proactive self-assessment can significantly improve security awareness and preparedness.

3 Industrial Needs

The increasing complexity of cybersecurity threats requires a multi-faceted approach that integrates threat modeling, automated security assessments, and proactive security strategies. Related research objectives are documented in Table 1 and explained in the following.

Organizations managing critical infrastructure in Operational Technology (OT) must balance security with uninterrupted functionality. Companies developing OT security solutions must ensure real-time threat detection within industrial control systems without causing operational disruptions. The convergence of IT and OT networks has introduced new vulnerabilities, which exploit weaknesses across interconnected systems. Additionally, strict regulatory requirements demand compliance-ready solutions that provide auditability and resilience against sophisticated cyber-attacks (O3).

Organizations developing secure hardware and software components in the automotive sector must meet stringent regulations. Security compliance standards, such as ISO/SAE 21434, require meticulous documentation of vulnerabilities, risk assessments, and mitigation strategies. The complexity of these assessments makes the process time-consuming and prone to inefficiencies. Automation of reporting can help address this. By streamlining security documentation through structured workflows and automated reporting tools, companies can efficiently integrate security assessments into the development cycle while ensuring regulatory compliance (O1, O4).

Companies must implement robust security measures in agile software development without hindering rapid development cycles. These organizations often handle highly sensitive data, including personal and corporate information, requiring strict adherence to privacy regulations such as GDPR. However, frequent software updates introduce potential vulnerabilities, which must be detected and mitigated to maintain system security. Integrating automated security assessments into the agile pipeline ensures vulnerabilities are identified and addressed without disrupting software delivery. Furthermore, modular security solutions allow rapid adjustments based on emerging threats, ensuring that security remains adaptable and scalable (O2, O5, O6).

Threat modeling techniques can support these challenges. Organizations need automated threat model generation that allows security professionals to extract security-relevant insights from existing software documentation. This involves generating structured threat models that reflect real-world attack vectors and system vulnerabilities (O3). Additionally, developing a domain-specific threat modeling language tailored to the needs of different industries allows for precise security assessments and simulations (O1, O4).

Organizations must ensure that security is integrated early in the development lifecycle. Embedding security practices into existing IT security management and software engineering processes ensures vulnerabilities are identified before deployment, reducing overall cybersecurity costs (O2, O5). This approach is reinforced through automated cost-benefit analysis, which optimizes security investment by balancing protection measures with economic feasibility (O4).

4 Research Design

The framework development follows the Action Design Research (ADR) [16] approach to iteratively develop, refine, and evaluate it to the needs of multiple industrial domains. ADR enables continuous stakeholder collaboration, ensuring the platform is technically sound and aligned with real-world security challenges.

The research begins with Problem Formulation, where security experts and industry partners in automotive, agile software development, and OT collaborate to identify key cybersecurity risks. We gather detailed security requirements, operational constraints, and regulatory considerations specific to each domain through workshops, interviews, and technical discussions. Additionally, we assess existing cybersecurity tools to identify gaps and determine how they can be improved or integrated into a more comprehensive framework. The outcome of this phase is a structured set of requirements outlining sector-specific challenges such as compliance automation in the automotive industry, security integration in agile workflows, and real-time monitoring in OT environments. This document serves as the foundation for the platform's design and development.

Following the problem formulation, the research moves into the Building, Intervention, and Evaluation (BIE) phase, which consists of two key sub-phases. First, we develop and customize the individual components of the cybersecurity platform. Security tools such as threat modeling, code analysis, penetration testing, and attack simulations are refined to address specific challenges within each domain. For example, threat modeling techniques are adapted to represent attacker-defender interactions in OT systems, while security assessment tools are tailored to facilitate structured compliance reporting in the automotive sector. Throughout this phase, industry stakeholders provide continuous feedback to ensure practical applicability.

Once the individual tools are customized, the next step in BIE involves integrating all components into a unified cybersecurity platform and conducting controlled testing within a sandbox environment. This approach allows us to simulate realistic cyber-attack scenarios without exposing sensitive operational data. The testing phase ensures all tools interact seamlessly, identifies potential usability issues, and allows for iterative refinements based on stakeholder feedback. The sandbox environment also enables safe and effective demonstrations of the platform's capabilities in academic and industrial settings.

The Reflection and Learning phase begins when the platform reaches a stable form. In this stage, stakeholders from each domain actively evaluate the system's performance, usability, and real-world effectiveness. Review sessions allow industry partners to discuss their experiences and suggest improvements. Simultaneously, empirical data from sandbox testing is analyzed to determine how well the platform meets its intended objectives. The insights gathered during this phase guide further refinements to ensure the platform remains aligned with practical security requirements and adaptable to emerging threats.

Finally, the Formalization of Learning and Final Evaluation phase marks the platform's deployment in live operational environments. Each use case presents unique security priorities: the automotive sector focuses on security compliance and automation, agile development emphasizes seamless security integration, and OT environments require real-time monitoring and resilience against cyber threats. The platform's effectiveness is assessed using well-defined performance metrics, including threat detection accuracy, efficiency improvements through automation, and compliance with regulatory frameworks. A comprehensive impact assessment follows, ensuring the platform delivers measurable security benefits while remaining adaptable to evolving cybersecurity challenges.

5 FreeCAT Design

The platform (cf. Fig. 1) is designed as a security assessment and improvement framework centering around its ability to automate the generation of structured threat models from software architecture descriptions and unstructured security-related data. By leveraging Large Language Models (LLMs), the platform converts documents and system descriptions into detailed threat models, allowing for a systematic security assessment without requiring extensive manual input. The LLM operates as an open-source solution and is deployed within the environments of industry partners, ensuring localized control over sensitive information while maintaining compliance with the European Artificial Intelligence Act, particularly in areas concerning transparency and data protection.

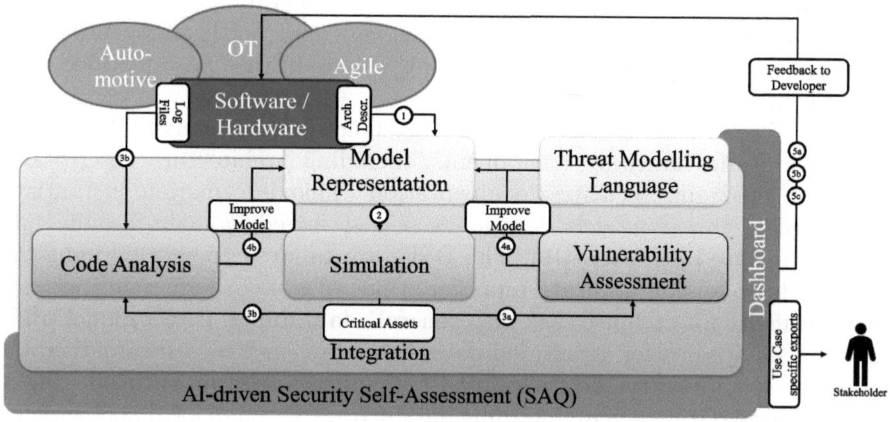

Fig. 1. FreeCAT Platform Outline

The generated threat models are formulated using MAL [21] and customized to each use case's specific vulnerabilities. By adapting MAL to various hardware and software architectures, the platform ensures that security assessments represent attack vectors relevant to each domain. Once threat models are established, they undergo automated security analysis through a simulation engine based on Stackelberg planning [19], a strategic decision-making model that simulates attacker-defender interactions. This technique allows the platform to recommend cost-effective defense strategies.

The simulation results identify high-risk software and hardware systems requiring further inspection. To prioritize security efforts, the platform directs penetration testing and code analysis toward the most critical system components, reducing security costs while ensuring protection where needed. The insights gained from these analyses are fed back into the threat models, enabling continuous refinement and dynamic risk assessment.

In addition to technical security evaluations, the platform incorporates AI-driven security self-assessments to address the human factor in cybersecurity. Recognizing that human error significantly contributes to security breaches; these assessments help organizations identify gaps in their teams' security awareness and practices, providing targeted training and policy improvement recommendations.

All assessment processes and results are presented through an interactive dashboard with a real-time security overview. This dashboard serves developers and decision-makers, enabling them to make informed security improvements based on live system insights. Additionally, the platform automates compliance documentation for partners with regulatory reporting requirements, such as Threat Analysis and Risk Assessment (TARA) reports, significantly reducing the time and effort required to meet industry regulations.

The cybersecurity assessment process follows a structured workflow that continuously integrates threat modeling, simulation, vulnerability assessment, code analysis, and feedback loops to improve software and hardware security. The platform follows an iterative cycle, ensuring vulnerabilities are identified, analyzed, prioritized, and addressed efficiently.

Step 1: The process starts by gathering structured and unstructured data from software and hardware components, including architecture descriptions, operational logs, and security documentation. This information instantiates domain-specific threat models, leveraging a customized Domain-Specific Language (DSL) based on MAL [10]. The DSLs are tailored to specific industrial environments to ensure accurate representations of system vulnerabilities, balancing specificity for each use case with general adaptability. Direct model transformations are applied for structured documentation, such as software diagrams or hardware specifications. Open-source LLMs extract relevant security insights for unstructured data while maintaining data privacy through local deployments.

Step 2: The generated threat models provide a structured representation of potential security threats within the system. These models are fed into a Stackelberg planning-based simulation engine [19], which simulates attacker-defender interactions to determine optimal defense strategies. The Stackelberg model allows defenders to anticipate attack vectors and plan cost-effective mitigation strategies, helping prioritize security actions based on risk exposure and resource constraints. This phase provides valuable insights into attack feasibility, likelihood, and potential impact, forming the basis for targeted security interventions.

Step 3a: The vulnerability assessment phase leverages simulation results to guide penetration testing efforts. Given the resource-intensive nature of penetration testing, only high-risk areas identified in the simulations are examined in detail, ensuring efficient resource allocation. The platform also incorporates LLM-powered automation to streamline penetration testing, allowing faster identification of vulnerabilities such as exploitable attack surfaces and misconfigurations. The output includes attack path analysis, risk assessments, and proof-of-concept exploits, enabling precise vulnerability mitigation.

Step 3b: Simultaneously, code analysis is conducted to detect software-level security vulnerabilities. Guided by simulation insights, the analysis focuses on critical code sections most susceptible to exploitation. Using LLMs trained on security libraries and best practices, the system identifies misuse of security APIs, unsafe coding patterns, and data flow vulnerabilities. Developers can refine the analysis by annotating security-critical elements, ensuring continuous improvement of security assessment capabilities.

Step 4a/4b: Penetration testing and code analysis findings are used to update and refine the threat models. This feedback ensures that newly discovered vulnerabilities and attack paths are accurately incorporated into the security framework. The threat modeling language is continuously updated to reflect generalizable insights, such as new attack techniques and mitigation strategies. At the same time, organization-specific findings remain within localized security assessments to preserve confidentiality.

Step 5a/5b/5c: Security insights gathered throughout the process are fed into software and hardware components, allowing targeted system updates and security patches. This feedback loop ensures that identified vulnerabilities are mitigated directly at the source, strengthening overall cybersecurity resilience.

The Meta Attack Language. MAL [21] is a formal modeling framework designed to represent and simulate complex cyber threats across digital systems. It provides a structured way to define attack paths, system components, and defense mechanisms, enabling static and dynamic vulnerability analysis. Initially applied in domains such as Operational Technology (OT) and core IT infrastructures [10], MAL has proven effective in modeling security scenarios in highly specialized environments.

A DSL based on MAL defines the fundamental components needed to model cybersecurity threats within a specific application domain. At the core of any MAL-based DSL are four key elements: Assets, Attack Steps, Defenses, and Associations. Assets represent entities that may be involved in or affected by an attack. These can be tangible components, such as servers, databases, or network devices, as well as more abstract entities like user accounts, passwords, or logical zones within a system. For organizational clarity, assets can be grouped into categories, such as different types of storage systems or user roles, depending on the domain.

Within each asset, one or more Attack Steps define specific malicious actions or changes in state that an attacker might attempt, such as exploiting a vulnerability, escalating privileges, or reading protected data. These steps are connected to form attack paths, modeling how an attack may progress through a system. The relationships between steps are described using logical operators: AND (&) indicates that all preceding steps must occur to enable the next. OR (|) allows any preceding steps to be sufficient for progression.

To counteract potential threats, Defenses can be defined for specific attack steps. These are modeled using a # symbol and represent mitigation measures that either block or reduce the impact of an attack.

Finally, Associations specify how assets are related or interact. These define the potential for attacks to spread from one asset to another through network access links or credential dependencies (e.g., a user account linked to a password or a device connected to a network). Through this structured and extensible approach, MAL enables detailed and scalable modeling of complex attack scenarios.

In FreeCAT, we extend MAL's capabilities by developing a DSL tailored to the needs of software architecture threat modeling. This new DSL will address the specific characteristics and security challenges inherent in software systems, which have not yet been fully explored within the MAL framework. We will iteratively refine and validate the DSL through real-world use cases by integrating insights from Model-Driven Engineering (MDE) and vulnerability detection techniques.

LLMs play a key role in automating the generation of MAL DSL instances by transforming structured and unstructured documentation into formal threat models. This capability significantly reduces the manual effort required to build and maintain security models, especially in complex or evolving systems.

For structured documentation, such as software architecture diagrams (e.g., UML), process models (e.g., BPMN), or configuration files, LLMs will assist in identifying and extracting relevant elements (e.g., components, data flows, user roles) and mapping them to corresponding Assets, Associations, and Attack Steps in the MAL DSL. This is done by recognizing established patterns and terminology in the input format and aligning them with domain-specific modeling rules defined within each DSL.

LLMs will be used to identify security-relevant entities and interactions based on natural language understanding for unstructured documentation, including technical reports, system descriptions, design documents, or even plain-text requirements. These insights are translated into structured representations by inferring which parts of the text correspond to MAL components, such as identifying a firewall as a defensive asset or recognizing a vulnerability description as an attack step.

To ensure privacy and regulatory compliance, especially regarding sensitive documentation, the LLMs will be deployed locally within the users' environments, avoiding transmitting proprietary or confidential data externally. This setup also allows for fine-tuning the models on domain-specific vocabulary and patterns, increasing accuracy and relevance.

Stackelberg Planning. To enrich FreeCAT's attack-simulation capabilities, we extend Stackelberg planning [19], a game-theoretic search technique that pits a defending "leader" against an attacking "follower." In a Stackelberg game, the defender selects a set of counter-measures subject to a cost budget; the attacker then observes that posture and seeks the cheapest sequence of steps that still reaches its objective. The planner, therefore, explores two intertwined state spaces: one describing alternative defence portfolios, the other describing the attacker's optimal path through each defended environment. By combining classical heuristic search (to prune inferior defence choices) with symbolic techniques that compactly store large state spaces, the engine produces a Pareto frontier showing, for every invested euro, how much additional effort the adversary must expend. This insight is invaluable for deciding whether isolating a subnet, patching a service, or hardening credentials yields the best return on security investment.

FreeCAT couples this planner directly to its MAL models. Each instantiated MAL diagram is translated into a planning representation: assets become objects, attack steps translate into attacker actions, and defensive controls appear as leader actions annotated with their deployment costs. A small library of translation rules covers standard MAL relations such as networkAccess or privilegeEscalation, while project-specific constructs are mapped automatically during model generation. Once the planner has computed the optimal attacker-defender interplay, its results—residual attack paths, critical assets, and expected time-to-compromise—are written back into the MAL model as annotations.

Code Analysis. To complement the planner-driven view of system-level risk, FreeCAT deepens its code-level insight by extending KLEE [7], a symbolic-execution engine built on the LLVM tool chain, to operate directly on the semantics contained in each MAL instance. Symbolic execution explores every feasible execution path of a program by treating inputs as symbolic variables and accumulating the constraints that govern those paths. When combined with an SMT solver, KLEE can automatically determine whether a path is feasible and, if so, produce concrete test vectors that trigger it.

In its original form, KLEE judges a path only against low-level correctness properties (e.g., absence of undefined behaviour). FreeCAT enriches the engine with model-aware guards: for every asset, attack step, and defence encoded in the current MAL model, a matching set of path predicates is generated. During execution, KLEE consults these predicates to decide whether a particular path (1) violates a confidentiality or integrity constraint implied by the model, (2) misuses a security API expected by a defensive control, or (3) opens a data-flow channel that the threat model flags as dangerous.

Whenever a path breaks one of these model-derived rules the engine emits a model-violation report that records the implicated code locations, the concrete exploit inputs, and the MAL elements that triggered the alert. These reports are automatically written back into the threat-model instance, where they (i) create new attack steps representing run-time exploits and (ii) inform the Stackelberg planner of fresh, code-level avenues available to an attacker. In parallel, developers receive ready-made test cases that reproduce the violation, enabling rapid triage and patching.

Penetration Testing. To complement automated analysis with real-world attack evidence, FreeCAT establishes a dedicated hacking-lab infrastructure that embeds classical penetration testing into the project's model-driven workflow. The lab mirrors the full attack chain: reconnaissance, scanning, exploitation, post-exploitation, and reporting—but executes each phase under the guidance of FreeCAT's analytic components.

Target Selection: After every Stackelberg-based simulation, the planner exports a ranked list of assets whose compromise yields the greatest attacker payoff. These high-priority assets and their predicted attack paths become the penetration-testing scope for the next cycle.

Automated Campaign Generation. The lab orchestrates commodity and custom tooling (e.g., Nmap, Metasploit, custom fuzzers) to create test campaigns that reproduce the planner's attack strategies. Parameter values such as payloads, credentials, or network routes are pulled directly from the current MAL model, ensuring each test reflects the system's most recent configuration.

Controlled Exploitation. Attacks execute inside an isolated, instrumented replica of the partner environment. Sensors capture run-time effects (i.e., file changes, privilege escalations, lateral moves) and map them back to MAL attack steps. When an exploit succeeds, the lab records the concrete conditions that enabled it (software versions, misconfigurations, timing windows).

Impact Analysis and Feedback. The evidence collected is fed into two channels: (1) Model refinement: successful exploits are inserted as confirmed attack steps with empirical likelihoods and time-to-compromise data, allowing future simulations to operate on measured rather than assumed parameters; (2) Defence validation: if a planned counter-measure fails to block an exploit, the discrepancy is flagged for immediate re-planning.

Reporting and Compliance. The lab automatically generates structured reports (e.g., TARA, ISO/SAE 21434 artefacts) that include exploit traces, risk ratings, and recommended fixes. These reports appear in the FreeCAT dashboard alongside symbolic-execution findings, giving stakeholders a single, coherent risk picture.

By closing the loop between model-based prediction and empirical verification, the hacking lab turns penetration testing into an adaptive, data-driven service: simulations decide where to probe, the lab supplies ground truth, and the updated evidence flows back to sharpen the threat model and the next simulation round. This synergy ensures that defenses are tested where they matter most, resources are used efficiently, and system resilience improves.

6 Conclusions

Cybersecurity threats are evolving at an unprecedented pace, so today's defenses must be continuous, proactive, and deeply embedded across the entire life cycle of a system. The FreeCAT framework answers this need by knitting together automated threat-model generation, Stackelberg-based attack simulations, LLM-driven vulnerability assessments, and compliance automation into a single, iterative loop that begins the moment code is written and persists while the system is in production.

By automatically extracting threat models from design artifacts and feeding the simulation results back to developers, FreeCAT exposes weaknesses early in the development stage, when fixes are cheapest (realizing O2 and O5), while its hacking-lab verification and live dashboard continue to scan, test and harden the running environment, proactively addressing threats during operational use. The framework's modular architecture ensures:

O1—Automation of security assessments and compliance reporting: LLM-powered document analysis and one-click generation of audit-ready artifacts slash the manual effort normally required for certification.

O2—Integration of security into agile development: Real-time feedback from simulations and code analysis is surfaced directly in CI/CD pipelines, turning every build into a security gate without slowing delivery.

O3—Automated threat-model generation: Domain-specific MAL dialects and local LLMs transform architecture diagrams and prose into executable threat models with minimal human input.

O4—Comprehensive cybersecurity framework: A unified platform links modeling, simulation, code analysis, penetration testing, and AI-driven self-assessment, giving stakeholders a single pane of glass for risk management.

O5—Reduction of costs through early security integration: Prioritized, model-driven testing focuses expensive expert effort only where simulations show the greatest risk, preventing late-stage rework and outages.

O6—Seamless interoperability of security tools: Standardized data exchange and feedback loops ensure that results from any component instantly refine the others, so each assessment cycle is smarter than the last.

In future work, because FreeCAT is currently a proposed framework rather than an operational platform, our first priority will be to implement and stitch together the modular services outlined above, validate them on representative systems, and iteratively refine the architecture from those findings. By building out these capabilities step-by-step, we intend to evolve the concept into a research prototype that can anticipate, verify, and mitigate threats throughout both development and operation.

Disclosure of Interests. The authors have no competing interests to declare that are relevant to the content of this article.

References

1. Abbaspour Asadollah, S., Imtiaz, S., Dehlaghi-Ghadim, A., Sjödin, M., Sirjani, M.: Enhancing cybersecurity through comprehensive investigation of data flow-based attack scenarios. J. Cybersecur. Priv. **4**(4), 823–852 (2024)
2. Andreoli, A., Lounis, A., Debbabi, M., Hanna, A.: On the prevalence of software supply chain attacks: empirical study and investigative framework. Foren. Sci. Int.: Digital Invest. **44**, 301508 (2023)
3. Ani, U.P.D., He, H., Tiwari, A.: Review of cybersecurity issues in industrial critical infrastructure: manufacturing in perspective. J. Cyber Secur. Technol. **1**(1), 32–74 (2017)
4. Bendovschi, A.: Cyber-attacks-trends, patterns and security countermeasures. Proc. Econom. Finan. **28**, 24–31 (2015)
5. Brickmann, M., Knoll, M., Steininger, P., Rappl, S.: Securing operational technology-course creation for SMEs. In: EDULEARN24 Proceedings, pp. 5347–5350. IATED (2024)
6. Burke, W., Stranieri, A., Oseni, T.: From dis-empowerment to empowerment: crafting a healthcare cybersecurity self-assessment. Comput. Secur. **148**, 104148 (2025)
7. Cadar, C., Dunbar, D., Engler, D.R., et al.: Klee: unassisted and automatic generation of high-coverage tests for complex systems programs. In: OSDI, vol. 8, pp. 209–224 (2008)

8. Crumpler, W., Lewis, J.A.: Cybersecurity workforce gap. JSTOR (2022)
9. Engebretson, P.: The basics of hacking and penetration testing: ethical hacking and penetration testing made easy. Elsevier (2013)
10. Hacks, S., Katsikeas, S.: Towards an ecosystem of domain specific languages for threat modeling. In: International Conference on Advanced Information Systems Engineering, pp. 3–18. Springer (2021)
11. Luttgens, J.T., Pepe, M., Mandia, K.: Incident response & computer forensics. McGraw-Hill Education Group (2014)
12. Mashkoor, A., Egyed, A., Wille, R., Stock, S.: Model-driven engineering of safety and security software systems: a systematic mapping study and future research directions. J. Softw.: Evol. Process **35**(7), e2457 (2023)
13. Mohammed, N.M., Niazi, M., Alshayeb, M., Mahmood, S.: Exploring software security approaches in software development lifecycle: a systematic mapping study. Comput. Stand. Interfaces **50**, 107–115 (2017)
14. Nguyen, P.H., Klein, J., Le Traon, Y., Kramer, M.E.: A systematic review of model-driven security. In: 2013 20th Asia-Pacific Software Engineering Conference (APSEC), vol. 1, pp. 432–441. IEEE (2013)
15. Potteiger, N., Samaddar, A., Bergstrom, H., Koutsoukos, X.: Designing robust cyber-defense agents with evolving behavior trees. In: 2024 International Conference on Assured Autonomy (ICAA), pp. 1–10. IEEE (2024)
16. Sein, M.K., Henfridsson, O., Purao, S., Rossi, M., Lindgren, R.: Action design research. MIS Quart. 37–56 (2011)
17. Shah, Y., Sengupta, S.: A survey on classification of cyber-attacks on Iot and Iot devices. In: 2020 11th IEEE Annual Ubiquitous Computing, Electronics & Mobile Communication Conference (UEMCON), pp. 0406–0413. IEEE (2020)
18. Siderova, A., Daneva, M., Bukhsh, F.A., Arachchige, J.J.: Security approaches in model-driven engineering for web applications: the state-of-the-art in the last 10 years. In: 2024 IEEE 32nd International Requirements Engineering Conference Workshops (REW), pp. 155–163. IEEE (2024)
19. Speicher, P., Steinmetz, M., Backes, M., Hoffmann, J., Künnemann, R.: Stackelberg planning: towards effective leader-follower state space search. In: Proceedings of the AAAI Conference on Artificial Intelligence, vol. 32 (2018)
20. Süren, E., Heiding, F., Olegård, J., Lagerström, R.: PatrIoT: practical and agile threat research for IoT. Int. J. Inform. Secur. (IJIS) **22**(1), 213–233 (February 2023)
21. Wideł, W., Hacks, S., Ekstedt, M., Johnson, P., Lagerström, R.: The meta attack language-a formal description. Comput. Secur. **130**, 103284 (2023)

Investigating the Role of FAIR Data Principles for Data Mesh Architecture

Khanh Nguyen(✉), João Luiz Rebelo Moreira, and Luiz Olavo Bonino da Silva Santos

University of Twente, Drienerlolaan 5, 7522 NB Enschede, The Netherlands
nguyenhoangnamkhanh@student.utwente.nl,
{j.luizrebelomoreira,l.o.boninodasilvasantos}@utwente.nl

Abstract. The Data Mesh paradigm has emerged as a promising response to the limitations of centralized data architectures by decentralizing ownership and promoting the principle of "Data as a Product". Although promising, its implementation hinges on the management of distributed data assets, particularly in terms of governance and interoperability. This paper investigates how the Findable, Accessible, Interoperable, Reusable (FAIR) data principles can address these gaps and strengthen the foundations of Data Mesh. Through a systematic literature review and the design science research methodology, we investigate the relation between the FAIR and the Data Mesh principles, revealing a strong conceptual alignment. Based on these findings, we extend a Data Mesh Reference Architecture using the ArchiMate enterprise modeling language, providing a blueprint that incorporates the FAIR data principles into organizational processes, data product lifecycles, and governance mechanisms. Our contributions are threefold: (1) a systematic mapping of FAIR principles to Data Mesh principles, (2) an extended reference architecture that demonstrates their integration in practice, and (3) concrete technical recommendations, such as the use of persistent identifiers and JSON-based semantic schema, to implement FAIR-compliant Data Products. Validation is done through schema testing, and a music streaming platform case illustrates the feasibility and benefits of the approach. This study offers to both scholars and practitioners actionable models and guidelines for designing FAIR Data Mesh architectures, paving the way for empirical research on real-world implementations.

Keywords: Data Mesh · FAIR Principles · Reference Architecture · Data Product

1 Introduction

The Data Mesh paradigm offers a promising approach to overcoming the limitations of traditional centralized data architectures by decentralizing data ownership and promoting data as a product [4]. However, the implementation of Data

J. Barateiro et al. (Eds.): EDOC 2025 Workshops, LNBIP 571, pp. 189–203, 2026.
https://doi.org/10.1007/978-3-032-16234-2_13

Mesh faces significant challenges, particularly in applying foundational principles to address the challenges of discoverability, access, semantic consistency, and governance among cross-domain data products. Although the core principles of Data Mesh provide a conceptual framework, they lack the prescriptive guidance needed for effective adoption. In contrast, the Findable, Accessible, Interoperable, Reusable (FAIR) data principles [30] provide a widely recognized set of guidelines that directly address the same types of challenges. Although previous work has demonstrated that the characteristics of a Data Product are extensively developed from the FAIR principles [6], there is still little clarity on how applying each of these principles can theoretically enhance a Data Mesh.

The primary goal of this research is to examine how the FAIR principles can enhance the Data Mesh architecture by extending a Data Mesh Reference Architecture (RA) proposed in our previous work [27]. We highlight how the adoption of the FAIR principles can provide a concrete framework for addressing challenges of cross-domain discovery, access, integration, and reusability. To achieve this research goal, we formulated three research questions aligned with the three core Data Mesh principles: *(Domain-owned) Data Product*, *Self-serve Data Platform*, and *Federated Governance*. The research approach used the Design Science Research Methodology, including a Systematic Literature Review (SLR) for problem investigation, RA development for treatment design, and validation through a prototype (a *Data Product* JSON Schema) combined with a use case about music streaming platform.

The paper is structured as follows. Section 2 presents the foundational concepts and theoretical background. Section 3 describes the research methodology. Section 4 introduces the Data Mesh RA extension, demonstrating how FAIR principles align with Data Mesh, represented through ArchiMate viewpoints. Section 5 validates the FAIR Data Mesh RA through a use case analysis. Section 6 discusses the implications of these findings, and Sect. 7 concludes the paper by summarizing the contributions and outlining avenues for future work. y materials are publicly available on Github[1].

2 Background

2.1 Data Mesh Architecture

Data Mesh represents the evolution of data architectures - from the centralized control of traditional data warehouses, through the scalable yet weakly governed data lakes, and the hybrid optimization of data lakehouses - towards a decentralized sociotechnical approach that manages analytical data at scale by treating data as a product [6]. The term *Data Mesh* was first defined in 2019 as a shift from monolithic data architectures to distributed architecture [4].

A strong analogy has been observed between the Data Mesh approach and microservice architectural style [1], where both architectures are influenced by domain-driven design [9,21]. Similarly to microservices, which decompose systems into loosely coupled components, Data Mesh decentralizes and distributes

[1] https://github.com/khanhnguyen7802/edoc-2025.

data responsibility to domain experts, i.e., people with deep knowledge of the data. Instead of flowing data from different domains into one centralized data platform, a specific domain will own and serve its data products, fostering accountability to ensure the quality of the output [4,27].

Dehghani (2022) proposed that every Data Mesh implementation should address four foundational principles: (1) domain-oriented, decentralized data ownership; (2) treating data as a product; (3) self-serve data platforms; and (4) federated computational governance [5].

The principle of domain-driven data ownership in a Data Mesh emphasizes decentralizing data responsibilities to the domains that generate and understand the data. Each domain, typically aligned with operational business functions, is responsible for producing, managing, and sharing analytical data as a Data Product according to organizational objectives [14,27]. The concept of Data as a Product applies product thinking to data, treating it as a valuable asset within a business model [6], and requires designing Data Products that integrate seamlessly across domains. The self-serve platform supports domain autonomy by providing shared infrastructure and tools to facilitate Data Product consumption. Federated computational governance ensures that all Data Products adhere to organizational standards, enabling interoperability and cohesion while complying with internal policies and industry regulations [6,22,27].

A Data Mesh use case can be seen at Zalando (Fig. 1), a European online fashion platform. Its previous Data Lake architecture (Fig. 1a) faced centralization challenges, prompting the adoption of a Data Mesh. Zalando maintains a processing platform (Fig. 1b), powered by Spark on Databricks, as the core of its data-agnostic central infrastructure [24]. Using the *"Bring Your Own Bucket"* paradigm, domain teams manage their datasets via Amazon S3, while a unified metadata layer enforces access control and delegates governance.

To promote a *Data as a Product* mindset, Zalando encourages behavioral shifts among teams, emphasizing that data quality represents a contract between producers and consumers. Its central platform supports this by providing self-service Spark clusters and seamless integration with tools such as Amazon Redshift, ensuring consistent interoperability across domains. This setup simplifies cross-domain data sharing while maintaining federated governance within the Data Product environment [13,25,26].

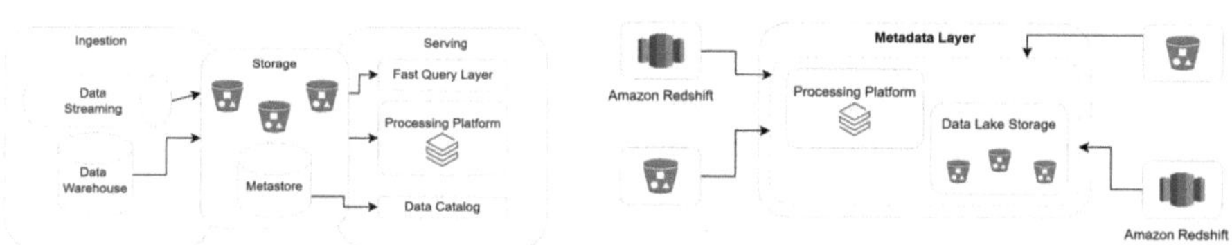

(a) Data Lake Architecture. (b) Data Mesh Architecture.

Fig. 1. Zalando shifting from Data Lake to Data Mesh. Adapted from [24,26].

2.2 FAIR Data Principles

The growing volume and variety of research data have underscored the need for effective data management and stewardship. Previously, the definition of good data management was often left to the data or repository owners. To address this, the FAIR data principles were introduced to improve long-term data discovery and reusability while clarifying the objectives of proper data stewardship. They also support automation, allowing systems to find, access, and reuse digital objects with minimal human intervention. FAIR is built on four core principles - Findable, Accessible, Interoperable, and Reusable - each with corresponding sub-principles [11,30]. In the following sections, shorthand notation (e.g., F1, A1.2) will be used to refer to these sub-principles.

3 Research Methodology

This study follows the SLR method of Carrera-Rivera et al. (2022) to systematically analyze existing research [3]. The method was slightly adapted to fit the scope of this study, while preserving its primary structure.

3.1 Planning

The review begins by clearly defining the research questions (RQs), followed by selecting databases that comprehensively cover the topic. All RQs and their associated sub-RQs are summarized in Table 1.

This study used ScienceDirect, IEEE Xplore, ACM, Springer, and Google Scholar databases, with Google Scholar yielding the broadest results. Inclusion and exclusion criteria were applied to focus on relevant and high-quality studies. Specifically, English-language books as well as rigorously peer-reviewed and non-peer-reviewed materials published between 2020 and 2025 were chosen, while documents deemed low-quality and irrelevant to the research objectives were excluded.

3.2 Conducting

In this phase, we constructed search strings for each database using the keywords "data mesh", "FAIR principle", and "reference architecture". As the study focuses on Data Mesh, "data mesh" was required and combined with either "FAIR principle" or "reference architecture" using Boolean OR and AND operators. Using these strings, we systematically queried the selected databases and applied predefined inclusion and exclusion criteria to ensure alignment with the study scope. This process yielded 1 journal article from ScienceDirect, 1 book and 1 journal article from IEEE, 1 book from ACM, 1 journal article and 1 conference proceeding from Springer, and 6 documents (including books, dissertations, and non-peer-reviewed papers) from Google Scholar. Although the time range focused on research from 2020, documents on FAIR principles were included regardless of the date, as they remain a foundational framework for current research and data management practices.

Table 1. Formulated Research Questions

RQ#	Main RQs	Sub-RQs
RQ1	How do the FAIR data principles contribute to the attributes of a *Data Product* for Data Mesh architecture to enable domain-owned Data Products?	a) What are the key characteristics and attributes of a *Data Product*? b) Which FAIR principles support these characteristics and attributes?
RQ2	How does the *Self-serve Data Platform* enable domain teams to implement the FAIR principles in their Data Products?	a) Which platform capabilities support identifier registration and rich metadata discovery (*Findability*)? b) Which platform capabilities ensure standardized and secure data access (*Accessibility*)?
RQ3	How does the governance mechanism ensure adherence to FAIR standards across distributed Data Products?	a) Which FAIR principles are supported by the *Federated Governance* concept? b) How can the Governance group leverage the structure of a Data Product to enforce standards and enhance interoperability?

4 FAIR Data Mesh Reference Architecture

Recent discussions on Data Meshes have highlighted potential synergies with established data management frameworks. In our preliminary research, we discussed the need to adopt the FAIR principles to facilitate Data Mesh implementation [27], while Dehghani (2022) noted that the core characteristics of a Data Product are largely derived from FAIR principles [6]. This section examines these claims by analyzing how each FAIR principle can be integrated into the foundational principles of Data Mesh.

4.1 Enabling Domain-Owned Data Products

We propose the FAIR Data Mesh RA, an extension of our previous work [27], as illustrated in Fig. 2. The RA emphasizes strong domain ownership, with each domain team accountable for its own Data Product. Within the Domain Team (top of the diagram), the roles of Data Product Owner and Data Product Development Team [14] are defined separately, with responsibilities aligned to the Data Product's life cycle. This cycle begins with the product's initial design and ends when the product is retired under specific conditions.

In the initial phases of the life cycle, Data Product Owners must define a clear business vision and strategic goals to identify the Data Products required for business cases and to clarify the architecture and meaning of the data they expose [8]. During development, the Data Product Development Team implements each Data Product (Fig. 2) as an autonomous, self-contained unit with three key interfaces: a Communication interface for data exchange, an Informa-

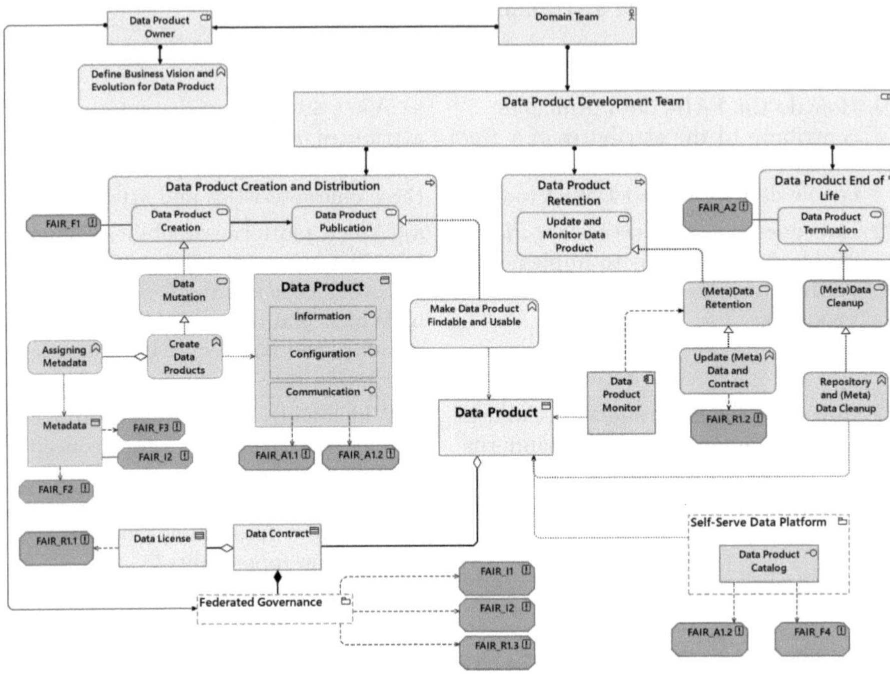

Fig. 2. Domain-owned Data Product in ArchiMate model, extended from [27].

tion interface for monitoring and metadata retrieval, and a Configuration interface for security and access control [14]. FAIR principle **F1** guides the creation of a globally unique identifier to facilitate discovery in the Data Product Catalog and prevent unintentional duplication, while **F3** complements Findability by ensuring data can be located even if the identifier is initially unknown.

Effective communication among Data Products relies on adherence to standardized protocols (**A1**). For example, data product names should use camel case, and versions should follow semantic versioning [19], formatted as MAJOR.MINOR.PATCH, to accurately track deployments, especially in production environments. To enforce these standards, Data Products must have fully defined metadata and data contracts before distribution in the Data Mesh, ensuring that they address the FAIR principles, i.e., have higher FAIRness [11]. The data contract, publicly available to meet governance requirements, specifies quality attributes, schema, and semantics, and includes a data license outlining usage terms, such as internal use only or compliance with regulations like GDPR. These practices support the fulfillment of **F2** and **R1.1**.

Majchrzak et al. (2022) recommend using a metadata-as-code approach in JSON format and define a Data Product as an autonomous, standardized unit containing at least one domain dataset, making the dataset its core component [14]. Listing 1 shows essential JSON properties required for interoperability within the Data Mesh, which addresses **I1** and **I3** (to some extent). For the complete version, see the JSON file (See footnote 1) on GitHub.

```
{
  "dataProduct": { // data product details
    "dataProductId": "10.17616/R3MW57",
    "pidType": "doi",
    "urlNamespace": "https://doi.org",
    "name": "fishBase",
    "description": "A database of searchable fish",
    "version": "4.0.0"
  },
  "domainDataset": {
    "datasets": [
        {
            "datasetId": "10.25504/FAIRsharing.db020e",
            "pidType": "doi",
            ...
        },
        ...
    ]
  }
}
```

Listing 1: Example of a Data Product in JSON format

When creating a Data Product, Majchrzak et al. (2022) used a URL with the Data Product's ID as a random alphanumeric string, whereas Gioia (2024) proposed using a version 5 UUID (Universally Unique Identifier) following RFC 4122 [8,12]. In Gioia's approach, the UUID serves as a persistent identifier (PID) derived from the Data Product's name string, making it ineffective for objects with different name forms. UUIDs also lack semantic value and do not support Findability, often yielding zero search results [18]. To address this, Digital Object Identifier (DOI) is recommended, providing Findability, in particular **F1**, and Accessibility through Crossref [16] and centralized resolution at doi.org. The main limitation of DOIs lies in Validability, as their pattern lacks strict constraints, making it difficult to reliably distinguish valid from invalid identifiers [17]. Listing 1 illustrates a Data Product composed of smaller domain datasets, each assigned a DOI. In addition, Listing 1 illustrates the use of URL namespace with the HTTPS protocol for universal standardization and open access. Consumers can access it through a public endpoint[2] [20], composed of *urlNamespace* and *dataProductId*. HTTPS also supports authentication and authorization, providing access control and satisfying principles **A1.1** and **A1.2**.

During the development phase, a Data Product must generate tangible value aligned with the organization's strategic objectives. Achieving this requires contextualizing and interpreting the collected information in light of the organization's domain knowledge. Ontologies play a critical role here by creating semantic links between exposed physical data and domain-aligned concepts, connecting

[2] https://doi.org/10.17616/R3MW57.

data, metadata, and conceptual knowledge. All metadata for the Data Product is defined using standard annotations within the schema, ensuring consistency, interoperability, and machine-readable understanding across the organization.

Gioia (2024) proposed an ontology represented as a JSON Schema [31], linking it semantically to *schema.org* [2] via the context definition. JSON Schema, a declarative language, defines structure and constraints for JSON data, while *schema.org* is a widely adopted standardized vocabulary that enables data exchange across domains, and enhances semantic search by connecting to other ontologies. This approach supports FAIR principle **I2**. Furthermore, the JSON for Linked Data (JSON-LD) [28], a W3C-standardized (World Wide Web Consortium) format of the RDF (Resource Description Framework) data model [29], expresses relationships between entities and clarifies the context defined by *schema.org*. Integrating JSON-LD positions the Data Product within the W3C-promoted semantic web "stack" (ecosystem). Listing 2 depicts an example of a schema of domain datasets defined in JSON Schema and JSON-LD (following the format of a complete Data Product). For a complete representation of the schema, refer to JSON file (See footnote 1).

```
{
  "$id": "https://example.com/schemas/domainDatasets.json",
  "$schema": "https://json-schema.org/draft/2020-12/schema",
  "properties": {
    "@context": { "type": "string", "const": "https://schema.org" },
    ...,
    "itemListElement": {
      "items": { "$ref": "#/$defs/Dataset" }
    }
  },

  "$defs": {
    "Dataset": {
      ...,
      "properties": {
        "@type": { "type": "string", "const": "Dataset" },
        "identifier": {
          "properties": {
            "value": { "type": "string", "pattern": "^10\\.[0-9]{4,}/\\S+$" }
          }
        },
        "version": {
          "pattern": "^(0|[1-9]\\d*)\\.(0|[1-9]\\d*)\\.(0|[1-9]\\d*)$"
        },
        ...
      }
    }
  }
}
```

Listing 2: Schema of domain datasets

In Listing 2, the JSON Schema illustrates linked data principles through its references and connections. Rather than redefining each dataset schema within a domain, the "*$ref*" field creates a formal semantic link to a reusable inline schema. By specifying *@context* as https://schema.org and *@type* as "Dataset", the schema provides semantic context and acts as a universal translator for the data. Additionally, following the DOI style, the *pattern* fields enforce adherence to predefined standard constraints. As represented in the JSON file (See footnote 1), the *required* field strictly guides which fields are mandatory to include in the *Dataset* instance. Furthermore, each field is strictly defined with a specific data type. This implementation strategy supports the FAIR principles **I1** and **I3**.

After deployment, a Data Product becomes operational and requires continuous governance, monitoring, and updates throughout its lifespan. As datasets evolve, provenance information must be captured and updated in the metadata, enabling members across domains to evaluate the Data Product's suitability for reuse and follow appropriate procedures. This practice supports the fulfillment of FAIR principle **R1.2**.

A Data Product may be dormant or extinct. During the termination phase, it is considered dormant as long as its past data are still in use, and extinct once fully retired. Even after retirement, FAIR principle **A2** requires that metadata remain available to document the product's characteristics or explain the reason for removal. For example, metadata from an old version should persist for reference and documentation in relation to the new version.

In summary, throughout the life cycle of a Data Product, certain FAIR principles play a central role in shaping the product's design and implementation.

4.2 Enabling Self-serve Data Platform

According to van der Werf et al. (2025), the Self-Serve Data Platform equips all domains with tools that enable domain teams to manage Data Products autonomously [6,13,14,27]. For example, in Fig. 3, the Data Product Catalog is implemented via an application interface, while access control is provided by an Authentication Engine, improving product search and protecting against unauthorized access [8,27].

The Data Product Catalog enables discovery of Data Products via identifiers and metadata [9], while the Authentication Engine validates credentials over HTTPS for authentication and authorization. Together, these services support FAIR principles **F4** and **A1.2**. Furthermore, principle **F1** underpins the requirement that a Data Product must be searchable by its identifier, a capability delivered through the catalog.

In essence, the *Self-Serve Data Platform* provides the core infrastructure that enables computational and automated aspects of the Data Mesh through standardized interactions. It also supports the application of additional FAIR principles within the broader framework of data governance (see Sect. 4.3).

4.3 Enabling Federated Governance

Although most elements of van der Werf et al.'s (2025) original model remain intact, we added the architectural principles to highlight how FAIR principles

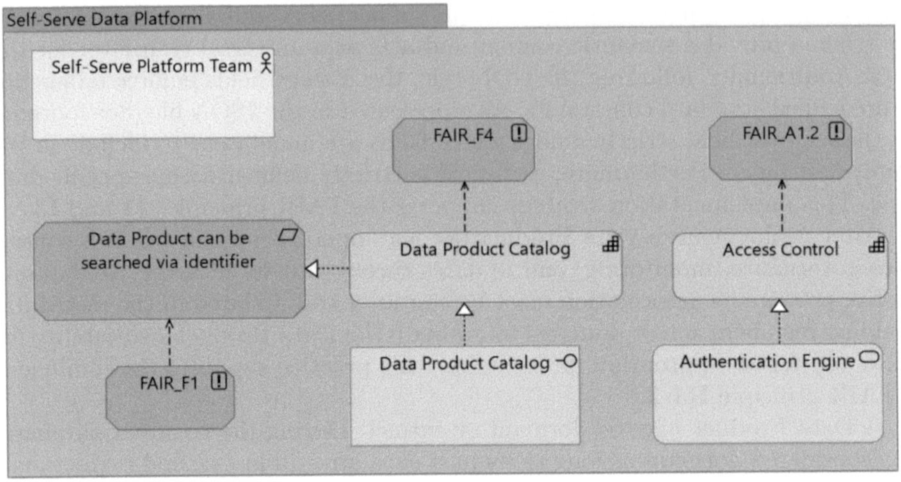

Fig. 3. Self-Serve Data Platform in Archimate model. Adapted from [27].

influence Data Mesh governance. The annotated diagram in Fig. 4 emphasizes Interoperability and Reusability among Data Products and policy compliance. The characteristics of a Data Product (see Sect. 4.1) aligns with FAIR principles **I1** and **I2**. To ensure this, the *Federated Governance* group enforces standardizations and organization-wide policies [9]. Security is equally critical: the Governance group defines access policies in data licenses, guided by principle **R1.1**, to safeguard data and ensure proper usage.

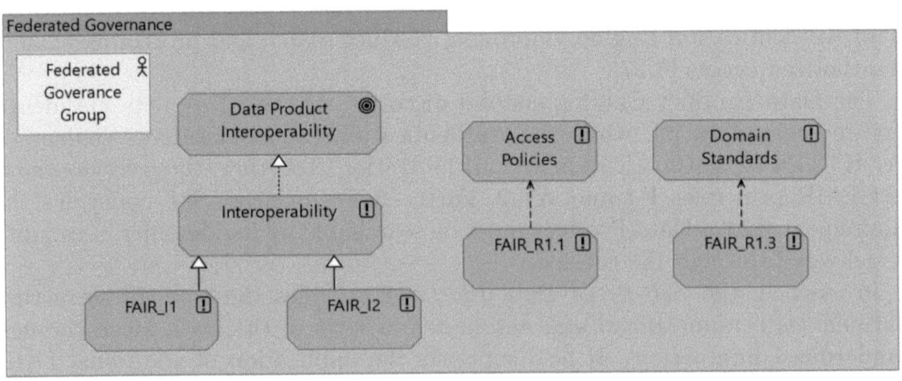

Fig. 4. Federated Governance in Archimate model. Adapted from [27].

FAIR principle **R1.3** requires Data Products to comply with domain standards. For example, in the JSON file (See footnote 1) on the context of marine life, the fifth dataset follows standards via a URL linked to the Ocean Biodiversity Information System, a global open-access resource on marine biodiversity. Adhering to domain-specific standards ensures community members can understand and integrate resources without manual curation.

5 Reference Architecture Validation

This section discusses the validation of the FAIR Data Mesh RA, which was performed through a use case analysis, and a JSON schema for the verification of Data Products.

5.1 Use Case Analysis

Dehghani (2022) introduces *Daff*, a music streaming platform with four domains: *Playlist*, *Artist*, *Media Player*, and *Listener*. A modified architecture diagram (Image (See footnote 1) on Github, adapted from [5]) illustrates how *Daff* can be structured as a Data Mesh. In this section, *Daff* serves as a running example to demonstrate how the RA applies in practice, i.e., how it captures the Data Product life cycle from an organizational perspective (Fig. 2), and then how the RA supports defining FAIR-based Data Product properties, focusing on the *Media Player* domain.

Based on the architecture illustrated in Image (See footnote 1) on Github and Fig. 2, the *Media Player* domain team, which comprises the Data Product Owner and Development Team, collects user operational data and enriches it with metadata to create a Data Product. This process is supported by Extract, Transform, Load (ETL) pipelines within the self-serve platform. The Data Product exposes metadata through its *Information interface*, exchanges data via the *Communication interface*, and manages access through the *Configuration interface*. Before distribution, each Data Product, including its data license, must be reviewed by the Governance team to ensure compliance with standards and access policies.

Throughout its life cycle, a Data Product evolves alongside emerging domains. New aggregated domains may be derived from foundational ones. For example, a *Listener Sessions* domain can be generated from *Media Player* to provide an analytical view of aggregated play events. The Archimate model illustrates this evolution by mapping the Data Product life cycle from creation to maturity (Fig. 2). Since the Data Product is the central element of this model, the following evaluation focuses on the *Media Player* Data Product and assesses its properties against FAIR principles.

1. **Findability**
   The product is assigned a globally unique *dataProductId* and its constituent datasets (e.g., playSessions) also have unique *datasetIds*. As argued in Sect. 4.1, using a resolvable DOI will further enhance Findability. The product will then be indexed in the central Data Product Catalog powered by the

Self-serve Data Platform (fulfilling **F4**), where data consumers can search for it using its identifier (**F1**), or by searching its rich metadata, such as the name and description (**F2**), or even the included product's identifier within the metadata (**F3**).

2. **Accessibility**
The designated *urlNamespace* (Listing 1) implies that the data product can be retrieved using a standardized protocol like HTTPS (**A1.1**). The Self-Serve Data Platform (Fig. 3) ensures that access requests are authenticated and authorized (**A1.2**) via Authentication Engine. Moreover, when a version of the product is deprecated, its metadata should remain accessible to inform about retirement and refer to a potential successor version (**A2**).
3. **Interoperability**
For the *mediaPlayer* product to interoperate with a *playlist* product, they must share a common language. By applying the combination of *JSON Schema*, *schema.org* and *JSON-LD* (Sect. 4.1), the domains can ensure semantic interoperability (**I1, I2**). Regarding data linkage across the mesh, each track in a playlist includes metadata referencing to related datasets, for example, the *track* field contains qualified links to the associated artist (**I3**).
4. **Reusability**
A data contract, enforced by Federated Governance, includes a data license (**R1.1**) and provenance information in the lineage section (**R1.2**), detailing how other aggregated data was generated. Adherence to domain-relevant standards, such as the inclusion of DDEX (Digital Data Exchange) standards [7] to satisfy the domain-relevant community standards, ensures that data consumers can confidently integrate and reuse domain-specific and widely accepted metadata vocabularies (**R1.3**).

5.2 Schema Verification

The schema provided in JSON file (See footnote 1) combines the benefits of *JSON Schema*, *JSON-LD* and *schema.org*. This unified schema can be used to verify JSON messages for syntactic and semantic correctness. For the following validation processes, a Data Product instance (JSON file (See footnote 1)) is used alongside and evidence of each validation process is documented in Image (See footnote 1), (See footnote 1) and (See footnote 1) on Github.

First, to verify syntactic adherence, the data instance was validated against this schema using the "JSON Schema Validator" tool [15]. The successful validation, accessible through the saved result[3], confirms that we can use the framework to programmatically enforce metadata consistency. Second, to assess semantic correctness and interoperability, we tested with the "Schema Markup Validator" [23]. The result confirms that structured data conforms to *schema.org* vocabulary and syntax, ensuring that the schema markup adheres to standards

[3] https://www.jsonschemavalidator.net/s/cnSI26wz.

recognized by search engines. Finally, Google's Rich Results Test [10] confirmed the submitted instance as a valid 'Dataset', successfully parsed without errors.

In summary, these validation steps confirm that the proposed schema provides reliable outlines towards implementation for the Data Product within the Application Layer of the Archimate language.

6 Discussion

The explicit linking of individual FAIR principles to components of the Data Mesh architecture via Archimate models provides a theoretical blueprint for practitioners. However, this study is primarily a theoretical and architectural investigation based on SLR and therefore requires empirical validation through real-world implementation. The technical overhead of implementing PIDs and rich semantic metadata, maintaining Data Products, and defining different concepts within a Data Mesh might present a hindrance to both product owners and development teams. Moreover, using DOIs as PIDs in a Data Product also incurs considerable costs associated with registration and maintenance, which poses a notable challenge for small-scale organizations. For example, the fee at the Crossref [16] registration agency starts with the minimum annual membership[4] of USD 200. Additional costs are incurred for content registration, and the total expense can vary depending on factors such as publisher revenue and associated support services.

7 Conclusion

This investigation demonstrates that the FAIR principles provide a mature and standardized framework that directly addresses some implementation challenges of Data Mesh by guiding the creation of interoperable Data Products. Three key lessons emerge from this study. First, the alignment between FAIR principles and Data Mesh reveals their inherent complementarity, showing that adopting FAIR can strengthen governance, interoperability, and usability within decentralized data architectures. Second, embedding FAIR principles requires careful consideration of both organizational roles and technical infrastructures, highlighting the importance of clearly defined responsibilities and standardized metadata. Third, the use of persistent identifiers, semantic metadata, and standardized schemas is essential to enable automation, reproducibility, and cross-domain integration.

The primary contributions of this work are threefold. First, it systematically mapped the FAIR principles to the core principles of Data Mesh, providing a conceptual framework for their integration. Second, it proposes an extended Data Mesh RA using ArchiMate, serving as a blueprint for implementation. Third, this study offers technical recommendations, including the use of DOIs as persistent identifiers and metadata schemas based on JSON Schema and JSON-LD, providing concrete guidance for achieving semantic interoperability in practice.

[4] https://www.crossref.org/fees/.

Among the main limitations, this study is primarily a theoretical and architectural investigation based on a SLR, and, therefore, requires empirical validation in real-world settings. The technical overhead of implementing PIDs, rich semantic metadata, and maintaining Data Products may challenge product owners and development teams, and the associated costs of DOI registration may be prohibitive for small-scale organizations. Future research should focus on empirical validation of the proposed RA through case studies of real-world Data Mesh deployments to evaluate performance, usability, and organizational impact. Additionally, considering Data Products as Digital Objects suggests the potential to adopt the FAIR Digital Object (FDO) framework, which may further enhance interoperability, governance, and lifecycle management within Data Mesh environments.

Disclosure of Interests. The authors have no competing interests to declare that are relevant to the content of this article.

References

1. Ashraf, A., Hassan, A., Mahdi, H.: Key lessons from microservices for data mesh adoption. In: 2023 International Mobile, Intelligent, and Ubiquitous Computing Conference (MIUCC), pp. 1–8 (2023). https://doi.org/10.1109/MIUCC58832.2023.10278300
2. Brickley, D.: Schema.org (2011). https://schema.org
3. Carrera-Rivera, A., Ochoa, W., Larrinaga, F., Lasa, G.: How-to conduct a systematic literature review: a quick guide for computer science research. MethodsX **9**, 101895 (2022)
4. Dehghani, Z.: How to move beyond a monolithic data lake to a distributed data mesh (2019). https://martinfowler.com/articles/data-monolith-to-mesh.html
5. Dehghani, Z.: Data mesh principles and logical architecture (2020). https://martinfowler.com/articles/data-mesh-principles.html
6. Dehghani, Z.: Data Mesh. Inc, O'Reilly Media (2022)
7. Digital Data Exchange, LLC: Digital data exchange (DDEX) (2020). https://ddex.net/standards/
8. Gioia, A.: Managing Data as a Product. Packt Publishing (2024)
9. Goedegebuure, A., et al.: Data mesh: a systematic gray literature review. ACM Comput. Surv. **57**(1) (2024). https://doi.org/10.1145/3687301
10. Google: Rich results test (2018). https://search.google.com/test/rich-results
11. Jacobsen, A., et al.: FAIR principles: interpretations and implementation considerations. Data Intell. **2**(1–2), 10–29 (2020). https://doi.org/10.1162/dint_r_00024
12. Leach, P.J., Salz, R., Mealling, M.H.: A Universally Unique IDentifier (UUID) URN Namespace. Technical report (2005). https://doi.org/10.17487/RFC4122, https://www.rfc-editor.org/info/rfc4122
13. Machado, I.A., Costa, C., Santos, M.Y.: Data mesh: Concepts and principles of a paradigm shift in data architectures. Procedia Comput. Sci. **196**, 263–271 (2022). https://doi.org/10.1016/j.procs.2021.12.013, https://www.sciencedirect.com/science/article/pii/S1877050921022365. International Conference on ENTERprise Information Systems / ProjMAN - International Conference on Project MANagement / HCist - International Conference on Health and Social Care Information Systems and Technologies 2021

14. Majchrzak, J., Siwiak, M., Balnojan, S., Sieraczkiewicz, M.: Data Mesh in Action. Manning Publications (2022)
15. Newton-King, J.: JSON Schema Validator (2015). https://www.jsonschemavalidator.net/
16. Pentz, E.: Crossref (2000). https://crossref.org
17. Philipson, J.: About a BUOI: Joint custody of persistent universally unique identifiers on the web, or, making PIDs more FAIR. In: González-Beltrán, A., Osborne, F., Peroni, S., Vahdati, S. (eds.) Semantics, Analytics, Visualization, pp. 33–48. Springer International Publishing, Cham (2018)
18. Philipson, J.: Identifying PIDs playing FAIR. Data Sci. **2**(1–2), 229–244 (2019)
19. Preston-Werner, T.: Semantic versioning (2010). https://semver.org/
20. re3data.org: Fishbase; editing status 2024-11-21. https://doi.org/10.17616/R3MW57 (2024). https://doi.org/10.17616/R3MW57, re3data.org - Registry of Research Data Repositories. Accessed 29 Jun 2025
21. Richardson, C.: Microservice Architecture Pattern (2018). https://microservices.io/patterns/microservices.html
22. Schemann, J., Zavgorodnia, L., Funke, S.: Data mesh architecture - data mesh from an engineering perspective (2022). https://www.datamesh-architecture.com/
23. Schema.org Organization: Schema.org validator (2021). https://validator.schema.org/
24. Schultze, M.: How Zalando built its data lake on Amazon S3. Technical Blog (2020). https://aws.amazon.com/blogs/storage/how-zalando-built-its-data-lake-on-amazon-s3/
25. Schultze, M., Izadi, A.: Data mesh in practice: how Europe's leading online platform for fashion goes beyond the data lake. Presentation Video (2020). https://www.youtube.com/watch?v=eiUhV56uVUc
26. Schultze, M., Izadi, A.: Data mesh in practice: how Europe's leading online platform for fashion goes beyond the data lake. Presentation Slide (2020). https://www.slideshare.net/slideshow/data-mesh-in-practice-how-europes-leading-online-platform-for-fashion-goes-beyond-the-data-lake-236728093/236728093
27. van der Werf, D., Moreira, J., Piest, J.P.S.: Towards a data mesh reference architecture. In: Kaczmarek-Heß, M., Rosenthal, K., Suchánek, M., Da Silva, M.M., Proper, H.A., Schnellmann, M. (eds.) Enterprise Design, Operations, and Computing. EDOC 2024 Workshops, pp. 339–353. Springer, Cham (2025). https://doi.org/10.1007/978-3-031-79059-1_21
28. W3C JSON-LD Community Group: JSON-LD (2011). https://json-ld.org
29. W3C JSON-LD Working Group: JSON-LD 1.1 (2020). https://w3.org/TR/json-ld11/
30. Wilkinson, M.D., Dumontier, M., Aalbersberg, I.J.: The FAIR guiding principles for scientific data management and stewardship. Sci. Data **3**(1), 160018 (2016)
31. Wright, A., Andrews, H., Hutton, B., Dennis, G.: JSON schema: a media type for describing JSON documents. Technical report (2020). https://json-schema.org/draft/2020-12/json-schema-core.html

Doctoral Consortium

A Method for Model-Driven Engineering of IoT-Based Digital Twins

Benjamin Nast(✉)

University of Rostock, Albert-Einstein-Street 22, 18059 Rostock, Germany
benjamin.nast@uni-rostock.de

Abstract. In recent years, interest in digital twins (DTs) has increased among both industry and academia. Consequently, various methods have been proposed to enhance the development and maintenance of DTs. The creation of DTs relies on integrating models and data from a variety of sources, including sensors, Internet of Things (IoT) devices, and other data streams. Model-driven engineering (MDE) is considered an effective approach for developing IoT applications. Previous research indicates that current methods focus primarily on software and systems perspectives, often overlooking the importance of organizational integration. Additionally, there is a growing need for approaches specifically designed to meet the needs of small and medium-sized enterprises (SMEs). This thesis project aims to develop (i) a method that includes clearly defined steps, (ii) a tool to assist SMEs in developing IoT-based DTs, and (iii) consider aspects of organizational integration in and following the development process.

Keywords: Model-driven engineering · Internet of Things · Method · Digital twin · Metamodel · Domain-specific modeling language

1 Introduction and Problem Statement

Digital twins (DTs) are virtual representations of physical or cyber-physical objects, systems, or processes [12] and are characterized by the automatic, bidirectional exchange of data between the virtual and physical instances [15]. The fundamental notion is to establish a comprehensible and adaptable virtual (digital) image of a tangible entity in the real world, with the objective of enhancing comprehension, observation, and control of its behavior [27].

Recently, there has been a notable increase in the attention and utilization of DTs across various industries [18,31]. The deployment of DTs offers a multitude of advantages, e.g., real-time monitoring, simulating and analyzing data, predictive analytics, remote control and automation, and facilitating life cycle management [1,18]. The development of DTs is contingent upon the integration of models and data derived from disparate sources, including sensors, Internet of Things (IoT) devices, and other data streams.

J. Barateiro et al. (Eds.): EDOC 2025 Workshops, LNBIP 571, pp. 207–215, 2026.
https://doi.org/10.1007/978-3-032-16234-2_15

Model-driven engineering (MDE) is considered an effective technique for addressing the challenges inherent in the development of IoT applications [4,30]. The automatic generation of code resulting from model transformations enhances productivity and ensures consistency through automation [3]. The complexity of development and the efficient and (partially) automated implementation can be addressed by metamodels for domain-specific applications. MDE can be enabled by defining a domain-specific modeling language (DSML) to describe system requirements [7]. The integrity of a model can be preserved by defining semantics or syntax, which also prevents nonsensical models. Specific graphical notations can provide a concrete syntax to improve the models' understanding and clarity.

Many companies face difficulties in extracting business value from IoT technology, while others hesitate to invest due to the challenges of organizational integration [29]. Fortino et al. [6] point out that existing development products primarily emphasize software components. In previous work, we have confirmed through systematic literature searches and a case study that MDE approaches for IoT applications tend to focus on technological aspects [21,23].

The prerequisites of small and medium-sized enterprises (SMEs) for developing IoT-based DTs differ from those of larger companies. In [23], we derived specifics of SMEs regarding the introduction of new technological innovations (such as the IoT and DTs) from the aspects of digital innovation readiness. There are notable differences regarding the available resources, IT structure, knowledge, and general aspects like the strategy or culture of the SME. Currently, available model-driven approaches do not specifically consider the special needs of SMEs. A recent literature survey by Van Bossuyt et al. [32] confirms these aspects for adopting DTs in manufacturing and concludes that clear guidelines for implementation are lacking and that the staff in those enterprises are often unable to face the resulting challenges. Lehner et al. [16] state in a systematic mapping study that most approaches for MDE of DTs are still to be evaluated in an industrial context, and their maturity should be advanced by application in new domains.

The method proposed in this work is grounded and evaluated in an industrial case study, and the application and evaluation is expanded to further domains. The research in this thesis project started with the formulation of research questions (RQs) derived from the aforementioned problem statements:

- RQ1: What should a method for MDE of IoT-based DTs look like?
- RQ2: What should the technological support look like?
- RQ3: Which organizational aspects need to be considered while and after the development of DTs?

2 Related Work

Plenty of existing work focuses on MDE of IoT applications. FRASAD [26] is a framework for model-driven software development to manage the complexity of IoT applications. In [4], a framework to support the modeling of things and the self-adaptation of emergent configurations in the IoT is presented. Sosa-Reyna et al. [30] present a methodology with different levels of abstraction, and a set of MDE methods for transforming models using formal rules is proposed. Hussein et al. [10] adopted SysML4IoT (an extension of SysML) to specify system functions and adaptations. They also adopted a publish/subscribe paradigm to model environment information and its relationship with the system.

Kirchhof et al. [14] suggest a model-driven approach combining MontiArc models and UML/P (a specialized UML language profile) class diagrams to address the need for methods to build DTs of cyber-physical systems. In a practical IoT application, it is shown that this can eliminate repetitive programming activities and promote the systematic engineering of DTs. In [5], an integrated method for MDE of low-code development platforms for DTs is introduced. It enables domain experts to create and operate customized DTs for cyber-physical systems for a variety of applications using the most appropriate modeling languages. A model-driven framework to automatically derive specific DT models from existing AutomationML files created during the development of a system is presented by Lehner et al. [17]. In their case study, this reduced the time and effort required by experts to set up the necessary infrastructure by about 50%.

The focus of the aforementioned works is to systematize, simplify, and thus accelerate the development of IoT applications and DTs. A validated method that integrates both technological and organizational aspects throughout all phases of and after the development process, which is tailored for SMEs, has not yet been identified.

3 Research Method

The overall research strategy follows the ideas and principles of design science research (DSR) [9], which aim to develop practical solutions by humans that professionals can use in their respective fields [13]. To fulfill the requirements of DSR, a viable artifact must be produced in the form of a construct, a model, a method, or an instantiation [9,13,19]. The artifact of the research presented here can be regarded as a method [19]. Our development procedure is oriented towards Peffers et al. [28]. The goal of the method (artifact) development can be described following the *design problem* template proposed by Wieringa [33]:

> ***Improve*** *the development of IoT-based DTs*
> ***by*** *engineering a method and tool support*
> ***that*** *are applicable by users in SMEs,*
> ***in order to*** *accelerate development processes, while considering both technological and organizational integration.*

A combination of literature study, descriptive case study, and argumentative-deductive work was applied to address the RQs defined in Sect. 1. Since our previous work [21,23] indicated that the specifics of SMEs were not sufficiently represented in existing work and not well understood, we decided to perform a case study to gather information pertinent to the subject area. A qualitative case study is a research approach that facilitates the exploration of a phenomenon within its context using various data sources [2]. This ensures that the subject under consideration is not explored from only one perspective but rather from various perspectives, allowing for multiple facets of the phenomenon to be revealed and understood. Within the case study, we used three different perspectives, which at the same time represent sources of data: we observed the activities during IoT development, examined the enterprise's business model, and interviewed people involved in different roles. The case study in which the initial version of the described method was developed [11,20,25] has to be considered descriptive, as it describes the phenomenon of process outsourcing and the real-life context in which it occurs [34].

Several iterations of the DSR process [28] have been conducted for the case study in the heating, ventilation, and air conditioning (HVAC) domain [11,20,25]. The objective was to enhance the efficiency of existing HVAC facilities by equipping them with a measurement case containing a minimal set of sensors. This would facilitate the analysis of data, enabling the optimization of energy consumption. Evaluation is a central and critical aspect of DSR [9,19] and is primarily concerned with assessing the outcomes (e.g., artifacts [19]). Therefore, the method and tool support were evaluated in terms of quality, usefulness, effectiveness [22,24], and digital innovation readiness aspects for SMEs [23], resulting in various improvements and confirming the expected contributions in this domain.

4 Preliminary Results

To reach the goal defined in Sect. 3, the thesis is expected to make the following contributions: **Contribution 1 (C1)** is to provide a method for developing IoT-based DTs with defined steps and guidelines on how to apply it. **Contribution 2 (C2)** is a tool to support the development process without needing specialized IT knowledge at the application level. **Contribution 3 (C3)** concerns the consideration of organizational aspects in and following the development process. To this end, we provide an overview of the expected changes resulting from the introduction, as well as implementation guidelines.

Figure 1 shows the proposed approach for MDE of DTs. The method is structured in accordance with the method conceptualization by Goldkuhl et al. [8]. They define a method as a set of interchangeable and reusable *method components* that address specific subproblems of the overall problem. Based on identified related work (e.g., [10,30]) and experiences from our first case study [11,20], it is divided into three phases representing different stages of the development process. The upper part of Fig. 1 shows the six components and a general execution flow (**C1**). Each phase creates outputs that are utilized in the subsequent phase. The whole method is triggered by identified problems or optimization potential in the physical world and aims to improve it.

Phase A: Preparation addresses the scope of the specific application, derives requirements, and prepares the tool support. The *1. Scoping* component is

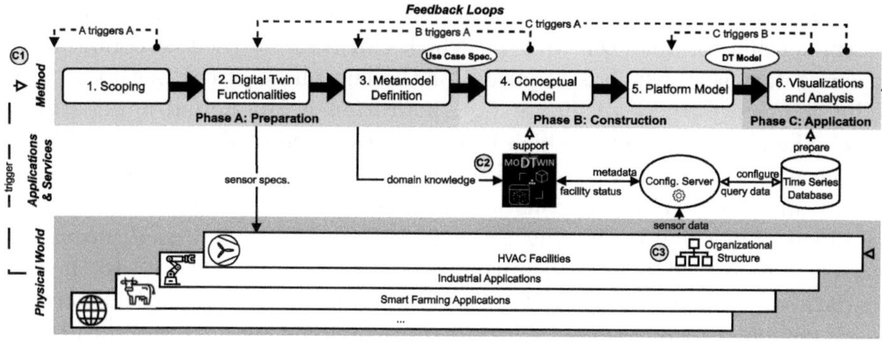

Fig. 1. Approach for model-driven engineering of digital twins.

responsible for determining the scope of the application. In order to gain a comprehensive understanding of the problem, a detailed analysis must be conducted. This analysis should identify the causes of the problem and define the problem domain, stakeholders, and individuals responsible for developing the application. It must be clarified which knowledge and resources are necessary. Once these elements have been established, the overall goals of the application can be defined. The objective of *2. Digital Twin Functionalities* is to identify the specific functionalities of the DT based on this. It must be clarified what's realistic to be implemented in the given situation, regarding the context and the enterprise. The available and required sensors or further data sources for the application can now be derived. In *3. Metamodel Definition*, domain experts can create the metamodel with the corresponding DSML and prepare the metadata collection using the *Modeling Digital Twins (MODTWIN)*[1] tool, which is based on the ADOxx metamodeling platform[2]. Based on the ADOxx metamodel, we defined the MODTWIN metamodel for IoT-based DTs. This allows for the simple creation of domain-specific metamodels using domain knowledge, and by adding graphical representations, the DSML can be created to generate conceptual models. The output of this phase is the defined *Use Case Specification.*

The objective of *Phase B: Construction* is to develop the DT. The MODTWIN tool used by the domain expert supports both components (**C2**). Component *4. Conceptual Model* aims to create a conceptual model of a facility using the implemented DSML with the domain-specific metamodel. In addition, the data required from the facilities (metadata) was determined in *Phase A* to implement the application. The retrieval of the metadata represents a significant portion of the development of the conceptual model of a facility (components and required sensors are created automatically for each facility type). The model can then be adjusted and converted into the platform model. For this, as well as further data exports, several functionalities are implemented to support the modeling process (e.g., checks for completeness or errors in the data). Component *5. Plat-*

[1] https://www.omilab.org/activities/projects/details/?id=510.
[2] https://www.adoxx.org/.

form Model is responsible for using the entered metadata to convert it into a platform-specific format (*DT Model*), which can then be used to configure the time series database, which is required for the last phase of the method.

The primary purpose of *Phase C: Application* is the actual application of the DT. The platform model, which is automatically created with the tool, combines the metadata with the requisite information to configure the time series database and create visualizations and analyses that are intended to optimize the problems identified in the physical world (Component *6. Visualizations and Analysis*). The metadata is transmitted as a JSON file via HTTPS to the time series database (currently InfluxDB). An API token is then automatically created for each customer or enterprise, and the corresponding buckets and dashboards are created based on the metadata. In addition, in this phase, it is necessary to assess whether the objectives of the use case are met by the DT, which must be maintained in a current state.

The method contains feedback loops that may occur during execution. They are important if the execution of a component generates knowledge that leads to the need to execute a previous component again. These are typical loops we identified while developing this method and applying it in the case studies. They are not intended to prevent users from executing other loops that may occur when the method is executed. Those feedback loops are, for example: *2. Digital Twin Functionalities* triggers *1. Scoping*: When it's realized that specific functionalities can't be realized (e.g., sensors can't be utilized or data sources are not available), the scope must be adjusted. *4. Conceptual Model* triggers *1. Scoping:* The defined scope is subsequently found to be incomplete or incorrect. *6. Visualizations and Analysis* triggers *4. Conceptual Model:* It may be realized that the objects created or metadata entered contain errors that need to be adjusted in the conceptual model.

5 Plan for Evaluation

The development of our approach was initially based on findings of literature searches and the case study in the HVAC domain, in which the complete approach was evaluated. In addition to **C1** and **C2**, we also looked at changes in the enterprise architecture and multi-perspective enterprise models in order to derive the effects of introducing IoT-based DTs and support the alignment with the business strategy (**C3**). Some method components generate outputs relevant to organizational considerations. This can be *goals* defined in *1. Scoping* (to derive requirements and use them as the interface to the organizational process of change), *technical components* created in the *Construction* phase, or *roles* that can be input for existing multi-perspective methods (e.g., 4EM).

It is planned to provide a slice of a high-level enterprise architecture and guidelines for integration into the existing one. The focus here is on the integration of the DT application, the required metadata, the necessary knowledge, and the technologies (modeling tool, config. server, and time series database). This enables the consideration of both the uncertainties of the organization and those of the DT. The method description is planned to be extended by adding the aspects requiring organizational consideration (e.g., goals, roles, or technical components).

In two further case studies (digital medical record for cows, and cranes and hoists in intralogistics), we were able to further evaluate our approach. This confirmed that our method (**C1**) and tool support (**C2**) are applicable in these domains. The evaluation of **C3** in these case studies will be the subject of the next research work to complete the answers to the RQs. This will be done by expert interviews and experiments. Before this, aspects such as the co-operation forms and parts of the method components (see Goldkuhl et al. [8]) must be further defined based on the experience gained so far.

Acknowledgements. This research work is supervised by Prof. Kurt Sandkuhl.

Disclosure of Interests. The author has no competing interests to declare that are relevant to the content of this article.

References

1. Attaran, M., Celik, B.G.: Digital twin: benefits, use cases, challenges, and opportunities. Decision Anal. J. **6**, 100165 (2023)
2. Baxter, P., Jack, S.: Qualitative case study methodology: study design and implementation for novice researchers. Qual. Report **13**(4), 544–559 (2008)
3. Brambilla, M., Cabot, J., Wimmer, M.: Model-driven software engineering in practice. Morgan & Claypool Publishers (2017)
4. Ciccozzi, F., Spalazzese, R.: MDE4IoT: supporting the internet of things with model-driven engineering. In: Intelligent Distributed Computing X, pp. 67–76. Springer International Publishing, Cham (2016)
5. Dalibor, et al.: Generating customized low-code development platforms for digital twins. J. Comput. Lang. **70**, 101117 (2022)
6. Fortino, G., Savaglio, C., Spezzano, G., Zhou, M.: Internet of Things as system of systems: a review of methodologies, frameworks, platforms, and tools. IEEE Trans. Syst. Man, Cybern.: Syst. **51**(1), 223–236 (2020)
7. Frank, U.: Domain-Specific Modeling Languages: Requirements Analysis and Design Guidelines, pp. 133–157. Springer (2013)
8. Goldkuhl, G., Lind, M., Seigerroth, U.: Method integration: the need for a learning perspective. IEE Proc.-Softw. **145**(4), 113–118 (1998)
9. Hevner, A.R., March, S.T., Park, J., Ram, S.: Design science in information systems research. MIS Q. **28**(1), 75–105 (2004)
10. Hussein, M., Li, S., Radermacher, A.: Model-driven development of adaptive IoT systems. In: MODELS (Satellite Events), pp. 17–23 (2017)
11. Ivanovic, N., Nast, B., Reiz, A., Sandkuhl, K.: Technologies for a diagnostic technique for HVAC systems using IoT and cloud-based architecture. In: 2023 International Interdisciplinary PhD Workshop (IIPhDW), pp. 1–6 (2023)
12. Javaid, M., Haleem, A., Suman, R.: Digital twin applications toward industry 4.0: a review. Cogn. Robot. **3**, 71–92 (2023)
13. Johannesson, P., Perjons, E.: An Introduction to Design Science. Springer, Cham (2021). https://doi.org/10.1007/978-3-030-78132-3_9

14. Kirchhof et al.: Model-driven digital twin construction: Synthesizing the integration of cyber-physical systems with their information systems. In: International Conference on Model Driven Engineering Languages and Systems, pp. 90–101 (2020)
15. Kritzinger, et al.: Digital twin in manufacturing: a categorical literature review and classification. Ifac-PapersOnline **51**(11), 1016–1022 (2018)
16. Lehner, D., Zhang, J., Pfeiffer, J., Sint, S., Splettstößer, A.K., Wimmer, M., Wortmann, A.: Model-driven engineering for digital twins: a systematic mapping study. Softw. Syst. Model. 1–39 (2025)
17. Lehner et al.: AML4DT: a model-driven framework for developing and maintaining digital twins with automationml. In: 26th IEEE International Conference on Emerging Technologies and Factory Automation (ETFA), pp. 1–8 (2021)
18. Liu, M., Fang, S., Dong, H., Xu, C.: Review of digital twin about concepts, technologies, and industrial applications. J. Manuf. Syst. **58**, 346–361 (2021)
19. March, S.T., Smith, G.F.: Design and natural science research on information technology. Decis. Support Syst. **15**(4), 251–266 (1995)
20. Nast, B., Reiz, A., Ivanovic, N., Sandkuhl, K.: A modeling approach supporting digital twin engineering: Optimizing the energy consumption of air conditioning facilities. In: 2023 ACM/IEEE International Conference on Model Driven Engineering Languages and Systems Companion (MODELS-C), pp. 479–483 (2023)
21. Nast, B., Sandkuhl, K.: Meta-model and tool support for the organizational aspects of Internet-of-Things development methods: organizational aspects of IoT development methods. In: 3rd International Conference on Advanced Information Science and System. AISS '21, ACM, New York, NY, USA (2021)
22. Nast, B., Sandkuhl, K.: Evaluation of the intuitiveness of MIoTA. In: BIR 2024 Workshops and Doctoral Consortium, 23rd International Conference on Perspectives in Business Informatics Research (BIR 2024), vol. 3804, pp. 225–237 (2024)
23. Nast, B., Sandkuhl, K.: A method for model-driven IoT application development. In: Evaluation of Novel Approaches to Software Engineering, pp. 141–164. Springer Nature Switzerland, Cham (2024)
24. Nast, B., Sandkuhl, K.: Quality evaluation of a DSML supporting model-driven IoT development for air conditioning facilities. In: Advances in Enterprise Engineering XVII, pp. 52–72. Springer, Cham (2024)
25. Nast, B., Sandkuhl, K., Paulus, S., Schiller, H.: MIoTA: modeling IoT applications for air conditioning facilities with ADOxx. In: 22nd International Conference on Perspectives in Business Informatics Research Workshops and Doctoral Consortium, BIR-WS 2023, vol. 3514, pp. 158–168. CEUR (2023)
26. Nguyen, X.T., Tran, H.T., Baraki, H., Geihs, K.: FRASAD: A framework for model-driven IoT application development. In: 2nd World Forum on Internet of Things (WF-IoT), pp. 387–392. IEEE (2015)
27. Ogunsakin, R., Mehandjiev, N., Marin, C.A.: Towards adaptive digital twins architecture. Comput. Ind. **149**, 103920 (2023)
28. Peffers, et al.: A design science research methodology for information systems research. J. Manag. Inf. Syst. **24**(3), 45–77 (2007)
29. Sandkuhl, K., Seigerroth, U.: Digital transformation of enterprises: case studies and transformation paths. In: PACIS, p. 35 (2021)
30. Sosa-Reyna, C.M., Tello-Leal, E., Lara-Alabazares, D.: Methodology for the model-driven development of service oriented IoT applications. J. Syst. Architect. **90**, 15–22 (2018)
31. Tao, F., Zhang, M.: Digital twin shop-floor: a new shop-floor paradigm towards smart manufacturing. IEEE Access **5**, 20418–20427 (2017)

32. Bossuyt, V., et al.: The future of digital twin research and development. J. Comput. Inf. Sci. Eng. **25**(8), 080801 (2025)
33. Design Science Methodology for Information Systems and Software Engineering. Springer, Heidelberg (2014). https://doi.org/10.1007/978-3-662-43839-8_20
34. Yin, R.K.: Case Study Research: Design and Methods, vol. 5. Sage (2009)

Adapting Conventional Business Process Management to Digital Process Innovation: A Comparative Study of China and Western Europe

Han Bingbing(✉)

Department of Business Informatics and Operations Management, Faculty of Economics and Business Administration, Ghent University, Tweekerkenstraat 2, 9000 Ghent, Belgium
Bingbing.Han@UGent.be

Abstract. The PhD research investigates how conventional Business Process Management (BPM) adapts to Digital Process Innovation (DPI) through a three-staged, mixed-method research design. Project 1 conducts a systematic literature review (SLR) to identify key challenges linked to BPM capabilities and organizational tensions in DPI contexts. It proposes a dual-path adaptation framework based on capability reconfiguration and tension resolution mechanisms. Project 2 builds on these insights by employing a multiple-case study design for comparing Chinese and Western European organizations. It investigates how organizations reconfigure their BPM capabilities and manage tensions to innovate their business processes, for uncovering distinct adaptation trajectories shaped by regional institutional logics. Project 3 adopts a quantitative approach using structural equation modeling (SEM) to statistically validate the proposed "tension–capability–adaptation" model. This study contributes to the theoretical understanding of dynamic BPM adaptation by integrating capability theory and paradox theory, while offering practical insights for organizations navigating DPI. By comparing institutional contexts, it focuses on how digital maturity, cultural norms, and governance structures can help shape BPM adaptation strategies in different regions.

Keywords: Business Process Management · Digital Technologies · Capability Reconfiguration · Organizational Tensions

1 Introduction

Digital technologies (DTs), ranging from established SMAC (social, mobile, analytics and cloud) [1] to emerging DARQ (distributed ledger, artificial intelligence, extended reality and quantum computing) [2], constitute the main forces driving comprehensive changes in management [3]. In response, organizations increasingly embed these technologies into their operations, giving rise to digital process innovation (DPI) [4]. DPI refers to new ways of conducting organizational activities enabled by or embodied in information technology [5]. By combining core technologies with organizational and

J. Barateiro et al. (Eds.): EDOC 2025 Workshops, LNBIP 571, pp. 216–223, 2026.
https://doi.org/10.1007/978-3-032-16234-2_16

technical elements, DPI not only enhances efficiency and flexibility but also lays the foundation for digital product and business model innovations [6]. Accordingly, DPI is widely regarded as a key driver of digital innovation [7] and a critical antecedent to digital transformation [8]. Amid the ongoing DPI wave, conventional Business Process Management (BPM) emphasizes modeling, executing, and optimizing business processes by emphasizing standardization, stability, and continuous improvement [9], but this control-oriented approach limits adaptability and innovation [10]. Therefore, organizations need to reconfigure their BPM capabilities, which are defined as the skills and resources for supporting process modeling, execution, optimization, management, as well as for cultural alignment, and structural redesign [11]. Prior research on BPM capabilities has mainly relied on maturity models (MMs) to identify capability areas or classify challenges that reveal limitations in existing practices [12]. To address these limitations, organizations draw on successful factors that act as enablers to strengthen or reconfigure BPM capabilities [13]. While useful, these categorizations remain descriptive and provide limited insight into how organizations dynamically reconfigure BPM capabilities during DPI, leaving BPM's adaptive trajectories insufficiently explored. Beyond capability challenges, DPI also intensifies paradoxical demands, conceptualized as tensions. Paradox theory suggests that organizations are inherently embedded in enduring yet contradictory interdependent demands [14]. Such tensions cannot be eliminated but require acceptance and dynamic responses [14]. Within the DPI context, organizations need to exploit existing technologies (i.e., exploitative BPM) while simultaneously exploring new digital opportunities (i.e., explorative BPM) [10]. This duality epitomizes the exploration–exploitation tension, often regarded as a manifestation of ambidextrous tensions [15]. Prior studies on BPM-related tensions have highlighted issues such as balancing analytical complexity with lifecycle agility or managing process model complexity while maintaining cost efficiency [1]. Coping approaches, including structural and contextual ambidexterity, offer mechanisms to separate or integrate explorative and exploitative activities [15]. However, this stream of work also remains descriptive, without uncovering how organizations dynamically navigate ambidextrous tensions during DPI. Existing BPM–DPI research has mainly examined single-country settings or comparisons in relatively homogeneous environments [12, 13], often treating capabilities and tensions separately. Capability studies span diverse contexts [10], while research on organizational tensions is concentrated in the United States and Western Europe, with limited evidence from Asia where China has only recently contributed [15]. To capture greater institutional heterogeneity, this PhD project compares Western Europe and China. Western Europe offers mature cases, whereas China presents a contrasting environment shaped by rapid policy-driven digitalization and distinctive practices. This comparison highlights divergent institutional logics-centralized, state-driven digitalization in China versus market-driven, regulation-intensive, and culturally diverse environments in Western Europe. Taken together, three gaps emerge: (1) BPM adaptation has been addressed mainly at the level of descriptive identification, not dynamic trajectories; (2) capabilities and tensions have been studied separately, lacking integration; and (3) cross-regional comparisons are scarce, particularly between China and Western Europe, limiting theorization of the institutional influence on BPM adaptation.

Accordingly, the research question is formulated as follows: "What conceptual and empirical framework can capture how organizations reconfigure BPM capabilities and resolve ambidexterity tensions in the context of Digital Process Innovation, and how are these adaptation trajectories shaped by contrasting institutional settings in China and Western Europe?" Theoretically, this study develops an integrative framework that reveals the dual-path evolution of BPM adaptation trajectories. Practically, it offers insights for firms in diverse institutional environments, guiding them in reconfiguring BPM capabilities and managing ambidextrous tensions to achieve successful DPI."

2 Research Design

This PhD research adopts the behavioral-science paradigm [16] and is designed as a coherent study unfolding across three sequential phases. Each phase builds on the outputs of the previous one, moving from theory building to empirical refinement and, finally, to statistical validation. (Table 1).

Table 1. PhD Research Roadmap.

Aspect	Phase 1	Phase 2	Phase 3
Steps	Identify BPM capabilities, challenges, success factors, and tensions in DPI	Trace adaptation trajectories and regional differences (China vs. Western Europe)	Validate dual-path framework and test institutional moderators
Method	Systematic Literature Review	Multiple Case Study	Structural Equation Modeling
Outcome	Dual-path framework (capability-driven vs. tension-driven)	Region-specific trajectories and propositions; adaptation across institutional contexts	Validated model; key mechanisms; cross-regional insights
Contributions	Link BPM capabilities and tensions in DPI	Reveal adaptation in distinct institutional settings (China vs. Western Europe)	Confirm validity, define key constructs, and provide actionable insights

2.1 Phase 1 (in Progress): A Structured Literature Review of BPM Capabilities and Tensions in DPI

This first Phase aims to categorize how conventional Business Process Management (BPM) has been applied in DPI projects, as reported in the body of knowledge. It seeks to identify the explorative variants of conventional (or exploitative) BPM capabilities, and the key organizational tensions faced when trying to combine exploitative with explorative BPM. This investigation is structured around four research questions:

- RQ1.1: How has research on DPI evolved over time, and why?
- RQ1.2: What BPM capabilities (as challenges or success factors) have been identified in the current literature in the context of DPI?
- RQ1.3: What tensions do organizations typically face during DPI projects, according to the literature?
- RQ1.4: How does China and Western Europe research differ in their approaches to DPI?

A Systematic Literature Review (SLR) addresses these questions [17]. Using the keywords "process innovation" AND ("case stud*" OR "field stud*"), an initial dataset of 803 articles is retrieved from Scopus, Web of Science, AIS eLibrary, and IEEE Xplore. After rigorous screening and following textual coding procedures, 60 relevant articles are selected for an in-depth analysis. This project adopts a dual-theoretical framework. First, we rely on a validated BPM Capability Framework [11]. This framework classifies the identified challenges and success factors into six main BPM capability areas (i.e., process modeling, deployment, optimization, management, culture, and structure) and seventeen sub-capabilities. Secondly, we rely on established Paradox Theory [14], which facilitates the analysis of contradictory, yet interdependent tensions faced by organizations during DPI. Accordingly, tensions are categorized into four types (i.e., performing, organizing, belonging, and learning). The expected outcomes for project 1 are: (1) a synthesized overview of BPM research trends within the context of DPI, (2) a conceptual framework that integrates challenges and success factors into a structured BPM capability configuration in capability framework, (3) an initial typology of tensions and resolutions (or coping mechanisms) grounded in paradox theory, and (4) a preliminary cross-regional DPI comparison in Chinese and West-European organizations, laying the foundation for empirical examination in the next projects.

2.2 Phase 2: A Multiple Case Study of BPM Adaptation Trajectories in Digital Process Innovation: Empirical Evidence from China and Western Europe

Building on the theoretical insights developed in Phase 1, this Phase will transition from a conceptual analysis to an empirical investigation. It will explore adaptation mechanisms focusing on two complementary trajectories: (1) reconfiguring capabilities to address DPI-related challenges, e.g., a Chinese manufacturer addressing fragmented process data by reconfiguring modeling and monitoring capabilities, resulting in greater agility; and (2) coping tensions arising from ambidextrous tensions, e.g., a European bank resolving the tension between regulatory control and innovation through structural ambidexterity, enabling compliance and digital service innovation.

The study will compare 5 Chinese and 5 Western European organizations to uncover a shared trajectory along regional differences. The investigation is structured around the following research questions:

- RQ2.1: What capability reconfigurations explain organizational responses to DPI-related challenges?
- RQ2.2: What mechanisms explain how organizations resolve ambidextrous tensions during DPI?

- RQ2.3: What similarities and differences exist between Chinese and Western European organizations in terms of BPM capability configurations and tension resolution mechanisms?

This study will adopt a multiple case study design [18]. The conceptual framework will integrate the BPM Capability Framework and Paradox Theory as the core lenses to guide data interpretation [11, 14]. To understand cross-regional differences, it will also draw on institutional theory to examine institutional influences (e.g., legal frameworks, cultural norms, government involvement) that shape adaptation outcomes [19]. Cases will be selected using theoretical sampling to ensure maximum variation in digital maturity, organization size and industry. This approach will enable theoretical replication and to reveal boundary conditions across institutional environments. Data will be collected through semi-structured interviews using an iteratively refined protocol. Each case includes respondents from BPM, IT, and innovation departments, including at least one senior executive. Additional data (e.g., publicly available documents, internal reports) are used where available to support data triangulation. The data analysis will follow a two-stage strategy. Within-case analysis first identifies key elements, including challenges, capability configurations, tensions, and tension-resolution mechanisms, thereby complementing and validating the findings of Project 1 and further exploring the adaptation outcomes (e.g., process agility, efficiency, innovation enablement), which will then be synthesized into two adaptation trajectories per case:

Trajectory 1: Challenge → Capability Configuration → Adaptation Outcome;

Trajectory 2: Tension → Tension Resolution Mechanism → Adaptation Outcome.

Cross-case comparisons will then explore commonalities and differences across cases in terms of challenges, tensions, capability responses, and adaptation outcomes.

Particular attention will be given to region-specific trajectories, focusing on institutional factors. The analysis will examine how institutional environments (e.g., regulation, policy, culture) influence organizations' strategic responses of capabilities and tension resolution.

The expected outcomes are: (1) an empirically refinement of the "capability-tension" framework proposed in Phase 1; (2) the identification of shared and region-specific BPM adaptation trajectories and theoretically grounded propositions specifying which BPM capabilities and tension-resolution mechanisms are most critical under DPI, thereby preparing hypotheses for Phase 3.

2.3 Phase 3: A Survey-Based Study of the Tension–Capability Trajectories in BPM Adaptation: Empirical Evidence from China and Western Europe

Building on the conceptual framework developed in Phase 1 and the empirical findings from Phase 2, Phase 3 will directly translate the constructs and mechanisms identified earlier into measurable survey items for quantitative validation. This phase will adopt a quantitative approach using Structural Equation Modeling (SEM) to validate how organizations adapt their Business Process Management (BPM) practices in the context of Digital Process Innovation (DPI). This phase will empirically validate the dual-path adaptation framework proposed earlier, which comprises two parallel trajectories:

- Trajectory 1: Challenge → Capability Configuration → Adaptation Outcome;

- Trajectory 2: Tension → Tension Resolution Mechanism → Adaptation Outcome.

In addition, the third project incorporates institutional theory to examine how macro-level national differences (e.g., legal systems, cultural norms, and government support) affect BPM adaptation and draws on organizational behavior theory to capture micro-level dynamics (e.g., employee motivation, resistance, and participation) that affects how capability configurations and tension mechanisms are enacted. These two adaptation paths are non-sequential and context dependent. Not all organizations necessarily experience tensions. Some may follow a capability-driven trajectory in response to DPI-related challenges. Others (when facing intensified contradictions between exploration and exploitation) may activate additional tension-resolution mechanisms. Purposive sampling will be used to obtain at least 150 valid responses per region (China and Western Europe), targeting mid-to-senior-level managers in BPM, IT, and digital innovation roles from organizations engaged in DPI initiatives. A pilot study will be conducted prior to a large-scale data collection to refine the questionnaire and mitigate non-response risk. The method will rely on an international survey to be analyzed using Structural Equation Modeling (SEM) [20]. The survey instrument will be explicitly grounded in Phases 1 and 2, ensuring that each item reflects either a capability configuration, a tension-resolution mechanism, or an institutional moderator identified earlier. The expected outcomes are: (1) a validated dual-path BPM adaptation framework; (2) identification of the most critical capability configurations and tension-resolution mechanisms supporting adaptation; and (3) a synthesis of cross-regional differences in adaptation logic, highlighting how institutional contexts shape BPM adaptation trajectories.

2.4 Intermediate Results

This PhD research is currently conducting the first project, focusing on the text coding analysis based on a Systematic Literature Review (SLR) protocol. The literature filtering and initial coding have been completed. Preliminary findings suggest notable regional differences in how organizations adapt their business processes in the context of DPI. In terms of capability development, the reported European organizations tend to emphasize not only technological innovation but also the coordinated evolution of management duties and organizational culture. In contrast, the reported Chinese organizations are primarily driven by efficiency goals and focus more on technology-centered innovation efforts. Regarding organizational tensions, European academic studies identify multiple tension types but provide limited concrete coping strategies. On the other hand, Chinese research tends to overlook the issue of organizational tensions, even though tensions may be encountered in real-world DPI implementation.

3 Conclusion and Future Steps

This PhD project investigates how organizations adapt conventional Business Process Management (BPM) practices to Digital Process Innovation (DPI), focusing on capability reconfiguration and tension management. The research is carried out in three stages, each as a sub-project. In the first year, project 1 conducts a systematic literature review to identify key capabilities and organizational tensions, leading to the development of a dual-trajectory adaptation framework. In the second year, project 2 uses multiple case studies to explore how organizations in China and Western Europe respond to DPI through an adaptation trajectory by: (1) reconfiguring their conventional BPM capabilities to address DPI challenges, and (2) managing related tensions through various resolution mechanisms. This project also highlights regional differences. In the third year, project 3 uses Structural Equation Modeling (SEM) to test and validate the two adaptation paths through a large-scale survey and examines how institutional factors influence their effectiveness. Future research can further refine the adaptation trajectory model, verify key relationships, and offer practical maturation guidance for organizations implementing BPM in the context of DPI, particularly across China and Western Europe. This project contributes to the BPM and digital innovation literature by bridging a static capability analysis with more dynamic tension resolution.

Acknowledgments. This PhD project is carried out under the supervision of Prof. Dr. Amy Van Looy at Ghent University. I gratefully acknowledge the financial support provided by the China Scholarship Council (CSC), which has been essential in enabling this research. I would also like to thank my family for their unwavering support throughout this journey.

Disclosure of Interests. The authors have no competing interests to declare that they are relevant to the content of this article.

References

1. Beverungen, D., et al.: Seven paradoxes of business process management in a hyper-connected world. Bus. Inf. Syst. Eng. **63**, 145–156 (2021). https://doi.org/10.1007/s12599-020-00646-z
2. Sehdev, V., Verma, A.: DARQ – distributed ledger technology, artificial intelligence, extended reality and quantum computing. In: ENCADEMS 2020 Conference Proceedings, Int. J. Eng. Res. Technol. (IJERT), vol. 8, issue 10, Special Issue, pp. 63–66. IJERT, Delhi (2020)
3. Nowicka, K.: Digital innovation in the supply chain management. Prace Nauk. Uniwersytetu Ekonomicznego we Wrocławiu **63**, 202–214 (2019). https://doi.org/10.15611/pn.2019.8.16
4. Duygan, M., Fischer, M., Ingold, K.: Assessing the readiness of municipalities for digital process innovation. Technol. Soc. **72**, 102179 (2023). https://doi.org/10.1016/j.techsoc.2022.102179
5. Makkonen, H., Komulainen, H.: Explicating the market dimension in the study of digital innovation: a management framework for digital innovation. Technol. Anal. Strateg. Manag. **30**, 1015–1028 (2018). https://doi.org/10.1080/09537325.2018.1433823
6. Fichman, R.G., Dos Santos, B.L., Zheng, Z.E.: Digital innovation as a fundamental and powerful concept in the information systems curriculum. MIS Q. **38**, 329–354 (2014). https://doi.org/10.25300/MISQ/2014/38.2.01
7. Yoo, Y., Henfridsson, O., Lyytinen, K.: Research commentary — the new organizing logic of digital innovation: an agenda for information systems research. Inf. Syst. Res. **21**, 724–735 (2010). https://doi.org/10.1287/isre.1100.0322
8. vom Brocke, J., Mendling, J. (eds.): Business Process Management Cases. Springer, Cham (2018). https://doi.org/10.1007/978-3-319-58307-5
9. Dumas, M., La Rosa, M., Mendling, J., Reijers, H.A.: Fundamentals of Business Process Management. Springer, Berlin (2018). https://doi.org/10.1007/978-3-662-56509-4
10. Ahmad, T., Van Looy, A.: Business process management and digital innovations: a systematic literature review. Sustainability **12**, 6827 (2020). https://doi.org/10.3390/su12176827

11. Van Looy, A., De Backer, M., Poels, G.: A conceptual framework and classification of capability areas for business process maturity. Enterp. Inf. Syst. **8**, 188–224 (2014). https://doi.org/10.1080/17517575.2012.688222
12. Szelągowski, M., Berniak-Woźny, J.: BPM challenges, limitations and future development directions – a systematic literature review. Bus. Process. Manag. J. **30**, 505–557 (2024). https://doi.org/10.1108/BPMJ-06-2023-0419
13. Putra, H., Er, M.: The role of business process management in digital innovation and digital transformation: a systematic literature review. Procedia Comput. Sci. **234**, 829–836 (2024). https://doi.org/10.1016/j.procs.2024.03.069
14. Smith, W.K., Lewis, M.W.: Toward a theory of paradox: a dynamic equilibrium model of organizing. Acad. Manag. Rev. **36**, 381–403 (2011). https://www.jstor.org/stable/41318006
15. Helbin, T., Van Looy, A.: Is business process management (BPM) ready for ambidexterity? Conceptualization, implementation guidelines and research agenda. Sustainability **13**, 1906 (2021). https://doi.org/10.3390/su13041906
16. Recker, J.: Scientific Research in Information Systems. Springer, Berlin (2013). https://doi.org/10.1007/978-3-642-30048-6
17. Boell, S.K., Cecez-Kecmanovic, D.: On being 'systematic' in literature reviews in IS. J. Inf. Technol. **30**, 161–173 (2015). https://doi.org/10.1057/jit.2014.26
18. Eisenhardt, K.M.: Building theories from case study research. Acad. Manag. Rev. **14**, 532–550 (1989). https://doi.org/10.5465/amr.1989.4308385
19. Armenakis, A.A., Bedeian, A.G.: Organizational change: a review of theory and research in the 1990s. J. Manag. **25**, 293–315 (1999). https://doi.org/10.1177/014920639902500303
20. Hair, J.F., Hult, G.T.M., Ringle, C.M., Sarstedt, M., Danks, N.P., Ray, S.: Partial least squares structural equation modeling (PLS-SEM) using R: a workbook. Springer, Cham (2021). https://doi.org/10.1007/978-3-030-80519-7

Industry 5.0 Performance Indicators for Sustainable Business Practices

Vânia Sousa[1,2(✉)]

[1] CCG/ZGDV Institute, University of Minho, Campus de Azurém, 4800-058 Guimarães, Portugal
vania.sousa@ccg.pt
[2] ALGORITMI Research Centre, University of Minho, Campus de Azurém, 4800-058 Guimarães, Portugal

Abstract. Industry 5.0 emphasizes resilience, sustainability, and human-centric approaches in industrial operations. However, a significant gap remains in integrating sustainability-related performance indicators into analytical systems. Many organizations lack essential data on aspects such as energy efficiency, material consumption, and operational costs, limiting their ability to evaluate and improve sustainable practices. This thesis aims to address this gap by proposing a methodological approach that incorporates Industry 5.0 performance indicators into analytical systems to support sustainable business practices. The approach includes the development of a meta-model that extends core analytical system concepts, integrating business, process, and sustainability indicators. Additionally, a taxonomy of relevant Industry 5.0 performance indicators will be created. To overcome data limitations, simulation-based scenarios aligned with sustainability goals will be designed and used to generate synthetic data. This research contributes to advancing data-driven sustainability by enabling better decision-making and aligning industrial analytics with the Sustainable Development Goals (SDGs) through integrated performance measurement.

Keywords: Industry 5.0 · Performance Indicators · Simulation · Sustainable Business Practices

1 Introduction

Industry 5.0 emerges as a complementary concept to Industry 4.0 by strengthening the collaboration between humans and machines, highlighting human-centered, resilient, sustainable approaches in industrial operations [4,21]. These approaches promote more inclusive industrial practices, aligning technological innovation with social and environmental goals. Performance indicators addressing sustainability are crucial to evaluating the environmental, social, and economic impacts, but their integration into analytical structures frequently lacks a systematic approach [7,14]. Moreover, the absence of operational data, such as energy consumption or the carbon footprint of processes, remains a significant

J. Barateiro et al. (Eds.): EDOC 2025 Workshops, LNBIP 571, pp. 224–231, 2026.
https://doi.org/10.1007/978-3-032-16234-2_17

barrier to aligning business practices with sustainable goals [8,9]. In addition, analytical systems often operate with differing focuses. While Business Analytics (BA) emphasizes historical and predictive performance metrics, Process Analytics (PA) tends to assess efficiency and identify optimization opportunities on the process level [1,11]. This fragmentation hinders an integrated analysis combining business, process, and sustainable perspectives, which is important to the transition to more responsible industrial practices.

Despite the proposal of such performance indicators, a strategy for integrating them into analytical systems remains lacking. Moreover, sustainability-related data is usually missing in organizational databases. From the business or process perspective, sustainable practices require data about, for instance, operating costs, material consumption, and energy efficiency, among others, which usually are not available. While some studies address integrating business and process perspectives for holistic performance evaluation [6,17,19,20], adding sustainable indicators alongside these perspectives would empower organizations to manage their operations more efficiently and sustainably.

The primary goal of this work is to advance sustainable business practices by integrating Industry 5.0 performance indicators into analytical systems. By addressing environmental, social, and economic dimensions, it seeks to provide organizations with the tools for making informed decisions, optimizing operations, and fostering efficiency aligned with sustainable and resilient practices. To address the objectives and conduct the research, a Design Science Research Methodology for Information Systems (DSR) by Peffers et al. [15] was adopted.

This work aims to enable organizations to harmonize operational efficiency with sustainable strategies, and boost responsible and resilient management strategies. By offering practical tools and guidelines, this research provides valuable insights for practitioners to incorporate sustainability into daily operations effectively. Furthermore, this work supports global efforts toward achieving the Sustainable Development Goals (SDGs), particularly in innovation, responsible production, and climate action. By integrating operational efficiency with sustainability, it fosters technological advancements that contribute to an industrial future where economic growth and environmental responsibility coexist.

The remainder of this paper is organized as follows. Section 2 discusses the background and research gap. Section 3 presents the research question and objectives. Section 4 addresses the adopted research method. Section 5 shows the expected outcomes and preliminary results. Section 6 summarizes the presented work and outlines the relevance of this work.

2 Background and Research Gap

The different focus between BA and PA challenges organizations that aim to optimize their performance holistically. BA emphasizes the analysis of large volumes of data from various sources, enabling organizations to monitor Key Performance Indicators (KPIs), both historical and predictive, and use a wide range of tools to support informed decisions, identify new opportunities, optimize processes, and support innovation [11]. PA focuses specifically on business process activities, evaluating the efficiency and effectiveness of these activities to understand and improve process performance through methods such as Process Mining [1]. This separation creates a lack of integration between business indicators and their supporting processes, hindering a broader analysis of organizations.

In the literature, there is a divergence between methodologies that emphasize BA and those that focus on PA. There are methodologies that prioritize BA, exploring optimization techniques and Data Warehousing to enhance efficiency and business decision-making [16,18], and others focusing on PA [3,13], with the aim of identifying bottlenecks, redundancies, and opportunities for improvement in the execution of organizational activities.

Notwithstanding, some authors have addressed the challenges of integrating BA and PA perspectives. Santos & Sá [17] suggested that process-oriented models unify process management and business intelligence but lack practical integration of detailed operational data with performance indicators. Similarly, Delgado & Calegari [6] emphasize the importance of inter-organizational collaboration to promote data integration but lack a detailed implementation structure.

To address this gap, Vieira et al. [20] proposed a Data Warehouse model that unifies business performance and process efficiency, enabling a comprehensive analysis that identifies what is happening in organizational processes and how these processes impact the overall organizational performance. In line with this work, Sousa et al. [19] proposed a structured and multidimensional approach to reinforce BA and PA integration, aligning business performance and operational processes for strategic decision support. Enhancing this line of research, Industry 5.0 has been gaining considerable relevance.

Unlike Industry 4.0, Industry 5.0 emphasizes human-machine collaboration, prioritizing human-centric, resilient, and sustainable approaches in industrial practices [4,12,21]. Sustainability indicators are crucial to this approach. Some studies have tackled the integration of sustainability indicators into organizational performance: Glišić et al. [7] highlight the difficulty of aligning sustainability with process and business goals. Medne and Lapina [14] note that existing frameworks fail to integrate these aspects efficiently; Hristov and Chirico [8] point out the difficulty of linking sustainable indicators to strategic objectives. Moreover, data related to sustainable practices, such as operating costs from water or energy consumption and the use of sustainable materials, are often missing from organizational databases [2,9]. This absence of data hinders the implementation of sustainable practices, underscoring the need for a systematic approach to integrate these indicators in analytical systems aligned with Industry 5.0.

This work addresses this gap by proposing a methodological approach combining operational and business data with sustainability indicators. Due to the aforementioned lack of data, this work also needs to include the ability to generate data, including certain scenarios of interest, thereby effectively expanding traditional analytical systems. For example, in an order management process, the delivery error rate (process indicator) can directly impact customer satisfaction (business indicator) since failed deliveries damage the consumer experience. In addition, the carbon footprint of deliveries (sustainability indicator) can be influenced by problems in the shipping process, such as multiple deliveries or inefficient routes, affecting both costs and the organization's environmental goals.

3 Research Question and Objectives

This thesis aims to contribute to sustainable business practices by integrating Industry 5.0 performance indicators into analytical systems, namely Data Warehouses, to evaluate these practices and foster more efficient and sustainable organizations. Given the increasing emphasis on sustainability and the pursuit of more sustainable industrial practices, the following research question arises: "*How can Industry 5.0 performance indicators be integrated into analytical systems to promote sustainable business practices?*" This question guides the development of this study, which focuses on identifying the most relevant performance indicators and how they may be explored through analytical systems to improve sustainable practices. To answer this research question and achieve the aim of this thesis, the following research objectives (RO) were defined:

1. Propose a meta-model that formalizes analytical systems with performance indicators aligned with Industry 5.0.
2. Propose a taxonomy of performance indicators for Industry 5.0, aligning business, process, and sustainable concerns.
3. Propose a methodological approach for the design and development of analytical systems for sustainable business practices in Industry 5.0.
4. Propose scenarios for implementing analytical systems that comply with sustainable business practices, using Discrete Event Simulation (DES) to test different alternatives and explore the impact of several decisions. Simulation, besides supporting what-if analyses for the scenarios, will support data generation, making available data that may be missing for the analysis.
5. Evaluate and discuss the proposed scenarios using synthetic data resulting from simulation.

4 Research Methodology

To address the research objectives and develop a unified approach for integrating sustainability, process, and business indicators, the DSRM by Peffers et al. [15] is used. The DSRM is divided into six distinct phases. Due to its flexibility, the project may start at one of four entry points. Once started, the process flows sequentially (Fig. 1). This method, known for its iterative and structured approach, ensures that solutions are developed and validated systematically.

The method's phases associated with this thesis are as follows:

1. **Identify Problem & Motivation**: Definition of the problem, namely the absence of a unified approach integrating sustainability, business, and process indicators into analytical systems, motivating a new innovative solution. This definition is based on a critical literature analysis and identified gaps, as presented in Sect. 2.

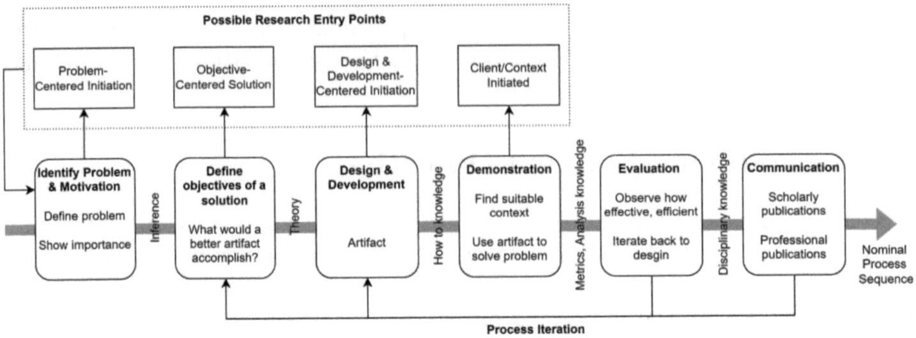

Fig. 1. Design Science Research for Information Systems. Adapted from Peffers et al. [15].

2. **Define Objectives of a Solution**: Characterization of the solution's objectives from the identified problem and the knowledge about what is possible and practicable. At this phase, the objectives of the solution (Sect. 3) are defined. These objectives should specify how the solution is to be built.
3. **Design & Development**: Design and development of the artifacts resulting from research, including the meta-model, taxonomy, and methodological approach, as well as the detailed integration of data from various perspectives into analytical systems.
4. **Demonstration**: Demonstration of the use of the artifacts to solve the problem identified. It will be conducted by proposing scenarios for implementing analytical systems aligned with sustainable business practices, using simulations to test alternatives and examine the effects of different decisions.
5. **Evaluation**: Observation and evaluation of the proposals' effectiveness in solving the identified problem. The evaluation will be carried out using simulation techniques, incorporating the synthetic data generated into analytical systems. This will enable testing of "what-if scenarios" and extend the capabilities of traditional analytical systems, including the integration of sustainability indicators in business and operational contexts.
6. **Communication**: Communicating and presenting the results and contributions of the work to all stakeholders, namely researchers and professionals in the field. This includes the writing and presentation of this thesis, as well as relevant scientific contributions that may arise from this work.

5 Expected Outcomes and Preliminary Results

This proposal addresses the literature gap identified, where a unified view fails to merge business, process, and sustainability perspectives. The expected outcomes are (1) the proposal of a meta-model providing a structure to integrated data analysis, supporting decision-making in organizational contexts aligned with Industry 5.0 principles; (2) the proposal of a taxonomy of performance indicators that will help to categorize and identify relevant indicators, enabling the adjustment of sustainable practices according to organizational needs; (3) a methodological approach, validated through applied scenarios and simulation techniques, to demonstrate its viability and impact.

The main contribution of this research is to enable organizations to align their operational efficiency with sustainable strategies, supporting more conscientious and resilient management. This is achieved via practical contributions to company leaders and information systems professionals, facilitating the implementation of analysis practices incorporating sustainability into daily operations.

By supporting the development of more robust and sustainable practices, this research contributes to the SDGs[1]. In particular, it addresses Goal 9 by promoting technological innovation and sustainable industrialization, thereby strengthening industrial infrastructure. It also supports Goal 12 by focusing on sustainable performance indicators that optimize resource use and reduce waste, aligning with sustainable production practices. Finally, it contributes to Goal 13 by leveraging performance indicators to monitor and reduce greenhouse gas emissions, thus fostering climate resilience in business operations.

To obtain preliminary results of two of the proposed artifacts (outcomes (1) and (3)), a use case for order management available at [10] has been used. This use case was already used in the works of Vieira et al. [20] and Sousa et al. [19], both serving as starting points for the artifacts proposed in this thesis. Vieira et al. [20] propose a Data Warehouse meta-model that unifies business performance and process efficiency but still does not consider the sustainability perspective considered in this proposal (RO1). Sousa et al. [19] propose a structured and multidimensional approach to reinforce BA and PA integration, but does not take into account the absence of sustainability-related data in the traditional analytical systems. In this thesis, this methodological approach is complemented with the use of simulation for both generating missing data and assessing alternative scenarios that implement sustainable business practices (RO3).

Moreover, a systematic literature review is in course to identify relevant performance indicators to include in the taxonomy (RO2). As simulation has been tested to define the scenarios, the what-if analyses, and to generate synthetic data (RO4), an extension of the iStar modeling language [5] is under development to enhance requirements modeling in simulation and to address the lack of a structured approach to define what should be simulated in alternative scenarios.

6 Evaluation and Validation of the Results

The evaluation of the proposed research artifacts will adopt a multi-layered strategy to ensure both scientific rigor and practical relevance. The meta-model will be assessed through a real-case implementation, verifying its ability to represent business, process, and sustainability indicators in an integrated way, considering criteria such as clarity, completeness, and applicability. The taxonomy will be

[1] https://sdgs.un.org/goals.

validated through a systematic literature review and expert assessment, ensuring that it captures the most important Industry 5.0 indicators while remaining usable and extensible. The methodological approach will be tested through what-if scenarios, using synthetic data for missing sustainability indicators. Validity will be ensured by comparing the synthetic data with real-world data, and evaluation criteria will include feasibility, decision utility, robustness, and contribution to sustainability goals.

7 Conclusions

The shift from Industry 4.0 to Industry 5.0 presents challenges, such as the lack of data related to sustainable practices. This PhD thesis explores the integration of sustainability, business, and process indicators into analytical systems to support more efficient business practices and align with Industry 5.0 pillars.

Sustainability indicators are crucial to this approach, and simulation plays a key role in generating synthetic data about performance indicators for Industry 5.0. This work proposes a methodological approach that combines operational and business data with sustainability indicators, generating data for various scenarios of interest. A meta-model formalizing analytical systems with performance indicators aligned with Industry 5.0 is being proposed, along with a taxonomy of these performance indicators. The work proposes scenarios for implementing analytical systems that comply with sustainable business practices, using simulation to test different alternatives and explore the impact of several decisions.

Acknowledgements. This work has been supported by *FCT Fundação para a Ciência e Tecnologia* within the R&D Units Project Scope: UID/00319/Centro ALGORITMI (ALGORITMI/UM).

I would like to express my gratitude to Prof. António Vieira and Prof. Maribel Santos for their invaluable guidance and support throughout this doctoral thesis.

Disclosure of Interests. The author has no competing interests to declare that are relevant to the content of this article.

References

1. van der Aalst, W.M.P.: Process Mining: Data Science in Action, 2nd edn. Springer, Heidelberg (2016)
2. Ahmad, S., Wong, K.Y., Rajoo, S.: Sustainability indicators for manufacturing sectors: a literature survey and maturity analysis from the triple-bottom line perspective. J. Manuf. Technol. Manag. **30**, 312–334 (2019)
3. Akhramovich, K., Serral, E., Cetina, C.: A systematic literature review on the application of process mining to industry 4.0. Knowl. Inf. Syst. **66**, 2699–2746 (2024)
4. Breque, M., Nul, L.D., Petridis, A.: Industry 5.0 – towards a sustainable, human-centric and resilient European industry. Publications Office of the EU (2021)

5. Dalpiaz, F., Franch, X., Horkoff, J.: ISTAR 2.0 language guide. CoRR abs/1605.07767 (2016)
6. Delgado, A., Calegari, D.: Towards a unified vision of business process and organizational data. In: 2020 XLVI Latin American Computing Conference (CLEI), pp. 108–117 (2020)
7. Glišić, M., Veluri, B., Ramanujan, D.: A bottom-up methodology for identifying key performance indicators for sustainability monitoring of unit manufacturing processes. Sustainability **16** (2024)
8. Hristov, I., Chirico, A.: The role of sustainability key performance indicators (KPIS) in implementing sustainable strategies. Sustainability **11** (2019)
9. Joung, C.B., Carrell, J., Sarkar, P., Feng, S.C.: Categorization of indicators for sustainable manufacturing. Ecol. Ind. **24**, 148–157 (2012)
10. Knopp, B., van der Aalst, W.M.: Order management object-centric event log in OCEL 2.0 standard. [Data set] (2023)
11. Krishnamoorthi, S., Mathew, S.K.: Business analytics and business value: a comparative case study. Inf. Manag. **55**, 643–666 (2018)
12. Leng, J., et al.: Industry 5.0: prospect and retrospect. J. Manuf. Syst. **65**, 279–295 (2022)
13. Lorenz, R., Senoner, J., Sihn, W., Netland, T.: Using process mining to improve productivity in make-to-stock manufacturing. Int. J. Prod. Res. **59**, 4869–4880 (2021)
14. Medne, A., Lapina, I.: Sustainability and continuous improvement of organization: review of process-oriented performance indicators. J. Open Innov.: Technol. Mark. Complex. **5**, 1–14 (2019)
15. Peffers, K., Tuunanen, T., Rothenberger, M.A., Chatterjee, S.: A design science research methodology for information systems research. J. Manag. Inf. Syst. **24**(3), 45–77 (2007)
16. Sakib, N., Jamil, S.J., Mukta, S.H.: A novel approach on machine learning based data warehousing for intelligent healthcare services. In: 2022 IEEE Region 10 Symposium (TENSYMP), pp. 1–5 (2022)
17. Santos, M.Y., Sá, J.O.: A data warehouse model for business processes data analytics. In: Computational Science and Its Applications – ICCSA 2016, pp. 241–256. Springer, Cham (2016)
18. Singh, M., Shukla, A.K.: Enhancing business intelligence and decision-making through big data analytics. In: 2023 3rd International Conference on Technological Advancements in Computational Sciences (ICTACS), pp. 319–323 (2023)
19. Sousa, V., Vieira, C., Lavalle, A., Vieira, A., Santos, M.Y.: Integrating business and process analytics for enhanced data-driven decision-making. In: The 43rd International Conference on Conceptual Modeling, vol. 3849, pp. 84–97 (2024)
20. Vieira, C., Sousa, V., Vieira, A., Santos, M.Y.: Convergence of business and their processes: a data analytics approach. In: Information Systems, vol. 536, pp. 94–109. Springer, Cham (2025)
21. Xu, X., Lu, Y., Vogel-Heuser, B., Wang, L.: Industry 4.0 and industry 5.0—inception, conception and perception. J. Manuf. Syst. **61**, 530–535 (2021)

Formal Foundations for Enterprise Ontology: *Ontologically Grounded Enterprise Information Systems*

Edwin de Haan(✉)

Maastricht University, Maastricht, The Netherlands
e.dehaan@maastrichtuniversity.nl

Abstract. Critical misalignments between ontological enterprise models and their implementations persist, causing behavioural inconsistencies and traceability gaps. To address this misalignment issue, the doctoral research presented in this paper develops a formal framework that refines ontological enterprise models into implementations with verifiable adherence to ontological constraints. The framework combines The framework combines (1) an ontological enterprise model, (2) its formally defined enterprise ontology, and (3) Correctness-by-Construction refinement. The framework, grounded in annotated first-order logic, is designed to ensure traceable correctness from an ontological enterprise model to an implementation. The anticipated results of the research are *reduced implementation deficits* and *improved expertise amongst Enterprise Ontology practitioners* through error-free refinements and enabling formal reasoning. Additionally, a formalised ontology is expected to strengthen model-driven development of Enterprise Ontology based information systems.

Keywords: Enterprise Ontology · Correctness-by-Construction · Enterprise Engineering

1 Introduction

Implemented business processes and their information systems, despite having explicit requirements, frequently fail to provide critical functionality [9]. Causes of these failures include incomplete requirements, insufficient collaboration, and insufficient system architecture knowledge [1], resulting in misrepresented operational logic, designer misinterpretations, and flawed code implementation. To address these causes, Enterprise Engineering (EE) employs theory-based methodologies that support adaptive design and evolution of enterprises.

Within EE, Dietz and Mulder [3] state that the ontological enterprise model of Enterprise Ontology (EO) enables rigorous software derivation that correctly supports business processes. However, the axioms of EO [3], while precise, are expressed in natural language rather than in formal machine-verifiable logic,

J. Barateiro et al. (Eds.): EDOC 2025 Workshops, LNBIP 571, pp. 232–240, 2026.
https://doi.org/10.1007/978-3-032-16234-2_18

making them semi-formal. EO's semi-formal axioms obstruct the rigorous use of the Correctness-by-Construction (CbC) principle [14] to ensure that an implementation verifiably adheres to an ontological enterprise model. To bridge this gap, the doctoral research presented in this paper enables refinement verification of ontological enterprise models by developing a formal framework for EO.

The remainder of this paper is organised as follows. Section 2 highlights the background of EO and CbC. Section 3 covers the problem statement, research questions, and related work. In Sect. 4 the research methodology and the expected results are discussed. Finally, Sect. 5 concludes the paper, including next steps of the research.

2 Background

2.1 Enterprise Ontology

In today's complex business environment, EE has emerged as a crucial discipline that models organisations as sociotechnical systems by integrating organisational science and computer science. EO [3] is a prominent methodology in this area, characterised by its practical method and published case studies in various domains.

With EO, Dietz and Mulder [3] base information systems, which are technical platforms that coordinate and integrate business processes, on an ontological enterprise model. The ontological enterprise model deliberately abstracts from material, documental, and informational aspects to focus on essential business coordination. Consequently, it enables EE experts to (re)design the construction of an enterprise and its accompanying information systems.

EO [3] posits that the construction of an enterprise involves actors who enter into and comply with social and business commitments. EO assumes that these actors try to reach social consensus, a concept derived from Habermas' theory of communicative action [12]. Commitments are coordinated through transactions concerning a product to be brought about. EO's ontological enterprise model is a network of transaction kinds, linked by dependencies. The following summary of EO axioms [3] explains the transaction concept in more detail:

- A transaction involves two actors, one as initiator and one as executor.
- Actors perform Coordination acts (C-acts) to enter into and comply with social commitments towards each other.
- A successful C-act creates a new commitment, a coordination fact.
- An event brings a fact into existence.
- An execution act brings about the requested product.
- The related product fact is created with an accept C-act.
- Each product kind has a one-to-one relationship with a transaction kind.
- Each transaction kind follows a universal pattern, see Fig. 1.
- An actor may initiate other transactions while performing an act.
- An actor may wait for events of other transactions before proceeding.
- An actor may seek to revoke a previous act.

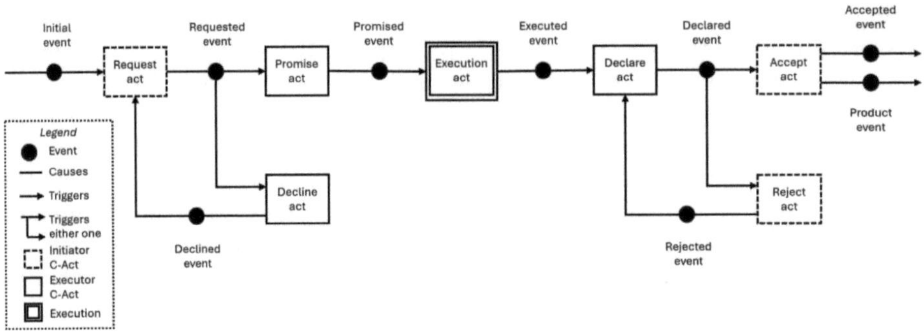

Fig. 1. Semi-formal presentation of the standard transaction pattern.

In formal terms, the ontological system of EO is a discrete event-driven system [3] whose axioms can be formalised in annotated first-order logic. EO states that an information system must adhere to the transaction concept and to the ontological constraints of each transaction kind, as specified in an ontological enterprise model [4]. For each transaction kind, implementing the technological support for actors requires adding informational, documental, and material aspects, from which the ontological enterprise model abstracts. Implementation steps must preserve ontological abstraction; for example, they cannot conflate transaction kinds with user-interface components.

2.2 Correctness-by-Construction

Historically, EE practitioners used EO's ontological enterprise model primarily to achieve a shared understanding before starting a traditional implementation process. However, advances in low-code/no-code platforms and generative AI now enable direct derivation of implementations from ontological models [8,15]. Although ontological models reduce ambiguities in specifications, they do not inherently ensure that an implementation adheres to ontological constraints. The CbC principle [14] mitigates this by enforcing verifiable adherence of an implementation to its specification. Unlike testing, which reveals errors but cannot prove their absence [5], CbC ensures reliability through formal refinement [14].

Starting with a specification, each CbC refinement step reduces its abstraction level by adding more details while adhering to the constraints of the previous refinement. CbC requires each refinement step to verifiably preserve validity relative to a specification [14]. Invariant enforcement, a key aspect of CbC, transforms business specifications into verifiable constraints, ensuring that they are followed rigorously rather than being treated as mere guidelines. The CbC refinement approach maintains mathematical traceability through verifiable refinements between a business specification and implementation artefacts.

For example, within the CbC refinement process, a constraint such as "payment must be received before delivery of the product" is verifiably preserved from the specification through each refinement step to its implementation. Although

CbC ensures that an implementation adheres to a specification, CbC fails to address vagueness and incompleteness issues of specifications [19], such as the omission of a payment transaction.

3 Problem Statement, Research Questions and Related Work

3.1 Problem Statement

EO provides a disciplined methodology for analysing complex organisational structures and obtaining precise specifications. However, shortcomings in its formalisation hinder its use for information system development. The primary problem that this research addresses is the inability to verifiably trace constraints from an ontological enterprise model to an implementation, a key issue in EO's application. Several barriers hinder the traceability of constraints through the refinement process:

1. Under-specified axioms: EO axioms are not explicitly axiomatised in logic [3], therefore, there is no direct means to check whether a statement is valid in its logic theory.
2. Non-isomorphic annotations: The non-isomorphic relation between EO linguistic terminology and EO concepts [3] makes a consistent interpretation difficult.
3. Different interpretation of ontological enterprise models: Although Dietz [3] provides Design and Engineering Methodology for Organisations (DEMO) so that practitioners can apply EO concepts, its syntax is ambiguous [6,16].

For example, a practical consequence of these barriers is that it is impossible to mathematically prove if a BPMN model, such as Guerreiro's model [10], adheres correctly to an ontological enterprise model. Furthermore, different interpretations of an ontological enterprise model hinder the validation of models such as Guerreiro's BPMN model [10] against it.

3.2 Research Questions

This research explores how to verifiably align an ontological enterprise model with its implementation, as outlined in the problem statement. Its main research question is as follows: "*How can EO's axioms be formalised to guarantee traceable correctness from an ontological enterprise model to an implementation?*". To address the primary research question, the following sub-questions are defined:

1. Formal foundations: What definitions and axioms are needed to develop a consistent and sound first-order logic theory of EO's ontological system?
2. Semantic alignment: What formal conditions ensure an isomorphic relationship between the concepts of EO's logic and their annotation?
3. Verifiable refinement: Which verification methods and tools can enforce CbC for refinements of EO's logic and ontological enterprise models?

4. Practical viability: What are the practical challenges and benefits of verifying refinements of ontological enterprise models and how can these challenges be overcome?

These sub-questions guide the development of a formal framework designed to overcome the barriers identified in Sect. 3.1.

3.3 Related Work

Enterprise Ontology-Driven Software Development. The gap between ontological enterprise models and low-code systems is bridged by the Enterprise Ontology-Driven Software Development (EODSD) method [15]. It is grounded in EO and ensures that enterprise systems can faithfully reflect the real-world semantics of organisations, avoiding ambiguities and misalignments common in ad-hoc software engineering practices. However, it fails to offer verification of its transformations and does not provide stepwise refinements.

Enterprise-Grade Tool Support for DEMO. Mulder and Proper [16] have developed a DEMO support tool that provides a standard for DEMO diagrams and syntax through a meta-model. The tool offers an exchange format that allows a suite of DEMO tools to work together and provides verification of DEMO models. The tool bridges the gap between the theoretical constructs of EO and the practical design of ontological enterprise models in complex, large-scale enterprises. Although the design tool solves ambiguities within the DEMO notation, it does not provide a consistent annotated logical theory. In addition, it does not offer a verifiable method to develop an implementation.

Unified Formal Ontology A foundational ontology such as Unified Foundational Ontology (UFO) [11] allows conceptual modelling across domains, e.g. finance, law, and organisations. UFO focusses on information models, checks model consistency through ontological antipattern detection, and is formalised in first-order logic. However, UFO does not provide mechanisms for refining an implementation and has an information focus versus EO's transactional commitments. UFO realism viewpoint cannot ontologically combine with EO's social constructivism. However, refinements adding informational aspects may leverage UFO as a complementary theory.

4 Methodology

4.1 Preliminary Artefact Design Approach

The objective of this research is to develop a formal framework that bridges the verification gap between EO's semi-formal ontological system and its implementations. Employing the Agile Design Science Research (ADSR) [2] methodology is instrumental in developing the formal framework, due to its iterative nature and ability to co-evolve problem and solution space. ADSR combines the artefact focus of Design Science Research [13] with adaptive sprints. This research began with an objective-centred initiation, which was followed by ADSR phases to identify the underlying problem and define objectives of its solution. To achieve the research objective, ADSR is tailored to ontology development through an adapted version of Agile Methodology for Ontology Development (AMOD) [17], as presented in Fig. 2.

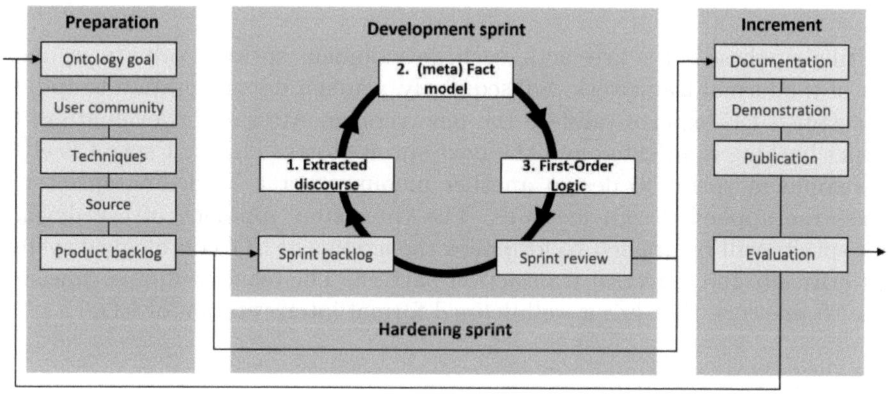

Fig. 2. Iterative artefact design approach, adopted from [17].

During AMOD's preparation phase, the product backlog is created, which is based on the goal of formalising an ontology. This involves certified EE experts as the intended ontology users, and uses the semi-formal version of EO [3] as the source of the discourse. Hardening sprints, which refine and validate the design approach, result in the selection of design techniques. The preparation phase ends with a product backlog aimed at formalising EO's ontological system. Every development sprint is based on items in the product backlog, for example, formalising the concept "Thing". Each development sprint creates three connected artefacts:

1. Extracted discourse: the Fact Oriented Modelling [20] protocol is used to capture knowledge from the discourse source. This ensures traceability between the current semi-formal EO version [3] and the formal framework.
2. (Meta) fact model: the collected discourse is used to create a normalised fact model. For example, the discourse "conceptual things are things in the mind" assert the fact "type conceptual thing is a specialisation of type thing". Well-defined semantics for each concept are created with Formal Concept Analysis (FCA) [7]. FCA ensures alignment between all EO examples, fact types, logic, and definition of concepts. This process also defines unnamed concepts from the original discourse, such as the concept "cognitive thing" that refers to "a thing in the mind".

3. First-order logic model: the (meta)fact model is transformed into an Event-B model [18]. Event-B was selected for its ecosystem of automated first-order logic proofs, CbC refinements, and code generators, such as Python and Java. For example, fact "type cognitive thing is a specialisation of type thing" implies that the extension of type cognitive thing is a subset of the extension of type thing. Formally in Event-B, $CognitiveThing \subseteq Thing$. Event-Bs ecosystem then verifies logical correctness and verifies adherence of refinements to ontological constraints.

Utilizing these three artefacts, each development sprint results in an increment of the formal framework. Subsequently, artefact documentation is updated and certified EE experts validate the new version. After sprint evaluation, the product backlog is adjusted and the next sprint starts. The next sprint is either a development sprint to design another increment or a hardening sprint that evolves the applied design methods. The three-step approach of the development sprints will be applied to formalise the axioms of EO's ontological system, most critically the universal transaction pattern. The result will be a consistent formal framework that has a well-defined formal interpretation of EO.

4.2 Expected Results

The presented research aims to deliver the following outcomes regarding ontological enterprise model-based implementations of an organisation:

- Enhanced organisation design knowledge: Improved conformity of interpretations of ontological enterprise models by EE practitioners.
- Reduced implementation errors due to verifiable correct refinements of ontological enterprise models. This aims to bridge the formalisation gap between EO's transaction theory and software engineering practice, strengthening the EODSD method [15].
- Reusable formal ontology for ontological enterprise models. This intends to formalise the theoretical constructs behind the DEMO notation, strengthening DEMO design tools.
- Re-formalised universal transaction pattern. The annotated first-order logic theory of EO is expected to improve the current formalisation [3] of the transaction pattern. This formal theory is designed to provide a foundation for follow-up research and practical work on implementations.

5 Conclusion and Next Steps

This research addresses a fundamental limitation in EE: the absence of verifiable correctness between EO theory, its ontological enterprise models, and their implementations. By formalising EO's axioms, in annotated first-order logic, and integrating CbC refinements, the modelling discipline of EO may be used in verifiable software engineering. Moving forward, the research follows a roadmap with measurable goals: (1) formalise EO's foundational ontology, (2) formalise the transaction pattern, (3) demonstrate refinement on an academic EO example, and (4) validate with real-world cases.

Acknowledgments. The author would like to thank Prof. Dr. A. F. Harmsen, Prof. Dr. H. A. Proper, and Dr. ir. M. R. Krouwel for sharing their insights and methodological guidance throughout this research.

Disclosure of Interests. The author has no competing interests to declare that are relevant to the content of this article.

References

1. Bergmane, L., Grabis, J., Žeiris, E.: A case study: software defect root causes. Inf. Technol. Manag. Sci. **20**(1), 54–57 (2017)
2. Conboy, K., Gleasure, R., Cullina, E.: Agile design science research. In: Donnellan, B., Helfert, M., Kenneally, J., VanderMeer, D., Rothenberger, M., Winter, R. (eds.) DESRIST 2015. LNCS, vol. 9073, pp. 168–180. Springer, Cham (2015). https://doi.org/10.1007/978-3-319-18714-3_11
3. Dietz, J.L.G., Mulder, H.B.F.: Enterprise Ontology - A Human-Centric Approach to Understanding the Essence of Organisation, 2nd edn. Springer, Cham (2024)
4. Dietz, J.L.G., Mulder, H.B.F.: Enterprise Design Fundamentals - Settling an Enterprise Business and Devising the Enterprise Organisation. Springer, Cham (2025)
5. Dijkstra, E.: Structured programming. In: Classics in Software Engineering, pp. 41–48. Yourdon Press (1979)
6. Figueira, C., Aveiro, D.: A new action rule syntax for DEmo MOdels based automatic workflow procEss geneRation (DEMOBAKER). In: Aveiro, D., Tribolet, J., Gouveia, D. (eds.) EEWC 2014. LNBIP, vol. 174, pp. 46–60. Springer, Cham (2014). https://doi.org/10.1007/978-3-319-06505-2_4
7. Ganter, B., Wille, R.: Formal Concept Analysis: Mathematical Foundations. Springer, Cham (2024)
8. Gazzawe, F.: Integrating ontology in information science and AI: evolution, applications, and future directions. In: Ontology in Computer Science - State of the Art and Its Future in AI. IntechOpen, Rijeka (2025)
9. Group, T.S.: Chaos report series (1994-). https://www.standishgroup.com/, Annual Report Series on Project Success Rates. Includes CHAOS Report (1994–2018), CHAOS Chronicles (2015–2018), and CHAOS (2020-present)
10. Guerreiro, S., Sousa, P.: A framework to semantify BPMN models using demo business transaction pattern. arXiv preprint arXiv:2012.09557 (2020)
11. Guizzardi, G., Wagner, G., Almeida, J.P.A., Guizzardi, R.S.: Towards ontological foundations for conceptual modeling: the unified foundational ontology (UFO) story. Appl. Ontol. **10**(3–4), 259–271 (2015)
12. Habermas, J.: The Theory of Communicative Action. No. v. 2, Beacon Press (1984)
13. Hevner, A., Chatterjee, S.: Design Research in Information Systems: Theory and Practice, 1st edn. Springer, Cham (2010)
14. Kourie, D.G., Watson, B.W.: The Correctness-by-Construction Approach to Programming. Undergraduate Topics in Computer Science, 1st edn. Springer, Cham (2012)

15. Krouwel, M.R., Op't Land, M., Proper, H.A.: From enterprise models to low-code applications: mapping DEMO to Mendix; illustrated in the social housing domain. Softw. Syst. Model. **23**(4), 837–864 (2024)
16. Mulder, M.A.T., Proper, H.A.: On enterprise-grade tool support for DEMO. Softw. Syst. Model. **21**(4), 1341–1361 (2022)
17. Peroni, S.: A simplified agile methodology for ontology development. In: Dragoni, M., Poveda-Villalón, M., Jimenez-Ruiz, E. (eds.) OWLED/ORE -2016. LNCS, vol. 10161, pp. 55–69. Springer, Cham (2017). https://doi.org/10.1007/978-3-319-54627-8_5
18. Russo, A.G.: Modeling in event-b - system and software engineering by Jean-Raymond Abrial. ACM SIGSOFT Softw. Eng. Notes **36**(2), 38–39 (2011)
19. Smith, B.: The limits of correctness. ACM Sigcas Comput. Soc. **14**, 18–26 (1985)
20. Zwart, J.P., Engelbart, M., Hoppenbrouwers, S.: Fact Oriented Modeling with FCO-IM: Capturing Business Semantics in Data Models with Fully Communication Oriented Information Modeling. Technics Publications (2015)

Towards a Knowledge Management Treatment for Design Thinking with the Help of Knowledge Graphs

Anca Moldovan(✉)

Faculty of Economics and Business Administration, Babeş-Bolyai University, 400591 Cluj Napoca, Romania
anca.moldovan@econ.ubbcluj.ro

Abstract. This Ph.D. project aims to develop a model-driven Knowledge Management treatment for Design Thinking (DT) workshops. DT is both a cognitive framework and a collaboration format structured into phases that produce diverse artifacts: empathy insights, idea catalogs, solution prototypes. DT workshops foster stakeholder commitment through iterative refinement of outcomes. However, current DT practices lack dedicated mechanisms to capture and structure content objects in the semantic context where they emerged. Consequently, Design Thinking knowledge often remains tacit, content remains untraceable, limiting possibilities for retrospective learning, idea evaluation, and strategic reuse. This doctoral project is organized as Design Science research that will engineer a model-driven approach to DT knowledge capture and management. The resulting artifact will streamline a Domain-Specific Modeling Language (DSML) and a Design Thinking Knowledge Graph. The DSML is intended to mimic the visual experience of ideation boards while preserving semantic distinctions in content and adding machine-readability, ultimately turning the visual designs into Knowledge Graphs. This will enable semantic and procedural traceability providing a core structure for potential DT knowledge management systems that can enable organizations to better govern and reuse innovation practices.

Keywords: Design Thinking · Knowledge Graphs · Domain-specific Modeling

1 Design Problem Motivation

In today's innovation landscape, organizations increasingly use Design Thinking (DT) to generate creative solutions in a participatory way. DT offers a structured yet flexible format following along phases such as Empathize, Define, Ideate, Prototype, and Test. Its strengths—empathy insights, interdisciplinary collaboration, divergent and convergent thinking, and rapid prototyping—are especially valuable in digital transformation, healthcare, and service design [12]. The shift to distributed teams and agile virtual work has further heightened the need for human-centered methods while business process perspectives are also applied to such work [18]. Yet, despite its effectiveness, DT lacks

J. Barateiro et al. (Eds.): EDOC 2025 Workshops, LNBIP 571, pp. 241–249, 2026.
https://doi.org/10.1007/978-3-032-16234-2_19

formal mechanisms for explicit knowledge capture, traceability, and reuse, a shortcoming that this PhD work aims to address from a method engineering perspective [3]. Workshop outputs—such as sticky notes, empathy maps, or digital boards (e.g., in tools like Miro[1])—are visual artifacts but lack any structured semantics outside the tacit knowledge of the facilitator, conveyed by social participation. Knowledge embedded in the facilitator's experience remains disconnected from long-term decision-making and reuse, depending on individual memory. As Wrigley et al. observe [20], this gap leads to "innovation blind spots" where rationale and design history are lost. Bridging this gap is essential to scale DT into sustainable, knowledge-driven practice.

This Ph.D. research vision proposes a Design Science Research (DSR) treatment to establish a model-driven DT knowledge management (KM) capability. By resorting to established approaches of knowledge engineering and method engineering disciplines and following Gregor and Hevner's guidelines on positioning DSR for maximum impact [6], the contributions are framed on two levels, technical artifacts and conceptual:

- The technical artifacts will be: (a) a *diagrammatic modeling tool* to balance the visual experience of on-line ideation boards with the rigor of conceptual modeling; (b) a *knowledge graph (and associated ontology)* to capture the diagrammatic structures and semantic distinctions into machine-readable form, thus enabling knowledge systems to leverage Design Thinking experience in a knowledge management context. Technologically, a DSR demonstrator is planned to be implemented using the ADOxx metamodeling platform[2] and its RDF[3] derivation mechanisms [9];
- The conceptual treatment will be a modeling method grounded on a *Domain-specific Modeling Language (DSML)* supported by the aforementioned modeling tool, expected to generate insights on patterns of applying Design Thinking in different innovation settings. BPMN[4] is planned to be adopted as a conceptualization entry point, by relaxing its imperative nature and aligning its core constructs to the specificity of the DT practice. The modeling method will be built according to the practices of both general Method Engineering [3] and the Agile Modeling Method Engineering approach specific to the OMILAB conceptualization ecosystem [1].

This work builds on practitioner insights from over 80 DT workshops facilitated by the author in product development and plans to reveal conceptual design principles that can inform knowledge management capabilities for participatory innovation practices.

2 Related Work

During the 1st year stage of the doctoral work, we have identified a research stream and relevant body of knowledge concerning the design-oriented research preoccupation with DT and problem-solving methodologies in general, and their occasional intersection with business process modeling for procedural framing (as also considered here).

[1] https://miro.com/.
[2] https://adoxx.org/.
[3] https://www.w3.org/RDF/.
[4] https://www.bpmn.org/.

Scene2Model [13] is a visual tool for designing and digitizing DT storyboards, typically used with SAP Scenes[5] and QR codes for capturing haptic objects in digital scenes. It links story sketches to BPMN models, however it lacks a granular traceability between them, and to the overall DT workshop execution and assets. A similar focus on visualization, but closer to our need to cover the DT problem solving experience, was reported in [7]. Tangible Business Process Modeling (TBPM) [5] uses physical objects to represent BPMN, making it more accessible to non-experts. Our DSML has the potential to reduce facilitator overhead by mimicking DT boards while adding semantic traceability. Problem–solution chains [8] act as boundary objects bridging business and IT. This inspires our objective of linking DT insights with BPMN process snippets, however the reference paper's proposition is agnostic of both the DT specificity and process modeling, maintaining a minimalist chaining and ramification approach. Participatory Enterprise Modeling [4] shares DT's collaborative nature but implies use of formal enterprise modeling methods. This contrast highlights the need to balance creativity and rigor, motivating our hybrid DSML–Knowledge Graph solution and a requirement to relax the imperative nature of BPMN to make it usable for DT. Knowledge conversion theory [10, 11] suggests a connection between DSMLs and Nonaka's model of knowledge creation - our project extends this by turning tacit DT outputs into explicit, machine-readable structures. Collaboration engineering [2] offers structured facilitation approaches, perspectives that can inform this project's evaluation design. The TRIZ methodology [16] is a systematic approach to innovation that emphasizes structured creativity, illustrating ways to balance creativity with method rigor.

Such prior work demonstrates interest in digital modeling of co-creation or process innovation but stops at visualization and participation management, while we are interested in semantic traceability over the DT experience and content.

3 Problem Statement and Research Questions

DT workshops generate valuable artifacts—empathy maps, personas, ideation boards, and prototypes—but these are often captured informally on physical or digital boards, lacking machine-readable semantics or structured content management. As a result, insights, decisions, and stakeholder contributions are not preserved for traceability, analysis, or reuse. Figure 1 illustrates typical artifacts from a physical workshop, such as color-coded post-its and voting dots distributed across boards and workspaces. Existing digital tools (e.g., Miro) support visual navigation and manipulation but lack structure and semantics for retrospective evaluation. On the other hand, modeling standards like BPMN offer formally grounded knowledge structures, but lack the human-centric and qualitative focus of DT. Alternatives such as CJML (Customer Journey Modeling Language)[6] and process-centric approaches like Signavio's customer journey mapping[7] move closer to non-imperative flexibility but still fall short of DT's knowledge management needs. These disconnects between creative ideation and structured representation lead to loss of rationale behind solution design decisions, inability to score ideas or lack

[5] https://apphaus.sap.com/resource/scenes.

[6] https://cjml.no/.

[7] https://www.signavio.com/post/customer-journey-mapping/ last accessed 2025/19/9.

of problem-solution traceability, redundant ideation efforts, dependence on facilitator's tacit knowledge and limited knowledge transfer.

Fig. 1. Exemplary objects from a Design Thinking setting (author's own archive)

Inspired by the Design Science research question taxonomy of [19], the research challenge is decomposed in two artifact-focused and one empirically focused question:

RQ1: *How can we preserve the DT digital board visual user experience, while adding to it an explicit semantics dimension* that recognizes DT assets, artifacts, tasks and their dependencies as first-class constructs? The envisioned solution is to adopt DSML metamodeling to reconcile the explicit conceptualization of existing standards (BPMN) and the tacit conceptualization of a DT facilitator.

RQ2: *How can DT ideation management leverage knowledge representation and reasoning to enable a KM capability* over accumulated DT experience, knowledge, and content? The envisioned solution is to adopt ADOxx-to-RDF for model-driven derivation of knowledge graphs [9], enabling reasoning scenarios and competency questions over a repository of diagrammatic models created with the DSML addressing RQ1.

RQ3: *What is the cognitive and operational overhead that the proposed treatment brings to DT facilitators and stakeholders compared to the traditional DT practices*? The envisioned answer to this will be empirically founded on quality frameworks such as SEQUAL [11] (demonstrated in [14]) in order to assess qualities of the proposed modeling method and demonstrator.

4 Preliminary Relevance Analysis Steps

Innovation management's key challenge is evaluating ideas under various constraints, falling back to alternatives and reuse. While portfolio-level decision frameworks exist, innovation knowledge management and idea evaluation are often neglected, leading to redundant ideation and poor solution–problem traceability. The author's DT facilitation experience motivated a SWOT analysis of lessons learned across business settings, summarized in Table 1 around the general characterization of DT strengths from [20].

Table 1. SWOT analysis on past DT deployments and learned lessons.

Category	Reflection
Strengths	• User-Centered: Focus on real user needs through empathy. • Collaborative & Creative: Promotes diverse thinking and teamwork. • Low-Risk Iteration: Prototyping cycles reduce costly failures. • Versatile: Applies across products, services, and business design.
Weaknesses	• No Structured Knowledge Capture: Outputs remain tacit and untraceable. • Ad Hoc Evaluation: Lacks formal idea scoring, leading to fickle decisions. • Dependent on expert facilitators: hard to scale or transfer knowledge. • Poor Traceability: Limited reuse of past ideas or rationale.
Opportunities	• Develop DT Knowledge Repositories: To enable learning and reuse. • Formalize Idea Scoring: To improve strategic decision-making. • AI Integration: To populate knowledge structures. • Link DT to BPMN: To ensure procedural governance over DT.
Threats	• Low KM Adoption: Organizations may omit long-term knowledge needs. • Cultural Resistance: Change from traditional models may face pushback. • Budget Limits: Investment in DT formalization may be deprioritized.

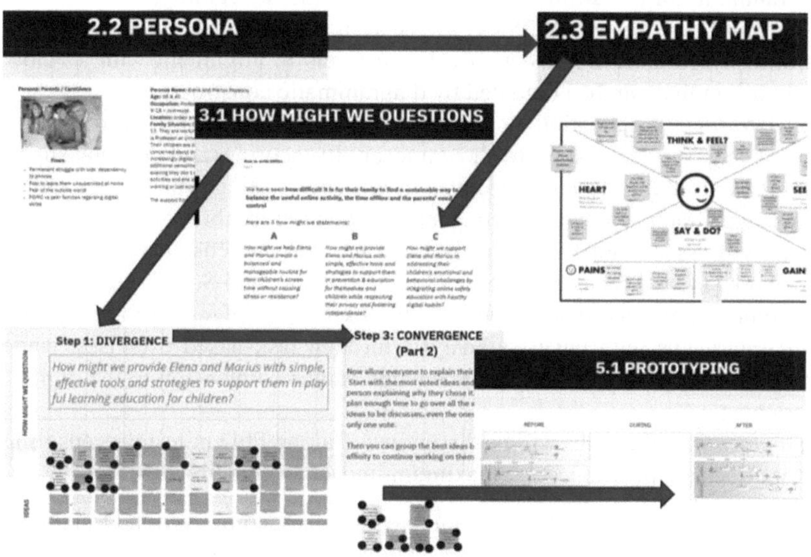

Fig. 2. Exemplary items from a Design Thinking digital board (Miro-based)

Figure 2 shows exemplary digital boards equivalent to the phases of a DT workshop, with the arrows suggesting their sequencing.

Persona boards define fictional user profiles combining demographic attributes with key concerns that frame the problem space. Empathy maps break these concerns into what the user sees, hears, thinks, says, and does—grouped into Pains and Gains. The

"How Might We" board turns these insights into actionable questions. DT participants refine and vote them to identify the most relevant needs. During Ideation, the Divergence board encourages broad idea generation, while the Convergence board helps narrow ideas down through evaluation and voting. The Prototyping board turns selected ideas into mockups (for digital solutions) or storyboards (for service scenarios), which can later be formalized in BPMN diagrams, as recommended by tools like Scene2Model [13]. While widely used, these boards are unified by a tacit conceptual model – we aim to make this explicit, into one that can be exposed to AI agents.

5 Research Methodology and Evaluation Vision

This research is guided by Peffers' DSR methodology [15] through the following iterative stages, for which three iterations are envisioned until the end of the engineering-evaluation cycle:

1. *Problem Identification and Motivation:* Facilitation experience in DT workshops provides the basis for observing future workshops to refine semantic distinctions and competency questions to be addressed by the proposed DSR treatment.
2. *Define Objectives:* Artifact requirements will be formulated to inform representation and granularity of DT artifacts, supporting semantic traceability.
3. *Design and Development:* A DSML will be designed and implemented on the ADOxx platform, hybridizing BPMN with DT constructs in alignment with a Knowledge Graph design that can be populated by diagrammatic constructs.
4. *Demonstration:* Application of the prototype in iterative DT workshops across domains (e.g. service design) to show traceability, scoring, and decision support.
5. *Evaluation:* Linking design objectives to artifacts, testing whether the DSML and Knowledge Graph achieve desired competency and traceability in real contexts. The project will assess modeling effectiveness and comprehension with the SEQUAL framework [11, 14] focusing on Semantic, Pragmatic, and Social dimensions. Methods include controlled experiments, meta-observation of workshop iterations, and expert interviews with business analysts through task-based exercises, while estimating the overhead of adding a knowledge capture dimension to the digital board experience;
7. *Communication:* Findings will be disseminated along PhD milestones ensuring DSR contributions are positioned for maximum impact as guided by [6].

Methodologically, our DSR approach may be upgraded by Action Design Research with its iterative cycles of building, intervention, and evaluation [17].

6 Preliminary Engineering Steps

Figure 3 suggests how DT phases and constructs can be structured into a Knowledge Graph in the form of RDF named graphs, which we are currently designing towards addressing initial competency questions derived from DT practitioner experience. The suggested BPMN descriptions of problem processes or solution processes can also be incorporated as its own named graph, by resorting to business process-to-RDF converters already available in both literature [9] and educational tooling[8], therefore we take BPMN as a key component to be extended with a DT conceptualization, to enable flexible shifting between process-centric rigor and flexible traceability of less constrained DT constructs. Exemplary competence questions to be addressed as semantic queries (or exposure to an AI agent, not currently in focus but potentially relevant) are listed as follows: (a) *Which ideas were most voted for by a particular stakeholder participating in multiple DT workshops*? (b) *Which were the alternate ideas, in case the selected one hits a feasibility obstacle*? (c) *What BPMN tasks are to be executed to enact the idea tackling a particular Pain of a particular Persona*?

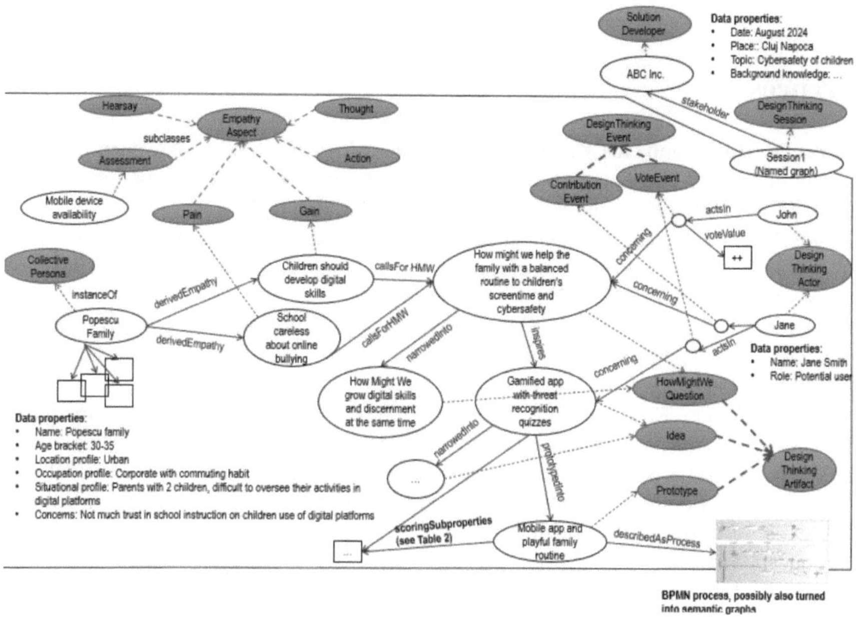

Fig. 3. Exemplary KG structure gleaned from DT digital boards

7 Conclusions and Next Steps

This PhD project pursues an approach for semantically integrating the tacit knowledge embedded in Design Thinking facilitation with BPMN-inspired procedural knowledge on semi-structured DT process deployment. Drawing on the author's extensive experience with both physical and digital workshop formats, a conceptual modeling effort is underway to granularly define and align these semantic structures. The work now focuses on designing the Knowledge Graph ontology, to be followed by the DSML metamodel as input for the subsequent DSR phases enumerated in Sect. 5.

[8] https://bee-up.omilab.org/activities/bee-up/

The contributions of this project can be summarized on two levels. At the artifact level, the DSML and Knowledge Graph demonstrator can provide a hybrid visual-semantic tool that preserves the familiar board experience while enabling traceability and reuse. At the knowledge level, the research aims to derive design principles for bridging the tacit, experience-based knowledge with machine-oriented knowledge engineering for the application domain of DT.

Acknowledgments. This PhD work is supervised by Prof. Dr. Robert Andrei Buchmann, at University Babeş-Bolyai, Romania, in the Information Systems domain.

The authors have no competing interests to declare that are relevant to the content of this article.

References

1. Bork, D., Buchmann, R., Karagiannis, D., Lee, M., Miron, E.-T.: An open platform for modeling method conceptualization: the OMiLAB digital ecosystem. Commun. Assoc. Inf. Syst. **44**, 673–697 (2019). https://doi.org/10.17705/1CAIS.04432
2. Briggs, R.O., De Vreede, G.J., Nunamaker Jr., J.F.: Collaboration engineering with ThinkLets to pursue sustained success with group support systems. J. Manag. Inf. Syst. **19**(4) (2003). https://doi.org/10.1080/07421222.2003.11045743.
3. Brinkkemper, S.: Method engineering: engineering of information systems development methods and tools. Inf. Softw. Technol. **38**(4), 275–280 (1996). https://doi.org/10.1016/0950-5849(95)01059-9
4. Godfrey, T., Batra, R., Douthwaite, S., Edgeworth, J., Miles, S., Zschaler, S.: A methodology for DSML-assisted participatory agent-based enterprise modelling. In: Proceedings of POEM 2022, pp. 201–215. Springer, Cham (2022). https://doi.org/10.1007/978-3-031-21488-2_13
5. Grosskopf, A., Edelman, J., Weske, M.: Tangible business process modeling – methodology and experiment design. In: Business Process Management Workshops 2009, pp. 489–500. Springer, Cham (2010). https://doi.org/10.1007/978-3-642-12186-9_46
6. Gregor, S., Hevner, A.R.: Positioning and presenting design science research for maximum impact. MIS Q. **37**(2), 337–355 (2013). https://doi.org/10.25300/MISQ/2013/37.2.01
7. Hawryszkiewycz, I.: Visualizations for addressing wicked problems using design thinking. In: Proceedings of ECIS 2014. Assoc. Inf. Sys. (2014). https://aisel.aisnet.org/ecis2014/proceedings/track13/2/
8. Hoppenbrouwers, S., Mulder, M.A., Sunnotel, J.: Conceptualisation and (meta)modelling of problem-solution chains in early business-IT alignment and system design. In: Proceedings of POEM 2024, pp. 207–223, Springer, Cham (2024). https://doi.org/10.1007/978-3-031-77908-4_13
9. Karagiannis, D., Buchmann, R.A.: A proposal for deploying hybrid knowledge bases: the ADOxx-to-GraphDB interoperability case. In: Proceedings of HICSS 2018 (2018). https://aisel.aisnet.org/hicss-51/ks/ks_creation/4/. https://doi.org/10.24251/HICSS.2018.510
10. von Krogh, G., Nonaka, I.: Tacit knowledge and knowledge conversion: controversy and advancement in organizational knowledge creation theory. Organ. Sci. **20**(3), 635–652 (2009). https://doi.org/10.1287/orsc.1080.0412
11. Krogstie, J., Sindre, G., Jørgensen, H.: Process models representing knowledge for action: a revised quality framework. Eur. J. Inf. Syst. **15**, 91–102 (2006). https://doi.org/10.1057/palgrave.ejis.3000598

12. Meinel, C., Leifer, L., Plattner, H.: Design Thinking: Understand-Improve-Apply, pp. 100–106. Springer, Cham (2011). https://doi.org/10.1007/978-3-642-13757-0
13. Muck, C., Palkovits-Rauter, S.: Conceptualizing design thinking artefacts: the scene2model storyboard approach. In: Domain-Specific Conceptual Modeling, pp. 567–587. Springer, Cham (2022). https://doi.org/10.1007/978-3-030-93547-4_25.
14. Nast, B., Sandkuhl, K.: Evaluation of the intuitiveness of MIoTA. In: Proceedings of BIR 2024 Workshops, CEUR-WS, vol. 3804 (2024). https://ceur-ws.org/Vol-3804/paper10o.pdf
15. Peffers, K., Tuunanen, T., Rothenberger, M.A., Chatterjee, S.: A design science research methodology for information systems research. J. Manag. Inf. Syst. **24**(3), 45–77 (2007). https://doi.org/10.2753/MIS0742-1222240302
16. Savransky, S.D.: Engineering of Creativity: Introduction to TRIZ Methodology of Inventive Problem Solving. CRC Press, Boca Raton (2000). https://doi.org/10.1201/9781420038958
17. Sein, M.K., Henfridsson, O., Purao, S., Rossi, M., Lindgren, R.: Action design research. MIS Q. **35**(1), 37–56 (2011). https://doi.org/10.2307/23043488
18. Thoring, K., Müller, R.M.: Understanding design thinking: a process model based on method engineering. In: Proceedings of E&PDE 2011, pp. 493–498 (2011). https://www.designsociety.org/publication/30932/
19. Thuan, N., Drechsler, A., Antunes, P.: Construction of design science research questions. Commun. Assoc. Inf. Syst. **44** (2019). https://doi.org/10.17705/1CAIS.04420
20. Wrigley, C., Nusem, E., Straker, K.: Implementing design thinking: understanding organizational conditions. Calif. Manag. Rev. **62**(2), 125–143 (2020). https://doi.org/10.1177/0008125619897606

Towards a Reference Ontology and -Architecture for Public-Private Learning Communities

Marcel Pertenbreiter(✉)

University of Twente, Drienerlolaan 5, 7522 NB Enschede, Netherlands
m.pertenbreiter@utwente.nl

Abstract. Public-Private Learning Communities (PPLCs) provide a collaborative environment where public and private organisations join forces to work, learn, and innovate together. Digital platforms can facilitate the primary processes in these networks. However, there are no design paradigms or reference architectures to support the development of a collaborative platform tailored to PPLCs. This doctoral consortium paper aims to introduce a novel design approach comprising two artefacts: a reference ontology that contains essential domain knowledge for a collaborative platform tailored to PPLCs and a reference architecture to guide platform development. A design science research approach is adopted, combining participatory research methods to explore the problem context of PPLCs and technical action research to iteratively design and evaluate prototypes of the artefacts. This doctoral research will generate new design knowledge regarding collaborative platforms for PPLCs and evaluate the reference ontology and -architecture using case study research in PPLCs.

Keywords: Reference Ontology · Reference Architecture · Public-Private Collaboration · Learning Community · Platform

1 Introduction

Companies' competitiveness relies strongly on their innovative capacity, but many companies lack the human resources with adequate competencies [9]. To address this issue, companies can participate in Public-Private Learning Communities (PPLCs). PPLCs describe a network in which both public and private actors come together to work, learn, and innovate [16]. PPLCs are characterised by four core themes. They are cross-sectional, multilayered, and designed to establish both intentional and shared benefits, as well as growth and development for all members [16]. Thus, PPLCs inherit the notion of open innovation by enabling the bidirectional flow of information across organisational boundaries [6] and "interactive, collaborative process of joint value creation" [14, p. 39]. Besides, PPLCs emphasise the learning of individual organisations and employees, focusing on how shared knowledge can be applied internally [16].

J. Barateiro et al. (Eds.): EDOC 2025 Workshops, LNBIP 571, pp. 250–257, 2026.
https://doi.org/10.1007/978-3-032-16234-2_20

Digital platforms offer the tools to strengthen collaboration and innovation within PPLCs [7]. However, research has not forwarded a paradigm or framework for designing a collaborative platform tailored specifically towards PPLCs. Moreover, the design knowledge that underpins platform-mediated PPLCs remains unclear. As a result, the design and implementation process is potentially unstructured, more time-consuming, and not aligned with the specific structures and processes of the respective community [12].

This project focuses on designing and evaluating a Reference Ontology (RO) and Reference Architecture (RA) for producing new design knowledge and a design paradigm for platform-mediated PPLCs, respectively. This PhD is part of the broader research project Smart4L, focusing on platform development for PPLCs. Two other work packages study the design and social dynamics of PPLCs. The project involves four PPLCs, which are a constellation of companies (logistics, manufacturing, and consulting), universities, sector organisations, and governments. Each PPLC is at a different stage of maturity, ranging from emerging to expanding to highly established, allowing the study of PPLCs at multiple stages of development.

The remainder of this paper is organised as follows. Section 2 introduces existing RA and RO developed for networks similar to PPLCs. Based on the existing research, Sect. 3 highlights the current knowledge gaps. Section 4 lists the objectives and research questions. Section 5 describes the methodology and the research methods employed. Finally, Sect. 6 presents the current state of the PhD.

2 Related Literature

An RO and RA can respectively provide the design knowledge and blueprint needed to develop collaborative platforms for PPLCs. While research has not yet produced an RO or conceptual framework that captures the design knowledge, some RAs and models already exist for networks similar to PPLCs. These RAs will be briefly reviewed to elaborate on the existing knowledge gaps.

[3] developed a reference model for an outside-in open innovation platform, thus enabling organisations to internalise external knowledge. The model comprises functional characteristics, actors, and scenarios, primarily centered on knowledge sharing and managing innovation processes. The actors within the model include innovators, innovation adopters, and innovation intermediaries who aid in the innovation process. [10] proposed a more niche RA targeting the innovation process. They demonstrate how computer-aided systems can support collaborative product design across companies and industries. With a greater focus on learning, [13] developed a reference framework for designing teaching-learning systems in education based on the notion of collaborative networks and open innovation. Their framework provides the instruction for determining students' learning needs and methods, as well as the ICT and physical infrastructure to realise the learning methods. [15] delivered a reference model for configuring the services that digital innovation hubs should offer. Their model encompasses

a comprehensive range of processes, including ecosystem building, knowledge sharing, learning, and innovation management, but does not offer guidance on developing an ICT architecture to deliver these services.

The results of these works can be leveraged to extract existing solutions and best practices that are also applicable to designing collaborative platforms for PPLCs. However, their analysis highlights existing knowledge gaps that must be addressed to tailor an RA and RO to the specific needs of PPLCs.

3 Knowledge Gaps

Existing reference models and architectures do not encompass all relevant processes of PPLCs and only briefly outline the architectural components required to support them. An updated and focused RA is needed to guide the design of collaborative platforms tailored towards PPLCs by combining collaborative learning, working, and innovating. Additionally, an RO is required to capture relevant design knowledge, providing PPLC stakeholders with a conceptual framework for a shared understanding. By operationalising the RO, it can also serve as a knowledge base for the platform and enable the integration of intelligent systems. The following specifies four knowledge gaps that need to be addressed to construct the RO and RA.

First, PPLCs encompass a range of processes, including collaboration, learning, working, and innovating. The existing architectures are not comprehensive enough, as they focus either on innovating or learning. Consequently, they might overlook the interplay between these processes and the unique design requirements attached to them.

Second, the models and architecture address learning mainly in an educational context [13]. The inclusion of distinct learning methods for competency acquisition in a workplace setting is overlooked. [16] also stresses that, beyond knowledge sharing, metalearning of individual employees should be facilitated through PPLCs. Hence, research is required to explore the mechanism through which platforms can optimise both network, intraorganisational, and individual learning [4].

Third, existing architectures and models typically focus on narrow user groups, such as students in educational contexts [13]. In contrast, PPLCs involve a diverse range of stakeholders and end-users, including researchers and students from academia, companies, consultants, and governments. To understand how platforms can support PPLCs, the needs and the (non) functional requirements of individual stakeholders and the community as a construct itself need to be explored.

Fourth, existing architectures and models are obsolete. They fail to consider the benefits and requirements of integrating modern technologies, such as AI [1]. Given the rapid pace of technological advancements [2], both the platform and the user must be resilient and adaptable to changes, for instance, by adopting the vision of Industry 5.0 and Education 5.0 [11], which emphasise human-centricity, resilience, and sustainability in technology development.

4 Research Objectives and Questions

This PhD project aims to achieve three objectives, enabling the design of a collaborative platform for PPLCs. The first two objectives are the RO and RA, which answer the main research question: "How to effectively design collaborative platforms for PPLCs?". Consequently, the third objective concerns their evaluation.

Objective 1 - RO: The RO serves as a knowledge base capturing the essential domain knowledge for platform-mediated PPLCs. Specifically, the RO should interrelate various concepts, such as actors, their requirements, and processes (PPLC context), with the most optimal platform functions, components, and technologies (platform design). Simultaneously, it can provide a shared semantic understanding for the various stakeholders involved in PPLCs. The RO can also be operationalised, enabling the integration of knowledge-based systems, such as AI retrieval agents. SABIOx will be used as a methodology, as it provides guidance for the development of reference and operational ontologies alongside OntoUML as a modelling language. The following research questions will be addressed:

RQ1.1: What domain knowledge is central for developing collaborative platforms for PPLCs?
RQ1.2: How to design an RO to model and interrelate the domain knowledge?
RQ1.3: How can the RO optimally serve as a shared conceptual understanding for stakeholders during the design and development of PPLC platforms?
RQ1.4: How can the RO be operationalised to facilitate the integration of knowledge-based and intelligent systems?

Objective 2 - RA: The second objective is the design of a utilitarian and effective RA by covering essential stakeholder requirements and supporting the core PPLC processes. Another key innovation of the RA is its emphasis on enabling interoperability with other platforms and technologies.

For the development of the RA, the six-step approach outlined in [5] will be followed. The design of the RA is both research- and practice-driven, as it involves researching the requirements and processes with the four PPLCs while extracting common components from their existing architectures. Various data collection methods will be employed, with the most effective ones being incorporated into the RA as best practices for architectural design. Furthermore, the RA should enable variability to allow for the instantiation of different kinds of concrete architectures. The following research questions will be answered:

RQ2.1: What are the requirements and components of an RA that facilitate the central processes of collaborative learning, working, and innovating in PPLCs?
RQ2.2: What are the requirements and components that ensure interoperability and adaptability with existing and future systems and technologies?

RQ2.3: Which data collection methods best enable the extraction of central architectural components and requirements from the PPLCs?
RQ2.4: How can the RA support variability in the instantiation of concrete architectures?

Objective 3 - Evaluating the constructed artefacts: The RO and RA will be assessed based on the evaluation criteria of Hevner [8]. These include utility and quality, efficacy, and generality. Variability is added as an additional criterion to assess the RA.

RQ3.1: Do the artefacts address the requirements, problems, and challenges of PPLCs?
RQ3.2: How effective are the artefacts in improving the processes relevant for PPLCs compared to existing architectures, frameworks, or models?
RQ3.3: What is the degree of variability of the RA?
RQ3.4: To what extent can the artefacts be generalised to other contexts?

5 Methodology

Given the aim of this PhD in designing and evaluating information system research artefacts, the Information System Research Framework (ISRF) of Hevner [8] will be followed. The ISRF integrates three cycles in design science research: the relevance cycle, design cycle, and rigor cycle. The following section provides a brief overview of the cycles and methods employed within each cycle in relation to the research questions (see Fig. 1 for a high-level illustration).

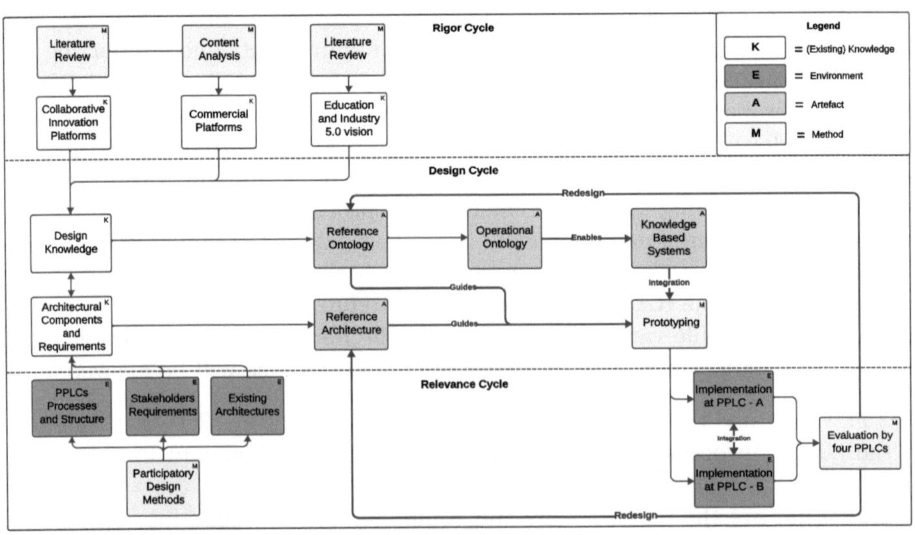

Fig. 1. Model of the Research Plan.

Rigor Cycle: The rigor cycle ensures that design science makes an innovative contribution to the research domain by considering past knowledge. Therefore, a Systematic Literature Review (SLR) will be conducted to identify existing research gaps in collaborative platforms used in innovation networks. The SLR will also partially answer *RQ1.1 and RQ1.2* by examining the platforms based on the stakeholders involved, their requirements, and the technologies implemented. Additionally, a content analysis of modern commercial platforms will be conducted to learn about new technologies such as AI that can interoperate with the PPLC platform (*RQ2.2*).

Design Cycle: The design cycle describes the produced artefacts and the methods used for their development. The RO will contain and interrelate design knowledge accumulated through data collection methods from both the rigor and relevance cycles (*RQ1.1 - RQ.1.2*). Furthermore, stakeholders will assess its effectiveness in providing a shared conceptual framework of the various concepts and components relevant in platform-mediated PPLCs (*RQ1.3*). The generated design knowledge can also be used to operationalise the RO, enabling the integration of knowledge-based and intelligent systems into the architecture *(RQ1.4)*.

The RA will be constructed based on central components of existing architectures and the requirements and processes relevant to PPLCs. These two knowledge streams will be synthesised to empirically ground the RA (*RQ2.1*). The RA also ensures interoperability between PPLC platforms, facilitating collaboration and knowledge exchange across communities (*RQ2.2*). Multiple methods will be used to collect data about and from PPLCs. The most suitable methods for data extraction can be included in the RA (and RO) as best practices for PPLCs to determine their platform requirements and needs (*RQ2.3*). Finally, the RA will ensure variability to guide the design of concrete architectures tailored to the specific needs and context of each PPLC (*RQ2.4*).

Relevance Cycle: The RO and RA need to provide utility by addressing relevant requirements and effectiveness in promoting core processes in PPLCs. By applying participatory research methods in use cases with the four partnering PPLCs, insights are gained into the PPLCs' existing requirements and processes (*RQ2.1*). A document analysis of their working processes can generate additional insights. These methods will also help develop a better understanding of how and which knowledge is shared within PPLCs (*RQ1.1 - RQ1.2*) and how systems used by the organisations in the PPLCs can interoperate with the PPLC platform (*RQ2.2*).

Besides, applying technical action research, platform architectures will be developed for the four PPLCs. These will guide prototype developments, which are then subsequently evaluated by stakeholders of the PPLCs (*RQ3.1 - RQ3.2*). Simultaneously, they demonstrate the variability of the RA through distinct concrete architectures (*RQ3.3*). The RO will be ontologically validated with experts and verified with PPLC stakeholders, focusing on its utility as a conceptual understanding *(RQ3.1-RQ3.2)*. The problem analysis, design, prototyping, and evaluation are repeated three times to ensure thorough validation and continuous refinement of the RO and RA. The generability can be tested in future iterations with a mature version of RA and RO with PPLCs from other industries or sectors *(RQ3.4)*.

6 Progress and Future Outlook

Throughout the course of the PhD, three contributions have been delivered. The first contribution is an SLR of collaborative innovation platforms (CIPs). The review represents the state-of-the-art of CIPs, consolidates various design ideas, and knowledge commonly shared on CIPs. A second contribution stemming from the SLR is a taxonomy of innovation mechanisms supported by CIPs. To construct said taxonomy, the functions and features of the reviewed platforms have been categorised. In total, four core mechanisms have been identified relating to collaboration, knowledge, learning, and innovation process management, with a total of 52 submechanisms. The taxonomy will serve as the basis for constructing the RO.

The third contribution is the RA. Two workshops have been conducted with stakeholders from the four PPLCs to gather their use cases. The insights gained from these workshops have been translated into both functional and non-functional requirements, which the stakeholders validated through a questionnaire. Besides, informal interviews and a content analysis of implemented information technologies have been conducted to unravel the baseline architecture in place at each PPLC. Building on the requirements and core processes of the PPLCs, target architectures (the envisioned future state) were developed for each PPLC. By synthesising common elements from the extracted baseline and target architectures, an application cooperation viewpoint has been developed, synthesising common application components for PPLC platforms. The application components can be sorted into components for social, engagement, idea, project, and knowledge management. Other components pertain to control mechanisms such as user management, intellectual property rules, and data and knowledge regulations. Furthermore, the RA prescribes a 10-step approach for PPLCs on how to apply the viewpoints and develop a platform, including stakeholder identification, data collection, requirements analysis, and determination of application components. Finally, a prototype has been developed that incorporates the application components and is currently being evaluated by stakeholders.

Future work will concentrate on utilising both the RO and RA to develop an intelligent tool that guides PPLCs through the platform design process, using the RA as guidelines and the RO as a domain understanding of contextual variables and platform design concepts.

Acknowledgements. I want to thank my supervisors, Dr. Sebastian Piest, Dr. Gayane Sedrakyan, and Prof. Martijn Mes, for their support and feedback on this paper.

Disclosure of Interests. The author has no competing interests to declare.

References

1. Broekhuizen, T., Dekker, H., de Faria, P., Firk, S., Nguyen, D.K., Sofka, W.: AI for managing open innovation: opportunities, challenges, and a research agenda. J. Bus. Res. **167**, 114196 (2023)
2. Clausen, R.T., Nielsen, J.A., Mathiassen, L.: Organising and managing digital platform renewal: the role of framing and overflowing. Inf. Syst. J. **34**(5), 1440–1465 (2024)
3. Cruz, P., Beroiza, F., Ponce, F., Astudillo, H.: A reference model for outside-in open innovation platforms, pp. 1–8 (2021)
4. De Faria, P., Noseleit, F., Los, B.: The influence of internal barriers on open innovation (2020)
5. Galster, M., Avgeriou, P.: Empirically-grounded reference architectures: a proposal, pp. 153–158 (2011)
6. Gassmann, O., Enkel, E.: Towards a theory of open innovation: three core process archetypes. In: R&D Management Conference, vol. 6, pp. 1–18. Lisbon (2004)
7. Grimpe, C., Sofka, W., Distel, A.P.: SME participation in research grant consortia–the emergence of coordinated attention in collaborative innovation. Small Bus. Econ. **59**(4), 1567–1592 (2022)
8. Hevner, A.R., March, S.T., Park, J., Ram, S.: Design science in information systems research. MIS Q., 75–105 (2004)
9. Hii, J., Neely, A.: Innovative capacity of firms: on why some firms are more innovative than others (2000)
10. Huang, C.Y., et al.: Reference architecture for collaborative design. Tech. Rep. 1 (2010)
11. Ivanov, D.: The industry 5.0 framework: viability-based integration of the resilience, sustainability, and human-centricity perspectives. Int. J. Prod. Res. **61**(5), 1683–1695 (2023)
12. Lyu, B., Lai, C.: Learners' Engagement on A Social Networking Platform: An Ecological Analysis (2022)
13. Miranda, J., Ramírez-Montoya, M.S., Molina, A.: Education 4.0 reference framework for the design of teaching-learning systems: two case studies involving collaborative networks and open innovation. In: Camarinha-Matos, L.M., Boucher, X., Afsarmanesh, H. (eds.) PRO-VE 2021. IAICT, vol. 629, pp. 692–701. Springer, Cham (2021). https://doi.org/10.1007/978-3-030-85969-5_65
14. Piller, F., West, J.: Firms, users, and innovation. New Front. Open Innov. **29**(1), 29–49 (2014)
15. Sassanelli, C., Terzi, S.: The D-BEST reference model: a flexible and sustainable support for the digital transformation of small and medium enterprises. Glob. J. Flex. Syst. Manag. **23**(3), 345–370 (2022)
16. Schipper, T.M., Mennens, K., Preenen, P., Vos, M., van den Tooren, M., Hofstra, N.: Interorganizational learning: a conceptualization of public-private learning communities. Hum. Resour. Dev. Rev. **22**(4), 494–523 (2023)

EA4AI - International Workshop on Enterprise Architecture for Augmented Intelligence

LLM4BPMN: A Prompting Approach with LLMs for BPMN Model Generation

Ana Costa(✉), Alena Wimmer(✉), and Luise Pufahl(✉)

School of Computation, Information and Technology, Technical University of Munich, Heilbronn, Germany
{a.costa,alena.wimmer,luise.pufahl}@tum.de
https://www.cs.cit.tum.de/infs/startseite/

Abstract. Recent advances in Natural Language Processing (NLP) and Large Language Models (LLMs) show significant potential for automating the extraction of process information and the generation of process models directly from descriptions. We present an approach that automatically generates Business Process Model and Notation (BPMN) from process descriptions using LLMs and Prompt Engineering. Our approach considers a large subset of BPMN elements for generation and focuses on the quality of the generated models that are evaluated with Graph Edit Distance. We propose a prompting strategy that serves as a guiding method to help researchers in the future use of LLMs in the field and provide a tool to support the approach. The results evaluated through a quantitative comparison show that our approach outperforms a state-of-the-art tool, especially for more complex processes.

Keywords: Large Language Model · Business Process Model Generation · Process Description · Natural Language Processing

1 Introduction

Business Process Management (BPM) is a broad discipline concerned with the identification, understanding, monitoring, standardization, and improvement of business processes within and across organizations [1]. A key activity across several stages of BPM is the modeling of business processes as they are performed ("as-is") and as they should be ("to-be") [2]. A process model–key artifact of BPM–is the abstracted visual representation of a business process for a specific modeling purpose, e.g., documentation or training. BPMN has emerged as the de facto industry standard for process modeling due to its ability to comprehensively communicate complex execution logic [3].

However, a significant challenge remains in practice: If process documentation exists, it is often not in the form of process models, rather it is available in unstructured text documents. Additionally, the process documentation is often outdated and incomplete [4,5]. In case that the processes are modeled, the individuals who have deep operational knowledge of a process are typically not the

J. Barateiro et al. (Eds.): EDOC 2025 Workshops, LNBIP 571, pp. 261–278, 2026.
https://doi.org/10.1007/978-3-032-16234-2_22

same individuals who are tasked with creating the process models and experts in modeling with BPMN [6]. This highlights the need for knowledge exchange between domain experts and process modelers, which traditionally involves several rounds of interviews, meetings, surveys, or workshops [7]. However, this process is prone to errors, ambiguities, misunderstandings, and loss of information. As a result, process modeling often takes up to 60% of the time spent on process management projects [6].

Therefore, BPM researchers have tested various NLP techniques to tackle the task of extracting process information from textual or oral process descriptions [8]. However, before the advent of LLMs, language-related tasks were approached using a modular, often linguistically inspired techniques, in scenarios involving standardized terminology and simple sentence structures [9]. Recent advancements in LLMs have substantially improved performance in handling complex and context-dependent textual and spoken data, demonstrating great capabilities in capturing implicit knowledge and process intricacies [10]. Given this, there is significant potential to improve the efficiency of process modeling through the use of LLMs [11].

Considering this, we propose LLM4BPMN, a prompting approach that leverages LLM techniques to generate BPMN diagrams covering an extended set of BPMN elements and producing syntactically and semantically correct BPMN XML files. The motivation for developing the proposed approach emerges from challenges encountered across distinct industry domains. First, processes in industry are documented in unstructured formats [4], such as textual documents, spreadsheets, or wikis. Second, standardizing communication between stakeholders remains difficult due to the complexity and limited accessibility of BPMN knowledge for industry domain experts [12]. Lastly, traditional NLP methods lack the contextual understanding necessary to accurately represent implicit, domain-specific knowledge [13]. By incorporating advanced LLM techniques, LLM4BPMN combines the capabilities from traditional NLP and contextual understanding from LLMs, accommodating varied complexity levels found in process descriptions. The main contributions of our approach in comparison with existing approaches using LLMs [13–19] include:

- Support of a large set of BPMN elements, such as intermediate events and data objects that are not addressed in previous research approaches. The choice of focusing on BPMN is driven by its wide industrial adoption, standardized notation, and integration with enterprise-level tools.
- Provision of a BPMN output in Extensible Markup Language (XML) format directly importable into tools supporting the BPMN XML standard.
- Robust evaluation of results based on quantitative measures that can be used as a benchmarking setup. This is a significant advantage, as current research works rely on case studies or expert evaluation, which do not facilitate a comparison of the quality of the generated models.

The paper is organized as follows. Section 2 describes recent achievements in literature for BPMN model generation. Section 3 describes the preliminaries.

Section 4 describes our approach, and Sect. 5 describes the experimental setup and evaluation results. Finally, Sect. 6 presents the conclusion and future work.

2 Related Work

Approaches for BPMN generation include traditional pipelines that rely on a combination of NLP tools, or alternatively on LLM-based methods. When extracting information from text, NLP tools were combined in pipelines for syntactic and semantic analysis [8], dependency parsing [20], rule-based pattern matching [21], or a combination of the three [22]. Standard NLP preprocessing was combined with pattern matching to extract domain-specific language [23,24], with tokenization [25], and with custom rule-based algorithms [9].

More recent approaches use LLMs like OpenAI's GPT-3, GPT-3.5, GPT-4, and others, for information extraction and BPMN model generation. Practically, LLMs are suitable for tasks like process modeling that require the generation of outputs from process description due to their capability to process and interpret natural language [15]. Techniques, such as in-context learning [14], multi-turn dialogue strategies, prompt engineering, and self-improving code generation [17] are used to extract process data. Since 2024, prompting techniques such as zero-shot, few-shot, and chain-of thought are introduced in literature [19].

Although LLMs are common for information extraction, there are few approaches that directly generate the process from text, since most of them make use of an intermediate representation. Honkisz et al. [8] use the `bpmn_python`[1] library to automatically transform their list into the corresponding BPMN file. The BPMN Sketch Miner first applies a process mining algorithm to generate the initial control flow, then uses a rule-based approach to define the element types and lanes, and finally applies a hierarchical layout algorithm to generate the additional diagram metadata [23,24]. Sonbol et al. [9] apply two rule-based steps to transform their graph-based concept map into the BPMN diagram. Process modeling with `ProMoAI` transforms the intermediate representation Partially OrderedWorkflow Language (POWL) into the corresponding BPMN diagram using the `pm4py`[2] library [13,17]. Daclin et al. [16] use a rule-based approach to transform their intermediate representation, a list called formalized process data, into a corresponding BPMN format. Nivon and Salaün [18] use a rule-based approach mapping patterns of their trees to BPMN flows. In contrast to these studies, our approach makes a direct transformation from text to BPMN diagram using LLMs.

For the sake of artifact development, it is common practice to limit the subset of supported BPMN elements. Table 1 shows the BPMN elements that are explicitly or implicitly supported by related work. The generic BPMN task is supported by many publications, but most of them only support start and end events. Only three studies support other events [23–25], with only two of them

[1] https://github.com/KrzyHonk/bpmn-python.

[2] https://github.com/process-intelligence-solutions/pm4py.

also including the specific types for intermediate events, such as time, error, send, receive, notify, publish, escalate, and terminate [23,24].

Table 1. Supported BPMN elements by the proposed solutions (✓ = column considered by a study)

Ref.	Task	Events		Gateways			Roles	Data
		Start, End	Other	XOR	AND	Event-based		
[8]	✓	✓		✓				
[24]	✓	✓	✓	✓	✓	✓	✓	
[25]	✓	✓	✓	✓	✓		✓	✓
[9]	✓	✓		✓			✓	
[16]	✓	✓		✓	✓			
[23]	✓	✓	✓	✓	✓	✓	✓	
[17]	✓	✓		✓				
[13]	✓	✓		✓	✓			
[19]	✓	✓		✓	✓		✓	
[18]	✓	✓		✓	✓			

Many studies support exclusive gateways. The parallel gateway is supported by seven studies. The least commonly supported gateway is the event-based gateway [23,24]. Pools and lanes (in Table 1 summarized as *Roles*) are supported by half of the studies. The *data* perspective (cf. Table 1) with data objects and stores is supported by only one study [25]. Furthermore, none of the publications claims to support sub-processes. In contrast to these studies, we aim to support all of the mentioned BPMN elements.

Besides that, our approach includes the possibility of using spoken process descriptions with audio files or direct recording to generate the model. This is not considered a research contribution, but adding a module that automatically describes speech-to-text into the approach was only presented in the literature by Daclin et al. [16].

3 Preliminaries

In this section, we define the main concepts used in our approach, such as process description, prompt, LLM, the imperative representation of a process model, and the process diagram in XML format.

A process description *PD* is defined as a tuple (pd_S, pd_T), which consists of a process description as speech pd_S and as text pd_T.

We define *PR* as a set consisting of all prompts included in our approach. The prompts used for generation (pr_{gen}), refinement (pr_{ref}), and completeness check (pr_{cc}) are therefore $\in PR$. Each of the prompts is given in different steps to an LLM, in order to generate, refine, and complete the process diagram. Furthermore, *LLM* is defined as a set consisting of all different models:

$$LLM = \{llm_1, llm_2, \ldots, llm_n\},$$

where $n \in \{1, \infty\}$. Two examples of *llms* are the `whisper-1` used for speech-to-text and the `o1` from OpenAI.

Following the definitions of Dijkman et al. [26] for a business process graph, let T be a set of types and Ω be a set of text labels. A business process graph is a tuple $(N, E, \tau, \lambda, \alpha)$ in which N is a finite set of nodes, $E : N \times N$ is a finite set of edges, $\tau : (N \cup E) \to T$ associates nodes and edges with types, $\lambda : (N \cup E) \to \Omega$ associates nodes and edges with labels, $\alpha : (N \cup E) \to (T \to \Omega)$ associates nodes and edges with attributes, where an attribute is always a combination of a type and a label. In our case, the attributes are defining the lanes and pools' names.

The design decisions on types T have been cast to include all the specific elements that we have defined. Therefore, $T = A \cup S \cup V \cup G \cup D$, with each element being a finite set of activities, collapsed subprocesses, events, gateways, and data, respectively. Then, V is the set of all events defined for our approach, so that V ={*start*, *messageStart*, *timerStart*, *throwingMessage*, *catchingMessage*, *timer*, *escalation*, *catchingIntermediate*, *throwingIntermediate*, *interruptingBoundary*, *end*, *messageEnd*} . G is the set of all gateways, so that G ={*exclusive*, *inclusive*, *parallel*} and D ={*dataObject*, *dataStore*} . Further, Ω ={*sequenceFlow*, *messageFlow*, *inputAssociation*, *outputAssociation*} . These elements are defined as input given in the prompts to the LLM for generation. With regard to the event types, the more general ones, such as start, end and intermediate catching and throwing, as well as interrupting boundary events, are supported, and a set of specific event types is often used [27]. We utilize these defined BPMN elements for prompting and the resulting quantitative evaluation; however, our approach allows the LLM to leverage the wide range of BPMN elements when following the standard.

A *bpmn* is a business process graph modeled using the Object Management Group (OMG) standard and represented as an XML. At each stage of our approach, transformations are performed in the *bpmn*. *BPMN* is defined as the set of all diagrams considered in our approach. Therefore, the generated $bpmn_{gen}$, refined $bpmn_{ref}$, and completed $bpmn_{cc}$ are $\in$ *BPMN*. The *bpmn* is the data storing format used in our approach, and it contains definitions, the process logic, the visual position and layout of elements called Diagram Interchange (DI), and other data such as name space or extensions.

In addition, the representation of the model in a process graph, defined by [26], enabled the Graph Edit Distance (GED) calculations of our evaluation.

4 Proposed Approach: LLM4BPMN

This section presents the LLM4BPMN, a prompting approach and architecture for building BPMN XML files from a given process description with an extended BPMN element set based on an LLM system. While the architecture and prompts apply to any LLM, one LLM was chosen for the implementation of the tool support. First, the approach of prompt engineering is presented in Sect. 4.1, followed by the architecture with its prompts in Sect. 4.2, and the tool support in Sect. 4.3.

4.1 Approach of Prompt Engineering

For developing the prompts of our approach and to be able to test different prompting techniques, we have set up a controlled testing environment. This approach was selected instead of ablation studies since the purpose is to design prompts so that the LLM produce more reliable output, and not to understand the contribution of each component. The first step was to create a controlled dataset consisting of four process descriptions and corresponding BPMN diagrams for testing different prompting techniques. The dataset was created based on a defined subset of BPMN elements and contains diagrams of varying size and complexity. The sizes of the processes range from 12 to 29 elements, and the pd_T range from 98 to 218 words. Further details of the dataset, can be found on HuggingFace[3].

Following prompting best practices, recommendations, and approaches proposed by Kourani et al. [17], prompting techniques were defined. By applying each prompting technique, three models for each process description were generated to account for the inherent randomness of the LLM. We calculated the similarity GED and averaged the metric per generated process. Based on these results, the prompting techniques are compared to determine which one produces the best results.

Initially, a simple instruction prompt and a more structured Chain-of-Thought (CoT) prompt were developed and evaluated. The instruction prompt includes a *task* description (i.e., transforming a given description into BPMN XML compliant with the BPMN 2.0 standard), and a *goal* (i.e., the output can be directly imported into tools such as *bpmn.io*). In addition, it contains more detailed *instructions and requirements*. These were informed by the process modeling steps and guidelines of Dumas et al. [28, Ch.3-5] as well as the instructions adopted from the OMG standard [29]. The instructions and requirements were refined iteratively through trial and error, based on observations of how the LLM responded to specific process descriptions and the related output. In contrast to the instruction prompt, the CoT prompt includes the instructions and requirements as a step-by-step instruction. Both prompts were constructed using role prompting, i.e., an expert in process management and BPMN 2.0 modeling.

As the results in Table 2 show, the CoT prompt performed better on all four processes. Therefore, the CoT prompt was selected as the base prompt pr_{gen}.

In the next step, we evaluated two possible extensions of the base prompt: The first one, two-shot, added two examples to the CoT prompt. Two examples were chosen because one example might have biased the LLM towards the exemplary process layout. These examples contain a process description and a

[3] https://huggingface.co/datasets/alenatz/controlled-environment-modified.

Table 2. The prompting techniques evaluation by averaged similarity GED.

Prompting Techniques	Process1	Process2	Process3	Process4	Avg.
Instruction Prompt	0.8781	0.5342	0.7194	0.5550	0.6717
CoT	**0.8968**	0.6141	0.7448	0.5777	0.7083
CoT two-shot	0.8720	0.7105	0.8043	0.7085	0.7738
CoT + Refinement	0.6401	**0.7722**	0.7406	0.5948	0.6869
CoT two-shot + Refinement	0.7920	0.7700	**0.8136**	**0.7571**	**0.7832**

corresponding BPMN XML. In the second extension, we added a refinement prompt asking the LLM to improve the previously generated process diagram. For the refinement prompt, we developed a checklist for potential corrections. These were collected based on several tests with the LLM and observations of typical errors.

The CoT base prompt was tested in combination with two-shot, with the refinement prompt, and with both options. As Table 2 shows, CoT with two-shot and the refinement prompt performed best on Processes 3 and 4, and very close to the best on Process 2. It also produced the highest average GED of 0.7832. Due to these results, we selected as the generation prompt pr_{gen} CoT with two-shot, and additionally, added the refinement prompt pr_{ref} to our approach.

During the testing, we observed that in some cases, the LLM generated the DI part of the XML-file incompletely, even though the prompts specifically instructed the LLM against it. To prevent incompletely generated XML files, we implemented a custom algorithm that checks whether the DI part is complete. We added another prompt to our overall approach, the completeness check prompt pr_{cc}, which is executed in cases where the diagram is incomplete. Next, the architecture and the detailed prompts are presented.

4.2 Architecture and Prompts

As shown in the high-level architecture of LL4BPMN in Fig. 1, the user provides a process description in natural language, which can alternatively be provided as an audio file or recording. This description is given to BPMN generation, which is connected with a prompt and receives information in the form of *bpmn* from the LLM. After the generation, the model in form of a BPMN XML file is refined, and, in a second step, a completeness check is performed to ensure that the number of visual elements in the diagram matches the logical process elements. In the following, the details of each step are provided.

BPMN Generation from Dual-Modal Input. The generation enables users to provide either audio or textual process descriptions as input. For audio, a speech recognition LLM is used to transcribe speech into text, supporting dual-modal input processing. The first step in the pipeline is the generation of

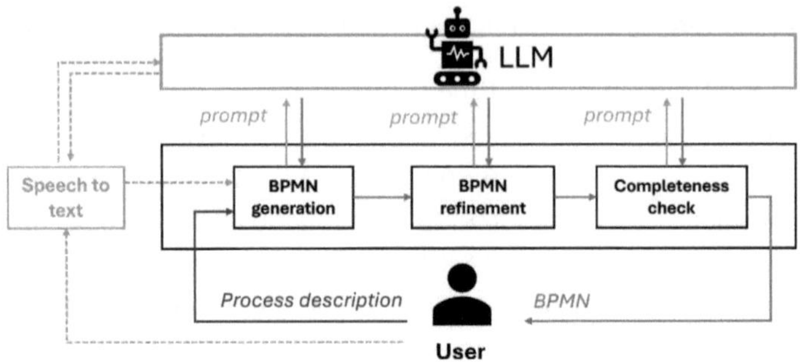

Fig. 1. A high-level system diagram of LLM4BPMN.

$bpmn_{gen}$, which uses the process description pd_T, and the prompt pr_{gen} as input.

$$BPMNGen(pd_T, pr_{gen}) = bpmn_{gen}.$$

The structure of pr_{gen} includes role assignment, task and goal, a step-by-step textual instruction, and two demonstration examples (in form of two process descriptions and their corresponding BPMN XML files) given as additional information to the prompt. The reduced version of the prompt[4] is provided in Table 3. The task aims to convert the process description pd_T into *bpmn* and does not include all the necessary knowledge about the problem. The LLM is therefore forced to use its own knowledge on the BPMN 2.0 standard to solve the conversion problem. The goal instructs on the output that should be given, in this case, the XML structure. When the task and goal are determined, five steps that actively guide the LLM on how to solve the task are given.

The first, second, and third steps involve extracting elements, such as tasks, events, process flows, and assignments to their corresponding roles, i.e., defining pools and lanes. The fourth step includes the *bpmn* construction with modeling requirements, such as that opened gateways must be closed, specific outgoing sequence flows must be labeled, communication between pools with throwing and catching events, and others. The last step instructs the LLM to complete the visual layout with assignment of coordinates and dimensions and alignment elements. In addition, two examples that include the process description and the BPMN XML is given in order to assist the LLM on answering the task.

LLM-Based Model Refinement. Once the first version of the BPMN model is generated, an LLM-refinement loop is implemented. The refinement step uses pd_T, pr_{ref}, and $bpmn_{gen}$, to improve the quality of the diagram.

$$BPMNRef(pd_T, pr_{ref}, bpmn_{gen}) = bpmn_{ref}$$

The prompt pr_{ref} directs the model to correct common modeling errors or semantic inconsistencies (Table 4). This feedback loop combines the generative capabilities of the LLM for self-correction and iterative enhancement. The

[4] The complete prompts can be accessed at https://github.com/alenatz/LLM4BPMN.

Table 3. The generation prompt (reduced).

Prompt
You are an expert in process management and BPMN 2.0 modeling. Task: Convert the following textual process description into a fully compliant BPMN 2.0 XML model. The final BPMN model should adhere strictly to the BPMN 2.0 standard. Do only output the final BPMN XML. ... Step 1: Process Element Extraction – Identify all tasks, events, and gateways in the text Step 2: Participant Extraction – Identify all participants in the text as candidates for pools and lanes, if applicable. ... Step 3: Define Process Flow – Use the identified elements, their lanes, and extract the correct flow in the text to construct a valid BPMN 2.0 XML representation. ... Step 4: BPMN XML Construction – Create a valid BPMN 2.0 XML representation from the identified elements, participants, and flow. ... Step 5: Complete the BPMN DI (Diagram Interchange) part – The diagram should be aligned horizontally: start events on the left, flow from left to right, and end events on the right. ...

approach is scalable and adaptive, which enables the system to incrementally improve the process diagram quality without manual intervention.

Taking into account this, pr_{ref} uses role assignment, task, goal, and checklist for potential corrections. While the task involves reviewing the LLM's own output to identify improvement potentials, the goal give instructions on the *bpmn* output. Then, the LLM checks specifications on the five steps presented in pr_{gen}, such as structural correctness, logical flow inconsistencies, layout considerations, and adherence to the BPMN standard.
The checklist makes use of domain-specific language within the BPMN standard, which encourages the LLM to produce output with the same nomenclature. By using specific checks, pr_{ref} guides the model toward automated validation that a human BPMN reviewer would perform. The initial version of *bpmn* is therefore refined by integrating the improvement solutions and producing $bpmn_{ref}$. In the last check, there is an emphasis on the completeness of the layout since the LLM was constantly omitting DI parts. To ensure the completeness of the BPMN XML files, particularly for more complex process scenarios, an algorithmic validation step is performed next.

Completeness Check. To ensure that the generated model is both logically and visually complete, the completeness check module includes our own devel-

Table 4. The refinement prompt (reduced).

Prompt
You are an expert in process management and BPMN 2.0 modeling. Task: Review the following BPMN XML output and identify potential issues or improvements and implement them based on the process description provided as additional information. Do only output the final BPMN XML. ... Check for: – Structural correctness (e.g., unclosed gateways, missing sequence flows, message events and flows) – Logical flow inconsistencies – Adherence to BPMN 2.0 standards – Ensure all special characters are escaped according to XML rules, if applicable. – For each laneSet and lane make sure all nodes are listed as flowNodeRef physically and logically in that lane. – Readability and layout considerations – Ensure full coverage of BPMN DI: every process element must have a corresponding BPMNShape or BPMNEdge in the BPMNDiagram section. Important: You must output your BPMN Diagram elements without omission!

oped validation algorithm. If the algorithm determines that the model is not complete, pd_T is used as input together with pr_{cc}, and $bpmn_{ref}$ to complete it.

$$BPMNCom(pd_T, pr_{cc}, bpmn_{ref}) = bpmn_{cc}$$

The validation algorithm of this step parses $bpmn_{ref}$ and defines the set of nodes (for elements like tasks, subprocesses, events, among others) and the set of logical flows. Then, it iterates through the element types, counting the corresponding visual elements of the BPMN diagram. The counts are compared in case logical elements lacks its visual representation. If, as a result of the validation algorithm, discrepancies are found (e.g., missing visual shapes or connectors), the system automatically advises the LLM to generate the missing visual elements, and the generated section is merged back into the final model. The prompt pr_{cc} is based on role assignment, and therefore, the LLM acts as an expert in process modeling (Table 5). Immediately after role assignment, the prompt provides context, informing that the previously generated model is missing or incomplete. This already directs the LLM to search for $bpmn_{ref}$ to resolve the task. The task involves generating solely the missing DI part, and the goal provides instructions on uploading the output. Since pr_{cc} was designed because the previous prompts were not generating complete *bpmn*, this prompt makes use of a more concrete task with clearer reasoning steps, which can provide less reasoning context and induce the LLM to generate a more direct prediction in comparison to the other prompts.

Table 5. The completeness check prompt.

Prompt
You are an expert in process management and BPMN 2.0 modeling.
The BPMN DI part of the following process BPMN XML is either missing or incomplete.
Task: Generate the BPMN DI part of the XML file. Output only the XML code for this part.
Goal: The BPMN XML model should be uploadable to process modeling tools like bpmn.io and signavio.
Ensure completeness. As information, you get the BPMN XML and a textual description of the process.

4.3 Tool Support

All processing steps are integrated into a Streamlit-based web interface[5], which allows for interactive input, Application Programming Interface (API) credential management, and real-time visualization of results. The final BPMN can be rendered with *bpmn.io* or exported directly to an external provider. Automated extraction and merging use standard XML parsing libraries and regular expressions to ensure robustness. The result is a user-friendly, end-to-end system that combines modern LLM-based process automation with traditional validation and error-handling strategies, as shown in Fig. 2. The tool utilizes the OpenAI API with the `whisper-1` model used to transcribe the audio and the `o1` GPT model used for three chained calls. All requests to the API are authenticated via a user-provided API key. Optionally, an external provider API can be used to visualize the generated model. In this case, the external providers' API is called to upload the model to the target directory and to download the corresponding image file, which can be displayed in the web application. Additionally, file downloading is implemented using Streamlit's standard download component, without the need for additional libraries.

[5] https://bpmn-generation.streamlit.app/.

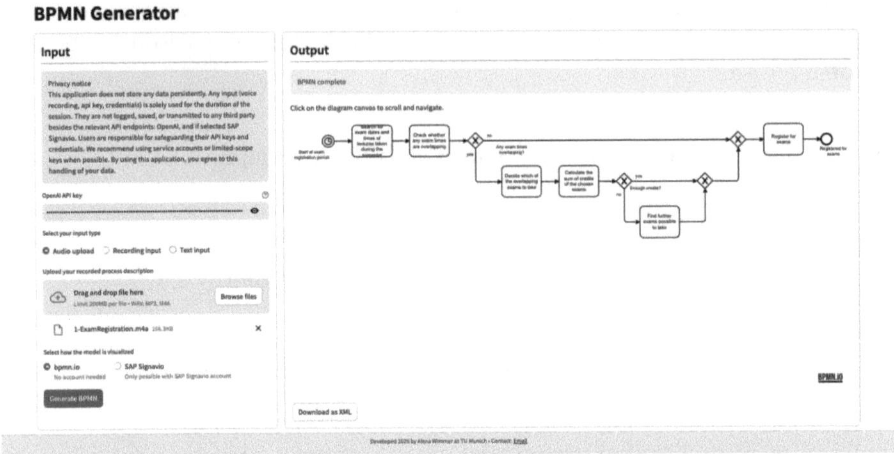

Fig. 2. The tool support after the generation of a process.

5 Evaluation

This section presents a quantitative comparison of LLM4BPMN approach of this paper and a current state-of-the-art solution, PromoAI, by Kourani et al. [13]. Conducting such an evaluation, however, is not straightforward, as most approaches are evaluated qualitatively, use different metrics, are based on unavailable datasets, or vary in generation tasks. PromoAI [13] is the closest in literature since they apply LLMs to solve the BPMN diagram generation task and provide an available tool that can be used for evaluation. Considering this, we evaluated both approaches using the GED metric and compared the results of the ground truth models with the generated ones. Firstly, we present the dataset used and the experimental setup, and then the results of the quantitative comparison.

5.1 Dataset

We created a dataset of 40 process descriptions paired with their corresponding ground truth BPMN models based on the dataset proposed by Friedrich et al. [30]. The dataset was created by domain experts from multiple sectors: academic (12), industry (8), textbook-based (7), and public sector (13).

The BPMN diagrams were remodeled and exported as BPMN 2.0 XML files. We created additionally audio recordings of each written process description so that the data set consists of 40 audio-text-process model triplets[6]. While the process descriptions vary between third-person and first-person descriptions, the

[6] The process descriptions and corresponding BPMN XML files can be accessed on HuggingFacehttps://huggingface.co/datasets/alenatz/friedrich_modified.

process models contain different elements and vary in length and complexity. This curated dataset allows a reliable comparison between the generated models by LLMs and the ground truth models created by human experts.

Most processes are described in fewer than 10 sentences, with only a few outliers being much longer. The processes have on average 7.5 different element types, ranging from 4 to 13 element types, 21.2 total elements, ranging from 8 to 73 total elements, and 21.5 connections, ranging from 6 to 84.

5.2 Experimental Setup

For each input, we let LLM4BPMN and PromoAI generate three BPMN models to account for inherent LLM randomness. The similarity GED was computed for each model and averaged over the three models for each process description. Additionally, the generated models were checked for completeness and uploadability to process visualization tools. The experimental setup involved matching the graph process elements and calculating the GED[7]. Since the process models may differ in characteristics and number of elements, the same process behavior may be represented by different types of elements or different labels. To match the individual elements of the ground truth and generated models, a greedy heuristic based on element similarity is applied [26].

For each element in the first process graph, we compute the similarity to each element in the second graph and match it to the most similar of those elements. To ensure that an element that is only included in one process is not matched to any element, a similarity threshold is introduced as a limit for elements to be considered similar enough to be matched.

The similarity of two nodes is calculated with four similarity measures: (1) Semantic label similarity sim_{sl}, (2) Attribute lane similarity sim_a, (3) Type node similarity sim_t, and (4) Positional similarity sim_p. This differs from the similarity measures proposed by [26] in two ways. First, they compare the labels by syntactic and semantic similarity, which we consider obsolete by using more recent NLP methods, and thus reduce them to the semantic label similarity measure. Second, instead of the positional similarity, they use a context similarity measure that takes into account not only the number of incoming and outgoing flows but also takes the corresponding node similarity.

$$sim(n_1, n_2) = w_{sl}sim_{sl}(n_1, n_2) + w_a sim_a(n_1, n_2) + w_t sim_t(n_1, n_2) + w_p sim_p(n_1, n_2)$$

The weights $w_{sl} = w_a = w_t = 0.3$, $w_p = 0.1$ were defined[8], since the semantic label, attribute, and type similarity are more relevant than the position of the

[7] The detailed definition approximations of the GED are available with DOI: 10.6084/m9.figshare.29312891.

[8] In the exception that only one of the three generated BPMN diagrams contains pools and lanes, the weights are defined as $w_{sl} = w_t = 0.4$ and $w_a = w_p = 0.1$, because the reduced similarity measure could compromise the element matching process.

nodes. As proposed by [26], we consider node deletion, node insertion, node substitution, edge deletion, and edge insertion. Any node that was not mapped in the process detailed in the previous paragraph is considered a deleted or inserted node. Furthermore, every node that was successfully mapped is considered a substitution, where the difference is $1 - sim(n_1, n_2)$. The edges are categorized by their type, and the difference in the number of edges from the ground truth and the generated models is considered as deleted or inserted edges. Due to the ambiguity of BPMN models, a model with a GED similarity to the ground truth model of less than 1 is not necessarily incorrect or less complying to the process description. We use the metric as a guide to assess the quality of the output model, but not with the intention that a GED similarity of 1 must be achieved.

5.3 Quantitative Comparison

In this subsection, we present the results of the quantitative comparison between PromoAI and our approach, LLM4BPMN. Conducting the experiments, 120 BPMN diagrams were generated and evaluated against their respective ground truth models. The same LLM was used for the generation of models in both approaches.

In Table 6, the average results per process description group is shown as well as the overall average for both BPMN diagram generation approaches based on LLMs. PromoAI generated models with an average similarity GED of 0.6020, which is outperformed by our approach with a GED of 0.6487. Despite generally performing more accurate representations, LLM4BPM generates simpler models with fewer elements in comparison to the ground truth process models. Processes of groups 1, 4, and 8 show significant improvements with LLM4BPM, which indicates that the tool handles more complex process descriptions more effectively. This is further observed in Fig. 3, in which our approach shows a higher performance for processes with a higher complexity (i.e., higher number of words in the description and the number of elements in the process).

LLM4BPM performs better in general, with exception for processes with a medium to low complexity, varying between 71 to 88 words in the process description and between 18 to 27 elements, which has a difference in GED values around 0.1. However, PromoAI outperformed in 5 of the 8 processes of group 3. This is the case since the ground truth models of these processes do not contain pools or lanes elements. Considering this, PromoAI has an inherent limitation in generating certain BPMN constructs, such as pools or lanes, making it unsuitable for process descriptions that require these elements. This is further observed for processes with difference of GED -0.25 (Fig. 3), since these processes contains more pools and lanes than others despite the lower number of elements and short description. Furthermore, the highest difference in GED value of around 0.15 considers processes that do not contain more than one pool or lane.

Moreover, despite some significant differences in individual cases, the general oscillation pattern in Fig. 3 remains synchronized, since both methods share similar sensitivities to certain complexity characteristics. Furthermore, the gap

Table 6. The results of PromoAI [13], and LLM4BPMN per process group.

Group	PromoAI [13]	LLM4BPMN
1	0.6416	0.7142
2	0.5891	0.6721
3	0.7032	0.6765
4	0.6199	0.7243
5	0.5628	0.6335
6	0.5767	0.6502
7	0.5725	0.6651
8	0.6277	0.7389
9	0.5526	0.6357
10	0.5598	0.5988
Avg	**0.6020**	**0.6487**

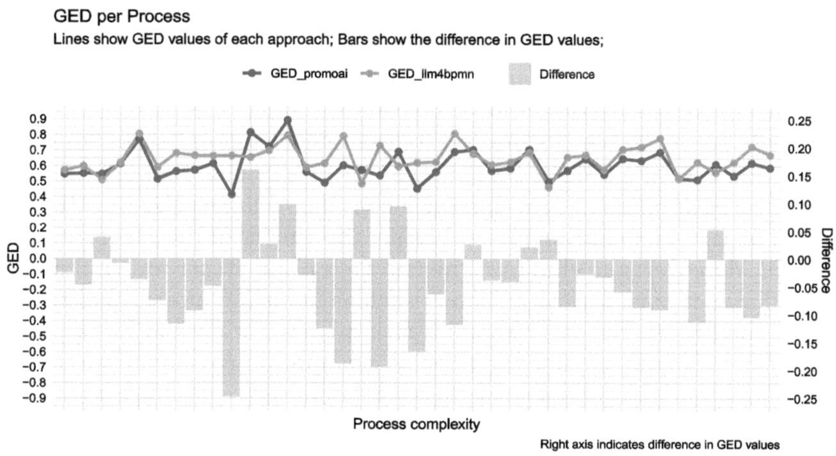

Fig. 3. GED values per process of both approaches and their difference.

between the two methods becomes smaller at both the lowest and highest complexity levels, with LLM4BPMN consistently achieving better results in these extremes. Thus, factors beyond complexity (e.g., specific BPMN element behavior or description patterns) influences the similarity.

When examining process models generated by LLM4BPM with a low similarity, it was observed that the main reason for the low similarity was the difference between the number of elements and connections. This was the case since the generated and ground truth models used pools and lanes in different ways, which affects how message flows and events interact between pools. These decisions often come down to modeling preferences. Therefore, even though some models might present a low similarity measure, these models are not necessarily syntactically or semantically incorrect.

6 Conclusion

This paper introduces LLM4BPMN, which uses LLMs to automatically generate process models from process descriptions. The selected prompting strategies for model generation enable language models to achieve a wide range of tasks in the BPMN field with high performance. With the customized generation prompts, a structure of *bpmn* is proposed. This structure can be used to accomplish process modeling and mining tasks such as process description, anomaly detection, fairness, and process improvement. The prompting strategies serves, therefore, as a guiding method that helps researchers in the future use of LLMs in the field. Furthermore, the paper provides a benchmarking setup for the quantitative evaluation of BPMN XML generation results for LLM as well as other NLP approaches.

Several limitations should be noted. The processes in the evaluation dataset consider a limited subset of BPMN elements, and the dataset covers only a limited amount of variety and ground truth models. Furthermore, the reliance on external LLM API and computational resources limits the accessibility when providers are not available. Future research should therefore benefit from a comparison of how several LLMs perform within the proposed framework. In contrast to the presented approaches, our approach considers a large subset of BPMN elements and focuses on quantitavely evaluating the quality of the generated models with GED. Moreover, the similarity metric focuses on structural similarity and therefore does not consider other factors such as modeling intent, quality, or layout, that could be further investigated with qualitative evaluation approaches. Overall, there is a tendency for the LLM to generate process models in a simpler way than presented in process descriptions. While this simplification does not always result in invalid models, it can reduce semantic completeness. To address these limitations, future research should focus on refining prompting strategies for generation or integrating domain-specific knowledge to enhance the accuracy of the model.

Disclosure of Interests. The authors have no competing interests to declare that are relevant to the content of this article.

References

1. Beerepoot, I., et al.: The biggest business process management problems to solve before we die. Comput. Ind. **146**, 103837 (2023)
2. zur Muehlen, M., Ho, D.T.: Service process innovation: a case study of BPMN in practice. In: Proceedings of the 41st Annual Hawaii International Conference on System Sciences (HICSS 2008). IEEE, 2008, pp. 372–372 (2008)
3. Recker, J.: Opportunities and constraints: the current struggle with BPMN. Bus. Process. Manag. J. **16**(1), 181–201 (2010)

4. Van der Aa, H., Carmona Vargas, J., Leopold, H., Mendling, J., Padró, L.: Challenges and opportunities of applying natural language processing in business process management. In: COLING 2018: The 27th International Conference on Computational Linguistics: Proceedings of the Conference: August 20–26, 2018 Santa Fe, New Mexico, USA. Association for Computational Linguistics, 2018, pp. 2791–2801 (2018)
5. Van Woensel, W., Motie, S.: Nlp4pbm: a systematic review on process extraction using natural language processing with rule-based, machine and deep learning methods, Enterprise Information Systems, p. 2417404 (2024)
6. Herbst, J., Karagiannis, D.: An inductive approach to the acquisition and adaptation of workflow models. In: Proceedings of the IJCAI, vol. 99. Citeseer, 1999, pp. 52–57 (1999)
7. Hvatum, L.B.: Requirements elicitation with business process modeling. In: Proceedings of the 21st Conference on Pattern Languages of Programs, 2014, pp. 1–9 (2014)
8. Honkisz, K., Kluza, K., Wiśniewski, P.: A concept for generating business process models from natural language description. In: Liu, W., Giunchiglia, F., Yang, B. (eds.) KSEM 2018. LNCS (LNAI), vol. 11061, pp. 91–103. Springer, Cham (2018). https://doi.org/10.1007/978-3-319-99365-2_8
9. Sonbol, R., Rebdawi, G., Ghneim, N.: A machine translation like approach to generate business process model from textual description. SN Comput. Sci. **4**(3), 291 (2023)
10. Zhou, Y., Muresanu, A.I., Han, Z., Paster, K., Pitis, S., Chan, H.: Large Language Models are Human-level Prompt Engineers.
11. Hörner, L.F., Reichert, M.: Generating process models by interacting with chatbots–a literature review. Future Internet **16**(10) (2024)
12. Klievtsova, N., Benzin, J.-V., Kampik, T., Mangler, J., Rinderle-Ma, S.: Conversational process modelling: state of the art, applications, and implications in practice. In: International Conference on Business Process Management. Springer, 2023, pp. 319–336 (2023)
13. Kourani, H., Berti, A., Schuster, D., van der Aalst, W.M.: Promoai: Process modeling with generative AI, arXiv preprint arXiv:2403.04327 (2024)
14. Bellan, P., Dragoni, M., Ghidini, C.: Extracting business process entities and relations from text using pre-trained language models and in-context learning. In: International Conference on Enterprise Design, Operations, and Computing. Springer, 2022, pp. 182–199 (2022)
15. —, "Process knowledge extraction and knowledge graph construction through prompting: A quantitative analysis. In: Proceedings of the 39th ACM/SIGAPP Symposium on Applied Computing, 2024, pp. 1634–1641 (2024)
16. Daclin, N., Mallek-Daclin, S., Zacharewicz, G.: Generative ai for business model generation (gai4bm): from textual description to business process model. In: The 10th International Food Operations and Processing Simulation Workshop. CAL-TEK SRL (2024)
17. Kourani, H., Berti, A., Schuster, D., van der Aalst, W.M.: Process modeling with large language models. In: International Conference on Business Process Modeling, Development and Support. Springer, 2024, pp. 229–244 (2024)
18. Nivon, Q., Salaün, G.: Automated generation of BPMN processes from textual requirements. In: International Conference on Service-Oriented Computing. Springer, 2024, pp. 185–201 (2024)

19. Wenger, S., Spahic-Bogdanovic, M., Martin, A.: Large language models for democratizing business process modeling: BPMN model generation and style guide adherence, In: Southern African Conference for Artificial Intelligence Research. Springer, 2024, pp. 372–389 (2024)
20. van der Aa, H., Di Ciccio, C., Leopold, H., Reijers, H.A.: Extracting declarative process models from natural language. In: Giorgini, P., Weber, B. (eds.) CAiSE 2019. LNCS, vol. 11483, pp. 365–382. Springer, Cham (2019). https://doi.org/10.1007/978-3-030-21290-2_23
21. van der Aa, H., Balder, K.J., Maggi, F.M., Nolte, A.: Say it in your own words: defining declarative process models using speech recognition. In: Fahland, D., Ghidini, C., Becker, J., Dumas, M. (eds.) BPM 2020. LNBIP, vol. 392, pp. 51–67. Springer, Cham (2020). https://doi.org/10.1007/978-3-030-58638-6_4
22. Quishpi, L., Carmona, J., Padró, L.: Extracting annotations from textual descriptions of processes. In: Fahland, D., Ghidini, C., Becker, J., Dumas, M. (eds.) BPM 2020. LNCS, vol. 12168, pp. 184–201. Springer, Cham (2020). https://doi.org/10.1007/978-3-030-58666-9_11
23. Ivanchikj, A., Serbout, S., Pautasso, C.: From text to visual BPMN process models: Design and evaluation. In: Proceedings of the 23rd ACM/IEEE International Conference on Model Driven Engineering Languages and Systems, 2020, pp. 229–239 (2020)
24. —, "Live process modeling with the bpmn sketch miner. Softw. Syst. Model. **21**(5), 1877–1906 (2022)
25. Sholiq, S., Sarno, R., Astuti, E.S.: Generating BPMN diagram from textual requirements. J. King Saud Univ.-Comput. Inform. Sci. **34**10,10 079–10 093 (2022)
26. Dijkman, R., Dumas, M., Van Dongen, B., Käärik, R., Mendling, J.: Similarity of business process models: Metrics and evaluation. Inf. Syst. **36**(2), 498–516 (2011)
27. Zur Muehlen, M., Recker, J.: We still don't know how much BPMN is enough, but we are getting closer. In: Seminal Contributions to Information Systems Engineering, J. Bubenko, J. Krogstie, O. Pastor, B. Pernici, C. Rolland, and A. Sølvberg, Eds. Springer, Berlin Heidelberg, pp. 445–451. [Online]. Available: http://link.springer.com/10.1007/978-3-642-36926-1_36
28. Dumas, M., Rosa, L.M., Mendling, J., Reijers, A.H.: Fundamentals of Business Process Management. Springer (2018)
29. I. O. Object Management Group, Business process model and notation (bpmn) version 2.0.2, (2014). [Online]. Available: https://www.omg.org/spec/BPMN
30. Friedrich, F., Mendling, J., Puhlmann, F.: Process model generation from natural language text. In: Mouratidis, H., Rolland, C. (eds.) CAiSE 2011. LNCS, vol. 6741, pp. 482–496. Springer, Heidelberg (2011). https://doi.org/10.1007/978-3-642-21640-4_36

Designing a Predictive Digital Twin Architecture for Smart Bridge Maintenance

Ali Sabzi Khoshraftar(✉), Berend Jan van der Zwaag, Duc V. Le, and Rob Bemthuis

University of Twente, Enschede, The Netherlands
{a.sabzikhoshraftar,b.j.vanderzwaag,v.d.le,r.h.bemthuis}@utwente.nl

Abstract. The growing number of aging bridges and their associated risks call for smarter, more cost-effective maintenance strategies. Digital twins (DTs) offer significant potential by enabling real-time monitoring, predictive analytics, and integrated decision-making. Although DTs are widely explored, their integration into enterprise architectures for infrastructure asset management remains limited. This paper presents a structured approach to architecting predictive DTs for bridge maintenance using the ArchiMate modeling language. Following a Design Science Research Methodology (DSRM), we: (1) analyze limitations in traditional maintenance workflows; (2) design reference enterprise architectures for DT integration; (3) propose a phased migration strategy toward prescriptive DTs; and (4) demonstrate practical feasibility through a requirement-based comparison and an illustrative implementation applied to a Dutch steel bridge. The architecture integrates IoT sensing, AI-based defect detection, and XR-based visualization. This work provides a blueprint for digital transformation initiatives in civil infrastructure.

Keywords: Digital twin · Bridge maintenance · Enterprise architecture · Archimate

1 Introduction

Many bridges in the Netherlands, and globally, are reaching the end of their design lifespan [6], with most constructed after the 1960s [3]. As structures age, the risk of failure increases, often with severe consequences. High-profile incidents such as the collapses of the I-35W bridge in Minneapolis (2007), the Polcevera viaduct in Genoa (2018) [33], and a Pittsburgh bridge in 2022 highlighted the inadequacy of current inspection and maintenance practices [2].

These bridges were not designed for today's traffic volumes or environmental stressors, such as climate change. Maintenance costs continue to rise, with annual expenses reaching up to 85% of total facility management budgets [8]. Predictive

J. Barateiro et al. (Eds.): EDOC 2025 Workshops, LNBIP 571, pp. 279–295, 2026.
https://doi.org/10.1007/978-3-032-16234-2_23

maintenance, supported by digital technologies, can reduce these costs by up to 50% while improving operational efficiency [23].

Digital twin (DT) technologies, recognized as a top strategic trend [7], offer a promising solution. They enable real-time data integration, system simulation, and predictive analytics. Yet, despite increasing adoption in manufacturing, their uptake in civil infrastructure adoption remains limited [25]. This is especially true for enterprise-wide applications, where DTs must integrate with existing information systems, legacy data, and asset management workflows.

Although previous work has proposed reference models for DTs in construction [1,4,11,27], these often lack integration across enterprise layers and often overlook governance structures essential for sustainable implementation. Bridging this gap, our study investigates how DTs can be embedded into the enterprise architectures of infrastructures.

To this end, we adopt the Design Science Research Methodology (DSRM) [26] to guide the development and evaluation of baseline and target enterprise architectures for bridge maintenance. The architectures distinguish between different maturity stages (monitoring-driven, predictive, and prescriptive) and include a phased migration strategy toward full DT integration. Following DSRM's six iterative steps, we identify limitations in current workflows, define stakeholder-informed objectives, design the architecture, and implement a functional prototype on a real bridge.

In addressing these challenges, our contributions are fourfold: (1) an architecture that links DT capabilities with enterprise-level systems and stakeholders; (2) a phased transformation roadmap; (3) an illustrative implementation for a real steel bridge, including monitoring and extended reality (XR)-enabled visualization; and (4) an initial evaluation of the architecture through a requirement-based comparison. This approach contributes to both scientific rigor and practical relevance for infrastructure stakeholders.

The remainder of this paper is structured as follows. Section 2 reviews related work. Section 3 presents the baseline architecture and identifies current integration challenges. Section 4 details the proposed DT architectures. Section 5 discusses the evaluation. We conclude in Sect. 6 with implications and directions for future work.

2 Related Work

This section reviews the conceptual evolution of DTs, their applications in infrastructure maintenance, and the role of enterprise architecture in supporting DT-enabled digital transformation.

2.1 Digital Twins in Infrastructure Maintenance

DTs are virtual representations of physical assets that enable continuous monitoring, simulation, and decision support through bidirectional data exchange. While the term was popularized by Grieves in 2002 [13], its conceptual origins trace back to NASA's Apollo program [11]. Definitions have since evolved, with recent work converging around the idea of an integrated model that updates in real time and interacts dynamically with its physical counterpart [4,30]. However, there remains no universally accepted definition, particularly in the context of smart infrastructures [5].

DTs in infrastructure are commonly applied to monitoring and predictive maintenance [10]. In this study, we focus on adopting DTs to support both condition-based and predictive maintenance, with a future trajectory toward prescriptive capabilities [9]. Compared with reactive or manually scheduled maintenance, these approaches enable earlier interventions, reduced costs, and improved structural integrity. Unlike in manufacturing, where DTs are often tied to product lifecycle stages [29], infrastructure-oriented DTs are better classified by functional goals such as anomaly detection, risk forecasting, and decision support [28].

2.2 Enterprise Architectures for Digital Twins

Digital transformation in asset-intensive sectors requires more than technical innovation; it demands integration across organizational layers. Enterprise architecture provides a foundation for such alignment. While DTs have gained traction across domains, few studies have examined their incorporation into EA frameworks [14].

Ilin et al. [14] explored EA transformations using Industry 4.0 technologies, including DTs. However, their models remain high-level and focused on manufacturing contexts. To our knowledge, no prior work provides a domain-specific reference enterprise architecture for DT adoption in the construction and infrastructure sectors.

This study addresses that gap by offering layered reference enterprise architectures tailored to bridge maintenance, using the ArchiMate modeling language [19]. Our work builds on prior DT research [27] but explicitly links DT functionalities to enterprise-level goals, capabilities, system components, a migration strategy, and a development roadmap, thereby supporting scalable and interoperable adoption across infrastructure asset owners.

3 Baseline Architecture

Bridge maintenance traditionally relies on periodic, on-site visual inspections to assess structural integrity, detect defects, and schedule interventions. These methods, although widespread, are slow, costly, and prone to human error, particularly in difficult-to-access areas or under resource constraints [18,21]. While some organizations have adopted digital tools such as mobile inspection apps [18], the underlying processes largely remain manual and disconnected from predictive analytics.

This research was conducted within a multi-stakeholder consortium. Most identified stakeholders contributed to the motivation, architectural design, and validation. This collaborative approach grounds the baseline in current practice and aligns the envisioned transition toward predictive DTs with stakeholder priorities and constraints.

To understand the transformation potential, we identify key stakeholders in the current bridge maintenance ecosystem. These include asset owners, inspectors, maintenance crews, data platform providers, and engineering consultancies (internal and represented in the consortium), as well as regulatory bodies, heritage authorities, and external system vendors (external).

As infrastructure ages and sustainability goals intensify, stakeholders increasingly seek to reduce costs, improve safety, and enable more data-driven and circular maintenance practices. Figure 1 illustrates these motivations and links them to strategic capabilities such as predictive maintenance, defect forecasting, and material reuse planning, capabilities not supported by current methods.

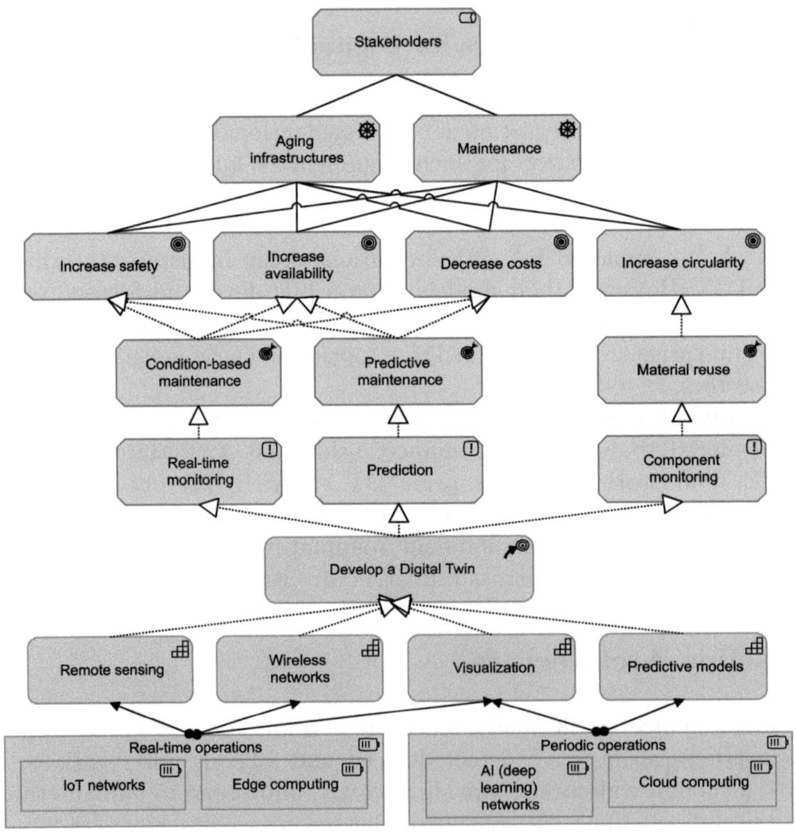

Fig. 1. Motivation and strategy for digital twin-enabled bridge maintenance.

A predictive DT can address these gaps by integrating sensor networks, AI-based analytics, and visualization tools into a unified architecture. To guide this transition, we derive a set of requirements (Table 1), reflecting both technical needs, such as anomaly detection and near real-time response, and organizational goals including traceability, usability, and long-term asset data continuity.

Table 1. Requirements of a predictive bridge assessment system.

#	Main requirements
R1	Structural integrity of the bridge shall be assessed.
R2	Surface defects of the bridge shall be detected.
R3	Surface defects shall be traceable spatially and temporally.
R4	Global anomalies in the bridge operation shall be detected.
R5	Anomalies shall be detected ahead of reaching a critical stage.
R6	Prediction range of the failures shall be acceptable.
R7	Preprocessed and processed data shall be retained.
R8	The interface of the system shall be accessible.
R9	Visualization schemes shall be suitably informative to capture and present the insights.
R10	Application response time of the system shall be near real-time.
R11	The state of bridge components and corresponding materials shall be accurately tracked.

Figure 2 illustrates the baseline enterprise architecture for bridge maintenance, modeled in ArchiMate [15]. It reflects the current state, where inspectors conduct field assessments. The proposed enterprise architecture is composed of three layers: business, application, and technology. The components enclosed within a red contour are only present in systems that are equipped with an installed sensor network and will be explained later. At the business layer, assessments are triggered periodically or by anticipated damage from events such as earthquakes and floods. Based on these assessments, the decision-makers, together with inspectors, decide on a course of action to maintain the asset, and the maintenance crew carries out that strategy. These inspectors use special equipment and software to conduct their assessment, which is presented in the application and technology layers. As presented in the application layer, the inspectors use a mobile application to record their findings in the field and input them into a digital inspection system. These findings, alongside the previous reports, are then used to collaborate with decision-makers to define the maintenance plans. Variability in systems across organizations, and reliance on non-standard documentation, often leads to fragmented data, limited historical traceability, and loss of assessment records over time.

To overcome the limitations of traditional bridge inspection, some asset owners have introduced sensor-based monitoring as a complementary process. In this setup (Fig. 2), sensors collect real-time data to support condition assessments or

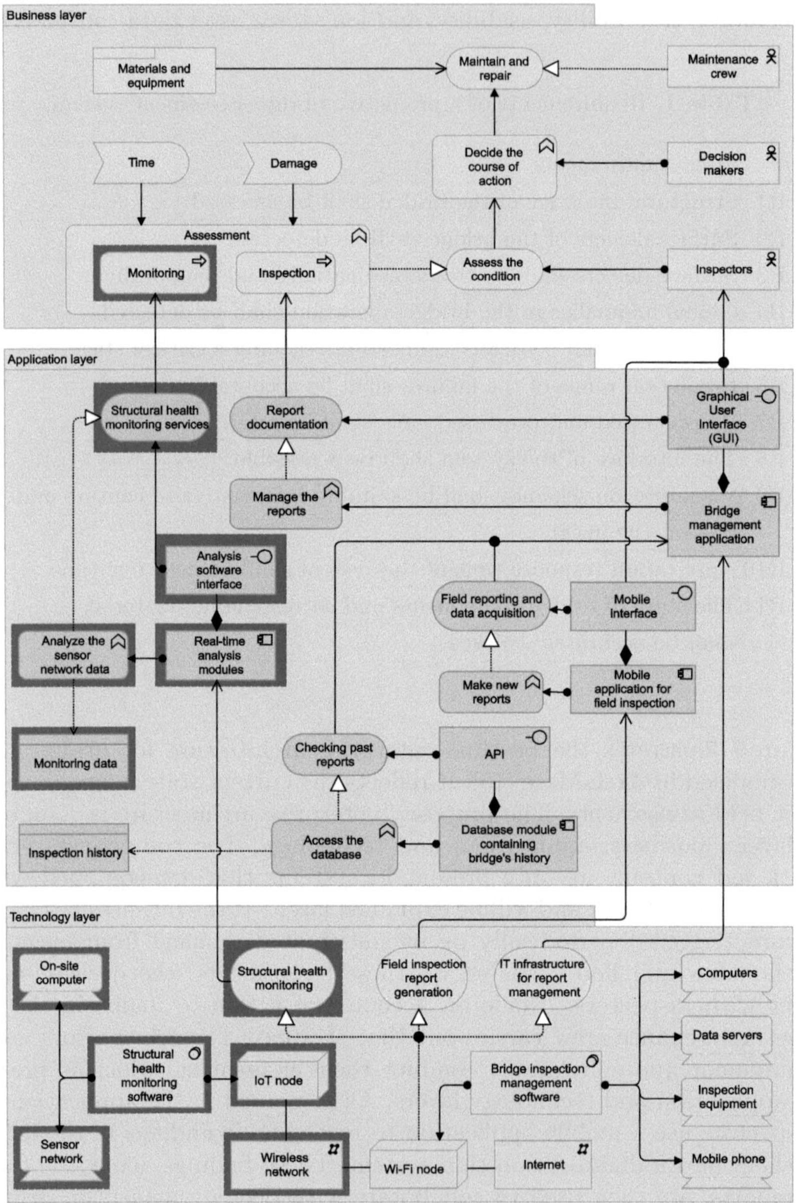

Fig. 2. Baseline enterprise architecture for bridge maintenance using inspection and monitoring. Components in red indicate monitoring-specific elements; others are standard in typical inspection systems. (Color figure online)

trigger alerts when predefined thresholds are breached [18]. In these systems, the business layer is mostly the same, but the monitoring theoretically allows assessments to be triggered by any damage to the asset. For example, when the sensor readings exceed a predefined threshold, inspectors will go to the site to conduct an inspection. In the application layer, components necessary for monitoring sensor readings are added to the architecture. These components are enclosed in a red polygon. In the technology layer, the sensor network and its network nodes are added. This sensor network may require preprocessing, so an on-site computer is included in the architecture Lastly, a router is necessary for sending these readings to the management system. However, these monitoring systems typically operate in isolation from inspection workflows, lack advanced analytics, and may not retain historical data for predictive use.

4 Digital Twin Architecture

To address the limitations of the baseline architecture, we propose an integrated predictive DT architecture (Fig. 3). This architecture integrates inspection data, real-time monitoring, and predictive analytics into a unified decision-support system. A combination of fixed sensors (e.g., accelerometers) and mobile data sources (e.g., UAV-mounted cameras) collect structural and surface-level data. Edge computing modules preprocess data locally, reducing latency and network load, before being uploaded to cloud-based storage and analytics platforms.

The business and technology layers in the DT-based architecture are similar to the baseline architecture, with some key differences that are enclosed by red lines in Fig. 3. In the business layer, the assessment is realized by a unified DT-based system rather than by fragmented inspection and monitoring assessments. In the technology layer, new hardware is required to conduct resource-intensive analysis and prediction. In this architecture, cloud resources are recommended for these tasks. However, what truly distinguishes this architecture from the baseline is the application layer. This layer is almost completely overhauled, as shown in Fig. 4. In this architecture, the data gathered from sensors and the field inspection reports are directly input into a unified DT-based system. This system stores the data in its database while utilizing sensor readings for real-time monitoring. The stored data is then processed periodically or on request to generate predictions and analyses. These analyses can include advanced AI components, including deep learning models used to detect surface anomalies [31] and classify structural components using point clouds [16,17]. Processed insights are then visualized through 3D models and dashboards that allow inspectors to verify results and decision-makers to formulate maintenance strategies. The XR modules are of special interest in this architecture as they can allow the inspectors to seamlessly utilize and connect with the DT in their field inspections. Using AR, inspectors can visualize insights from the DT while interacting with it and inputting their observations. VR can also enable virtual remote inspections or the presentation of insights to decision-makers. In this architecture, the DT platform acts as an interface between different modules, connecting them.

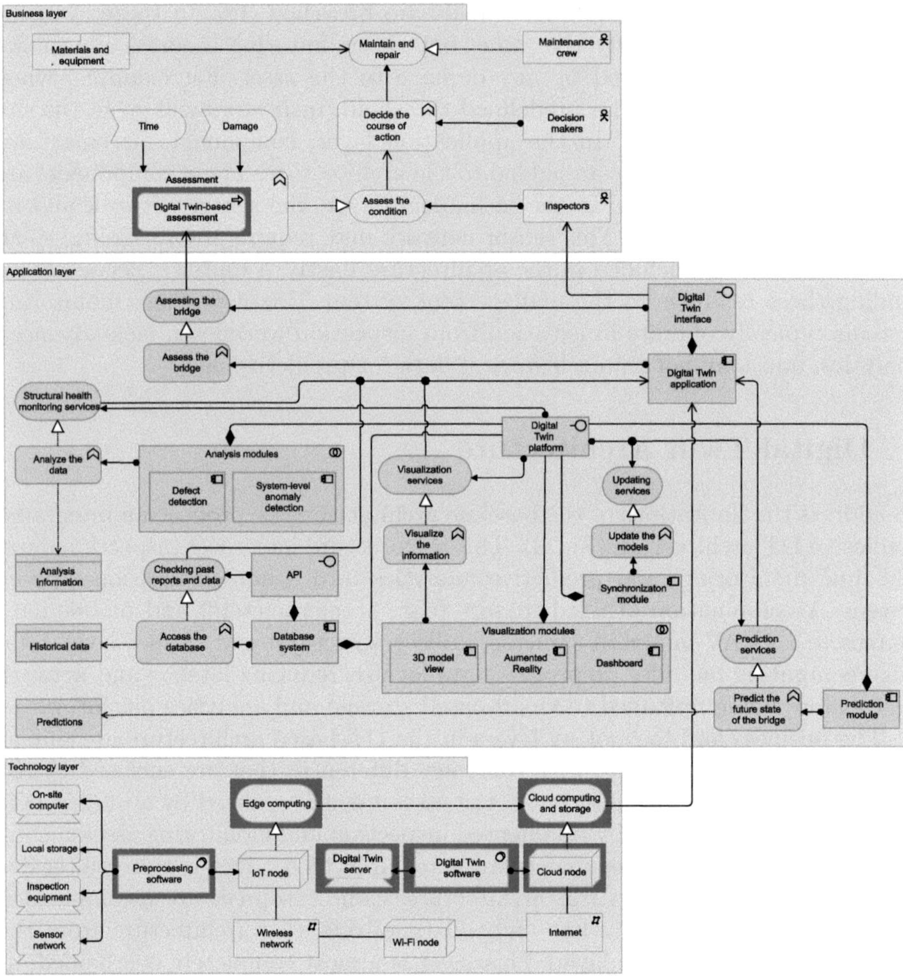

Fig. 3. Enterprise architecture of bridge maintenance using predictive digital twins. Red-highlighted components indicate changes from the baseline in the business and technology layers; the application layer is fully redesigned. (Color figure online)

The data and insights from different components are first fed to the platform, where the platform stores them in the database if required. Any component that requires data requests it via the platform. Importantly, the DT maintains digital assets over time (e.g., FEMs, inspection histories), supporting organizational knowledge continuity even as service providers change. Figure 5 summarizes the data and control flows within the proposed architecture.

While this study focuses on predictive DTs, an evolution toward prescriptive DTs, which are capable of autonomous recommendation or actuation of mainte-

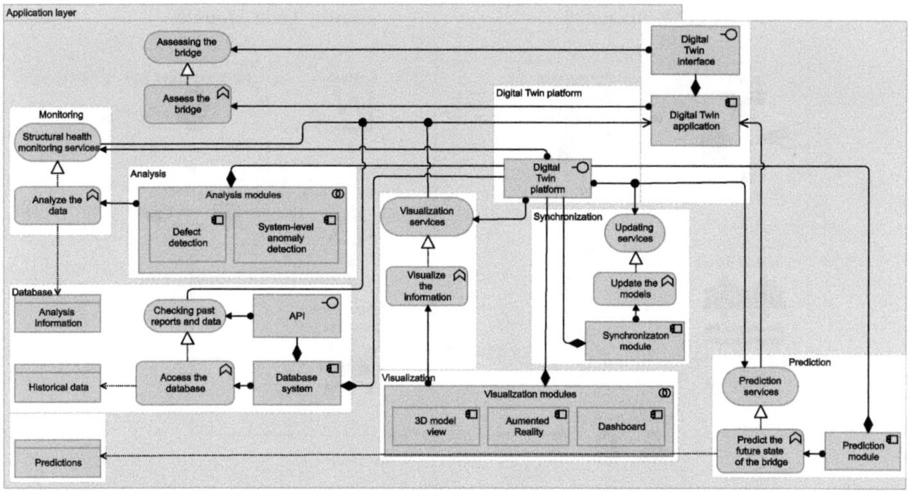

Fig. 4. The component groups of the application layer of the enterprise architecture of bridge maintenance using predictive digital twins.

nance actions, represents a promising direction for future research. Such systems would further reduce human workload and enable closed-loop decision-making.

4.1 Migration Strategy

Transitioning from traditional inspection to predictive DTs requires a phased strategy. We adopt the conceptual framework by Fuller et al. [12], distinguishing between three evolutionary stages:

1. **Digital Model**: A static representation of the physical asset.
2. **Digital Shadow**: A periodically updated model without feedback loops.
3. **Digital Twin**: A dynamically updated, bi-directional system capable of informing or influencing physical processes.

Figure 6 illustrates our proposed migration path–from current practices to predictive and eventually prescriptive systems. This path emphasizes modular upgrades, stakeholder readiness, and progressive capability integration.

4.2 Roadmap

To operationalize the migration strategy, we define a roadmap that outlines the evolution of software components and system capabilities across transformation stages (Fig. 7). The roadmap may guide practitioners in planning and executing staged upgrades–from isolated inspection apps to integrated, AI-powered DT platforms.

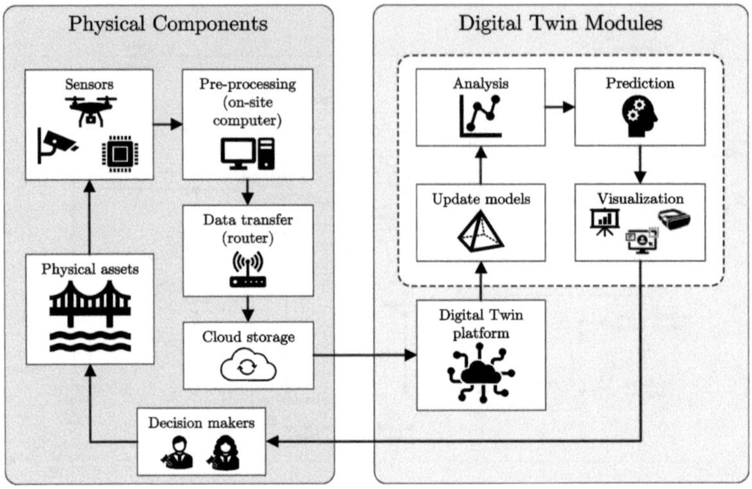

Fig. 5. Data and control flows of a predictive digital twin for bridge maintenance (adapted from [27]).

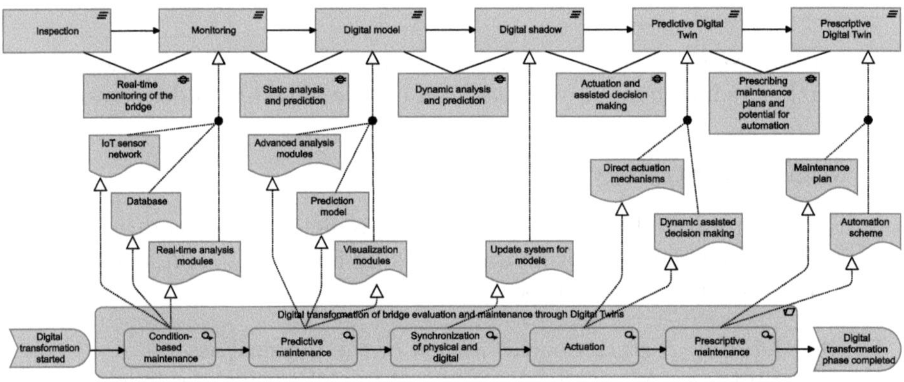

Fig. 6. Implementation strategy and migration path for digital twins in bridge maintenance.

5 Evaluation

While a comprehensive implementation and deployment of the proposed architecture is beyond the scope of this study, we provide a multi-level evaluation in line with design science research principles. This includes: (1) a qualitative comparison of the proposed architecture compared to the baseline based on the requirements in Table 1, and (2) an illustrative implementation for a real bridge in the Netherlands based on our earlier work [27].

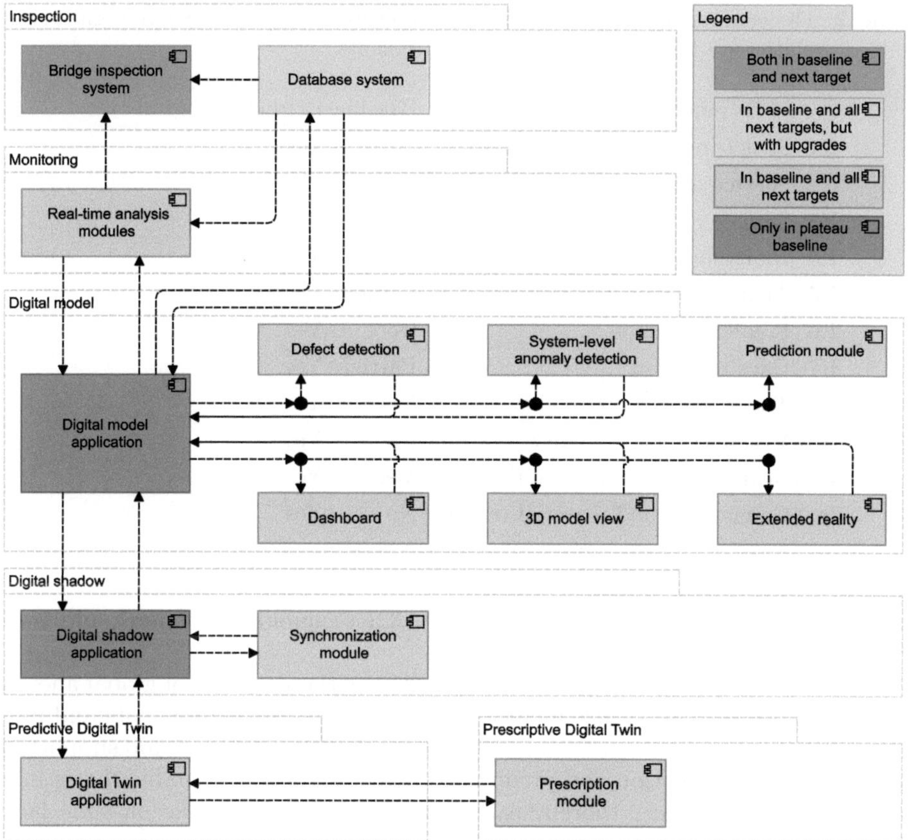

Fig. 7. Software development roadmap from inspection to predictive digital twins.

5.1 Requirement-Based Comparison

In this section, we compare the proposed predictive DT-based architecture with the baseline architecture based on their potential to meet the requirements outlined in Table 1. A summary of this comparison is provided in Table 2. Studies such as [20,22] show that while general anomalies, like paint failure and corrosion, are identified by more than 50% of inspectors during manual visual inspections, local anomalies such as weld cracks and bolt defects are identified far less frequently. However, computer vision techniques have been shown to enhance visual inspection accuracy [24,32]. Therefore, the proposed architecture, which incorporates such methods, is better positioned to satisfy requirement R2. This improved anomaly detection also supports requirement R1 by providing inspectors and engineers with more accurate insights.

Locating previously identified anomalies, especially after a long time or if they have been painted over, is particularly challenging. The proposed architecture

Table 2. The comparison of the baseline architecture and the predictive digital twin-enabled architecture based on the target requirements.

#	Main requirements	Baseline	Predictive digital twin
R1	Structural integrity assessment	Partial	Yes
R2	Surface defects detection	Limited	Yes
R3	Surface defects tracing	No	Yes
R4	Global anomalies detection	Partial	Yes
R5	Anomalies detected on-time	Limited	Yes
R6	Prediction range	No	Yes
R7	Data retention	Partial	Yes
R8	The interface accessibility	Yes	Yes
R9	Visualization suitability	No	Yes
R10	Near real-time response time	Yes	Yes
R11	Component and material tracking	No	Yes

addresses this by leveraging 3D models and XR technologies to mark and track anomalies over time, thereby satisfying R3.

While baseline monitoring services may detect the presence of global anomalies, the proposed architecture includes dedicated analysis components and integrated monitoring services, offering more comprehensive coverage and supporting R4. Its improved detection and prediction capabilities further enable the estimation of anomaly severity, thereby satisfying R5. In contrast, the baseline lacks predictive capabilities and therefore does not fulfill R6.

While the baseline model can retain the SHM data, manual inspection data (reports) is not effectively stored and only partially satisfies R7. Requirements R8 and R10 can be met by both architectures. However, the baseline lacks adequate visualization tools for 3D data, immersive remote inspection, and real-time on-site visualization, particularly critical for effective visualization during on-site inspections. The proposed architecture, using XR technologies, is better equipped to meet R9 in this context.

Moreover, the baseline system does not track the condition or materials of bridge components in detail. The proposed architecture incorporates this functionality, which can reduce maintenance costs and enhance circularity by optimizing component lifespan and material reuse, thus supporting R11. In summary, the proposed architecture has the potential to fully satisfy all identified requirements, whereas the baseline architecture falls short on several and only partially fulfills some others.

5.2 Illustrative Implementation: Tankinkbrug

In our earlier work [27], we presented a partial implementation of a predictive DT on the Tankinkbrug, a 58.96 m steel arch bridge in the Twente region of the

Netherlands (Fig. 8). Building on that work, we have extended their design into a fully formalized reference enterprise architecture. Accordingly, we use that case study here to partially illustrate our proposed DT framework. As shown in Fig. 4, the architecture's components are organized into seven groups: monitoring, analysis, prediction, database, visualization, DT platform, and synchronization. In this implementation, the core platform is developed in C# (Fig. 9). Figure 9a shows the platform's backend implementation in Visual Studio, while Fig. 9b presents the Windows Presentation Foundation (WPF)-based frontend. Within the first tab (Fig. 10a), two visualization modules are embedded: an interactive 3D model and an immersive XRbased remote inspection interface. This tab also demonstrates an analysis module that invokes a Python script directly from the platform, thereby integrating analysis and prediction workflows into the platform. A snapshot of the XR-based inspection experience is provided in Fig. 10b. The second tab of the platform is devoted to real-time monitoring of the bridge. Although a cloud-based database was not integrated in this prototype, we simulated a real-time database by feeding accelerometer readings, obtained during a prior measurement campaign, from an Excel sheet into the platform via a Python script. The synchronization module remains to be implemented in future work.

Fig. 8. Tankinkbrug (case study bridge).

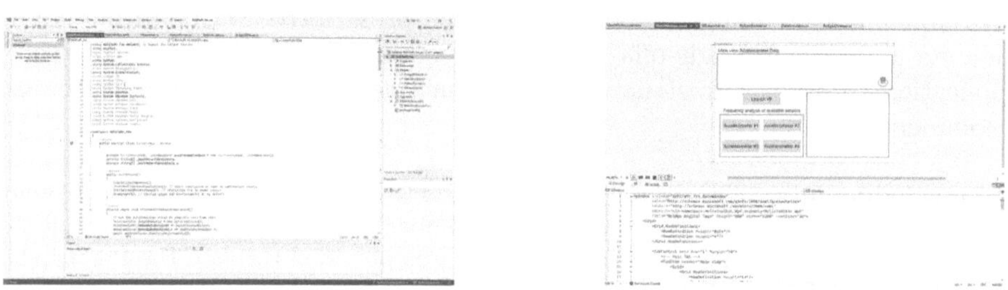

(a) (b)

Fig. 9. C#-based digital twin platform for bridges: (a) Backend of the digital twin platform (b) Frontend of the digital twin platform.

(a) (b)

Fig. 10. Illustrative partial implementation of the digital twin-based architecture: (a) The interactive 3D model component, the launcher of the VR-based immersive remote inspection component, and the Python-based analysis component are shown in this tab. (b) After clicking the "Launch VR" button, the application for immersive remote inspection will start.

6 Conclusion

This study proposed DT architectures to address the increasing maintenance demands of aging bridges. By integrating sensor networks, AI-based analytics, and XR-enabled visualization into a structured enterprise architecture, we offer a baseline for more efficient, data-driven maintenance workflows. The proposed architectures illustrated how DTs can be embedded into infrastructure practices.

To evaluate feasibility, we conducted a multi-level assessment comprising: (1) a requirement-based comparison of the baseline architecture with the proposed one; and (2) an illustrative implementation on a Dutch steel bridge, including real-time monitoring and 3D visualization. The results suggest that predictive DTs offer benefits over conventional systems, particularly in terms of long-term cost-effectiveness, decision support, and architectural interoperability.

While full-scale deployment and comparative studies are future work, our results indicate promise for predictive twins, especially in high-density bridge environments. Extending this work to include prescriptive DTs and human-in-the-loop automation trade-offs is a key direction for future research. Broader application to other infrastructure types, such as quay or piling walls, is also recommended.

Acknowledgments. This work was supported by the Dutch Research Council (NWO) under the SUBLIME project (grant number KICH1.ST01.20.008), as part of the NWO KIC programme. Additional support was provided through the Partnership Program of the Materials innovation institute (M2i) (N21007d).

Disclosure of Interests. The authors have no competing interests to declare that are relevant to the content of this article.

References

1. Alam, K.M., Saddik, A.E.: C2ps: a digital twin architecture reference model for the cloud-based cyber-physical systems. IEEE Access **5**, 2050–2062 (2017). https://doi.org/10.1109/ACCESS.2017.2657006
2. Andone, D., Afshar, P.: Bridge in Pittsburgh collapses hours before scheduled Biden visit to talk infrastructure (2022)
3. Bleijenberg, A.N.: Renewal of Civil Infrastructure. Dutch national forecast for replacement and renovation. Technical report, TNO (2021)
4. Broo, D.G., Bravo-Haro, M., Schooling, J.: Design and implementation of a smart infrastructure digital twin. Autom. Construct. **136**, 104171 (2022). https://doi.org/10.1016/j.autcon.2022.104171
5. Broo, D.G., Schooling, J.: Digital twins in infrastructure: definitions, current practices, challenges and strategies. Int. J. Constr. Manag. **23**, 1254–1263 (2023). https://doi.org/10.1080/15623599.2021.1966980
6. Bukhsh, Z.A., Stipanovic, I., Saeed, A., Doree, A.G.: Maintenance intervention predictions using entity-embedding neural networks. Autom. Constr. **116**, 103202 (2020). https://doi.org/10.1016/J.AUTCON.2020.103202
7. Cearley, D., Burke, B., Velosa, A., Kerremans, M.: Top 10 strategic technology trends for 2019: Digital twins (2019)
8. Chen, W., Chen, K., Cheng, J.C., Wang, Q., Gan, V.J.: BIM-based framework for automatic scheduling of facility maintenance work orders. Autom. Construct. **91**, 15–30 (2018). https://doi.org/10.1016/J.AUTCON.2018.03.007
9. Consilvio, A., et al.: Prescriptive maintenance of railway infrastructure: from data analytics to decision support. In: 2019 6th International Conference on Models and Technologies for Intelligent Transportation Systems (MT-ITS), pp. 1–10 (2019). https://doi.org/10.1109/MTITS.2019.8883331
10. Errandonea, I., Beltrán, S., Arrizabalaga, S.: Digital twin for maintenance: a literature review. Comput. Ind. **123**, 103316 (2020). https://doi.org/10.1016/J.COMPIND.2020.103316
11. Ferko, E., Bucaioni, A., Behnam, M.: Architecting digital twins. IEEE Access **10**, 50335–50350 (2022). https://doi.org/10.1109/ACCESS.2022.3172964
12. Fuller, A., Fan, Z., Day, C., Barlow, C.: Digital twin: enabling technologies, challenges and open research. IEEE Access **8**, 108952–108971 (2020). https://doi.org/10.1109/ACCESS.2020.2998358
13. Grieves, M., Vickers, J.: Digital twin: mitigating unpredictable, undesirable emergent behavior in complex systems. In: Transdisciplinary Perspectives on Complex Systems: New Findings and Approaches, pp. 85–113 (2016). https://doi.org/10.1007/978-3-319-38756-7_4
14. Ilin, I., Levina, A., Borremans, A., Kalyazina, S.: Enterprise architecture modeling in digital transformation era. Adv. Intell. Syst. Comput. **1259 AISC**, 124–142 (2021). https://doi.org/10.1007/978-3-030-57453-6_11
15. Josey, A.: Archimate® 3.0. 1-A pocket guide. Van Haren (2017). http://pubs.opengroup.org/architecture/archimate3-doc/toc.html
16. Kim, H., Kim, C.: Deep-learning-based classification of point clouds for bridge inspection. Remote Sens. 2020 **12**, 3757 (2020). https://doi.org/10.3390/RS12223757
17. Kim, H., Yoon, J., Sim, S.H.: Automated bridge component recognition from point clouds using deep learning. Struct. Contr. Health Monitor. **27**, e2591 (2020). https://doi.org/10.1002/STC.2591

18. Kruachottikul, P., Cooharojananone, N., Phanomchoeng, G., Chavarnakul, T., Kovitanggoon, K., Trakulwaranont, D.: Deep learning-based visual defect-inspection system for reinforced concrete bridge substructure: a case of Thailand's department of highways. J. Civil Struct. Health Monitor. **11**, 949–965 (2021). https://doi.org/10.1007/S13349-021-00490-Z
19. Lankhorst, M.: Enterprise Architecture at Work. Springer Berlin Heidelberg, Berlin, Heidelberg (2017). https://doi.org/10.1007/978-3-662-53933-0
20. Middleton, C., Lea, F.: Reliability of visual inspection of highway bridges. Tech. rep., Turner-Fairbank Highway Research Center (2002). https://www.academia.edu/33376499/Reliability_of_Visual_Inspection_of_Highway_Bridges
21. Mirzaei, K., Arashpour, M., Asadi, E., Masoumi, H., Bai, Y., Behnood, A.: 3d point cloud data processing with machine learning for construction and infrastructure applications: a comprehensive review. Adv. Eng. Inform. **51**, 101501 (2022). https://doi.org/10.1016/J.AEI.2021.101501
22. Moore, M., Phares, B.M., Graybeal, B., Rolander, D., Washer, G.: Reliability of visual inspection for highway bridges, Volume I: Final report. Research Paper FHWA-RD-01-105, Turner-Fairbank Highway Research Center (2001). https://rosap.ntl.bts.gov/view/dot/33883
23. Mourtzis, D., Angelopoulos, J., Panopoulos, N.: Intelligent predictive maintenance and remote monitoring framework for industrial equipment based on mixed reality. Front. Mech. Eng. **6**, 578379 (2020). https://doi.org/10.3389/FMECH.2020.578379/BIBTEX
24. Mundt, M., Majumder, S., Murali, S., Panetsos, P., Ramesh, V.: Meta-learning convolutional neural architectures for multi-target concrete defect classification with the concrete defect bridge image dataset. In: Proceedings of the IEEE Computer Society Conference on Computer Vision and Pattern Recognition, pp. 11188–11197 (2019). https://doi.org/10.1109/CVPR.2019.01145
25. Opoku, D.G.J., Perera, S., Osei-Kyei, R., Rashidi, M.: Digital twin application in the construction industry: a literature review. J. Build. Eng. **40**, 102726 (2021). https://doi.org/10.1016/J.JOBE.2021.102726
26. Peffers, K., Tuunanen, T., Rothenberger, M.A., Chatterjee, S.: A design science research methodology for information systems research. J. Manag. Inf. Syst. **24**, 45–77 (2007). https://doi.org/10.2753/MIS0742-1222240302
27. Sabzi, A.K., van der Zwaag, B.J., Le, D.V., Özlem Durmaz-Incel: Digital twins for bridge assessment and maintenance. In: International Conference on Smart Applications, Communications and Networking (SmartNets) (2025). https://doi.org/10.1109/SmartNets65254.2025.11106891
28. Segovia, M., Garcia-Alfaro, J.: Design, modeling and implementation of digital twins. Sensors **22**(14) (2022). https://doi.org/10.3390/S22145396
29. Tao, F., Zhang, H., Liu, A., Nee, A.Y.: Digital twin in industry: State-of-the-art. IEEE Trans. Indust. Inform. **15**, 2405–2415 (2019). https://doi.org/10.1109/TII.2018.2873186
30. VanDerHorn, E., Mahadevan, S.: Digital twin: generalization, characterization and implementation. Decis. Support Syst. **145**, 113524 (2021). https://doi.org/10.1016/J.DSS.2021.113524
31. Xu, Y., Bao, Y., Chen, J., Zuo, W., Li, H.: Surface fatigue crack identification in steel box girder of bridges by a deep fusion convolutional neural network based on consumer-grade camera images. Struct. Health Monitor. **18**, 653–674 (2019). https://doi.org/10.1177/1475921718764873

32. Zakaria, M., Karaaslan, E., Catbas, F.N.: Real-time AI-based bridge inspection using mixed reality platform. In: Structures Congress 2023, pp. 120–131 (2023)
33. Zinno, R., Haghshenas, S.S., Guido, G., Vitale, A.: Artificial intelligence and structural health monitoring of bridges: a review of the state-of-the-art. IEEE Access **10**, 88058–88078 (2022). https://doi.org/10.1109/ACCESS.2022.3199443

CLAIR: Generating On-Demand Low-Code Application Documentation Through Knowledge Graph and LLM-Based Multi-agent System Integration

Tim Eichhorn[1,2], Luís Ferreira Pires[1(✉)], Gayane Sedrakyan[1], and Ruben ten Asbroek[2]

[1] University of Twente, Drienerlolaan 5, 7522 NB Enschede, The Netherlands
l.ferreirapires@utwente.nl
[2] CAPE, Transportcentrum 16, 7547 RW Enschede, The Netherlands
tim.eichhorn@cape.nl
https://www.utwente.nl/

Abstract. Low-Code is an approach to application development that enables rapid application creation with minimal coding effort. However, as Low-Code applications scale, challenges related to documentation, maintainability, and technical debt become increasingly prevalent. Inadequate documentation hampers collaboration, maintenance, troubleshooting, and knowledge retention, particularly in agile development environments where documentation is often neglected. Fragmented knowledge, poor traceability, and missing documentation sources are the main challenges for low-code documentation. To address these issues, we developed CLAIR (*Connecting Low-Code and Artificial Intelligence for RAG*), which is an AI-driven documentation assistant that leverages a knowledge graph and an LLM-based Multi Agent System to generate on-demand, context-aware documentation for Low-Code applications. CLAIR was validated through expert evaluations and a series of test cases, demonstrating its ability to generate accurate, usable, and context-aware documentation. Therefore, our main contribution is a novel approach that combines knowledge graphs and LLMs to improve documentation processes. By bridging the gap between Low-Code application development and AI-driven automation, CLAIR sets the foundation for future advancements in intelligent Low-Code maintainability solutions.

Keywords: Low-Code · Documentation · Knowledge Graphs · Large Language Models · LLM-based Multi Agent System

1 Introduction

Low-Code is an approach to application development that enables rapid application creation with minimal coding effort by using graphical tools and/or scripting [4,19]. This approach is supported by Low-Code Development Platforms

J. Barateiro et al. (Eds.): EDOC 2025 Workshops, LNBIP 571, pp. 296–312, 2026.
https://doi.org/10.1007/978-3-032-16234-2_24

(LCDPs), like, e.g., Mendix[1], which empower developers (often non-technical users) to swiftly design, deploy, and maintain applications through visual modeling and automated code generation [8]. Initially attractive due to their ease of use and reduced reliance on specialised technical skills, LCDPs promise enhanced productivity, quicker time-to-market, and improved alignment between business requirements and IT implementation [2].

However, as Low-Code applications grow in complexity, developers and stakeholders increasingly encounter significant challenges [19]. Comprehensive and accurate documentation is considered vital in software development as it supports maintainability, scalability, and effective collaboration [28], but it is often perceived as a secondary activity in Low-Code due to the abstract nature of development [2] and the frequent use of agile methodologies [36] that discourage documentation. Consequently, documentation becomes fragmented, incomplete, or outdated. In traditional application development, documentation processes are often costly, time-consuming, and prone to human error, making it difficult for organisations to produce high-quality documentation [10]. In Low-Code application development, the unpredictability of documentation needs exacerbates the issue, as documentation that is created is often not used in practice [28]. This makes traditional documentation approaches inefficient, as they often lead to over-documentation or critical gaps [1].

While the visual abstraction provided by Low-Code accelerates the early stages of development, it often inadvertently conceals the underlying complexity as applications scale. In addition, the agile practice of prioritising working software over comprehensive documentation used in Low-Code application development aggravates the challenges of producing and maintaining proper documentation [36]. This documentation gap leads to increased technical debt, higher cognitive load during maintenance, difficulties in onboarding new team members, and overall decreased maintainability and sustainability of Low-Code applications. Therefore, this research aimed to improve the documentation process and quality for Low-Code applications. We addressed the identified gap by developing an innovative automated documentation assistant, which we called CLAIR (*Connecting Low-Code and Artificial Intelligence for Retrieval-Augmented Generation*). CLAIR leverages state-of-the-art Artificial Intelligence (AI) techniques, namely Knowledge Graphs and Large Language Model (LLM)-based Multi-Agent Systems, to generate precise, context-aware, and on-demand documentation tailored to the stakeholders' specific needs.

In this study, we applied the Design Science Methodology (DSM) [38] to systematically design, develop, and validate CLAIR within the context of Low-Code application documentation. To identify and define requirements for improving Low-Code documentation, we undertook a literature review alongside an industry-focused survey distributed within CAPE[2], which is a consultancy company specialised in Low-Code development. With our literature review, we identified key documentation challenges such as fragmentation, inconsistency, and

[1] https://www.mendix.com/.
[2] https://cape.nl/.

inadequacy, emphasising that documentation must be accurate, complete, accessible, and up-to-date [1]. Our survey within CAPE validated these literature findings, highlighting that Low-Code practitioners face issues due to outdated, incomplete, and hard-to-access documentation. CLAIR was validated through expert opinion and Technical Action Research (TAR) [38], involving industry experts evaluating CLAIR's effectiveness, accuracy, and usability in generating automated documentation. We selected Mendix as platform for our case study due to its widespread use [35] and for being considered as a typical LCDPs [8].

This paper focuses on the design, implementation and validation of CLAIR, and its potential benefits for Low-Code development and maintenance. This paper is further structured as follows: Sect. 2 discusses related work, Sect. 3 discusses the CLAIR solution architecture, Sect. 4 presents the Knowledge Graph Database component, Sect. 5 discusses the LLM-based Multi-Agent System that is the core component of our solution, Sect. 6 discusses the procedures we performed to validate CLAIR, and Sect. 7 gives our final remarks.

2 Related Work

In a literature review, we investigated many attempts that have been made to generate documentation automatically, as reported in [7]. This section presents our main findings.

Automated documentation generation has been a prominent theme in Software Engineering [22], particularly due to the increasing complexity of software systems and the burden of maintaining comprehensive documentation manually. Existing studies propose diverse techniques, ranging from algorithm-driven to model-driven methods, as well as modern AI integrations that address multiple aspects of documentation challenges. A substantial body of work focuses on generating automatic comments and summaries directly from source code [22,23,31]. These techniques often have limited scalability and emphasise code summarisation rather than generating contextually rich or purpose-driven descriptions [21].

Low-Code documentation generation is closely related to model-driven documentation, which leverages structured templates and mappings to create various artifacts such as requirements, design specifications, and system overviews directly from underlying software models. Wang et al. [37] present a model-driven documentation generator integrated into the SmartOSEK IDE [40], aiming to bridge the gap between software models and their corresponding documentation. This tool ensures consistency across artifacts by using a hierarchical documentation model. Other frameworks, such as the one proposed in [10], further extend the scope of model-driven documentation by aggregating UML, BPMN, and GSN model information into ISO-compliant documents. These approaches rely on model consistency and on predefined outputs, limiting flexibility, and responsiveness in rapidly changing projects or user requirements [28].

More recently, Large Language Models (LLMs) have shown considerable potential for automating software documentation [14,24,32]. Tools like Codex excel at generating context-aware descriptions across multiple programming languages [14]. These tools significantly reduce manual effort, but several issues remain, including the tendency toward verbose outputs, limited domain specificity, hallucination, and reliance on proprietary large-scale infrastructures that can pose data privacy risks [14]. Retrieval-Augmented Generation (RAG) addresses these challenges by coupling LLMs with external knowledge sources, allowing them to query and incorporate relevant information in real time [3]. This approach significantly improves accuracy, adaptability, and context-awareness, making it highly valuable for software development tasks [29]. Finally, graph-based RAG methodologies have emerged as a compelling paradigm for enhancing the interaction between LLMs and external knowledge, such as GraphRAG [6,27], which leverages the structural relationships between entities to enhance retrieval precision and depth, effectively capturing relational knowledge and enabling more accurate, context-aware responses [27].

3 CLAIR Architecture

To achieve the primary goal of this research of improving the documentation quality and process for Low-Code applications, we propose an AI-driven assistant, which we named CLAIR that integrates knowledge graphs and LLM agents for Retrieval-Augmented Generation to automate and support on-demand documentation for Low-Code applications.

3.1 Functional Requirements

Although the CLAIR design principles and architecture are quite general and can be applied to any Low Code platform, for the current implementation we targeted data and application logic elements of Mendix applications. This means that CLAIR extracts and processes components such as modules, domain models, and microflows, which form the foundation of application logic and data

Table 1. CLAIR Functional requirements

ID	Requirement	Description
FR1	Knowledge Extraction	Extract components like domain models, microflows, and their relationships from Mendix applications.
FR2	Store Retrievable Knowledge	Store extracted knowledge of components in a graph repository, retrievable by the documentation assistant.
FR3	On-Demand Documentation Generation	Automatically generate dynamic context-aware documentation based on user queries.
FR4	Chat Interface	Provide a chat interface for intuitive user interaction
FR5	Multi-Purpose Functionality	Provide various types of documentation to support different purposes across the development lifecycle, including design, development, and maintenance.

relationships. At this stage, UI-related elements such as pages, and custom code components, including Java actions, scheduled events, and other advanced customisations, have been excluded, but can added in future CLAIR extensions.

To achieve its intended goals, CLAIR must satisfy the functional requirements shown in Table 1. The CLAIR functional requirements were captured based on a combination of literature review, empirical research through a survey, stakeholder analysis and the gaps we identified in currently available solutions [7], in line with DSM [38].

3.2 Components

CLAIR bridges low-code applications and LLMs through a knowledge graph interface, chosen for its ability to provide a structured, queryable representation of complex interrelated application data. By leveraging a data pipeline, CLAIR transforms structured data extracted from Mendix applications into a knowledge graph database, serving as a central knowledge repository that supports efficient and dynamic information retrieval.

Figure 1 shows the CLAIR architecture, which also includes an LLM-based Multi-Agent System (MAS) [9] to process user queries. This MAS was implemented for its capability to interpret natural language queries, generate graph queries, and retrieve relevant insights from the knowledge graph, providing accurate, context-aware responses tailored to users' needs. The modular and scalable design ensures flexibility and adaptability, allowing users to access up-to-date, dynamic, and context-aware documentation on-demand.

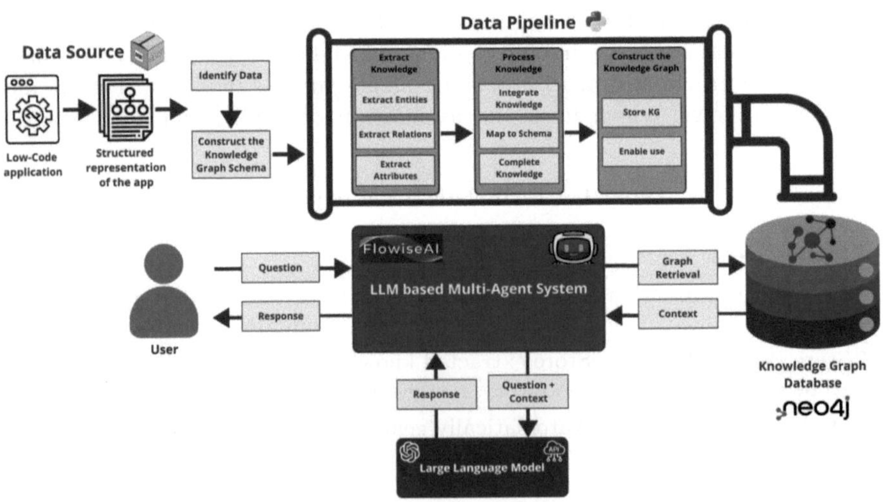

Fig. 1. CLAIR architecture

4 Knowledge Graph Database

The Knowledge Graph serves as the data storage component of the CLAIR architecture, structuring and storing detailed application information extracted directly from Low-Code platforms. This database captures entities, logic, dependencies, and interactions, of the essential elements in a Low-Code application enabling efficient querying and retrieval. Furthermore, the Knowledge Graph facilitates multi-hop reasoning [18], crucial for dynamically constructing precise documentation tailored to user queries.

To construct a knowledge graph schema for a Mendix application, we combined the components extracted from the application with the publicly available Mendix Metamodel[3]. This approach ensured that the schema not only reflected the specific structure of the application but also adhered to the general Mendix model structure and relationships defined by the platform. By following this method, we adhered to a top-down knowledge graph construction process [33]. The top-down approach leverages an existing domain metamodel or structured dataset, both of which are available, to guide the development of the knowledge graph schema [33]. The schema specifies the categories of nodes, edges, and their properties, which dictate how the graphs are structured and stored within the graph database [33]. Figure 2 shows the knowledge graph schema.

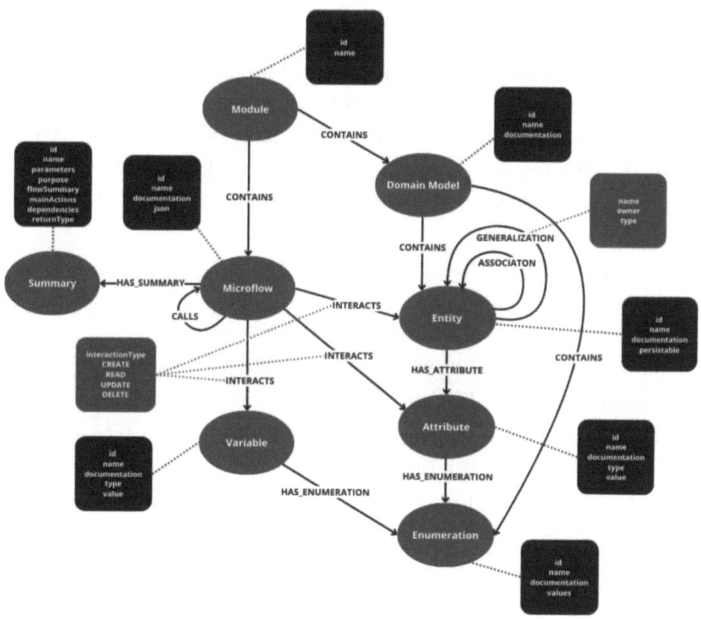

Fig. 2. Knowledge Graph schema

[3] https://docs.mendix.com/apidocs-mxsdk/mxsdk/mendix-metamodel/.

Our knowledge graph database was built using Neo4j[4], a graph database platform designed to store and manage highly connected data. Neo4j is commonly used in research [17,25] and offers several benefits, including scalability, flexibility in modelling relationships, and performance for graph-based queries, making it well-suited for representing the intricate dependencies and interactions within applications. Furthermore, Neo4j uses the Cypher query language[5], which is a declarative language specifically designed for querying and manipulating graph data. This is another great benefit because research has shown that state-of-the-art LLM models have high accuracy in generating correct Cypher queries to interact with graph databases, especially OpenAI's GPT model [11].

5 LLM-Based Multi-agent System

The LLM-based Multi-Agent System (MAS) [9] is the core component of the CLAIR architecture, enabling intelligent interaction with the Knowledge Graph. It has been implemented using Flowise[6], which is a low-code orchestration platform. The MAS integrates specialised agents operating in a structured workflow, and combines natural language interaction, role-specific expertise, and iterative refinement to form a scalable and flexible interface for querying complex Low-Code application structures.

In CLAIR, agents are LLM-driven units capable of managing control flow. Agents are either *single-task* or part of a collaborative MAS [12]. For complex tasks, decomposing responsibilities across multiple agents improves accuracy and efficiency [11,18]. Therefore, we designed a hierarchical architecture where a *Supervisor Agent* manages communication and task delegation among *Worker Agents*, fostering dynamic, natural language-based coordination [16,39]. Table 2 lists the CLAIR MAS specialised agents and their responsibilities. Figure 3 shows the CLAIR agents in Flowise.

Table 2. MAS agents and their responsibilities

Supervisor Agent	Central coordinator that manages workflow and integrates outputs from other agents.
Information Assessor Agent	Parses user input to identify required data points.
Cypher Query Generator Agent	Converts identified information into valid Cypher queries using zero-shot prompting [15].
Query Executor Agent	Executes queries via a custom JavaScript interface and retrieves relevant graph data.
Critic Agent	Validates response quality and completeness. If issues are detected, feedback is relayed for refinement.

[4] https://neo4j.com/.
[5] https://neo4j.com/docs/getting-started/cypher/.
[6] https://flowiseai.com/.

Fig. 3. LLM-based Multi-Agent System Design in Flowise

In the MAS design, we strove for: a) *efficient communication,* by implementing robust protocols for agent coordination [12], b) *effective data transformation,* by minimising information loss while optimising token cost [16], and c) *high scalability,* by supporting dynamic expansion and real-time processing [12].

To improve prompt quality, we applied iterative LLM-driven prompt generation and optimisation. Prompt engineering remains a high-effort task, but recent models can assist in refining task-specific prompts [5].

6 Validation

Although originally developed for automated documentation, CLAIR's architecture supports a wider range of applications due to the flexibility of LLM-based agents. Inspired by retrieval-augmented and graph-integrated systems such as REDCODER [26], REPOGRAPH [25], and CodexGraph [18], CLAIR leverages its knowledge graph and multi-agent reasoning capabilities to address various challenges in Low-Code development.

6.1 Use Cases

The following use cases have been performed to validate CLAIR:

On-Demand Documentation Generation. CLAIR generates structured, context-aware documentation for Mendix applications by querying the knowledge graph. It provides tailored documentation for microflows, domain models, and modules, improving accessibility and reducing the need for manually maintained wikis. Unlike traditional documentation, the output adapts to user intent and avoids issues of irrelevance or excessive detail [1].

Annotation Generation. CLAIR can produce annotations similar to in-code comments, attached directly to model elements. These support maintainability and collaboration, addressing the frequent absence or inconsistency of inline documentation observed in practice.

Debugging and Troubleshooting. By processing stack traces and inspecting application structure, CLAIR can assist in identifying root causes of errors. It supports queries targeting specific components, highlights relevant dependencies, and proposes actionable fixes [18,25].

New Logic Generation. Based on user requirements, CLAIR generates textual descriptions of microflow logic using components already present in the application. This aids both novice and experienced developers, reduces cognitive load, and enhances learning through visual and textual representations [12,20].

High-Level Overview Generation. Employing a hierarchical summarisation approach inspired by GraphRAG [6], CLAIR aggregates microflow summaries into module- and application-level descriptions. This enables users to answer broad, strategic questions, supporting better architectural insight and alignment with business processes.

We performed testing to evaluate CLAIR's effectiveness, usability, and adaptability in the real-world Low-Code development scenarios mentioned above. Effectiveness refers to the quality of the generated documentation, usability concerns how intuitive and user-friendly the system is, and adaptability refers to other user needs in addition to generating documentation.

During testing sessions, participants were instructed to complete five different test scenarios designed to evaluate the different capabilities of CLAIR discussed earlier. The participants were 10 Mendix developers from CAPE's development and support teams, covering a range of expertise from junior to senior levels. This diverse group was chosen to ensure a balanced evaluation of CLAIR's capabilities and to gather both quantitative and qualitative feedback. The selection aligns with the principles of Technical Action Research (TAR) [38], which emphasize stakeholder diversity to validate practical utility in real-world settings.

Due to page limitations, we only discuss the validation of the first use case in this paper. A detailed discussion of the validation process can be found in [7].

6.2 Data Collection and Analysis

To collect data to validate CLAIR we performed interviews, a post-scenario survey and a post-test survey. We performed semi-structured interviews during the testing sessions to gather qualitative feedback on both user experience and CLAIR's effectiveness. For the post-scenario survey, following each test scenario each participant answered 6 questions designed to assess various quality aspects based on the CLAIR requirements. The participants could add comments to each answer to clarify the answer or suggest improvements. For the post-test survey, participants responded to statements using a Likert scale (1 = Strongly Disagree, 5 = Strongly Agree) to assess usability and satisfaction.

The evaluation metrics used in the surveys were determined using the Goal Question Metric method (GQM) [30]. Data analysis involved: statistical evaluation analysis of qualitative feedback to identify strengths and areas for improvement, and comparative analysis of performance across different developer skill levels.

6.3 Test Case 1 Documentation Generation

In this test case, we evaluated CLAIR's ability to generate documentation for microflows in Mendix applications. Participants were instructed to generate documentation for three microflows, each with increasing size and complexity. Table 3 shows the quantitative results of the evaluation.

Table 3. Test Case 1 - Quantitative results

Aspect	Score (0-10)
Correct	8.8
Complete	8.1
Relevant	8.5
Understandable	9.2
Readable	8.5
Useful	7.5

Each aspect of this evaluation is briefly discussed below:

Correctness. CLAIR demonstrated a high degree of accuracy in generating documentation, with most participants agreeing that the outputs were technically correct and aligned with the provided input. However, occasional issues arose, such as minor errors in interpreting meaning from naming conventions or misrepresenting relationships between entities. While these errors were not frequent, they highlighted a need for refining the system's dependence on naming conventions. This suggests that CLAIR could benefit from additional logic to validate inferred relationships and names, or the injections of semantics to reduce misinterpretation. Inconsistencies in user-defined names could also be an indication of improper naming conventions applied by developers, thereby highlighting an area of improvement for the application.

Completeness. While CLAIR's outputs were generally comprehensive, providing detailed responses, including multi-layered documentation, participants noted that the system sometimes lacked high-level context, focusing more on technical details ("what" happens) in the microflow rather than providing deeper insights into the rationale ("why" something happens). It was pointed out that this could potentially be improved by including business context into the system. Apart from this, participants expressed that the combination of high-level summaries and detailed information was really helpful. However, for larger and more complex microflows, the generated documentation occasionally missed critical interactions with other components.

Relevance. The system scored well in terms of relevance, with participants finding that the generated documentation typically aligned with their queries and provided meaningful information. Various participants praised CLAIR's ability to provide purpose and explain relationships between microflows, especially if they tailored their queries. However, feedback suggested that the system could benefit from prioritising essential details over exhaustive coverage, which sometimes diluted the relevance of the output. Furthermore, some participants remarked that while the generated documentation was relevant, much of the information could be retrieved directly from the microflow. However, this comment was mainly given by the more experienced developers, indicating a difference in perception of ease of understanding complex logic.

Understandability. This was the strongest metric for this test scenario, as participants praised the clarity of the generated documentation. The use of consistent terminology and alignment with Mendix's model structure contributed to its high understandability. Suggestions for improvement included organising information chronologically to enhance logical flow and ensuring that the most critical details are presented first.

Readability. Participants found the documentation easy to read, with bullet points and structured outputs contributing to its readability. However, the ordering of information could be improved, particularly for complex microflows where chronological ordering of sub-microflows and actions within the flow was suggested to improve logical flow and readability further.

Usefulness. Although usefulness received the lowest score among the metrics, a 7.5 score for a prototype system is an encouraging result, especially given CLAIR's complexity and experimental nature. Participants consistently highlighted the tool's value for onboarding new developers and team members, making it a valuable asset for simplifying complex applications or understanding unfamiliar models. CLAIR's functionality for breaking down the purpose and inner workings of large and complex microflows was especially appreciated, with participants recognising its ability to clarify intricate workflows. Furthermore, the "purpose" section in the documentation stood out as a key feature, offering valuable insights into the rationale and logic behind microflows. Participants noted that this section should remain constant over time for a microflow, serving as a stable reference point for making changes in the future. Experienced developers, who are already familiar with the application, found CLAIR less impactful. However, this was also expected, given that for the test scenarios the participants were very familiar with the application, therefore reducing the need for documentation in general.

From this test case we concluded that CLAIR performs well for generating technically correct documentation, but further development is needed to eliminate a few edge-case inaccuracies. While CLAIR provides granular detail, completeness could be improved by integrating application-wide context and offering explanations for design choices, although participants did indicate this might be difficult to infer solely from the application structure. CLAIR's relevancy could be improved by balancing the depth of information with the specific focus of the query. CLAIR excels in delivering clear and comprehensible documentation, but improved information hierarchy and structure would make the documentation even more user-friendly. Finally, CLAIR is highly effective as a tool documentation creation and for onboarding, especially for new developers or those tackling complex workflows. However, its utility could be broadened to better serve experienced developers and business stakeholders by incorporating additional features, such as business context and coverage of elements beyond the current scope, such as REST services and Java actions.

6.4 Usability and User Experience

To evaluate CLAIR's usability and user experience, we considered how the participants scored on a Likert scale statements concerning various aspects of the system's performance, user-friendliness, and its perceived value in a real-world Mendix development workflow (post-test survey mentioned in Sect. 6.2), in line with the extended Technology Acceptance Model (TAM) [34]. Table 4 summarises the results.

Table 4. Usability results

Statement	Score
The system was easy to use.	3.8
The system is able to provide the requested information.	3.8
The documentation/responses are helpful.	4.4
The system accurately provides the requested information.	3.6
The system would save me time writing documentation.	4.2
The system improves the organisation of the documentation.	3.7
The system was easy to learn how to use.	4.0
The system improves traceability of the documentation.	3.6
I would use this tool in my workflow.	3.9

Participants found CLAIR relatively easy to use (3.8) and learn (4.0). The lower score for ease of use compared to ease of learning suggests that while the system is easier to understand with some guidance, some friction points remain in usage, such as crafting effective prompts or navigating complex outputs. Participants appreciated the chat-based interface but some suggested the addition of predefined query templates to streamline interactions and reduce user effort when crafting effective prompts.

CLAIR performed well in providing helpful (4.4) and relevant (3.8) responses, with participants particularly praising the clarity and structure of its outputs. However, slightly lower scores for accuracy (3.6) indicate occasional issues, such as fabricated details, reliance on naming conventions, or incomplete context integration. While participants highlighted its helpfulness, ensuring precise and context-aware outputs remains critical for building trust and reliability, which is essential for AI adoption [13].

The system demonstrated clear time-saving potential (4.2), with participants noting its ability to generate structured documentation and annotations that would otherwise require significant effort. However, the lower scores for improving organisation (3.7) and traceability (3.6) highlight a need for enhanced features, such as integration with existing documentation workflows or Mendix Studio Pro.

Participants were generally positive about incorporating CLAIR into their workflows, especially for onboarding, troubleshooting, and generating documentation for complex applications. Furthermore, the system's appeal as a co-developer tool for brainstorming or validating ideas was also highlighted. However, some participants noted its limited added-value for experienced developers, who may already have in-depth knowledge of their applications.

6.5 Requirements Satisfaction

We also evaluated to what extent CLAIR fulfils its functional and non-functional requirements, but we refrain from discussing this evaluation here due to page limitations. Details can be found in [7]. Scores in this evaluation ranged between 7.5 and 8.7 in a scale from 0 to 10, so we concluded that CLAIR covers its requirements quite sufficiently.

7 Final Remarks

The main initial objective of this research has been to improve the documentation process and indirectly the quality of Low-Code applications. The enhanced documentation should lead to improved system understandability, maintainability, sustainability, and knowledge retention. This objective was achieved through the development of CLAIR, which automates the generation of context-aware, up-to-date documentation, helping address the broader challenges identified in our literature review and survey.

This research provides contributions to both academia and practice in the domain of Low-Code development and automated documentation. To our knowledge, this is the first research to focus on documentation in Low-Code environments, to reduce technical debt and improve collaboration. We identified documentation challenges in Low-Code platforms, like a lack of robust documentation practices, fragmented documentation, and inadequate traceability, Through a survey and a case study, we identified low code documentation challenges perceived by practitioners, particularly on issues such as knowledge retention, maintainability, and accessibility. CLAIR provides a practical, automated solution to improve the documentation process of Low-Code applications, especially Mendix applications, addressing issues such as fragmented, out-dated documentation, and manual effort by offering context-aware, query-based insights tailored to diverse stakeholder needs. To our knowledge, CLAIR is the first solution to combine Low-Code, knowledge graphs, and LLM agents into a unified and novel approach to address documentation challenges in Low-Code environments. CLAIR's solution architecture is not only adaptable to other Low-Code platforms beyond Mendix but also to traditional software development environments. Its graph-based design and reliance on semi-structured data ensure flexibility for a wide range of applications. Furthermore, the integration of LLM-based Multi-Agent reasoning enhances the system's adaptability, enabling potential applications in domains outside software development, provided the input data is (semi-)structured and relational.

Limitations of this research come mainly from the survey and the case study being performed by a small research team and based on a simple (but representative) Low-Code platform (Mendix). CLAIR was validated in a testing environment with a limited sample size of 10 participants, who were known to one of the authors before the validation. Consequently, the controlled testing environment and the limited scope of use cases may not fully capture the variability in challenges and scenarios encountered in broader industry contexts or other organisations. Furthermore, due to time constraints and a lack of a validated data set, we did not employ a data-driven systematic analysis of the outputs generated by CLAIR, so we have no quantitative evidence that validates the consistency of the generated documentation. However, the consistency of the outputs was qualitatively validated by one of the authors by examining the outputs across the different testing sessions. The validation results show that improving the usability of CLAIR is a key area for future development, which could include the use of predefined query templates to guide users in framing their queries more effectively, and embedding CLAIR directly into development environments.

In CLAIR's current implementation, the knowledge graph is statically updated, requiring manual intervention to synchronise with application changes, so future work could address the integration of CLAIR with deployment or CI/CD pipelines to automate this process. Porting CLAIR to other Low-Code platforms, such as OutSystems or Microsoft PowerApps, remains an interesting direction for future research, which would require tailoring the knowledge graph schema and data extraction pipelines to accommodate different platform-specific structures. Deploying CLAIR in real-world development environments and gathering longitudinal feedback from users is required to evaluate its long-term impact, usability, and effectiveness. The inherent flexibility of the LLM-based MAS can also be explored to extend CLAIR's use cases beyond the cases we have already investigated. For instance, CLAIR could potentially be extended to actively assist application developers by offering intelligent recommendations of reusable components or design optimisations. Finally, the development of a validated documentation dataset can be a crucial step toward systematically improving and evaluating CLAIR's outputs. This dataset would contain high-quality, thoroughly reviewed documentation samples, providing a benchmark for measuring CLAIR's outputs. By comparing CLAIR-generated documentation against these validated samples, researchers could obtain quantitative metrics on clarity, accuracy, and completeness using data-driven analysis, in contrast to our reliance on expert validation.

Disclosure of interests. Tim Eichhorn has performed this work during an internship at CAPE. Ruben ten Asbroek works at CAPE.

References

1. Aghajani, E., Nagy, C., Linares-Vásquez, M., Moreno, L., Bavota, G., Lanza, M., Shepherd, D.C.: Software documentation: The practitioners' perspective. In: Proceedings of the ACM/IEEE 42nd International Conference on Software Engineering, pp. 590–601. ACM (6 2020). https://doi.org/10.1145/3377811.3380405
2. Alamin, M.A.A., Malakar, S., Uddin, G., Afroz, S., Haider, T.B., Iqbal, A.: An empirical study of developer discussions on low-code software development challenges. In: 2021 IEEE/ACM 18th International Conference on Mining Software Repositories (MSR), pp. 46–57 (2021). https://doi.org/10.1109/MSR52588.2021.00018
3. Arslan, M., Ghanem, H., Munawar, S., Cruz, C.: A survey on rag with llms. Procedia Comput. Sci. **246**, 3781–3790 (2024). https://doi.org/10.1016/j.procs.2024.09.178, https://www.sciencedirect.com/science/article/pii/S1877050924021860, 28th International Conference on Knowledge Based and Intelligent information and Engineering Systems (KES 2024)
4. Bock, A.C., Frank, U.: Low-code platform. Bus. Inf. Syst. Eng. **63**(6), 733–740 (2021). https://doi.org/10.1007/s12599-021-00726-8
5. Cui, W., Zhang, J., Li, Z., Sun, H., Lopez, D., Das, K., Malin, B., Kumar, S.: Phaseevo: Towards unified in-context prompt optimization for large language models (2024). https://arxiv.org/abs/2402.11347
6. Edge, D., Trinh, H., Cheng, N., Bradley, J., Chao, A., Mody, A., Truitt, S., Larson, J.: From local to global: A graph rag approach to query-focused summarization (2024). https://arxiv.org/abs/2404.16130
7. Eichhorn, T.: CLAIR: Generating On-Demand Low-Code Application Documentation through Knowledge Graph and LLM-based Multi-Agent System Integration. Master's thesis, University of Twente (March 2025). https://essay.utwente.nl/106037/
8. Frank, U., Maier, P., Alexander, B.: Low code platforms: Promises, concepts and prospects: A comparative study of ten systems (12 2021). https://doi.org/10.17185/duepublico/75244, https://doi.org/10.17185/duepublico/47018
9. Guo, T., Chen, X., Wang, Y., Chang, R., Pei, S., Chawla, N.V., Wiest, O., Zhang, X.: Large language model based multi-agents: A survey of progress and challenges (2024). https://arxiv.org/abs/2402.01680
10. Henzgen, A., Strey, L.: Model-driven approach for automatic model information aggregation in structured documents. In: 2023 ACM/IEEE International Conference on Model Driven Engineering Languages and Systems Companion (MODELS-C), pp. 403–413. IEEE, October 2023.https://doi.org/10.1109/MODELS-C59198.2023.00072

11. Hornsteiner, M., Kreussel, M., Steindl, C., Ebner, F., Empl, P., Schönig, S.: Real-time text-to-cypher query generation with large language models for graph databases. Future Internet **16**, 438 (2024). https://doi.org/10.3390/fi16120438
12. Jeong, C.: Beyond text: Implementing multimodal large language model-powered multi-agent systems using a no-code platform (2025). https://arxiv.org/abs/2501.00750
13. Kelly, S., Kaye, S.A., Oviedo-Trespalacios, O.: What factors contribute to the acceptance of artificial intelligence? a systematic review. Telematics Inform. **77**, 101925 (2023). https://doi.org/10.1016/j.tele.2022.101925, https://www.sciencedirect.com/science/article/pii/S0736585322001587
14. Khan, J.Y., Uddin, G.: Automatic code documentation generation using gpt-3. In: Proceedings of the 37th IEEE/ACM International Conference on Automated Software Engineering, pp. 1–6. ACM (10 2022). https://doi.org/10.1145/3551349.3559548
15. Li, Y.: A practical survey on zero-shot prompt design for in-context learning. In: Proceedings of the Conference Recent Advances in Natural Language Processing - Large Language Models for Natural Language Processings, pp. 641–647. INCOMA Ltd., Shoumen, BULGARIA (2023). https://doi.org/10.26615/978-954-452-092-2_069, http://dx.doi.org/10.26615/978-954-452-092-2_069
16. Liang, Y., et al.: Taskmatrix.ai: Completing tasks by connecting foundation models with millions of apis (2023). https://arxiv.org/abs/2303.16434
17. Liu, S., Chen, Y., Xie, X., Siow, J., Liu, Y.: Retrieval-augmented generation for code summarization via hybrid gnn (2021). https://arxiv.org/abs/2006.05405
18. Liu, X., et al.: Codexgraph: Bridging large language models and code repositories via code graph databases (2024). https://arxiv.org/abs/2408.03910
19. Luo, Y., Liang, P., Wang, C., Shahin, M., Zhan, J.: Characteristics and challenges of low-code development: The practitioners' perspective. In: Proceedings of the 15th ACM / IEEE International Symposium on Empirical Software Engineering and Measurement (ESEM), pp. 1–11. ACM (10 2021).https://doi.org/10.1145/3475716.3475782
20. Mayer, R.E.: Multimedia Learning. Cambridge University Press, 3 edn. (2020). https://doi.org/10.1017/9781316941355
21. McBurney, P.W., McMillan, C.: Automatic documentation generation via source code summarization of method context. In: Proceedings of the 22nd International Conference on Program Comprehension, pp. 279–290. Association for Computing Machinery (2014). https://doi.org/10.1145/2597008.2597149, https://doi.org/10.1145/2597008.2597149
22. Moreno, L., Marcus, A.: Automatic software summarization: the state of the art. In: 2017 IEEE/ACM 39th International Conference on Software Engineering Companion (ICSE-C), pp. 511–512. IEEE, May 2017. https://doi.org/10.1109/ICSE-C.2017.169
23. Moser, M., Pichler, J.: eknows: Platform for multi-language reverse engineering and documentation generation. In: 2021 IEEE International Conference on Software Maintenance and Evolution (ICSME), pp. 559–568. IEEE (9 2021). https://doi.org/10.1109/ICSME52107.2021.00057
24. Naimi, L., Bouziane, E.M., Jakimi, A., Saadane, R., Chehri, A.: Automating software documentation: employing llms for precise use case description. Procedia Comput. Sci. **246**, 1346–1354 (2024). https://doi.org/10.1016/j.procs.2024.09.568
25. Ouyang, S., et al.: Repograph: enhancing ai software engineering with repository-level code graph (2024). https://arxiv.org/abs/2410.14684

26. Parvez, M.R., Ahmad, W.U., Chakraborty, S., Ray, B., Chang, K.W.: Retrieval augmented code generation and summarization (2021). https://arxiv.org/abs/2108.11601
27. Peng, B., et al.: Graph retrieval-augmented generation: A survey (2024). https://arxiv.org/abs/2408.08921
28. Robillard, M.P., et al.: On-demand developer documentation. In: 2017 IEEE International Conference on Software Maintenance and Evolution (ICSME), pp. 479–483. IEEE (9 2017). https://doi.org/10.1109/ICSME.2017.17
29. Shin, J., Aleithan, R., Hemmati, H., Wang, S.: Retrieval-augmented test generation: How far are we? (2024). https://arxiv.org/abs/2409.12682
30. van Solingen (Revision), R., Basili (Original article, 1994 ed.), V., Caldiera (Original article, 1994 ed.), G., Rombach (Original article, 1994 ed.), H.D.: Goal Question Metric (GQM) Approach. John Wiley & Sons, Ltd (2002). https://doi.org/10.1002/0471028959.sof142
31. Song, X., Sun, H., Wang, X., Yan, J.: A survey of automatic generation of source code comments: Algorithms and techniques. IEEE Access **7**, 111411–111428 (2019). https://doi.org/10.1109/access.2019.2931579, http://dx.doi.org/10.1109/ACCESS.2019.2931579
32. Su, C.Y., McMillan, C.: Distilled gpt for source code summarization. Automated Softw. Eng. **31**, 22 (2024). https://doi.org/10.1007/s10515-024-00421-4
33. Tamašauskaitė, G., Groth, P.: Defining a knowledge graph development process through a systematic review. ACM Transactions on Software Engineering and Methodology **32**, 1–40 (1 2023). https://doi.org/10.1145/3522586
34. Venkatesh, V., Davis, F.D.: A theoretical extension of the technology acceptance model: Four longitudinal field studies. Management Science **46**(2), 186–204 (2000). https://doi.org/10.1287/mnsc.46.2.186.11926, https://doi.org/10.1287/mnsc.46.2.186.11926
35. Vincent, P., Lijima, K., Driver, M., Wong, J., Natis, Y.: Magic quadrant for enterprise low-code application platforms (8 2019)
36. Wagenaar, G., Overbeek, S., Lucassen, G., Brinkkemper, S., Schneider, K.: Working software over comprehensive documentation – rationales of agile teams for artefacts usage. J. Softw. Eng. Res. Dev. **6**, 7 (2018). https://doi.org/10.1186/s40411-018-0051-7
37. Wang, C., Li, H., Gao, Z., Yao, M., Yang, Y.: An automatic documentation generator based on model-driven techniques. In: 2010 2nd International Conference on Computer Engineering and Technology, vol. 4, pp. V4–175–V4–179 (2010). https://doi.org/10.1109/ICCET.2010.5485654
38. Wieringa, R.J.: Design Science Methodology for Information Systems and Software Engineering. Springer, Heidelberg (2014). https://doi.org/10.1007/978-3-662-43839-8
39. Wu, Q., et al.: Autogen: Enabling next-gen llm applications via multi-agent conversation (2023). https://arxiv.org/abs/2308.08155
40. Zhao, M., Wu, Z., Yang, G., Wang, L., Chen, W.: Smartosek: a real-time operating system for automotive electronics. In: Embedded Software and Systems, pp. 437–442. Springer, Heidelberg (2005). https://doi.org/10.1007/11535409_63

iRESEARCH - 3rd Workshop on Empirical Methodologies for Research in EA and Service/Data-oriented Computing

Machine Learning-Based Enhancement of Access Control in ERP Systems Using Real-World Data

Jonas Schnepf[1(✉)], Simon Anderer[2], Boris Grothues[2], and Bernd Scheuermann[1]

[1] Faculty of Management Science and Engineering, University of Applied Sciences Karlsruhe, Karlsruhe, Germany
{jonas.schnepf,bernd.scheuermann}@h-ka.de
[2] Pointsharp AB, Karlsruhe, Germany
{simon.anderer,boris.grothues}@pointsharp.com

Abstract. The security of IT systems faces substantial risks from external and internal threats, emphasizing the need for access control. Role-based access control is widely used in IT systems, where permissions are assigned to users via roles. However, insufficient permission concepts and dynamic changes in user responsibilities often lead to errors in permission assignments. These issues can undermine key security principles such as Least Privilege and Segregation of Duties. Therefore, this study explores the application of machine learning-based access control (MLBAC) to address these challenges in the context of enterprise resource planning (ERP) systems. For this purpose, different ERP data sources, including permission concept data and records of user behavior, are described, and their suitability for MLBAC is investigated. This study further highlights the significant potential of MLBAC for predicting access decisions to evaluate existing permissions concepts and to assign permissions to new users. Moreover, this study demonstrates how combining permission concept data and records of user behavior can validate access decisions.

Keywords: Machine Learning-based Access Control · Enterprise Resource Planning Systems · Gradient Boosted Decision Trees · CatBoost

1 Introduction

IT systems, which allow multiple users to access shared resources, face significant risks and must therefore be secured against external and internal threats. Permission management and access control are essential to mitigate these crucial risks. A commonly adopted approach is role-based access control (RBAC), especially in enterprise resource planning (ERP) systems, which are used to support and automate business processes. In RBAC, users are assigned permissions through predefined roles [1]. A permission corresponds to the authorization to perform an operation on an object, e.g., to access a file or to write in a table.

J. Barateiro et al. (Eds.): EDOC 2025 Workshops, LNBIP 571, pp. 315–332, 2026.
https://doi.org/10.1007/978-3-032-16234-2_26

The responsibilities of employees change over time. As part of the identity lifecycle management (ILM), the digital identities of employees must be continuously adapted to reflect these changes. ILM covers the entire lifecycle of a digital identity, from its creation and ongoing updates to its termination. Therefore, a critical component of ILM is ensuring that users of ERP systems have the appropriate permissions to perform their jobs [10]. In ERP systems, users are often assigned more permissions than needed, creating potential for accidental damage, error, and fraud, which can lead to high financial losses [1]. Incorrect permission assignments and changes as part of the ILM highlight the ongoing need to adapt permission concepts, ensuring that these are as accurate as possible so that every user is assigned exactly the permissions needed. The manual adaptation of permission concepts in ERP systems is a highly time-consuming, cost-intensive, and error-prone activity, as, in addition to the difficulty of the task itself, qualified personnel are also lacking to implement it correctly [12]. Therefore, data-driven approaches are required for generating recommendations on permission assignments and revocations to adapt the permission concept. Besides rule-based and manual approaches, recent research has explored the application of machine learning (ML) for this purpose, e.g. [17].

Within this study, the use of ML for access control, referred to as machine learning-based access control (MLBAC) [18], is to be adapted to ERP systems, as MLBAC has not yet been applied in this context. This study focuses on the ERP systems of SAP SE, the market-leading provider of ERP software [22]. The objective of this study is to adapt MLBAC for ERP systems in order to assess the permission assignments of existing users and to recommend initial permissions for new users. The remainder of this study is structured as follows: Sect. 2 provides the problem description. The related work is reviewed in Sect. 3. Section 4 presents the fundamentals of access control in SAP ERP systems. Additionally, the necessary steps to process SAP ERP data for MLBAC are described. Section 5 analyzes the real-world data utilized in the experiments, which are then described in Sect. 6. Section 7 summarizes the main findings and provides an outlook on future research. Comprehensive implementation details, including the developed code and all results, are available on GitHub[1].

2 Problem Description

IT systems must be secured against internal and external threats. Therefore, a permission concept must be defined in which permissions are assigned to users to restrict access. For a set of M users $U = \{u_1, ..., u_M\}$ and N permissions $P = \{p_1, ..., p_N\}$, the permission concept can be represented by a permission-to-user assignment matrix $UPA \in \{0,1\}^{(M \times N)}$, where $UPA_{i,j} = 1$ indicates that permission p_j is assigned to user u_i. In the following, the implemented permission concept is referred to as UPA_I. As part of the identity lifecycle management (ILM), UPA_I must continuously be adapted to protect IT systems while ensuring that users are assigned the needed permissions [10]. Thereby, three phases in

[1] https://github.com/JSch25/ERP_MLBAC.

ILM can be distinguished: (1) create, (2) update, and (3) terminate. (1) The creation of new users necessitates the assignment of initial permissions. (2) The permission concept must be continuously updated as user responsibilities change over time to remove excessive permissions and assign needed permissions. (3) The termination of users requires the removal of all assigned permissions.

A widely used access control model is role-based access control (RBAC) [8,9], particularly for enterprise resource planning (ERP) systems [1]. In RBAC, users are assigned permissions via roles. As these assignments are often erroneous, users are assigned more permissions than needed, leading to Type I errors. This issue is further exacerbated by how permissions in SAP ERP systems are defined: Instead of exact values, entire value ranges or wildcards are used [1,2]. This may lead to users utilizing permissions that are not needed to perform their jobs, violating the Principle of Least Privilege (PoLP), which stresses that users should only be given the permissions needed [11]. It may also conflict with the Segregation of Duties (SoD), which requires separating the responsibilities for critical actions among users [8,21]. Type II errors occur if users are assigned insufficient permissions, hindering them from completing their jobs [2]. Figure 1 highlights assigned, needed, and used permissions, as well as Type I and II errors.

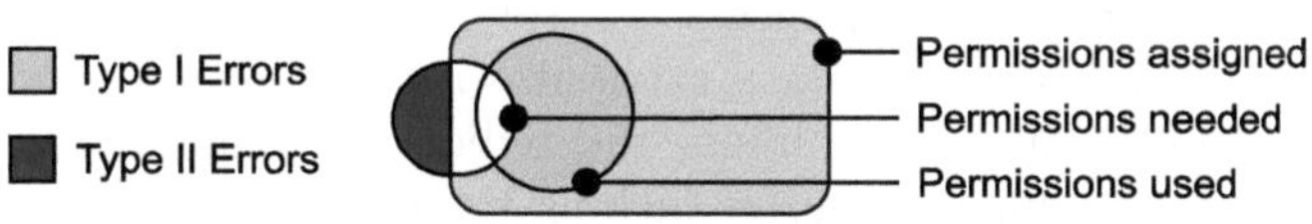

Fig. 1. Venn diagram depicting assigned, needed, and used permissions.

The different phases of ILM and erroneous permission assignments necessitate the continuous adaptation of UPA_I. At any time, the UPA_I must represent the current permission needs while respecting security principles such as SoD.

3 Related Work

Recent literature suggests the use of machine learning (ML) in access control. This section focuses on ML-driven access decisions, referred to as machine learning-based access control (MLBAC) [18]. In MLBAC, access decisions are provided by an ML model, which is trained on permission data consisting of the requesting user u_i, the requested permission p_j, user and/or permission attributes, and the access decision (target) [17]. Given the practical focus of this study, a comprehensive literature review is not intended. For a comprehensive review on the use of ML in access control, readers are referred to Nobi et al. [17].

Cappelletti et al. [4] utilize different ML algorithms to predict access decisions based on public data sets, including the Amazon employee access challenge[2] and

[2] https://www.kaggle.com/competitions/amazon-employee-access-challenge.

the Amazon access samples[3]. The results indicate that symbolic ML models, such as decision trees or random forest (RF), perform better than non-symbolic models, like support vector machines (SVM) or neural networks (NN).

Chang et al. [5] utilize SVMs to predict access decisions with time constraints. As an example, the authors consider access to a resource outside of office hours, which is not permitted. The approach involves dividing users into groups based on their passwords and login times and assigning the corresponding permissions. The process is structured into three stages: (1) The input (password and timestamp) is transformed into a 9-dimensional vector. (2) The SVM is trained on these preprocessed input vectors, and (3) the SVM divides the users into groups and assigns permissions according to security levels. The authors do not provide details about the data set used. Srivastava et al. [25] propose risk-adaptive access control (RAdAC) to address scenarios where access to resources may be necessary, which would be denied under the current permission concept. An ML model verifies the authenticity of the requester and evaluates the risk of the request based on time, location, access frequency, and resource sensitivity. For their experiments, the authors compare NN and RF, with the RF demonstrating superior performance. The data sets used are not detailed and are not provided.

Karimi et al. [12] suggest the use of reinforcement learning (RL) for the improvement of attribute-based access control (ABAC) and address key challenges of ABAC: (1) A system with n attributes results in 2^n rule combinations, making it error-prone, time-consuming, and tedious to manage. (2) Access control models are often defined by users lacking the expertise to ensure efficiency, effectiveness, and accuracy. (3) Modern IT systems rapidly evolve, requiring continuous permission management. Therefore, the authors develop an RL-based system that learns access decisions through user interactions. The system is evaluated using the Amazon employee access challenge data set and two synthetic data sets. Outchakoucht et al. [20] also propose an RL approach. In combination with blockchain technologies, decentralized access control is to be created for devices in the Internet of Things. RL enables knowledge to be adapted step by step through trial and error to learn from experience. The presented approach is not practically implemented as the authors keep it for future work.

Khilar et al. [14] propose trust-based access control for cloud computing systems to evaluate access based on users' access history and behavior. Parameters such as bogus requests, unauthorized requests, forbidden requests, and range specifications are considered. The authors utilize various ML models (k-nearest neighbor, nearest centroid, Gaussian naive bayes, decision tree, SVM, logistic regression, and ridge classifier) and ensemble techniques. They evaluate the performance of the different models, demonstrating the superior performance of trust-based access control for cloud computing systems compared to traditional access control models. The authors do not specify the data set used.

Liu et al. [16] introduce the Efficient Permission Decision Engine based on ML (EPDE-ML). The framework utilizes an RF to predict access decisions based on permission data. The authors evaluate EPDE-ML on the Amazon employee

[3] http://archive.ics.uci.edu/dataset/216/amazon+access+samples.

access challenge data set. They compare their method against different ML algorithms such as LightGBM, logistic regression, k-nearest neighbor, SVM, and decision trees. EPDE-ML achieves scores that differ only slightly depending on the size of the permission concept and thus exceed other approaches.

Nobi et al. [19] propose deep learning-based access control (DLBAC) to address the challenges of creating and maintaining a permission concept. The authors use the two mentioned Amazon data sets and synthetic data to demonstrate the effectiveness of DLBAC, reporting that DLBAC balances the trade-off between over-provisioning (allowing unauthorized access) and under-provisioning (denying legitimate access). In addition, the authors propose different methods to provide explanations for the system's outputs. Further, Nobi et al. [18] examine the issues of access control administration[4]. When a permission concept changes, the model must adapt accordingly. The authors compare symbolic (RF) and non-symbolic models (NN), indicating that the non-symbolic models outperform symbolic models in adapting to changes in the permission concept.

For practical users, numerous literature, such as [15], provides guidance on best practices for defining permission concepts in SAP systems. However, to our knowledge, MLBAC has not yet been applied to ERP systems, nor have any studies considered the specific characteristics of ERP data for MLBAC.

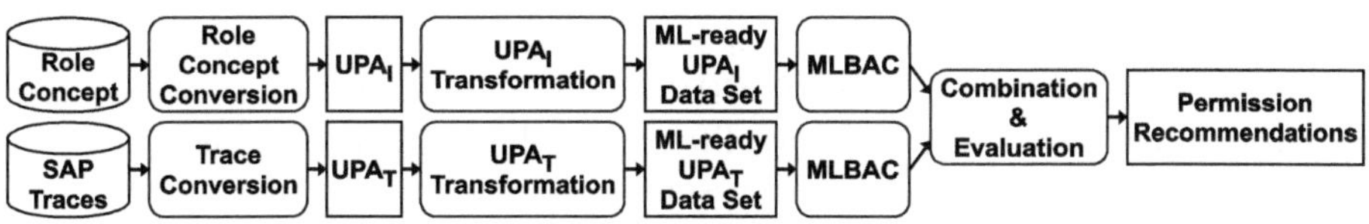

Fig. 2. Overview of the presented approach for MLBAC in SAP ERP systems.

4 Processing ERP Data for MLBAC

A particularity of enterprise resource planning (ERP) systems is the availability of different data sources for machine learning-based access control (MLBAC): the implemented permission concept, referred to as UPA_I, and records of used permissions, so-called traces. UPA_I can be derived from the role concept, indicating the assigned permissions. Traces, in turn, enable the derivation of a matrix UPA_T based on the permissions actually used. Therefore, Sect. 4.1 depicts the fundamentals of access control in SAP ERP systems. To enable the application of MLBAC to ERP data, Sect. 4.2 explains how the role concept and traces can be converted into UPA_I and UPA_T. Furthermore, Sect. 4.3 illustrates the transformation of UPA_I and UPA_T into ML-ready data sets. Afterwards, it is shown

[4] https://github.com/dlbac/MLBAC-Administration.

how MLBAC can be applied to predict access decisions, supporting the assignment of initial permissions to new users and the evaluation of existing users. Thereby, the combination of UPA_I and UPA_T, although not yet considered in the literature, is taken into account as it offers valuable opportunities to assess the predictions of access decisions. These can be used to derive permission recommendations that enhance the permission concept currently implemented. The outlined approach is summarized in Fig. 2.

4.1 Access Control in SAP ERP

Access control mechanisms are implemented to ensure that users perform only authorized actions [15,23]. In contrast to role-based access control (RBAC) in its original form, a two-level role concept is used in SAP systems, consisting of single and composite roles. Single roles typically represent specific, limited responsibilities within companies. In contrast, composite roles encompass broader responsibilities [1]. Two-level role concepts comprise the assignment of composite roles to users (UCA), the assignment of single to composite roles (CSA), and the assignment of permissions to single roles (SPA). Analogous to the permission-to-user assignment matrix UPA_I, these can be represented by binary matrices.

In SAP systems, a permission consists of one object and up to ten field definitions. Each field definition is a tuple (N_i, V_i), where N_i is a field name and V_i is a field value. The field value V_i can be a single value, a value range, or a wildcard [24]. A special type of permission is one that defines access to transactions. Transactions in SAP ERP are executable business processes or tasks that allow users to create, modify, or display data within the system by calling transaction codes. These permissions are defined by the object S_TCODE, the field TCD, and a field value containing one or more alpha-numeric keys called transaction codes [1], such as ME21N (a transaction for creating a purchase order). This study investigates MLBAC based on permissions with the object S_TCODE, as they refer to transactions, which are crucial for executing business activities.

For each transaction a user wants to perform, it is evaluated whether the user has the needed permissions. Therefore, a comparison is made between the permissions assigned and the permissions requested. These checks, referred to as traces, are recorded to monitor user behavior and actually used permissions [24].

4.2 Generation of UPA Matrices

In SAP systems, the permission concept can be derived from the implemented role concept. In addition, traces are available that record user behavior and provide an indication of the permissions actually used. Both role concept and trace data can be converted into permission-to-user assignment matrices UPA_I and UPA_T, which constitute the basis for the application of MLBAC.

Role Concept Conversion - Generation of UPA_I. As aforementioned, two-level role concepts can be represented by three matrices: UCA, CSA, and SPA.

From this, further assignment matrices can be derived using Boolean matrix multiplication. For $A \in \{0,1\}^{m \times k}$ and $B \in \{0,1\}^{k \times n}$, it is defined as follows:

$$(A \otimes B)_{i,j} := max_{l \in \{1,\ldots,k\}}(A_{i,l} \cdot B_{l,j})$$

The assignment of permissions to composite roles (CPA) results from $CPA = CSA \otimes SPA$, whereas the assignment of single roles to users (USA) results from $USA = UCA \otimes CSA$. In particular, the actual assignment of permissions to users $\text{UPA}_I \in \{0,1\}^{M \times N}$, which constitutes the main data for MLBAC, can be derived from the implemented two-level role concept: $UPA_\text{I} = UCA \otimes CSA \otimes SPA$.

Trace Conversion - Generation of UPA$_T$. Traces can be exploited to derive an assignment matrix $\text{UPA}_T \in \{0,1\}^{M \times N}$ from the permissions actually used. For each permission $p_j \in P$, $(\text{UPA}_T)_{i,j} = 1$, if permission p_j was used by user u_i. If permisison p_j was not used by user u_i, $(\text{UPA}_T)_{i,j} = 0$. This approach is detailed in [2]. It should be noted that UPA_T has a significantly lower number of ones, as not all permissions that are assigned to a user are actually used by him or her. In particular, there may be permissions that have not been used by any user. As a result, the corresponding columns in UPA_T only contain zeros.

4.3 UPA Transformation for MLBAC

MLBAC can be used to predict access decisions, determining the initial permission needs of new users and evaluating the permission assignments of existing users, reducing Type I and II errors. In order to make UPA_I and UPA_T applicable for MLBAC, both matrices must be transformed. Each matrix element becomes a separate row in the corresponding MLBAC data set. E.g., if $(UPA_I)_{i,j} = 1$ (user u_i is assigned permission p_j), the target is labeled 1. Analogously, for $(UPA_I)_{i,j} = 0$, the target is labeled 0. The same transformation is applied for UPA_T. The emerging rows are supplemented with user and permission attributes. User attributes are defined once new users are created in an SAP system. The decision as to which attributes should be used and maintained is dependent on the respective company. The attributes include, e.g., personal information, but also information about the department, the cost center, or

Permission-to-User Assignment Matrix

	p_1 ME29N	p_2 ME21N	p_3 ME51N
u_1	0	1	1
u_2	1	0	1

+ User Attributes
+ Permission Attributes

MLBAC-ready Data Set

User	Permission	Target	User Attributes	Permission Attributes
u_1	ME29N	0	user attributes of u_1	permission attributes of ME29N
u_1	ME21N	1	user attributes of u_1	permission attributes of ME21N
u_1	ME51N	1	user attributes of u_1	permission attributes of ME51N
u_2	ME29N	1	user attributes of u_2	permission attributes of ME29N
u_2	ME21N	0	user attributes of u_2	permission attributes of ME21N
u_2	ME51N	1	user attributes of u_2	permission attributes of ME51N

Fig. 3. Exemplary transformation of a permission-to-user assignment matrix for two users and three permissions into an MLBAC-ready data set.

a natural language function description. Permission attributes describe transactions in more detail. These attributes are referred to as components and subcomponents. The transaction ME21N (create purchase order) can be assigned to the materials management (MM) component and the materials management purchasing (MM-PUR) subcomponent. Figure 3 depicts the transformation process. The abbreviations ME29N, ME21N, and ME51N refer to permissions required to execute the corresponding transactions: release purchase order (ME29N), create purchase order (ME21N), and create purchase requisition (ME51N).

5 Analysis of Real-World Use Case Data

The experiments utilize data from two companies, which provide their role concept, traces, as well as user and permission attributes. Due to confidentiality reasons, the companies are referred to as company A and company B and are not further detailed. Table 1 summarizes the data sets derived from UPA_I and UPA_T. Within a company, the number of users M, the number of permissions N, and the number of data points $M \cdot N$ are the same for both data sets. The ratio of data points with a target of 1 to all data points, referred to as the positive class ratio (R^+), is provided as well. For the UPA_I data set, R^+ corresponds to the ratio of assigned permissions to all possible assignments of permissions to users, analogous for UPA_T with regard to the used permissions. The data sets indicate a significant class imbalance, as many permissions are only assigned to a small number of users. Further, only a fraction of the assigned permissions is used and therefore recorded in the traces and included in UPA_T.

Table 1. Data sets derived from UPA_I and UPA_T for company A and company B.

	Company A	Company B
Users (M)	399	3232
Permissions (N)	4,628	17,781
Data Points ($M \cdot N$)	1,846,572	57,468,192
R^+(UPA_I data set)	13.6%	4.8%
R^+(UPA_T data set)	0.4%	0.2%

All permissions considered are transaction permissions and are grouped according to the SAP component to which the included transaction code belongs. To speed up the calculations, the two data sets are split based on these components. The data sets for the five most relevant components, based on the number of users and permissions, are selected: Financial Accounting (FI), Controlling (CO), Materials Management (MM), General Logistics (LO), Sales & Distribution (SD). Tables 2 and 3 summarize the resulting data sets for both companies. In addition to the known key figures from Fig. 1, the number of SAP subcomponents is reported. Each SAP component comprises multiple subcomponents to which transaction codes are assigned, as described in Sect. 4.3.

Table 2. Divided data sets derived from UPA_I and UPA $_T$ for company A.

	FI	CO	MM	LO	SD
Users (M)	334	156	141	120	46
Permissions (N)	1,469	906	174	83	141
Data Points ($M \cdot N$)	490,646	141,336	24,534	9,960	6,486
Subcomponents	41	20	7	9	13
R^+(UPA_I data set)	7.9%	32.7%	33.1%	14.5%	39.4%
R^+(UPA_T data set)	0.5%	0.4%	1.6%	2.0%	5.7%

Table 3. Divided data sets derived from UPA_I and UPA $_T$ for company B.

	FI	CO	MM	LO	SD
Users (M)	2,200	752	1,671	1,851	1,649
Permissions (N)	2,212	1,205	1,090	1,245	835
Data Points ($M \cdot N$)	4,866,400	906,160	1,821,390	2,304,495	1,376,915
Subcomponents	69	19	19	40	27
R^+(UPA_I data set)	2.2%	9.3%	16.7%	11.7%	9.3%
R^+(UPA_T data set)	0.2%	0.4%	0.9%	0.6%	1.0%

Besides the role concept and traces, user and permission attributes are also available. Six user attributes are provided by both companies. Table 4 gives an overview of the user attributes, including the attribute name, a brief description, the number of distinct values, and the ratio of non-missing values to all values.

Table 4. Overview of the user attributes for company A and company B.

Attribute	Description	Company A		Company B	
USTYP	user type	1	100.0%	5	100.0%
FUNCTION	job title	90	99.5%	210	15.0%
COMPANY	company code	40	100.0%	23	99.9%
DEPARTMENT	department name	114	98.5%	355	98.6%
KOSTL	cost center	52	96.4%	362	97.8%
CLASS	user group in user master	8	100.0%	105	90.3%

The six user attributes are well-maintained for both companies, as they only contain a few missing values. Furthermore, company B provides an additional 14 user attributes that are more technical, such as the SAP license type, the system language of the user, the time zone, and different ID numbers. Of these attributes, three are sparsely maintained (<5%), one is moderately maintained (~65%), and 10 are well-maintained (>85%). Company A does not provide these attributes. Besides the user attributes, permission attributes are available for both companies. These include the aforementioned attributes "component" and "subcomponent", indicating which SAP component and subcomponent the transaction code belongs to. As the data is already partitioned according to components, only the subcomponent attribute is used in the experiments conducted.

6 Enhancing ERP Access Control Through MLBAC

This section outlines the experiments and key findings. The experimental setup is depicted in Sect. 6.1. Section 6.2 provides the results based on the UPA_I data sets, while Sect. 6.3 presents the findings based on the data sets derived from UPA_T. Finally, Sect. 6.4 discusses how combining UPA_I and UPA_T data sets can be used to generate permission recommendations. The complete results of the experiments and the corresponding code are provided on GitHub[5].

6.1 Experimental Setup

The data sets are split into training, validation, and test data sets, considering two approaches according to the phases of identity lifecycle management (ILM), see Sect. 2. (1) In the create phase, permissions are initially assigned to new users. These new users are therefore not part of the training data set. 60% of the users are included in the training set, 20% in the validation set, and 20% in the test set. This approach ensures that each set contains only users who are not present in the other two sets. (2) In the update phase, users' permissions are evaluated, and new permissions are assigned or unneeded permissions are revoked. Therefore, a random split is applied, where 60% of the data points are randomly assigned to the training set, 20% to the validation set, and 20% to the test set. This enables the evaluation of the permissions of existing users. As the termination phase only consists of permission removal, it is not considered.

As a classification algorithm, the gradient boosted decision tree (GBDT) CatBoost is selected. GBDT algorithms consist of a sequence of decision trees, where each tree attempts to minimize the loss of the previous one using gradient descent algorithms [7]. Compared to other GBDT algorithms like XGBoost [6] and LightGBM [13], CatBoost is noted for its minimal performance differences between default and tuned settings [3]. CatBoost further provides the ability to handle categorical variables natively [7], and is frequently used in related problems like the Amazon employee access challenge. Additionally, symbolic algorithms like GBDTs are considered well-suited for providing access decisions [4], underlining CatBoost's practical relevance. CatBoost's *cat_features* parameter is specified to encode the categorical attributes. The value of the *iterations* parameter is selected to be 1,000 to achieve early stopping in the majority of the experiments, enabling training until no further improvement of the validation score is observed. Early stopping is enabled after 100 iterations (*early_stopping_rounds*).

[5] https://github.com/JSch25/ERP_MLBAC.

The F1 score is used to evaluate the potential of MLBAC for predicting access decisions in SAP systems. Furthermore, the macro F1 score is given. As a baseline, the F1 score is calculated using a random classifier that predicts class labels based on the observed class distribution in the data set. For example, if 10% of the data points belong to the positive class and 90% to the negative class, the random classifier predicts class 1 with a probability of 0.1 and class 0 with a probability of 0.9. Each experiment is conducted ten times with different random seeds. Therefore, the mean value and the standard deviation are reported.

6.2 MLBAC Based on UPA_T Data Sets

The data sets derived from UPA_I are utilized for the first experiment. For company A, five data sets are available according to the five SAP components considered. These data sets contain seven attributes: six user attributes and one permission attribute. For company B, the same five data sets are used but in two variants due to the availability of further attributes: one consisting of seven attributes (six user attributes and one permission attribute) and the other of 21 attributes (20 user attributes and one permission attribute). Table 5 shows the results for the materials management (MM) component. The results are separated by the examined ILM phase: ILM phase create (user split), and ILM phase update (random split). As performance metrics, the F1 score baseline, the F1 score of the positive class, and the macro F1 score are given. Since similar results are obtained for the other SAP components, they are provided on GitHub.

Table 5. Results for the MM component based on the data sets derived from UPA_I.

Metric	Company A (7 Attributes)	Company B (7 Attributes)	Company B (21 Attributes)
ILM Phase: Create (User Split)			
Baseline	0.3307 ± 0.0179	0.1686 ± 0.0041	0.1680 ± 0.0047
F1 Score	0.9569 ± 0.0182	0.9069 ± 0.0119	0.9083 ± 0.0107
Macro F1	0.9678 ± 0.0132	0.9445 ± 0.0071	0.9452 ± 0.0064
ILM Phase: Update (Random Split)			
Baseline	0.3271 ± 0.0111	0.1675 ± 0.0019	0.1676 ± 0.0013
F1 Score	0.9886 ± 0.0025	0.9727 ± 0.0004	0.9735 ± 0.0004
Macro F1	0.9915 ± 0.0019	0.9836 ± 0.0002	0.9841 ± 0.0002

The results demonstrate strong performance across all five components, highlighting the suitability of UPA_I data sets for MLBAC in SAP systems. Applying the user split, the F1 score for the positive class exceeds 63% and reaches up to 98%, with over 78% achieved in 12 out of 15 experiments. The F1 score for the negative class surpasses 97% in all but one experiment (89%). As expected, tuples with target 0 are identified with higher accuracy due to their higher prevalence. Consequently, MLBAC reveals significant potential for the create phase of ILM. For the experiments utilizing random split, the F1 score for the positive class exceeds 91% and reaches up to 99%, while the F1 score for the negative class surpasses 98%. The values indicate that MLBAC can propose the necessary changes in the update phase of ILM. Minor differences can be observed when comparing the five components. For company A, the highest macro F1 score is achieved on the controlling component, and company B's highest score for both attribute sets is observed on the logistics general component. However, the differences between the components are negligible. The inclusion of additional attributes for company B leads to minor improvements. Improvements are limited to 0.8% points across all metrics, except for the controlling component, where the F1 score for the positive class increases by 8.0% points for the user split. Even if the use of the six attributes leads to good results, consideration can be given to include further attributes, if available.

6.3 MLBAC Based on UPA_T Data Sets

The experiment outlined in Sect. 6.2 is similarly performed on the UPA_T data sets, which are derived from the recorded traces. Table 6 shows the results for the MM component for both companies. Since similar results are obtained for the other components, they are again available in the GitHub repository.

Table 6. Results for the MM component based on the data sets derived from UPA_T.

Metric	Company A (7 Attributes)	Company B (7 Attributes)	Company B (21 Attributes)
ILM Phase: Create (User Split)			
Baseline	0.0158 ± 0.0119	0.0101 ± 0.0019	0.0096 ± 0.0018
F1 Score	0.6063 ± 0.0432	0.4964 ± 0.0611	0.5471 ± 0.0393
Macro F1	0.8003 ± 0.0216	0.7464 ± 0.0306	0.7718 ± 0.0197
ILM Phase: Update (Random Split)			
Baseline	0.0217 ± 0.0163	0.0084 ± 0.0018	0.0092 ± 0.0011
F1 Score	0.5620 ± 0.0936	0.5854 ± 0.0071	0.6021 ± 0.0067
Macro F1	0.7782 ± 0.0470	0.7911 ± 0.0035	0.7995 ± 0.0034

The experiments based on the UPA_T data sets yield significantly poorer results compared to those in Sect. 6.2. Applying the user split, the F1 scores for the positive class range from 21% to 85%, while for the random split, the F1 scores for the positive class range from 40% to 88%. The UPA_T data sets do not appear suitable for MLBAC due to the high number of incorrect predictions.

The UPA_T matrix has the exact dimensions as the corresponding UPA_I matrix but contains significantly fewer elements with value 1. This difference arises because some permissions assigned are not used and thus are not recorded in the traces. This non-use of transactions can be utilized to improve the prediction: The UPA_T matrices can be simplified by removing columns with only zeros, excluding transactions unused by any user. These reduced matrices can then be transformed according to Sect. 4 and utilized for MLBAC, while the eliminated tuples can be manually labeled as 0, as these transactions are known to be unused. The model is therefore trained using a less imbalanced data set. The reduced matrix is referred to as UPA_R. Table 7 provides the results for the MM component. The F1 score for the positive class and the Macro F1 score for the data sets derived from both UPA_T and UPA_R are provided for comparison. The complete results are again presented on GitHub.

Table 7. Results for the MM component based on the data sets derived from UPA_T and UPA_R.

Data	Metric	Company A (7 Attributes)	Company B (7 Attributes)	Company B (21 Attributes)
ILM Phase: Create (User Split)				
UPA_T	F1 Score	0.6063 ± 0.0432	0.4964 ± 0.0611	0.5471 ± 0.0393
	Macro F1	0.8003 ± 0.0216	0.7464 ± 0.0306	0.7718 ± 0.0197
UPA_R	F1 Score	0.6244 ± 0.0650	0.5217 ± 0.0430	0.5362 ± 0.0305
	Macro F1	0.8094 ± 0.0329	0.7591 ± 0.0215	0.7664 ± 0.0153
ILM Phase: Update (Random Split)				
UPA_T	F1 Score	0.5620 ± 0.0936	0.5854 ± 0.0071	0.6021 ± 0.0067
	Macro F1	0.7782 ± 0.0470	0.7911 ± 0.0035	0.7995 ± 0.0034
UPA_R	F1 Score	0.6700 ± 0.0592	0.5990 ± 0.0082	0.6111 ± 0.0080
	Macro F1	0.8325 ± 0.0299	0.7980 ± 0.0041	0.8041 ± 0.0040

Despite the use of the data sets derived from UPA_R, the results remain significantly worse compared to UPA_I while slightly improving compared to UPA_T. Applying the user split (ILM phase create), the F1 scores for the positive class range from 20% to 86%, while with the random split (ILM phase update), the scores vary between 45% and 89%. For the macro F1 score, only marginal changes are observed, as the F1 score for the negative class improves only slightly. Hence, both UPA_T and UPA_R data sets do not appear to be suitable for MLBAC. Nevertheless, when combined with UPA_I, trace data can serve as a valuable source for generation permission recommendations to enhance the permission concept.

6.4 Combining UPA_I and UPA_T Data Sets for MLBAC Validation

The combined use of UPA_I and UPA_T data sets appears promising, as transactions can only be used and recorded if the corresponding permission is assigned. Of particular interest are four scenarios where the prediction is incorrect. These predictions can be validated using the true target of the other data source to derive permissions recommendations and corresponding further actions. To address an incorrect prediction considering user u_i and permission p_j on the data sets derived from UPA_I, two scenarios S1 and S2 can be distinguished.

Scenario S1: The prediction on UPA_I is false negative. The model predicts that p_j should not be assigned to u_i. The question is whether p_j is actually needed by u_i. This cannot be definitively answered, however UPA_T provides supporting information: (a) If $(UPA_T)_{ij} = 1$, u_i has actually used p_j. This indicates that p_j is needed by u_i, and therefore, no further action is required. (b) If $(UPA_T)_{ij} = 0$, u_i has not used p_j. This indicates that p_j is not needed by u_i, resulting in a Type I error. Therefore, p_j may be revoked from u_i.

Scenario S2: The prediction on UPA_I is false positive. The model predicts that p_j should be assigned to u_i. Again, the question is whether p_j is actually needed by u_i. In this case, no additional information can be derived from UPA_T, as $(UPA_I)_{ij} = 0$ implies $(UPA_T)_{ij} = 0$ (if a permission is not assigned, it cannot be used). However, the prediction can indicate that this permission might be needed in the future, resulting in a Type II error.

Analogously, the scenarios S3 and S4 refer to an incorrect prediction considering user u_i and permission p_j on the data sets derived from UPA_T.

Scenario S3: The prediction on UPA_T is false negative. The model predicts that p_j has not been used by u_i, although p_j has been used by u_i according to UPA_T. The question is whether the usage was actually necessary, such that p_j is needed by u_i. No additional information can be derived from UPA_I, as $(UPA_T)_{ij} = 1$ implies $(UPA_I)_{ij} = 1$ (if a permission has been used, it must be assigned). However, the prediction can indicate that this permission might not be needed in the future, resulting in a Type I error.

Scenario S4: The prediction on UPA_T is false positive. The model predicts that p_j has been used by u_i, although p_j has not been used by u_i according to UPA_T. The question is whether the permission will be needed in the future, resulting in a Type II error. Here, UPA_I provides supporting information: (a) If $(UPA_I)_{ij} = 1$, this means that p_j is already assigned to u_i, supporting the prediction that p_j may be needed in the future. (b) If $(UPA_I)_{ij} = 0$, no additional information can be derived for verification.

Table 8 depicts the total number of data points matching the four scenarios S1-S4 for the MM component and the ILM phase update (random split). All data points matching the scenarios are summed up over the 10 runs conducted. As comparable results are obtained for the different components considered, the complete results are again provided in the GitHub repository. Alongside the high number of correctly predicted permissions, these four scenarios provide actionable recommendations that could further enhance the permission concept.

The results of this experiment indicate that combining UPA_I and UPA_T data sets provides opportunities for validating the prediction results. For company A, 49,080 data points are predicted for the MM component in 10 runs for the UPA_I data set (ILM phase update). Of these, 48,710 are correctly predicted as true positives and true negatives, while 370 (0.8%) are misclassified. Seven data points are related to scenario 1a, indicating that these permissions are actually needed and should therefore not be revoked. Scenario 1b includes 195 data points, suggesting that these permissions are not needed (type I error), which means they

Table 8. Data points matching the scenarios S1 - S4 for the MM component based on UPA_I and UPA_T data sets. Results only relate to the ILM phase update.

Scenario	Company A (7 Attributes)	Company B (7 Attributes)	Company B (21 Attributes)
Incorrect Prediction on UPA_I			
Scenario S1a	7	942	921
Scenario S1b	195	19,375	18,982
Scenario S2	168	12,773	12,220
Incorrect Prediction on UPA_T			
Scenario S3	417	16,850	16,376
Scenario S4a	125	5,402	4,963
Scenario S4b	12	674	680

could be revoked. Scenario 2 accounts for 168 data points, where no immediate action is advised, but adaptation may be necessary in the future. For the misclassified data points, practical recommendations can be provided through the combined use of data sets derived from UPA_I and UPA_T, which could further enhance the permission concept. By comparing the permission tuples' true and predicted target with the true target of the other data source, the prediction outcome can be verified, recommendations can be derived, and confidence in the ML-based predictions can be enhanced.

7 Conclusion and Future Works

This study demonstrated the applicability of machine learning-based access control (MLBAC) for enterprise resource planning (ERP) systems from SAP SE, which, to our knowledge, has not been considered in recent literature. Incorrect permission assignments and changes as part of the identity lifecycle management (ILM) necessitate the continuous adaptation of the implemented permission concept. By leveraging MLBAC to provide access decisions, the initial permission needs of new users can be determined, and current assignments of permissions to already existing users can be reevaluated. As the approach solely relies on data available in ERP systems, the feasibility and transferability of the presented approach within further real-world enterprise environments are emphasized.

The application of the implemented permission concept UPA_I combined with user and permission attributes for MLBAC was examined in this study. The results demonstrated strong performance, both in the creation phase and the update phase of ILM, supporting the assignment of permissions to new users and the evaluation of existing users. Besides the implemented permission concept UPA_I, ERP systems provide records of actually used permissions referred to as traces (UPA_T). Previous studies relied solely on a single type of data for MLBAC, whereas this study leverages the advantages of UPA_I and UPA_T. It was revealed that traces alone, whether unmodified (UPA_T) or modified (UPA_R), are not reliable due to the high number of incorrect predictions. However, combining UPA_T with UPA_I provides valuable opportunities to validate the predictions, generate actionable recommendations, and ultimately enhance confidence in the model's predictions. Furthermore, the impact of ERP-specific user and permission attributes on the performance of MLBAC was addressed. Experiments with seven attributes (six user attributes and one permission attribute) were conducted for both companies, while the data sets of company B were further combined with 21 attributes (20 user attributes and one permission attribute). The results showed minimal performance improvement with the additional attributes, additionally highlighting the transferability of the approach to use cases with different attribute sets. In the experiments conducted, the original number of six user attributes appears sufficient to provide the necessary information. However, the consideration of further attributes, if available, may improve the performance. Within this context, analyzing the impact of individual attributes on the prediction results could provide valuable insights. Future research could further consider the incorporation of single roles, composite roles, or additional permissions. These elements are more complex and provide additional attributes. Evaluating which attributes are maintained across different companies would also enhance practical applicability. Furthermore, future experiments could investigate alternative classification algorithms and the application of over- and undersampling techniques to improve prediction accuracy.

Disclosure of Interests. The authors have no competing interests to declare that are relevant to the content of this article.

References

1. Anderer, S.: Role mining for industrial-strength ERP systems using evolutionary algorithms. Phd thesis, Otto von Guericke University, Magdeburg, Germany (2023). https://doi.org/10.25673/103421
2. Anderer, S., Sahin, A., Scheuermann, B., Mostaghim, S.: On using authorization traces to support role mining with evolutionary algorithms. In: Proceedings of the 14th International Joint Conference on Computational Intelligence, pp. 121–132. SCITEPRESS (2022). https://doi.org/10.5220/0011539300003332
3. Bentéjac, C., Csörgő, A., Martínez-Muñoz, G.: A comparative analysis of gradient boosting algorithms. Artif. Intell. Rev. **54**(3), 1937–1967 (2020). https://doi.org/10.1007/s10462-020-09896-5
4. Cappelletti, L., Valtolina, S., Valentini, G., Mesiti, M., Bertino, E.: On the quality of classification models for inferring ABAC policies from access logs. In: 2019 IEEE International Conference on Big Data, pp. 4000–4007. IEEE (2019). https://doi.org/10.1109/bigdata47090.2019.9005959
5. Chang, C.C., Lin, I.C., Liao, C.T.: An access control system with time-constraint using support vector machines. Int. J. Netw. Secur. **2**(2), 150–159 (2006)
6. Chen, T., Guestrin, C.: XGBoost: a scalable tree boosting system. In: Proceedings of the 22nd ACM SIGKDD International Conference on Knowledge Discovery and Data Mining, pp. 785–794. ACM (2016). https://doi.org/10.1145/2939672.2939785

7. Dorogush, A.V., Ershov, V., Gulin, A.: CatBoost: gradient boosting with categorical features support (2018). https://doi.org/10.48550/arXiv.1810.11363
8. Ferraiolo, D.F., Kuhn, D.R.: Role-based access controls. In: Proceedings of the 15th National Computer Security Conference. US Department of Commerce, National Institute of Standards and Technology (2009). https://doi.org/10.48550/arXiv.0903.2171
9. Ferraiolo, D.F., Sandhu, R., Gavrila, S., Kuhn, D.R., Chandramouli, R.: Proposed NIST standard for role-based access control. ACM Trans. Inf. Syst. Secur. **4**(3), 224–274 (2001). https://doi.org/10.1145/501978.501980
10. Ghadge, N.: Enhancing identity management: best practices for governance and administration (2024). https://doi.org/10.2139/ssrn.4877656
11. Hu, V.C., Ferraiolo, D.F., Kuhn, D.R.: Assessment of access control systems. US Department of Commerce, National Institute of Standards and Technology (2006). https://doi.org/10.6028/nist.ir.7316
12. Karimi, L., Abdelhakim, M., Joshi, J.: Adaptive ABAC policy learning: a reinforcement learning approach (2021). https://doi.org/10.48550/arXiv.2105.08587
13. Ke, G., et al.: LightGBM: a highly efficient gradient boosting decision tree. In: Advances in Neural Information Processing Systems, vol. 30. Curran Associates, Inc. (2017). https://doi.org/10.5555/3294996.3295074
14. Khilar, P.M., Chaudhari, V., Swain, R.R.: Trust-based access control in cloud computing using machine learning, pp. 55–79. Springer International Publishing (2019). https://doi.org/10.1007/978-3-030-03359-0_3
15. Lehnert, V., Stelzner, K., John, P., Otto, A.: SAP-Berechtigungswesen, 3rd edn. SAP PRESS, Rheinwerk (2016)
16. Liu, A., Du, X., Wang, N.: Efficient access control permission decision engine based on machine learning. Secur. Commun. Netw., 1–11 (2021). https://doi.org/10.1155/2021/3970485
17. Nobi, M.N., Gupta, M., Praharaj, L., Abdelsalam, M., Krishnan, R., Sandhu, R.: Machine learning in access control: a taxonomy and survey (2022). https://doi.org/10.48550/arXiv.2207.01739
18. Nobi, M.N., Krishnan, R., Huang, Y., Sandhu, R.: Administration of machine learning based access control. In: Computer Security – 27th European Symposium on Research in Computer Security, pp. 189–210. Springer Nature Switzerland (2022). https://doi.org/10.1007/978-3-031-17146-8_10
19. Nobi, M.N., Krishnan, R., Huang, Y., Shakarami, M., Sandhu, R.: Toward deep learning based access control. In: Proceedings of the 12th ACM Conference on Data and Application Security and Privacy, pp. 143–154. ACM (2022). https://doi.org/10.1145/3508398.3511497
20. Outchakoucht, A., Es-Samaali, H., Philippe, J.: Dynamic access control policy based on blockchain and machine learning for the internet of things. Int. J. Adv. Comput. Sci. Appl. **8**(7), 417–424 (2017). https://doi.org/10.14569/ijacsa.2017.080757
21. Sandhu, R., Ferraiolo, D., Kuhn, R.: The NIST model for role-based access control: towards a unified standard. In: Proceedings of the 5th ACM Workshop on Role-Based Access Control, pp. 47–63. ACM (2000). https://doi.org/10.1145/344287.344301
22. Sarferaz, S.: ERP-software: Funktionalität und Konzepte: Basierend auf SAP S/4HANA. Springer Fachmedien Wiesbaden (2023). https://doi.org/10.1007/978-3-658-40499-4

23. Schnepf, J., Scheuermann, B., Vetter, P.: Analyzing data sets for ML-driven fraud detection in sap systems. In: 2023 IEEE International Conference on Big Data, pp. 3314–3324. IEEE (2023). https://doi.org/10.1109/bigdata59044.2023.10386379
24. Schnepf, J., Vetter, P., Temel, T., Scheuermann, B., Schmidt-Thieme, L.: On the potential of using ERP business and system data for fraud detection. In: 2022 IEEE International Conference on Big Data, pp. 3081–3091. IEEE (2022). https://doi.org/10.1109/bigdata55660.2022.10020785
25. Srivastava, K., Shekokar, N.: Machine learning based risk-adaptive access control system to identify genuineness of the requester, pp. 129–143. Springer International Publishing (2020). https://doi.org/10.1007/978-3-030-38445-6_10

From Process Mining to Simulation: A Systematic Review of Data Quality Issues in Event Logs for Business Process Simulation

Samira Khraiwesh[1(✉)], Enkhtuya Seseer[1], Finn Klessascheck[1,2], and Luise Pufahl[1,2]

[1] School of CIT, Technical University of Munich, Bildungscampus 2, 74076 Heilbronn, Germany
{samira.khraiwesh,finn.klessascheck,luise.pufahl}@tum.de
[2] Weizenbaum Institute, Berlin, Germany

Abstract. Business Process Simulation (BPS) offers organizations a risk-free environment to evaluate process changes and support decision-making. However, the quality and reliability of simulation outcomes are highly dependent on the quality of event logs used to derive BPS models via process mining techniques. Although data quality issues in event logs, such as missing, incorrect, or inconsistent data, have been extensively discussed in the context of process mining, their specific impact on BPS remains underexplored. This study systematically investigates the intersection of event log data quality and BPS by reviewing 22 relevant papers. We systematically investigate which event log data quality issues have been addressed in existing studies and assess how these issues have been managed, particularly in the context of BPS. Specifically, we identify the types of data imperfections that have been explored in the literature, determine which quality issues relevant to BPS remain insufficiently studied, and analyze the approaches used to detect and mitigate these problems. Through this analysis, the study provides a structured foundation for understanding current research coverage and highlights opportunities for advancing data quality support tailored to BPS needs.

Keywords: Business process simulation · Business process management · Literature review

1 Introduction

Business Process Simulation (BPS) provides organizations with a powerful, risk-free environment to evaluate process changes, predict outcomes, and support operational decision-making [18]. Traditionally, BPS requires manual modeling by domain experts, which is a time-consuming and assumption-heavy approach [30]. With the advancement of *process mining* techniques [47], simulation

J. Barateiro et al. (Eds.): EDOC 2025 Workshops, LNBIP 571, pp. 333–350, 2026.
https://doi.org/10.1007/978-3-032-16234-2_27

models can now be derived automatically from event logs [6,39], reducing modeling effort and improving accuracy by using real-life process data.

However, new challenges arise due to a shift towards data-driven approaches, chief among them being the quality of the input event logs [27]. Event logs generated by information systems often contain various data imperfections [22] such as missing timestamps, incorrect activity labels, inconsistent case IDs, or imprecise durations. These data quality issues can severely affect the accuracy and realism of BPS model [23], potentially leading to misleading or invalid conclusions.

The importance of event log data quality has been widely acknowledged in the context of process mining, and it was highlighted early in the Process Mining Manifesto [48], which outlined maturity levels of event logs, ranging from poor-quality (incomplete or inaccurate) to high-quality (trustworthy and comprehensive). Still, there is limited research examining how these imperfections specifically impact simulation models.

Moreover, much of the academic work that relies on synthetic log generation assumes that event logs are initially clean and complete [44]. Tools and frameworks are frequently tested using idealized datasets with complete start and end timestamps, structured attributes, and minimal noise. In practice, however, analysts often work with raw, real-world logs that may be incomplete, inconsistent, or contain artifacts from legacy systems and manual entries. This disconnect between research assumptions and operational reality limits the practical applicability and adoption of BPS tools.

While many studies have focused on event log quality in the context of process mining, much less attention has been given to how these issues affect BPS. This is a critical oversight, as BPS requires not only the structural aspects of a process (i.e., control-flow) but also behavioral data, including activity durations, resource assignments, and probabilistic routing decisions. Even minor data issues can introduce major distortions into simulation outputs. For example, missing timestamps or incorrect durations may lead to inaccurate performance estimates, while misassigned resources can skew workload distribution analyses.

Recent works have highlighted the need to extend current research by systematically addressing data quality issues in event logs used for simulation modeling [20]. As Khraiwesh and Pufahl [20] argued, improving the input quality of event logs is a necessary step toward developing more accurate, reliable, and decision-supportive BPS models. Despite the growing recognition of the importance of data quality, the literature still lacks a comprehensive overview of event log imperfections from a simulation perspective. While Liu et al. [23] highlight the absence of a structured overview of preprocessing tasks in process mining, this gap is even more pronounced when considering event logs specifically for simulation purposes. This gap may partly explain the limited adoption of data-driven BPS in practice [38], as organizations are often reluctant to rely on simulation-based decision-making when the underlying event data are incomplete, ambiguous, or semantically inconsistent, which undermines trust in the simulation outcomes. To address this gap, this study aims to systematically investigate the intersection of event log data quality and BPS by focusing on the following research questions:

RQ1: Which event log data quality issues have been addressed in existing studies? and Which quality issues relevant to BPS remain insufficiently explored in the current literature?
RQ2: How have existing studies addressed these data quality issues?

The rest of the paper is structured as follows: Sect. 2 provides background information regarding BPS and data quality for event logs. We then present the research method of our study in Sect. 4. In Sect. 5, we present our main findings. We further discuss these in Sect. 6, where we also provide impulses for further research and conclude the article.

2 Background

2.1 Business Process Simulation

BPS is a widely adopted technique for conducting quantitative analyses of business processes [12]. BPS uses a *simulator* to generate hypothetical instances of a process [12], providing insights into the expected performance of a process design through measures such as the overall cycle time, resource utilization, or waiting time for a given activity [6]. This capability allows organizations to conduct what-if analyses, comparing alternative process designs without implementing actual changes in a real environment.

The usefulness of BPS hinges on the accuracy of the simulation model, which should faithfully represent the real-world behavior of the business process [33]. The BPS model is a process model enhanced with simulation parameters to enable the simulation of real-world process behavior [6]. Traditionally, these models are constructed manually by domain experts using qualitative methods such as interviews, observations, and contextual inquiries [31]. While effective, this manual approach is time-consuming and prone to bias or incomplete coverage.

Therefore, *process mining* techniques have emerged as a promising foundation for automated simulation model discovery [6,39]. Process mining is a data-driven discipline that enables the extraction of structured process knowledge from event logs–digital footprints recorded by information systems during process execution [17]. These logs contain sequences of events, each associated with a case ID, activity name, timestamp, and potentially additional attributes such as resource identifiers or cost. However, as any piece of data, event logs can also suffer from issues in data quality; this requires further elaboration on what data quality means specifically for event logs.

2.2 Event Log Data Quality

The concept of data quality is fundamentally linked to its "fitness for use," a definition introduced by Wang and Strong [52]. They emphasized that data quality is inherently contextual, and classified data quality into four dimensions: intrinsic (e.g., accuracy, objectivity), contextual (e.g., completeness, timeliness), representational (e.g., interpretability, consistency), and accessibility (e.g., ease of access, security). Rahm et al. [36] further elaborated on this by differentiating between single-source and multi-source quality issues. Single-source issues typically involve schema inconsistencies, duplicate entries, or erroneous data within a single system, while multi-source issues arise when integrating heterogeneous data sources, potentially causing semantic mismatches and inconsistencies.

In the context of process mining, data quality challenges manifest in event logs, that is, structured records containing event identifiers, timestamps, activities, and associated resources. While traditional data quality dimensions are applicable, event logs exhibit domain-specific issues not fully addressed by generic classifications [28]. Poor-quality event logs can lead to inaccurate simulation models, undermining decision-making and model trustworthiness.

The *IEEE Task Force on Process Mining* introduced a five-level maturity model to assess the quality of event logs [48]. At Level 1, logs are manually created, incomplete, and may not correspond to reality. Level 2 logs are generated automatically but lack standardized procedures, often resulting in missing or imprecise information. Level 3 represents a moderate level of quality with automated, more consistent logging, though occasional errors remain. Level 4 involves systematically recorded and complete event data, offering reliable input for analysis. Finally, Level 5 logs are characterized by well-structured, semantically enriched, and privacy-compliant data–ideal for process mining applications. While the classification of event logs in process mining focuses on how well and reliably events are recorded, BPS places additional demands on event logs, requiring not only correct event recording, but also a sufficient level of detail and accurate attributes (e.g., timestamps, activity names, resources) to support structurally and temporally accurate simulation.

2.3 Data Quality in BPS

BPS depends heavily on the availability of high-quality input data to ensure reliable and interpretable results. While process mining and BPS share a reliance on event logs, their data quality requirements diverge significantly. Process mining generally emphasizes structural accuracy and completeness, such as valid case IDs, consistent activity labels, and correct timestamps [48]. In contrast, BPS extends these expectations by requiring detailed and context-rich parameters, such as activity durations, routing probabilities, and resource allocations. As a result, even data considered "fit" for process mining may prove inadequate for simulation due to lack of realism or insufficient semantic granularity.

To systematically explore and compare data quality concerns in process mining and BPS literature, this study used the framework proposed by Vanbrabant et al. [49], which was specifically designed for simulation contexts. Their taxonomy identifies 14 distinct data quality issues, organized into three overarching categories: missing data, wrong data, and non-missing but not directly usable data (see Fig. 1). These include challenges such as missing attributes or cases, violated logical dependencies, inaccurate timestamps, and implicit or embedded values–all of which can severely compromise the fidelity of BPS models. It begins with the distinction between missing and non-missing data. If data is missing, issues such as missing case IDs, missing timestamps, or incomplete logs may arise, preventing the reliable reconstruction of process instances or execution times. If data are present, the framework distinguishes between wrong and not-wrong data.

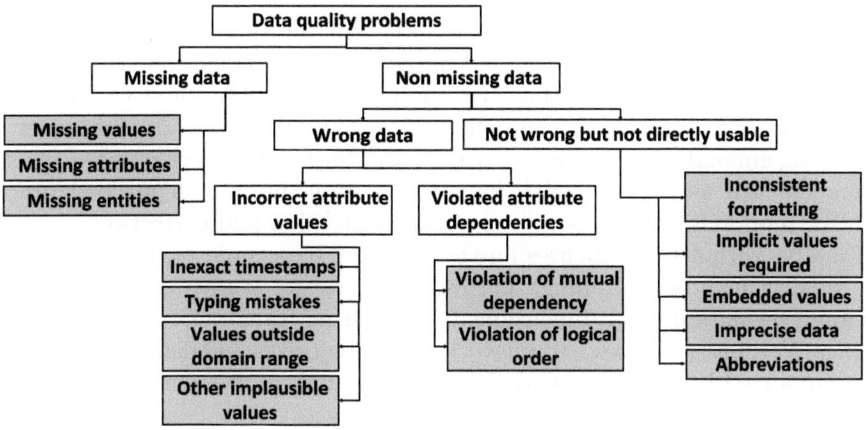

Fig. 1. Data quality framework from Vanbrabant et al. [49].

This structured taxonomy supports systematic identification and remediation of data quality problems in event logs.

3 Related Work

Data quality in event logs is a recurring concern in both process mining and BPS, and various studies related to ours have investigated data quality issues the two fields face. In the following, we provide a brief overview of the insights offered by these studies.

Dakic et al. [10] examine data quality problems in event logs and corresponding preprocessing techniques. They categorize common issues such as missing, incorrect, imprecise, or irrelevant data and link these to patterns like scattered events, elusive cases, and distorted activity labels. Their review classifies preprocessing methods into trace clustering, event filtering, log repair, AI-based methods (e.g., neural networks), alignment-based techniques, and embedded preprocessing in mining tools. The study also presents findings from expert surveys, highlighting a gap between perceived importance and actual occurrence of data issues and providing practical guidance on technique selection. Bertrand et al. [4] investigate data quality issues in process mining with IoT data. They identify six recurring sensor-level problems, such as noise and missing values, that directly affect event log quality and stress the importance of preprocessing in ensuring reliable outcomes.

Ter Hofstede et al. [46] also discuss challenges encountered when analyzing event logs in business process contexts. They highlight problems such as, e.g., distorted labels, incorrect timestamps (e.g., 'time travel' cases), and inconsistent activity naming, all of which can significantly affect the accuracy of process mining results. In the context of large-scale cyber-physical systems, Alwan et al. [1] analyze Intelligent Transportation Systems and identify 13 recurring data quality problems, including missing values and incorrect timestamps. These issues are classified by type, root cause, and impact on downstream processing.

Anomaly detection is another area closely tied to data quality in BPS. Ko and Comuzzi [21] provide a comprehensive systematic review of techniques for identifying anomalies in business process event logs. Their work emphasizes how anomalies–such as unexpected behavior or system faults–can mislead process analysis, reinforcing the importance of early detection and correction.

Finally, Verhulst [50] focuses on the need for structured evaluation of event data quality in process mining. Through a literature study, Verhulst compiles and analyzes data quality dimensions from existing frameworks. Based on these findings, Verhulst proposes a framework that categorizes and defines each dimension, supported by practical guidelines to help analysts systematically evaluate and manage event data quality.

Therefore, while related work has addressed data quality issues in event logs, the focus has largely been on process mining—data quality issues in the context of BPS remains underexplored. Many of the existing frameworks focus on general data quality dimensions or propose data cleaning methods, but they rarely highlight the issues that affect the reliability or accuracy of simulation models. Moreover, the number of literature reviews targeting BPS in general remains limited [38], and to the best of our knowledge, no prior study has systematically reviewed data quality issues specific to BPS.

To address this gap, we herein conduct a targeted literature review to (1) identify which event log data quality issues, specifically those that impact BPS, have been recognized or addressed in existing research and (2) analyze how these issues are addressed in existing research.

4 Research Method

To address the research questions outlined above, we conducted a systematic review of the literature (SLR) using the eight-step method described in Okoli's methodology [34]. In doing so, our review represents a *descriptive* literature review as defined by Paré et al. [35], aiming to systematically categorize and assess the current state of research on event log data quality issues in the context of BPS.

For the *protocol and training* steps, we defined inclusion and exclusion criteria. The search was conducted using five databases: *Scopus, ACM Digital Library, IEEE Xplore, ScienceDirect*, and *SpringerLink*.

To achieve the objective of this SLR, we conducted a search using specific keywords such as *data quality* AND *event logs* in combination with *business process simulation* OR *process mining*. This strategy was designed to identify studies that address event log data quality issues in the context of BPS, particularly those constructed using process mining techniques.

The resulting search string, "*data quality* AND *event log* AND (*Business Process simulation* OR *Process Mining*)", was applied across the five databases mentioned above to the title and abstract fields. Furthermore, we filtered the results by publication date, considering papers published starting from 2015. The reason to start the review from 2015 is based on the findings of Marin-Castro [27], who shows that data cleaning and quality management became central research topics after that year. This period also marks a surge in the volume of available event logs and the widespread adoption of process-aware information systems, which led to an increase in relevant studies. Consequently, starting from 2015 reflects both the topic's growing relevance and the feasibility of conducting an SLR, in line with the recommendation of vom Brocke et al. [5] to build on an amount of identified studies that appropriately (and not necessarily exhaustively) covers the literature.

For the *practical screening*, we defined a set of inclusion *(IN)* and exclusion *(EX)* criteria to ensure the relevance and quality of the selected studies. We included only papers that directly address data quality issues, particularly in event logs for business processes (IN1). The selected papers focus on BPS, process mining, or both (IN2). Furthermore, only peer-reviewed journal articles and conference papers (IN3) published between 2015 and 2024 (IN4) were considered. We excluded papers that do not contribute to understanding or improving data quality in event logs for BPS (EX1), papers not written in English (EX2), and publications that are review articles, case studies without methodological contributions, or general surveys (EX3). To maintain a general perspective on event log data quality, papers focusing on highly domain-specific applications (EX4) such as hospitals, electronic health records, smart home environments, or IoT devices were also excluded. The literature search was conducted in October 2024, and only papers published up to that date were considered for inclusion. Table 1 presents the number of papers retrieved in the initial search and those remaining after applying the inclusion criteria. Out of a total of 528 papers initially identified, 22 were ultimately included in the study.

Table 1. Number of papers identified, filtered, and included in this study

Source	Initial Search	Search results after applying IN3, IN4, EX2
ACM Digital Library	56	23
IEEE Xplore	19	17
ScienceDirect	123	103
SpringerLink	263	184
Scopus	67	56
Total	**528**	**383**
After deduplication		347
After title and abstract screening for all IN and EX		44
Final set *after full-text screening for all IN and EX*		**22**

For the *quality appraisal*, we conducted a title and abstract screening to exclude papers that were clearly out of scope, such as those that did not address data quality or were unrelated to process mining or BPS. Next, we carried out a full-text screening to ensure that the remaining studies provided a substantive discussion of data quality issues in event logs, specifically within the context of process mining or BPS. Only studies that explicitly addressed these aspects were retained. Finally, we conducted backward and forward snowballing on the included papers to identify any additional relevant studies. Although backward and forward snowballing did not result in the inclusion of new papers, it supported the comprehensiveness and robustness of our literature coverage.

For *data extraction*, we applied a mixed strategy combining both deductive and inductive coding. For the first research question, identifying event log data quality issues that impact BPS and have been recognized or addressed in existing research, we began with a *deductive approach* based on the data quality taxonomy proposed by Vanbrabant et al. [49]. Since BPS models are commonly derived from event logs via process mining, we extracted quality issues from the selected studies that were either (1) explicitly related to BPS, or (2) identified in the process mining literature and corresponded to one or more categories in the Vanbrabant taxonomy. In cases where quality issues described in the papers did not perfectly align with a single predefined category, we first coded them based on their descriptive characteristics (e.g., identical timestamps, missing durations, or vague labels) and then aggregated them into one or more appropriate categories of the taxonomy based on their conceptual alignment. This mapping allowed us to systematically assess which predefined quality categories have received attention in the literature.

To complement this structured view and add interpretive depth, we then conducted an *inductive coding phase*. In this phase, we developed thematic categories grounded in how the selected studies discussed, interpreted, and addressed specific quality issues. These categories–such as *activity label issues*, *timestamp issues*, and *missing values*, enabled a more nuanced exploration of how different types of data quality problems influence BPS. Papers belonging to these categories are those that focus mainly on them as their main contribution. Papers that introduce methods or tools to detect or fix quality issues in general, and do not focus primarily on one or two specific issues, are assigned to the *general* category. Together, the deductive and inductive phases provided a comprehensive understanding of both the coverage and treatment of data quality issues in the existing body of research.

To address the second research question, which explores how existing studies address data quality issues, we employed an inductive approach. We analyzed the main contributions of each paper to identify emerging patterns and strategies used to address data quality problems in event logs. Through this open coding process, we developed two categories: (1) Detection and Assessment, which includes studies that aim to detect or identify data quality problems and those that assess their impact, and (2) Mitigation-Oriented, which includes studies that propose methods to resolve or mitigate such issues. This inductive analysis enabled us to capture the diversity of research responses and to develop a grounded classification of methodological efforts in the field. The results of our analysis and coding procedure are displayed in the form of a concept matrix [53] in Table 2. Therein, we present the distribution of data quality concerns, affected BPS phases, and whether the approaches contribute to detecting or mitigating the corresponding quality issues.

Table 2. Concept matrix of selected studies on data quality in BPS.
(*) Papers address data quality issues in a general manner.

#	Author and Reference	Missing data			Wrong data						Not wrong but not directly usable					Contribution Type	
		Missing values	Missing attributes	Missing entities	Violation of logical order	Violation of mutual dep.	Inexactness of timestamps	Typing mistakes	Outside domain range	Other implausible values	Inconsistent formatting	Implicit value needed	Embedded values	Abbreviations	Imprecise data	Mitigation	Detection
P01	Sadeghianasl et al. [42]							x			x					x	
P02	Schmid et al. [43]				x		x									x	
P03	Lu et al. [26]	x														x	
P04	Chen et al. [7]							x			x						x
P05	Martin et al. [29]	x	x		x		x	x			x			x	x		x
P06	Goel et al. [16]	x					x								x		x
P07	Fischer et al. [15]				x		x										x
P08	Ramos-Gutierrez et al. [37]							x		x	x	x	x	x	x	x	x
P09	Ziolkowski et al. [54]	x	x		x		x	x			x		x	x			x
P10	Vugs et al. [51]	x	x		x		x	x					x		x		x
P11	Conforti et al. [8]				x		x									x	
P12	Sadeghianasl et al. [40]							x			x					x	x
P13	Fischer et al. [14]				x		x										x
P14	Andrews et al. [2]	x		x			x								x		x
P15	Sadeghianasl et al. [41]							x			x						x
P16	Nguyen et al. [32]	x			x		x	x							x	x	x
P17	Ekici et al. [13]	x			x		x				x					x	x
P18	van Cruchten [9]*															x	x
P19	Dixit et al. [11]				x		x				x					x	x
P20	Andrews et al. [3]						x				x				x		x
P21	Lu et al. [24]							x			x				x	x	
P22	Lu et al. [25]				x			x				x	x		x		x

Further, a more detailed version of the concept matrix, which maps the reviewed studies to the identified data quality issues as well as mitigation strategies, is provided in the supplementary material.

5 Findings

In the following, we present our findings based on the data extraction process described above.

5.1 Data Quality Issues in Event Logs Impacting BPS (RQ1)

First, we observe that all 22 papers focused exclusively on data quality issues in the context of process mining. None of the papers specifically addressed data quality from a simulation-oriented perspective.

To identify which event log quality issues, from a BPS perspective, have received greater attention in the literature and which remain underexplored or insufficiently developed, we mapped the quality issues reported in the selected papers to the data quality taxonomy defined by [49], as illustrated in Fig. 2. The figure illustrates various BPS data quality issues, with the blue numbers representing the number of studies that have addressed each issue. Among the categories, issues related to timestamps were most frequently addressed in the literature, appearing in twelve publications. In contrast, half of the quality issues (7 out of 14) were either not addressed at all or mentioned in fewer than four papers. Overall, "wrong data" emerged as the most commonly discussed type of quality problem. This suggests that the literature has largely concentrated on observable errors in recorded data, while less emphasis has been placed on more "subtle" or implicit quality challenges.

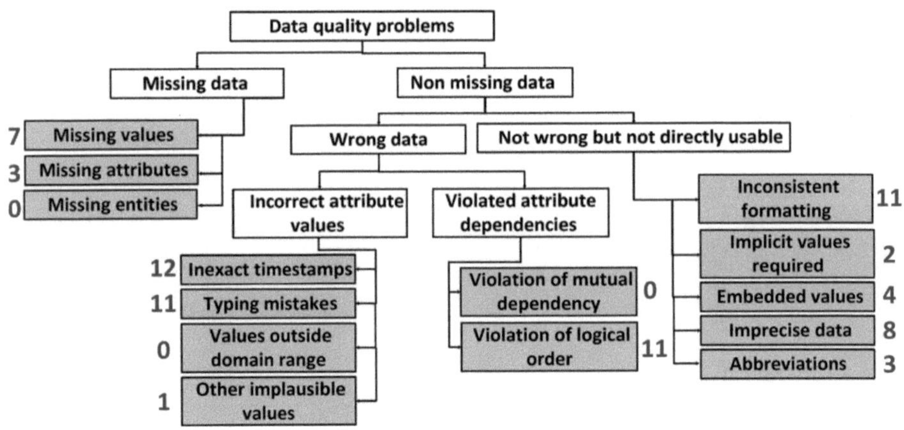

Fig. 2. Data quality framework from Vanbrabant et al. [49], with blue numbers showing how many publications address each issue.

While the mapping of studies to different types of data quality issues, presented in Fig. 2, provides a structured overview of the frequency and types of BPS data quality issues addressed in the literature, the ways in which these issues are interpreted and handled by researchers deserve further attention. To add depth to our analysis, we further categorized the selected studies according to the specific nature of the issues they addressed, i.e. whether they focused on activity label issues, timestamp issues, missing values, or general data quality problems. This classification enables a more detailed exploration of how different quality problems impact BPS. In the following, we present each category individually.

Activity Label Issues. These include imprecise, synonymous, polluted, redundant, or missing activity labels. Lu et al. [24] highlight the challenge of imprecise labels where identical activity names represent different process steps, leading to overgeneralized models. Andrews et al. [3] discuss "synonymous labels" (e.g., "Medical Assign" vs. "DrSeen") and "homonymous labels" (e.g., multiple uses of "Triage Assessment" with different meanings). Sadeghianasl et al. [40,41] examine synonymous and polluted labels and propose gamified crowdsourcing to support label correction. Chen et al. [7] introduce a multi-view framework to detect redundant labels caused by inconsistencies from various data sources. Lu et al. [26] address missing labels using an LSTM-based deep learning approach to repair gaps based on control-flow and attribute data.

Timestamp Issues. Timestamp inaccuracies included incorrect ordering, identical timestamps, imprecise granularity, and "inadvertent time travel". Andrews et al. [3] describe patterns such as form-based event capture and the Query Language for Event Identification (QUELI) for detecting timestamp imperfections. Dixit et al. [11] introduce indicators for detecting ordering violations and propose domain knowledge-based repair strategies. Conforti et al. [8] address "same-timestamp" where multiple events within the same process instance have the same timestamp issues affecting ordering and performance analysis. Fischer et al. [14,15] propose metrics and imperfection detection patterns, including inconsistent formats, overlapping events, and mixed granularity. Schmid et al. [43] explain how identical timestamps distort event order and model interpretation.

Missing Values. Nguyen et al. [32] propose using autoencoders to reconstruct missing or anomalous attribute values. Their method avoids process model dependency by learning from inter-attribute relationships, enhancing robustness in incomplete logs.

General Issues. Some studies aim to identify and address a wide range of imperfections rather than focusing on specific types of issues. The work by Martin et al. [29] introduces DaQAPO, an open-source R package that enables flexible, fine-grained analysis of event log quality. DaQAPO supports the detection of various quality problems. Its customizable testing framework allows context-specific evaluations, making it a robust tool for supporting reliable process mining outcomes. One study adopts a general perspective on event log data quality. Concretely, van Cruchten [9] proposes a rule-based framework for systematically identifying and repairing event data imperfections. Building on broad classifications of event data quality issues, the framework is designed to be systematic, automated, domain-agnostic, and transparent. Because these categories are too coarse-grained compared to Vanbrabant's detailed taxonomy of simulation-specific issues, we did not perform a direct mapping of the study to it, but still keep the study in our set of papers for completeness.

5.2 Research Contributions Addressing Data Quality Issues (RQ2)

To explore how data quality issues are addressed, we categorized the papers based on their contributions into two main types, as shown in Fig. 3.

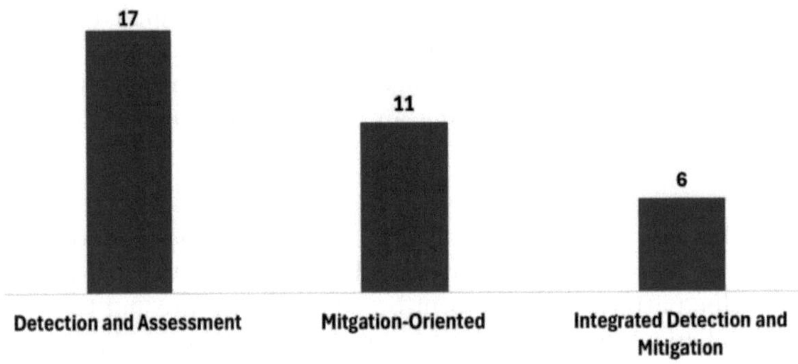

Fig. 3. Distribution of papers by focus: detection vs. mitigation. Counts are non-exclusive, with papers contributing to both included in each category.

Detection and Assessment. These studies focus on identifying, quantifying, and evaluating data quality problems. Andrews et al. [3] propose query languages (QUELI) and frameworks to detect known imperfection patterns such as inadvertent time travel, synonymous labels, and form-based event capture. Other papers [14,15] develop quality metrics that are aligned with multi-dimensional data quality frameworks, offering structured assessments along accuracy, precision, and consistency. Fischer et al. [14] developed a tool-supported approach for fine-grained assessment of event logs across event, activity, trace, and log levels. Their work is particularly notable for addressing timestamp validity through 15 specific metrics, which are systematically mapped to known imperfection patterns, enabling structured evaluation of temporal data quality. Goel et al. [16] introduce a quality annotation scheme for event logs, allowing analysts to score events based on time accuracy and label reliability.

Mitigation-Oriented. These papers propose methods or tools for correcting identified data quality issues. A number of studies adopt *human involvement* as a core strategy. For instance, Dixit et al. [11] present an interactive repair method where users apply their domain knowledge to model process fragments and guide corrections of event ordering imperfections. Other papers turn to *neural networks* for automated correction. Nguyen et al. [32] use autoencoders to reconstruct missing or anomalous values in activity labels and timestamps, training the model to recognize and repair abnormal patterns. Lu et al. [26] work on refining imprecise labels using LSTM models. Their approach leverages deep learning to restore missing activity labels based on context within a trace, improving the precision of process models. Similarly, Schmid et al. [43] employ *Generative Adversarial Networks* (GANs) to repair identical timestamp errors by learning from correct temporal patterns and generating plausible replacements. Another group of works applies *algorithmic* methods. Conforti et al. [8] address the same-timestamp issues using *Integer Linear Programming* (ILP) to reorder events and estimate new timestamps based on activity durations and control-flow confidence. Additionally, less traditional approaches include gamification and crowdsourcing, as seen in Sadeghianasl et al. [40], where domain experts are engaged in repairing semantically identical labels using a gamified interface to enhance participation and accuracy. Figure 4 illustrates the number of papers corresponding to each solution category.

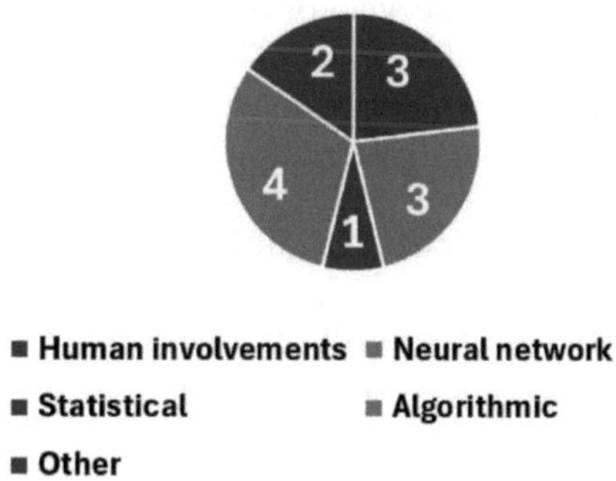

Fig. 4. Types of solutions proposed for mitigation of data quality issues

A small portion of papers make contributions in **both** detecting and mitigating data quality problems. For example, Dixit et al. [11] introduce concrete indicators such as timestamp granularity mismatches and ordering anomalies to detect event ordering issues, and provide an interactive repair approach using Petri net fragments and alignment techniques. Similarly, van Cruchten [9] presents a rule-based framework that detects inconsistencies using conditional functional dependencies and supports mitigation through rule-guided data transformation and abstraction. These studies offer integrated solutions that address the full lifecycle of data quality management in process mining.

6 Discussion and Conclusion

In this study, we have identified a significant and underexplored challenge in the field of BPS: the quality of event logs as a foundation for building accurate and reliable simulation models. Through an SLR of 22 papers, we have presented key insights relevant to researchers in the field of BPS and process mining.

First, our review has revealed an important gap in the literature, as none of the selected papers address data quality from a *simulation-specific* perspective. This indicates a need for data quality metrics and methods tailored specifically to BPS contexts. Additionally, mapping the literature to Vanbrabant's taxonomy has shown that only a subset of the 14 data quality issues known in the literature are actively being addressed in the context of BPS. Among these, timestamp-related issues dominate, reflecting their central role in both process mining and simulation.

Second, we have observed that human involvement plays an important role for addressing complex data quality issues, especially those involving semantic ambiguity or domain-specific logic. While fully automated approaches are ideal, they often fail to account for nuanced interpretations of process behavior. Hybrid methods, where automated techniques are combined with expert validation, offer a practical and effective solution [20].

Third, our review has shown that the number of papers offering integrated solutions that address the full lifecycle of data quality management in process mining is limited. Most works focus on either detecting or mitigating quality issues. This lack of integration poses challenges, as undetected issues can propagate and negatively affect downstream analysis. The importance of such end-to-end approaches is emphasized by Suriadi et al. [45], who argue for a systematic method that not only identifies but also guides the repair of event log imperfections.

Fourth, we have assessed the usability of tools for detecting data quality issues of event logs by selecting a subset of papers that addressed timestamp-related issues and provided publicly accessible implementations. Although eight papers met these criteria, we observed that only two tools could be practically used and replicated with real-life event logs. The rest were limited by technical complexity, missing components, or reliance on unavailable ground-truth data. This highlights a disconnect between research outputs and practical application—while the number of expert users is limited [19], many tools are still designed for technically advanced users. Their steep learning curves, rigid configurations, and non-standard input formats make them inaccessible to non-technical stakeholders who most frequently rely on BPS insights. This reinforces earlier findings [19,38] that one of the core barriers to broader BPS adoption is the lack of usable tools for non-expert users. While this evaluation is not a central focus of the paper, and it was conducted with only a subset of the available tools, we still believe that our observations provide fruitful impulses for research and practice. Additional details regarding the evaluation we sketched above are available in the supplementary material.

Threats to Validity. There are several limitations that threaten the validity of our findings, which we need to acknowledge. First, in terms of search and selection bias, our systematic review relied on specific keywords and databases, which may have excluded relevant studies that used different terminology or were published in other venues. To mitigate this, we refined our search strings iteratively before the search reported herein, and used backward and forward snowballing to identify additional papers. Second, the time span of our review, covering the literature up to October 2024, may limit the inclusion of more recent contributions. Third, classifying and coding the studies involved interpretive decisions, particularly in distinguishing between types of data quality issues and solution approaches. Although a structured coding process was used and disagreements were resolved through discussion, some degree of subjectivity remains.

Future Work. Our findings point to several promising directions for future research: First, there is a need to develop BPS-specific data quality metrics that extend beyond process mining concerns to address how issues such as imprecise durations, missing timestamps, or inconsistent event sequences affect simulation accuracy. Second, researchers should focus on designing semi-automated, explainable repair methods that incorporate human feedback, enabling guided corrections with transparency and interpretability. Third, benchmark datasets containing known imperfections and validated simulation outputs are essential for comparative evaluation of cleaning techniques. Fourth, the development of user-friendly, guided tools is crucial–particularly those that empower non-experts, such as business analysts, to assess and repair data quality issues without requiring technical expertise. Fifth, assessing the usability of existing tooling for detecting data quality issues of event logs in a more structured and comprehensive manner could uncover further avenues for additional research. Finally, empirical studies that quantify how different types of imperfections influence simulation outcomes would help build an evidence-based foundation for preparing event logs in BPS settings.

Data Availability Statement. Supplementary data are available in a FigShare repository at https://doi.org/10.6084/m9.figshare.29328731.

Disclosure of Interests. The authors have no competing interests to declare that are relevant to the content of this article.

References

1. Alwan, A.A., Ciupala, M.A., Brimicombe, A.J., Ghorashi, S.A., Baravalle, A., Falcarin, P.: Data quality challenges in large-scale cyber-physical systems: a systematic review. Inf. Syst. **105**, 101951 (2022)
2. Andrews, R., van Dun, C.G., Wynn, M.T., Kratsch, W., Röglinger, M., ter Hofstede, A.H.: Quality-informed semi-automated event log generation for process mining. Decis. Support Syst. **132**, 113265 (2020)
3. Andrews, R., Suriadi, S., Ouyang, C., Poppe, E.: Towards event log querying for data quality. In: Panetto, H., Debruyne, C., Proper, H.A., Ardagna, C.A., Roman, D., Meersman, R. (eds.) OTM 2018. LNCS, vol. 11229, pp. 116–134. Springer, Cham (2018). https://doi.org/10.1007/978-3-030-02610-3_7
4. Bertrand, Y., Van Belle, R., De Weerdt, J., Serral, E.: Defining data quality issues in process mining with iot data. In: International Conference on Process Mining, pp. 422–434. Springer (2022). https://doi.org/10.1007/978-3-031-27815-0_31

5. vom Brocke, J., Simons, A., Niehaves, B., Riemer, K., Plattfaut, R., Cleven, A.: Standing on the shoulders of giants: challenges and recommendations of literature search in information systems research. Commun. Assoc. Inf. Syst. **37**(1), 9 (2015)
6. Camargo, M., Dumas, M., González-Rojas, O.: Automated discovery of business process simulation models from event logs. Dec. Support Syst. (2020)
7. Chen, Q., Lu, Y., Tam, C.S., Poon, S.K.: A multi-view framework to detect redundant activity labels for more representative event logs in process mining. Future Internet **14**(6), 181 (2022)
8. Conforti, R., La Rosa, M., ter Hofstede, A.H.M., Augusto, A.: Automatic repair of same-timestamp errors in business process event logs. In: Fahland, D., Ghidini, C., Becker, J., Dumas, M. (eds.) BPM 2020. LNCS, vol. 12168, pp. 327–345. Springer, Cham (2020). https://doi.org/10.1007/978-3-030-58666-9_19
9. Cruchten, R.: Data quality in process mining: A rule-based approach (2019)
10. Dakic, D., Stefanovic, D., Vuckovic, T., Zizakov, M., Stevanov, B.: Event log data quality issues and solutions. Mathematics **11**(13), 2858 (2023)
11. Dixit, P.M., et al.: Detection and interactive repair of event ordering imperfection in process logs. In: Krogstie, J., Reijers, H.A. (eds.) CAiSE 2018. LNCS, vol. 10816, pp. 274–290. Springer, Cham (2018). https://doi.org/10.1007/978-3-319-91563-0_17
12. Dumas, M., Rosa, L.M., Mendling, J., Reijers, A.H.: Fundamentals of business process management. Springer (2018)
13. Ekici, B., Tarhan, A., Ozsoy, A.: Data cleaning for process mining with smart contract. In: 2019 4th International Conference on Computer Science and Engineering (UBMK), pp. 1–6. IEEE (2019)
14. Fischer, D.A., Goel, K., Andrews, R., van Dun, C.G.J., Wynn, M.T., Röglinger, M.: Enhancing event log quality: detecting and quantifying timestamp imperfections. In: Fahland, D., Ghidini, C., Becker, J., Dumas, M. (eds.) BPM 2020. LNCS, vol. 12168, pp. 309–326. Springer, Cham (2020). https://doi.org/10.1007/978-3-030-58666-9_18
15. Fischer, D.A., Goel, K., Andrews, R., van Dun, C.G., Wynn, M.T., Röglinger, M.: Towards interactive event log forensics: detecting and quantifying timestamp imperfections. Inf. Syst. **109**, 102039 (2022)
16. Goel, K., Leemans, S.J., Martin, N., Wynn, M.T.: Quality-informed process mining: a case for standardised data quality annotations. ACM Trans. Knowl. Dis. Data (TKDD) **16**(5), 1–47 (2022)
17. van Hulzen, G., Martin, N., Depaire, B.: The need for interactive data-driven process simulation in healthcare: a case study. In: Leemans, S., Leopold, H. (eds.) ICPM 2020. LNBIP, vol. 406, pp. 317–329. Springer, Cham (2021). https://doi.org/10.1007/978-3-030-72693-5_24
18. Jansen-Vullers, M., Netjes, M.: Business process simulation–a tool survey. In: Workshop and Tutorial on Practical Use of Coloured Petri Nets and the CPN Tools, Aarhus, Denmark, vol. 38 (2006)
19. Khraiwesh, S., Pufahl, L.: Automated business process simulation studies: Where do humans fit in? In: WSC. Accepted, in Press (2025)
20. Khraiwesh, S., Pufahl, L.: Review of design of business process simulation models. In: International Conference on Research Challenges in Information Science, pp. 452–469. Springer (2025). https://doi.org/10.1007/978-3-031-92474-3_27
21. Ko, J., Comuzzi, M.: A systematic review of anomaly detection for business process event logs. Bus. Inform. Syst. Eng. **65**(4), 441–462 (2023)
22. Landauer, M., Onder, S., Skopik, F., Wurzenberger, M.: Deep learning for anomaly detection in log data: a survey. Mach. Learn. Appli. (2023)

23. Liu, Y., Stein Dani, V., Beerepoot, I., Lu, X.: Turning logs into lumber: preprocessing tasks in process mining. In: International Conference on Process Mining, pp. 98–109. Springer (2023). https://doi.org/10.1007/978-3-031-56107-8_8
24. Lu, X., Fahland, D., van den Biggelaar, F.J.H.M., van der Aalst, W.M.P.: Handling duplicated tasks in process discovery by refining event labels. In: La Rosa, M., Loos, P., Pastor, O. (eds.) BPM 2016. LNCS, vol. 9850, pp. 90–107. Springer, Cham (2016). https://doi.org/10.1007/978-3-319-45348-4_6
25. Lu, X., Fahland, D., Van Der Aalst, W.M.: Interactively exploring logs and mining models with clustering, filtering, and relabeling (2016)
26. Lu, Y., Chen, Q., Poon, S.K.: A deep learning approach for repairing missing activity labels in event logs for process mining. Information **13**(5), 234 (2022)
27. Marin-Castro, H.M., Tello-Leal, E.: Event log preprocessing for process mining: a review. Appl. Sci. **11**(22), 10556 (2021)
28. Martin, N.: Data quality in process mining. In: Fernandez-Llatas, C. (ed.) Interactive Process Mining in Healthcare. HI, pp. 53–79. Springer, Cham (2021). https://doi.org/10.1007/978-3-030-53993-1_5
29. Martin, N., Van Houdt, G., Janssenswillen, G.: Daqapo: supporting flexible and fine-grained event log quality assessment. Expert Syst. Appl. **191**, 116274 (2022)
30. Măruşter, L., Van Beest, N.R.: Redesigning business processes: a methodology based on simulation and process mining techniques. Knowl. Inform. Syst. **21** (2009)
31. Măruşter, L., Van Beest, N.R.: Redesigning business processes: a methodology based on simulation and process mining techniques. Knowl. Inf. Syst. **21**, 267–297 (2009)
32. Nguyen, H.T.C., Lee, S., Kim, J., Ko, J., Comuzzi, M.: Autoencoders for improving quality of process event logs. Expert Syst. Appl. **131**, 132–147 (2019)
33. Oberle, L.J., van der Aa, H.: Ddps: a project methodology for data-driven process simulation. In: AMCIS (2023)
34. Okoli, C., Schabram, K.: A guide to conducting a systematic literature review of information systems research (2015)
35. Paré, G., Trudel, M.C., Jaana, M., Kitsiou, S.: Synthesizing information systems knowledge: a typology of literature reviews. Inform. Manag. **52**(2), 183–199 (2015)
36. Rahm, E., Do, H.H., et al.: Data cleaning: problems and current approaches. IEEE Data Eng. Bull. **23**(4), 3–13 (2000)
37. Ramos-Gutiérrez, B., Varela-Vaca, Á.J., Ortega, F.J., Gómez-López, M.T., Wynn, M.T.: A NLP-oriented methodology to enhance event log quality. In: Augusto, A., Gill, A., Nurcan, S., Reinhartz-Berger, I., Schmidt, R., Zdravkovic, J. (eds.) BPMDS/EMMSAD -2021. LNBIP, vol. 421, pp. 19–35. Springer, Cham (2021). https://doi.org/10.1007/978-3-030-79186-5_2
38. Rosenthal, K., Ternes, B., Strecker, S.: Business process simulation: a systematic literature review. In: ECIS, p. 199 (2018)
39. Rozinat, A., Mans, R.S., Song, M., van der Aalst, W.M.: Discovering simulation models. Inform. Syst. (2009)
40. Sadeghianasl, S., ter Hofstede, A.H., Suriadi, S., Turkay, S.: Collaborative and interactive detection and repair of activity labels in process event logs. In: 2020 2nd International Conference on Process Mining (ICPM), pp. 41–48. IEEE (2020)
41. Sadeghianasl, S., ter Hofstede, A.H.M., Wynn, M.T., Suriadi, S.: A contextual approach to detecting synonymous and polluted activity labels in process event logs. In: Panetto, H., Debruyne, C., Hepp, M., Lewis, D., Ardagna, C.A., Meersman, R. (eds.) OTM 2019. LNCS, vol. 11877, pp. 76–94. Springer, Cham (2019). https://doi.org/10.1007/978-3-030-33246-4_5

42. Sadeghianasl, S., Ter Hofstede, A.H., Wynn, M.T., Türkay, S.: Humans-in-the-loop: gamifying activity label repair in process event logs. Eng. Appl. Artif. Intell. **132**, 107875 (2024)
43. Schmid, S.J., Moder, L., Hofmann, P., Röglinger, M.: Everything at the proper time: repairing identical timestamp errors in event logs with generative adversarial networks. Inf. Syst. **118**, 102246 (2023)
44. Sommers, D., Sidorova, N., van Dongen, B.: A ground truth approach for assessing process mining techniques. arXiv preprint arXiv:2501.14345 (2025)
45. Suriadi, S., Andrews, R., ter Hofstede, A.H., Wynn, M.T.: Event log imperfection patterns for process mining: towards a systematic approach to cleaning event logs. Inf. Syst. **64**, 132–150 (2017)
46. Ter Hofstede, A.H.: Process-data quality: the true frontier of process mining. ACM J. Data Inform. Q. **15**(3), 1–21 (2023)
47. Van Der Aalst, W.: Process mining: overview and opportunities. ACM Trans. Manag. Inform. Syst. (TMIS) **3**(2), 1–17 (2012)
48. van der Aalst, W., et al.: Process mining manifesto. In: Daniel, F., Barkaoui, K., Dustdar, S. (eds.) BPM 2011. LNBIP, vol. 99, pp. 169–194. Springer, Heidelberg (2012). https://doi.org/10.1007/978-3-642-28108-2_19
49. Vanbrabant, L., Martin, N., Ramaekers, K., Braekers, K.: Quality of input data in emergency department simulations: framework and assessment techniques. Simul. Model. Pract. Theory **91**, 83–101 (2019)
50. Verhulst, R.: Evaluating quality of event data within event logs: an extensible framework. Eindhoven University of Technology, Eindhoven, The Netherlands (2016)
51. Vugs, L., van Asseldonk, M., van Son, N.: Lumigi: Shining light on your process data (2021)
52. Wang, R.Y., Strong, D.M.: Beyond accuracy: what data quality means to data consumers. J. Manag. Inf. Syst. **12**(4), 5–33 (1996)
53. Webster, J., Watson, R.T.: Analyzing the past to prepare for the future: writing a literature review. MIS Q., xiii–xxiii (2002)
54. Ziolkowski, T., Brandt, L., Koschmider, A.: Elogqp: an event log quality pointer. In: ZEUS, pp. 42–45 (2021)

A Design Method for Intelligence Amplification

Jean Paul Sebastian Piest(✉)

University of Twente, Drienerlolaan 5, 7522 Enschede, NB, The Netherlands
j.p.s.piest@utwente.nl

Abstract. Designing applications to amplify human intelligence is non-trivial. Although relevant design knowledge exists, a comprehensive design approach for practitioners is lacking. This short paper presents a novel design method for intelligence amplification for practitioners. Action design research has been utilized to iteratively design, implement, and evaluate its use within 27 organizations. The design method effectively supports the design and development of intelligence amplification prototypes and provides guidance for implementation.

Keywords: Design Method · Intelligence Amplification · Action Design Research

1 Introduction

Industry 5.0 and Society 5.0 emphasize the human centered use of Artificial Intelligence (AI) [1], often referred to as Intelligence Amplification (IA). IA originates from the 1950s and can be traced back to the seminal works of Asby [2, 3]. Over time, various definitions of IA emerged, including synonyms such as augmented intelligence, hybrid intelligence, and cognitive extension. In this paper, IA is defined as *"the effective use of information technology in augmenting human intelligence in a given context"* [4].

Designing applications that amplify human intelligence is non-trivial. Earlier work systematically mapped existing design knowledge related to IA and identified 4 constructs, 23 methods, 29 models, and 4 design theories [5]. However, this Systematic Literature Study (SLR) concluded that existing design theories are either outdated or lack detailed guidance for application by practitioners. Similarly, existing methods provide either high-level guidance or focus on specific tasks or domains.

The aim of this short paper is to present a new design method for IA (hereafter IADM) and the results and findings of its evaluation in different empirical settings. The IADM is iterative designed, implemented, and evaluated using the Action Design Research (ADR) method of Sein et al. [6]. The application of ADR and its guiding principles is described in [5]. Supplementary materials are made available at [7].

The remainder of this paper is structured as follows. Section 2 presents the IADM. Section 3 presents the evaluation results of the IADM. Section 4 concludes the paper and outlines directions for future research.

J. Barateiro et al. (Eds.): EDOC 2025 Workshops, LNBIP 571, pp. 351–356, 2026.
https://doi.org/10.1007/978-3-032-16234-2_28

2 Intelligence Amplification Design Method

2.1 Overview

The IADM consists of four phases, as shown in Fig. 1.

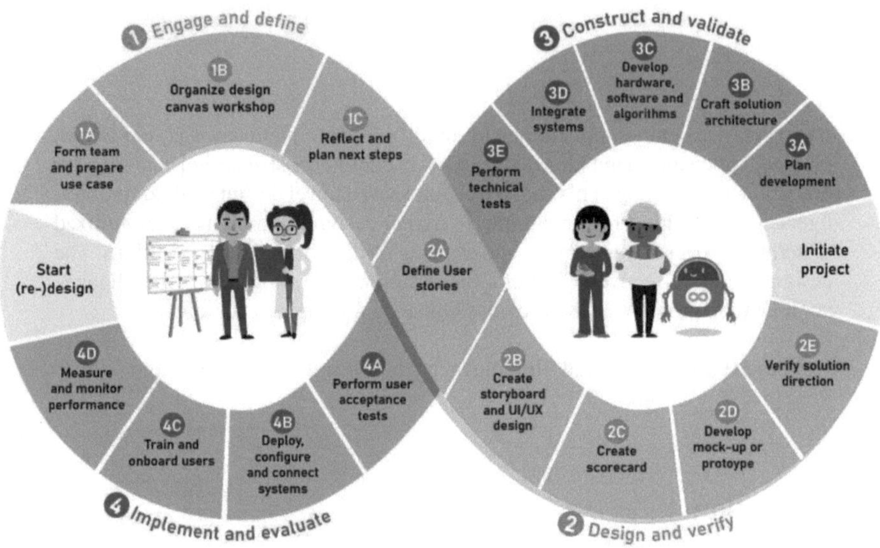

Fig. 1. Overview of the IADM and its four phases.

The IADM utilizes the IA design canvas [4] to define the core concepts of IA [1, 5] and prescribes design activities based on the principles of design thinking [8], addressing the needs of practitioners, and design science evaluation (e.g., ex-ante verification, ex-post validation and evaluation) for rigor [9]. A lemniscate representation is selected to emphasize an iterative design process and position the central role of user stories for human-centered design [8]. The main activities, required input, and output of the four phases are described in Table 1. Detailed descriptions of each phase, including supporting materials and (suggestions for) software support, are made available at [7].

Table 1. Main activities, required input, and output of the four phases.

ID	Phase	Description	Input	Output
1	Engage and define	Start an initiative to explore use cases for IA and plan a design canvas workshop.	Ideas. For re-designs: user reports and system performance.	Initiation document(s), workshop planning, software support, budget.

(*continued*)

Table 1. (*continued*)

ID	Phase	Description	Input	Output
2	Design and verify	Plan a design sprint to define user stories and develop a mock-up / prototype IA application.	Results phase 1.	Design brief, sprint planning, solution concept and UI/UX design, prototype.
3	Construct and validate	Initiate a project to realize the IA application.	Results phase 2.	Business case, project plan(ning), contracts, repository, instantiation.
4	Implement and evaluate	Implement the IA application for operational use.	Results phase 3.	Test–/acceptance plan(ning), roll-out plan(ning), end-user training, situated instantiation.

2.2 Phase 1: Engage and Define

Phase 1 consists of three activities to start a (re-)design trajectory and organize a design canvas workshop. Activity 1.A starts by forming a team and preparing use cases for IA. This activity can best be done in pairs or groups (led by a facilitator) and requires at least one use case. It is important to involve design thinkers from the beginning and try to extend the team with external experts and stakeholders [8]. Activity 1.B concerns the organization and execution of a design canvas workshop. Use cases are defined using the IA design canvas in four iterations using the guiding principles, as described in [4], and presented for ex-ante verification [8]. Activity 1.C concludes phase 1 with reflection and determining next steps. The results of phase 1 serve as input for phase 2.

2.3 Phase 2: Design and Verify

Phase 2 covers five activities and aims to start a small design sprint to experiment early and often [8]. Activity 2.A starts by defining user stories, emphasizing human-centricity [8]. Based on the completed IA design canvas, the main user stories are derived and described. Activity 2.B builds upon the user stories by creating a storyboard and user interface and -experience design using guidelines for human-AI interaction [10] and the related toolkit [11]. The envisioned future use is visualized in a storyboard and sketches are made of the IA application its form and function(s). Activity 2.C then creates a scorecard for ex-ante verification of the solution direction [9]. The main metrics are determined and a user survey is prepared. Activity 2.D focuses on developing a mock-up or clickable prototype. Here, various tools are available (e.g., Figma, Lovable). Activity 2.E concludes phase 2 by verifying the solution direction. This involves presenting the solution design and IA prototype to stakeholders to obtain feedback from intended users and refine the design. More specifically, the feasibility, desirability, and viability are assessed as part of the design thinking approach [8] and an initial risk assessment can be conducted. Based on phase 2, a decision is made to initiate a project.

2.4 Phase 3: Develop and Validate

Phase 3 encompasses five activities to blend the short design sprint within a larger project with a clear innovation budget and multidisciplinary team [8]. Activity 3.A starts with planning the development of the IA application. Assuming an agile development approach, the user stories are planned a in product backlog, sprints, and complemented with a definition of done. Activity 3.B focuses on crafting a solution architecture. Here, a detailed solution design is produced, including architecture representations as well as ex-post validation and evaluation criteria [9]. In activity 3.C, the hardware, software, and algorithms are developed/acquired. A repository and a (local) development environment are created to instantiate the IA application and run (local) technical tests. Activity 3.D realizes systems integrations. Source and target systems are configured for data exchange and connectors are deployed to integrate the IA application. Activity 3.E concludes phase 3 with technical tests for ex-post validation [9]. Here, units, assemblies, and integrations are merged and technical tests are conducted using the ex-post validation criteria.

2.5 Phase 4: Implement and Evaluate

Phase 4 covers four activities to implement and evaluate the IA application. Activity 4.A extends the technical tests with user acceptance tests for further ex-post validation [9]. The IA application, developed in phase 3, is staged to an acceptance environment for user testing following the user stories and definition of done. After user acceptance, activity 4.B deploys, connects, and configures the IA application for operational use. Activity 4.C provides training to onboard users. This includes organizing training sessions, updating work instructions, and providing users access to the IA application. Activity 4.D contains the continuous performance measurement and monitoring of the IA application for ex-post evaluation [9]. This also includes periodical user surveys to gather user experience feedback and input for improvement. Based on this activity, a re-design trajectory can be initiated following the lemniscate of the IADM.

3 Evaluation

Based on the ADR method, the IADM and supporting tools have been evaluated in a Community of Practice (CoP) in three cycles involving 27 organizations active in transportation, logistics, manufacturing, and IT. The aim of the CoP was to guide practitioners to design, develop, and implement IA applications in a series of monthly workshops (one for each of the four phases and an evaluation session) and collaboratively develop the IADM and supporting tools (14 tools were developed and evaluated).

Overall, practitioners were positive about the CoP (average score of 8/10). The use of the IADM was evaluated per phase. Phase 1, including the use of the IA design canvas and four guiding principles, was evaluated by practitioners with an average score of 4.52

out of 5. Phase 2, including the use of the human-AI guidelines and the related toolkit, was positively evaluated with an average score of 4.16 out of 5. Phase 3, including tools for project management and the development of IA applications, was evaluated with an average score of 3.78 out of 5. Phase 4, providing tools for implementation and evaluation, was evaluated with an average score of 4.12 out of 5. The use of the 14 developed tools was individually evaluated. Evaluation data are described in more detail in [5].

Based on reflection, learning, and abstraction, three design principles were derived, namely: joint inquiry, collaborative design inquiry, and IA measurement. These three design principles are described in more detail in [5]. Joint inquiry is essential for phase 1 and the effective use of the IA design canvas whereas practitioners lack technical expertise and IT professionals lack domain knowledge [4, 5]. Based on reflection and learning between the ADR cycles, the efforts to organize and conduct a design workshop were reduced from a workshop of a full day to a workshop of three hours (depending on the facilitator) [5]. Collaborative design inquiry during phase 2 effectively supports the initiation of a design sprint to produce and verify a solution direction and prototype IA application in 3–5 days. Exemplar prototype IA applications include solutions to support commercial planners with empty mileage reduction in transportation, provide dynamic refueling decision support for drivers, and support warehouse managers to forecast demand spikes and required resources. The SLR provided two approaches for the measurement of IA: comparing the current performance without IA to the performance with the IA application and/or use information representation theory to measure cognitive work of humans and measure cognitive gains realized by AI agents to determine the IA effects [1, 5]. These measurement approaches were used to estimate IA effects during phase 1 and refine the estimates during phase 2–4 based on verification, validation, and evaluation. An important finding is that the CoP mainly supported the practitioners during phase 1 and 2 to produce prototypes of IA applications based on the four monthly workshops. The actual implementation and empirical evaluation was not feasible for most practitioners within the timeframe of four months. However, practitioners emphasized that the IADM provides guidance for implementation.

4 Conclusion

This short paper presented a new design method for IA applications, the IADM, addressing the lack of a comprehensive design approach for practitioners. The IADM provides practical guidance to define, design, develop, and implement IA applications. Based on the evaluation by practitioners from 27 organizations in the CoP, the IADM has proven to be effective to develop prototypical IA applications and provide guidance for implementation. Evaluation is limited to IA applications in transportation, logistics, manufacturing, and IT. Future research will evaluate the IADM in other domains (e.g., healthcare, education) and explore how the IADM can be augmented using AI agents.

Acknowledgments. The author thanks Bas Groot, Marcel Wouterse, and participants of the community of practice for AI for their support and participation in this research. Additionally, the author thanks dr.ir. M.J. van Sinderen, prof.dr. M.E. Iacob, dr. K. Karaca, and prof.dr. Y. Masuda for their supervision during the PhD trajectory and fruitful discussions about the IADM.

Disclosure of Interests. The author has no competing interests to declare.

References

1. Huang, S., Wang, B., Li, X., Zheng, P., Mourtzis, D., Wang, L.: Industry 5.0 and society 5.0—comparison, complementation and co-evolution. J. Manuf. Syst. **64**, 424–428 (2022). https://doi.org/10.1016/j.jmsy.2022.07.010
2. Ashby, W.R.: An Introduction to Cybernetics (1956)
3. Ashby, W.R.: Design for an intelligence-amplifier. In: Automata studies, vol. 34, pp. 215–234. Princeton University Press (1956b)
4. Piest, J.P.S., Iacob, M.E., Wouterse, M.J.T.: Designing intelligence amplification: a design canvas for practitioners. In: Ahram, T., Taiar, R. (eds.) Human Interaction & Emerging Technologies (IHIET 2022): Artificial Intelligence & Future Applications. AHFE, vol. 68. International Conference. AHFE Open Access (2022).: https://doi.org/10.54941/ahfe1002714
5. Piest, J.P.S.: A design science research knowledge base for intelligence amplification. University of Twente doctoral thesis. pp. 18–83, pp. 204–275 (2024). https://doi.org/10.3990/1.9789036557542
6. Sein, M.K., Henfridsson, O., Purao, S., Rossi, M., Lindgren, R.: Action design research. MIS Q., 37–56 (2011). https://doi.org/10.2307/23043488
7. Piest, J.P.S.: Review of design theories, methods, frameworks and case studies for intelligence amplification (2023). https://doi.org/10.17605/OSF.IO/BVKXZ.
8. Brown, T.: Design thinking. Harv. Bus. Rev. **86**(6), 84 (2008)
9. Vom Brocke, J., Hevner, A., Maedche, A.: Introduction to design science research. In: Vom Brocke, J., Hevner, A., Maedche, A. eds. Design Science Research. Cases. Progress in IS. Springer, Cham (2020) https://doi.org/10.1007/978-3-030-46781-4_1
10. Amershi, S., et al.: Guidelines for human-AI interaction. In: Proceedings of the 2019 CHI Conference on Human Factors in Computing Systems (CHI '19). Association for Computing Machinery, vol. 3, pp. 1–13, New York, NY, USA (2019). https://doi.org/10.1145/3290605.3300233
11. Microsoft HAX: Toolkit. Available online: https://www.microsoft.com/en-us/haxtoolkit/.

Optimization of Care Pathways with the Use of Process Mining and Text Mining Techniques: Combining PM2 and CRISP-ML Methodologies

Cheng Qi Wang[1], Vera Bulsink[2], Reini Bretveld[2], Rogier Krom[2], Shiva Faeghi[3], and Faiza Bukhsh[1](✉)

[1] Department of Computer Science, University of Twente, Enschede, The Netherlands
f.a.bukhsh@utwente.nl

[2] Medisch Spectrum Twente, Enschede, The Netherlands

[3] Health Technology and Services Research, TechMed Center, University of Twente, Enschede, The Netherlands

Abstract. Healthcare systems under increasing pressure require innovative strategies to optimize care delivery and reduce waiting times. This study presents a dual-method approach combining process mining and text mining to enhance insight into clinical workflows and support value-based healthcare. Process mining techniques are used to map diagnostic and treatment pathways, identifying inefficiencies, bottlenecks, and process variations across patient trajectories. By analyzing event logs extracted from electronic health records, patterns and deviations are uncovered, enabling targeted improvements in care coordination and resource planning. Text mining, particularly with domain-specific natural language processing models, is leveraged to extract unstructured information from clinical narratives. A deep learning classification model trained on medical texts was refined using techniques such as data filtering, class balancing, early stopping, and decision threshold optimization to identify specific complications from reports with high accuracy. Integrating structured event data with insights drawn from clinical notes creates a richer understanding of why certain process deviations occur, supporting the development of predictive models and personalized care strategies. Together, these methodologies illustrate the power of data-driven analysis in healthcare, providing the foundation for operational improvements and better patient outcomes. The study also demonstrates how combining structured and unstructured data enables a more complete representation of clinical workflows and informs future deployment of machine learning models in clinical environments.

Keywords: PM2 · CRISP-ML · Care Pathways

J. Barateiro et al. (Eds.): EDOC 2025 Workshops, LNBIP 571, pp. 357–367, 2026.
https://doi.org/10.1007/978-3-032-16234-2_29

1 Introduction

Healthcare is facing high pressure as our aging society encounters multiple complications that require different treatments [1,2]. Increasing cancer cases demand more staff, however, the shortage of experienced professionals is growing [3]. In the Netherlands, this gap is predicted to widen from 3,800 individuals in 2023 to 26,500 in 2033 [4], while current oncologists are experiencing high burnout load [5]. These pressures result in longer waiting times for patients and compromised care quality. [1,2].

Additionally, hospitals often encounter significant administrative challenges in managing and recording post-surgical complications, particularly for conditions like lung cancer. Inefficient data recording systems requires considerable manual effort to evaluate surgical performance and identify complications, placing an administrative burden on healthcare professionals. This, of course, hinders timely insights. Addressing these challenges requires a structured approach to both process optimization and data-driven analysis. Therefore, this research combines PM2 methodology with the CRISP-ML framework. PM2 Methodology [6] is a process mining project methodology aiming to improve process performance and compliance and supports diverse analysis techniques, and CRISP-ML is the Cross-Industry Standard Process for Data Mining, which outlines a project phases for data-driven modeling and deployment [7]. This combination offers a strong foundation for improving care delivery and reducing administrative load in data evaluation, and thus supporting Value-Based Healthcare.

In this research, the main emphasis is put on process mining (PM) within PM2 and text mining within (TM) the PM2 and CRISP-ML frameworks, respectively, and how they can complement each other in the healthcare domain. With PM we can systematically identify process inefficiencies and with TM we can gain insights from clinical text data. As a result, the following research questions (RQ) have been formulated:

1. *How can the diagnosis and treatment process for cancer patients be evaluated through process mining by using PM2 methodology?*
2. *How can postoperative complications for cancer patients be detected through text mining by using CRISP-ML methodology?*
3. *What opportunities exist to enhance insights into care pathways in hospitals by integrating process mining and text mining techniques?*

The structure of this paper is as follows. Section 2 provides a brief literature review. Section 3 describes the methodology. The results are discussed in Sect. 4, and finally the paper is concluded in Sect. 5.

2 Related Work

While process mining and text mining have independently demonstrated significant value, an emerging field of research is where text mining is used to enrich data for process mining. Several studies have investigated the use of text mining in process mining. The activities in the event log sometimes miss critical context information that is stored in unstructured data. Therefore, [8] introduces a framework for event log annotation, where additional information found in unstructured data is added to the event. Additionally, [9] introduces an approach to systematically transform unstructured data into Object-Centric Event Logs (OCELS) using a collector and a refiner for extracting OCELS from unstructured data.

Limited research has been conducted on how this can be utilized in the healthcare sector. However, there is evidence that it supports better insights and better understanding of process deviations. [10] highlights the potential of LLMs in discovering pathways. For process mining, the event logs are not always complete or immediately available in the EHR. Therefore, SQL scripts or manual analysis are required to obtain the relevant data. Techniques such as named entity recognition (NER) and classification, combined with prompt engineering, allow the identification of key medical terms related to diagnoses and treatments. It will be able to retrieve the relevant information from a large dataset. These data can be organized to generate event logs, allowing for further analysis and identification of trends and relationships [11]. The results can be integrated with process mining techniques to identify deviations, bottlenecks, and inefficiencies and streamline care pathways. This will help find exception cases and other dependencies. [12] proposed an architecture to extract essential information from unstructured data through data pre-processing and rule-based semantic parsing, transforming it into structured data events suitable for process mining [11]. Hence, using text mining and process mining can help better understand the process in practice and identify the underlying reasons behind deviations. This will also minimize the need for domain expertise [8,13].

3 Overview Research Methodology

In this paper, we explore the application of process mining and text mining in the healthcare sector. To answer our research questions, an approach has been designed, as illustrated in Fig. 1. The approach consists of two components: process mining and text mining. These will be further elaborated in the following sections and is visualized in Fig. 2. By applying these techniques, our aim is to develop practice recommendations to improve the care pathways of cancer patients. In addition, for the research field, we want to provide insight into the feasibility and effectiveness of these techniques in hospitals. PM was applied to patients with pancreatic cancer and TM was used to treat patients with lung cancer.

3.1 Data Collection and Processing

Data was sourced from the HiX Electronic Health Record (EHR) system from Medisch Spectrum Twente (MST), a clinical hospital located in the Netherlands.

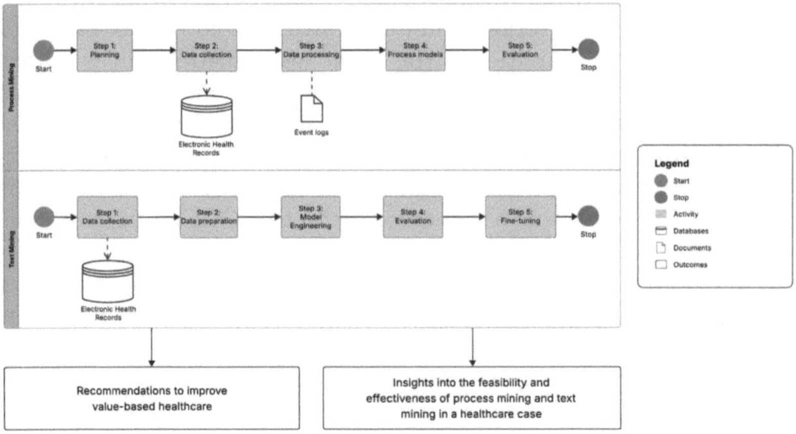

Fig. 1. Overview Method

- For Process Mining, columns relevant to constructing an event log were selected. The data underwent cleaning and clustering to ensure integrity.
- For Text Mining, preprocessing involved removing empty entries, punctuation, and duplicates. Multiple tables were merged to yield a structured dataset suitable for analysis.

3.2 Methodology Process Mining

For process mining, the PM2 methodology has been followed. First, together with MST, the scope and objectives will be discussed to achieve consensus on which steps of the pancreatic cancer care pathways are relevant to this research, as well as their desired granularity. Subsequently, the next phase involves aggregating data from their existing databases based on some pre-specified criteria. The data was processed to ensure that only relevant data was retained and could be transformed into an event log. This results in an event log, where each data entry includes at least a patient ID, an activity, a timestamp, and the referral type for diagnosis and treatment type. Using this event log, process models were generated using the ProM tool, an established open-source framework offering diverse plug-ins for analysis. Data was handled with strict confidentiality protocols. A process discovery analysis was performed using the "Mine with Inductive Visual Miner" and "Mine with Directly Follows Visual Miner" plug-ins to map the processes, assess step durations, and identify bottlenecks. The results from these analyses are presented and discussed in the subsequent section.

3.3 Methodology Text Mining

For the second part of this research, a Natural Language Processing (NLP) tool was trained to identify postoperative complications for lung cancer patients. For this, the CRISP-ML methodology has been followed. First, the problem goals are identified. Following data extraction and data preparation, we performed model engineering, where the NLP algorithm was selected, and the model was trained using the prepared data. The deployment and maintenance phases of CRISP-ML are outside the scope of this research.

The dataset obtained after the data preparation was annotated and labeled in order to train the model. The Dutch Institute for Clinical Auditing (DICA) data has been retrieved to evaluate whether a patient has a complication or not. However, it only contains patients who were treated between 2021 and 2024. For those patients not included in the DICA dataset, reports were labeled manually. As the dataset contains a vast amount of data, a rule-based algorithm was first applied to filter the reports that mention keywords indicating possible complications. Then, the filtered data was manually checked and modified if needed to ensure that the complications are accurately classified. These annotated reports serve as the "gold standard" for evaluating the NLP model's performance. This research focuses specifically on complications related to air leaks that persisted for longer than five days. There are three categories in which an NLP model can be developed. In this study, MedRoBERTa.nl, a deep learning model pre-trained on medical data, has been selected, as it is trained on Dutch medical texts, which enhances its capability for domain-specific language understanding and classification tasks for this case study. This ensures that the model can capture terminology and medical language more effectively. Texts and labels were tokenized and split into training (80%) and testing (20%) sets. Due to class imbalance, Cross-Entropy Loss with class weighting was applied to prevent bias toward the majority class. The model was trained over a maximum of five epochs, with early stopping triggered if the F1 score plateaued over two consecutive epochs. Evaluation metrics include accuracy, precision, recall, and F1-score, alongside a plotted confusion matrix. The classification threshold was fine-tuned to maximize F1 performance.

4 Results and Discussions

4.1 Process Mining Results for Diagnosis

The cohort consists of 200 patients with a total of 11,239 events. Following data cleaning and preparation, as described in Sect. 3, 1,924 events remained, representing 23 unique events.

The diagnostic process reveals high variability and complexity, with over 82.7% of GP-referred patients following unique pathways. The most frequently observed patterns can be found in Table 1. Although MST has shortened overall diagnosis times from 36 to 27 days (2022–2024), only in early 2025 does the process meet the recommended target of 21 days or less for completing diagnostics. Major bottlenecks include long waits for endoscopic ultrasound and infrequent but impactful events like esophagogastroduodenoscopy with biopsy. Urgency-based analysis shows patients with lower urgency experience notably prolonged

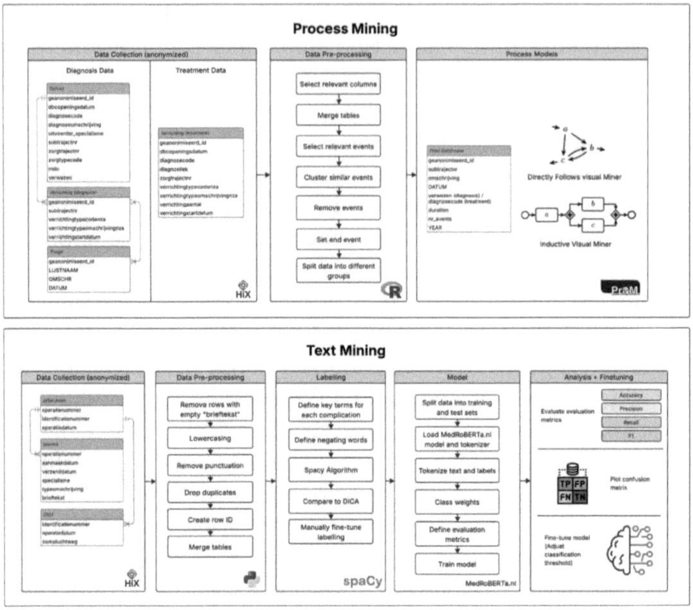

Fig. 2. Detailed Method for Process Mining and Text Mining

delays, particularly before initial clinical evaluation. Despite efforts to streamline processes, core activities like imaging remain sensitive to scheduling delays, especially in endoscopic procedures.

In order to develop an overview of the process, a process model has been constructed. This model was generated using the Inductive Visual Miner plugin, which allows the creation of models with the most frequent activities and paths. The resulting model is illustrated in Fig. 3. The process begins with a referral, followed by diagnostic tests such as CT scans and endoscopic ultrasound, as well as a clinic visit. Patients may also require further examination, including endoscopic retrograde cholangiopancreatography (ERCP) and biopsy. Each case is discussed during the MDO to determine whether additional tests are necessary for a diagnosis or whether it can be referred for an outpatient clinic visit. The process will stop if the patient is discussed during MDO or has visited the outpatient clinic.

4.2 Process Mining Results for Treatment

In treatment, surgery and chemotherapy pathways also demonstrate unique trajectories for each patient. Surgery shows consistent delays with a median of 31 days, driven largely by unexpected repeat outpatient visits and additional CT scans not covered in standard protocols. In contrast, chemotherapy treatment aligns better with recommended expectations, with a median of 15 days from outpatient visit to first session. Yet, a subtle upward trend, from 10 days in

2022 to 19 days in 2024, hints at potential emerging inefficiencies. Although, chemotherapy generally performs well, the increasing duration warrants closer attention to avoid future deviations from clinical norms.

Table 1. Most Common Traces for Diagnosis

Nr.	Trace	Occurrence
1	Triage - CT scan - MDO - First outpatient clinic visit	8 (9.9%)
2	Triage - CT scan - First outpatient clinic visit - MDO	3 (3.7%)
3	Triage - CT scan - First outpatient clinic visit - MDO - Repeat outpatient clinic visit	2 (2.5%)
4	Triage - MDO - CT scan - First outpatient clinic visit	2 (2.5%)
5	Triage - First outpatient clinic visit - CT scan - Repeat outpatient clinic visit - MDO	2 (2.5%)

4.3 Text Mining Results MedRoBERTa.nl

MedRoBERTa.nl was utilized as a text classification model trained on Dutch clinical texts. This model was trained on 2,336 clinical texts from 780 patients who were treated between 2018 and 2025. There were 187 samples that mentioned the complication “air leak longer than 5 days”, showing a class imbalance.

To evaluate the model's performance, the classification metrics accuracy, precision, recall and F1-score were used. Due to the class imbalance, precision, recall, and F1 were prioritized over accuracy, as accuracy could result in misleading conclusions regarding the model's effectiveness.

In order to train and fine-tune the MedRoBERTa.nl model for optimal performance, several methods were employed. Initially, a baseline model was trained on the labeled data, where the data was classified as “air leak” or “no complication". However, the model exhibited low performance, particularly in recall. After evaluating the misclassified records, some records were ambiguous as to whether they had a persistent air leak. To address this ambiguity and enhance the model's capacity to differentiate uncertain cases, we introduced an additional category labeled “maybe", which was excluded from the training data.

After iterative enhancements, the optimized MedRoBERTa.nl model reached strong performance metrics—accuracy of 0.97, precision of 0.86, recall of 0.86, and an F1-score of 0.86 (see Table 2). A threshold of 0.8 yielded the best balance between precision and recall. The final confusion matrix revealed only seven false positives and seven false negatives, confirming the model's reliability and stability in classifying medical reports. Overall, the combination of strategic filtering, data balancing, and threshold tuning demonstrated the feasibility of using domain-specific deep learning for clinical text classification in Dutch-language healthcare data.

Table 2. Results MedRoBERTa.nl model

	Accuracy	Precision	Recall	F1
Baseline	0.96	0.59	0.77	0.67
Exclude maybes	0.97	0.89	0.78	0.83
Handling class imbalance	0.97	0.83	0.86	0.84
Optimize threshold	0.97	0.86	0.86	0.86

4.4 Insights Into Care Pathways in Hospitals by Integrating Process Mining and Text Mining Techniques

Although process mining and text mining were analyzed separately, there was evidence that these methods are helpful for hospitals like MST by offering a deeper understanding of care pathways and supporting value-based healthcare. Combining event logs with information extracted from clinical notes enriches process mining outcomes, making it possible to interpret real-world deviations more effectively. For instance, unusual sequences such as MRIs appearing early in the diagnostic timeline were clarified through text mining of referral notes, revealing that prior imaging often occurred abroad or for other purposes. This fusion of structured and unstructured data improves the accuracy of care models and allows for detection of patient-specific characteristics mentioned in referrals. However, this fusion poses some methodological challenges in aligning heterogeneous data. EHR data are typically standardized and structured data based on which event logs can be extracted for process mining, while clinical texts are narrative and variable in format. One possible solution is to use Named Entity Recognition (NER). NER is the problem of identifying and classifying important nouns and proper nouns in a text into categories. In the context of this research these categories could be patient names, organizations or departments within the healthcare institution, dates and times or medical codes or diagnosis. NER can help link them to specific events in a patient's care pathway. Ultimately, incorporating these insights enriches the process models and enables hospitals to identify pathway variations among subgroups. This paves the way for predictive modeling using machine learning, paving the way for more personalized and efficient healthcare delivery.

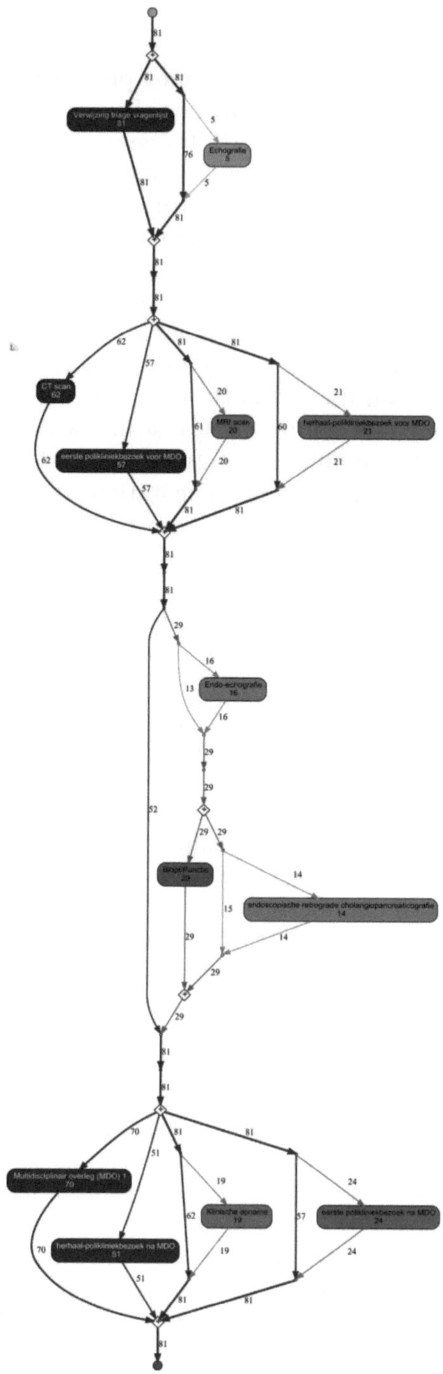

Fig. 3. Diagnosis Process for Pancreatic Cancer Patients

5 Conclusions

This study demonstrates the value of combining process mining and text mining to support data-driven, value-based healthcare. By applying the PM2 methodology for process mining and the CRISP-ML framework for text mining, the paper leverages structured and unstructured clinical data to uncover bottlenecks, classify complications, and interpret deviations within care pathways. Their integration yields richer process insights and enhances the accuracy and interpretability of clinical workflows. The RQs of this research could be answered as follows: **RQ1**: Process mining revealed that most pancreatic cancer patients follow individualized diagnostic and treatment paths, often deviating from established protocols. Over time, improvements in communication and care coordination have led to shorter diagnostic durations. Bottlenecks were identified in specific steps such as endo-echography and additional CT scans, which were often linked to resource constraints and scheduling limitations. **RQ2**: Text mining successfully addressed the issues of inconsistent documentation of postoperative complications in lung cancer patients. Using the MedRoBERTa.nl model, complications were extracted with high accuracy (F1-score: 0.86). **RQ3**: Text mining can enrich process models by explaining deviations and uncovering patient-specific traits from clinical notes. This fusion of structured and unstructured data enhances the interpretability of care pathways and supports the development of predictive models for personalized healthcare.

The findings show strong potential to improve operational efficiency, support clinical decision-making, and enable cross-institutional comparisons. These scalable methodologies go beyond specific use cases and can be adapted to optimize diverse healthcare processes. There are limitations to this work. Regarding the PM part there were issues such as data quality, DBC code inaccuracy and incomplete process traces which call for better data capturing at hospitals. Moreover, only 81 patients were analyzed for diagnosis and 34 for treatment which restricts the ability to detect rare but important pathway variation and may skew the results. In the TM part the annotation was only validated with clinical experts which introduces potential errors and reduces model reliability. Additionally, the model was trained only on clinical notes, which may lack sufficient detail to identify complications. Excluding other sources like lab results limits the model's ability to handle complex cases, reducing precision and recall. Regarding the integration of PM and TM, further research is needed to explore the effective integration of process mining and text mining within hospital settings. Applying both techniques for a use case can provide insights into the feasibility, interpretability, and clinical utility. Ultimately, this approach contributes to more personalized, timely, and effective patient care by minimizing delays, reducing redundancies, and delivering greater value to both clinicians and patients.

Disclosure of Interests. The authors have no competing interests to declare that are relevant to the content of this article.

References

1. Dekker, L., Busch, M., Rözer, J., Janssen-van Eijndt, T., Uiters, E.: Zorg en sociaal domein, Themaverkenning bij de Volksgezondheid Toekomst Verkenning 2024 (2024). https://www.rivm.nl/bibliotheek/rapporten/2024-0047.pdf
2. Ministerie van Volksgezondheid, Stand van de zorg 2024 (2024). https://www.nza.nl/onderwerpen/stand-van-de-zorg-2024
3. CBS, Vacatures in de sector zorg en welzijn (2024). https://www.staatvenz.nl/kerncijfers/vacatures-in-de-sector-zorg-en-welzijn
4. Prognosemodel Zorg en Welzijn, Ziekenhuizen en overige medisch specialistische zorg – Nederland (2022). https://prognosemodelzw.nl/dashboard/stories-dashboard/4--ziekenhuizen-en-overige-medisch-specialistische-zorg
5. Centraal Bureau voor de Statistiek, Helft zorgwerknemers vindt werkdruk te hoog (2022). https://www.cbs.nl/nl-nl/nieuws/2022/46/helft-zorgwerknemers-vindt-werkdruk-te-hoog
6. European Commission, PMÂš Project Management Methodology Guide, Publications Office of the European Union (2023). https://pm2.europa.eu/index_en
7. Shearer, C.: The CRISP-DM model: the new blueprint for data mining. J. Data Warehousing **5**(4), 13–22 (2000)
8. Benton, G., Flokas, L., Yu, C.: Disentangling event logs with large language models. J. Name, **x**(Y), Z–Z (2025)
9. Buss, A., Kecht, C., Kratsch, W., Röglinger, M., Sadeghianasl, S., Wynn, M.T.: From words to workflows: extracting object-centric event logs from textual data. In: Pufahl, L., Rosenthal, K., España, S., Nurcan, S. (eds.) Intelligent Information Systems, pp. 37–44. Springer Nature Switzerland, Cham (2025)
10. Muyama, L., Neuraz, A., Coulet, A.: Machine learning approaches for the discovery of clinical pathways from patient data: a systematic review. J. Biomed. Inform., **160** (2024). https://doi.org/10.1016/j.jbi.2024.104746
11. Stein Dani, V., et al.: Event log extraction for process mining using large language models, in cooperative information systems. In: Comuzzi, M., Grigori, D., Sellami, M., Zhou, Z., Eds., Cham: Springer Nature Switzerland, pp. 56–72 (2025)
12. Barbieri, L., Madeira, E.R.M., Stroeh, K., van der Aalst, W.M.P.: Towards a natural language conversational interface for process mining. In: Process Mining Workshops, Munoz-Gama, J., Lu, X., Eds., Lecture Notes in Business Information Processing, vol. 433, pp. 268–280. Springer, Cham (2022). https://doi.org/10.1007/978-3-030-98581-3_20
13. Park, J.I., Park, J.W., Zhang, K., Kim, D.: Advancing equity in breast cancer care: natural language processing for analysing treatment outcomes in under-represented populations. BMJ Health Care Inform., **31**(1) (2024). https://doi.org/10.1136/bmjhci-2023-100966

SoEA4EE'2025 - 16th Workshop on Service oriented Enterprise Architecture for Enterprise Engineering

Dematerializing Promissory Notes: A Service-Oriented Blockchain Architecture and Web Platform for Secure Financial Document Management

Filipe Quina[1(✉)], Henrique Silva[1(✉)], Sérgio Guerreiro[1,2(✉)], and Miguel Matos[1,2(✉)]

[1] INESC-ID, Lisbon, Portugal
{filipe.d.l.quina,henrique.c.silva}@tecnico.ulisboa.pt
[2] Instituto Superior Técnico, University of Lisbon, Lisbon, Portugal
{sergio.guerreiro,miguel.marques.matos}@tecnico.ulisboa.pt

Abstract. Promissory Notes (PN) remain a cornerstone of formal financial commitments but are still predominantly managed using paper-based processes. This leads to operational inefficiencies, elevated compliance burdens, and data accessibility challenges. This paper presents a digital platform built on a permissioned blockchain infrastructure that replaces paper-based PN workflows with secure, scalable, and verifiable digital services. The platform includes a blockchain backend based on Cosmos and CometBFT, a modular web frontend developed in React, and a RESTful middleware API built in Go. Core functionalities include role-based onboarding, PN issuance and signing, data encryption, lifecycle management, and real-time PN observation. The platform supports all processes present in the lifecycle of paper based PN while providing mechanisms to meet the legal requirements, reduce processing times, and improve governance in institutional and enterprise contexts, and is currently entering a testing phase in a pre-production environment.

Keywords: Promissory Note · Blockchain · Digital Platform · React · REST API · Institutional Workflows · Cosmos SDK

1 Introduction

Promissory Notes (PN) are widely recognized legal-financial instruments that document a commitment by one party to repay a defined amount to another [1]. In Portugal, PN are frequently used in both corporate and institutional financial operations, such as supplier agreements, short-term loans, and asset trading. Despite their legal relevance, the handling of PN continues to rely heavily on paper-based processes. This reliance introduces numerous drawbacks, including inefficiency, high compliance overhead, vulnerability to document loss or forgery, and limited traceability.

J. Barateiro et al. (Eds.): EDOC 2025 Workshops, LNBIP 571, pp. 371–385, 2026.
https://doi.org/10.1007/978-3-032-16234-2_31

To address these challenges, we have developed a digital platform that manages the complete lifecycle of PN using a distributed architecture. The platform provides a secure, verifiable, and role-aware environment for creating, signing, transferring, and archiving PN. It is specifically tailored to meet the legal, operational, and security needs of regulated financial institutions and public entities.

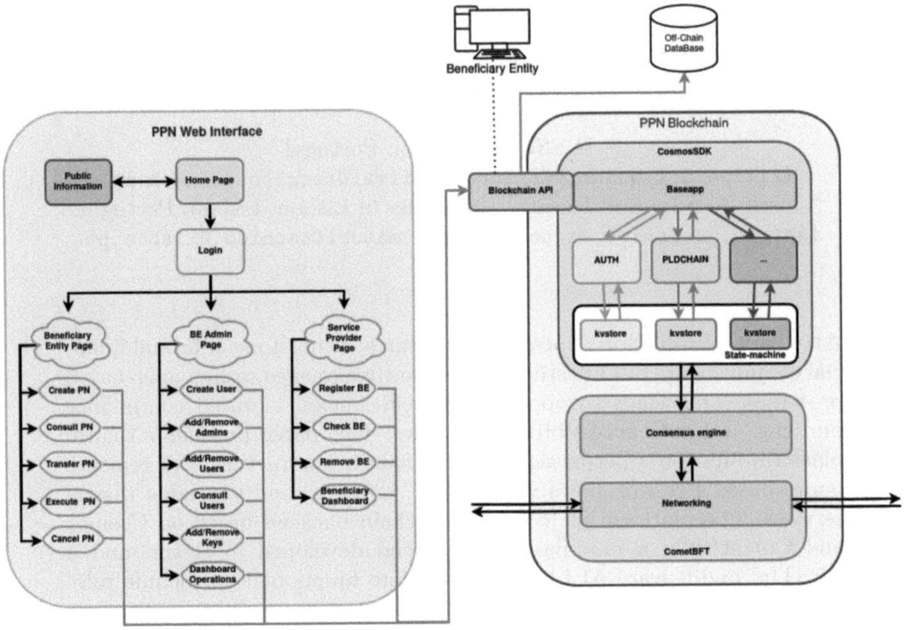

Fig. 1. Portal of Promissory Notes components.

The system is composed of four main components Fig. 1:

- A **permissioned blockchain** that functions as a distributed ledger, constructed using the Cosmos SDK framework and utilizing CometBFT as its consensus engine. It records all operations performed on the PN in a chronological and immutable manner, while ensuring data integrity, privacy, and traceability among participants.
- A **client API** implemented in Go, which serves as an intermediary between user-facing applications and the blockchain. This API acts as a facilitator for the blockchain component, managing role-based authorization, input validation, and the signing and broadcasting of transactions.
- A **react-based web application** that provides tailored interfaces for all actors in the platform, including Service Providers (SP), Beneficiary Entities (BE), and their internal users. The frontend supports features such as user management, digital signature collection (manual and via national authentication systems), PN creation, transfer, and real-time consultation.

- A **off-chain database** responsible for storing off-chain data, such as contracts/agreements, among other data types. It operates independently of the rest of the infrastructure and is referenced as an address to which data will be sent, remaining agnostic.

Each operation in the platform is encapsulated as a modular service exposed via the API and reflected in the user interface. This service-based structure enables automation of complex workflows while maintaining human oversight and legal accountability. The platform's design ensures strong guarantees of confidentiality, integrity, and availability, while offering usability and extensibility for real-world institutional deployment.

Furthermore, the platform adopts a modular and non-prescriptive architecture that promotes interoperability with existing institutional systems. Participants in the network are not constrained to a specific user interface or data storage implementation. Instead, they retain the flexibility to utilize or develop web interfaces and databases that align with their internal infrastructure and operational requirements. The only mandatory components are the blockchain and the client API, which constitute the canonical sources of truth and the exclusive gateway for authorized interactions with the distributed ledger. By decoupling the presentation and data persistence layers from the core transaction logic, the platform enables seamless integration with pre-existing enterprise systems, minimizes disruption to established workflows, and supports institution-specific customization without compromising the integrity or security of the overall network.

2 Use Cases and Requirements for the Platform

The system distinguishes between several types of actors, these roles and interactions are all defined at a blockchain layer through the application logic, each with specific access permissions and responsibilities:

- **Service Provider (SP):** Operates as the governance authority responsible for onboarding and managing BE. SP administrators powers are limited to registering and removing BE from the blockchain.
- **Beneficiary Entities (BE):** These represent institutional users (e.g., financial institutions, agencies). BE are granted isolated administrative domains and can autonomously manage their users permissions, cryptographic keys and PN.
- **BE Admins and Users:** Internal actors of a BE. Admins manage access controls and keys, while standard users can initiate PN, perform signature operations, transfer notes, or consult note histories.
- **Signatories (Guarantor and Subscriber):** Individuals or institutions who commit to or receive payment under a PN. Their participation is formalized through digital signatures, which are enforced and validated by the system.

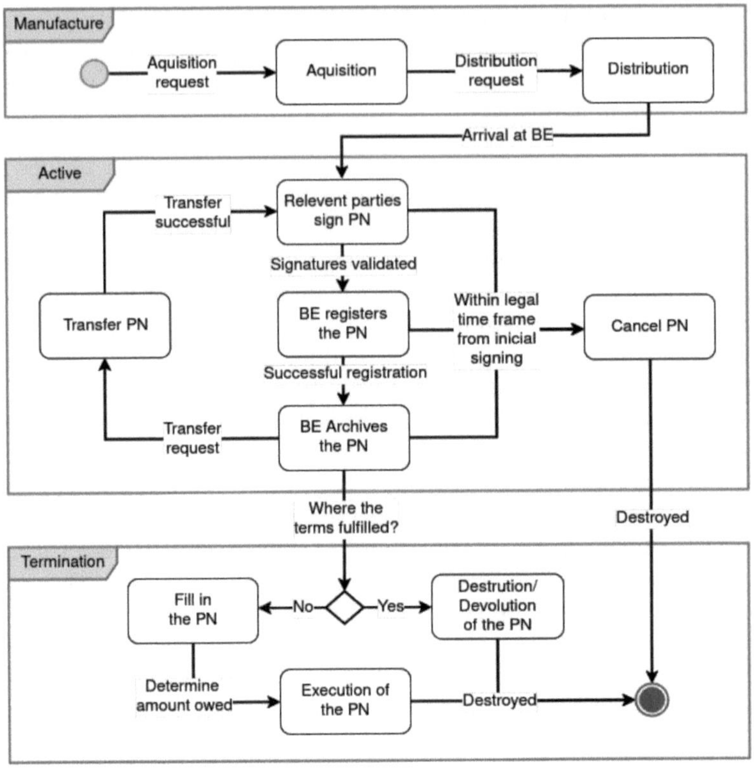

Fig. 2. Current lifecycle of promissory notes.

Each role is enforced at both the API and blockchain levels, ensuring that all operations are traceable, verifiable, and authorized.

The platform automates the end-to-end lifecycle of PN Fig. 2, structuring interactions according to the roles and responsibilities of participating entities. Participants may access the system via the provided web interfaces, develop custom interfaces, or interact directly with the Client API through authenticated requests to invoke predefined operations. All interactions are immutably recorded on the blockchain.

Central to the platform is a governance model in which the SP functions as a trusted authority responsible for registering and removing BE from the network. Once registered, each BE gains the ability to manage internal users independently, issue PN, and perform legally binding actions such as signing, transferring, and executing PN.

All operations are captured as discrete service calls and mapped to the blockchain as transactions. Confidential data involved in sensitive operations is cryptographically secured, ensuring data privacy while maintaining full auditability and verifiability of all interactions.

The platform supports the following capabilities: Role-based user management, Digital PN creation and metadata validation, Manual and identity-based signature workflows, Secure transfer and revocation of PN, and On-chain consultation of active or historical PN.

3 Blockchain Infrastructure

The platform operates a sovereign permissioned blockchain, which functions as a distributed and immutable ledger. In this system, blocks are cryptographically linked to their predecessors and store transactions in a strictly ordered sequence [2]. Unlike permissionless blockchains that permit open participation, permissioned blockchains restrict access to a defined set of authorized entities, thereby enhancing security and enabling structured governance.

Consensus within the blockchain is achieved using an algorithm that provides strong transaction finality, such as CometBFT. This Byzantine Fault Tolerant (BFT) mechanism, derived from Tendermint, operates under a Proof-of-Stake (PoS) model in which a set of validators propose and vote on blocks through sequential rounds [3]. Each round includes a pre-vote and pre-commit phase to establish agreement before a block is finalized. This procedure ensures that at most one block is committed at each height. In cases where consensus is not achieved, the process restarts with a new proposal round [4,5].

A sovereign permissioned blockchain offers several advantages. The restricted validator set improves security by relying on known and vetted participants. Efficiency is enhanced by avoiding the resource-intensive consensus mechanisms required in permissionless environments. Governance policies can be enforced directly through the system's rules, facilitating compliance with regulatory and institutional requirements. Furthermore, the BFT consensus ensures strong finality, eliminating the risk of forks and preserving data consistency, which is critical in enterprise and institutional contexts.

Transactions are defined and handled through a custom Cosmos module that encodes all PN lifecycle events, along with administrative operations performed by the SP and BE. Supported operations include the creation, signature registration, transfer, cancellation, and execution of PN. The module also supports administrative functions such as BE registration and removal, user management, permission assignment, and public key updates.

Data privacy is preserved through encryption mechanisms. Sensitive transaction data, including the identities of the Guarantor and Subscriber and the associated debt amount, is encrypted using asymmetric cryptography. The encrypted payload is then secured using the public key of the initiating BE. Moreover, the format of transaction broadcasts is uniform across all application workflows, preventing external observers from distinguishing between different types of operations.

By integrating a permissioned blockchain architecture with a fault-tolerant consensus mechanism, the platform achieves enhanced security, transaction integrity, and operational efficiency. These properties make it a suitable foundation for enterprise-level management of Promissory Notes.

Key properties of the blockchain layer include:

- **Immutable Record keeping:** All operations are permanently stored and indexed.
- **Secure Access Model:** Participators are authenticated and governed centrally by the SP.
- **Finality and Fork Prevention:** Achieved through CometBFT's three-phase consensus.
- **Data confidentiality:** Sensitive information is encrypted before being broadcast across the network.

4 Middleware and Client API Services

The client API, implemented in Go, functions as an intermediary layer between user-facing applications and the blockchain infrastructure. It is designed to abstract the complexity of blockchain interactions by providing a programmatic interface that supports secure and scalable communication with the distributed ledger. The API is responsible for validating request formats, enforcing role-based access control, signing transactions with the user's cryptographic credentials, and submitting them to the blockchain for processing. Simultaneously, it records the operation's result in the off-chain database to ensure real-time synchronization between the ledger and local data systems [10].

The off-chain database stores:

- **User accounts and roles:** Including hashed credentials, assigned permissions, and display names.
- **Beneficiary Entity metadata:** Human-readable identifiers, contact information, registration status.
- **Session state and logs:** Used for tracking login activity, token validity, and action history.
- **Temporary mappings:** Such as Cosmos addresses to usernames or key ownership, which are not directly stored on-chain.

Operationally, the API behaves as a blockchain client, encapsulating the necessary procedures for transaction creation, validation, and broadcasting. This includes verifying the structure of requests and checking user credentials. Although these mechanisms provide strong guarantees regarding the formal correctness and authorization of transactions, it remains the user's responsibility to ensure the semantic validity of the submitted data. This design choice aligns with current institutional practices and preserves the accountability of the originating entity.

Supported operations include:

- **GET:** Query PN, BE, keys, and related metadata.
- **POST:** Add new users, initiate PN, or submit transactions.

- **DELETE:** Revoke users or deactivate notes while preserving audit history.

It is particularly important to emphasize that the immutability of the blockchain implies that any transaction submitted and successfully processed becomes permanently recorded. Therefore, incorrect or invalid submissions, even if syntactically correct and authorized, cannot be reversed. The system architecture reflects this constraint by encouraging rigorous validation prior to transaction issuance, while the off-chain database supports local consistency and efficient access to replicated operational data.

Security policies include strict field validation, TLS enforcement, and CORS configuration for frontend communication.

Each interaction initiated from the frontend results in a JSON-formatted request handled by the RESTful API. For instance, when a BE user fills in the form to create a PN, the frontend sends a POST request to the API with the necessary fields (e.g., guarantor, subscriber, amount, due date). The API validates this input, serializes it, and forwards it to the blockchain interface for commitment. The entire flow is protected by Transport Layer Security (TLS), and the backend uses public key credentials to ensure that transactions are submitted only by authorized users.

Figure 3 illustrates this operation workflow, from frontend input to blockchain processing, including the payload structure and endpoint used.

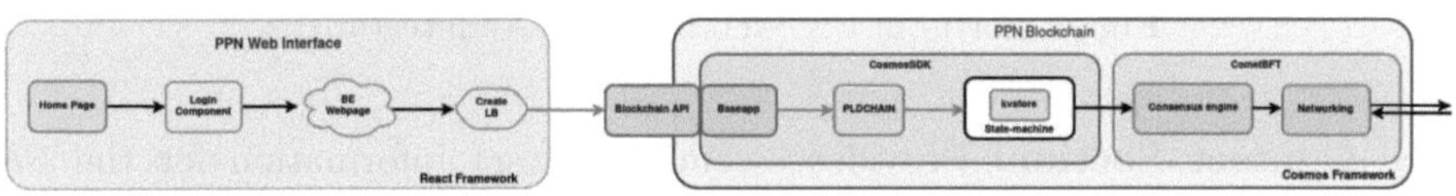

Fig. 3. Information flow of a *PN*.

5 Web Application and User Interfaces

The user interface layer is implemented as a single-page application (SPA) using React [6,7]. Although structured into distinct routes, all views are rendered dynamically within the same client-side environment. This architecture supports fast transitions, modular development, reactive UI updates, and enhanced performance, eliminating the need for full-page reloads. Figure 4 illustrates the structure of the web application.

The web interface, named the Portal of Promissory Notes (PPN), is divided into four logically distinct modules, each tailored to a specific user role:

- **Home Page:** Serves as the platform's entry point, offering general information and an overview of the PPN's features. It includes:
  - **Public Information Section:** Displays details about the system's purpose and functionality, including an overview of the *SP*.

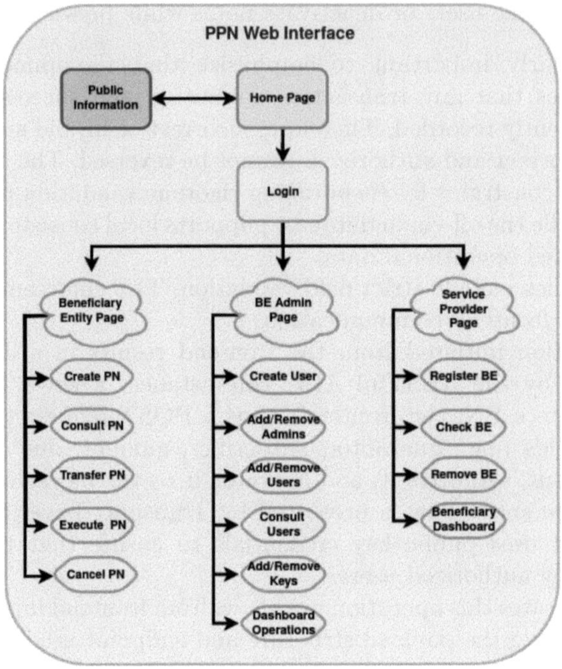

Fig. 4. Portal of PN Web Interface Architecture

  - **Contact Section:** Provides essential contact information for the *SP*, ensuring support transparency.
  - **Login Component:** A secure authentication interface that allows registered users to access their respective dashboards while enforcing session control and data protection.
- **Service Provider Page:** Grants SP administrators full control over Beneficiary Entity (BE) access. The interface supports:
  - **Registering BE:** To onboard new entities and generate access credentials.
  - **Consulting BE:** To inspect existing BE data, ensure compliance, and validate operational status.
  - **Removing BE:** To revoke access rights in accordance with administrative or legal requirements.
  - **Beneficiary Dashboard:** A unified view where SP administrators can register, remove, and consult BE in a single interface.
- **BE Admin Page:** Available to administrators within each BE, this interface supports the internal management of users, roles, and public keys. Components include:
  - **Create User:** To generate new user credentials within the BE environment.
  - **Add Admins / Remove Admins:** To assign or revoke administrative roles from users.

  - **Add Users / Remove Users:** To manage user-level access for standard BE operations.
  - **Consult Users:** To review user accounts and their associated roles within the BE.
  - **Dashboard Operations:** A unified interface enabling bulk creation of users, direct role assignment, and role revocation through a streamlined UI.
  - **Add Keys / Remove Keys:** To manage the BE's cryptographic key pair by registering or revoking public keys used for encryption and identity verification on-chain.
- **BE User Page:** Provides standard BE users with access to promissory note (PN) workflows. Available operations include:
  - **Create *PN***: To initiate new digital promissory notes in a standardized and verifiable format.
  - **Consult *PN***: To inspect details of existing PN for auditability and validation.
  - **Transfer *PN***: To securely reassign PN between entities under legally binding agreements.
  - **Execute *PN***: To finalize and execute PN when mandated by regulatory or financial conditions.
  - **Remove *PN***: To invalidate outdated or obsolete PN, ensuring data cleanliness and legal compliance.

The frontend implements controlled form inputs, custom confirmation modals, and toast-based notifications for real-time user feedback. Authentication state is securely managed via session storage, while role-based access controls dynamically enable or disable UI elements. All components follow a modular design and interact exclusively with scoped API endpoints to ensure isolation, scalability, and maintainability.

This design guarantees that users can only access features permitted by their assigned roles, enhancing both usability and security across the platform.

6 Security and Privacy Architecture

The security and privacy strategy of the platform is designed to reflect its modular architecture, which consists of three main components: a blockchain backend, a middleware API, and a web-based frontend application. A fourth component, the off-chain database, supports secure storage of authentication and session data, and BE-specific user and PN metadata. This layered structure ensures end-to-end integrity, confidentiality, and interoperability across diverse institutional contexts.

6.1 Blockchain Layer: Immutable and Cryptographically Protected Ledger

The Cosmos-based blockchain functions as the immutable ledger for all operations concerning PNs, ensuring data traceability, cryptographic non-repudiation, and regulatory compliance. The blockchain's architectural design mandates that only encrypted data is stored on-chain, thereby preventing the exposure of sensitive information in plaintext [11]. This design principle aligns with privacy-by-design methodologies for distributed ledger technologies.

Security features of this layer include:

- **Public Key Infrastructure (PKI):** Each participating Beneficiary Entity (BE) registers a unique public key within the platform. This public key is subsequently utilized in the encryption of sensitive PN attributes, such as involved parties, digital signatures, and transactional amounts.
- **User digital Signatures:** Every operation initiated by a user at the blockchain layer is cryptographically signed using the user's private key. This process establishes a robust mechanism for authenticating user identity and ensuring the integrity of the submitted transaction.
- **Domain-bound Access Control:**The application layer rigorously enforces access controls, restricting user operations strictly to the scope of permissions pre-assigned by their respective BE or SP. This implements a principle of least privilege, enhancing overall system security.

Sensitive data encryption is performed client-side using a hybrid encryption scheme. Initially, a symmetric Advanced Encryption Standard (AES) key is generated to encrypt the private information pertaining to the PN. This ephemeral AES key is then itself encrypted using the Business Entity's (BE) public RSA key. This ensures that only the designated BE, possessing the corresponding private RSA key, can decrypt the AES key and subsequently access the sensitive information contained within the public blockchain element.

6.2 Middleware API Layer: Centralized Validation and Secure Mediation

The RESTful API layer, developed in Go, acts as the secure intermediary between client-facing applications and the blockchain backend. All operations related to the PN lifecycle (e.g., creation, transfer, execution, revocation) are exposed via authenticated API endpoints [12].

This design enables two distinct modes of interaction:

1. **Direct API Integration:** Institutional systems with integration capabilities can interact with the API directly, using standardized JSON-format messages.
2. **Web Application-Driven Operations:** Institutions without backend integration capabilities can use the PPN web interface, which relies on the same API endpoints.

Security mechanisms at this layer include:

- **Role-based Access Control (RBAC):** Enforced per endpoint based on user role and domain.
- **Transport Layer Security (TLS):** Ensures encrypted communication between clients and the API.

- **Multi-Factor Authentication (MFA):** Supported via external services such as Chave Móvel Digital for critical operations.

6.3 Frontend Web Application: Access-Controlled Interface for End Users

The Portal of Promissory Notes (PPN) is a React-based single-page application designed for institutions that prefer or require a user-friendly web interface. It provides secure role-based access to key features—such as managing PN, BE, and administrators, and interacts exclusively with the REST API to perform operations.

Frontend-level protections include:

- **Session Isolation and Management:** Login credentials are validated via the API and securely stored in the browser's session state using encrypted handlers to prevent tampering or leakage.
- **Access-Gated UI Components:** The interface dynamically renders components based on user roles, preventing unauthorized actions.
- **Real-Time Feedback and Validation:** Controlled form inputs, modals, and toast notifications guide users securely through workflows.

6.4 Off-Chain Database: Secure Identity and Credential Management

The off-chain database supports the web frontend by persisting user account data, session tokens, and registration metadata. It is not exposed directly to the blockchain and is accessed only via the API.

It implements the following safeguards:

- **Password Hashing:** User credentials are stored using bcrypt, ensuring strong resistance to brute-force attacks.
- **Encrypted Storage:** Data at rest is protected with encryption standards.
- **Audit Logging:** All login attempts and administrative actions are tracked for auditing and compliance.

This multi-tiered architecture ensures that operations are secure regardless of the access point, whether via direct API, the web interface, or future third-party integrations, while upholding privacy and trust across all interested parties involved in the PN lifecycle.

7 Validation and Evaluation

The platform was successfully validated in a controlled environment using a virtualized network setup that included one Service Provider (SP) and seven distinct Beneficiary Entities (BEs), simulating a realistic multi-actor institutional scenario. The tests covered all operational layers: back-end block chain, middleware API, front-end application, and off-chain database, verifying functional correctness, performance stability, and resistance to security threats [9].

These results confirm an initial readiness to transition the testing into a enterprise-scale pre-production environment involving real financial institutions and real word operational workloads.

7.1 Functional Validation in Simulated Multi-actor Setup

All core workflows were validated across eight actors using role-specific interfaces and API requests. The validation confirmed the correct implementation of:

- Secure user registration, login, and session management
- Role-based access to features based on SP, BE Admin, and BE User roles
- Full lifecycle operations: PN creation, signing, consultation, transfer, execution or cancellation
- Synchronization between the different nodes on blocks committed and translation ordering

Transactions initiated from both the web frontend and direct API interaction were consistently processed, validated, and committed to the blockchain. Cross-role operations, such as PN signing between entities, were enforced according to governance and access rules. No logic inconsistencies were found across layers. Note that these tests were conducted in both a local environment and a virtualized network setup consisting of six virtual machines (VMs): three running blockchain nodes and three hosting the web application deployments.

7.2 Performance Evaluation in Virtual Network Conditions

Stress testing was carried out within a virtualized network environment to simulate operational conditions representative of enterprise-level deployments, in line with the methodology described in [8]. All actors engaged in concurrent permissioned network (PN) operations—including creation, transfer, and digital signing—exercising both backend consensus mechanisms and frontend synchronization components.

The observed performance metrics are summarized as follows:

- **Latency:** The average end-to-end latency per operation remained under 1.5 s under nominal load, with maximum latency not exceeding 3 s during peak concurrent activity.
- **Throughput:** The system successfully committed over 100 transactions within a 2.5 min window, without observable functional degradation and while preserving total order semantics.
- **Stability:** Both latency and resource utilization exhibited consistent behavior as the number of active nodes scaled to 8, indicating stable operational characteristics under moderate load.

These initial results indicate that it is well-suited for environments where transaction integrity, deterministic execution, and fault tolerance are critical. This aligns with its applicability in permissioned consortium chains and enterprise applications, where strict performance is not the primary bottleneck, but consistency, auditability, and security guarantees are vital. Note that this initials tests were conducted in a local environment with a AMD Rysen5 5600X and 16 GB of RAM.

7.3 Readiness for Enterprise-Scale Testing

The outcomes of local and virtualized environment testing confirm the platform's stability, correctness, and maturity. Its modular architecture, layered security controls, and scalable components make it suitable for integration and validation in real-world institutional environments.

The next phase will involve pilot testing with financial institutions, targeting production-like usage scenarios, user onboarding at scale, and end-to-end validation under regulatory conditions and improvements to the transaction latency by fine tuning the consensus engine metrics.

8 Technical Observations and Development Challenges

The implementation of this platform uncovered a number of critical insights and areas of complexity:

- **Synchronization Between Layers:** Ensuring consistency between frontend UI state, API responses, and blockchain confirmations required robust coordination and transaction state tracking.
- **Address and Role Resolution:** Correctly mapping blockchain addresses to human-readable usernames and associated roles required the implementation of indexing and lookup logic across both on-chain and off-chain layers.
- **Error Handling and Feedback:** Handling blockchain validation errors - such as consensus failures or contract logic rejections - and translating them into actionable and user-friendly messages required a layered error handling strategy.

9 Conclusion and Future Work

This work presents a modular, secure, and service-oriented platform for managing Promissory Notes in a fully digital and legally compliant environment. By combining blockchain-based record keeping with API-driven orchestration and role-based web interfaces, the platform replaces inefficient paper-based processes with transparent, traceable, and auditable digital workflows.

The underlying architecture leverages a permissioned Cosmos blockchain with CometBFT consensus, eliminating the need for a native currency while ensuring tamper-proof record keeping. Centralized governance by a trusted authority (the SP) enhances system integrity and supports regulatory alignment. A custom built-in React front-end, supported by an RESTful Go-based API and an optional off-chain database, enables both institutional integration and usability for stakeholders with varying levels of digital maturity.

This infrastructure not only streamlines the PN lifecycle, removing the need for physical manufacturing and manual record keeping, but also introduces secure identity management, access control, and cryptographic data protection.

The planned future work includes:

1. Expanding support for digital identity providers to streamline secure authentication and signature workflows.
2. Conducting performance benchmarks and stress tests under real institutional deployment conditions.
3. Enhancing observability with real-time dashboards to monitor PN flows and system compliance.
4. Improve latency and performance values under real institutional deployment and enterprise conditions.
5. Performing in-depth security and vulnerability testing in collaboration with financial institutions in Portugal.

Acknowledgments. This work was supported by national funds through Fundação para a Ciência e a Tecnologia (FCT), under project UIDB/50021/2020 (INESC-ID), and by the PLD-INCM initiative for the dematerialization of Promissory Notes, developed in partnership with INESC-ID Lisboa and Imprensa Nacional–Casa da Moeda (2023–2024).

References

1. Barone, A.: Promissory Note: What It Is, Different Types, and Pros and Cons. Investopedia (2024). https://www.investopedia.com/terms/p/promissorynote.asp
2. Tripathi, G., Ahad, M.A., Casalino, G.: A comprehensive review of blockchain technology: Underlying principles and historical background with future challenges. Decision Anal. J. **9**, 100344 (2023). https://www.sciencedirect.com/science/article/pii/S2772662223001844
3. Nico: Proof-of-stake (PoS). Ethereum.org (2024). https://ethereum.org/en/developers/docs/consensus-mechanisms/pos/
4. Kwon, J., Buchman, E.: Cosmos whitepaper. A Netw. Distrib. Ledgers **27**, 1–32 (2019)
5. CometBFT: GitHub - cometbft/cometbft: CometBFT (fork of Tendermint Core): A distributed, Byzantine fault-tolerant, deterministic state machine replication engine (2022). https://github.com/cometbft/cometbft
6. Miguel, P.G.: 24 Best Web Development Tools for 2024. The CTO Club (2024). https://thectoclub.com/tools/best-web-development-tools/
7. Spotlight, S.C.: API Types and Protocols. BrowserStack (2024). https://www.browserstack.com/guide/angular-vs-react-vs-vue

8. Hasan, M.M., Rahman, M.A., Chowdhury, M.S., Rahman, M.H., Abdulle, K.H., Hasan, M.: Testing React single-page web applications using automated testing tools. https://www.researchgate.net/publication/360230007_Testing_React_Single_Page_Web_Application_using_Automated_Testing_Tools
9. Bajenaru, L., et. al.: Modern single-page application architecture: A case study. https://www.researchgate.net/publication/334150777_Modern_Single_Page_Application_Architecture_A_Case_Study
10. Joseph, W., Lamidi, H.: Modern API security frameworks for enterprise systems. https://www.researchgate.netpublication/389380711_Modern_API_Security_Frameworks_for_Enterprise_Systems
11. Springer, T., Haindl, M.: Blockchain-based PKIs: Overcoming trust anchor limitations with decentralized certificate issuance and auditability. ResearchGate (2024). https://www.researchgate.net/publication/382066062_Blockchain-based_PKI_within_a_Corporate_Organization_Advantages_and_Challenges
12. Medium: Role-Based Access Control (RBAC) vs Attribute-Based Access Control (ABAC): Simplifying permissions in microservices. Medium (2024). https://medium.com/globant/attribute-based-access-control-in-a-microservices-architecture-7c68f633b2d3

Investigating Future Viability in Enterprise Architecture: A Qualitative Content Analysis Approach

Christoph Rosenau[1](✉), Kurt Sandkuhl[1,2], and Benjamin Nast[1]

[1] Rostock University, Albert-Einstein-Str. 22, 18059 Rostock, Germany
{christoph.rosenau,kurt.sandkuhl,benjamin.nast}@uni-rostock.de
[2] Jönköping University, Box 1026, 55111 Jönköping, Sweden

Abstract. Enterprise Architecture (EA) aims to align IT with business goals, but the concept of "future viability" remains academically abstract and practically elusive, creating a significant theory-practice gap. This study addresses this gap through a qualitative content analysis of semi-structured interviews with seasoned EA practitioners. Our findings reveal that practitioners define future viability not as a technical property, but as a direct outcome of business strategy, making its assessment highly context-dependent. While confirming that business capabilities serve as a "central anchor point" for translating strategy into design, the analysis also shows that the primary obstacles are not technical but organizational: the significant impact of technical debt and pervasive institutional inertia. By empirically validating and nuancing theoretical concepts, this paper contributes a practitioner-grounded understanding of future viability, offering actionable insights into the real-world challenges and strategic imperatives for building resilient and adaptable enterprise architectures.

Keywords: Enterprise Architecture · Future Viability · Qualitative Content Analysis · Business Capabilities · Expert Interviews

1 Introduction

In theory, Enterprise Architecture (EA) is a strategic management discipline. Its purpose is to ensure that an organization's sprawling IT landscape remains coherent, aligned with business goals, and capable of adapting to relentless technological and market shifts. In practice, however, it often devolves into a technical record-keeping exercise, disconnected from the very business goals it's meant to support. As companies grapple with digital transformation, new regulations, and market disruptions, the ability to design an architecture that is genuinely future-viable isn't just an academic ideal, it's a condition for survival. In this paper, *future viability* denotes an enterprise's capacity to sustain success by being scalable, flexible, and adaptable.

This practical problem motivated our previous study, a Structured Literature Review (SLR) that explored the role of business capabilities in this equation [18].

J. Barateiro et al. (Eds.): EDOC 2025 Workshops, LNBIP 571, pp. 386–400, 2026.
https://doi.org/10.1007/978-3-032-16234-2_32

That work confirmed several of the authors own observations from industry, but grounded them in academic literature:

1. **Business capabilities appear to be the bedrock.** They offer a stable way to anchor IT in business strategy, providing a structure that can outlast specific technologies or organizational charts.
2. **Scalability and flexibility are non-negotiable.** Any architecture aiming for longevity must be designed to handle growth and absorb change without collapsing under its own weight.
3. **Existing frameworks like TOGAF are insufficient.** While they touch upon adaptability, they offer frustratingly little in the way of concrete methods for actually measuring or systematically achieving future viability. It's often implied, but never explicitly engineered. However, it lays in the nature of a framework to be as abstract as possible to achieve general applicability.
4. **The theory-practice gap is real.** The literature agrees that business capabilities are important, but there is a striking lack of empirical evidence showing how-or even if-they are used effectively in real-world organizations to achieve this goal.

While the SLR gave us a solid theoretical map, it also highlighted a vast, uncharted territory: the practical reality of how organizations define and implement future viability. The term itself is often used loosely in research, bundled with concepts like agility or adaptability without clear distinction. For practitioners, this is a real pain point. Without standardized metrics or methods, how can they assess if their architecture is truly built to last, or just propped up by wishful thinking?

This is the gap this study aims to fill. We need to move beyond theory and empirically test these ideas. To do that, we conducted a series of expert interviews with Enterprise Architecture practitioners. The goal was to understand how they perceive, measure, and implement future viability in their daily work and to find out if business capabilities are the powerful tool we believe them to be. By bridging this gap between theory and practice, we aim to provide actionable insights that help Enterprise Architects and decision-makers build EA frameworks that do more than just document the present-they enable long-term adaptability in a world that refuses to stand still.

The remainder of this paper is structured as follows. Section 2 outlines the background and related work. Section 3 describes the research methodology. Section 4 presents the interview guide. The results of our analysis are presented in Sect. 5, followed by the conclusions in Sect. 6. Finally, Sect. 7 discusses the implications of our findings, their limitations, and derives requirements for future work.

2 Background and Related Work

2.1 Enterprise Architecture Management

Enterprise Architecture Management (EAM) is a strategic discipline aimed at aligning an organization's business objectives with its IT landscape. It ensures that the underlying architecture remains scalable and adaptable in the face of evolving business environments. EAM adopts a comprehensive framework that integrates business processes, information systems, and technological infrastructure with the organization's strategic goals [15]. This alignment enhances decision-making and supports organizational agility. One of the most commonly used frameworks in EAM is TOGAF (The Open Group Architecture Framework), which provides standardized methodologies and tools for designing and managing enterprise architectures [12].

While the terms "IT Architecture" and "Enterprise Architecture" are sometimes used interchangeably, IT Architecture is actually a subset of EA. It concentrates on the technical components of architecture-such as software systems, networks, and hardware-and their role in supporting organizational objectives [5]. Both terms are closely related and have a complementary nature: IT Architecture underpins the technical infrastructure, whereas EAM encompasses the broader strategic alignment between business and IT.

A foundational element of EAM is the concept of business capability, which has its roots in strategic management [21]. Within the context of EAM, business capabilities are defined as an organization's fundamental abilities to achieve specific outcomes by leveraging a combination of people, processes, and technology. These capabilities represent essential business functions, irrespective of execution methods or responsible parties. Incorporating business capabilities into EAM enables the development of modular and adaptable architectures capable of responding to both internal shifts and external pressures [4].

To support this integration, business capability maps are widely employed within EAM frameworks. These maps visually depict the alignment between capabilities and IT systems, as well as other business components. They enhance communication between business and IT stakeholders by clarifying the interdependencies and relationships among business functions and the supporting technology. This visualization helps to uncover redundancies, identify gaps, and highlight opportunities for improvement, thereby contributing to the creation of a more scalable and responsive architecture [11].

2.2 Viability of EA Architectures

In the context of IT Architecture, future viability is primarily characterized by scalability and flexibility. These attributes are essential for ensuring that an architecture can accommodate future business and technological developments. A future-oriented system should be capable of incorporating new functionalities and technologies while maintaining stable and reliable performance [20].

Within IT Architecture, scalability and adaptability are critical components of an effective and future-proof Enterprise Architecture Management (EAM) strategy. Scalability enables an architecture to support increased demand or organizational growth without necessitating major structural changes. Frameworks such as TOGAF facilitate this by offering a systematic approach to the continuous evolution of IT systems, ensuring their alignment with changing business needs [2]. Flexibility, on the other hand, is vital for responding to technological innovation and market dynamics, making it easier to adopt emerging technologies such as artificial intelligence and cloud computing [9].

In summary, EAM - particularly when guided by frameworks like TOGAF - equips organizations with the methodologies and tools required to design architectures that are flexible, scalable, and resilient to future change. By emphasizing business capabilities, enterprises can ensure their IT systems remain strategically aligned, technologically adaptable, and capable of supporting sustainable business growth [1]. Future viability is a quality characteristic of enterprise architectures that, guided by business capabilities, expresses the capacity to, over time, remain flexible, scalable, and resilient to future change under expected and unforeseen conditions.

2.3 Related Work on Viability of EA

A review of the literature on Enterprise Architecture (EA) viability, which we previously conducted, reveals a consistent pattern: the concept is almost always explored through the lenses of scalability and flexibility [18]. This creates a dichotomy between abundant theoretical discussion and a shortage of actionable, empirically-supported guidance for those in the field.

One of the prevailing threads in this theoretical landscape is the notion of leveraging business capabilities to make an EA more responsive. The groundwork was laid by Brits et al. [7], who designed a framework for modeling capabilities to create a more agile IT architecture, complete with feedback mechanisms for continuous improvement. This perspective was later refined by Freitag et al. [10], who deepened the model by adding a method to analyze the intricate dependencies between capabilities and other EA elements.

Within these discussions, scalability is consistently flagged as a key determinant of future viability, defined as the ability of a system to accommodate growth and shifting loads [6]. The argument advanced by scholars is that architectural scalability is not just a technical feature but is fundamentally linked to the business model itself; a truly scalable model that integrates economic and social goals is seen as essential for competitive advantage [13,16]. Furthermore, the work of Ashrafi et al. [3] provides a mechanism for this, demonstrating that robust business analytics capabilities are a key enabler of the agility and performance that scalability requires.

Flexibility stands as a complementary, yet equally critical, attribute. It represents the capacity to incorporate new requirements and technologies-facilitated by modularity, adaptability, and integrability-without necessitating complete overhauls [8]. In essence, while the literature provides a strong conceptual blueprint linking these ideas to future viability, the practical application and understanding of these concepts by practitioners remains an underexplored territory, a key finding from our earlier review [18].

3 Research Methodology: Qualitative Content Analysis

3.1 Introduction to QCA

To move beyond academic theory and capture the messy reality of EA practice, we needed a method that balances rigor with interpretive depth. This is why we chose Mayring's Qualitative Content Analysis (QCA). It provides a structured and systematic way to analyze text - in our case, expert interviews-that maintains methodological discipline without sacrificing the nuance of human experience [17].

Unlike traditional quantitative analysis, which might simply count keywords, QCA is about context-dependent interpretation. It gives us a replicable, theoretically grounded process for extracting meaning. One of its greatest strengths, and a key reason for its selection here, is its integration of both deductive and inductive reasoning. This allows us to start with the theoretical constructs from our literature review but remain open to discovering new, unexpected insights from the practitioners themselves [19].

For this study, QCA is the ideal analytical tool. We have a conceptual foundation from our SLR, but we need to see how it holds up in the real world. QCA allows us to empirically test our assumptions about future viability and business capabilities while simultaneously exploring how industry context shapes these very concepts.

3.2 Justification for the Use of QCA in This Study

The decision to use Mayring's QCA is directly tied to the exploratory and theory-validating nature of this research. Our previous SLR laid the theoretical groundwork, showing that business capabilities should, in principle, enhance the future viability of EA. However, it also left us with critical, unanswered questions:

1. How do practitioners on the ground actually interpret a term like "future viability"?
2. To what extent are business capability models really being used to assess an architecture's ability to scale and adapt?
3. What are the real-world barriers and frustrations that get in the way of implementing these future-proof frameworks?

These questions can't be answered with a survey or quantitative data. We need to understand the nuances, the "why" behind the "what," which demands a qualitative approach. The structured nature of QCA is perfect for this. It allows us to use theory-driven (deductive) coding to examine literature-based propositions, while its inductive component gives us the freedom to identify novel, industry-specific themes that we hadn't anticipated. It's a balanced approach for a balanced, practitioner-academic study.

3.3 Research Design and Application of QCA

Our application of Mayring's QCA follows a deliberate, multi-step process designed to ensure our analysis is both consistent and rigorous. The process unfolds in several key phases:

Step 1: Select Materials and Triangulation The empirical data consists exclusively of the transcribed conversations conducted for this research. The findings from our prior SLR [18] were used for methodological triangulation, informing the development of the interview guide and the initial deductive coding categories, thereby enhancing the validity of our interpretations.

Step 2: Definition of Research Questions and Analytical Focus The entire investigation is guided by a set of core research questions. These are the practical problems we aim to solve:

RQ1: How do Enterprise Architects define future viability in their organizations?
RQ2: How do they go about assessing it?
RQ3: Do they connect future viability to scalability, flexibility, and adaptability? And if so, how do they measure these attributes?
RQ4: What role, if any, do business capabilities play in making an EA truly future-viable?
RQ5: What are the practical, everyday challenges they face when trying to implement future-proof architectures?
RQ6: What is the perceived utility of tools like Business Capability Maps?

These questions form the backbone of our QCA process, directly shaping the coding categories we use to analyze the interview data.

Step 3: Data Collection – Semi-structured Expert Interviews.

- **Participant Selection:** We used a purposive sampling approach. This means we specifically sought out three experienced Enterprise Architects and IT strategists from a range of industries to ensure we captured a breadth of perspectives for this exploratory study.
- **Interview Methodology:** We conducted semi-structured interviews. This format provided a consistent guide for our conversations while allowing the flexibility to chase down interesting, emergent themes. Each interview lasted between 45 and 60 min and was fully transcribed for analysis.
- **Data Format:** The raw material for our analysis is the collection of transcribed interview responses. This text is the dataset we feed into the QCA process.

Step 4: Deductive Category Formation (Theory-Driven Coding). A core strength of QCA is its dual-coding approach. We began by developing deductive categories derived directly from our SLR findings. This ensures our analysis is firmly anchored in existing research and directly examines our initial literature-based propositions. These categories (see Table 1) act as our first-pass coding framework, which we then refine based on what the interview data tells us.

Table 1. Deductive Categories Derived from SLR Findings

Category	Theoretical Basis (SLR Findings)
Definition of Future Viability	In terms of EA, the concept is often addressed implicitly through scalability and flexibility but lacks a standard, actionable definition.
Scalability & Flexibility Criteria	Scalability is typically linked to architectural modularity, integration capacity, and resource elasticity.
Role of Business Capabilities	Business capabilities are positioned as a key strategic tool for linking IT systems to organizational adaptability.
Assessment Methods	The literature points to a significant lack of standardized metrics for evaluating future viability in EA.
Implementation Challenges	Commonly cited barriers include regulatory constraints, technical debt, and organizational resistance to change.

Step 5: Inductive Category Formation (Emergent Themes). After the initial deductive coding, we shifted to an inductive approach. This is where we listen closely to the data itself, identifying emergent themes, ideas, and challenges that were not anticipated in the literature. This allows for genuine discovery.

Step 6: Data Interpretation and Thematic Analysis. The final phase is an iterative process of refining the categories and interpreting the results. Our goal here is to ensure our findings are solidly grounded in both our theoretical framework and the empirical evidence, to clearly articulate commonalities and divergences among the experts, and to systematically derive practical implications.

3.4 Coding Procedure and Quality Assurance

To ensure a systematic and rigorous analysis, the coding of the transcripts was conducted by the first author following a structured procedure grounded in Mayring's QCA. A detailed codebook was developed to guide the process, containing clear definitions, application rules, and anchor examples for each category. This ensured coding consistency across all interviews and throughout the analysis.

The analysis was performed iteratively. Following an initial coding of the material, the data was reviewed in multiple cycles to refine categories, consolidate themes, and ensure that the interpretations remained grounded in the data. Memoing was used throughout this process to document analytical decisions, reflect on emerging patterns, and track the evolution of the coding scheme. This practice created a transparent audit trail from the raw data to the final results, enhancing the dependability and traceability of the findings.

4 Interview Guideline: Semi-structured Interview Questions

The following interview guide was designed to spark a focused yet open-ended conversation with each expert. The questions are directly linked to our research questions and the deductive categories from our QCA framework. They are deliberately phrased to be non-leading, aiming to elicit genuine perspectives rather than confirming the interviewers own biases. For the same reason, only the first seven questions were handed to the interviewees upfront. The remaining questions were presented to them one by one - to keep a good interview flow without anticipating things.

Section 1: Background and Context (To Understand Their Professional World and How it Shapes their Views.)

1. Could you start by briefly describing your current role and your main responsibilities related to Enterprise Architecture?
2. How many years have you been working with Enterprise Architecture, and in what kinds of industries or companies?
3. From your perspective, how important is Enterprise Architecture for the long-term success of a business?

Section 2: Defining "Future Viability" (RQ1).

4. When you hear the term "future viability" in the context of Enterprise Architecture, what does that mean to you personally?
5. In your view, what are the absolute must-have characteristics of a future-viable architecture?

Section 3: Assessment and Measurement (RQ2).

6. What specific criteria or factors do you look at when you're trying to judge the future viability of your architecture?
7. Are there any specific methods, models, or frameworks you actually use to measure or evaluate this?

Section 4: The Core Attributes (RQ3).

8. How closely do you link concepts like scalability, flexibility, and adaptability to the overall future viability of an EA?
9. How do you specifically measure or assess the scalability, flexibility, or adaptability of your architecture? Are there KPIs or is it more of a qualitative judgment?
10. Do you make a conscious distinction between scalability, flexibility, and adaptability? If so, what is it?

Section 5: The Role of Business Capabilities (RQ4).

11. First off, what does the term “Business Capabilities” mean to you?
12. Does your organization use Business Capabilities as a tool in EA? If so, can you describe exactly how?
13. In your experience, what role do Business Capabilities play in ensuring the future viability of your architecture?
14. How do you know if your Business Capabilities are actually helping to achieve long-term future viability? What are the signs of success?

Section 6: The Real-World Challenges (RQ5).

15. What are the most common or frustrating challenges you face when trying to develop and implement future-viable architectures?
16. How does your organization deal with the elephant in the room: integrating legacy systems into these new, future-viable designs?
17. What impact do regulatory requirements or compliance mandates have on your ability to design a truly adaptable architecture?

Section 7: The Value of Capability-Based Approaches (RQ6).

18. What has been your direct experience with capability-based approaches, like creating Business Capability Maps?
19. Do you see these approaches as a genuinely useful tool for structuring and improving an EA's future viability? Why, or why not?
20. Can you give me any practical examples-good or bad-where a capability-based approach made a real difference to future viability?

Section 8: Closing Thoughts and Advice.

21. If you could advise a company on what to change to focus more on future viability in their EA, what would you tell them?
22. Do you have any suggestions for how existing EA frameworks could be improved to provide better support for long-term adaptability?
23. Is there anything else you think is important on this topic of Business Capabilities and future viability that we haven't covered?

5 Results: A Qualitative Analysis of Practitioner Perspectives

The interviews with three highly experienced EA practitioners provided a clear and candid answer to what happens when the theoretical concept of future viability meets the real world. This section synthesizes their perspectives, structuring them thematically to map directly to our research questions. To protect confidentiality, the interviewees are anonymized as P1, P2, and P3.

5.1 Profile of the Interviewed Experts

To ground these findings, it's important to know who we talked to. The panel consists of practitioners with deep, multi-year experience across a variety of industries and company sizes. The first expert (P1) is a strategic EAM consultant who advises a wide range of organizations, from the German *Mittelstand* (medium-sized companies) to large multinational corporations. The second (P2) is a consulting Principal Director with over a decade in EA, specializing in guiding large transformation programs. The third expert (P3) is a Lead Project Architect operating in a highly complex software environment, responsible for architecting solutions across more than 400 applications.

5.2 Defining and Assessing Future Viability (RQ1, RQ2)

A clear message emerged from all three practitioners: future viability is not a technical quality. It is a direct reflection of an architecture's ability to contribute to long-term business success. As P3 put it, the assessment of whether an architecture is future-viable "is derived directly from the goals and the strategy of the company." This anchors EA firmly as a strategic management function.

While this strategic anchor was undisputed, the assessment methods varied, revealing a spectrum from structured models to intensely context-specific analysis. P1 uses a repeatable set of criteria-including *Functional Fit*, *Technology Fit*, and resource availability-to create a consistent assessment. In contrast, P2 takes a more problem-oriented approach, quantifying *technical debt* and overlaying IT quality onto a business capability map to highlight organizational "pain points." P3 argues against any fixed checklist, emphasizing that the critical factors are entirely situational. For a company aiming for deeper customer integration, the decisive criterion might be the decoupling of its front- and backend systems. This indicates that while the goal is clear, the specific yardstick must be tailored to the business context.

5.3 Core Attributes of a Future-Viable Architecture (RQ3)

When asked to make the abstract goal of future viability more concrete, the experts consistently identified a core set of architectural attributes. A sharp distinction emerged between scalability on one hand, and the intertwined concepts of flexibility and adaptability on the other. Scalability was defined more narrowly as the ability to handle more load.

The priority and measurement of these attributes, however, were not uniform. P2 classified scalability as a "level-2" property-important, but often a non-functional requirement at the solution level rather than a primary driver at the EA level. A particularly insightful point was about the pragmatism required when communicating with senior management (P3). To sidestep overly technical jargon, abstract terms are often translated into business-friendly language, focusing on "changeability" (*Änderbarkeit*) and "cost." This practitioner (P3) also reported using a specific KPI for "modifiability," derived from an ISO standard and composed of "analyzability" and "modularity."

5.4 The Role and Utility of Business Capabilities (RQ4, RQ6)

A strong consensus emerged on the role of business capabilities. They are seen as the fundamental instrument for building the bridge between business strategy and IT architecture. Practitioners described capabilities as the *"Dreh- und Angelpunkt"* (pivot point) (P1) and the *"zentraler Ankerpunkt"* (central anchor point) (P3) of any strategic EA practice. This approach provides a stable, abstract model of the enterprise-what the business does, independent of who does it or how.

Despite this widespread agreement, practitioners pointed out practical hurdles. P2 observed that business stakeholders are often more comfortable with process maps, and shifting the organization's mindset to capability-based thinking can be a strenuous process. P3 added a critical nuance: in highly complex transformations, a capability map alone isn't enough. It's the essential starting point, but must be reinforced with deeper architectural layers-like reference architectures or design guidelines-to effectively steer implementation.

5.5 Practical Challenges: Technical Debt and Organizational Inertia (RQ5)

The path to a future-viable architecture is, in practice, littered with obstacles. The experts consistently sorted these challenges into two main buckets: technical debt and organizational inertia.

The primary technical roadblock is the impact of legacy systems. All three practitioners named monolithic, tightly-coupled, and poorly documented applications as the single biggest barrier to flexibility. Dealing with this reality requires deliberate strategies, from containment via APIs to more aggressive approaches like the "strangler fig pattern" or a full replacement (P2, P3).

Perhaps even more difficult to overcome are the organizational and strategic hurdles. Practitioners are in a constant battle against siloed thinking, departmental turf wars, and a management culture focused on short-term "firefighting" (P1). Securing resources to tackle deep-rooted technical debt is a significant challenge, often made worse by a corporate aversion to risk (P2). The most fundamental challenge is creating strategic awareness at the executive level (P3). Without a clear mandate, any effort to build a truly future-viable enterprise is a considerable challenge. Regulatory requirements were also mentioned as powerful external forces that both compel change and constrain architectural freedom (P1, P3).

6 Conclusions

The central finding of this study is unequivocal: future viability is not an inherent technical property of an architecture, but an emergent quality of its alignment with business strategy. The expert interviews dismantle the notion of a universal, one-size-fits-all definition and instead anchor the concept firmly in the specific competitive context of an organization. This practitioner-grounded perspective allows us to provide clear answers to the research questions that motivated this investigation.

This research set out to understand how practitioners define and assess future viability. The answer is clear: its definition is entirely context-dependent, derived directly from an organization's strategic goals (RQ1). Consequently, its assessment is not a standardized procedure but a pragmatic and situational exercise (RQ2). When translating this strategic alignment into architectural characteristics, flexibility and adaptability emerge as paramount, often viewed as more critical than pure scalability (RQ3). The most resounding finding is the central role of business capabilities in this process (RQ4). Described as the "central anchor point," they are confirmed as the indispensable instrument for translating strategic intent into architectural design. Capability maps, in particular, are seen as vital tools for this translation (RQ6).

Finally, the study sought to identify the primary obstacles to achieving a future-viable state (RQ5). The interviews reveal that the greatest barriers are not technical puzzles but human and historical ones: the significant weight of legacy systems and the deep-rooted organizational inertia that favors short-term fixes over long-term strategic investment. These findings empirically validate the link between business strategy, articulated through capabilities, and a modular architectural design as the key to future viability.

7 Discussion

The interviews paint a compelling picture, but they also force us to ask some difficult questions. This is where we step back and critically examine what these findings mean for the EA discipline, acknowledging both the powerful consensus that emerged and the practical limitations that came with it.

7.1 The Primacy of Business Strategy and the Situational Nature of Future Viability

The unanimous agreement that future viability is dictated by business strategy reinforces the view of EA as a management discipline. But this has a profound implication: any attempt to create a universal, one-size-fits-all framework for assessing future viability is probably doomed to fail. The interviews strongly suggest that the *process* of deriving assessment criteria from a company's unique strategic context is far more important than any predefined checklist. This means any useful framework must be inherently adaptable - a guide to contextual analysis, not a rigid set of rules.

7.2 The Business Capability "Gospel" and Its Practical Limits

The study reveals a strong belief in the utility of business capabilities, empirically confirming their role as the essential bridge between strategy and execution. This aligns with prior research on capability-oriented EA [7, 10]. However, the friction one expert (P2) described when introducing capability maps to stakeholders steeped in process thinking is a real and significant hurdle. It highlights that these abstract models require dedicated change management and education to gain traction.

Furthermore, the insight from P3 that capabilities alone can be insufficient in complex transformations is a vital, grounding nuance. They are the necessary starting point for defining the "what," but a truly future-viable architecture also needs detailed guidance on the "how"-through reference architectures, design patterns, and concrete standards. This suggests a critical need to seamlessly integrate high-level, capability-based planning with the more granular level of architectural governance.

7.3 The Challenge of Measurement: From Qualitative Assessment to Quantitative Metrics

A subtle but critical tension surfaced in the interviews: the gap between the desire to "assess" future viability and the ability to truly "measure" it. Practitioners are using structured tools like heatmaps and fit-gap analyses, but these methods remain largely qualitative. They depend heavily on expert judgment. The mention of a specific KPI for "modifiability" (P3) is a notable exception and points toward the future of the discipline. This gap between qualitative assessment and quantitative measurement is a massive opportunity for research. Developing and validating reliable metrics for architectural qualities is a promising direction for design-oriented research.

7.4 Limitations and Avenues for Future Research

These findings must be viewed in light of the study's limitations. As an exploratory study, a primary limitation is the small sample size of three participants. Although the experts provided deep insights, the findings are not generalizable. Future research should aim to validate these findings with a larger, more diverse sample.

Furthermore, our sample draws heavily from a consulting perspective, which may favor the use of structured, methodical tools like capability mapping. Future work should actively seek to mitigate this potential bias by including the perspectives of in-house strategists or Heads of EA who have stewarded a single enterprise's architecture over many years. This was also a cross-sectional study; a longitudinal case study that tracks a single organization's multi-year journey could yield far deeper insights into the dynamic interplay between strategic pivots, architectural choices, and organizational learning.

Future work should also investigate the impact and potential of new concepts in EAM, such as Enterprise Architecture as-a-Service (EAaaS) [14], on future viability. EAaaS refers to the provision of Enterprise Architecture capabilities and expertise as a service offering to external stakeholder groups (e.g., customers).

7.5 From Findings to Design: Requirements for a Supporting Artifact

The challenges identified by practitioners point toward a clear need for concrete support that helps EA professionals navigate these issues. Based on the interview findings and the preceding discussion, we derive five core requirements for an artifact to guide future design-oriented research. These requirements (see Table 2) synthesize the interview results and related work.

Table 2. Requirements for supporting future viability in EA

Req. ID	Requirement (neutral formulation)	Rationale (link to evidence)
REQ-01	Provide a method to *contextualize and operationalize* future viability from business strategy (organization-specific criteria and targets).	Sec. 5.2, 7.1; Related work [18].
REQ-02	Ensure *traceability* from capabilities to architectural decisions, complemented by reference architectures/patterns.	Sec. 5.4, 7.2; Related work [4].
REQ-03	Define *assessment instruments* for architectural qualities (e.g., modifiability), supporting qualitative judgments with operational indicators where feasible.	Sec. 5.3, 7.3; Related work [20].
REQ-04	Provide decision support to *analyze and mitigate technical debt* at capability level (e.g., containment, replacement, staged modernization).	Sec. 5.5, 7.2.
REQ-05	Include *change management guidance* to facilitate adoption of capability-based planning in process-centric organizations.	Sec. 5.4, 7.2.

Disclosure of Interests. The authors have no competing interests to declare that are relevant to the content of this article.

References

1. Aleatrati Khosroshahi, P., Hauder, M., Volkert, S., Matthes, F., Gernegroß, M.: Business capability maps: current practices and use cases for enterprise architecture management (2018)
2. Alm, R., Wißotzki, M.: TOGAF adaption for small and medium enterprises. In: Abramowicz, W. (ed.) BIS 2013. LNBIP, vol. 160, pp. 112–123. Springer, Heidelberg (2013). https://doi.org/10.1007/978-3-642-41687-3_12

3. Ashrafi, A., Ravasan, A.Z., Trkman, P., Afshari, S.: The role of business analytics capabilities in bolstering firms' agility and performance. Int. J. Inf. Manage. **47**, 1–15 (2019)
4. Barroero, T., Motta, G., Pignatelli, G.: Business capabilities centric enterprise architecture. In: IFIP International Conference on Enterprise Architecture, Integration and Interoperability, pp. 32–43. Springer (2010)
5. Booch, G.: Enterprise architecture and technical architecture. IEEE Softw. **27**(2), 96–96 (2010)
6. Brataas, G., Hughes, P.: Exploring architectural scalability. In: Proceedings of the 4th international workshop on Software and performance, pp. 125–129 (2004)
7. Brits, J., Botha, G., Herselman, M.: Conceptual framework for modeling business capabilities. Ph.D. thesis, Tshwane University of Technology (2006)
8. De Neufville, R., Scholtes, S.: Flexibility in engineering design. MIT Press (2011)
9. Fitriani, L., Khodra, M.L., Surendro, K.: Togaf-based enterprise architecture framework for utilizing artificial intelligence. In: 2023 International Conference on Computer, Control, Informatics and its Applications (IC3INA), pp. 90–95. IEEE (2023)
10. Freitag, A., Matthes, F., Schulz, C., Nowobilska, A.: A method for business capability dependency analysis. In: International Conference on IT-enabled Innovation in Enterprise (ICITIE2011), Sofia (2011)
11. Hanschke, S., Ernsting, J., Kuchen, H.: Integrating agile software development and enterprise architecture management. In: 2015 48th Hawaii International Conference on System Sciences, pp. 4099–4108. IEEE (2015)
12. Harrison, R.: TOGAF® 9 Foundation Study Guide. Van Haren (2016)
13. Jabłoński, A.: Scalability of sustainable business models in hybrid organizations. Sustainability **8**(3), 194 (2016)
14. Kaddoumi, T., Tambo, T.: Enterprise architecture as a service: agile transformation driven by technology services providers. Available at SSRN 4683825 (2024)
15. Lankhorst, M., et al.: Enterprise architecture at work, 4th Edition, vol. 352. Springer (2017)
16. Lund, M., Nielsen, C.: The concept of business model scalability. J. Bus. Models **6**(1), 1–18 (2018)
17. Mayring, P.: Qualitative content analysis. Online PDF (2024). https://www.researchgate.net/publication/215666096_Qualitative_Content_Analysis. Updated on October 22, 2024. Accessed on 26-11-2024
18. Rosenau, C., Sandkuhl, K., Nast, B.: The role of business capabilities for future viability in enterprise architecture - a structured literature review. In: Practice of Enterprise Modeling Forum, M4S, FACETE, AEM, Tools and Demos, Stockholm, Sweden, December 3-5, 2024. CEUR-WS (2024)
19. Schreier, M.: Introduction: What is qualitative content analysis? In: Qualitative Content Analysis in Practice. SAGE Publications, Inc. (2012). https://methods.sagepub.com/book/mono/qualitative-content-analysis-in-practice/chpt/1-introduction-what-is-qualitative-content-analysis. Accessed on 26-11-2024
20. Shashi, A.: Future-proofing your architecture: Embracing scalability and flexibility (2024). https://medium.com/@ashutoshshashi/future-proofing-your-architecture-embracing-scalability-and-flexibility-c1204927995a
21. Wernerfelt, B.: A resource-based view of the firm. Strateg. Manag. J. **5**(2), 171–180 (1984)

A Decade of Challenges: A Practitioners Exploratory Study of Microservices Operational Stability

Gabriel Morais[1(✉)], Mehdi Adda[1], and Dominik Bork[1,2]

[1] Université du Québec à Rimouski, Lévis, QC, Canada
{gabrielglauber.morais,mehdi_adda}@uqar.ca, dominik.bork@tuwien.ac.at
[2] Business Informatics Group, Technische Universität Wien, Vienna, Austria

Abstract. Microservices have been around for a decade, but operational challenges remain unsolved. The complexity of operating them has been a persistent issue among practitioners, being a barrier to the proper adoption of the Microservices Architecture (MSA) paradigm. In some extreme cases, this situation led to the failure of MSA adoption and a return to monolithic architectures. Throughout a longitudinal exploratory case study conducted at a large financial organization with over 40 years of experience in developing and operating complex distributed systems, we examine the factors influencing the dependability and sustainability at runtime, i.e., the operational stability of microservices. Our findings highlight the need for systematic approaches to define realistic service-level targets, design cohesive and robust stability strategies, and establish optimal resource utilization, thereby framing a research agenda aligned with industry needs. Ultimately, we ensure the quality of our study by adopting a multivocal approach to data collection, employing systematic data triangulation during analysis, and ensuring transferability by relating our findings to previous studies and collecting feedback from non-participants from a different domain.

Keywords: Microservices Architecture · Operational Stability · Software Dependability · Software Sustainability

1 Introduction

Over the last decade, microservices architecture (MSA) has driven a paradigm shift in the design and deployment of large, distributed systems, aligning with the continuum of Internet services and inheriting their objectives and challenges [33]. MSA has focused on coping with barriers that prevent fast adaptation to market conditions and evolution [26,52]. It has fostered independence at all levels as the backbone of adaptable, reusable, scalable and resilient applications, impacting the technology, development and operation processes used when developing software systems [4,29]. MSA has demonstrated significant benefits in system

J. Barateiro et al. (Eds.): EDOC 2025 Workshops, LNBIP 571, pp. 401–419, 2026.
https://doi.org/10.1007/978-3-032-16234-2_33

design and development, but it remains a complex paradigm when in operation [17,43,51]. Due to this complexity, organizations have reverted to monolithic approaches, primarily because of the operational costs and issues with system performance, scalability, and management [44].

The lack of governance and the presence of organizational silos in MSA development, combined with its operational complexity, may cause misalignments that hinder the effective use of this service-oriented paradigm in enterprise architecture (EA) for engineering reliable enterprise systems, leading to weaknesses in EA design, governance, and its ability to support evolving business needs [24,29]. Besides, migration to microservices may produce hybrid systems composed of microservices and non-microservices components, which are developed and operated using disparate practices [5,17]. This context leads to specific challenges, such as defining system dependability strategies or determining thresholds for automatic recovery mechanisms that accommodate different architectural paradigms deployed in heterogeneous infrastructures, and using different appraoches [29,51].

These challenges influence the operational dependability and sustainability of systems, as well as their ability to maintain them at expected levels over time, thereby ensuring their stability. Indeed, systems *operational stability* is achieved through *dependability*, including fault tolerance and avoidance, systems performance and robustness aspects, and *sustainability*, including services' social impact, economic viability, resource consumption optimization, portability, evolvability, and maintainability [1,22,23]. Realizing dependability and sustainability requires strategies, measurements, and coordination to be effective [1,9,23]. However, these aspects have been overlooked, highlighting the current need for developing novel approaches to handling them within MSA [19,43,44].

This research aims to identify the goals, factors, challenges and improvement perspectives related to operational stability of microservices in a microservices migration context, from a practitioner's perspective. We conducted a twelve-month exploratory case study in collaboration with an industrial partner from the finance services domain. Findings reveal that MSA operational stability depends on cross-service coordination and requires holistic approaches to design pragmatic system-wide operational stability strategies, displaying the practical limitations of MSA's core tenets of independence and autonomy. Specifically, practitioners pointed out the challenges of defining realistic end-user service levels, achieving cohesive stability strategies, assessing the robustness of resilience mechanisms, and optimizing resource consumption. These insights contribute to shaping a research agenda grounded in practitioners' latent needs.

Besides, we offer a working definition of operational stability to support understanding stability in this context. Eventually, we evaluated our research against its multivocality, rigour, reflexivity, credibility, and transferability. Artifacts used in and produced by this research are available at this paper's companion repository [28].

The remainder of this paper is organized as follows: Sect. 2 presents foundational concepts related to operational stability and MSA, as well as a summary of related works. Section 3 presents the research design. Section 4 reports the findings, and Sect. 5 discusses their implications and lessons learned. We discuss evaluation in Sect. 6, and we conclude with final remarks and research perspectives in Sect. 7.

2 Background and Related Work

This section provides foundational knowledge and related work necessary to understand the research problem and its implications, as well as to contextualize its findings. First, we introduce a working definition of operational stability, followed by the principles and challenges of microservices operations. Finally, we present related work.

2.1 A Working Definition of Operational Stability

Operational stability has been considered a purpose within software stability. It aims to stabilize systems' runtime behaviour, encompassing software evolution, maintenance and runtime aspects [41]. However, a unique definition of operational stability may be inaccurate or incomplete because stability is context-specific and multi-dimensional [40]. A trade-off is to use a working definition built from properties related to the context or case where the stability abilities should be observed. Such a definition provides a conceptual framework to support the understanding of specific stability tenets within the context [41].

In the scope of this paper, we are concerned with operation control processes [49], notably the control of the system's capacity to face failures and service degradation. Focusing on the purpose of stability during the software systems' operation, we constructed a definition for *operational stability* (Definition 1) based on the system's ability to achieve dependability and sustainability.

In this context, the dimensions of dependability and sustainability have specific properties. *Operational dependability* is the ability to avoid system failures that violate established service-level duties. Indeed, dependability is considered the background of building system trustworthiness [11,45]. *Operational sustainability* is the ability to operate systems cost-effectively, relying on adequate resource consumption. Sustainability encompasses the social, economic, technical, and environmental perspectives of a system, which may support or conflict, requiring their accommodation [12,23]. Based on this context and dimensions, we define operational stability as follows:

Definition 1. *Operational stability is the ability of a system to maintain its behaviour at a fixed operation level under varying internal and external conditions.*

Here, *system* denotes a software architecture comprising components that interact to deliver a service [1]. *Behaviour* denotes the set of states the system exposes when delivering a service [1]. *Operation level* denotes the degree of compliance with operational specifications, which represent runtime boundaries defined from operational dependability and sustainability attributes for a specific use environment, establishing the acceptable tolerance threshold for deviation from expected runtime behaviour. The system's *environment* is the set of other systems with which the considered system interacts [1]. The system's structure defines the *varying internal conditions*. The variability in the operational stability of the system environment defines the *varying external conditions*. These properties are often defined throughout contracts that establish the system performance targets as service-level agreements (SLAs) and objectives (SLOs) [10].

2.2 Operating Microservices

Contemporary systems based on cloud microservices adhere to recovery-driven computing (ROC) principles, which focus on building fault-tolerant systems [9, 34]. Microservices are built based on the isolation principle and operated in a scalable infrastructure that enhances redundancy [13,52]. They are developed in short cycles and rely on approaches that foster automation and tight collaboration between developers and operators, such as DevOps [4,47]. However, practitioners have identified challenges in handling operational concerns, such as evaluating, establishing baselines and metrics, and effectively monitoring microservices [18,51].

MSA complexifies system operation due to its distributed nature, which impacts resource consumption, system management, and monitoring [43,48]. This complexity has been exacerbated by the proliferation of microservices resulting from the MSA migration process [51]. Additionally, organizations transitioning from legacy to MSA systems must manage different paradigms and operational practices in parallel and address the incompatibilities that may arise from operating such hybrid systems. For instance, DevOps has a positive impact on system operational performance and is considered complementary to MSA; however, the adoption of DevOps may not be entirely achieved, and challenges to adopting MSA and DevOps may arise concurrently, influencing each other [3,47,51].

The difficulty in comprehensively monitoring microservices leads to the challenge of defining their operational behaviour, which is paramount to supporting automatic resilience mechanisms and assessing performance [48,51]. It has been achieved by aggregating its historical operation data using application performance monitoring tools and modelling supposed baselines, which are used as comparison points in monitoring activities [18]. Resource usage, load balancing, and availability are the most frequently used monitoring metrics for microservices systems, supporting continuous analysis of application stability and estimation of operational costs [47]. However, frequent microservice releases, fault tolerance, and resilience mechanisms make modelling a microservice's operational normal behaviour difficult [18,51]. Besides, the monitoring is achieved atomically, i.e., for each microservice individually, which makes establishing the expected behaviour and monitoring microservices compositions complex [18,29,47].

2.3 Related Work

In 2017, Soldani et al. [43] reviewed 51 non-academic industrial studies published between 2014 and 2017 to identify the gains and pains of adopting MSA. They unveiled challenges in handling the complexity of distributed systems, data management, and consistency, as well as increased resource consumption. In 2020, Waseem et al. [48] surveyed 106 practitioners using a questionnaire and interviewed six practitioners to identify standard practices and challenges associated with designing, monitoring, and testing microservices. They confirmed the previous challenges and unveiled others related to fault detection and isolation, log exploration, performance assessment and monitoring, and the lack of tools to support operations activities. Between 2021 and 2022, Zhou et al. [51] revisited these challenges to document their evolution. They interviewed 20 practitioners from various industries to analyze their current practices and challenges. Their findings showed that challenges identified by Soldani et al. and subsequent studies remain unresolved. They also elaborated on practical issues in operating microservices, such as excessive technology diversity, difficulties in automating operational processes, and setting thresholds to trigger operational tasks, e.g., recovery mechanisms, calling for formal and methodical approaches.

Previous studies did not focus on runtime dependability and sustainability, and lack a longitudinal, immersive approach, which limits the depth of their observations. Our study complements these prior works by targeting operational stability concerns and considering the extended context of microservices operation within hybrid systems. We also bring depth to the study of these aspects in a real-world scenario through a longitudinal on-site study, enabling a comprehensive understanding and revealing insights that may be previously inaccessible.

3 Case Study Design

We followed the guidelines for the design and execution of observational case studies proposed in [50] and the standard for conducting empirical case studies proposed in [38] to structure this research execution. We engaged with practitioners to incrementally build knowledge about the operational stability challenges they face, using a combination of literature review, interviews, document exploration, and observations, similar to the approach adopted in [31] and [39].

3.1 Objectives and Research Questions

We aimed to qualitatively explore *how* practitioners address MSA operational stability in the context of hybrid systems and *what* challenges they encounter. To meet this goal, we explored the following research questions:

RQ1. Which factors influence the operational stability of hybrid systems?
RQ2. How do these factors influence operational stability?
RQ3. How operational stability practices should be enhanced?

3.2 Defining a Conceptual Framework

We conducted a literature review of taxonomies, ontologies and conceptual frameworks in the fields of MSA and software stability, dependability, and sustainability. Based on them, we built a conceptual framework that bounded our exploration and served as a classification schema to categorize our findings.

3.3 Data Collection

We grounded our study in a critical realism stance, recognizing the role of subjective information from actors while acknowledging the independent structures that influence their actions. We relied on interviews and observations, and approached the research questions from two epistemological perspectives: constructivism and pragmatism [25]. The constructivist perspective ensured the reflection of the role of individual and collective experiences in building an understanding of operational stability, serving as a guideline for interviews. The pragmatic perspective ensured that the role of operational stability practice in extending practitioners' knowledge was considered, guiding our observations.

The first time we met participants, we presented our definition of operational stability (cf. Sect. 2) to avoid any ambiguity or misunderstanding, and asked demographic questions. Table 1 provides a summary of participants' demographics.

Table 1. Participants Demographics

Gender	*Males*												*Females*		
Role	*Business*			*Developer*			*Operator*					*Process Owner*			
YoE-SO	15+		5-10	10-15		15+	10-15			15+		10-15		15+	5-10
YoE-MSA	2-5	5-10	2-5	2-5	5-10	5-10	0-2	2-5	5-10	2-5	5-10	0-2		2-5	5-10
Number	*2*	*1*	*1*	*3*	*1*	*3*	*1*	*2*	*1*	*3*	*4*	*1*	*1*	*1*	*1*
Total Role	**4**			**7**			**11**					**4**			
Total Gender	**23**												**3**		
Total	**26**														

Abbreviations: Years of experience in software operation (YoE-SO), Years of experience in MSA (YoE-MSA).

Interviews – We conducted semi-structured interviews (cf. [28] for interview guides). Each interview involved an interviewee and a researcher who discussed for a duration of at least 30 min and a maximum of 60 min. Minutes were created and sent to the interviewees for review and validation. Any questions that emerged were recorded in a *questions backlog* to be addressed in subsequent sessions, as in [39]. We conducted four interview cycles from June to November 2024. The number of sessions per cycle varied according to the number of questions in the *questions backlog*.

Observations – We conducted the observations from November 2024 to May 2025 using the protocol proposed in [39], recording the observation period, details, quotes, and follow-up questions. We observed practitioners as they executed the process of defining system SLAs for eight business functions, each with 4 to 13 services. Stakeholders, operators, and developers varied by function, but the process owner remained the same. Table 2 summarizes our observation execution.

Table 2. Observations Execution

Observed Task	Participants	Duration	Times	Recurrence
Process improvement	PO(3)	60 min	3	monthly
SLA definition kick-off	B(1), PO(1), O(1), D(1)	60 min	8	1 / BF
Definition of capability	O(1), D(1)	≈90 min	27	≈3 / BF
SLA negotiation	B(1), PO(1), O(1)	60 min	16	2 / BF
SLA tasks alignment	PO(1), O(1)	60 min	8	1 / BF
Operators-Business alignment	B(4), PO(1), O(11)	60 min	14	2 / month
SLA enactment	PO(1), B(1), O(1)	60 min	8	1 / BF

Abbreviations: Business stakeholders (BS), Process owners (PO), Operators (O), Developers (D), Business functions (BF).

During individual observations, we spent at most 90 min with participants, with the duration varying according to the tasks they had to perform. One observer conducted each observation session. We began by asking participants to describe the task they would perform, and then we followed its execution, asking questions throughout the performance. We kept 15 min after each session for an open discussion with the participants, during which we collected their thoughts about the tasks they had just performed, their perception of the tasks' utility and effectiveness, as well as the improvements they foresaw. During group meetings, we observed the dynamics of the group as participants aligned their tasks and progressed toward achieving the process. Our goal was to identify how the individual perceptions and improvement ideas observed during individual sessions were conveyed to the group.

3.4 Data Analysis

We conducted a triangulation of the data collected. We compared facts acquired during the interviews against what we observed when practitioners execute operational stability tasks. Then, we examined the organization's documents, including processes documentation, EA-related documents, and architecture decision and operations guides, to corroborate our observations. We sought to confirm perceptions and claims, as well as identify gaps between what practitioners see and do and what is expected. Besides, we reviewed the literature and updated the conceptual framework when we encountered novel insights. We used the framework suggested in [23] to support the data analysis process. This framework identifies factors holistically, relating them to the dimensions under study. It supports the identification of how factors influence each other, representing dependencies and characterizing them, as dependency can be supportive or conflictual. We relied on UML class diagrams to convey our findings, complementing them with textual descriptions. The final version of the conceptual framework is available at this paper companion [28].

3.5 The Case Studied

To align with our goals, the case study had to encompass complex systems, including microservices that operate concurrently with legacy systems. Additionally, it had to have a significant number of microservices, above 100, and be substantial in the system; thus, we target systems comprising at least 25% of microservices implementing business functionalities.

The selected case is a section of a financial services organization, a concentration of technologies and practices that encapsulate 40 years of system development and operation in a single location. They started MSA-migration in 2018, nowadays, they operate 234 complex business services, comprising 5 to 32 functionalities, totalling 1,300 components, which include legacy services (480 or 69% of business services), microservices (220 or 31% of business services), and infrastructure services (600), such as gateways, databases, and monitoring services. These services are arranged to compose a transactional website serving approximately 1 million users and a transactional intranet portal used by the organization's staff (approximately 20,000 users). We cannot share detailed case information due to the organization's confidentiality policy, but we facilitate some details upon request to assist with reproducing the study.

4 Findings

The findings reveal that operational stability in microservice architectures cannot be achieved in isolation—it demands coordination across system components, directly challenging the MSA principles of independence and autonomy. This tension is evident in the difficulty of defining realistic service-level targets, a problem exacerbated by current methods that rely on localized thresholds rather than system-wide metrics and fail to integrate non-MSA components. These limitations constrain the adoption of advanced dependability techniques, exposing a gap between the capabilities of existing tools and their practical application. Furthermore, the prevalence of longstanding operational challenges in software engineering, as observed in the studied case, such as defining achievable operational targets and developing cohesive strategies, suggests that addressing them requires more than a commitment to MSA tenets and the availability of advanced recovery mechanisms.

Table 3. Summary of Key Findings

Observation	***#PA***	***#NPA***
Realistic End-user SLAs	16	2
(G1) End-user satisfaction	23	2
(G2) Optimize operation costs	7	2
(F1) End-user expectations	16	2
(F2) IT capabilities	16	2
(F3) Feasibility of SLA-SLOs	16	2
(F4) Instability level	19	2
(C1) Accommodate end-user expectations and IT capabilities	10	2
(C2) Define operational normal behaviour	10	2
(P1) Systematic approach to establish operation profile	10	2
Cohesive Strategies	26	2
(G3) Design complementary stability strategies	22	1
(F5) Services' dependencies	22	2
(F6) Services' disruption point	22	2
(F7) Available stability mechanisms	22	2
(F8) Stability mechanisms interplay	22	2
(F9) Compatibility of services and stability mechanisms	13	2
(C3) Assess strategy complementarity	26	2
(C4) Establish operational stability profiles	26	2
(C5) Align stability strategies	26	2
(P2) Methodical approach to align stability strategies	19	2
(P3) Simulation-projection mechanisms	9	1
Robustness of Resilience Mechanisms	17	2
(G4) Choose the right mechanism for the right scenario	17	2
(F10) Mechanism configuration	15	2
(F11) Mechanism reliability	17	2
(C5) Benchmark robustness	15	2
(C6) Evaluate mechanisms in real-life conditions	15	2
(C7) Assess the mechanism's robustness when facing cascading failures	15	1
(P4) Methods to identify mechanisms disruption points	17	2
Optimal Resource Consumption	22	2
(G5) Saving on stability mechanisms costs	8	2
(F12) Billing model	4	1
(F13) Consumption goals-limits	22	2
(F14) Outages-failure resource costs	8	1
(C8) Accommodate SLAs-SLOs and resource consumption	22	2

Abbreviations: Operational stability goal (G), factors (F), challenges (C), propositions (P), participants (PA), non-participant (NPA).

Below, we examine these findings through four themes—service level, strategies, mechanisms, and resources—by first identifying the underlying factors (F) shaping stability (RQ1), then analyzing their relationship with stability goals (G) and challenges (C) (RQ2), and finally proposing concrete improvements (P) to address these issues (RQ3) (Table 3).

4.1 Realistic End-User Service Level Agreements

Participants (16) highlighted the theme of service level as a central component in understanding and achieving operational stability. Notably, the importance of defining realistic service level targets that align with end-user expectations (F1) and IT capabilities (F2), as well as setting feasible targets (F3), is emphasized. All operators and business participants (19) indicated service instability level (F4) as the main factor considered when defining a service level target. In this context, the instability level acts as a risk indicator. By doing so, the objective is to achieve high end-user satisfaction (G1) while optimizing costs (G2).

The factors associated with the need for realistic end-user service level agreements align with what the literature identified as the need to unveil and understand the goals and requirements related to operational stability concerns [41]. It involves identifying stakeholders and their goals to derive views, requirements, and stability strategies, aiming to reach a consensus by accommodating stakeholders' needs, objectives and IT capabilities. Once a common view is reached, implementation strategies can be derived [11,20]. These end-user SLAs are then transformed into local SLOs, which must be met to comply with the agreed SLAs [16,46]. This factor aligns with the social perspective on sustainable systems [23], as the systems provide trustworthy services to end-users.

Participants (10) stressed the challenges of balancing end-user expectations and IT capabilities (C1), which necessitate baselining system capabilities (C2), aligning with longstanding issues in MSA [18,43,51]. A proposition is to develop systematic approaches to establish local and system operation profiles, which requires benchmarking SLAs-SLOs by defining rules and baselines, allowing them to measure their achievement system-wide, similar to requests made in [51].

4.2 Cohesive Strategies

All process owners, operators, and developers emphasized the importance of unveiling service dependencies at runtime (F5), arguing that services, both legacy and microservices, are often developed in silos with limited interaction between teams, resulting in recurring mismatches in architectural documents between development and operations, as noted in [29,30]. Similarly, they pointed out the services' stability profile (F6), the available stability mechanisms (F7), and their interplay (F8) as unavoidable factors in designing complementary stability strategies (G6). They consider aligned objectives as essential because the predominance of disparate stability objectives within services may prevent the achievement of dependability and sustainability at the system level. Furthermore, they noted that the service nature, i.e., legacy or microservice, introduces compatibility concerns (F9). Operators (7) and developers (6) indicated that assessing stability strategies is a challenge (C3) that requires reliable system runtime models, identifying the trigger patterns of stability mechanisms, and a dedicated test environment, aligning with known limitations in testing microservices and runtime architecture [18,29,35,43].

All participants emphasized understanding the system stability profile (C4), which identifies service properties that affect operational stability. While C4 is related to C2 in terms of modelling service runtime behaviour, C2 focuses on the system's standard operational capabilities without considering SLA and SLO targets, while C4 examines behaviour changes leading to SLA and SLO violations. In all, they are concerned with the negative impact of contradictory stability actions (C5).

The case primarily relies on a 'fix-as-fails' strategy, addressing faults as they occur. It manages operational stability within the ITIL framework for service operations, particularly through incident management and problem management practices [2]. Automatic and manual monitoring are key elements of its operational strategy, which focus on the velocity of detecting, alerting, classifying, and fixing outages. Two operators mentioned the low level of "intelligent monitoring" and advocated for the adoption of observability practices [27]. Besides, six operators pointed out the annoyance caused by improper alert thresholds, relating this issue to the lack of practical guidance and operational knowledge required to set the fit values when configuring them. Preventive strategies using automatic resilience processes were observed; however, four operators noted that they have, occasionally, been a source of instability, as reported in [51].

Generally, participants (19) emphasized the lack of systematic and objective methods, such as data-based or test-based approaches, indicating that current practices foster ad-hoc and approximate solutions, which we observed when they executed operational stability-related processes. To address these challenges, they proposed benchmarking strategies for alignment and complementarity. Thus, the proposition of developing a methodical approach to align stability strategies (P2) emerged. Some of the participants (9) envisioned a simulation system (P3) that could project operational behaviour without deploying the system, resilience and recovery mechanisms in a physical structure, which would allow them to conduct tests and experiment with stability strategy variants. P2 closely align with recent research on applying Digital Twins techniques to MSA and cloud applications to avoid infrastructure costs during test activities [7,36].

4.3 Robustness of Resilience Mechanisms

The robustness of resilience mechanisms encompasses their adaptability, strength, and capacity to keep the system in the desired state when activated. Robust resilience mechanisms within cohesive stability strategies relate to technical sustainability [23]. It directs the design of adaptable and resilient systems, influencing their long-term use [12]. Participants (15) were concerned with the adequacy of resilience mechanism configurations (F10), mainly in how minimal and maximal values are established and in identifying variations between expected and actual mechanisms' behaviour, echoing the challenge of defining adequate triggers identified in [51]. Besides, participants (17) identified the reliability of resilience mechanisms (F11) as a critical decision factor. Indeed, considering that stability mechanisms can face disruption helps practitioners analyze and make informed decisions when designing stability strategies and defining realistic SLAs.

These considerations remained theoretical in the case without practical application. Developers (7) and operators (8) acknowledged their importance but indicated that they did not apply any specific method to assess them. They argued that they face a lack of standards to benchmark robustness (C5) and the need for a test environment representative of real-life conditions (C6) to conduct mechanism evaluation in a trial-and-error approach, which is the ad-hoc technique we observed some of them used (2 operators). They also indicated the challenge of assessing mechanisms' robustness when facing cascading failures (C7), from the viewpoint of mechanisms' interaction. This perspective differs from the one identified in [43] and [51], where participants were concerned with the cascading effect of service failures.

Therefore, participants (17) identified the need to pinpoint disruption points in mechanisms (P4), i.e., when mechanisms are overwhelmed, and to track variations over time, allowing them to evaluate the mechanism's reliability and outage risks. Similar to experimenting with stability strategies, they suggested using simulators (P3) in place of real test environments to enhance mechanisms manipulation and experiments.

4.4 Optimal Resource Consumption

Business participants pointed out the cost of stability mechanisms as a critical factor in ensuring the economic sustainability of stability strategies. This cost is directly related to resource consumption and the platform provider's billing model (F12). Operators and developers noted the case of using autoscaling resilience mechanisms, where the costs vary depending on the type of service being scaled. Also, resource consumption is budgeted yearly, imposing a consumption limit goal (F13). However, operators and developers noted the lack of knowledge of real costs as they are managed outside their teams.

Nevertheless, all operators noted that they have extensive knowledge of normal resource consumption levels, which they use to optimize operations. We observed the practical use of this knowledge when operators manually adjust resources in production to adapt to usage peaks. Similarly to the definition of stability strategies, all operators and developers highlighted the influence of connections between microservices and legacy services on resource consumption induced by inadequate choices (F9 and C5). For instance, we observed that operators closely follow the scalability of microservices that depend on legacy parts that are not scalable, both for technical and business reasons. All developers and operators noted the impracticability of generalizing autonomous resource management through the auto scale-up and down practice in this context.

Building dependable systems is considered a priority by business and process owners to achieve end-user satisfaction (G1). However, it is likely to conflict with resource savings and consumption limits aimed by the same business participants (G5). Indeed, the activation of stability mechanisms helps ensure dependability, but it also increases operational costs (F14). Operators and developers nuanced this conflict; for them, these costs depend on the number and activation rate of stability mechanisms, which in turn depend on the particularities of the service and its operational stability profile (F6).

Operators, developers, and process owners highlighted the alignment between SLAs, strategies, and implemented mechanisms and their consumption levels as essential conditions for achieving operational stability but acknowledged the difficulty in concretizing this alignment (C8). They emphasized that these conditions are addressed individually within each service. It is worth noting that in this case study, resource consumption limits are allocated to each service individually, but SLAs may overlap between services. The lack of wide alignment at the system level is considered a source of fragility for operators and an economic risk for process owner participants. One operator summarized the situation: "*The biggest challenge I face is trusting resilience mechanisms. I lack a complete understanding of the interplay between all the system's parts, I cannot ensure these mechanisms will align with what is required when handling a service disruption, in both their capability to keep the service up and to fit in the expected costs.*"

These factors echo the challenges of managing microservice resource consumption unveiled by previous research [43,48,51]. Yet, here, we observed this concern in the context of supporting processes, not within microservices. Again, the proposal of a simulation and projection mechanism (P3) to support the design and assessment of resource consumption was mentioned, which reinforces previous findings on the practitioners' need for systematic and virtualized approaches to design effective MSA operational strategies [19,35].

5 Discussion

The findings of this study suggest a continuity in the operational challenges experienced by practitioners, aligning with existing literature in software systems operations and MSA challenges. The need for reachable targets, systematic approaches and assessment methods as fundamental elements for building customers' trustworthiness has been suggested as a paramount factor in designing, implementing and operating reliable systems since the 1990s [11]. Similarly, economic sustainability is a constant in product development and operation [42]. The novelty lies in the perspective of resource consumption optimization due to environmental concerns. However, even here, the results have a direct impact on the economics of the product, thus on business motivations.

Also, we unveiled novel insights into MSA and hybrid-system interplay, notably the significant role of cohesion between these system parts, which may, in some cases, be unattainable due to their intrinsic characteristics. This insight allows us to advance the theoretical understanding of microservices operations within hybrid systems by linking this phenomenon to two theorized phenomena in distributed software engineering: the consensus problem [6,15] and the mixed-criticality problem [8]. On the one hand, system parts are independent components that collaborate to achieve a goal, requiring consensus when deciding on an event. On the other hand, each of these parts may be characterized by a different business or technical criticality. Beyond that, we identified collaboration and coordination factors behind those pointed out by the participants. The central place of coordination and the need for enforced alignment between the system's parts may encounter the organizational silos observed in MSA practices [29]. Therefore, questions arise about the practicability of the MSA's share-nothing philosophy.

Besides, we found that the concept of resilience in MSA extends beyond the technical implementation of mechanisms such as autoscaling or redundancy [18]. Here, the critical issue is not the availability of advanced resilience mechanisms but the lack of a unified approach to define, quantify, and enforce reliability objectives across a multi-service and multi-architecture system. Therefore, the challenge lies not in deploying resilience mechanisms, but in designing them to operate as a cohesive whole—a problem that existing practices and tools alone do not fully address. The shift from technical capability to systemic alignment represents the unaddressed frontier in MSA operational stability, where the complexity stems less from tooling and more from architectural and organizational misalignment. This frontier affects the EA's ability to effectively build service-oriented systems that align with the enterprise's goals.

We interpreted our study findings from the perspective of engineering practices. Therefore, there is room for alternative explanations. One plausible alternative is the effect of using a specific instance or combination of methodologies and frameworks, e.g., Agile, DevOps, and Waterfall, as the common factor identified in the above challenges is the coordination of system parts that directly depends on teams' coordination, which is influenced by the development and operation methodology adopted [37]. Indeed, the operational challenges observed may originate from insufficient DevOps adoption or its fragmented implementation. While DevOps, with its emphasis on cross-functional collaboration, is often viewed as synergistic with MSA, it is not inherently required for microservice development and operation [47,51]. The case studied exemplifies this: the organization's partial adoption of DevOps with a segregation of development and operations teams may amplify coordination challenges. In such contexts, the overlapping struggles of MSA and DevOps adoption may create a feedback loop, where gaps in one domain exacerbate difficulties in the other [44,47]. Nevertheless, a system-wide practices alignment seems required, which necessitates adapting development methods to encompass the entire system, including non-microservices components.

Another perspective for explanations may be the lack of literacy among practitioners on specific aspects of MSA [32]. Likewise, the impact of transferring practices from previous paradigms to MSA may influence some of the identified issues, as this practice may generate MSA anti-patterns [14].

A key lesson in conducting this study is flexibility, as the unpredictable nature of software failures, the substantial workload of operators, and the tight schedules of business stakeholders often disrupted this research execution, leading to context-shifting that needed restarting interviews and observations, which demanded patience and rigour. A second lesson is transparency. Industrial studies may face issues of secrecy that restrict researchers' access to precise descriptions of processes, goals, or motivations [21]. Software operation is sensitive to them, as they fear reputational damage by exposing weaknesses. Despite having worked with this organization on other research projects, building confidence and trust with participants remained a pivotal and time-consuming process. At the first contact with participants, we conveyed that our purpose was not to criticize individual practices or spy but to understand their reality and unveil the causes of the challenges they face, which they could assess by reviewing anonymized interview minutes, observation protocols, and this paper. Some initially reticent participants became more open to the study's conclusions, thanks to the policy of transparency we adopted. A third lesson is managing participants' subjective perceptions. We must distinguish between criticisms driven by discontent with the organization and objective assessments of operational reality. Data triangulation and immersive, on-site observations have proven essential in navigating this issue.

6 Evaluation

We relied on the quality criteria for evaluating exploratory case studies proposed in [38]. Therefore, we evaluated our study against its multivocality, rigour, reflexivity, credibility, and transferability.

We achieved *multivocality* by including participants with both technical and non-technical profiles, different backgrounds, and diverse viewpoints on operational stability-related processes. We maintained *rigour* by employing a systematic data collection and analysis approach, including a data triangulation strategy. Additionally, we maintained a "questions backlog," which gauged the need for more data and analysis; thus, being our saturation indicator. We achieved *reflexivity* by continuously auto-analyzing our interactions with participants, particularly considering the risks of unintentionally influencing their responses or actions, as we brought external knowledge and experience that may not have been present in the case. When in doubt, we cross-checked interview minutes and observation journals with those of other participants. If uncertainty persisted, we re-interviewed the participant to check for any influence; as a final recourse, we excluded the data from the analysis. We maintained the *credibility* of our conclusions through the multivocal and triangulated data collection and analysis approach we employed. Finally, *transferability* refers to the ability of a study's results to plausibly apply to other contexts. Indeed, case studies aim to produce theoretical generalizations, creating transferable concepts applicable to various contexts. To assess transferability, we first related our findings to existing literature. We then shared our results with non-participant practitioners from the health insurance (1) and real estate (1) domains to check whether our insights were recognizable and familiar to them. Their feedback confirmed that our findings resonated, unveiling a set of common concerns in the industry.

7 Conclusion and Future Work

This study examined challenges to the operational stability of microservices within hybrid systems through a longitudinal exploratory case study. We found that the coherence and coordination of stability attributes among a system's components are the primary factors influencing the effectiveness of operational stability strategies. Additionally, operational stability attributes are complex to estimate, underscoring the need for systematic approaches. Without such systematic approaches to translate high-level operational stability goals and requirements into cohesive, cross-service strategies, even well-implemented stability mechanisms risk failing to deliver effective system dependability and sustainability. This gap between localized stability tactics and holistic stability governance is where the next frontier of microservice operation lies. Future work will focus on developing metrics, indicators and interpretation models to support operational stability decisions in MSA.

Disclosure of Interests. The authors have no relevant financial or non-financial interests to disclose.

References

1. Avizienis, A., Laprie, J.C., Randell, B., Landwehr, C.: Basic concepts and taxonomy of dependable and secure computing. IEEE Trans. Dependable Secure Comput. **1**(1), 11–33 (2004)
2. AXELOS: Itil foundation, itil 4 edn. (2019)
3. Azad, N., Hyrynsalmi, S.: Devops critical success factors–a systematic literature review. Inf. Softw. Technol. **157**, 107150 (2023)
4. Balalaie, A., Heydarnoori, A., Jamshidi, P.: Migrating to cloud-native architectures using microservices: an experience report. In: Advances in Service-Oriented and Cloud Computing: Workshops of ESOCC 2015, Taormina, September 15-17, 2015, Revised Selected Papers 4, pp. 201–215. Springer (2016)
5. Balalaie, A., Heydarnoori, A., Jamshidi, P., Tamburri, D.A., Lynn, T.: Microservices migration patterns. Softw. Pract. Experience **48**(11), 2019–2042 (2018)
6. Barborak, M., Dahbura, A., Malek, M.: The consensus problem in fault-tolerant computing. ACM Comput. Surv. **25**(2), 171–220 (1993). https://doi.org/10.1145/152610.152612
7. Borsatti, D., et al.: Modeling digital twins of kubernetes-based applications. In: 2023 IEEE Symposium on Computers and Communications (ISCC), pp. 219–224 (2023).https://doi.org/10.1109/ISCC58397.2023.10217853
8. Burns, A., Davis, R.I.: A survey of research into mixed criticality systems. ACM Comput. Surv. (CSUR) **50**(6), 1–37 (2017)

9. Candea, G., Brown, A.B., Fox, A., Patterson, D.: Recovery-oriented computing: building multitier dependability. Computer **37**(11), 60–67 (2004)
10. Comuzzi, M., Kotsokalis, C., Spanoudakis, G., Yahyapour, R.: Establishing and monitoring slas in complex service based systems. In: 2009 IEEE International Conference on Web Services, pp. 783–790. IEEE (2009)
11. Dale, C.: Software reliability assessment-the need for process visibility. IFAC Proc. Vol. **23**(6), 77–82 (1990)
12. David, I., Bork, D., Kappel, G.: Circular systems engineering. Softw. Syst. Modeling, 1–15 (2024)
13. Dragoni, N., Lanese, I., Larsen, S.T., Mazzara, M., Mustafin, R., Safina, L.: Microservices: how to make your application scale. In: Perspectives of System Informatics: 11th International Andrei P. Ershov Informatics Conference, PSI 2017, Moscow, June 27-29, 2017, Revised Selected Papers 11, pp. 95–104. Springer (2018)
14. Farsi, H., Allaki, D., En-Nouaary, A., Dahchour, M.: Dealing with anti-patterns when migrating from monoliths to microservices: challenges and research directions. In: 2023 IEEE 6th International Conference on Cloud Computing and Artificial Intelligence: Technologies and Applications (CloudTech), pp. 1–8. IEEE (2023)
15. Fischer, M.J.: The consensus problem in unreliable distributed systems (a brief survey). In: Karpinski, M. (ed.) FCT 1983. LNCS, vol. 158, pp. 127–140. Springer, Heidelberg (1983). https://doi.org/10.1007/3-540-12689-9_99
16. Frey, S., Reich, C., Lüthje, C.: Key performance indicators for cloud computing slas. In: The Fifth International Conference on Emerging Network Intelligence, EMERGING, pp. 60–64 (2013)
17. Fritzsch, J., Bogner, J., Wagner, S., Zimmermann, A.: Microservices migration in industry: intentions, strategies, and challenges. In: 2019 IEEE International Conference on Software Maintenance and Evolution (ICSME), pp. 481–490. IEEE (2019)
18. Heinrich, R., et al.: Performance engineering for microservices: Research challenges and directions. In: Proceedings of the 8th ACM/SPEC on International Conference on Performance Engineering Companion, pp. 223–226. ICPE '17 Companion, Association for Computing Machinery, New York (2017). https://doi.org/10.1145/3053600.3053653
19. Jagadeesan, L.J., Mendiratta, V.B.: When failure is (not) an option: reliability models for microservices architectures. In: 2020 IEEE International Symposium on Software Reliability Engineering Workshops (ISSREW), pp. 19–24 (2020). https://doi.org/10.1109/ISSREW51248.2020.00031
20. Kieninger, A., Westernhagen, J., Satzger, G.: The economics of service level engineering. In: 2011 44th Hawaii International Conference on System Sciences, pp. 1–10. IEEE (2011)
21. Kontio, J., Bragge, J., Lehtola, L.: The focus group method as an empirical tool in software engineering. In: Guide to Advanced Empirical Software Engineering, pp. 93–116. Springer (2008)
22. Koziolek, H.: Sustainability evaluation of software architectures: a systematic review. In: Proceedings of the joint ACM SIGSOFT conference–QoSA and ACM SIGSOFT symposium–ISARCS on Quality of software architectures–QoSA and architecting critical systems–ISARCS, pp. 3–12 (2011)
23. Lago, P., Koçak, S.A., Crnkovic, I., Penzenstadler, B.: Framing sustainability as a property of software quality. Commun. ACM **58**(10), 70–78 (2015)
24. Lankhorst, M.: Enterprise architecture at work: modelling, communication, and analysis. Springer (2017)

25. Lawani, A.: Critical realism: what you should know and how to apply it. Qual. Res. J. **21**(3), 320–333 (2021)
26. Lewis, J., Fowler, M.: Microservices (2014). https://martinfowler.com/articles/microservices.html
27. Li, B., Peng, X., Xiang, Q., Wang, H., Xie, T., Sun, J., Liu, X.: Enjoy your observability: an industrial survey of microservice tracing and analysis. Empir. Softw. Eng. **27**, 1–28 (2022)
28. Morais, G., Adda, M., Bork, D.: Companion repository. https://bit.ly/edoc87, companion repository for the paper titled "a decade of challenges: a practitioners exploratory study of microservices operational stability"
29. Morais, G., Adda, M., Bork, D.: Breaking down barriers: building sustainable microservices architectures with model-driven engineering. In: Proceedings of the ACM/IEEE 27th International Conference on Model Driven Engineering Languages and Systems, pp. 528–532 (2024)
30. Morais, G., Lemelin, E., Adda, M., Bork, D.: Enhancing API labelling with Bert and GPT: an exploratory study. In: International Conference on Enterprise Design, Operations, and Computing, pp. 169–182. Springer (2024)
31. Morais, G., Lemelin, E., Adda, M., Bork, D.: Large language models for API classification: an explorative study. In: 2025, EASE (2025)
32. Nogueira, V.L., Felizardo, F.S., Amaral, A.M., Assunção, W.K., Colanzi, T.E.: Insights on microservice architecture through the eyes of industry practitioners. In: 2024 IEEE International Conference on Software Maintenance and Evolution (ICSME), pp. 765–777. IEEE (2024)
33. Oppenheimer, D., Patterson, D.A.: Architecture and dependability of large-scale internet services. IEEE Internet Comput. **6**(5), 41–49 (2002)
34. Patterson, D., et al.: Recovery-oriented computing (roc): motivation, definition, techniques, and case studies. Tech. rep, Citeseer (2002)
35. Pietrantuono, R., Russo, S., Guerriero, A.: Testing microservice architectures for operational reliability. Softw. Test. Verification Reliabil. **30**(2), e1725 (2020)
36. Raghunandan, A., Kalasapura, D., Caesar, M.: Digital twinning for microservice architectures. In: ICC 2023 - IEEE International Conference on Communications, pp. 3018–3023 (2023). https://doi.org/10.1109/ICC45041.2023.10279802
37. Raj, P., Sinha, P.: Project management in era of agile and devops methodlogies. In: International Conference on Applied Sciences. vol. 9, pp. 1024–1033 (2015)
38. Ralph, P., et al.: Empirical standards for software engineering research (2020). https://arxiv.org/abs/2010.03525
39. Roehm, T., Tiarks, R., Koschke, R., Maalej, W.: How do professional developers comprehend software? In: 2012 34th International Conference on Software Engineering (ICSE), pp. 255–265. IEEE (2012)
40. Salama, M., Bahsoon, R.: A taxonomy for architectural stability. In: Proceedings of the 31st Annual ACM Symposium on Applied Computing, pp. 1354–1357 (2016)
41. Salama, M., Bahsoon, R., Lago, P.: Stability in software engineering: survey of the state-of-the-art and research directions. IEEE Trans. Softw. Eng. **47**(7), 1468–1510 (2019)
42. Sauvé, J., Marques, F., Moura, A., Sampaio, M., Jornada, J., Radziuk, E.: SLA design from a business perspective. In: Schönwälder, J., Serrat, J. (eds.) DSOM 2005. LNCS, vol. 3775, pp. 72–83. Springer, Heidelberg (2005). https://doi.org/10.1007/11568285_7
43. Soldani, J., Tamburri, D.A., Van Den Heuvel, W.J.: The pains and gains of microservices: a systematic grey literature review. J. Syst. Softw. **146**, 215–232 (2018)

44. Su, R., Li, X., Taibi, D.: From microservice to monolith: a multivocal literature review. Electronics **13**(8), 1452 (2024)
45. Tsiakis, T., Katsaros, P.: Hands on dependability economics. In: 2009 Second International Conference on Dependability, pp. 117–121 (2009). https://doi.org/10.1109/DEPEND.2009.24
46. Walter, J., Okanović, D., Kounev, S.: Mapping of service level objectives to performance queries. In: Proceedings of the 8th ACM/SPEC on International Conference on Performance Engineering Companion, pp. 197–202 (2017)
47. Waseem, M., Liang, P., Shahin, M.: A systematic mapping study on microservices architecture in devops. J. Syst. Softw. **170**, 110798 (2020)
48. Waseem, M., Liang, P., Shahin, M., Di Salle, A., Márquez, G.: Design, monitoring, and testing of microservices systems: the practitioners' perspective. J. Syst. Softw. **182**, 111061 (2021)
49. Washizaki, H.: Guide to the software engineering body of knowledge (SWEBOK). IEEE Comput. Soc. version 4.0 edn. (2024). https://www.computer.org/swebok
50. Wieringa, R.: Design science methodology for information systems and software engineering. Lecture Notes in Computer Science, Springer, Heidelberg (2014). https://doi.org/10.1007/978-3-662-43839-8_20
51. Zhou, X., et al.: Revisiting the practices and pains of microservice architecture in reality: an industrial inquiry. J. Syst. Softw. **195**, 111521 (2023)
52. Zimmermann, O.: Microservices tenets: agile approach to service development and deployment. Comput. Sci. Res. Dev. **32**, 301–310 (2017)

Discovery Rules Related to Acquiring Stakeholders for the Fractal Enterprise Model

Ilia Bider[1,2(✉)] and Erik Perjons[1]

[1] Stockholm University, Borgarfjordsgatan 12, Kista, 164 55 Stockholm, Sweden
{ilia,perjons}@dsv.su.se
[2] University of Tartu, Ülikooli 18, 50090 Tartu, Estonia

Abstract. The paper introduces rules that help identify and depict in a model enterprise elements that are aimed at acquiring stakeholders, e.g., customers, employees, and partners. Without these activities, a business service cannot be provided. The modeling is done using a specific enterprise modeling technique called Fractal Enterprise Model (FEM). However, the result can be of interest to researchers and practitioners using other modeling techniques. Though the processes of acquiring stakeholders are discussed in the literature, not all important elements of these processes are depicted. The type of rules presented in this paper follows our suggestion to consider the so-called discovery power of enterprise modeling languages alongside their expressive power.

Keywords: stakeholder · autopoiesis · discovery power · enterprise model · Fractal Enterprise Model · FEM

1 Introduction

For a service to be operational, it needs to have customers. In addition, most services require engagement of people, be it the employees of the company that provide the service, or employees of a partner. Without proper management of these stakeholders, the service cannot be provided. This work is devoted to modeling activities related to acquiring stakeholders. Such a model can help to detect problems in these activities and find a way to correct them.

The paper explores the concept of discovery power introduced in our previous paper [1]. The concept is informally defined as the "Degree of help provided by the structure of enterprise modeling language to expand a partly built model or fill gaps in it." What the enterprise modeling language helps to discover depends on the language, as the discovery power differs for different languages. For practical purposes, the discovery power of an enterprise modeling language can be represented as a set of rules that guide the modeler on what else can be found and depicted based on what is already depicted in the model[1].

[1] The term degree used in the informal definition does not imply that discovery power is a quantitative parameter. As the discovery power of different modeling languages lies in different

J. Barateiro et al. (Eds.): EDOC 2025 Workshops, LNBIP 571, pp. 420–434, 2026.
https://doi.org/10.1007/978-3-032-16234-2_34

In this paper, we investigate only one enterprise modeling language, the so-called Fractal Enterprise Model (FEM) [2, 3], and only in one aspect of discovery power - adding to the model activities that are related to the environment. FEM was chosen because it is our invention; thus, we have enough knowledge about its structure, and we have experience in using it in enterprise modeling. Connection to the environment was chosen because activities related to it are seldom depicted in enterprise models. This work continues our efforts to create a set of discovery rules that were formulated in [1]. This work is not the first one in this direction, as we already have one paper devoted to the topic of discovery rules, where we have presented the rules for adding elements related to tacit knowledge [4].

FEM has a form of a directed graph with two main types of nodes, *processes,* and *assets*, where the arrows (edges) from assets to processes show which assets are used in which processes, and arrows from processes to assets show which processes help to have specific assets in "healthy" and working order. The arrows are labeled with meta-tags that show how a given asset is used, e.g., *workforce, reputation, infrastructure*, etc., or how a given process helps to have the given assets "in order", i.e., *acquire, maintain*, or *retire.*

An organization normally has many connections with the environment in which it operates. In this paper, we will consider a special type of connection to the environment related to the organization being an autopoietic system. Autopoiesis is a process of a system constantly rebuilding itself from the elements taken from its environment. This process exists in living systems [5] and organizational systems. For example, an organization should substitute workers who leave it, e.g., retire or move to a different geographical region. It should also substitute its equipment when it no longer satisfies production.

The environment for a given organization includes components from which the organization can obtain elements to substitute the elements that disappear or those that can no longer function properly. If the supply of materials to rebuild itself is limited, there can be competition for the resources. In such a case, competitors are part of the organization's environment and must be represented in its model. Competition can be, for example, for customers or workers to employ. The discovery rules presented in this paper guide the FEM modeler to add elements related to the environment in order for an organization to be able to rebuild itself. In particular, in this paper, we will discuss the rules of adding elements connected to acquiring stakeholders – customers, employees, and partners.

The rest of the paper is structured according to the following plan. In Sect. 2, we give a background to our research, i.e., knowledge base, research approach, and introduction to FEM. In Sect. 3, we discuss the types and the format of discovery rules. In Sect. 4, we present and discuss the discovery rules related to acquiring stakeholders. In Sect. 5, we give an overview of related literature. In Sect. 6, we draw some conclusions and suggest future directions for our research.

---

areas, a quantitative description does not make much sense. The high discovery in the area that lies outside the current project goals will be irrelevant to the project. For example, a language with good discovery power related to the business environment may not be useful for a project that is not intended to depict the environment.

2 Research Background

2.1 Autopoiesis

We give a very short introduction to the topic using the work of Zeleny [6]. There are three general types of processes in an autopoietic system: (1) Degradation, (2) Production, and (3) Bonding. Production is a process of creating new components. Bonding is a process of introducing new components into the system structure. Degradation is a natural process of components aging and falling out of the system structure, which requires the production of new components to be bound into the structure. The specific meaning of these generic processes depends on the system in question. In a post-review by Zeleny [7], there are several examples of the instantiation of the generic process.

2.2 Introduction to Fractal Enterprise Model

As FEM is not a widely spread enterprise modeling technique, we will present the basic concepts and the relations between them used in this technique based on an example represented in Fig. 1. This example is a partial model of the company called *IbisSoft*, which was co-founded by the first author in 1989. The model reflects the company in its first years when it functioned as a distributor of the high-level software development tool called JAM from the US-based company called JYACC. The main business was selling JAM licenses and helping customers with software development projects that used JAM. The simplified model in Fig. 1 concerns only sales and support of JAM licenses.

FEM has four concepts represented by shapes, two of which are used to present internal elements of the enterprise, and two are used to represent the environment. The shapes used for representing internal elements are *process* and *asset*, and there could be two types of relations between them: *used in* and *managed by*.

A process, depicted as an oval, represents a repetitive behavior (see Fig. 1), i.e., a business process or a service. A process can be marked as a primary process – a behavior that produces some value for external stakeholders and for which the organization gets paid in one way or another. Such a process is visually represented with a double line border (see Fig. 1). An asset, depicted as a rectangle, represents a set of things that are engaged in the behavior and play a specific role in it, thus ensuring that the behavior continues to be repetitive (see Fig. 1). An asset can be marked as tacit – something that resides in the heads of people related to the given process. Such an asset is visually represented as having a dashed border (see Fig. 1). A process or an asset has a label attached to it that explains the kind of behavior that the process represents or the kind of elements the asset has. The labels are not standardized and are set by the modeler. Visually, the label is placed inside the shape that represents a process or asset.

A *used in* relation between a process and an asset means that the asset plays a certain role in the process. The relation is visually represented by an arrow with a solid line that goes from the asset to the process (see Fig. 1). A *managed by* relation between an asset and a process means that the process changes the set, i.e., adds or removes elements or changes their properties (see Fig. 1). The relation is visually represented by an arrow with a dashed line that goes from the process to the asset. To identify which role the asset plays in the process or how the process changes the asset, a label is added to the relation. The set of labels is standardized; more exactly, there are eight labels that can be added to a *used in* relation and three labels that can be added to a *managed by* relation. The latter are *Acquire*, *Maintain*, and *Retire*. *Acquire* means, as mentioned above, that new elements are added to the asset, *Retire* means that elements are removed from the asset, and *Maintain* means that elements are changed so that they can continue to be part of the asset engaged in the respective process.

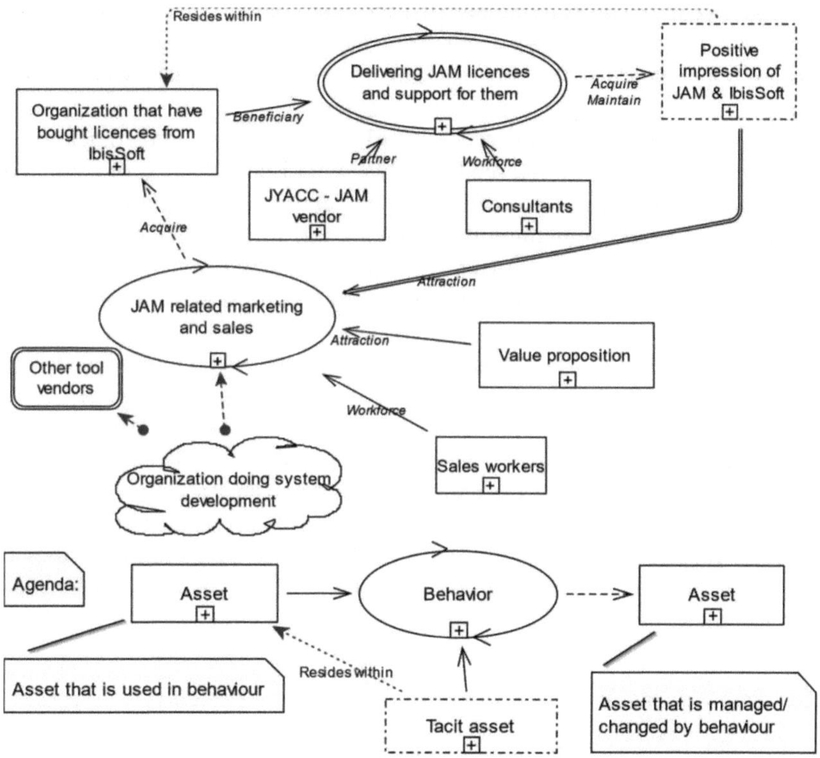

Fig. 1. An example of a FEM diagram

Note that the relation that connects the asset "*Positive impression of JAM & IbisSoft*" with the process "*Positive impression of JAM & IbisSoft*" has a double line. A double line means a transitive relation, e.g., there are some elements and connections that are not shown in the diagram.

The two concepts that are introduced to represent the organizational environments are:

- External pool – a set of the same type of elements as in assets, which is represented by a cloud shape, see Fig. 1. The label inside the external pool describes its content.
- External actor, which is represented by a rectangle with rounded corners. An external actor is an agent, like a company or person, acting outside the boundary of the organization in question. It can be a competitor or collaborator. The label inside the

external actor describes its nature. If the shape represents a set of external actors, the box has a double line, see Fig. 1.

To connect the environmental concepts to other elements of a model, a new relation *drawing/adding* has been introduced. It can connect a process to a pool, an external actor to a pool, or connect two pools. The visual representation is an arrow with a dashed blue line and a rounded tail; see Fig. 1. If the arrow points to a pool, the arrow tail shows who added elements to the pool. In the opposite direction, it shows who draws elements from the pool to convert them to their assets. This kind of relation can also connect two pools to show the movement of elements from one pool to another. The labels on these relations are not standardized; a modeler can set any text to explain what the relation represents.

Besides the *drawing/adding* relation, FEM introduces two other relations: *inspects/monitors* and *association*, see Fig. 1. We will discuss the first of them in one of the next sessions. The relation *association* has no definite meaning; it is used whenever there is a need to express something that is impossible to express with other relations. Visually, an *association* is represented by an arrow with a blue dotted line. This relation can be symmetrical – an arrow on both sides of the connection, or asymmetrical – an arrow only on one side.

A straightforward way of building an FEM that represents the internal structure of an organization is to start from a primary process, find all assets engaged in it, find processes that manage these assets, and repeat the search for assets for the management processes. Thus, building the model can be viewed as alternatively applying two types of archetypes (or patterns): a process-assets archetype and an asset-processes archetype. The archetypes will be discussed in more detail in one of the next sessions. In the end, we will get a recursively built graph that represents the operational activities of the organization in question. The idea of *recursion* is represented by the term *fractal* in the modeling technique name; see [2, 3].

2.3 Research Approach

The goal of this research is to develop a set of rules that can help a FEM modeler discover and depict activities related to acquiring stakeholders. Therefore, it is quite natural to choose the Design Science (DS) paradigm [8, 9] as a research approach. DS focuses on looking for generic solutions for problems, known and unknown. The result of a DS research project can be a "solution" to a problem in the terminology of [9] or an "artifact" in the terminology of [8]. Alternatively, the result can be in the form of "negative knowledge", stating that a particular approach is not appropriate for solving certain kinds of problems.

The artifact/solution that we want to develop – a set of rules – is a complement to FEM that allows a modeler who uses this modeling technique to find and add to the model new elements related to acquiring stakeholders. The knowledge base that we use for this DS project was obtained during our engagement in building FEM models for various domains and various purposes.

Roughly speaking, a DS project can be represented as an iterative two-phase process, where in each iteration, the design phase is followed by the testing phase of the design in practice. The testing phase provides the basis for the design phase in the next iteration. The work presented in this paper covers the *design phase* of the *first iteration.*

2.4 The Discovery Power of FEM

As was stated in the introduction, the discovery power is connected to specific means to express ideas in the given enterprise modeling language. In FEM, to such specific ideas belong the central concepts, such as *process* – repetitive behavior, *asset* – a set of things or actors that participate in the behavior, as well as specific labels on the relations, e.g., *Workforce, Partner, Acquire*, etc. In addition, there are essential subclasses for the central concept, e.g., tacit assets, that can increase the discovery power of FEM.

3 Types and Format of Discovery Rules

3.1 FEM Archetypes as Discovery Rules

To make the work of building a fractal model more systematic, [2] has introduced archetypes (or patterns) as fragments from which a particular model can be built. An archetype is a template defined as a fragment of a model where labels inside ovals (processes) and rectangles (assets) are omitted, but arrows are labeled. Instantiating an archetype means putting the fragment inside the model and labeling ovals and rectangles; it is also possible to add elements absent from the archetype or omit some elements that are present in the archetype.

FEM has two types of archetypes: the process-assets archetypes and the asset-processes archetype. A process-assets archetype represents the kinds of assets that can be used in a given category of processes. There are several archetypes of this sort. Figure 2 presents a so-called generic process-assets archetype, which can be applied to any process. There are also specific process-assets archetypes [2].

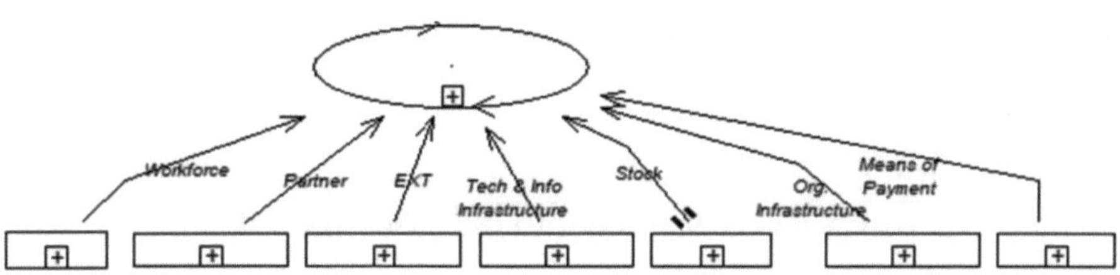

Fig. 2. A generic process-assets archetype

The asset-processes archetype shows the kinds of processes that are aimed at changing the given category of assets. There is only one such archetype, which is presented in Fig. 3.

The whole FEM graph can be built by the alternative application of these two types of archetypes, representing self-similar patterns on different scales. A modeler usually starts with a *primary* process – a process that produces value for an external beneficiary, and

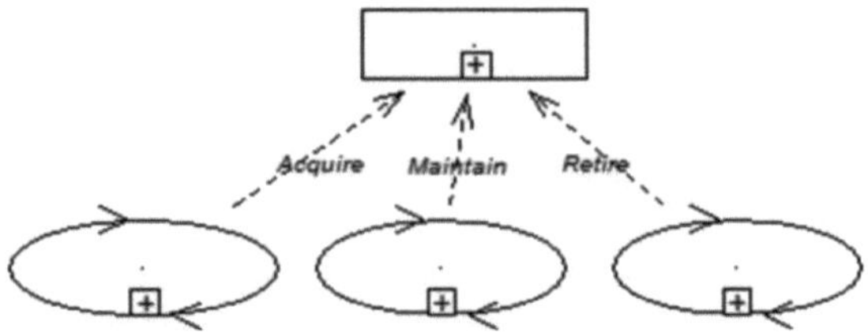

Fig. 3. Asset-processes archetype

continues down with finding assets needed for this process and then finding *supporting* processes aimed at managing these assets.

An archetype can be considered a discovery rule. Having a process of a certain type in a model, an archetype can be used to find all assets that are needed for it to run smoothly. Alternatively, having an asset in the model, the asset-processes archetype can be used to find all processes that are needed for maintaining this asset. Also, having an asset in the model can initiate a search for where else it can be used, having some process-asset archetype in mind. In this paper, we will not be looking at discovery rules that can be derived from the archetypes, but will consider rules that are not connected to them.

3.2 Format of Discovery Rules

In this paper, we use the discovery rules format that was introduced in [4]. Namely, a discovery rule represents a fragment of FEM, where elements that should be added are highlighted. An example of such a rule that will be explained in the next section is presented in Fig. 4. Concepts that should be added have the rose background, and relations that should be added are represented by thicker arrows.

Note that labels in the shapes of a discovery rule are generic. They are used to make the rules understandable. When applying the rule, these labels should be disregarded and substituted with more specific labels already assigned to the elements of the model being built. The rule should be complemented by discussing how to find out whether the addition exists in reality. Typical methods for getting relevant information are interviews, surveys, and facilitating workshops.

4 Discovery Rules Related to Acquiring Stakeholders

Stakeholders in FEM are assets that can fulfill the role of *Beneficiary* (e.g., a customer), *Workforce*, or *Partner*, see [2]. A stakeholder can be acquired from outside or from the inside of an organization. In this paper, we consider acquiring stakeholders from outside, as it is related to the autopoietic nature of an organization. A generic pattern of acquiring stakeholders from outside is presented in Fig. 5, left side.

This pattern can be derived from the FEM archetypes and the fact that the stakeholders need to be acquired from outside the organization. As we can see from Fig. 5 left side, the essential asset for acquiring stakeholders is "*Value proposition*", which is managed by the process of "*Managing value proposition*". Not all connections of this process can be derived from archetypes; thus, there is a need for discovery rules. As the rules differ depending on the type of stakeholder, we split the pattern in Fig. 5, left side, into three different patterns, one of which is shown in Fig. 5, right side, and the other two are shown in Fig. 6. We discussed the discovery rules for each of them in the subsections below.

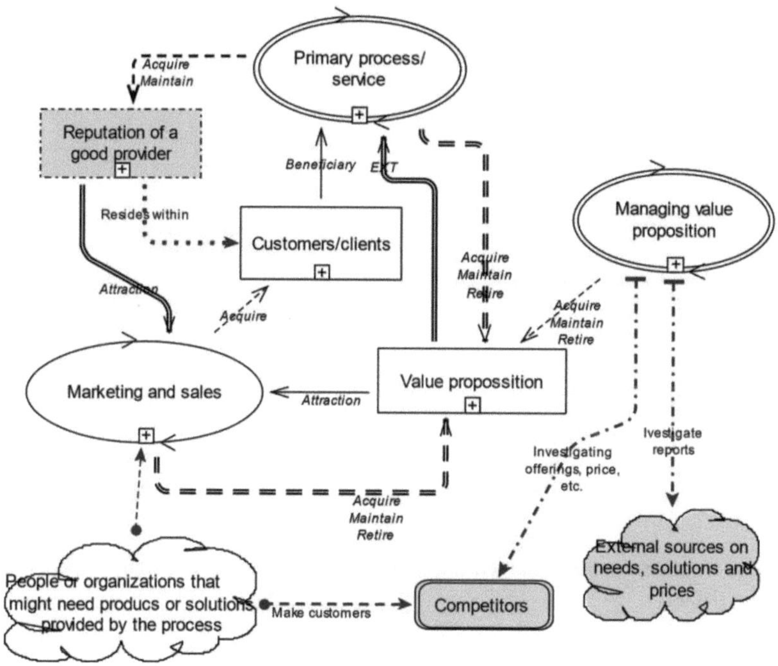

Fig. 4. Acquiring customers

4.1 Acquiring Customers

A discovery rule that concerns acquiring customers is presented in Fig. 4. Besides the elements that exist in Fig. 5 on the right, there are additional elements that can be added to the model. These elements consist of three additional concepts: (1) Tacit asset – "Reputation of a good provider"; (2) External actor – "Competitors"; and (3) External pool – "External sources on needs, solutions, and prices".

"Reputation of a good provider" resides in the "heads" of the asset "Customer/clients," which is shown by the association arrow, and it is acquired and maintained by the "Primary process/service", which is shown by the corresponding *managed by* link. Both links are highlighted, which means that they should be added when the rule is applied. Before adding this tacit asset, the modeler should investigate whether the existing customers are quite satisfied and are ready to talk about their satisfaction. If the fact is established, then this tacit asset can be used in the process "Marketing and sales" as an *Attraction.* This is shown by the transitive *used in* arrow with the label *Attraction.* The factual existence of this arrow should be verified by talking with existing customers to determine whether they are talking about their satisfaction with the representatives of other organizations. A more detailed model of how it can happen is presented in [4], which presents one way in which this transitive relation can appear.

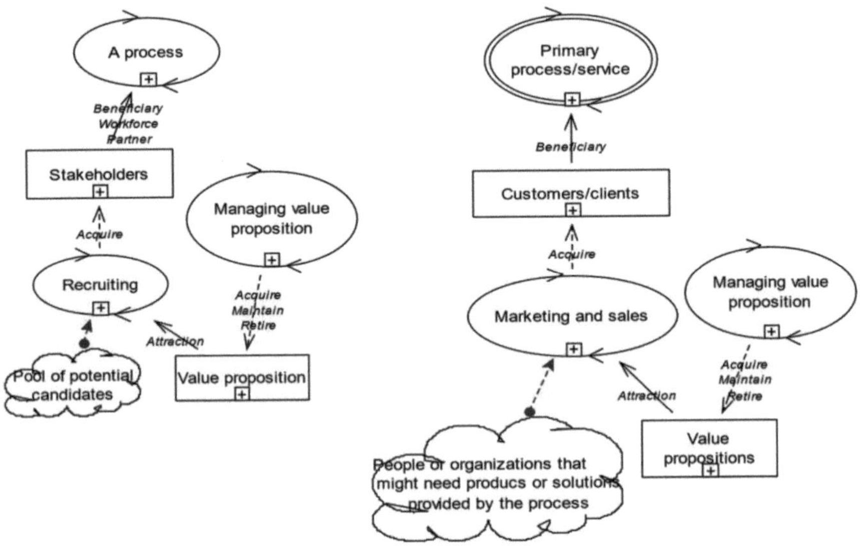

Fig. 5. Left - a generic model of acquiring stakeholders from outside; right – specialization of the model on the left

The external actor "Competitors" is an important element of the environment, as it draws new customers from the same pool as the enterprise that we model. Therefore, it is important to understand what the competitors deliver and at what price. The investigation of competitors is represented by a new type of arrow, *Inspects/Monitors,* that goes from the process "Managing value proposition" to the external actor "Competitors". This arrow shows that the process observes the element to which the arrow points to get some information needed for decision-making. The arrow is dash-dotted and is blue. The starting point is always a process, while the arrow can point to any concept that the process investigates. Investigation is done in a way that does not change the object of investigation. The presence of such a relationship can be established by talking to people who are engaged in the development of a value proposition.

Information on what competitors offer can be obtained not only from observing the competitors' offers but also from literature, e.g., professional periodicals. This fact is represented in Fig. 4 by the pool "External sources on needs, solutions and prices" and an *Inspects/Monitors* arrow from the process "Managing value proposition" to this pool. Whether these elements should be added to the model needs to be verified by talking to the people responsible for creating the value proposition.

Besides three new concepts and related to them arrows, Fig. 4 has three additional highlighted transitive arrows: (1) the *managed by* arrow between the process "Marketing

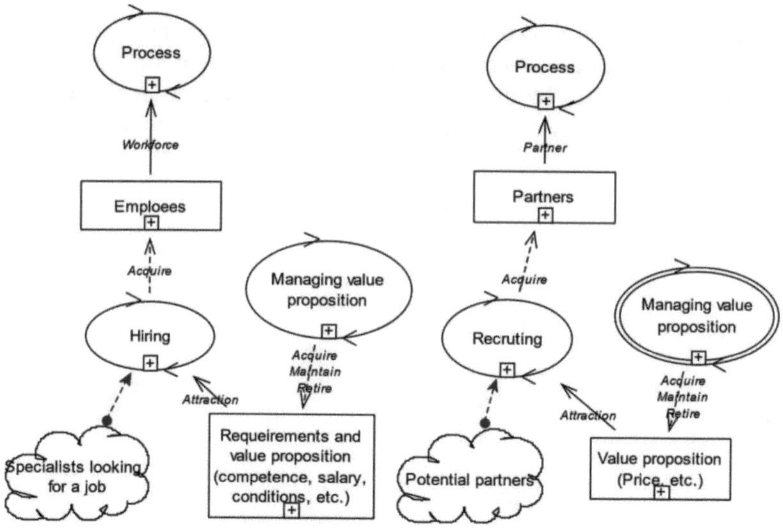

Fig. 6. Two more specializations for the generic model from Fig. 5, left.

and sales" and the asset "Value proposition"; (2) the *used in* arrow between "Value proposition" and "Primary process/service" labeled as EXT; (3) the *managed by* arrow between "Primary process/service" and "Value proposition". These arrows can be added to the model if their existence is established. While establishing that these arrows exist, the way in which they can be realized can also be established. Thus, instead of putting transitive arrows in the model, the dependencies can be shown in a normal way, i.e., having a set of concepts connected by nontransitive arrows.

The transitive arrow (1) means that marketing and sales people can have suggestions on changing the "Value proposition" based on their talking to potential customers. The transitive arrow (2) means that "Value proposition" should indirectly function as *EXT* - EXecutable Template - for "Primary process/service". If this is not the case, the enterprise has a problem in that what it delivers is not the same as what it promises. The transitive arrow (3) means that the experience of delivering products/services may affect the value proposition. Whether this is a fact and how it is done is for the modeler to establish. The modeler should substitute the transitive arrow with a chain of nontransitive arrows connecting intermediate processes and assets.

Note that Fig. 4 presents a generalized discovery rule that can be split into several rules. This is because even when one of the suggested additions does not prove to be true, other suggestions can still be incorporated into the model under development.

4.2 Acquiring Employees

The rule concerning employees is presented in Fig. 7. It has one new concept and two arrows that connect it to other concepts, and two additional *Inspects/Monitors* arrows that connect already existing concepts.

The new concept represents indirect competitors that are also looking for employees of the same kind. This is represented by the external actor "Other companies that look for the same kind of people" who is drawing elements from the common pool "Specialists looking for a job". The external actors should be investigated on the issue of what they offer to potential employees by the process "Managing value proposition" to create a value proposition that is not worse than the ones that are offered by the competitors.

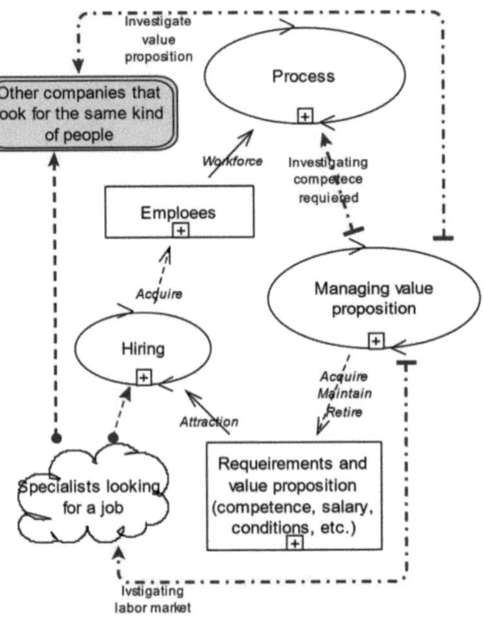

Fig. 7. Acquiring employees (workforce)

One *Inspects/Monitors* arrow concerns the investigation of what kind of expertise is required to be able to define the value proposition properly. The other arrow is the investigation of the labor market. Both arrows are attached to the process "Managing value proposition". The investigation of the labor market gives information on whether there is a lack of people with the expertise required or the market is oversaturated, e.g., in the case of depression. This information can be used in formulating the value proposition. For example, the requirement for expertise can be reduced, and education for new employees can be arranged. If the market is oversaturated, there is no need to define a salary higher than what competitors offer.

4.3 Acquiring Partners

Figure 8 presents a discovery rule for partners. The discovery rule suggests adding two arrows to the model; both are of the *Inspects/Monitors* type. The first arrow goes from the process "Managing value proposition" to the process "Process," and it aims to investigate the needs for a partner. The second goes from the process "Managing value proposition" to the pool of "Potential partners", and it aims at investigating offerings on the market.

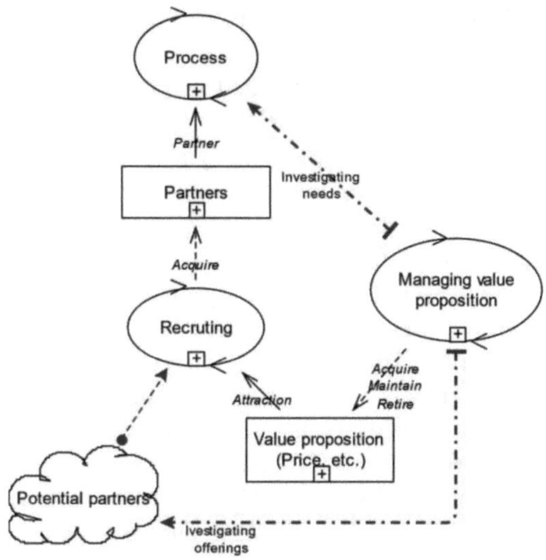

Fig. 8. Acquiring Partners

5 Related Literature

Several conceptual and analysis patterns have been proposed for representing stakeholders and their roles in enterprise models. In Fowler's analysis patterns [10], the concept Party Type represents stakeholders as parties assuming context-dependent roles. Hay's enterprise data model patterns [11] take a similar approach, using constructs such as Party, Party Role, and Party Relationship to capture stakeholders and their interactions. Sharp et al. [12] complement these structural approaches by offering practical techniques for identifying and classifying stakeholders in the early phases of system development, particularly in requirements engineering. While valuable for stakeholder recognition and prioritization, these approaches stop short of providing modeling constructs for how stakeholders are acquired and engaged over time.

OntoUML, based on the Unified Foundational Ontology (UFO) [13], provides ontologically rigorous constructs for modeling roles, relators, objects, and events. The underlying ontologies allow for precise representation of stakeholders, their context-dependent roles, and the events that establish stakeholder relationships. While OntoUML supports semantically robust modeling, it lacks reusable patterns specifically addressing stakeholder acquisition and engagement processes.

Enterprise architecture (EA) frameworks offer structured ways to describe organizations and their systems. One of the most widely used frameworks, ArchiMate [14], provides a modeling language for describing business, application, and technology layers. ArchiMate includes stakeholders as modeling elements and allows linking them to goals, requirements, and concerns. However, it mainly focuses on existing stakeholder relationships and strategic alignment. It does not show how changes in artefacts—such as adding digital features—can be used to attract or involve stakeholders. Other frameworks, such as TOGAF [15], include stakeholder analysis in planning phases, but primarily for communication purposes. Overall, EA frameworks describe stakeholders, but do not support modeling how these stakeholders are acquired, which is the focus of this paper.

The use of patterns is also well established in process modeling. The Workflow Patterns Initiative [16] and Event-Process Chains (EPC) [17] identify recurring process structures such as sequences, choices, and synchronizations. Pattern-Based Business Process Modeling [18] promotes constructing and evolving process models using reusable patterns. However, these patterns primarily address control flows and resource management, not stakeholder-related dynamics.

REA (Resources, Events, Agents) is an ontology-based model for enterprise systems, first proposed by McCarthy [19] and later developed further by scholars such as Hruby [20], Geerts and McCarthy [21]. The model structures business phenomena around three major concepts: resources (assets with economic value), events (changes in control over resources), and agents (parties exchanging resources). In Hruby's book Model-Driven Design Using Business Patterns [20], REA is presented not only as an accounting model but as a domain ontology and a pattern-based framework for building enterprise applications that are semantically rich, consistent, and reusable.

Although REA was primarily developed for modeling internal business processes and transactions, the model includes concepts that can be used to represent how stakeholders from the external environment are integrated into the organization, directly related to the discovery rules for acquiring customers, employees, and partners as discussed in FEM.

In Hruby's framework, this is handled through the following concepts:

- Economic Agents – actors external to the organization (e.g., customers, suppliers, workers) who can be engaged through contracts and commitments.
- Commitment and Contract Patterns – patterns used to model future obligations and relationships with external actors, which are central to stakeholder acquisition. An example is a contract where an external actor commits to delivering labor or receiving a service, representing an early phase of stakeholder engagement.
- Exchange and Conversion Process Patterns – patterns that allow modeling of how value exchanges (e.g., marketing and sales) are used to attract and transform external actors into internal assets.

What is missing in REA—but made explicit in FEM—is the representation of the external environment as a modeling entity, through concepts such as "external pools" and "external actors," and relationship types like draws from, adds to, and monitors. These are central to identifying how an organization, as an autopoietic system, interacts with its environment to continuously replenish and enhance its resources (e.g., workforce, customers).

While REA is often used as a stable foundational model for infrastructure and business logic, FEM's discovery rules aim to guide the modeler in uncovering what should be modeled in a given context, especially regarding the organization's relationships with its environment and stakeholder acquisition.

Stakeholder theory [22] has provided a foundational understanding of how organizations interact with diverse stakeholder groups. It conceptualizes organizations as networks of relationships between various actors—such as customers, employees, suppliers, and communities—and emphasizes the need to create value across this broader stakeholder ecosystem. While originally developed as a strategic and normative theory, its core premise has influenced fields such as business modeling and information systems.

In this paper, we build on this relational perspective by focusing not on managing existing stakeholder relationships, but on modeling how stakeholders are acquired and engaged over time. We do this by introducing a set of practical modeling rules based on the FEM. These rules help identify key elements like value propositions, external resources, and activities that bring in new stakeholders such as customers, employees, or partners. While existing modeling approaches often describe how things are today or show general process steps, our rules go further by showing how organizations can actively attract and involve new stakeholders acquired from their environment.

6 Conclusion and Plans for the Future

In this paper, we consider interactions between an enterprise and its environment when the enterprise needs to acquire some elements essential for its internal structure. The importance of such interactions was first understood in biological cybernetics under the concept of autopoiesis [5]. After that, the notion of autopoiesis was transferred to the world of enterprises by several authors, including Milan Zeleny [6].

Despite the importance of the concept of autopoiesis for business, this notion has not been extensively researched in the business literature in an explicit form. As far as enterprise modeling is concerned, we could not find any work that deals with this notion explicitly. However, as our literature analysis shows, some aspects of autopoiesis are discussed without introducing the term.

Our goal with this paper is to ensure that issues related to autopoiesis are not missed in enterprise models. Thus, we created a number of discovery rules that can help the modeler to properly represent these issues in the enterprise model. In this paper, we use a specific modeling technique to formulate the discovery rules. However, we believe that the rules presented can be used as an example of what needs to be depicted in an enterprise model, even when a modeler uses some other modeling language.

In this paper, we presented only the rules related to acquiring stakeholders. Stakeholders are not the only thing that an enterprise acquires from the environment. It also needs equipment, parts, etc. Creating discovery rules for other elements related to autopoiesis, as well as testing the rules while creating a model of an enterprise, is planned for the near future. The authors fully understand that without the rules having been successfully applied in the situation of modeling, their usefulness is just a hypothesis.

Acknowledgment. The authors are grateful to the anonymous reviewers whose comments helped improve the text. The work of the first author was partly supported by the Estonian Research Council (grant PRG1226).

Disclosure of Interests. The authors have no competing interests to declare that are relevant to the content of this article.

References

1. Bider, I., Perjons, E.: On the concept of discovery power of enterprise modeling languages and its relation to their expressive power. In Malinova Mandelburger, M., Guerreiro, S. (eds.) Advances in Enterprise Engineering XVII. EDEWC 2023, LNBIP, vol. 510, pp. 92–106 (2024)
2. Bider, I., Perjons, E., Elias, M., Johannesson, P.: A fractal enterprise model and its application for business development. SoSyM **16**(3), 663–689 (2017)
3. Bider, I., Perjons, E., Klyukina, V.: Tool support for fractal enterprise modeling. In: Domain-Specific Conceptual Modeling, pp. 205–229. Springer, Heidelberg (2022)
4. Bider, I., Perjons, E.: Discovery rules for depicting tacit knowledge usage and management in fractal enterprise models. In Řepa, V., Matulevičius, R., Laurenzi, E. (eds.) Perspectives in Business Informatics Research. BIR 2024. LNBIP, vol. 529, pp. 209–224. Springer, Heidelberg (2024)
5. Maturana, H.R., Varela, F.J.: Autopoiesis and Congnition: The Realization of the Living, Reidel, Dordrecht (1980)
6. Zeleny, M.: On social nature of autopoietic system. In Boulding, K., Khalil, E. (eds.) Evolution, Order and Complexity, pp. 122–145. Taylor & Francis Group (1996)
7. Cadenas, H., Arnold, M.: The autopoiesis of social systems and its criticisms. Constr. Found. **10**(2) (2015)
8. Hevner, A., March, S.T., Park, J.: Design science in information systems research. MIS Q. **28**(1), 75–105 (2004)
9. Bider, I., Johannesson, P., Perjons, E.: Design science research as movement between individual and generic situation-problem-solution spaces. In: Organizational Systems. An Interdisciplinary Discourse, pp. 35–61. Springer, Heidelberg (2013)
10. Fowler, M.: Analysis Patterns: Reusable Object Models. Addison-Wesley Professional, Boston (2015)
11. Hay, D.: Data Model Patterns: Conventions of Thought. Dorset House (2011)
12. Sharp, H., Finkelstein, A. ., Galal, G.: Stakeholder identification in the requirements engineering process. In: 10th International Workshop on Database and Expert Systems Applications, DEXA'99, pp.387–391 (1999)
13. Guizzardi, G., Wagner, G., Almeida, J., Guizzardi, R.: Towards ontological foundations for conceptual modeling: the unified foundational ontology (UFO) story. Appl. Ontol. **10**(3–4), 259–271 (2015)
14. The open group: ArchiMate® 3.2 Specification. In: The Open Group (2022). https://publications.opengroup.org/standards/archimate/specifications/c226
15. The open group: TOGAF Standard, Version 9.2. Van Haren Publishing (2018)
16. Russell, N., van der Aalst, W., Ter Hofstede, A.: Workflow Patterns: The Definitive Guide. MIT Press, Cambridge (2015)
17. Scheer, A.-W.: ARIS - Business Process Modeling. Springer, Heidelberg (2000)
18. Weber, B., Reichert, M., Rinderle-Ma, S.: Change Patterns and Change Support Features in Process-Aware Information Systems (2008)
19. McCarthy, W.: The REA accounting model: a generalized framework for accounting systems in a shared data environment. Account. Rev. **57**(3), 554–578 (1982)
20. Hruby, P.: Model-Driven Design Using Business Patterns. Springer, Heidelberg (2006)
21. Geerts, G., McCarthy, W.: An ontological analysis of the economic primitives of the extended-REA enterprise information architectures. Int. J. Account. Inf. Syst. **3**(1), 1–16 (2002). https://doi.org/10.1016/S1467-0895
22. Freeman, R.: Strategic Management: A Stakeholder Approach. Pitman Publishing, Boston (1984)

Tool Presentations

FEM Viewer Version 2: How Much Functionality Should Be Given to the Experts?

Ilia Bider[1,2(✉)] and Joonatan Ehlvest[2]

[1] Stockholm University, Borgarfjordsgatan 12, Kista, 164 55 Stockholm, Sweden
ilia@dsv.su.se

[2] University of Tartu, Ülikooli 18, 50090 Tartu, Estonia

Abstract. The paper discusses the new version of the FEM viewer, which gives business experts the possibility to change the package of models created by a modeling expert(s). The paper concerns a special kind of models, so-called Fractal Enterprise Models (FEM); however, the functionality given to business experts can be reproduced for other modeling languages/techniques. The new version of FEM viewer, which runs on the web and does not require any installation on the experts' computers, allows them to assign characteristics to elements of models by using background colors and border colors. What each color represents is agreed upon between modeling experts and business experts; the meaning of the colors is fixed by creating special sheets that explain the meaning of each color. The authors consider that this functionality could be used by business experts, even those who are not acquainted with enterprise modeling. The only requirement is that they understand the models created for their own business by a modeling expert(s).

Keywords: Modeling tools · Fractal Enterprise Model · FEM

1 Introduction

This paper discusses the functionality of the new version of the FEM viewer [1, 2], where FEM stands for Fractal Enterprise Model [3]. This version gives the business experts some functionality to change the model. This functionality is quite limited, based on the assumption that the business experts may not be familiar with modeling languages and have no time to learn sophisticated tools. The only requirement for them is that they understand the model of their own business, built by the business modeling experts, in cooperation with them.

The functionality given to business experts, for example, allows them to decide which component of the business does not work satisfactorily, and how many resources, in terms of money, time, and effort, are needed to improve the situation. The FEM viewer version 2 [4] extends the functionality of the previous version of the FEM viewer [2], which only allowed the business experts to study the package of interconnected models built by modeling experts without producing any changes in them.

The FEM viewer is a web-based tool that does not require installing any software on the computers used by the business experts. It, however, requires a Linux server running

J. Barateiro et al. (Eds.): EDOC 2025 Workshops, LNBIP 571, pp. 437–447, 2026.
https://doi.org/10.1007/978-3-032-16234-2_36

the software available from GitHub [2, 4]. It allows exporting models from the FEM toolkit [5] and importing them to the FEM viewer. The first version of FEM viewer required exporting an XML file, plus graphical representations of all exported models in the SVG format. Version 2.0 requires exporting only an XML file, and it builds all models from information in it. FEM viewer 2 also allows exporting the XML file that includes the changes made in the viewer, and importing it back to the FEM toolkit.

The FEM toolkit [5] is a workstation-based tool that allows the modeling expert to build a package of FEM models that represent the whole or a part of the business. FEM toolkit is a Windows-based tool, but it can also run under MAC and Linux operating systems. The FEM toolkit can be freely downloaded and used [6].

The goal of this paper is to present new functionality of the FEM viewer, which allows business experts to change the models created by the modeling experts. This functionality is not tightly coupled with the Fractal Enterprise Model, and can be applied to any enterprise modeling language and a tool that supports it. However, to be understood, we include in this paper the minimum description of FEM, which is needed to understand the ideas behind the new version of the FEM viewer.

The rest of the paper follows the following plan. In Sect. 2, we describe the relevant features of FEM and the FEM toolkit using an example. In Sect. 3, we describe the functionality of the FEM viewer that allows a business expert to change the models. Section 4 contains concluding remarks and plans for the future.

2 Fractal Enterprise Model and FEM Toolkit

2.1 Short Overview of Fractal Enterprise Model

In this chapter, we will give the readers some ideas on the Fractal Enterprise Model using the model presented in Fig. 1. The model represents the activities of internal IT support expressed in FEM. FEM has four shapes and several types of connections between them. Two of the shapes represent internal elements of the organization being modeled, and the other two represent the context. In this paper, we will only use the internal elements, which is enough for our task to show which editing possibilities exist in FEM viewer version 2.

The shapes used for representing internal elements are *process* and *asset*, and there could be two types of relations between them: *used in* and *managed by*. A process, depicted as an oval, represents a repetitive behavior (see Fig. 1). An asset, depicted as a rectangle, represents a set of things that are engaged in the behavior and play a specific role in it, thus ensuring that the behavior continues to be repetitive (see Fig. 1). An asset can be marked as tacit – something that resides in the heads of people related to the given process. Such an asset is visually represented as having a dashed border (see Fig. 1). A process or an asset has a label attached to it that explains the kind of behavior that the process represents or the kind of elements the asset has. The labels are not standardized and are set by the modeler. Visually, the label is placed inside the shape that represents a process or asset.

A *used in* relation between a process and an asset means that the asset plays a certain role in the process. The relation is visually represented by an arrow with a solid line that goes from the asset to the process (see Fig. 1). A *managed by* relation between an asset and a process means that the process changes the set that is represented by the asset, i.e., adds or removes elements or changes their properties (see Fig. 1). The relation is visually represented by an arrow with a dashed line that goes from the process to the asset. To identify which role the asset plays in the process or how the process changes the asset, a label is added to the relation. The set of labels is standardized; more exactly, there are eight labels that can be added to a *used in* relation and three labels that can be added to a *managed by* relation. The latter are *Acquire*, *Maintain*, and *Retire*.

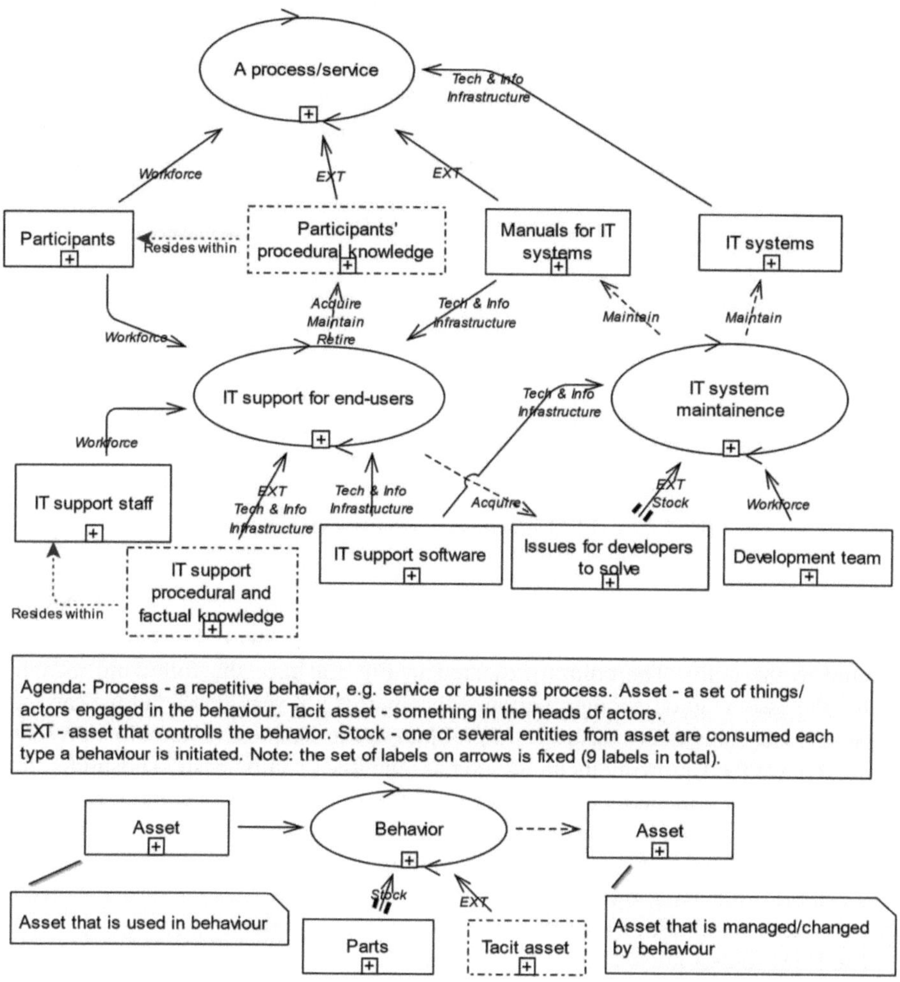

Fig. 1. FEM of IT support

If a *used in* relation has a label *Stock*, the arrow's tail gets two additional vertical lines, see Fig. 1. This label means that for each process run, the run consumes one or several elements of the assets. Thus, this asset requires constant filling up. Label *EXT* (EXecutable Template) means that the asset is a control element for the process, i.e., it has some instructions on completing the process runs. Other labels are self-explanatory. With this, we are finished with introducing FEM, more information on it can be found in [3, 5].

2.2 FEM Toolkit

The FEM toolkit is a tool for drawing FEM models and connecting them together that was created based on the ADOxx environment [7]. The connection between the models in the package is done through the elements that are repeated in more than one model using the so-called ghost feature, see [5]. In this paper, we are interested in other properties of the FEM toolkit, which make it tunable for different purposes. Namely, besides the models that can be created with the help of the FEM toolkit, it allows the creation of two other objects called: (1) *FEM subclassing*, and (2) *Border subclassing*. The examples of objects of these classes are presented in Fig. 2.

Fig. 2. (a) - FEM subclassing; (b) - Border subclassing

On the *FEM subclassing* object, the modeler can drop any shape and choose a background color for it. Then, using the label inside the shape he/she can assign a meaning to the color. The colors presented in Fig. 2a have the following meaning: green – the asset is good enough; yellow – the asset is not very good, but we can leave it as it is; rose – the asset constitutes a problem in the business. The colors presented in Fig. 2b have the following meaning: green – the asset can be easily substituted for a better one; yellow – the asset is difficult to substitute for a better one, but it is possible; red – the asset is difficult to substitute, i.e., the substitution requires a lot of resources (e.g., time and money). As we can see from the interpretation, we have two different ways to look at the asset: one concerns whether the asset satisfies the business, and the other concerns whether the asset is easy or difficult to substitute.

The FEM toolkit allows the modeler to attach a FEM subclass to any shape of the same sort, i.e., subclasses defined in Fig. 2a are related to assets. The same is true for subclasses in Fig. 2b. Note that nothing prevents us from defining subclasses for other shapes, e.g., processes. When the subclass is attached, the background color of the shape changes to the one defined in the subclass. If the modeler decides to change the background color of the subclass, all background colors of the shapes attached to this subclass automatically change to the new color. The same is true for the border color defined in border subclassing.

The package of models may include many FEMs connected to one another. However, in this package there can be max one object of the type *FEM subclassing* and max one object of the type *Border subclassing*. This is a natural decision, as models in the same package should follow the same rules. With this, we finish our descriptions of FEM and FEM toolkit. For additional information, see [3, 5, 8].

3 FEM Viewer Version 2.0

FEM viewer version 1.0 [2] allows a business user to investigate a package of models created by a modeler who used the FEM toolkit to create the package. This is done in the web environment using a standard browser. e.g., *Chrome* or *Firefox*. To allow a user to investigate the package, the modeler needs to export it from the FEM toolkit and import it into the FEM viewer, as well as define the users and give them access to the package.

FEM viewer version 2.0 extends the functionality of the original FEM viewer, allowing the business user to change the models. The changed models could be exported from the FEM viewer and imported back to the FEM toolkit, if needed.

After export/import of the package, we will get the models imported into the FEM viewer as shown in Fig. 3. In the left column, it shows the list of models (objects) included in the package. In the right column, it shows the model (object) from this list that was chosen for the view. In the case of Fig. 3, the model represented in Fig. 1 was chosen. This model is a bit different from Fig. 1, as the explanatory part of the model in Fig. 1 was deleted.

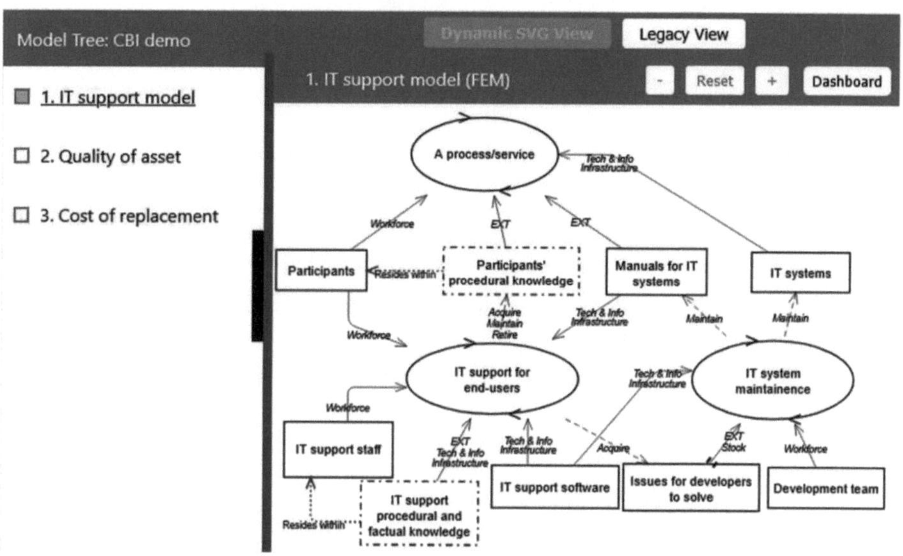

Fig. 3. The model of Fig. 1 in the FEM viewer

The other two objects in the list are shown in Fig. 4; they just repeat Fig. 3. Let us discuss the functionality given to the experts in the new version of the FEM viewer. If he/she wants to change the object in the model shown in Fig. 3, he/she needs to click on this object. As a reaction, a pop-up menu appears, as shown in Fig. 5, and the element on which the user clicked is highlighted. In the pop-up menu, there are three elements that have a pen symbol on the right. This symbol means that these elements can be changed by the user in the FEM viewer.

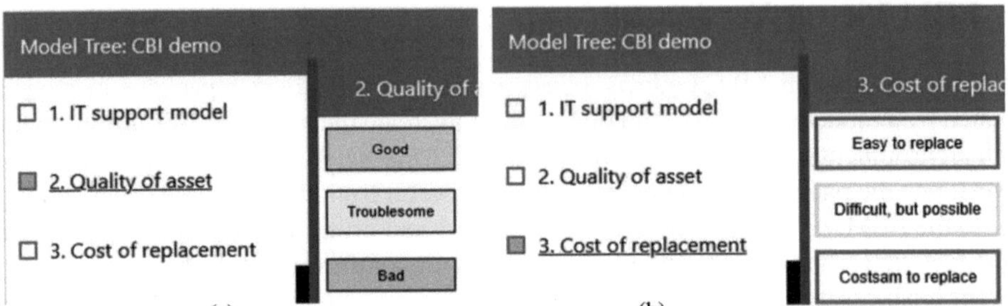

(a) (b)

Fig. 4. (a) - FEM subclassing; (b) - Border subclassing

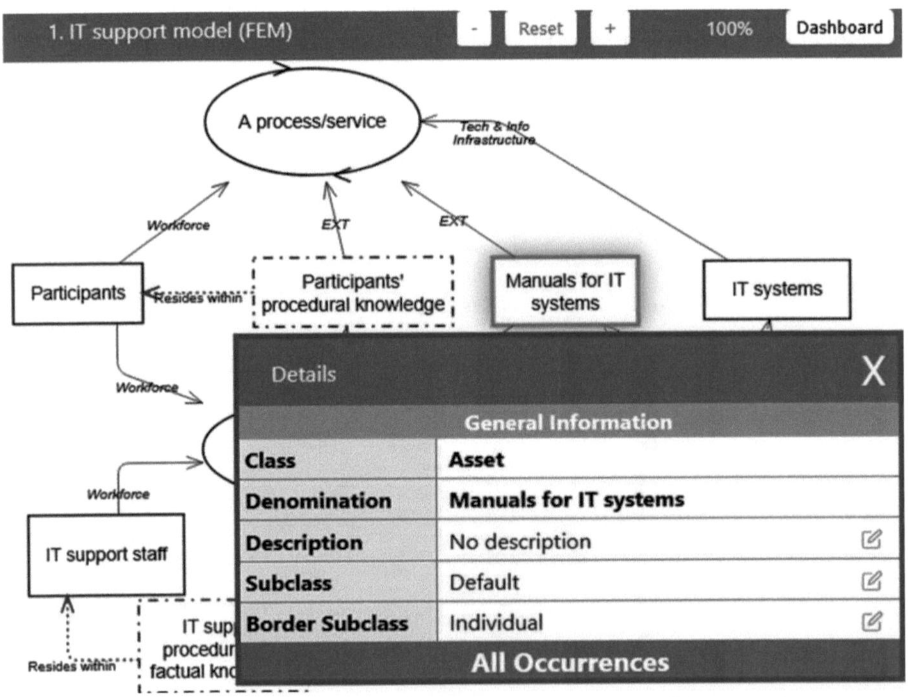

Fig. 5. A pop-up menu appears after we have clicked on the asset "Manuals for IT systems"

Let us click on the pen symbol for *Subclass*; then the pop-up menu is changed to what is presented in Fig. 6. Let us choose the element *Subclass*, then a menu shown in

Fig. 7 appears. The elements of this menu are taken from Fig. 4a. Let us choose *Bad* in the menu and press the *Update* button. Then the background color of the chosen asset is changed to the color that corresponds to the item *Bad* in Fig. 4a, see Fig. 8.

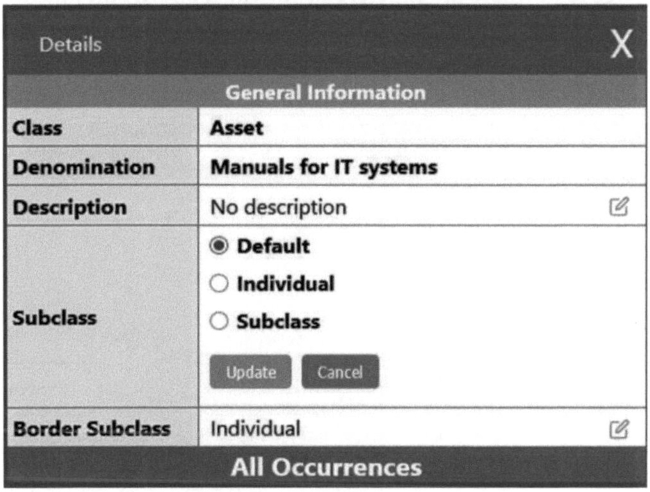

Fig. 6. Subclass menu

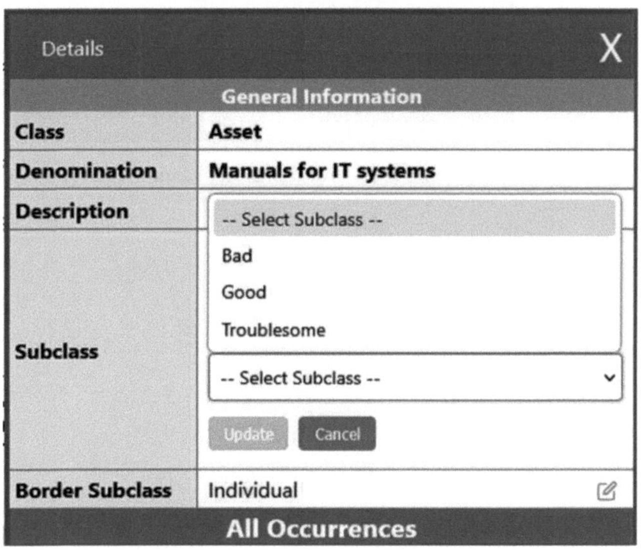

Fig. 7. Menu when the subclass is chosen

In the same way, we can choose the Border subclass. The result of choosing the border subclass *Easy to replace* (see Fig. 4b) for the asset *Manuals for IT systems* is shown in Fig. 9, where the asset got the green border. One more element that the FEM viewer user is allowed to change is the description attached to the shape, see Fig. 5. The description is a free text, where the experts can put a note on why they have chosen certain colors for the given shape, and give estimates of cost and time to make the changes, see Fig. 10.

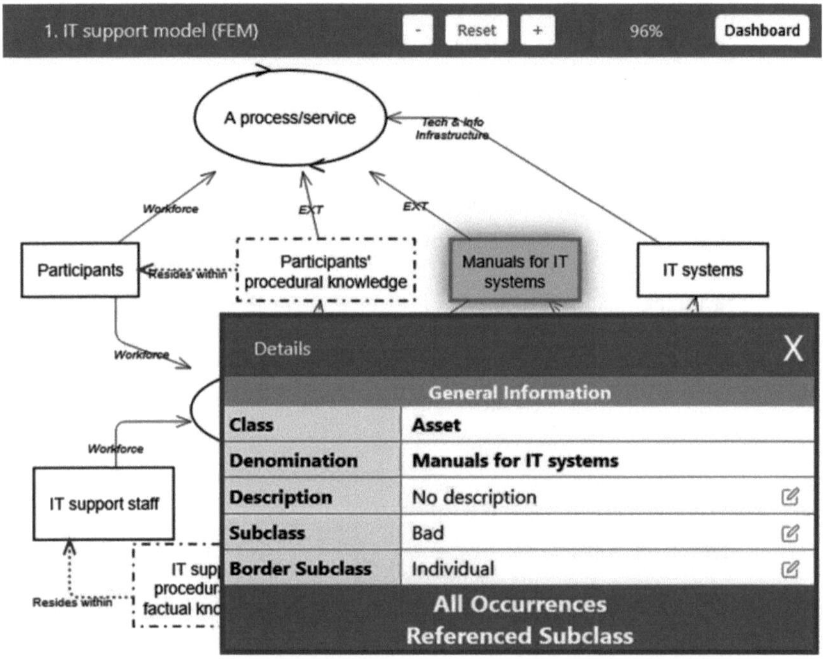

Fig. 8. The result of choosing *Bad* for the asset "Manuals for IT systems"

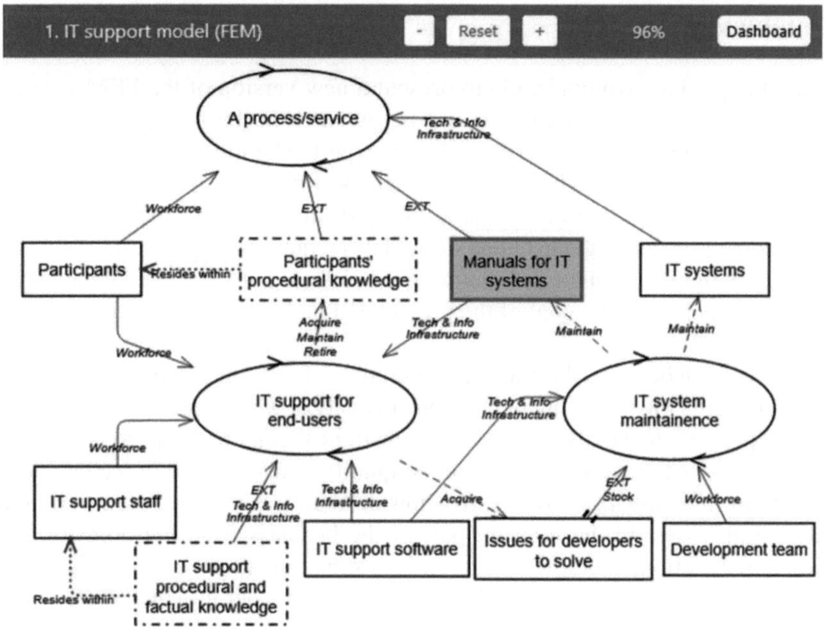

Fig. 9. The result of choosing "Easy to replace" as a *Border subclass*

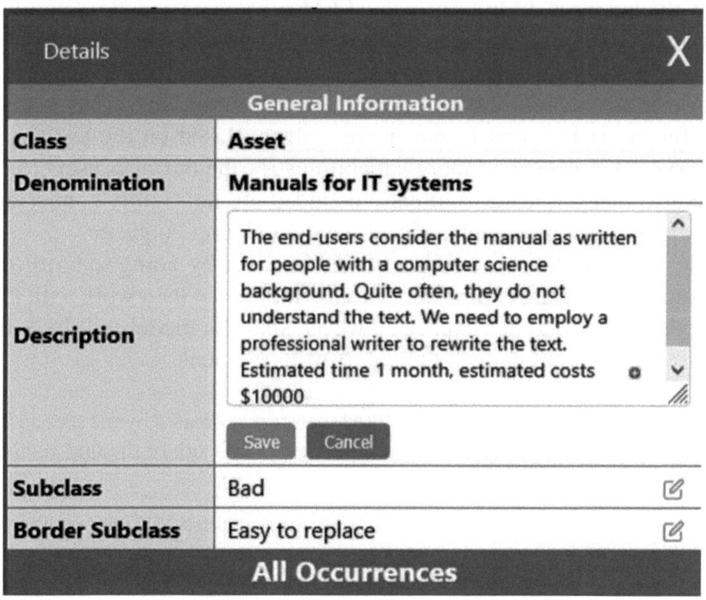

Fig. 10. Entering a description for the asset "Manuals for IT systems"

4 Conclusion

The current paper has two goals: (1) to present a new version of the FEM viewer, and (2) to discuss which functionality should be given to business experts, so that they can use the modeling tool without a modeling expert. The modeling expert may be an external consultant, and when he has left, it might be difficult to use the models. The new functionality included in the new version of FEM viewer allows the business experts to change some aspects of the package of models created by the modeling expert. This functionality is tightly coupled with defining subclasses that have special meaning, and this meaning depends on the goal of the project that includes creating the models of the business.

The models can be created for different purposes. The example that was discussed in this paper concerns the modeling that is done to analyze which elements of the business do not work properly and make a decision to substitute them. For this purpose, we created FEM subclasses that were used to assign the quality to assets used in the business. We also created *Border subclasses* to identify how difficult it is to substitute a certain asset. Considering all assets in the relevant part of the business from the point of view of how well they function, and how difficult it is to substitute them, can be done without a modeling expert. If needed, additional information can be put into the description of an asset as free text.

Note, however, that the purpose discussed above is not the only purpose of modeling; for example, modeling can be done with the purpose of finding a way of radically transforming the business. In this case, the *FEM subclasses* and *Border subclasses* are defined differently, see, for example, [5]. Actually, the idea behind subclasses is that they could be adjusted to various purposes.

The FEM viewer version 2.0 is a completely new tool, and it has not been tested in practice. Testing is included in our nearest plans. Based on the testing, a decision can be made on the inclusion of more capabilities for the business users to change the model. Note also that the features already included are not tightly connected to FEM. Analogous capabilities may be introduced in any modeling language.

The reader can test the new version of FEM viewer by going to https://femviewer server.cloud.ut.ee/ and using expert/trepxe to log in. He can then work with the example presented in this paper. Do not expect, however, that the model will look like Fig. 3; somebody else could have changed the colors of its elements.

Acknowledgments. The new version of the FEM viewer was created by the second author as his BS thesis work. The first author served as his supervisor. The work of the first author was partly supported by the Estonian Research Council (grant PRG1226).

Disclosure of Interests. The authors have no competing interests to declare that are relevant to the content of this article.

References

1. Bider, I., Langel, S.: Creating a web-based viewer for an ADOxx-based modeling toolkit. In Araújo, J., de la Vara, J.L., Santos, M.Y., Assar, S., (eds.) Research Challenges in Information

Science. RCIS 2024. LNBIP, vol. 514, pp.65–73 (2024). https://doi.org/10.1007/978-3-031-59468-7_8
2. Langel, S.: FEM viewer version 1.0. https://github.com/siimlangel/FEM (Accessed June 2025)
3. Bider, I., Perjons, E., Elias, M., Johannesson, P.: A fractal enterprise model and its application for business development. SoSyM **16**(3), 663–689 (2017)
4. Ehlvest, J.: FEM viewer version 2.0. (Accessed June 2025) https://github.com/JoonatanEhlvest/FEM
5. Bider, I., Perjons, E., Klyukina, V.: Tool support for fractal enterprise modeling. In: Domain-Specific Conceptual Modeling, pp. 205–229 Springer (2022). https://doi.org/10.1007/978-3-030-93547-4_10
6. Fractalmodel.org: FEM toolkit. (Accessed March 9, 2025). https://www.fractalmodel.org/fem-toolkit/
7. ADOxx.org: ADOxx. https://www.adoxx.org (Accessed January 2024)
8. Bider, I., Perjons, E., Bork, D.: Towards on-the-fly creation of modeling language jargons. In : ICTERI 2021: 17th International Conference on ICT in Education, Research, and Industrial Applications, CEUR, vol. 3013 (2021)

DISME: A DEMO Based Model-Driven Low-Code/No-Code Platform

David Aveiro[1,2,3], Vítor Freitas[1,3](✉), and Duarte Pinto[1,2]

[1] ARDITI – Regional Agency for the Development of Research, Technology and Innovation, 9020-105 Funchal, Portugal
daveiro@staff.uma.pt, duarte.nuno@arditi.pt
[2] NOVA-LINCS, Universidade NOVA de Lisboa, Campus da Caparica, 2829-516 Caparica, Portugal
[3] Faculty of Exact Sciences and Engineering, University of Madeira, Caminho da Penteada, 9020-105 Funchal, Portugal
vitor.freitas@staff.uma.pt

Abstract. This paper presents the Dynamic Information System Modeller and Executor (DISME), a low-code/no-code platform designed to help bridge the gap between enterprise modeling and their implementation into information systems. Grounded in the Design and Engineering Methodology for Organizations (DEMO), DISME allows domain experts to specify and execute organizational models through a visual, interface without writing any traditional code. The platform supports the modeling of processes, information structures, coordination acts, and business rules, which are immediately implemented into the runtime environment using its interpretation engine. DISME architecture includes a modular System Modeller and a live System Executor. In this paper we cover the key components such as action rule design, REST API integration, form building and designing and UI adaptivity that enable the real-time system configuration and interaction. Two real-world use cases are presented, highlighting some significant reductions in development time and system complexity, as well as improved usability outcomes.

Keywords: low-code · no-code · enterprise engineering · DEMO · information systems · modelling · UX · gendermag

1 Introduction

Information systems development still faces multiple challenges in aligning technical implementations with the evolving semantics of the organizations. Model-driven approaches have been promising to improve this alignment and reduce the implementation gaps. However, many of those approaches either remain too theoretical for practical deployment or rely on static code generation pipelines that limit adaptability and, in many cases, promote vendor lock in situations. This paper presents DISME (Dynamic Information System Modeler and Executor), a low-code/no-code platform that tried to operationalize enterprise models

J. Barateiro et al. (Eds.): EDOC 2025 Workshops, LNBIP 571, pp. 448–473, 2026.
https://doi.org/10.1007/978-3-032-16234-2_37

based on the Design and Engineering Methodology for Organizations (DEMO). With DISME, domain experts can model organizational processes, facts, actions, and user interactions using visual interfaces that are not only descriptive models, but can also be executed, forming the core of a system that directly interprets and enacts enterprise logic in real time. We begin by establishing the theoretical foundations for executable enterprise modeling, focusing on DEMO's aspect models. We then describe the architecture of DISME, covering both the modeling and execution environments. The platform's components are presented in detail, showcasing the most relevant features such as the rule-based logic, dynamic search, forms creation, and REST integration. The paper also includes two use cases, one in healthcare and another in public administration, where we conducted empirical validation of usability and efficiency. We then reflect on the platform's limitations and propose directions for further development, including semantic validation, scalability, and collaborative modeling support.

2 Enterprise Modeling Foundations

The DISME platform builds on the foundations of the discipline of Enterprise Engineering, that tells us that the implementation of enterprises as systems must be both coherent and purposeful. The Design & Engineering Methodology for Organizations (DEMO) then provides us with a formal and ontologically grounded approach to modeling the essence of organizations [7]. In DEMO, organizations are modeled using four interrelated aspect models:

- The Construction Model (CM), that captures the actor roles and transactions within the organization.
- The Process Model (PM), that contains the causal and conditional relations between transactions.
- The Fact Model (FM), where are represented the object classes and fact types relevant to the organization.
- The Action Model (AM), where are specified the business rules that govern the decisions and behavior between the transactions.

These models, grounded by Enterprise Ontology, promote a platform-independent, human-centric understanding of how organizations operate [7]. DISME tries to put these aspect models into practice, providing a platform where users can both define and execute the organizational artifacts, in an attempt to bridge the gap between enterprise modeling in theory, and, in practice. One of the biggest challenges with traditional DEMO adoption is the perceived complexity and learning curve, particularly if the practitioners are unfamiliar with its formal structures. To mitigate this, along with DISME, there were also introduced new visual notations for the Process and Fact Models [8,16], as well as an alternative Action Rule Specification grammar [3]. These new notations were validated through user studies that revealed increased usability and modeling accuracy in [2]. In DISME, the models serve as more than only descriptive representations, they also act as the direct enablers of the system behavior, ensuring that all modeling decisions are reflected immediately at runtime. The alliance of the DEMO-based models with a low-code/no-code runtime engine with no compilation or code generation allows DISME to maintain the continuous transformation between modeling, specification, and operational execution.

3 Architecture

DISME is implemented as a web-based, open-source low code/no-code platform with the goal of supporting the modeling, configuration, and execution of organizational information systems. Technology wise, DISME is built upon a PHP backend using the Laravel Framework[1] that gets its data from a MySQL database. The front end is handled by Angular and written in typescript. Then there were also integrated multiple other open-source components to improve the behavior of the platform such as Blockly (for action rule definitions), Form.io (for form layout and input handling), or Draw.io (for diagram generation). The platform can be divided into two main components: the System Modeller, that is responsible for the design and specification of organizational artifacts, business rules and overall behavior; and the System Executor, which interprets what is defined in the system modeler and runs those specifications in a live environment. At the core of DISME we have an ontology-driven database following the DEMO principles, with a fixed structure, where the organizational data is then dynamically introduced shaped by the parametrization defined through the System Modeller. As the database itself doesn't change with the parametrization, DISME can make them instantly reflect on run time without any need of compilation or other complicated procedures that would involve, for example, code generation as it's usual in these kinds of platforms. The structure of the database follows the Type Square pattern, inspired by the Adaptive Object Model (AOM) architectural style [18], where meta-definitions like, transaction types or entity types are defined in the parametrization and interpreted at runtime, originating when the system is being executed artifacts that derived from their meta definition namely transactions or entities.

4 System Modeller

The System Modeller is the core of the DISME platform, and it is used for the specification and configuration of the organizational information systems. Grounded in the principles of Enterprise Ontology and the DEMO methodology [7], and aligned with the Adaptive Object Model paradigm [19], the System Modeller acts as the design interface of the platform, enabling users to model the structure, behavior, and operational logic of the system without writing traditional code. This parametrization is then interpreted and ran by the platform engine in real time, allowing the users to organically change their processes on

[1] Laravel Framework - https://laravel.com.

the fly. Using a modular and visual interface, users define the organizational processes and transactions, as well as the rules governing their execution. Steps in these rules can be then associated with forms through which users interact with the system, and the queries and services used to retrieve or exchange information. DISME's system modeler requires no programming expertise, just knowledge of the business domain and some basic DEMO notions. With those, and taking advantage of high-level constructs and graphical tools such as Blockly[2] Form.io[3] and Draw.io[4], it allows the parametrization and maintenance of the organizational processes. The System Modeller is composed of eleven key components, each addressing a distinct concern of the system's specification:

- The **Diagram Editor** for a visual specification of DEMO's Process and Fact Models.
- The **Parametrization** to detail the core elements of the organization, including types of transactions, processes, entities, and their properties and relationships.
- The **Action Rules Management** for the definition of business rules and operational logic through a visual rule editor based on Blockly and an EBNF grammar.
- The **Forms Management** based on Form.io for users to customize the layouts of the interfaces associated with the multiple task steps.
- The **User Dependent Interface Management** that allows for the dynamic adaptation of the user interface based on specific user attributes or profiles. Leveraging concepts inspired by the GenderMag framework and other inclusive design approaches.
- The **Dynamic Search** for a graphical specification of advanced queries and filtering logic across the modeled domain, supporting any information needs.
- The **REST API** Integration to facilitate the exposure of internal resources as REST endpoints and the consumption of external APIs, supporting data exchange and interoperability across systems.
- The **Documentation Generation** that provides automatic Swagger/OpenAPI documentation for the system, promoting transparency, consistency, and ease of integration.
- The **Apps Manager** that enables the creation of modular, reusable application views composed of multiple forms, queries, and visual elements. These applications can serve as customized dashboards or specialized data entry modules, composed by assembling existing forms and search components in a layout defined by the user.
- The **Template Management** allows the creation and customization of system-generated outputs such as notifications, pop-ups, and formal documents—using a visual, no-code editor. It supports dynamic content insertion from the Fact Model and integrates with document management tools for archiving and compliance.

---

[2] Blockly - https://developers.google.com/blockly.
[3] Form.io - https://form.io/.
[4] Draw.io - https://www.drawio.com/.

- And finally, the **Business Intelligence Component** provides the organization analytical capabilities by giving them the ability to define exportable data templates and configure dashboards using model-driven queries with the help of Knowage[5]

Each of these components will be described in the following subsections. The combined use of these modules enables the creation of run time executable models that reflect the organization's operational logic and support the continuous adaptation.

4.1 Diagram Editor

The Diagram Editor is based in DISME and was originally inspired by the Universal Enterprise Adaptive Object Model [4]. This component uses both Draw.io as a full capable editor and Graphviz[6] for diagram generation as a way to help the users both model and visualize the enterprise models of their organization following the notations proposed in [16] for the process model and in [8] for the fact model. In Fig. 1 an example of a process model designed with the Diagram Editor can be seen, as well as the existent shapes for appliable in a process model on the left side.

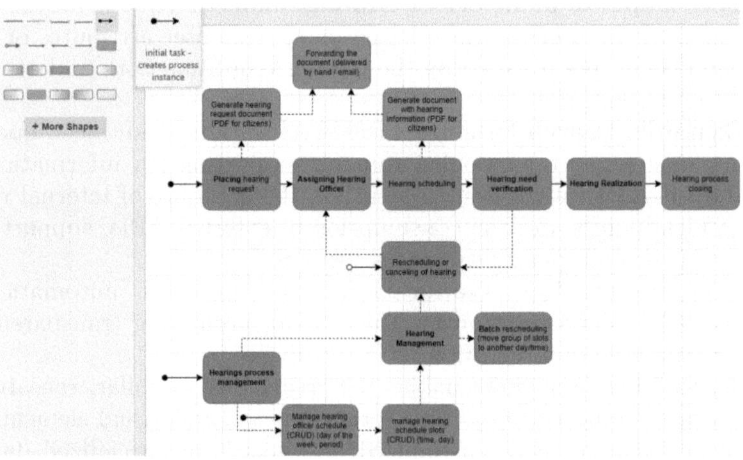

Fig. 1. Process Model of a municipality hearing processes.

The component is still undergoing some developments but, when completed, it is intended to be used in the parametrization process for both the visualization, by automatically generating the diagrams based on the existing system parameters on the platform, and for the modification, by allowing users to change names,

[5] Knowage - https://www.knowage-suite.com/.
[6] Graphviz - https://graphviz.org/.

add, change or remove elements and connections as they please. These visual representations can facilitate the onboarding of new members into the organization by providing a simple, although detailed, overview of any given process and their flow as well as aid them in knowing what information is needed for any given artifact or how they connect with each other. It can also help stakeholders get a full picture of the organization and, with that, facilitate the implementation of changes and optimizations.

4.2 Parametrization

Parametrization (formerly known as System Specifier) is where users define the core of the organizational artifacts. It was renamed to better reflect its broader scope. The artifacts in the parametrization are represented in tables where users can add, edit, remove and view the existing artifacts of each type. This component is subdivided into nine parts, namely:

- **Language**: Where users and add or remove languages to the system and change their state (e.g., active, inactive).
- **Users**: Where the system participants can be defined and managed.
- **Roles**: Where users can create the necessary organizational roles to interact with the transactions or processes. These roles are not the traditional DEMO roles and thus do not have limitations such as being limited to the execution of one transaction. That definition would only cause excessive clutter in the system as well as unnecessary complexity, therefore, even though they can be used in the traditional DEMO actor role way, it is recommended they are used as organizational capabilities, that often involve a cluster of responsibilities. Within the roles it is also determined the User Roles, where users and roles can be associated determining who can play a specific function within the organization.
- **Process Types**: Where the meta processes, composed by multiple transactions, are defined. Users can also define specific properties as descriptive metadata for a process, which are displayed when a process needs to be selected.
- **Transaction Types**: Where users define the meta transactions that can take place in the system. Each of this transaction needs to be associated with an existing process and existing executing role. Users also define if this transaction initiates or concludes a process.
- **Entity Types**: Where all relevant entities are defined and associated with the transactions.
- **Property Types**: Where users define the properties present at each entity as well as their kind (e.g., Text, Boolean, Integer, Date, Reference, File, amongst others). In this section users can also create unit kinds (e.g., Kilograms, Kilometers, Euros).
- **Constants**: Where property types with fixed values can be created or, the lists for the enumerations.
- **Waiting Links**: Where users can define that a specific step, including declines and cancellations, of one transaction waits for another step of the other transaction to conclude, as well as the cardinality of this relationship.

Changes in this parametrization, when set to active, are automatically applied to the runtime environment, although some might require additional steps like adjustments of the action rules or inclusion in forms. While these parameters are the organization business elements, they don't define the business rules on how they interact with each other and the users, for that Action Rules need to be created.

4.3 Action Rules Management

The Action Rules Management component allows the specification of how the transactions behave with each other and within themselves, including the conditions, the validations, the presentation and the responses to each action. This functionality is grounded in the principles of the DEMO Action Model, and takes place using a visual and user-friendly interface. We adopted an alternative syntax for Action Rule Specification (ARS), formally defined using an Extended Backus-Naur Form (EBNF) grammar [15]. This syntactic definition supports the creation of executable rules that are syntactically constrained and semantically aligned with the ontological commitments of the DEMO methodology. The adopted grammar and supporting notation are detailed in previous work [3], and were designed to improve clarity and reduce the cognitive strain associated with DEMO's traditional ARS formulations.

The specification of rules follows a triplet structure of the Action Model: an ***event*** part, describing the triggering coordination act(s); an ***assess*** part, comprising logical conditions and optional validations; and a ***response*** part, which defines the actions to be executed. This ***event-assess-response*** paradigm is consistent with the foundational DEMO coordination pattern and allows flexibility in expressing the organization's decision-making logic. To support rule specification by users with different levels of expertise and technical knowledge, a visual programming interface based on Blockly was integrated into the platform. Blockly allows users to construct rules using interlocking graphical blocks, thus abstracting from the DEMO's standard textual syntax and promoting error-free modeling. Rule blocks include constructs for conditional branching, iteration, data manipulation, and user interaction amongst other things, as can be seen in Fig. 2. Additionally, in the future, we plan on adding reusable rule templates can be defined and instantiated across multiple transactions to facilitate consistency and reduce redundancy.

All defined action rules are directly interpreted by the System Executor at runtime, without requiring compilation or code generation. This integration between modeling and execution guarantees immediate feedback and gives support to the creation of a dynamic, adaptive enterprise system.

DISME provides a robust library of custom blocks, tailored to support the modeling of complex organizational logic/actions in a declarative and visual way. These actions include:

- **Assign Expression:** Assign a value or fact to a context variable or property, including dynamic expressions based on user input or prior state.

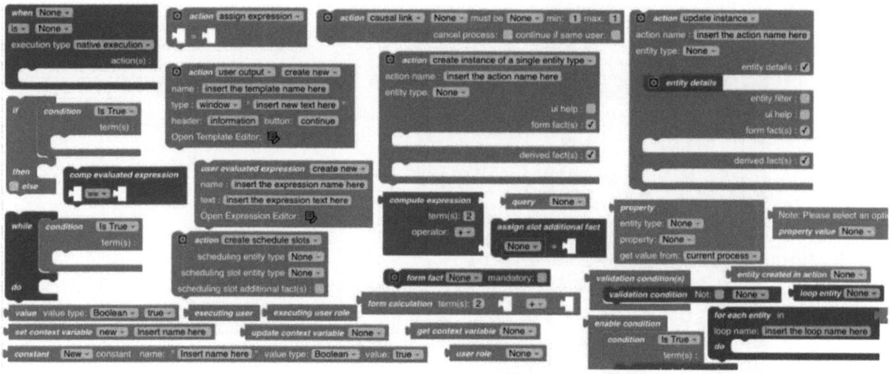

Fig. 2. DISME's custom Blockly blocks.

- **Causal Link:** Trigger or influence the initiation or state transition of another transaction, supporting inter-process coordination in line with DEMO's ontological model.
- **User Output:** Present information to users via notifications, modal windows, or auto-generated documents. This allows for feedback, alerts, or informative guidance during the task flow.
- **Create Instance:** Instantiate a new entity in the system, based on form submissions and/or derived facts from previous user actions.
- **Update Instance:** Modify an existing instance with updated information from user input or calculated values, maintaining data integrity and traceability.
- **Create Schedule Slots:** Automatically generate time slots linked to a specific entity type with all required properties, supporting scheduling processes such as hearings or appointments.
- **External API Call:** Integrate with third-party systems by sending requests and handling responses, enabling interoperability and automation of external processes.

Figure 3 shows an example of an action rule created using the visual programming interface for the `Create Citizen` transaction type. In this case, the rule is triggered upon the execution of the transaction and performs a **Create Instance** action using facts collected through a form filled by the user. The rule also includes **validation conditions** to ensure data integrity—such as verifying mandatory fields or checking for invalid inputs before allowing the transaction to complete. This example illustrates how business rules, data validation, and model-driven execution are cohesively expressed in a user-friendly, declarative format.

This component also addresses several limitations observed in earlier versions of DEMO's Action Model, particularly the ambiguity of structured English formulations and the limited support for validation and exception handling logic. Although the rules are directly implemented, some of the defined logic may need

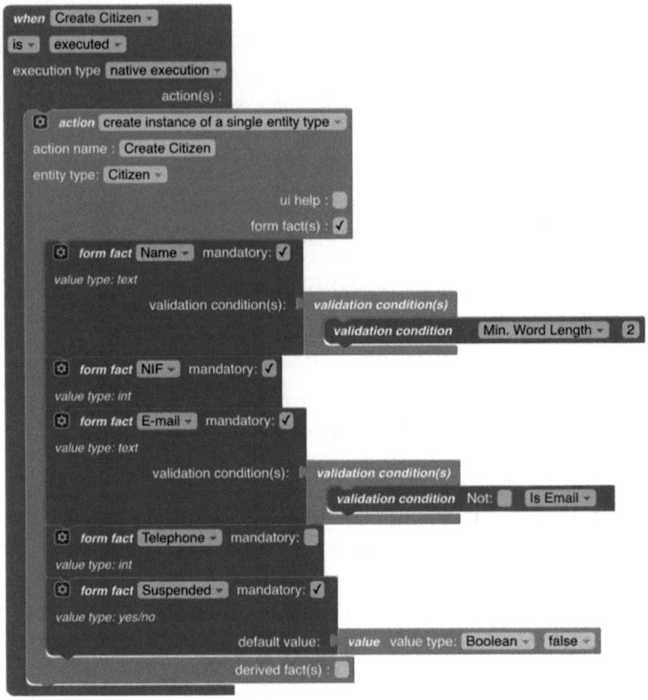

Fig. 3. Example of an Action Rule defined in DISME.

additional specification. One of those cases are the Forms where their layout and behavior also needs to be defined.

4.4 Forms Management

The Forms Management component allows users to create and manage the interfaces that end-users interact with in their day-to-day work to support transactional activities within the system. These forms are critical when an *action rule* specifies actions of type `create instance` or `update instance`, and are required whenever *form facts* are involved.

When creating or editing a form, users are redirected to the *Form Editor*, which leverages the **Form.io** framework to provide a WYSIWYG (What You See Is What You Get) environment. This editor allows users to design form layouts visually and intuitively, without requiring programming expertise.

Each form corresponds to a specific set of *properties*, derived from the **Fact Model** and associated with entity types and transactions via the **Parametrization** component. These properties are automatically retrieved based on the form facts defined in the associated *action rule*, and their possible input types are determined by their parameterized value types. Users are responsible for placing and organizing each property in the form layout and can complement the design with additional layout elements—such as *panels*, *columns*, *tables*, and *tabs*—to improve clarity and aesthetics, as can be seen in Fig. 4.

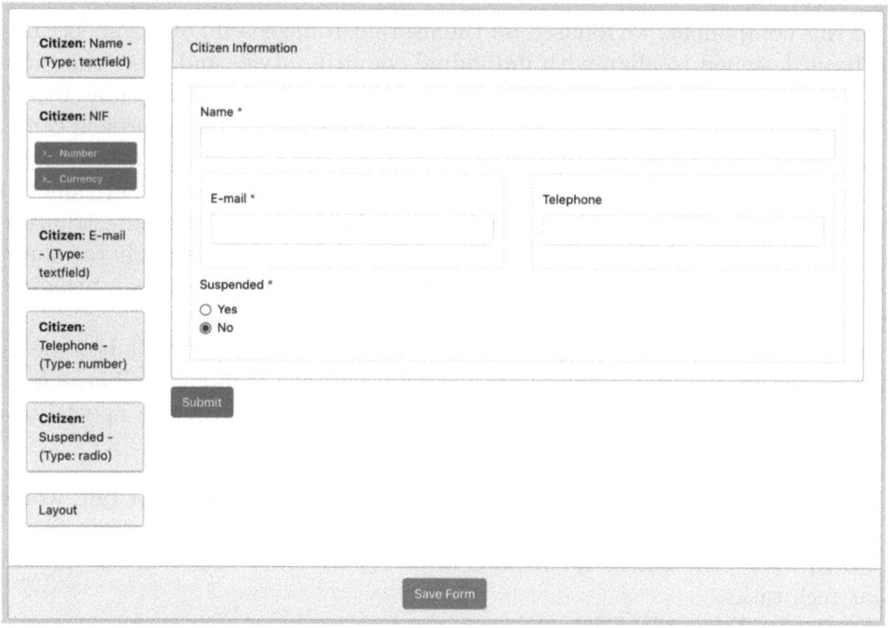

Fig. 4. Form's layout editor.

Forms are composed of individual fields, automatically mapped to system properties, and adapt their input types accordingly (e.g., text, date, number, dropdown). The editor also supports advanced field types such as *file uploads* and *nested inputs*. The *tooltips*, *validation rules*, and *custom display logic* associated with each property are defined in the corresponding action using the Blockly interface. Once the user places the property in the form layout, the system automatically enforces these configurations to guide user input and ensure data integrity.

This combination of data-driven form structure and flexible presentation ensures that each user experiences an interface optimized for their preferences and needs—boosting usability, reducing errors, and aligning with the broader goals of inclusive system design.

4.5 User Dependent Interface Management

User characteristics have long been a focal point in usability research. One key area of exploration is adaptive user interface (UI) design, which can be broadly categorized into two types: user-customized interfaces, where users explicitly tailor the interface to their preferences or needs, and dynamically adaptive interfaces, which modify themselves automatically in response to user behavior or context [11,13].

In this component, we focused on the user-customized end of the spectrum—interfaces designed to align with individual cognitive styles and user traits identified in advance. While systems like Supple [17] have demonstrated how UIs can adapt automatically based on user profiles and constraints, our approach centers on cognitive style-based customization guided by the GenderMag framework.

The GenderMag method supports developers and usability practitioners in identifying and addressing gender-related usability issues through structured cognitive walkthroughs [6,9]. As these issues have become increasingly recognized as a form of non-functional requirements [12], GenderMag provides a principled approach to assess and improve gender inclusiveness in software.

At the core of GenderMag are five cognitive facets that reflect how people process information, make decisions, and interact with technology. These facets tend to cluster statistically by gender, though individuals span a spectrum of behaviors:

- **Motivation**: Men are more likely to engage with technology for fun; women tend to be more goal-oriented.
- **Computer Self-Efficacy**: Women often report lower confidence in unfamiliar tech tasks.
- **Attitude Towards Risk**: Women tend to be more risk-averse, exploring new features less readily.
- **Information Processing Style**: Men often follow a selective, trial-and-error approach; women tend to prefer a comprehensive, detail-gathering style.
- **Learning Style**: Men are more likely to tinker; women often prefer structured learning—but benefit greatly from exploration when they do engage in it.

GenderMag operationalizes these facets through three personas: **Abi**, who favors structured, risk-averse strategies and is easily discouraged by vague interfaces (typically aligned with traits more common among women); **Tim**, who is confident, experimental, and comfortable with uncertainty (traits more commonly found in men); **Pat**, who blends these approaches depending on the context. As the facets define a spectrum, it is common for real users to often exhibit a mix of these facets, e.g., being like Tim in risk tolerance but like Abi in information processing.

The GenderMag Cognitive Walkthrough method uses these personas in step-by-step evaluations of software tasks, asking critical usability questions like: Will this persona form the correct goal? Will they know what to do? Will they recognize and understand the feedback? This process reveals cognitive-style-related usability issues, supporting more inclusive design practices [5,10,14]. Additionally, GenderMag includes a design catalog of known usability bugs and associated fixes. These are not one-size-fits-all solutions but provide inspiration for addressing cognitive-style barriers discovered through walkthroughs.

In our implementation within the DISME platform, we applied GenderMag's methodology to guide the possibility of design of user-customized interfaces. Specifically, we used the Abi and Tim personas to inform interface variants and employed the cognitive walkthrough method to allow evaluation and refinement of the user experience based on different cognitive styles. Our goal was to create interfaces that not only acknowledge but actively support diverse user problem-solving strategies, and their evolution, according to user evaluation capabilities integrated in the platform.

Our system implements user-customized interfaces through a two-part architecture: the first is the **User Profile** component, which is accessible to all end users and allows them to manage their personal interaction preferences; the second is the **User-Dependent Interface Management** component, which is accessible only to modelers or administrators and is responsible for configuring and managing adaptive interface behaviors based on user profiles.

Every user can access a "Customize My Experience" feature in their profile component. This allows them to complete a structured GenderMag Facets questionnaire, designed to assess their cognitive style across the five GenderMag facets: Motivation, Computer Self-Efficacy, Risk Aversion, Information Processing Style, and Learning Style. Once submitted, the system calculates individual facet scores and stores them in the user's profile. These scores serve as the basis for tailoring the UI experience, either directly (in a user-customized setting) or indirectly (through administrator-driven A/B testing).

Administrators have access to a dedicated interface for managing cognitive-style-based customizations. This User-Dependent Interface Management panel includes several key functions:

- **Facet Median Calculation**: The system computes and maintains up-to-date median values for each cognitive facet, aggregated across users. These serve as dynamic thresholds between *Abi-like* (lower range) and *Tim-like* (higher range) cognitive profiles. This classification establishes a reference point for user segmentation.
- **A/B Testing Classification**: Based on users' facet scores and the current medians, the system will assign users to different interface variants: Group A - Users interact with a version of the application that includes only the 'Abi' alternative of the UI features; and Group B - Users interact with a version that includes only the 'Tim' alternative. To ensure a balanced distribution of participants of each facet extreme across the groups and avoid selection bias, an algorithm is used that considers the users' facet scores for learning style and computer self-efficacy. This approach ensures that the groups are evenly distributed across different cognitive profiles, preventing over-representation of one type of user and enabling a fair comparison of the two UI versions.
- **Toggle A/B Testing**: Admins can enable or disable A/B testing functionality at any time, allowing the system to switch between active experimentation, where the classification evaluation's results are used, and stable configuration, where only the users scores and Gendermag default thresholds are used.

- **User Insights and History**: For each user, admins can view: current facet scores, a complete score history over time, current classification and classification history and current facet medians and their evolution over time.

This historical insight supports longitudinal analysis of user behaviour and adaptation effectiveness, and allows for auditing and refinement of the customization logic.

In addition to user profiling and administrative classification, the system supports run-time UI adaptation based on either the user's facet scores or their assigned A/B testing group. These adaptations aim to align the user interface with cognitive styles modeled by the GenderMag personas, thereby improving usability for diverse user types. Currently, the following UI elements adapt dynamically:

- **Forms Layout**: Abi users see a continuous, non-tabbed layout where all form fields are displayed on a single scrollable page. Tim users interact with a tabbed interface, where form sections are separated across different tabs.
- **Field Help Tooltips**: For Abi, help text is always visible directly beneath or beside each form field. For Tim, tooltips are hidden behind a "?" icon and only appear on hover or focus.
- **Task Button Tooltips**: In the Abi variant, tooltips are shown by default on all task-related buttons to provide additional guidance. In the Tim variant, tooltips are not displayed, assuming prior familiarity and reducing visual clutter.
- **Component Grouping**: Abi's interface includes clearly defined grouping panels that organize related UI elements under labeled sections. Tim's layout removes these groupings for a flatter, more compact presentation.

These adaptations are activated at run-time, ensuring that the user interface is automatically aligned with either the user's facet-based scores or their A/B classification assignment. By tailoring these subtle interface features, the system supports more inclusive interaction styles and enables empirical evaluation of design effectiveness across cognitive profiles.

4.6 Dynamic Search

The *Dynamic Search* component provides a visual and intuitive way for the users to define advanced queries across the organizational data without having to write them in SQL. This functionality is particularly useful for the non-technical users who need to retrieve, filter, or visualize data on demand, directly from the system while in execution.

With a drag-and-drop interface, as seen in Fig. 5, users can create query conditions based on the Fact Model, by applying logical operations, grouping rules, and various data filters. The existing filters automatically adapt to the data types defined in the model (e.g., text, dates, numbers, enumerations), and can be combined to express complex information if needed. Users can define one

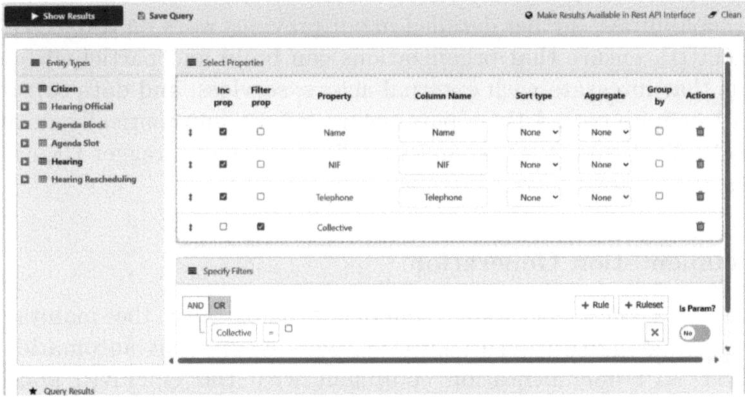

Fig. 5. Creating a dynamic search.

or more search criteria blocks, and chain them together with logical operators (AND, OR), as well as apply ordering or limits if needed.

The defined searches are reusable across multiple parts of the platform. For instance, they can be included into dashboards for contextual insights, linked to buttons or form components for task related lookup necessities, or even associated with API endpoints for external system integration. Furthermore, search outputs can be dynamically included into templates for document generation or reporting purposes, thus allowing personalized or context-aware outputs.

4.7 REST API Integration

The REST API Integration component allows users to expose or consume services via RESTful endpoints without requiring programming knowledge. This functionality is essential to ensure that the systems modeled within DISME can interoperate with external services, platforms, and applications, and be used in real-world scenarios where data must be shared across organizational and technical boundaries.

Regarding the API exposure, this integration enables the automatic generation of REST endpoints from existing entities, transactions, and processes defined in the parametrization. These endpoints follow the REST principles and are configured directly through the user interface, specifying the allowed operations such as Create, Read, Update, and Delete (CRUD). Users can define the path parameters, the filtering logic, and the response structures through graphical configuration in the Action Rules Manager, without writing a single line of backend code.

On the consumption side, the same interface allows users to point to external APIs that the system should call during specific process executions or validations. These integrations are defined visually by mapping external request/response schemas to the internally used Fact Model structure. Authentication mechanisms such as API keys or token-based headers are also supported.

These capabilities, further detailed in our previous work on Rapid REST API Management [1], ensure that organizations can build and participate in digital ecosystems that integrate with external actors, services, and data sources.

All API endpoints and their parameters can be automatically documented using the OpenAPI specification and visualized through Swagger UI, as detailed in the next subsection.

4.8 Documentation Generation

The Documentation Generation component helps with the maintainability, transparency and integration of DISME. This component automatically produces REST API documentation compliant with the OpenAPI specification through Swagger UI, offering an interactive and developer-friendly interface for inspecting and testing the system's available endpoints.

This documentation is generated directly from the organizational parametrization specified within the platform. As users define which of their entities, properties and transactions are exposed in the endpoints for the REST API Integration in the Action Rules, these elements are immediately reflected in the generated specification and easily accessible for the documentation. Other than the information that is being exposed, the documentation also includes all the other relevant details such as available operations, schemas, data types, authentication requirements as well as example payloads.

This automatic processing of this API documentation ensures that it remains consistent with the current parametrization at all times, reducing the risk of outdated or incomplete descriptions.

Beyond APIs, this component in the future will also be extended to include internal documentation resources such as transaction tables, business process overviews, or coordination structures.

4.9 Apps Manager

The *Apps Management* component enables administrators to build and manage customized application screens that serve as alternatives to the native DISME dashboard. These custom apps provide focused, task-specific interfaces designed to improve navigation, user experience, and organizational clarity.

Each app can consist of multiple screens (or views), with each screen tailored to a specific domain, such as managing citizens, officials, scheduling blocks, or hearings. The design of these screens is driven by reusable components: forms, tasks, and data lists—each one tied to organizational roles and preconfigured queries.

Administrators begin by accessing the "App Management" tab and selecting "New App." The app creation environment is divided into five main configuration areas, as can be seen in Fig. 6:

- **App Configuration:** Define the app's name and assign which organizational roles can access it.

- **Screens Configuration:** Name and manage the app's screens. Each screen corresponds to a user-facing view within the app.
- **Variants Configuration:** In addition to standard screen creation, administrators can define two alternative layout variants—Variant A (Abi) and Variant B (Tim)—for each screen. These variants are automatically selected at runtime based on the user's cognitive facet scores or A/B testing classification, as defined by the User-Dependent Interface Management module. This allows the same screen to be presented differently depending on the user's interaction style—e.g., showing a grouped layout for more structured users, and a more condensed layout for exploratory users—enhancing usability across diverse cognitive profiles.
- **Layout Configuration:** Specify layout dimensions and choose device-specific grid previews (e.g., Desktop, Tablet, or Mobile), assisting responsive design choices.
- **Components:** Insert various UI elements such as forms (linked to process-starting tasks), task buttons, data lists (driven by pre-existing queries), and even raw HTML templates for advanced customization. Some forms may be excluded due to action rule restrictions—only forms initiating standalone processes are eligible for inclusion.

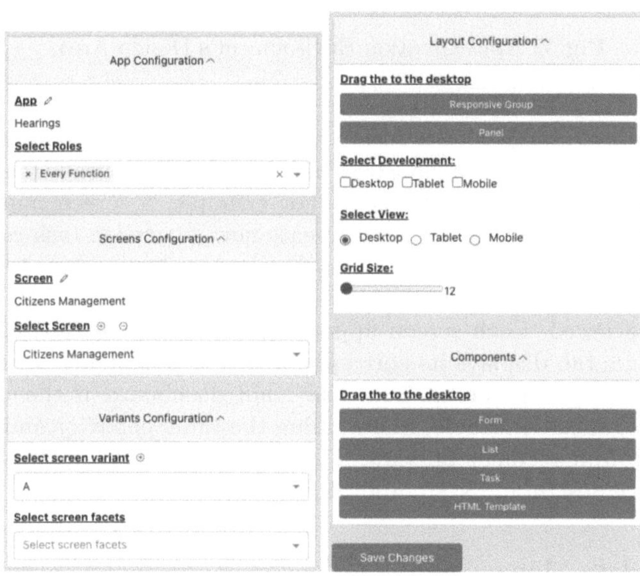

(a) App, screens and variants configuration. (b) Layout and components configuration.

Fig. 6. App Creation Environment's Configuration Areas.

Only components linked to roles configured in the App Settings tab are available for insertion, ensuring role-based access control is maintained.

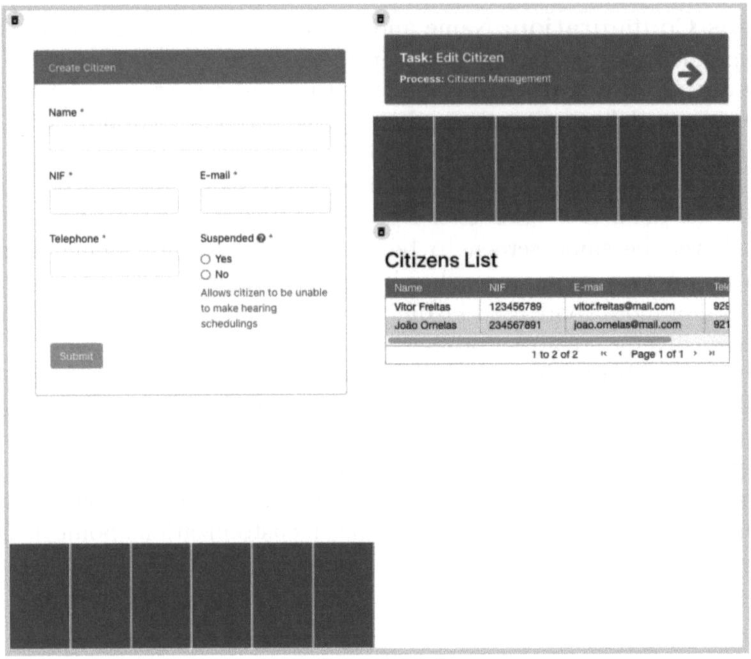

Fig. 7. Apps Creation Environment's Design Area.

Components are added to a screen using drag-and-drop onto a grid-based layout. Once placed, components can be resized and positioned according to design needs, as can be seen in Fig. 7. For example, a screen named "Citizen Management" might include a form to create new citizens, a task component to edit citizen details, and a list component displaying the registered citizens.

Once all desired screens and components are configured, the app can be saved and previewed. Each screen appears as a navigation tab below the app title. Selecting a tab displays its corresponding screen content, as seen in Fig. 8.

Apps can also be rendered from the main dashboard if the user has the appropriate organizational role, maintaining the same behavior and appearance as in the App Management preview. This allows seamless integration between user experience design and system-level permissions.

4.10 Template Management

The *Template Management* component in DISME provides comprehensive support for creating, styling, and delivering system-generated outputs, such as notifications, pop-up windows, and official documents, all without requiring any programming knowledge from the user.

Output actions are defined using the *User Output* custom block in the Blockly-based Action Rules specification. To fully customize the appearance and

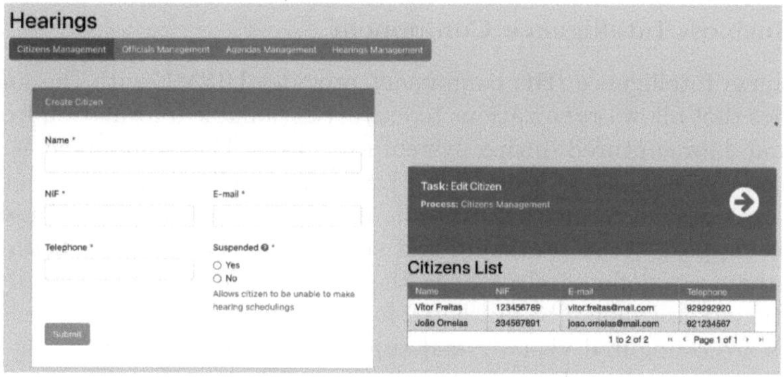

Fig. 8. Rendered App.

structure of these outputs, users can access the *Template Editor* component. This visual editor supports a WYSIWYG (What You See Is What You Get) interface, enabling users to design layouts for each output type: notifications, windows, or documents. Depending on the type selected, the interface adapts the required configuration fields—such as notification severity (e.g., warning, info), window headers and buttons, or document formatting preferences.

Within the editor, users can freely stylize text, insert tables and layout structures, and most importantly, embed dynamic values retrieved at runtime from the system's fact base. These values can include constants, properties of the current transaction instance, or the result of queries executed over the current process context. This allows templates to reflect real-time system information, improving their relevance and clarity to end-users.

The template content can be fully customized, including the use of HTML formatting for users who prefer finer control to layout, and style. This enables highly stylized and branded outputs, supporting advanced formatting requirements where needed.

When the user output type is a document, DISME leverages an integration with **Mayan EDMS**, a powerful open-source electronic document management system. Mayan is responsible for generating the final document file (e.g., PDF), handling its storage, indexing, and later retrieval. Documents generated through this integration are presented to users at runtime within the DISME interface, while also being archived in the system's document repository to ensure traceability and compliance.

This approach enables organizations to deliver tailored, high-quality outputs—ranging from interactive pop-ups to formal documents—within the same unified modeling and execution environment, maintaining full consistency with the underlying process model and information structure.

4.11 Business Intelligence Component

The Business Intelligence (BI) component provides DISME with the analytical capabilities that allow organizations to extract actionable information from their operational data captured during system execution. This component is divided in two main elements, Data Export and Dashboard Definition, and uses the data recorded by the Fact Model, transaction steps and connections, and user interactions to support decision-making and strategic analysis. In the Data Export module, the users define and manage the export templates that specify which organizational data should be extracted for reporting or external analysis. These templates are configured visually and support filtering and formatting rules in order to guarantee that the exported datasets are aligned with organizational requirements. The system then generates CSV or JSON exports that can be analyzed by an integrated deployment of Knowage or with resource to external tools such as Excel, Power BI, or statistical environments like R and Python-based analytics. The Dashboard Definition allows users to configure their dashboards composed of tiles that display the aggregate metrics or charts. These tiles are backed by queries defined via the Dynamic Search component, meaning no SQL or programming is required. Users can select which search to associate with each tile component, apply filters, and choose how the data should be rendered (e.g., counts, percentages, line charts, bar graphs). For more advanced users, the BI component also offers support for the definition of computed indicators, where users can define aggregation functions based on the existing queries and fact model properties (e.g., average session time, approval rate per role). These dashboards can also be embedded into apps built with the Apps Manager or displayed within the main user Dashboard, depending on role permissions.

5 System Executor

The System Executor is the runtime engine of DISME that is responsible for interpreting the specifications defined in the System Modeller. Instead of a more traditional compilation and code generation for the execution, in DISME, the System Executor gets its information directly from the model definitions stored in the platform's database. This allows for changes made to transactions, roles, forms, or rules to be immediately reflected in the live system, supporting the continuous adaptation and an iterative development. End-users interact with the system mainly through the System Executer's only component, the platform's dashboard.

5.1 Dashboard

The **Dashboard** is the central interface where DISME's end-users interact with the platform to carry out their daily organizational tasks. It serves as the runtime environment that adapts dynamically to each user's profile, offering access to task execution, process initiation, and monitoring functionalities based on the roles and permissions defined during system parametrization.

By default, the Dashboard presents a general-purpose interface that includes these components, as seen in Fig. 9:

- **Task Summary Panel**: Displays a real-time count of completed, pending, and delegated tasks, giving users an overview of their workload.
- **Pending Tasks Section**: Lists all tasks awaiting user action, color-coded by process type to help distinguish their context and origin.
- **Initiate Process Tasks**: Presents tasks that can initiate new transactions or business processes. The availability of these is determined by the user's competence and authorization.
- **In-Process Task Initiation**: Enables users to launch tasks within existing process instances by selecting the appropriate process context.

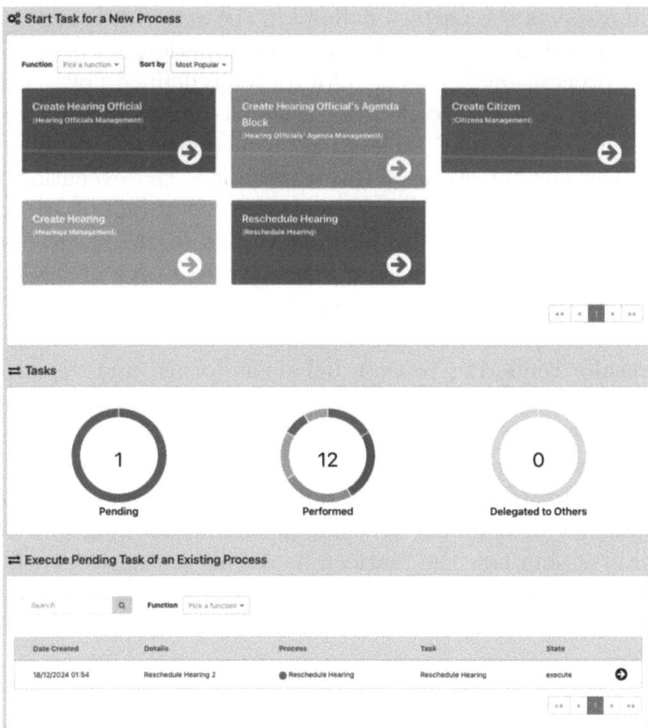

Fig. 9. Part of the default dashboard interface.

Each task tile includes indicators such as the process type, current step (e.g., *request*, *execute*, *state*), facilitating efficient process navigation and execution.

All these elements are automatically filtered according to the user's organizational roles and competences, ensuring that each individual sees only the tasks and process types they are authorized to act upon. Each task is also color-coded based on its associated process type, which is defined during process configuration, making navigation more intuitive and contextual.

In addition to this default configuration, DISME allows users to operate through **custom Apps**, as previously seen in Fig. 8, designed using the Apps Management component. When such Apps are defined and associated with a user's roles, the Dashboard can render these tailored interfaces instead of the default one. Each App can contain one or more screens that embed specific tasks, forms, and data visualizations (via dynamic searches), offering a focused and streamlined experience aligned with a particular business area or user need. These Apps provide greater visual flexibility and can be designed to better support domain-specific processes or usability preferences.

When a user initiates or executes a task—whether from the default Dashboard or within a custom App—the platform invokes the **Execution Engine**, which interprets the action rule defined for the corresponding transaction type. This execution respects the pattern defined in the action rule logic, determining the workflow and system behavior for each coordination act or fact.

Unlike rigid process engines that follow only predefined flows, DISME's Execution Engine supports a flexible transactional model based on the DEMO methodology. This means that, depending on the defined actions, their internal workflow, and the current state of the transaction, the execution may transition to any valid organizational state—not just the standard *request*, *promise*, *execute*, *state*, and *accept*, but also alternative paths such as *decline*, *cancel*, or others. This flexibility allows for comprehensive coverage of both normal and exceptional organizational behavior, ensuring that task execution aligns with the organization's rules and contingencies.

By dynamically rendering process behavior, forms, and visual components based on the underlying model, the Dashboard bridges the gap between high-level enterprise modeling and day-to-day user interaction. It acts as the operational layer, where the models defined by designers and analysts are enacted by the people responsible for carrying out real work in the organization. This runtime interplay between model-driven logic and actual usage provides a strong foundation for assessing how the platform performs under real-world conditions, both in terms of usability and organizational effectiveness.

6 Use Cases and Validation

To evaluate the usability and effectiveness of DISME, the platform has been applied and assessed in two real-world scenarios where it was also subject to both qualitative and quantitative validation.

6.1 Cognitive Rehabilitation Support System

In the Cognitive Rehabilitation Support System case [2] the study focused on the development of a support system for cognitive rehabilitation tasks in the health domain context that included user management, patient management, neuropsychological assessment management and training program management.

The organizational structure was modeled two ways: the first, the traditional approach with a dedicated platform being developed from scratch, and the second using DISME instead. In both cases, the goals and expected behaviors were the same, to manage patient sessions and evaluations.

In DISME, transactions were used to manage the organizational flow, forms supported data collection, and dynamic search queries powered therapist dashboards. Action Rules were employed to conduct patient and cognitive assessment sessions, orchestrate the execution of tests within each session, and compute the patient's cognitive profile based on their responses across multiple tests. These rules also enabled the design of personalized Training Programs tailored to assessment results. The entire system was configured without the need for manual coding, except for the layout customization of the generated documents containing the patient's information and cognitive profile.

Table 1. Traditional development time vs DISME deployment time.

Traditional Approach	Tasks	DISME Approach	
Total (hours)		Total (hours)	Relative %
108	**User Management**	5.7	**5.28%**
150	**Patient Management**	12.7	**8.47%**
420	**Neuropsychological Assessment Session Management**	19	**4.52%**
210	**Training Program Management**	10	**4.76%**
888	**Total**	**47.4**	**5.3%**

The development time of the DISME implementation was greatly inferior to the other approach as shown in Table 1 and the further usability testing with end-users (therapists and support staff) also demonstrated a substantial reduction in user errors, while preserving alignment with operational requirements.

Usability wise, DISME averaged 89,25% while the traditional implementation averaged 92%, both far above the acceptable threshold although with a small preference towards the traditional approach.

6.2 Municipality Hearings

The second case study had as the main objective the modernization of the digital support in a public hearing process in a local municipality. Here, DISME was customized to support the scheduling, coordination, and management of hearings, in order to replace the old system still in active use. In this deployment, we also integrated adaptive user interfaces guided by the GenderMag framework. UI variants were dynamically generated to match the user's cognitive styles, focusing on the Learning Style and Computer Self-Efficacy facets that were in turn captured through a structured questionnaire in the DISME user profile.

Qualitative Evaluation. The study involved 23 municipal officers that comprised the complete team responsible for managing hearings, and was conducted on-site during working hours. Participants executed tasks within two interface variants: one designed for Abi-like users (structured, risk-averse) and another for Tim-like users (exploratory, confident). A think-aloud protocol took place while they performed the tasks, and a post task qualitative survey followed. These were used to identify usability challenges, particularly with task discoverability (e.g., locating the "Edit" option). However, the participants consistently described the system as "intuitive" and "well-structured," expressing motivation to adopt it in their day-to-day workflow. Most interface difficulties they faced were during the initial tasks, with their confidence improving as familiarity increased.

Quantitative Evaluation. A controlled A/B test was conducted where participants were assigned to either the Abi or Tim interface variant. System Usability Scale (SUS) scores averaged 86.15 for Version A (Abi) and 88.25 for Version B (Tim), indicating an overall excellent usability perception. The NASA-TLX workload scores were also comparable, with minor differences across cognitive profiles.

The Task success rates, while unassisted, varied across them, with simpler tasks like profile creation showing success rates above 80%, and more complex scheduling operations showing lower rates (e.g., 35% for rescheduling). Users with lower computer self-efficacy (Abi-like) performed slightly better with the Abi variant, but the differences were not statistically significant. Process-oriented users (Abi) took longer on some of the tasks than tinkerers (Tim), particularly when facing UI navigation challenges. This supports partial evidence for differentiated interface impact based on cognitive style.

Overall, while we lacked statistical significance across most metrics that we measure, the results still suggest that interface adaptation based on GenderMag facets had the potential to enhance usability and reduce the issues for certain user types, particularly in structured, form-heavy environments.

7 Discussion and Limitations

DISME is a platform that shows the potential of the integration of theoretically grounded enterprise modeling with information systems through low-code/no-code, model driven approach. We have identified several strengths in our approach throughout the deployment and evaluations, being that, maybe the most relevant, is the integration of modeling and execution, enabling the implementation of organizational changed into the executable system in real time. Having the organizational logic specified through visual rules and diagrams, also lowers the barrier to participation in the information system design to users with no programming skills, which is further helped by the simple and intuitive interfaces like the action rules management, form management or app creation components. In the background, DISME guarantees that everything remains semantically correct between the multiple components, making it easier to maintain and use. The accessibility efforts further promote inclusiveness and a faster interaction with the organizational environment. However, some limitations still remain. With the growth of the modeled processes within the organization in both size and complexity, the cognitive effort to navigate and manage them also increase. The visual interfaces that greatly benefit novice users may become problematic in large scale deployments, indicating a likely need for the introduction of some scalability mechanisms. Performance wise, DISME still needs some optimization, specially regarding data intensive scenarios, and this is something that needs to be tackled in a near future. Regarding the diagram modeling, further work also needs to take place to both increase the semantic validation of the models while being created and guarantee their consistency with the already existing artifacts. This last step requires fully automation, which is something that is not yet implemented. Looking into the future, there are other key areas where we intend to improve and extend the platform's capabilities. These include:

- Simulation and analytics capabilities to evaluate model behavior before deployment.
- Multi-user model collaboration, including real-time co-editing and change tracking.
- Model and System versioning features such as diffing, rollback, and validation reports.

By continuing to evolve DISME, the platform can expand its utility across a broader range of organization processes and organizations with further complexity levels, while maintaining its core mission of bridging the gap between enterprise modeling theory and operational information system practice.

8 Conclusion

This paper presented DISME, a low-code/no-code platform that aims to bridge the gap between enterprise modeling and execution in the form of an information system through the use of organizational specifications. Grounded in the DEMO methodology and the Adaptive Object Model paradigm, DISME supports both the design definition and execution of the organizational logic without relying on any traditional programming or code generation. We described the system architecture and detailed the main components of the platform, including action rule specification, visual form editing, REST integration, and adaptive user interface management. Each component contributes to creating semantically coherent and directly executable models that can be adjusted during runtime, offering high flexibility as well as a closer alignment with the organizational needs. Two real-world use cases, one in the healthcare domain, and another in municipal governance, show DISME's applicability in multiple domains. The healthcare domain in particular shows substantial reductions in development time and complexity when compared to traditional approaches, and both cases also validated the platform's usability through both qualitative and quantitative evaluations. The results, although still very limited in scope, tend to suggest that DISME is a viable option for organizations seeking to model and maintain their processes and rules in a transparent and adaptable way. At the same time, several areas for future improvement remain. These include scalability mechanisms for managing large models, performance optimization under data-intensive conditions, enhanced semantic validation of diagrams and business logic, and expanded support for collaborative modeling, simulation, and version control. As the platform evolves, the focus will also remain on enabling inclusive, runtime-adaptable systems that maintain a close and traceable connection between enterprise design and operational reality.

Disclosure of Interests. The authors have no competing interests to declare that are relevant to the content of this article.

References

1. Aveiro, D., Caires, V.: DEMO model based rapid REST API management in a low code platform. In: Proceedings of the 22nd CIAO! Doctoral Consortium, and Enterprise Engineering Working Conference Forum 2022 co-located with 12th Enterprise Engineering Working Conference (EEWC 2022) **3388** (2022). https://ceur-ws.org/Vol-3388/paper2.pdf
2. Aveiro, D., Freitas, V.: Evaluating the usability of a system implemented on a DEMO-based low-code platform. In: Companion Proceedings of the 16th IFIP WG 8.1 Working Conference on the Practice of Enterprise Modeling and the 13th Enterprise Design and Engineering Working Conference: BES, DTE, FACETE, Tools & Demos, Forum, EDEN Doctoral Consortium co-located with PoEM 2023 **3645** (2023). https://ceur-ws.org/Vol-3645/forum9.pdf
3. Aveiro, D., Freitas, V., Pinto, D., Caires, V., Pacheco, D.: Extending DEMO action rule specifications' syntax in a low code platform based municipality hearing system implementation. In: Proceedings of the 16th International Joint Conference on Knowledge Discovery, Knowledge Engineering and Knowledge Management. pp. 243–251. SCITEPRESS - Science and Technology Publications, Porto, Portugal (2024). https://doi.org/10.5220/0013068800003838
4. Aveiro, D., Pinto, D.: Universal enterprise adaptive object model: a semantic web-based implementation of organizational self-awareness. Intell. Syst. Account. Finance Manage. **22**(1), 3–28 (2015). https://doi.org/10.1002/isaf.1363
5. Burnett, M., Peters, A., Hill, C., Elarief, N.: Finding gender-inclusiveness software issues with GenderMag: a field investigation. In: Proceedings of the 2016 CHI Conference on Human Factors in Computing Systems, pp. 2586–2598. CHI '16, Association for Computing Machinery, New York, USA (May 2016). https://doi.org/10.1145/2858036.2858274

6. Burnett, M., et al.: GenderMag: a method for evaluating software's gender inclusiveness. Interact. Comput. **28**(6), 760–787 (2016). https://doi.org/10.1093/iwc/iwv046
7. Dietz, J.L.G., Mulder, H.B.F.: Enterprise Ontology: A Human-Centric Approach to Understanding the Essence of Organisation. The Enterprise Engineering Series, Springer International Publishing, Cham (2020). https://doi.org/10.1007/978-3-030-38854-6
8. Gouveia, B., Aveiro, D., Pacheco, D., Pinto, D., Gouveia, D.: Fact model in DEMO - urban law case and proposal of representation improvements. In: Aveiro, D., Guizzardi, G., Pergl, R., Proper, H.A. (eds.) EEWC 2020. LNBIP, vol. 411, pp. 173–190. Springer, Cham (2021). https://doi.org/10.1007/978-3-030-74196-9_10
9. Hamid, M.M., et al.: How to measure diversity actionably in technology. In: Equity, Diversity, and Inclusion in Software Engineering: Best Practices and Insights, pp. 469–485. Apress Berkeley, CA (2024)
10. Hilderbrand, C., et al.: Engineering gender-inclusivity into software: ten teams' tales from the trenches. In: Proceedings of the ACM/IEEE 42nd International Conference on Software Engineering, pp. 433–444 (2020)
11. Lavie, T., Meyer, J.: Benefits and costs of adaptive user interfaces. Int. J. Hum Comput Stud. **68**(8), 508–524 (2010)
12. Makri, S.: Gendermag - a process to find and fix gender barriers in technology design. https://www.city.ac.uk/research/impact/case-studies/gendermag-a-process-to-find-and-fix-gender-barriers-in-technology-design
13. Miraz, M.H., Ali, M., Excell, P.S.: Adaptive user interfaces and universal usability through plasticity of user interface design. Comput. Sci. Rev. **40**, 100363 (2021)
14. Murphy-Hill, E., et al.: Gendermag improves discoverability in the field, especially for women: an multi-year case study of suggest edit, a code review feature. In: Proceedings of the IEEE/ACM 46th International Conference on Software Engineering, pp. 1–12 (2024)
15. Organization, I.S.: ISO/IEC 14977 - Information technology |Syntactic metalanguage| Extended BNF. Standard, International Organization for Standardization, Geneva, CH (Dec 1996)
16. Pinto, D., Aveiro, D., Pacheco, D., Gouveia, B., Gouveia, D.: Validation of DEMO's conciseness quality and proposal of improvements to the process model. In: Aveiro, D., Guizzardi, G., Pergl, R., Proper, H.A. (eds.) EEWC 2020. LNBIP, vol. 411, pp. 133–152. Springer, Cham (2021). https://doi.org/10.1007/978-3-030-74196-9_8
17. Weld, D., Gajos, K.: Supple: automatically generating user interfaces. In: Proceedings of the 9th International Conference on Intelligent User Interfaces, pp. 93–100. Association for Computing Machinery (2004). https://doi.org/10.1145/964442.964461
18. Yoder, J.W., Balaguer, F., Johnson, R.: Architecture and design of adaptive object-models. ACM SIGPLAN Not. **36**(12), 50–60 (2001). https://doi.org/10.1145/583960.583966
19. Yoder, J.W., Johnson, R.: The adaptive object-model architectural style. In: Bosch, J., Gentleman, M., Hofmeister, C., Kuusela, J. (eds.) Software Architecture: System Design, Development and Maintenance, pp. 3–27. IFIP – The International Federation for Information Processing, Springer US, USA (2002). https://doi.org/10.1007/978-0-387-35607-5_1

KPI-Driven Visualizations for Root Cause Analysis in Manufacturing Processes

Kacper Mucha[1(✉)], Kristof Böhmer[1], and Maria Leitner[1,2]

[1] Faculty of Computer Science, Research Group Workflow Systems and Technology, University of Vienna, Vienna, Austria
{kacper.mucha,kristof.boehmer}@univie.ac.at

[2] Faculty of Informatics and Data Science, Chair of Artificial Intelligence in IT Security, University of Regensburg, Regensburg, Germany
maria.leitner@ur.de

Abstract. In the past years, process mining has been a key technology to improve business processes. For example, through outlier, often also referred to as anomalies, detection and root cause analysis. However, visualizations for root cause analysis and anomaly detection have often been missing. Hardening it to follow up on anomalies through adaptive decision-making. Such visualizations aim at helping manufacturing professionals analyze this data on their own - without a need for a data expert. Existing works exploring this topic do not focus on the manufacturing domain, thereby missing the unique complexities inherent to this sector. We bridge this gap by introducing an interactive KPI-driven dashboard with two views: one for the overall material overview and one for the detailed analysis. This dashboard provides understandable KPI-driven visualizations for detecting anomalies and supports the identification of their root causes. Enabling the identification and assessment of unplanned, ad hoc, production approaches. The dashboard's benefits were validated by two focus groups. Both focus groups confirmed the dashboard's usefulness, highlighting its ability to reveal optimization opportunities through understandable visualizations. For future work, we aim to support variants and investigate its applicability to other domains.

Keywords: Anomaly Detection · Manufacturing · Process Mining · Root Cause Analysis

1 Introduction

In large manufacturing enterprises with diverse and parallel production processes, it poses a significant challenge to determine in which workflows or production processes certain Key Performance Indicators (KPIs) [13] perform below or above average. Such production steps, for which the KPI values deviate from the norm, we consider as anomalies [4]. Understanding the potential root causes of such anomalies could provide valuable insights for process improvement and security [10]. In the world of Industry 4.0, we are able to solve this problem

J. Barateiro et al. (Eds.): EDOC 2025 Workshops, LNBIP 571, pp. 474–489, 2026.
https://doi.org/10.1007/978-3-032-16234-2_38

by harnessing the data generated by factories through process mining (PM). However, the results obtained from PM are often complex and not everyone can interpret them on their own [17]. The lack of specialized technical and analytical skills presents a barrier for wider PM adoption within the organizations [11].

This work employs design science research methodologies [22]. In this context, the challenges of understanding complex PM data and codifying tacit expert knowledge for efficient transfer have been identified (Sect. 3). To address this issue, we have developed and evaluated a prototype dashboard, which can transform this data into intuitive visualizations, facilitating anomaly detection, root cause analysis and documentation of context-specific adaptations (e.g., temporary production workarounds during machine breakdowns). The dashboard is interactive, allowing users to select KPIs, define time periods, and filter data by material number and specific anomalies. The primary aim of this prototype is to enable manufacturing planning and control experts to conduct independent process analyses and institutionalize operational know-how, mitigating risks of knowledge loss when experienced personnel retire. The key stakeholders for this tool include process experts, planners, and shop floor workers.

We developed and evaluated the dashboard with input from multiple domain experts (Sect. 4). The development was based on a real-world dataset describing an entire manufacturing production process for about 4000 different materials, provided by our esteemed partners specializing in IT solutions for manufacturing enterprises. Each row corresponds to an activity with a unique activity number, linked to specific production process and material number.

The effectiveness of our visualization tool was assessed through a series of focus group interviews with experts from manufacturing and software domains (Sect. 5). Positive feedback underscores the tool's efficacy in streamlining root cause analysis within large-scale production environments. Key findings include the confirmation of KPI utilization in manufacturing processes, interest in data-driven optimizations, and positive impressions of the visualizations.

This paper is organized as follows: Sect. 2 discusses related works and showcases the existing research gap. Section 3 presents the requirements and concepts. The used technology, proposed approach, dataset and implementation are detailed in Sect. 4. Section 5 covers the evaluation process and discusses the results. Finally, conclusions, and future work are outlined in Sect. 6.

2 Related Work

Visualization of Anomalies in Business Processes. The need for easy-to-interpret visualizations that are able to explain information resulting from process mining has been identified, for example in [3,21]. Both of them acknowledge that the mined data is often challenging to understand quickly due to its representation in numerical form or complex process maps. They emphasize the need to complement process mining with various visualization techniques that would support the specialists in analysing the data, which they subsequently propose.

In the scope of anomaly detection, it has also been shown how good visualizations of process mining data can help the analysts [7]. The work of [5], although not focused on process mining, notices that: *"an anomaly can only be truly resolved by understanding and addressing its cause"* [5, p. 8].

To the best of our knowledge, current literature on visualization techniques for root cause analysis is not focused on the manufacturing domain [8,14,24]. We have experienced that the specific intricacies and complexities inherent in manufacturing processes are important to investigate, as they impact the effectiveness of process mining visualizations. For instance, let's consider the difference between a knowledge worker, such as someone processing insurance claims, and a manufacturing worker in a factory which produces metal parts. These individuals deal with vastly different process lengths, quantities and process lead times (processing a single insurance claim versus 10,000 gears). Consequently, these two groups may have varying levels of understanding when it comes to visualizations. Knowledge workers may be more accustomed to interpreting data visualizations related to their field, while manufacturing workers may find those same visualizations less familiar or relevant, as confirmed by domain experts.

Anomaly Detection and Process Mining. On the other hand, the works that lay in this scope and analyze the anomaly detection capabilities of the data resulting from process mining, do not focus on providing visualizations that would help in explaining the root cause e.g., [12,15,16]. This is also a limitation, because without effective visualization techniques to explain the root cause of anomalies, analysts may struggle to understand underlying issues and take appropriate corrective actions. As a result, the potential benefits of process mining for anomaly detection may not be fully realized, leading to inefficiencies and missed opportunities for improvement [2,5]. The importance of visualization techniques in the context of smart manufacturing is voiced in [24], where the authors advocate for leveraging domain-specific knowledge in interactive visualization systems.

Moreover, a systematic literature review on the application of process mining in manufacturing highlights the need for research that goes beyond simple process discovery, focusing on the important areas of process enhancement and conformance checking [6]. This work also points out, that traditional process mining tools often struggle with the complex and varied nature of event logs in the manufacturing sector, making effective analysis and process management more difficult. These challenges are further complicated by the non-linear aspects of many manufacturing processes, which make it harder to connect process instances with real-world results. As a result, the shortcomings of current solutions prevent organizations from fully utilizing the potential of process mining, ultimately hindering their ability to manage and improve processes effectively.

Considering this, we propose an interactive dashboard as *a business application with a rich user interface for users to interact with data*, based on [23], and presenting data through various visualization forms. Through this dashboard, we bridge the outlined research gap by providing an interactive tool for anomaly detection and root cause analysis in the manufacturing sector.

3 Concept and Requirements

In this section, we outline the essential requirements (**R1** to **R4**, see below) and the key concepts used to implement them. These requirements were discussed with domain experts and validated during the evaluation (cf. Sect. 5).

- **R1: Efficient Data Extraction:** A robust method for extracting footprints from process logs for large-scale analysis. This requirement is motivated by the high-volume, high-velocity nature of industrial data streams, where traditional extraction methods fail to scale.
- **R2: Graphical Representation:** The ability to create intuitive graphs and scatter plots tailored to domain-specific needs. While complex visualizations (e.g., Sankey diagrams) are common in research, domain experts emphasized that shop-floor workers require simplified, standardized representations to avoid misinterpretation of process flows.
- **R3: Interactive Visualization Interface:** An interactive, user-friendly, and visually engaging interface for all users. This was driven by feedback from plant operators, who noted that overly intricate tools lead to disengagement.
- **R4: Comprehensibility:** Clear dynamic representations to ensure insights are easily understood by individuals at all expertise levels. Experts highlighted that insights must be immediately actionable – even for workers without data literacy – to support real-time decision-making in production environments.

3.1 Concepts

In this section, we explain the concepts used and how they were applied to meet our selected requirements. This includes KPI usage, footprint analysis, dashboard design, and anomaly detection methods.

Usage of Key Performance Indicators. The selection of KPIs was informed by industry experts and deliberately chosen to enable precise validation of the framework's analytical accuracy during evaluation. These KPIs are widely used in manufacturing optimization, facilitating direct comparisons with existing benchmarks while allowing the framework to be extended to other metrics as needed. The chosen KPIs were: *Lead Time*, *Duration of Malfuntion*, *Rejections* and *Overall Equipment Effectiveness* (OEE). The OEE KPI is a standard in production environments [19].

KPI-driven Footprint Analysis. To calculate the KPI values of production steps, we utilized a KPI-driven footprint analysis. A footprint is "*a matrix that displays the causal dependencies between activities*" [1, p. 7]. This matrix aids in the identification of activity sequences that could potentially pose challenges. The calculation of these KPI values involves several steps. First, we iterate over all process instances in the given process execution log. For each process instance, we extract all footprints. Then we calculate the user-chosen KPI values related to each footprint (e.g., Lead Time or OEE). Finally, we take the average of the KPI values across extracted footprints. This process enables us to evaluate the impact of specific process activity interaction orders on KPIs and compare different activity orders used by various production processes for the same material.

Interactive Multi-view Dashboard Design. Our dashboard design incorporates a set of interactive options (see Sect. 4.3) through which we specify which visualization to display. There are two main views: (1) a view for the overview of all materials allowing swift identification of outliers across the production site utilizing a scatter plot (see Sect. 4.4) and (2) a view for the detailed analysis of a single material, leveraging scatter plots and directly follows graphs (DFG), for the detailed root cause analysis (see Sect. 4.5).

Usage of Colors to Enhance Visibility. To make data points with deviating performance immediately noticeable, different markings were introduced. Data points in scatter plots and paths in DFGs with KPI values deviating by more than one standard deviation from the average (indicating worse performance) were highlighted in red. Conversely, data points and paths were marked in green if their KPI values deviated by more than half of the standard deviation from the average (indicating better performance). The standard deviations and mean were marked as dotted blue and red lines respectively. A color scale was introduced for a nuanced representation, where a gentle red or gentle green represented a deviation of one standard deviation, more intense shades represented two, three and four (or more) standard deviations. Additionally, in scatter plots, the shape of the data points is dynamic: a triangle indicates worse, a circle - normal, and a square - better performance.

Standard Deviation as Anomaly Detection Mechanism. After the discussion with domain experts, it was decided to utilize standard deviation as a method for detecting anomalies. Although there is a risk using this method that we may miss out on some other types of anomalies, such as non-conformant behaviors or unseen variants like concept drift, the experts concluded that variant detection and concept drift are not of the highest priority for our current needs. Therefore, we aimed for simplicity of the solution, prioritizing ease of implementation. This approach allows us to quickly identify and address common anomalies without the complexity and resource demands of more advanced techniques.

4 Proof-of-Concept Implementation

This section details the implementation of the interactive dashboard[1], including the utilized dataset and technical aspects. We also explain the motivation behind each view, its implementation and an example from the real-world dataset.

[1] The source code is publicly available at: https://github.com/KEJEMIK/dashboard-for-root-cause-analysis-in-manufacturing.

4.1 Dataset

The backbone of our analysis is a rich dataset generously provided by our esteemed partner, a Manufacturing Execution System (MES) provider. The dataset, presented in CSV format, captures the manufacturing process completely, with around 30000 unique activities, 4000 different processes and 1000 materials. Each row represents a distinct activity, identified by an activity number and associated with a specific production process and material number. The materials represent final products, such as brake pads, and can be produced through one of many concurrently used alternative production processes. For instance, machine failure or maintenance can require applying an alternative production process. Hence, a single material can be the outcome of one of many chosen (by production planning staff) processes, each consisting of various activities executed in various orders. On average, there were 8 to 9 activities per process in our dataset. We will further use this dataset as our running example.

The dataset includes timestamps, enabling the computation of KPIs chosen in Sect. 3.1. The *Lead Time* KPI is derived from the interval between start and end times, while the *Duration of Malfunction* KPI is calculated from malfunction duration data. Additionally, information on the number of rejected materials is used to compute the *Rejections* KPI. Furthermore, rows detailing *Performance*, *Quality*, and *Availability*, ranging from 0 to 1, were utilized to calculate the *OEE* KPI. The dataset was anonymized to align with research partner requirements.

4.2 Architecture and Technology

Web Application Framework. In the exploration of state-of-the-art technologies for data visualization, the *Mercury Framework*[2] was selected for its ability to convert *Jupyter Notebooks* into interactive web applications using widgets. This aligns with the requirements R3 and R4.

Process Mining. We opted to utilize *PM4Py*[3] because of its extensive support for various process discovery methods. Notably, *PM4Py* offers a flexible and robust toolkit with pre-configured implementations of popular process discovery and conformance checking techniques. The footprints matrix methods, proved particularly suitable to fulfill requirement R1. Process mining is especially valuable in manufacturing, as it reconstructs actual process flows from event data rather than relying on predefined models. This enables the identification of inefficiencies, deviations, and root causes of production issues, facilitating data-driven process optimization.

Visualization. To fulfill the requirements R2 and R4, our visualization strategies were mainly anchored in the use of *Graphviz*[4] for visualizing Directly Follow Graphs (DFGs). Furthermore, for crafting scatter plots, we employed *Matplotlib*[5], a versatile and widely-used plotting library in Python.

[2] https://runmercury.com/, last accessed: 2025-06-25.
[3] https://processintelligence.solutions/, last accessed: 2025-06-25.
[4] https://graphviz.org/, last accessed: 2025-06-25.
[5] https://matplotlib.org/, last accessed: 2025-06-25.

4.3 Dashboard: General Overview

The primary goal of creating this dashboard was to allow users to interactively engage with the data. To achieve this, we implemented a selection of options that users can configure on the left, while on the right, the chosen views are displayed. The dashboard can be seen in Fig. 3 and interactive options are:

- **"Select a KPI"**: The user can choose which KPI to analyze.
- **"Select a time period"**: Filters the dataset for a selected time period.
- **"Select a material number"**: The user can choose one of the material numbers from the dataset in order to filter the dataset to include only the process instances associated with the selected material number. Selection of a material number triggers view (2) described in Sect. 4.5. The option **"All"** can also be chosen, which triggers the view (1) described in Sect. 4.4.
- **"Select analysis mode"**: This option allows the selection of an analysis mode. Currently, only one analysis mode is supported, *"Footprints"*.
- **"Select an outlier footprint"** - This option further filters the dataset and is available only when the **"Select material number"** option is not set to *"All"*. Users can choose one of the identified outlier footprints, which trigger the view visible on Fig. 4. Two additional options are also available, the option *"All"*, which triggers a view visible in Fig. 3 and option *"None"*, which triggers the view visible on Fig. 2.

4.4 Dashboard View 1: Production Overview

In the first view, our idea was to develop a dashboard that immediately allows an overview of the production side and consists of all materials present in the selected time frame. Given the substantial number of process logs in manufacturing companies, having a clear overview indicating which materials exhibit significantly better or worse KPIs compared to others is crucial. This overview enables quick identification of materials that require a thorough examination to determine the causes and apply measures to improve processes in the future.

View 1 Implementation. A scatter plot was created for all materials present in the selected production period. These materials are listed on the x-axis of the scatter plot. Then on the y-axis of the plot, the chosen KPI values are displayed for each of the materials, with applied to them different shapes and color markings as described in Sect. 3.1. The KPI values for the material are calculated by taking a mean over all activities linked to the material.

Running Example. To illustrate, we examine the data (see Sect. 4.1) from the last 2 weeks for the KPI *Lead Time* (Fig. 1). We can see in the figure that the scatter plot visualizes the outliers which can be quickly spotted and marked for further investigation. In this example, material number *7742719* (highlighted with a red ellipse in the bottom right) exhibits a particularly poor average lead time across all processes (highlighted with a red ellipse in the top right corner). After identifying such an anomaly, the material in question can be discussed at the next production meeting, and optimization possibilities can be explored.

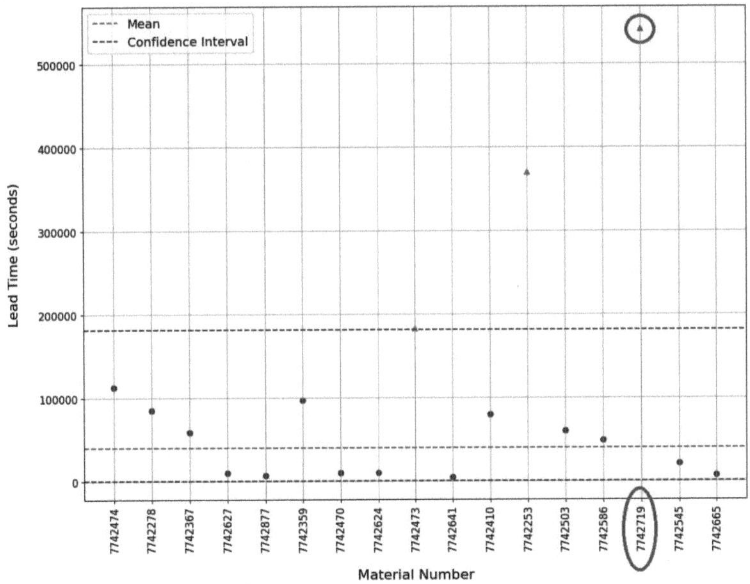

Fig. 1. Scatter Plot Visualization for KPI Lead Time (Screenshot).

4.5 Dashboard View 2: Detailed Analysis of a Material

The primary objective of this view is to equip users with the tools necessary to conduct a deeper analysis of outliers identified in View (1). When designing this view we had two goals in mind. The first was to provide an overview of all production steps involved in the selected material, with particular emphasis on under- and overperforming activities. This would facilitate swift detection of outliers and provide users with the option to examine process instances containing these outlier activities in greater detail. The second goal was to enable users to review the paths taken during the execution of process instances for a material. This would allow users to determine whether the outlier KPI value for an activity was influenced by preceding activities, enabling root cause analysis.

View 2 Implementation. This view provides a comprehensive overview of all production steps involved in the creation of a material, facilitating the identification of outliers. This is achieved through a scatter plot, where the x-axis displays the extracted footprints and the y-axis represents the corresponding KPI values. The details of footprint extraction, KPI calculation, and the use of shapes and color markings are discussed in Sect. 3.1. Additionally, **View 2 Implementation** offers a Directly-Follows Graph (DFG) visualization, which varies depending on the user's selection from the **"Select an outlier footprint"** dropdown. If *All* is selected, the DFG reflects all process instances for the material; if a specific outlier footprint is chosen, the DFG focuses on instances containing that outlier. The paths in the DFG corresponding to outlier footprints are highlighted in the same color as in the scatter plot.

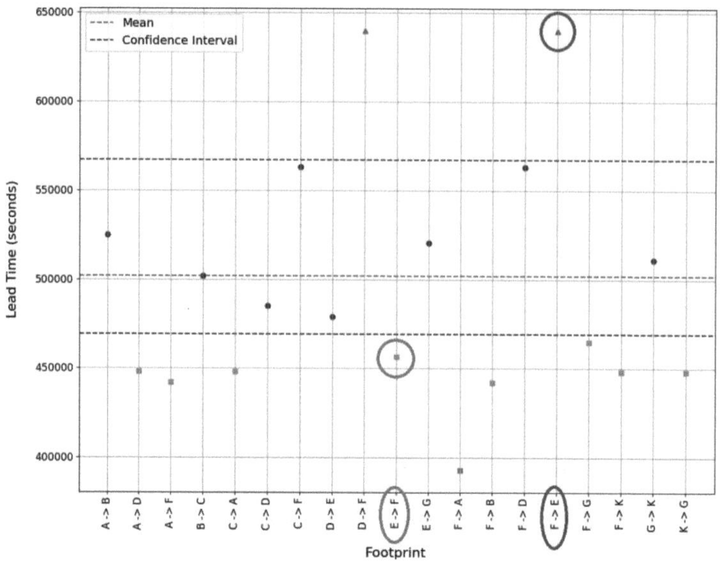

Fig. 2. Scatter Plot for a Material over all footprints (Screenshot). The Footprints of interest are highlighted.

Running Example. Let's take a closer look at the previously identified outlier material number *7742719* for the selected KPI *Lead Time*. The option **"Select an outlier Footprint"** is set to *"None"*, and in the dashboard, a scatter plot (see Fig. 2) is shown. Here, two footprints *(D → F)* and *(F → E)* stand out, showing a worse average performance, while several footprints have slightly better average lead times (e.g. *(F → K)*, *(F → G)*, *(A → D)*).

By activating a DFG view for all footprints (option **"Select an outlier Footprint"** set to *"All"*), we get a detailed representation (see Fig. 3). Here, we see that the path with normal performance for all footprints is used most frequently (the black, thick path *(A → B → C → F → D → E → G → K)*). Furthermore, we can also identify several alternative paths where lead time is better but less frequently used (the green paths (e.g. *(A → D)*, *(F →* K *→ G)*). There was also a red path which led to an increase in lead time *(D → F → E)*.

By examining the DFG, we may think that footprint *(F → E)* was influenced by the footprint *(D → F)*. We may check our hypothesis by filtering the DFG. We can do it by selecting the outlier footprint from the **"Select an outlier Footprint"** dropdown (Footrpint*(F → E)* in our case). This would draw a DFG only for processes containing the selected outlier footprint *(F → E)* (Fig. 4a). Indeed, the footprint *(D → F)* occurs before the footprint *(F → E)*, indicating that *(D → F)* may be the **root cause** and requires further analysis.

We can also examine the paths that have better lead times. In the DFG in Fig. 3, it can be seen that the path with a positive footprint *(E → F)* was used

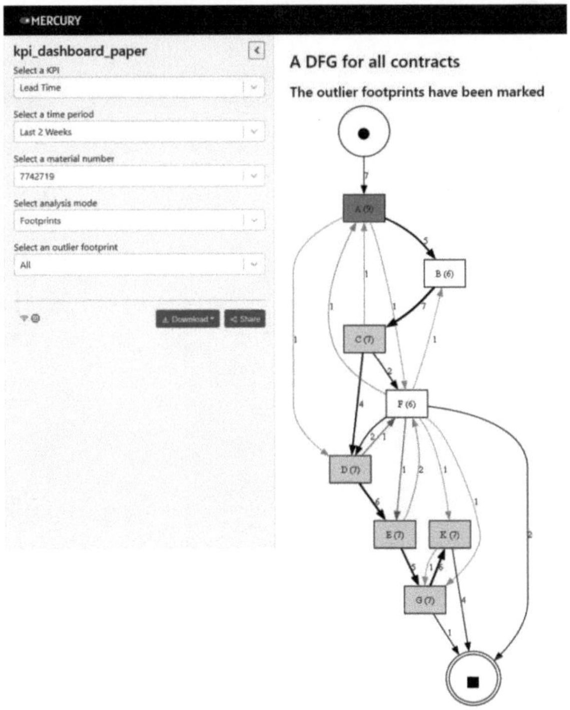

Fig. 3. Dashboard screenshot for a material number 7742719 over all Footprints (DFG) for "Lead Time" KPI. (Color figure online)

twice. A closer look in Fig. 4b suggests that the green paths represent a better alternative to the black paths, which were used more frequently.

To illustrate the practical benefits, let's consider the scenario of machine breakdowns. The colored segments, which deviate from the standard path, could signify workarounds implemented due to equipment failure. Recognizing these adaptations not only helps in understanding the direct impact of machine breakdowns on lead times but also in identifying potential best practices that could be standardized to enhance overall productivity (for example with green paths).

5 Evaluation

This section describes the evaluation of our approach. In particular, we conducted two focus groups to discuss and identify the potential intuitiveness and usefulness of visualizations for root cause analysis in the manufacturing domain. Focus groups are a good method to analyze the results from different points of view in a short period of time [9,18].

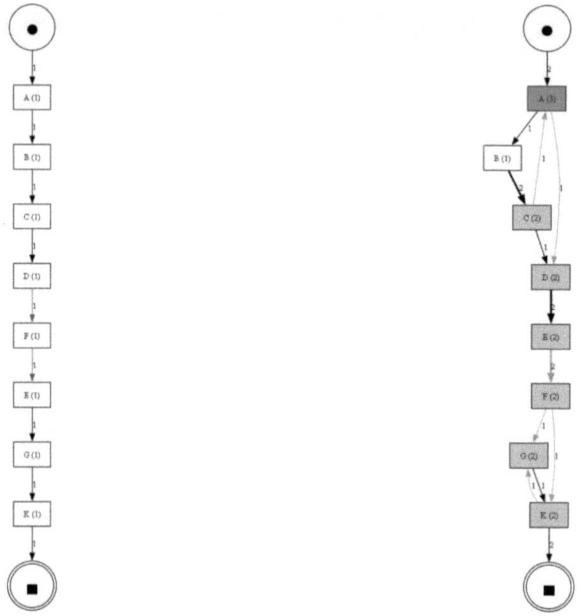

(a) DFG over all processes containing the footprint (F → E).

(b) DFG over all processes containing the footprint (E → F).

Fig. 4. Comparison of outlier footprints for material number 7742719 and KPI *Lead Time*. (Color figure online)

5.1 Participants and Procedure

For the main evaluation, we organized two focus group interviews, each scheduled to last approximately 90 min. The first focus group session was focused on assessing the software aspects of the dashboard, while the second session addressed usability aspects.

The initial focus group session, held on November 15, 2023, as an online meeting, included four experts from the manufacturing software domain: a product manager, a testing specialist, a software architect and a software engineer. They were selected based on their extensive industry experience and their roles in implementing software solutions for manufacturing enterprises.

A second session was conducted on March 25, 2024, in person, with three experts from the manufacturing field: a vision inspection specialist, a shop floor data collection expert, and a team supply chain manager. Their participation was crucial due to their in-depth knowledge of operational challenges and their experience in introducing new manufacturing technologies into production environment. Each of the listed experts brought over 10 years of practical experience, making them well-suited to provide valuable insights during the discussions.

The structure of each focus group was consistent: an introduction round was followed by hands-on demonstrations of the dashboard. During the presentations, three materials (from the experts organizations) were showcased, allowing participants to engage directly with the tool. Following the presentation of the results of each material, the results were openly discussed by the experts.

5.2 Goals and Questions

The focus groups were conducted with the following goals in mind: to assess current practices and challenges in production optimization using key performance indicators (KPIs), to explore the adoption and motivations behind data-driven workflows and process optimizations, and to evaluate the effectiveness and user experience of selected visualizations. To achieve these goals, the focus groups addressed and discussed the following questions (Q):

- **Q1:** How do you utilize key performance indicators to optimize production?
- **Q2:** How are you carrying out data-driven workflow optimizations?
- **Q3:** How useful and intuitive are the selected visualizations?

Question Q1 is designed to understand the extent to which KPIs are currently being used to optimize production processes. Additionally, this question aims to uncover how KPIs are used and which KPIs are the most important. Question Q2 seeks to determine whether data-driven approaches are being utilized to optimize workflows and processes. It aims to provide insight into what motivates organizations to pursue data-driven strategies and what benefits they hope to achieve. Question Q3 focuses on assessing the usefulness and intuitiveness of the selected visualizations. It aims to evaluate how effectively these visualizations convey information and to determine whether similar tools are already in use within the organizations. Additionally, it seeks feedback on how the visualizations can be improved for better usability and comprehension.

5.3 Findings

We analyzed the insights provided by the participants. Key findings:

Q1 and Q2: Participants utilize various KPIs like *Lead Time*, *OEE*, *Mean Time Between Failure*, and *Rejection Rate*, with *Lead Time* and *OEE* being the most important. They stressed the need for high data quality to avoid the "*garbage in, garbage out*" problem and suggested improvements such as automatic piece count recording and standardized calculations per VDMA guidelines [20]. Currently, data-driven optimizations are not implemented, relying instead on the experience of senior employees. This approach lacks evidence and risks knowledge loss if experienced employees leave. Experts acknowledged the sub-optimal nature of this situation, emphasizing the need for dedicated data-driven analysis tools.

Q3: During the interview, participants found the first view particularly helpful for identifying processes requiring closer analysis (Fig. 1). They especially applauded the DFG view of the production process with marked outlier footprints (Figs. 3 and 4). During the interview, using this view, experts were able to directly pinpoint long running activities in the production process and formulate hypotheses regarding the underlying issues. Also, the ability to filter processes based on them containing a specific outlier footprint was also met with positive feedback, with them noting that it really eases the analysis process.

On the other hand, the scatter plot view of the footprints has garnered in general criticism (Fig. 2). The experts stated that on the DFG they can clearly see on which production step a problem occurs, while on the scatter plot view, it was not easily noticeable, mainly due to footprints being described in textual form at the x-axis of the plot. Another aspect has been raised by the focus group about calculating KPIs such as *Lead Time* at the footprint level. The dashboard currently computes the average out of all the footprints, but some footprints are designed to take way shorter time as some others and can be marked as outliers by our dashboard. Noise reduction could be implemented to hinder this effect.

Furthermore, it was noted that the manufacturing organization represented by the experts does not utilize similar visualization techniques to those employed by our implementation. They find the prospect of having such a tool highly motivating, because it could help the employees and influence the quality of reporting. Would the workers be able to see that a process looks bad, they would feel affected and would try to fix it. This would also save monitoring time, as the employees would be able to monitor the processes themselves.

Overall the experts in both focus groups were able to analyze and identify the anomalies on their own and state reasons about potential root causes. In addition, the visualizations on the dashboard were understandable and useful to the experts and provided a useful benefit in future manufacturing environments.

5.4 Discussion

The overall positive feedback from domain experts underscores the benefits of the dashboard in addressing the challenge of losing an overview due to the vast amount of data that can quickly overwhelm users. Experts have emphasized that the tool's simple visualizations are essential for effective planning and discussions around production processes. The challenge of identifying root causes is also addressed by providing the ability to drill down into specific processes. They noted that this capability is not just beneficial but considered mandatory, as it allows stakeholders to substantiate their observations with concrete evidence. This is crucial for persuading individuals to adopt new work methodologies.

Another key takeaway is the importance of simplicity in visualizations. The clear DFG views of outlier footprints enabled all participants to quickly analyze production processes and draw their own conclusions regarding performance variations. One expert noted that individuals responsible for planning and monitoring production processes may be disinclined to engage with complex visualizations, emphasizing the need for clarity and ease of interpretation.

Furthermore, experts have raised a crucial point about the integration of new employees into the workforce. Unlike seasoned employees who often rely on extensive experience and intuition to make decisions, newcomers face challenges due to their limited exposure to the field. The impending retirement of the baby boomer generation exacerbates this issue, as a significant amount of expert knowledge is at risk of being lost. This underscores the necessity for a tool that provides a structured and documented approach to decision-making, reducing reliance on intuition. Such a tool would be very helpful in preserving and transferring knowledge within manufacturing environments, ensuring that the expertise of retiring employees is captured and made accessible to new hires. Moreover, the feedback highlighted the significant role of user involvement in the tool's development process. Incorporating suggestions and insights from users, such as enhancing KPI calculations at the footprint level to address outliers more effectively, is vital for refining the tool's usability and functionality. Additionally, it's worth emphasizing the motivational aspect highlighted by the experts. The prospect of having such a tool was found to be highly motivating for employees. The main reason for this was that it could enhance their understanding and influence the quality of reporting. When employees can directly observe the performance of processes, they are more likely to engage with improving them, thus fostering a culture of continuous improvement and efficiency.

Overall, the positive reception of the tool's visualizations and functionality indicates its potential to support decision-making processes and improve efficiency in manufacturing environments but could be also leveraged in other domains (e.g., administration, information security etc.) as future work.

6 Conclusion and Future Work

This paper identified a lack of effective visualization techniques for identifying anomalies and understanding their root causes in manufacturing domain. To address this gap, we developed and evaluated an interactive dashboard specifically designed to fit this purpose. Our approach included providing multiple visualizations and configuration options for data analysis, incorporating various KPIs such as *OEE* and *Lead Time*. To evaluate our approach, we conducted two focus groups where we showcased how the dashboard simplifies the analysis process. The results showed that our dashboard helps analysts to easily identify materials and their anomalies requiring in-depth investigation. The feedback gathered from the experts underscores the crucial importance of rendering every significant detail visibly and promptly, ensuring that analysts can interpret results without ambiguities. Moving forward, we plan to conduct a comprehensive study to assess the user-friendliness of our dashboard by interviewing a larger sample size. Furthermore, we plan to enhance the dashboard by incorporating a variant analysis mode as outlined in the feedback from the focus groups.

Acknowledgments. This research was partly funded by the Austrian Research Promotion Agency, project 907709.

Disclosure of Interests. The authors have no competing interests to declare that are relevant to the content of this article.

References

1. van der Aalst, W.: Process mining: overview and opportunities. ACM Trans. Manage. Inf. Syst. **3**(2) (2012). https://doi.org/10.1145/2229156.2229157
2. van der Aalst, W.M.e.a.: Process mining and visual analytics: breathing life into business process models. BPM Cent. Rep. **17**, 699–730 (2011)
3. Aguirre, J.A., et al.: Evaluation of operational process variables in healthcare using process mining and data visualization techniques. Health **7**, 19 (2019)
4. Bezerra, F., Wainer, J., van der Aalst, W.M.: Anomaly detection using process mining. In: BPMDS, pp. 149–161 (2009)
5. Böhmer, K., Rinderle-Ma, S.: Mining association rules for anomaly detection in dynamic process runtime behavior and explaining the root cause to users. Inf. Syst. **90**, 101438 (2020)
6. Dreher, S., Reimann, P., Gröger, C.: Application fields and research gaps of process mining in manufacturing companies. In: INFORMATIK 2020, pp. 621–634 (2021)
7. Huynh, V.H., Le, A.N.T.: Process mining and security: visualization in database intrusion detection. In: Intelligence and Security Informatics, pp. 81–95 (2012)
8. Ko, J., Comuzzi, M.: A systematic review of anomaly detection for business process event logs. Bus. Inf. Syst. Eng. **65**(4), 441–462 (2023). https://doi.org/10.1007/s12599-023-00794-y
9. Kriglstein, S., Leitner, M., Kabicher-Fuchs, S., Rinderle-Ma, S.: Evaluation methods in process-aware information systems research with a perspective on human orientation. Bus. Inf. Syst. Eng. **58**(6), 397–414 (2016)
10. Leitner, M., Rinderle-Ma, S.: A systematic review on security in process-aware information systems - constitution, challenges, and future directions. Inf. Softw. Technol. **56**(3), 273–293 (2014)
11. Martin, N., et al.: Opportunities and challenges for process mining in organizations: results of a Delphi study. BISE **63**, 511–527 (2021)
12. Nieves Avendano, D., et al.: Anomaly detection and event mining in cold forming manufacturing processes. Int. J. Adv. Manuf. Technol. **115**, 837–852 (2021)
13. Parmenter, D.: Key performance indicators: developing, implementing, and using winning KPIs. John wiley & sons (2015)
14. Pietsch, D., Matthes, M., Wieland, U., Ihlenfeldt, S., Munkelt, T.: Root cause analysis in industrial manufacturing: a scoping review of current research, challenges and the promises of AI-driven approaches. J. Manuf. Mat. Process. **8**, 277 (2024). https://doi.org/10.3390/jmmp8060277
15. Rudolf, N., Böhmer, K., Leitner, M.: BAnDIT: business process anomaly detection in transactions. In: CoopIS, pp. 405–415. Springer, Cham (2024)
16. Saraeian, S., Shirazi, B.: Process mining-based anomaly detection of additive manufacturing process activities using a game theory modeling approach. Comput. Ind. Eng. **146**, 106584 (2020)
17. Stein Dani, V., et al.: Progressing from process mining insights to process improvement: Challenges and recommendations. In: EDOC, pp. 152–168 (2024)
18. Stewart, D.W., Shamdasani, P.N.: Focus Groups: Theory and Practice. SAGE Publications (2014)
19. VDI Verein Deutscher Ingenieure e.V.: Technical availability of machines and production lines - Terms, definitions, determination of time periods and calculation. VDI - GESELLSCHAFT PRODUKTION UND LOGISTIK, Düsseldorf (2011)
20. Verband Deutscher Maschinen- und Anlagenbau e.V.: VDMA-Einheitsblatt 66412-1 – "Manufacturing Execution Systems (MES) – Kennzahlen" (2009)

21. Werner, M.: Materiality maps: process mining data visualization for financial audits. In: HICSS, pp. 1045–1054 (2019)
22. Wieringa, R.J.: Design science methodology for information systems and software engineering. Springer, Heidelberg (2014). https://doi.org/10.1007/978-3-662-43839-8
23. Zheng, J.G.: Data visualization for business intelligence. Global Business Intelligence, pp. 67–82 (2017)
24. Zhou, F., Lin, X., Liu, C., Zhao, Y., Xu, P., Ren, L., Xue, T., Ren, L.: A survey of visualization for smart manufacturing. J. Visual. **22**, 419–435 (2019)

Atlas: the Enterprise Architecture and Cartography Tool

Pedro Sousa[1,2](✉)

[1] University of Lisbon, Lisbon, Portugal
[2] Link Consulting, Av. Duque Ávila 23, 1000-123 Lisboa, Portugal
pedro.manuel.sousa@tecnico.ulisboa.pt

Abstract. The need to maintain up-to-date architectural representations of enterprises is an indescribable fact nowadays given their constant evolution. However, despite the large number of enterprise architecture tools available, organizations cannot maintain updated architectural models,the effort it entails. Atlas is an Enterprise Architecture tool conceived to reduce the effort needed to keep architectural models updated, by feeding into the architecture the pipeline of transformation initiatives. Atlas (https://atlas-eu.linkconsulting.com). from Link Consulting (www.linkconsuling.com) is a tool designed to produce TO BE diagrams for organizations in a decentralized, distributed, and asynchronous design process using multiple design tools.

Keyword: Enterprise Architecture

1 Enterprise Cartography

Enterprise Cartography (EC) is a discipline that focuses on systematically observing, abstracting, and representing the current state of an enterprise and the changes it is undergoing. Unlike Enterprise Architecture (EA), which is primarily prescriptive, aiming to define and design a future state for the organization, Enterprise Cartography is fundamentally descriptive. It seeks to map the enterprise "as it is," based on factual, observable data, and to do so continuously, even as the enterprise evolves.

The core objective of EC is to construct and maintain up-to-date representations of the enterprise that reflect both its operational reality and the expected trajectory of its evolution. This includes not only static elements such as organizational units, processes, and systems, but also the dynamics introduced by ongoing transformation initiatives, which are treated as observable artifacts in their own right. In this way, EC introduces the concept of the "emerging AS-IS": a view of the enterprise's expected future state based on current plans and initiatives, assuming no countervailing actions are taken.

To support this, EC relies on formal constructs such as the *enterprise model*, a graph of artifacts and their interrelations; the *enterprise meta-model*, which

J. Barateiro et al. (Eds.): EDOC 2025 Workshops, LNBIP 571, pp. 490–495, 2026.
https://doi.org/10.1007/978-3-032-16234-2_39

defines the valid types and states of these elements; and *architectural sentences*, which are time-stamped assertions about the state or structure of the enterprise. These allow EC to track not just the existence of artifacts, but also their lifecycle across five distinct states: conceived, gestating, productive (alive), retired, and removed.

What sets EC apart is its ability to offer a coherent and consistent view of the enterprise from diverse and distributed sources, enabling fact-based decision-making. It serves as the foundation for enterprise governance and systemic steering, particularly in complex organizations where change is constant and decentralized. EC empowers organizations to make better-informed decisions by providing a clear understanding of their current configuration, as well as a projection of where they are headed if current plans unfold as expected.

Ultimately, Enterprise Cartography complements traditional Enterprise Architecture by making the actual architecture of the enterprise visible, traceable, and navigable—much like a map does for physical space. It enables organizations to shift from designing in abstraction to managing transformation grounded in reality, offering both clarity and control in an era of accelerating complexity.

2 Leveraging Enterprise Cartography with Project Pipeline

An enduring challenge in enterprise architecture (EA) is the effort required to maintain a continuously up-to-date repository of architectural models. In large and complex organizations, where change is frequent and distributed, the architectural representations tend to become obsolete shortly after they are created. This paper proposes that a feasible and rigorous solution to this problem lies in the integration of Enterprise Cartography (EC) with the organization's transformation project pipeline.

Transformation initiatives are the primary mechanism through which enterprises evolve. Each approved initiative—whether it involves launching a new product, reengineering a business process, or modernizing an application landscape—introduces changes to the enterprise's architecture. We argue that these initiatives can and should be treated as primary sources of architectural change information. In particular, the moment a transformation project is approved and enters the organizational project pipeline—even if no concrete execution date is yet scheduled—it carries architectural implications that are both identifiable and relevant.

Before approval, transformation project sponsors must present key indicators to the organization's governance structures: namely, the estimated time, cost, and risk of the proposed project. These indicators are essential for decision-making and prioritization. However, deriving such estimates depends on having at least a high-level understanding of the architecture to be modified. In other words, the project must be described in architectural terms—what will be built, what will be changed, and what will be decommissioned. This is precisely where Enterprise Cartography provides a structured, formal foundation.

Under the EC approach, any architectural transformation can be summarized through three core lists of architectural artifacts:

1. the list of artifacts that will become productive ("becomes alive").
2. the list of artifacts that will be discontinued ("the dead list").

Artifacts, in this context, are instances of concepts defined in the organization's architectural metamodel—such as business processes, application components, data entities, or infrastructure elements. Because these lists must be produced to evaluate project feasibility and governance risks, they necessarily exist at the time of project approval, long before the actual implementation begins.

These three lists are not only sufficient for project planning—they are also sufficient to infer the architectural state of the enterprise after the completion of the project. When consolidated across the project pipeline, they allow enterprise architects and cartographers to compute the "emerging AS-IS" state of the organization: the expected configuration of the enterprise assuming all ongoing and approved transformations are completed as planned.

Consequently, EC enables organizations to maintain an architectural repository that is both current and forward-looking, without requiring continuous manual modeling. By integrating architectural projections derived from project pipeline data, EC shifts the architectural repository from being a retrospective documentation artifact to becoming a dynamic strategic asset—one that reflects both current and near-future configurations of the enterprise.

This approach reduces the effort of manual model updates, increases architectural accuracy, and ensures alignment between strategic planning and operational transformation. More importantly, it establishes a systematic, governance-driven mechanism to maintain architectural coherence in rapidly evolving organizational contexts.

3 Atlas: Tool for Living Enterprise Cartography

To operationalize the integration between Enterprise Cartography and the transformation project pipeline, we introduce Atlas, a purpose-built tool designed to support the continuous evolution of an enterprise architecture repository. Atlas was developed from the ground up to embody the principles of cartographic representation described in the previous sections, particularly those related to the representation of architectural change over time.

3.1 Diagrams as Time-Based Models

The fundamental innovation of Atlas lies in its treatment of architectural diagrams not as static images but as temporal sequences of states. In Atlas, every diagram is inherently time-aware: it includes a timeline navigation interface that allows the user to scroll through past, present, and future configurations of the enterprise model. This transforms diagrams into dynamic visualizations that reflect the enterprise's state at any point in time—from historical configurations (AS-WAS), to current operational states (AS-IS), and future planned configurations (TO-BE).

This concept is based on the temporal modeling framework introduced in Enterprise Cartography concept, where the TO-BE state of an enterprise at a future time where the TO-BE state of an enterprise at a future time Tn is defined as the union of the current AS-IS state and the set of changes introduced by all transformation initiatives in the pipeline scheduled to complete before or at Tn

In Atlas, this computation is performed automatically, allowing the user to simulate enterprise evolution by selecting a point in time on the timeline. The system aggregates the baseline architecture and applies the planned changes incrementally, producing a real-time rendering of the emerging TO-BE state.

3.2 Pipeline-Aware Projections

Every time a new project enters the pipeline, Atlas can ingest the three key architectural lists associated with it: the artifacts to be created (become alive), those to be decommissioned (retired), and those to be altered. These lists, submitted by the project sponsor at the time of project approval, are stored as structured metadata and timestamped in the system.

Atlas uses these lists to project the evolving state of the enterprise. By correlating each project's timeline with its impact on the architecture, the system generates emerging architectural views. These allow enterprise architects and decision-makers to preview the cumulative impact of the transformation roadmap on various architecture layers, such as business capabilities, applications, data, or infrastructure.

3.3 Metamodel Mapping and Model Importation

Another significant challenge in maintaining a coherent and consistent architecture repository is the diversity of modeling practices across teams and departments. Different teams may use standards like BPMN or ArchiMate in ways that reflect local conventions or assumptions. For instance, a "Data Store" in a BPMN diagram might be interpreted by one department as a logical placeholder for an information object, while another team may model it as a reference to an actual implemented application.

To address this heterogeneity, Atlas includes a metamodel transformation engine that supports semantic mapping during model import. When diagrams modeled in BPMN or ArchiMate are imported into the centralized repository, Atlas applies a set of transformation rules that interpret the meaning of elements according to the importing team's local conventions. These rules are configurable per department or project, allowing Atlas to accommodate multiple viewpoints without compromising the semantic integrity of the global architectural model.

This capability ensures that Atlas functions not only as a central repository but also as a federated integration platform, where diverse models can be harmonized into a unified, time-aware representation of the enterprise. The ability to resolve semantic differences during import is crucial to supporting large organizations where modeling is distributed and contextual.

3.4 LLM Driven Automation of BPMN Models

In addition to supporting time-aware modeling and federated model integration, Atlas introduces a novel and powerful feature: the automation of BPMN workflows through Large Language Model (LLM) execution engines. This functionality transforms BPMN diagrams from static process descriptions into dynamic, executable workflows powered by generative AI.

In this approach, Atlas interprets each activity in a BPMN model not merely as a task to be manually executed or mapped to traditional system functions, but as an invocation of an LLM engine. Specifically, the textual description of the activity is treated as a prompt. When the process is executed, Atlas passes this prompt to the LLM, along with the relevant data, automatically extracted from the associated data objects and data stores defined in the BPMN model.

This enables Atlas to orchestrate intelligent behavior within workflows without requiring low-level scripting or rigid application logic. For example, an activity labeled *Generate a personalized response to customer complaint* can trigger an LLM call where the prompt is derived from the activity label and the complaint content is drawn from the linked data objects. The LLMs output can then be stored, visualized, or passed on to subsequent activities in the process flow.

Because data context is automatically managed by Atlas, ensuring that inputs and outputs are passed correctly and securely between BPMN constructs and the LLM , users are freed from the complexity of manually handling variable binding or API integration. This allows non technical users to design and execute smart, data-driven processes using only high level modeling abstractions.

This integration of LLMs into BPMN execution brings several advantages:

- It enables low-code automation of knowledge-intensive tasks (e.g., summarization, content generation, decision support).
- It leverages existing enterprise data artifacts, increasing the reuse of structured models.
- It maintains architectural traceability, as each automated activity is still modeled, annotated, and timestamped within the cartographic representation.

By enabling the direct execution of modeled activities via LLMs, Atlas closes the gap between modeling and automation, turning enterprise cartographic models into live, intelligent systems that not only describe the enterprise but actively participate in its operation.

3.5 A Living Repository

In summary, Atlas is more than an enterprise architecture tool—it is a living cartographic system. It provides an operational framework where architectural models are no longer snapshots in time, but evolving maps synchronized with the organization's transformation initiatives. By aligning the repository with the project pipeline and supporting semantic interoperability across teams, Atlas enables organizations to maintain architectural consistency, support informed decision-making, and manage change systematically.

This approach realizes the core vision of Enterprise Cartography: to transform architectural documentation into an active, time-aware, and decision-relevant asset that reflects both the structure and the dynamics of the modern enterprise.

Disclosure of Interests. The author declare that there are no conflicts of interest.

Journal-first Papers

Decentralized Proof-of-Location Systems for Trust, Scalability, and Privacy in Digital Societies [1]

Eduardo Brito[1,2(✉)], Amnir Hadachi[2], Liina Kamm[1], and Ulrich Norbisrath[2]

[1] Cybernetica AS, Mäealuse 2/1, 12618 Tallinn, Estonia
eduardo.brito@cyber.ee, liina.kamm@cyber.ee

[2] University of Tartu, Narva mnt 18, 51009 Tartu, Estonia
amnir.hadachi@ut.ee, ulrich.norbisrath@ut.ee

Abstract. Verifying physical presence in digital systems is essential for secure authentication, authorization, and accountability. Proof-of-Location (PoL) systems address this need by enabling verifiable, tamper-resistant claims of location and time, particularly in adversarial environments where traditional localization methods such as GPS fall short. While recent efforts have explored decentralized PoL architectures, existing systems often lack a unified model that integrates spatio-temporal synchronization, distributed consensus, and cryptographic attestation. In this paper, we formalize the architectural foundations of decentralized PoL systems by introducing a composable model based on fault-tolerant witnessing zones. We define core components for synchronization and collective attestation, integrating primitives such as distributed digital signatures, distance bounding protocols, and consensus mechanisms. We contextualize the model across diverse application domains that necessitate digital trust, such as civic processes, content authentication, infrastructure auditing, and supply chain tracking, and argue for a shared, interoperable decentralized PoL infrastructure. To validate our design, we implement and emulate a reference protocol instance, analysing scalability, synchronization behaviour, and timing misalignment under varied conditions. We also outline its security model and discuss limitations and future directions in privacy, interoperability, and real-world deployment. Our contributions lay a formal and practical foundation for scalable, secure, and general-purpose decentralized PoL systems.

Keywords: Proof-of-Location · Decentralized Systems · Trustworthy Location Verification

Disclosure of Interests. The authors have no competing interests to declare that are relevant to the content of this article.

J. Barateiro et al. (Eds.): EDOC 2025 Workshops, LNBIP 571, pp. 499–500, 2026.
https://doi.org/10.1007/978-3-032-16234-2_40

References

1. Brito, E., Hadachi, A., Kamm, L., Norbisrath, U.: Decentralized proof-of-location systems for trust, scalability, and privacy in digital societies. Sci. Rep. **15**(1), 1–20 (2025)

How Can Cryptography Secure Online Assessments Against Academic Dishonesty?

Aarav Ashish Mehrishi[1], Dipti Kapoor Sarmah[2(✉)], and Maya Daneva[3]

[1] Times Network, AI Engineer, Mumbai, Maharashtra, India
[2] Semantics, Cybersecurity and Services, University of Twente, Enschede, Netherlands
d.k.sarmah@Utwente.nl
[3] Semantics, Cybersecurity and Services, University of Twente, Enschede, Netherlands
m.deneva@Utwente.nl

Abstract. Online learning systems such as Canvas, Moodle, and Google Forms are widely used for teaching and examinations, especially after the COVID-19 pandemic. However, these platforms still face major challenges in maintaining exam integrity and data security. Issues like cheating, impersonation, unauthorized access, and manipulation of answers have become common. This study focuses on identifying the main vulnerabilities in these systems and developing a secure and practical solution to make online assessments more reliable. The proposed prototype introduces multiple layers of security using encryption, digital signatures, and two-step authentication to protect exam content and verify the identity of users. It also integrates browser controls that block copying, pasting, or switching tabs to prevent cheating during tests. The system is built using secure coding practices that help defend against common attacks such as SQL Injection and Cross-Site Scripting. Performance tests show that the system runs efficiently, with fast encryption and decryption times, ensuring smooth operation even with larger data. Automated security scans confirmed that there were no serious vulnerabilities, showing the reliability of the design. Statistical analysis further indicated that performance remains stable across different data sizes. The approach is simple to integrate into existing learning platforms and complies with privacy regulations like GDPR. Although future work will focus on adding features such as grading support, automated key management, and privacy-aware proctoring, the current results clearly demonstrate that the proposed solution can significantly reduce cheating and strengthen trust in online education. By combining strong authentication, data encryption, and controlled browser environments, this study offers a secure, efficient, and user-friendly way to protect online examinations and promote academic honesty in digital learning environments.

Keywords: Online Assessments · Canvas LMS · Moodle · Google Forms · Two-Factor Authentication · Digital Signature

Disclosure of Interests. The authors have no competing interests to declare that are relevant to the content of this article.

J. Barateiro et al. (Eds.): EDOC 2025 Workshops, LNBIP 571, pp. 501–502, 2026.
https://doi.org/10.1007/978-3-032-16234-2

Reference

1. Mehrishi, A.A, Sarmah, D.K., Daneva, M.: How can cryptography secure online assessments against academic dishonesty?. Secur. Priv. **8**(4), e70065. (2025) https://doi.org/10.1002/spy2.70065

Building Trust in Predictive Analytics: A Review of ML Explainability and Interpretability

Shruthi Sajid[1,2], Jeewanie Jayasinghe Arachchige[2], Faiza Allah Bukhsh[1(✉)], Abhishta Abhishta[3], and Faizan Ahmed[2]

[1] EEMCS, University of Twente, Enschede, Netherlands
s.sajid@utwente.nl, shruthisajid97@gmail.com, f.a.bukhsh@utwente.nl
[2] Department of Computer Science, Vrije University, Amsterdam, Netherlands
faizan.ahmed@utwente.nl
[3] BMS, University of Twente, Enschede, Netherlands
s.abhishta@utwente.nl

Abstract. Purpose – The purpose of the manuscript is to explore the previous literature to reveal the trust and interpretability of predictive analytical models that use ML /AI techniques. Method – The methodology applied for the study is the guidelines of Kitchenham. Results – The results reveal that past research explicitly discussed the usage of predictive analytics. However, ML models are considered black boxes and suffer from transparency. The study proposed a typical process to ensure that predictions made by AI/ML models can be interpreted and trusted. Conclusion – The literature review conducted predictive analytics and AI/ML techniques in business decision-making, highlighting their usage in industries. The study reveals a significant gap exists in research on the explainability and interpretability of these ML models within a business context. Recommendations – Recommended the need for more research on transparency and interpretability of ML models by developing sector-specific explainability frameworks to bridge technical insights and business decisions. Further, it is recommended to integrate ethical and regulatory considerations into explainability frameworks and study collaboration methods between AI/ML experts and business leaders to align ML models with business goals. Research Implications – The research highlights the significant gap in the literature explainability and interpretability of ML and AI models in the business context. Therefore the research stresses the need for future investigations into improving model transparency and creating industry-specific and ethical frameworks that help organizations derive more meaningful, trusted, and interpretable insights from data-driven models. Practical Implications – It should focus on improving transparency, trust, and collaboration in using predictive analytics. By addressing explainability issues and incorporating ethical, regulatory, and industry-specific considerations, businesses can more effectively use the power of AI and ML to drive data-informed decisions. Social Implications – This study highlights the importance of ethical and regulatory concerns related to AI and ML, such as data privacy, and fairness.

J. Barateiro et al. (Eds.): EDOC 2025 Workshops, LNBIP 571, pp. 503–504, 2026.
https://doi.org/10.1007/978-3-032-16234-2_42

Keywords: explainability · interpretability · machine learning · predictive analytics · trust

Disclosure of Interests. The authors declare that they have no known competing financial interests or personal relationships that could have appeared to influence the work reported in this paper.

References

1. Sajid, S., Arachchige, J.J., Bukhsh, F.A., Abhishta, A., Ahmed, F.: Building trust in predictive analytics: a review of ML explainability and interpretability. Int. J. Comput. Sci. Res. **9**, 3364–3391 (2025). https://doi.org/10.25147/ijcsr.2017.001.1.223

Author Index

J. Barateiro et al. (Eds.): EDOC 2025 Workshops, LNBIP 571, pp. 505–506, 2026.
https://doi.org/10.1007/978-3-032-16234-2

MIX
Papier aus verantwortungsvollen Quellen
Paper from responsible sources
FSC® C105338

If you have any concerns about our products,
you can contact us on
ProductSafety@springernature.com

In case Publisher is established outside the EU,
the EU authorized representative is:
Springer Nature Customer Service Center GmbH
Europaplatz 3, 69115 Heidelberg, Germany

Printed by Libri Plureos GmbH
in Hamburg, Germany